KT-156-117

THIRD EDITION

Fundamentals of Management

Core Concepts and Applications

Ricky W. Griffin

Texas A & M University

Houghton Mifflin Company

Boston   New York

BROMLEY COLLEGE LIBRARY
B45340

BROMLEY COLLEGE LIBRARY
B50562

CD0333

WITHDRAWN

For all those who helped sustain me through 2001,
a time of personal challenge, trial, and endurance.

Executive Editor: George T. Hoffman
Associate Editor: Damaris R. Curran
Project Editor: Tracy Williams
Senior Production/Design Coordinator: Sarah Ambrose
Senior Manufacturing Coordinator: Priscilla Bailey
Marketing Manager: Steven W. Mikels

Cover illustration © Nicholas Wilton.

Credits may be found on page 480.

BROMLEY COLLEGE OF FURTHER & HIGHER EDUCATION

ACCN.	B45340
CLASSN.	658
CAT.	LOCN. TH

Copyright © 2003 by Houghton Mifflin Company. All rights reserved.

No part of this work may be reproduced or transmitted in any form or by any means, electronic or mechanical, including photocopying and recording, or by any information storage or retrieval system without the prior written permission of Houghton Mifflin Company unless such copying is expressly permitted by federal copyright law. Address inquiries to College Permissions, Houghton Mifflin Company, 222 Berkeley Street, Boston, MA 02116-3764.

Printed in the U.S.A.

Library of Congress Control Number: 2001133286

ISBN: 0-618-203397

3456789—QWV—05 04 03 02

Brief Contents

Contents

5 Entrepreneurship and New Venture Management 120

PART THREE

Organizing 152

6 Organization Structure and Design 154

12 Communication in Organizations   *332*

13 Managing Groups and Teams   *360*

PART FIVE

Controlling **388**

Managing the Control Process *390*

Managing Operations, Quality, and Productivity *422*

APPENDIX

Tools for Planning and Decision Making   452

Preface

Over the last four decades, literally hundreds of books have been written for introductory management courses. As the body of material comprising the theory, research, and practice of management has grown and expanded, textbook authors have continued to mirror this expansion of material in their books. Writers have understood the importance of adding new material pertinent to traditional topics, like planning and organizing, while simultaneously adding coverage of emerging topics, such as diversity and information technology. As a by-product of this trend, our textbooks have grown longer and longer, making it difficult to cover all the material in one course.

Another emerging trend in management education is a new focus on teaching in a broader context. That is, introductory management courses are increasingly being taught with less emphasis on theory alone and more emphasis on application of concepts. Teaching how to successfully apply management concepts often involves focusing more on skills development and the human side of the organization. This trend requires that textbooks cover theoretical concepts within a flexible framework that allows instructors to make use of interactive tools such as case studies, exercises, and projects.

This text represents a synthesis of these trends toward a more manageable and practical approach. By combining concise text discussion, standard pedagogical tools, lively and current content, an emphasis on organizational behavior, and exciting skills-development materials, *Fundamentals of Management* answers the call for a new approach to management education. This book provides an almost infinite flexibility, a solid foundation of knowledge-based material, and an action-oriented learning dimension that is unique in the field. Indeed, almost 100,000 students gained their first exposure to the field of management using the first two editions of this book. This third edition builds solidly on the successes of the earlier editions.

Organization of the Book

Most management instructors today organize their course around the traditional management functions of planning, organizing, leading, and controlling. *Fundamentals of Management* uses these functions as its organizing framework. The book consists of five parts, with fifteen chapters and one appendix.

Part One introduces management through two chapters. Chapter 1 provides a basic overview of the management process in organizations, while Chapter 2 introduces students to the environment of management.

Part Two covers the first basic management function, planning. Chapter 3 introduces the fundamental concepts of planning and discusses strategic management. Managerial decision making is the topic of Chapter 4. Finally, Chapter 5 covers entrepreneurship and the management of new ventures.

The second basic management function, organizing, is the subject of Part Three. In Chapter 6 the fundamental concepts of organization structure and design are introduced and discussed. Chapter 7 discusses organization change and innovation. Chapter 8 is devoted to human resource management.

Many instructors and managers believe that the third basic management function, leading, is especially important in contemporary organizations. Thus Part Four devotes five chapters to this management function. Basic concepts and processes associated with individual behavior are introduced and discussed in Chapter 9. Employee motivation is the subject of Chapter 10. Chapter 11 discusses leadership and influence processes in organizations. Communication in organizations is the topic of Chapter 12. The management of groups and teams is covered in Chapter 13.

The fourth management function, controlling, is the subject of Part Five. Chapter 14 introduces the fundamental concepts and issues associated with the management of the control process. A special area of control today, managing for total quality, is discussed in Chapter 15.

Finally, the Appendix provides coverage of important tools for planning and management.

Skills-Focused Pedagogical Features

With this text I have been able to address new dimensions of management education without creating a text that is unwieldy in length. Specifically, each chapter in this book is followed by an exciting set of skills-based exercises. These resources were created to bring an active and behavioral orientation to management education by requiring students to solve problems, make decisions, respond to situations, and work in groups. In short, these materials simulate many of the day-to-day challenges and opportunities faced by real managers.

Among these skills-based exercises are three different *Building Management Skills* organized around the set of basic management skills introduced in Chapter 1 of the text. The *Skills Self-Assessment Instrument* exercise helps readers learn something about their own approach to management. Finally, an *Experiential Exercise* provides additional action-oriented learning opportunities, usually in a group setting.

New to each chapter of the Third Edition is a *Management InfoTech* boxed feature. This feature is intended to briefly depart from the flow of the chapter to highlight or extend especially interesting or emerging points and issues relating to new technology and its role in management.

The Third Edition now also includes an icon that refers students to the new Knowledgebank on the Real Deal Upgrade CD-ROM. The Knowledgebank offers additional information about particular topics in the text. It can be used to gain further management knowledge or for a research project, and it can be found only on the Real Deal Upgrade CD-ROM.

In addition to the end-of-chapter exercises, every chapter includes important standard pedagogy: learning objectives, chapter outline, opening incident, boldface key terms, summary of key points, questions for review, questions for analysis, and an end-of-chapter case with questions.

An Effective Teaching and Learning Package

For Instructors

■ *Instructor's Resource Manual* (Margaret Hill, Texas A&M University). This resource includes suggested class schedules, detailed teaching notes for each chapter of this text, and a video guide. The teaching notes for each chapter include: chapter summary; learning objectives; detailed chapter lecture outline, including opening incident summary, highlighted key terms, teaching tips, group exercise ideas, discussion starters, and references to the transparencies; responses to review, analysis, and case questions; and information to help facilitate the skills development exercises.

■ *Videos.* An expanded video program will accompany *Fundamentals of Management*, Third Edition. Most chapters will now have their own text-specific video designed to illustrate the concepts discussed in the chapter by applying the discussion of the text to real-world case examples presented in the video. The video segments are designed to be shown for classroom discussion. The video guide for instructors can be found in the Instructor's Resource Manual.

■ *HMClassPrep™ CD-ROM.* This new CD-ROM, which replaces the Second Edition Instructor CD, is designed to assist the instructor with in-class lectures. The CD includes Lecture Outlines, PowerPoint slides, and text art, as well as material from the Real Deal Upgrade CD such as Knowledgebank, Chapter Outlines, and Learning Objectives.

■ *Test Bank* (Margaret Hill, Texas A&M University). The *Test Bank* includes over 2000 questions, 130 questions per chapter and 60 in the appendix. Each question is identified with the corresponding learning objective and page numbers for reference. In addition, the questions have an estimate of the level of difficulty and are identified by type of question—knowledge, understanding, or application.

■ *HMTesting.* This feature of the Computerized Test Bank allows instructors to administer tests via a network system, modem, or personal computer and includes a grading function that lets them set up a new class, record grades from tests or assignments, analyze grades, and produce class and individual statistics.

■ *Transparencies.* Approximately 80 full-color transparencies illustrate major topics in the text. Two types of transparencies are included: highlights of key figures from the text and additional images that can be used to enhance lecture presentation.

■ *Instructor Web Site.* This rich resource offers valuable information for instructors including PowerPoint slides, Lecture Outlines, and Instructor Solutions for Exercises in Management.

■ *Blackboard Course Cartridges.* This online course allows flexible, efficient, and creative ways to present learning materials and opportunities. In addition to course management benefits, instructors may make use of an electronic grade book, receive papers from students enrolled in the course via the Internet, and track student use of the communication and collaboration functions.

■ *WebCT e-Packs.* This online course provides instructors with a flexible, Internet-based education platform. These Internet-based e-Packs provide multiple ways to present learning materials. The WebCT e-Packs come with a full array of features to enrich the online learning experience.

For Students

■ *Real Deal Upgrade CD-ROM.* This student CD is carefully tailored to supplement and enhance the content of the text. The Knowledgebank, a feature new to the Third Edition, offers additional information about particular topics in the text. In addition, the CD also includes selected videos, Chapter Outlines, Company Web Links, a Glossary, Learning Objectives, Ready Notes, Self-Assessment Exercises, and Chapter Summaries.

■ *Student Web Site.* This site offers students ACE self-testing, Management Skills Assessments, Ready Notes, Flashcards, Term Paper Help, web activities and resources, Learning Objectives, Outlines, and Company Web Links. In addition, the site will feature links to important job and career sites.

■ *Manager: A Simulation.* This business simulation, developed by the successful team of Jerald R. Smith and Peggy Golden, allows student players to make business decisions through simulated real-world experiences.

■ *The Ultimate Job Hunter's Guidebook*, Third Edition. This practical, how-to handbook by Susan Greene and Melanie Martel is a concise manual containing abundant examples, practical advice, and exercises related to each of the job hunter's major tasks.

I invite your feedback on this book. If you have any questions, suggestions, or issues to discuss, please feel free to contact me. The most efficient way to reach me is through e-mail. My address is rgriffin@tamu.edu.

R.W.G.

Acknowledgments

I would like to acknowledge the many contributions that others have made to this book. My faculty colleagues at Texas A&M University have contributed enormously both to this book and to my thinking about management education. At Houghton Mifflin, an outstanding team of professionals, including George Hoffman, Damaris Curran, and Tracy Williams, has made more contributions to this book than I could even begin to list. A special thanks is also due the many reviewers who helped shape the content and form of the materials in this book.

While any and all errors are of course my own responsibility, thanks to Sally Alkazin (Linfield College), Sherryl Berg-Ridenour (DeVry College–Pomona), Alain Broder (Touro College), Sam Chapman (Diablo Valley College), Elizabeth Anne Christo-Baker (Terra Community College), Dr. Anne Cowden (California State University), Joe Dobson (Western Illinois University), Joseph S. Hooker, Jr. (North Greenville College), George W. Jacobs (Middle Tennessee State University), Ranjna Patel (Bethune-Cookman College), Dr. Joan Rivera (Angelo State University), Roberta B. Slater (Pennsylvania College of Technology), and Sheryl A. Stanley (Newman University) for their help. I would also like to thank Margaret Hill. Margaret has become an integral part of this project as well as my other Houghton Mifflin textbooks. I sincerely appreciate the high level of professionalism that she brings to her work.

My wife, Glenda, and our children, Dustin and Ashley, are, of course, due the greatest thanks. Their love, care, interest, and enthusiasm help sustain me in all that I do.

PART ONE

An Introduction to Management

CHAPTER 1

Understanding the Manager's Job

CHAPTER 2

The Environment of Organizations and Managers

3

1 Understanding the Manager's Job

When Leslie Wexner opened the first The Limited clothing store in an Ohio shopping mall in 1963, he had no idea that his fledgling business would grow to include thousands of specialty stores comprised of such well-known brands as Express, Abercrombie & Fitch, and Victoria's Secret. But by 1993 his firm was running out of steam, and rivals like Gap and J. Crew were attracting more and more attention. Now, though, The Limited seems to have righted itself and is again moving toward the forefront of the specialty retailing industry. The reasons for the decline and rebirth of The Limited underscore the importance of maintaining compatibility between a manager's style and the organization's situation.

When Wexner started The Limited, he was clearly an entrepreneur, and his focus was primarily on business growth and expansion. He pursued this growth in two ways. First, he continually looked for ways to branch out and systematically launched several different chains. Second, he grew each chain rapidly by opening new stores at a breakneck pace. Part of Wexner's strategy was to place his stores adjacent to one another in large shopping malls. Thus customers might walk from The Limited to Express to Lerner, buying clothes at each without realizing that they were actually buying from the same company.

Wexner created or bought several major chains, including The Limited, Express, Lerner New York, Lane Bryant, Henri Bendel, Victoria's Secret, Bath & Body Works, Structure, and Abercrombie & Fitch. Wexner himself also jumped from business to business, leaving the day-to-day operations in the hands of others. His focus, meanwhile, continued to be on growth and expansion as he continued to buy other chains, retool his existing chains, and build more and more stores. In some malls, for instance, The Limited stores might comprise as much as 25 percent of total square footage.

But in the early 1990s troubles began to surface. Sales declined in some markets, for example, and costs and operating expenses began to creep up. Moreover, competitors such as Gap and Old Navy started attracting more customers and increasingly became the stores of choice for hip young consumers. Investors also began to get nervous, and the company's stock price plummeted. And some experts openly questioned whether or not The Limited could be turned around.

Wexner recognized that he had a problem, but he also didn't know quite how to define it. So, starting in the mid-1990s he began to visit sev-

> *"I was an entrepreneur. . . . I think what went wrong was the . . . entrepreneurial style wasn't working."*
>
> —Leslie Wexner,
> founder and CEO of The Limited

After studying this chapter, you should be able to

- Define management, describe the kinds of managers found in organizations, and identify and briefly explain the four basic management functions.

- Justify the importance of history and theory to management, and explain the evolution of management thought.

- Discuss contemporary management issues and challenges.

eral of the very best managers in the United States, including such luminaries as Sam Walton (founder of Wal-Mart), Jack Welch (CEO of General Electric), and Wayne Calloway (former CEO of PepsiCo). And he gradually began to recognize the problem: The Limited had stopped being an entrepreneurial startup operation and had evolved into a mature major business operation, yet he was still trying to run it using the same managerial style he had used when he had only a few dozen stores. Clearly, he realized, running a global company with more than 5,000 stores, generating annual revenues of $9.3 billion, and employing 127,000 people required a different approach than the one he had been using.

So Wexner immersed himself in a crash course on how to manage a mature business. He learned about operations and financial control, revamped the firm's organization design, and implemented a more professional approach to human resource management. He also began to focus more on profit margins and acknowledged that sometimes you have to close or sell underperform-

ing stores and businesses. And he learned the difference between competitive strategy and growth strategy.

By the end of the decade, signs were clearly pointing to a resurgence at The Limited. For example, same-store sales are again increasing, and the firm's stock price reached a record high in mid-2000. But Wexner is quick to point out that, even though he has helped reinvent his company, he doesn't want to make the same mistake again. He has committed himself to staying abreast of modern management techniques and contemporary management thought.[1]

This book is about managers like Leslie Wexner and the work they do. In Chapter 1, we examine the nature of management, its dimensions, and its challenges. We explain the concepts of management and managers, discuss the management process, and summarize the origins of contemporary management thought. We conclude by introducing critical contemporary challenges and issues.

An Introduction to Management

management A set of functions directed at the efficient and effective utilization of resources in the pursuit of organizational goals

efficient Using resources wisely and in a cost-effective way

effective Making the right decisions and successfully implementing them

Management is the set of functions directed at the efficient and effective utilization of resources in the pursuit of organizational goals. By **efficient**, we mean using resources wisely and in a cost-effective way. By **effective**, we mean making the right decisions and successfully implementing them. In general, successful organizations are both efficient and effective.

Today's managers face a variety of interesting and challenging situations. The average executive works 60 hours a week, has enormous demands placed on his or her time, and faces increased complexities posed by globalization, domestic competition, government regulation, and shareholder pressure. The task is further complicated by rapid change, unexpected disruptions, and both minor and major crises. The manager's job is unpredictable and fraught with challenges, but it is also filled with opportunities to make a difference.

Kinds of Managers

Many different kinds of managers are at work in organizations today. Figure 1.1 shows how managers within an organization can be differentiated by level and area.

top managers The relatively small set of senior executives who manage the overall organization

Levels of Management   One way to differentiate managers is by their level in the organization. **Top managers** make up the relatively small group of executives who manage the overall organization. Titles found in this group include president, vice president, and chief executive officer (CEO). Top managers create the organization's goals, overall strategy, and operating policies. They also officially represent the organization to the external environment by meeting with government officials, executives of other organizations, and other individuals and groups.

Howard Schultz, CEO of Starbucks, is a top manager, as is Deidra Wager, the firm's senior vice president for retail operations. Top managers make decisions about such activities as acquiring other companies, investing in research and development, entering or abandoning various markets, and building new plants and office facilities. They often work long hours and spend much of their time in meetings or on the telephone. In most cases, top managers are also very well paid. In fact, the elite top managers of very large firms sometimes make several million dollars a year in salary, bonuses, and stock.[2]

middle managers The relatively large set of managers responsible for implementing the policies and plans developed by top managers and for supervising and coordinating the activities of first-line managers

Middle management is probably the largest group of managers in most organizations. Common middle-management titles include plant manager, operations manager, and division head. **Middle managers** are primarily responsible for im-

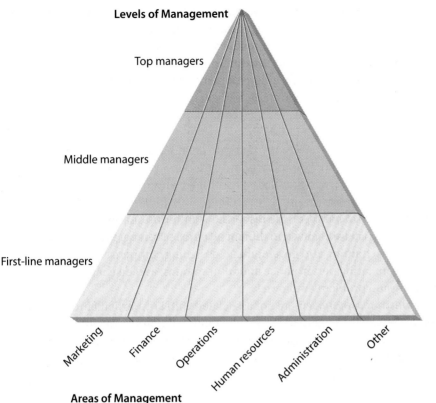

Levels of Management

Top managers

Middle managers

First-line managers

Marketing

Finance

Operations

Human resources

Administration

Other

Areas of Management

Figure 1.1

Kinds of Managers by Level and Area

Organizations generally have three levels of management, represented by top managers, middle managers, and first-line managers. Regardless of level, managers are also usually associated with a specific area within the organization, such as marketing, finance, operations, human resources, or administration.

plementing the policies and plans developed by top managers and for supervising and coordinating the activities of lower-level managers. Plant managers, for example, handle inventory management, quality control, equipment failures, and minor union problems. They also coordinate the work of supervisors within the plant. Jason Hernandez, a regional manager at Starbucks responsible for the firm's operations in three eastern states, is a middle manager.

First-line managers supervise and coordinate the activities of operating employees. Common titles for first-line managers are supervisor, coordinator, and office manager. Positions like these are often the first held by employees who enter management from the ranks of operating personnel. Wayne Maxwell and Jenny Wagner, managers of Starbucks coffee shops in Texas, are first-line managers. They oversee the day-to-day operations of their respective stores, hire operating employees to staff them, and handle other routine administrative duties required of them by the parent corporation. In contrast with top and middle managers, first-line managers typically spend a large proportion of their time supervising the work of subordinates.

first-line managers Managers who supervise and coordinate the activities of operating employees

Areas of Management   Regardless of their level, managers may work in various areas within an organization. In any given firm, for example, areas of management may include marketing, finance, operations, human resources, administration, and other areas.

Marketing managers work in areas related to the marketing function—getting consumers and clients to buy the organization's products or services, be they Nokia digital cell phones, Ford automobiles, *Newsweek* magazines, Associated Press news reports, flights on Southwest Airlines, or cups of latte at Starbucks. These areas include new product development, promotion, and distribution.

Financial managers deal primarily with an organization's financial resources. They are responsible for activities such as accounting, cash management, and investments.

Operations managers are concerned with creating and managing the systems that create an organization's products and services. Typical responsibilities of operations managers include production control, inventory control, quality control, plant layout, and site selection.

Human resource managers are responsible for hiring and developing employees. They are typically involved in human resource planning, recruiting and selecting employees, training and development, designing compensation and benefit systems, formulating performance appraisal systems, and discharging low-performing and problem employees.

Administrative managers are not associated with any particular management specialty. Probably the best example of an administrative management position is that of a hospital or clinic administrator. Administrative managers tend to be generalists; they have some basic familiarity with all functional areas of management rather than specialized training in any one area.[3]

Basic Management Functions

Regardless of level or area, management involves the four basic functions of planning and decision making, organizing, leading, and controlling. This book is organized around these basic functions, as shown in Figure 1.2.

planning Setting an organization's goals and deciding how best to achieve them

decision making Part of the planning process that involves selecting a course of action from a set of alternatives

Planning and Decision Making   In its simplest form, **planning** means setting an organization's goals and deciding how best to achieve them. **Decision making**, a part of the planning process, involves selecting a course of action from a set of alternatives. Planning and decision making help maintain managerial effectiveness by serving as guides for future activities. Part II of this text is devoted to planning and decision making.

organizing Grouping activities and resources in a logical fashion

Organizing   Once a manager has set goals and developed a workable plan, the next management function is to organize people and the other resources necessary to carry out the plan. Specifically, **organizing** involves determining how activities and resources are to be grouped. Although some people equate this function with the creation of an organization chart, we will see in Part III that it is actually much more.

leading The set of processes used to get members of the organization to work together to further the interests of the organization

Leading   The third basic managerial function is leading. Some people consider leading to be both the most important and the most challenging of all managerial activities. **Leading** is the set of processes used to get people to work together to advance the interests of the organization. We cover the leading function in detail in Part IV.

Controlling The final phase of the management process is **controlling**, or monitoring the organization's progress toward its goals. As the organization moves toward its goals, managers must monitor progress to ensure that it is performing in such a way as to arrive at its "destination" at the appointed time. The control function is explored in Part V. *Management InfoTech* discusses how these functions have helped United Parcel Service remain competitive.

Fundamental Management Skills

To carry out these management functions properly, managers rely on a number of specific skills. The most important management skills are technical, interpersonal, conceptual, diagnostic, communication, decision-making, and time management skills.[4]

Technical Skills **Technical skills** are the skills necessary to accomplish or understand the specific kind of work being done in an organization. Technical skills are especially important for first-line managers. These managers spend much of their time training subordinates and answering questions about work-related problems. They must know how to perform the tasks assigned to those they supervise if they are to be effective managers.

Interpersonal Skills Managers spend considerable time interacting with people both inside and outside the organization. For obvious reasons, then, the manager also needs **interpersonal skills**—the ability to communicate with, understand, and motivate individuals and groups. As a manager climbs the organizational ladder, he or she must be able to get along with subordinates, peers, and those at higher levels of the organization. Because of the multitude of roles managers must play, a manager must also be able to work with suppliers, customers, investors, and others outside of the organization.

Conceptual Skills **Conceptual skills** depend on the manager's ability to think in the abstract. Managers need the mental capacity to understand the overall workings of the organization and its environment, to grasp how all the parts of the organization fit together, and to view the organization in a holistic manner. This allows them to think strategically, to see the "big picture," and to make broad-based decisions that serve the overall organization.

Diagnostic Skills Successful managers also possess **diagnostic skills**, or skills that enable a manager to visualize the most appropriate response to a situation. A physician diagnoses a patient's illness by analyzing symptoms and determining

Figure 1.2
The Management Process
Management involves four basic activities—planning and decision making, organizing, leading, and controlling. Although there is a basic logic for describing these activities in this sequence (as indicated by the solid arrows), most managers engage in more than one activity at a time and often move between the activities in unpredictable ways (as shown by the dotted arrows).

controlling Monitoring organizational progress toward goal attainment

technical skills The skills necessary to accomplish or understand tasks relevant to the organization

interpersonal skills The ability to communicate with, understand, and motivate both individuals and groups

conceptual skills The manager's ability to think in the abstract

diagnostic skills The manager's ability to visualize the most appropriate response to a situation

MANAGEMENT INFOTECH

MANAGING E-COMMERCE DELIVERIES

When a consumer clicks to make a purchase online, United Parcel Service (UPS) wants to deliver the package. Because other shippers are also jockeying for position in e-commerce delivery, UPS's managers will need skillful planning, organizing, leading, and controlling to stay ahead of the pack.

UPS ships more than half of all consumer e-commerce purchases, whereas the U.S. Postal Service ships about one-third and FedEx ships just one-tenth. But all three companies want more of this fast-growing market, which could top 4.2 million packages daily within a few years.

Knowing that the stakes are high, UPS CEO James Kelly starts the planning process by setting strategic goals. A top priority is building UPS into the leading shipper of online purchases to any destination. From there, other management decisions—such as investing in sophisticated technology to track packages—are designed to bring UPS closer to its goals.

Organizing to implement these decisions, UPS has combined its air express and ground shipping businesses so that customers can arrange for any delivery with one phone call. Kelly, like nearly every top manager, started his career driving a UPS truck, so he has firsthand knowledge of what employees can and should be doing to stay ahead of competitors.

As Kelly and his top managers rose through the ranks, they forged connections with other managers and employees, and learned what works (and doesn't work) when leading and motivating the UPS workforce. Profit sharing is a powerful incentive, for example, as is the opportunity to own company stock now that UPS has gone public.

Controlling is vital in the shipping business, where customers demand on-time delivery. UPS managers use technology to track every shipment and to analyze the productivity of personnel and other resources. The system runs so smoothly that UPS now offers a money-back guarantee for ground shipments. By monitoring progress and making corrections as needed, Kelly and his managers are keeping UPS on course to remain the leader in e-commerce delivery.

> *We are going to involve ourselves in global commerce more deeply and more extensively than ever.*
>
> —*James Kelly, CEO, United Parcel Service**

References: Brian O'Reilly, "They've Got Mail!" *Fortune,* February 7, 2000, pp. 100–112 (*quote on p. 103); David Rocks, "Going Nowhere Fast in Cyberspace," *Business Week,* January 31, 2000, pp. 58–59.

---

their probable cause. Similarly, a manager can diagnose and analyze a problem in the organization by studying its symptoms and then developing a solution.

communication skills The manager's abilities to both effectively convey ideas and information to others and to effectively receive ideas and information from others

Communication Skills   **Communication skills** refer to the manager's abilities to effectively convey ideas and information to others and to effectively receive ideas and information from others. These skills enable a manager to transmit ideas to subordinates so that they know what is expected, to coordinate work with peers and colleagues so that they work well together properly, and to keep higher-level managers informed about what is going on. In addition, they help the manager listen to what others say and to understand the real meaning behind letters, reports, and other written communication.

decision-making skills The manager's ability to correctly recognize and define problems and opportunities, and then to select an appropriate course of action to solve problems and capitalize on opportunities

Decision-making Skills   Effective managers also have good decision-making skills. **Decision-making skills** refer to the manager's ability to correctly recognize and define problems and opportunities and to then select an appropriate course of action to solve problems and capitalize on opportunities. No manager makes the right decision all the time. However, effective managers make good decisions most of the time. And, when they do make a bad decision, they usually recognize their mistake quickly and then make good decisions to recover with as little cost or damage to their organization as possible.

Time Management Skills Finally, effective managers usually have good time management skills. **Time management skills** refer to the manager's ability to prioritize work, to work efficiently, and to delegate appropriately. As already noted, managers face many different pressures and challenges. It is all too easy for a manager to get bogged down doing work that can easily be postponed or delegated to others. When this happens, unfortunately, more pressing and higher-priority work may get neglected.

The Science and the Art of Management

Given the complexity inherent in the manager's job, a reasonable question relates to whether management is a science or an art. In fact, effective management is a blend of both science and art. And successful executives recognize the importance of combining both the science and the art of management as they practice their craft.[5]

Management is an important part of any organization, regardless of its size or mission. Luke Davis combines his business acumen with technical skills as he reaches out to a wide array of different kinds of organizations and offers his services as a web site designer. Here, for instance, he is demonstrating the new web site he designed for the Tyburn Convent in London. Davis has become quite successful by focusing on diverse kinds of religious, civic, and social organizations.

time management skills The manager's ability to prioritize work, to work efficiently, and to delegate appropriately

The Science of Management Many management problems and issues can be approached in ways that are rational, logical, objective, and systematic. Managers can gather data, facts, and objective information. They can use quantitative models and decision-making techniques to arrive at "correct" decisions. And they need to take such a scientific approach to solving problems whenever possible, especially when they are dealing with relatively routine and straightforward issues. When Starbucks considers entering a new market, its managers look closely at a wide variety of objective details as they formulate their plans. Technical, diagnostic, and decision-making skills are especially important when practicing the science of management.

The Art of Management Even though managers may try to be scientific as much as possible, they must often make decisions and solve problems on the basis of intuition, experience, instinct, and personal insights. Relying heavily on conceptual, communication, interpersonal, and time management skills, for example, a manager may have to decide between multiple courses of action that look equally attractive. Further, at any given time, as illustrated in the cartoon, a manager is

Managers are constantly engaged in many different activities. The types and sequences of activities are often difficult to predict from one day to the next, however, and managers often do their work in impromptu settings or on airplanes, in taxis, over meals, or even when walking down the street. The manager shown here, for example, may be helping a colleague develop goals for the next quarter (planning), discussing a proposed company restructuring (organizing), praising a subordinate for outstanding performance (leading), or checking on last month's sales information (controlling). The pace of this work may be stressful for some people, and exhilarating for others.

"*Do you mind? I happen to be on the phone!*"

© The New Yorker Collection 1996 Sam Gross from cartoon bank.com. All rights reserved.

likely to be engaged in several different activities simultaneously. And even "objective facts" may prove to be wrong. When Starbucks was planning its first store in New York, market research clearly showed that New Yorkers preferred drip coffee to more exotic espresso-style coffees. After first installing more drip coffee makers and fewer espresso makers than in their other stores, managers had to backtrack when New Yorkers lined up clamoring for espresso. Starbucks now introduces a standard menu and layout in all its stores, regardless of presumed market differences, and then makes necessary adjustments later. Thus managers must blend an element of intuition and personal insight with hard data and objective facts.

The Evolution of Management

Most managers today recognize the importance of history and theory in their work. For example, knowing the origins of their organization and the kinds of practices that have led to success—or failure—can be an indispensable tool in managing the contemporary organization. Thus in our next section we briefly trace the history of management thought. Then we move forward to the present day by introducing contemporary management issues and challenges.

The Importance of Theory and History

Some people question the value of history and theory. Their arguments are usually based on the assumptions that history has no relevance to contemporary society and that theory is abstract and of no practical use. In reality, however, both theory and history are important to all managers today.

A theory is simply a conceptual framework for organizing knowledge and providing a blueprint for action. Although some theories seem abstract and irrelevant, others appear very simple and practical. Management theories, used to build organizations and guide them toward their goals, are grounded in reality.[6] In addition, most managers develop and refine their own theories of how they should run their organization and manage the behavior of their employees.

An awareness and understanding of important historical developments are also important to contemporary managers.[7] Understanding the historical context of management provides a sense of heritage and can help managers avoid the mistakes of others. Most courses in U.S. history devote time to business and economic developments in this country, including the Industrial Revolution, the early labor movement, and the Great Depression, and to such captains of U.S. industry as Cornelius Vanderbilt (railroads), John D. Rockefeller (oil), and Andrew Carnegie (steel). The contributions of these and other industrialists left a profound imprint on contemporary culture.[8] And in recent years, new business history books have appeared that are directed more toward women managers and the lessons they can learn from the past.[9] Wells Fargo & Company, Polaroid, Shell Oil, Levi Strauss, Ford, Lloyd's of London, Disney, Honda, and Unilever all maintain significant archives about their past and frequently evoke images from that past in their orientation and training programs, advertising campaigns, and other public relations activities.

The Historical Context of Management

The practice of management can be traced back thousands of years. The Egyptians used the management functions of planning, organizing, and controlling when they constructed the great pyramids. Alexander the Great employed a staff organization to coordinate activities during his military campaigns. The Roman Empire developed a well-defined organizational structure that greatly facilitated communication and control.

In spite of this history, however, the study of management did not begin until the nineteenth century. Two of its first true pioneers were Robert Owen and Charles Babbage. Owen (1771–1858), a British industrialist and reformer, was one of the first managers to recognize the importance of an organization's human resources and the welfare of workers. Babbage (1792–1871), an English mathematician, focused his attention on efficiencies of production. He placed great faith in the division of labor and advocated the application of mathematics to problems such as the efficient use of facilities and materials.

The Classical Management Perspective

At the dawn of the twentieth century, the preliminary ideas and writings of these and other managers and theorists converged with the emergence and evolution of large-scale businesses and management practices to create interest and focus attention on how businesses should be operated. The first important ideas to emerge are now called the **classical management perspective**. This perspective actually includes two different viewpoints: scientific management and administrative management.

classical management perspective Consists of two distinct branches: scientific management and administrative management

Scientific Management   Productivity emerged as a serious business problem during the first few years of the twentieth century. Business was expanding and capital was readily available, but labor was in short supply. Hence, managers began to search for ways to use existing labor more efficiently. In response to this need, experts began to focus on ways to improve the performance of individual workers. Their work led to the development of **scientific management**. Some of the earliest advocates of scientific management included Frederick W. Taylor (1856–1915), Frank Gilbreth (1868–1924), and Lillian Gilbreth (1878–1972).[10]

scientific management Concerned with improving the performance of individual workers

One of Taylor's first jobs was as a foreman at the Midvale Steel Company in Philadelphia. It was there that he observed what he called **soldiering**—employees' deliberately working at a pace slower than their capabilities. Taylor studied and timed each element of the steelworkers' jobs. He determined what each worker should be producing, and then he designed the most efficient way to do each part of the overall task. Next, he implemented a piecework pay system. Rather than paying all employees the same wage, he began increasing the pay of each worker who met and exceeded the target level of output set for his or her job.

soldiering Employees' deliberately working at a slow pace

After Taylor left Midvale, he worked as a consultant for several companies, including Simonds Rolling Machine Company and Bethlehem Steel. At Simonds he studied and redesigned jobs, introduced rest periods to reduce fatigue, and implemented a piecework pay system. The results were higher quality and quantity of output, and improved morale. At Bethlehem Steel, Taylor studied efficient ways of loading and unloading rail cars and applied his conclusions with equally impressive results. During these experiences, he formulated the basic ideas that he called "scientific management." Figure 1.3 illustrates the basic steps Taylor suggested. He believed that managers who followed his guidelines would improve the efficiency of their workers.[11]

Taylor's work had a major impact on U.S. industry. By applying his principles, many organizations achieved major gains in efficiency. Taylor did have his critics, however. For instance, organized labor argued that scientific management was just a device to get more work from each employee and to reduce the total number of workers needed by a firm. There was a congressional investigation into Taylor's ideas, and evidence suggests that he falsified some of his findings.[12] Nevertheless, Taylor's work left a lasting imprint on business.[13]

Frank and Lillian Gilbreth, contemporaries of Taylor, were a husband-and-wife team of industrial engineers. One of Frank Gilbreth's most interesting contribu-

Figure 1.3

Steps in Scientific Management

Frederick Taylor developed this system of scientific management, which he believed would lead to a more efficient and productive workforce. Bethlehem Steel was among the first organizations to profit from scientific management and still practices some parts of it today.

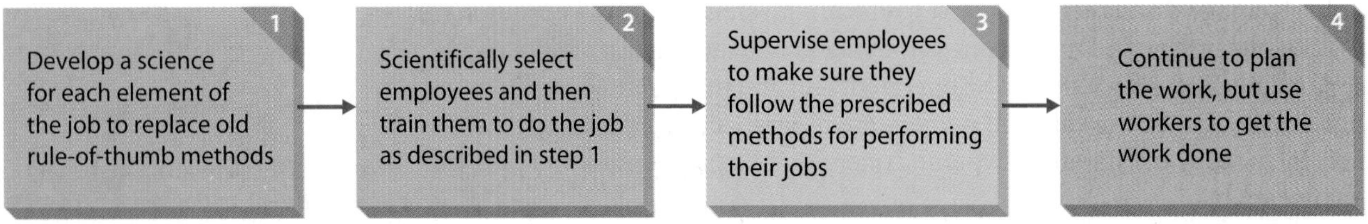

1	2	3	4
Develop a science for each element of the job to replace old rule-of-thumb methods	Scientifically select employees and then train them to do the job as described in step 1	Supervise employees to make sure they follow the prescribed methods for performing their jobs	Continue to plan the work, but use workers to get the work done

tions was to the craft of bricklaying. After studying bricklayers at work, he developed several procedures for doing the job more efficiently. For example, he specified standard materials and techniques, including the positioning of the bricklayer, the bricks, and the mortar at different levels. The results of these changes were a reduction from 18 separate physical movements to 5 and an increase in output of about 200 percent. Lillian Gilbreth made equally important contributions to several different areas of work, helped shape the field of industrial psychology, and made substantive contributions to the field of personnel management. Working individually and together, the Gilbreths developed numerous techniques and strategies for eliminating inefficiency. They applied many of their ideas to their family and documented their experiences raising 12 children in the book and movie *Cheaper by the Dozen.*

Administrative Management   Whereas scientific management deals with the jobs of individual employees, **administrative management** focuses on managing the total organization. The primary contributors to administrative management were Henri Fayol (1841–1925), Lyndall Urwick (1891–1983), and Max Weber (1864–1920).

administrative management
Focuses on managing the total organization

Henri Fayol was administrative management's most articulate spokesperson. A French industrialist, Fayol was unknown to U.S. managers and scholars until his most important work, *General and Industrial Management*, was translated into English in 1930.[14] Drawing on his own managerial experience, he attempted to systematize the practice of management to provide guidance and direction to other managers. Fayol also was the first to identify the specific managerial functions of planning, organizing, leading, and controlling. He believed that these functions accurately reflect the core of the management process. Most contemporary management books (including this one) still use this framework, and practicing managers agree that these functions are a critical part of their job.

After a career as a British army officer, Lyndall Urwick became a noted management theorist and consultant. He integrated scientific management with the work of Fayol and other administrative management theorists. He also advanced modern thinking about the functions of planning, organizing, and controlling. Like Fayol, he developed a list of guidelines for improving managerial effectiveness. Urwick is noted not so much for his own contributions as for his synthesis and integration of the work of others.

Although Max Weber lived and worked at the same time as Fayol and Taylor, his contributions were not recognized until some years had passed. Weber was a German sociologist, and his most important work was not translated into English until 1947.[15] Weber's work on bureaucracy laid the foundation for contemporary organization theory, discussed in detail in Chapter 6. The concept of bureaucracy, as we discuss later, is based on a rational set of guidelines for structuring organizations in the most efficient manner.

The Classical Perspective Today   The classical management perspective provides many techniques and approaches to management that are still relevant today. For example, thoroughly understanding the nature of the work being performed, selecting the right people for that work, and approaching decisions rationally are all useful ideas—and each was developed during this period. Similarly, some of the core concepts from Weber's bureaucratic model can still be used in the design of modern organizations, as long as their limitations are recognized. Managers should also recognize that efficiency and productivity can indeed be measured and controlled in many situations. On the other hand, managers must also recognize the limitations of the classical perspective and avoid its narrow focus on efficiency to the exclusion of other important perspectives.

The Behavioral Management Perspective

behavioral management perspective Emphasizes individual attitudes and behaviors and group processes

Early advocates of the classical management perspective essentially viewed organizations and jobs from a mechanistic point of view; that is, they essentially sought to conceptualize organizations as machines and workers as cogs within those machines. Even though many early writers recognized the role of individuals, their focus tended to be on how managers could control and standardize the behavior of their employees. In contrast, the **behavioral management perspective** placed much more emphasis on individual attitudes and behaviors and on group processes, and recognized the importance of behavioral processes in the workplace.

The behavioral management perspective was stimulated by a number of writers and theoretical movements. One of those movements was industrial psychology, the practice of applying psychological concepts to industrial settings. Hugo Munsterberg (1863–1916), a noted German psychologist, is recognized as the father of industrial psychology. Munsterberg suggested that psychologists could make valuable contributions to managers in the areas of employee selection and motivation. Industrial psychology is still a major course of study at many colleges and universities.

Another early advocate of the behavioral approach to management was Mary Parker Follett (1868–1933).[16] Follett worked during the scientific management era but quickly came to recognize the human element in the workplace. Indeed, her work clearly anticipated the behavioral management perspective, and she appreciated the need to understand the role of behavior in organizations.

The Hawthorne studies were a series of early experiments that focused on behavior in the workplace. In one experiment involving this group of workers, for example, researchers monitored how productivity changed as a result of changes in working conditions. The Hawthorne studies and subsequent experiments led scientists to the conclusion that the human element is very important in the workplace.

The Hawthorne Studies Although Munsterberg and Follett made major contributions to the development of the behavioral approach to management, its primary catalyst was a series of studies conducted near Chicago at Western Electric's Hawthorne plant between 1927 and 1932. The research, originally sponsored by General Electric, was conducted by Elton Mayo and his associates.[17] The first study involved manipulating illumination for one group of workers and comparing their subsequent productivity with the productivity of another group whose illumination was not changed. Surprisingly, when illumination was increased for the experimental group, productivity went up in both groups. Productivity continued to increase in both groups, even when the lighting for the experimental group was decreased. Not until the lighting was reduced to the level of moonlight did productivity begin to decline (and General Electric withdrew its sponsorship).

Another experiment established a piecework incentive pay plan for a group of nine men assembling terminal banks for telephone exchanges. Scientific management would have predicted that each man would try to maximize his pay by producing as many units as possible. Mayo and his associates, however, found that the group itself informally established an acceptable level of output for its members. Workers who overproduced were branded "rate busters," and underproducers were labeled "chiselers." To be accepted by the group, workers produced at the accepted level. As they approached this acceptable level of output, workers slacked off to avoid overproducing.

Other studies, including an interview program involving several thousand workers, led Mayo and his associates to conclude that human behavior was much more important in the workplace than had been previously believed. In the lighting experiment, for example, the results were attributed to the fact that both groups received special attention and sympathetic supervision for perhaps the first time. The incentive pay plans did not work because wage incentives were less important to the individual workers in determining output than was social acceptance. In short, individual and social processes played a major role in shaping worker attitudes and behavior.

Human Relations   The **human relations movement**, which grew from the Hawthorne studies and was a popular approach to management for many years, proposed that workers respond primarily to the social context of the workplace, including social conditioning, group norms, and interpersonal dynamics. A basic assumption of the human relations movement was that the manager's concern for workers would lead to increased satisfaction, which would in turn result in improved performance. Two writers who helped advance the human relations movement were Abraham Maslow and Douglas McGregor.

In 1943 Maslow advanced a theory suggesting that people are motivated by a hierarchy of needs, including monetary incentives and social acceptance.[18] Maslow's hierarchy, perhaps the best-known human relations theory, is described in detail in Chapter 10. Meanwhile, Douglas McGregor's Theory X and Theory Y model best represents the essence of the human relations movement (see Table 1.1).[19] According to McGregor, Theory X and Theory Y reflect two extreme belief sets that different managers have about their workers. **Theory X** is a relatively negative view of workers, consistent with the views of scientific management. **Theory Y** is more positive and represents the assumptions that human relations advocates make. In McGregor's view, Theory Y was a more appropriate philosophy for managers. Both Maslow and McGregor notably influenced the thinking of many practicing managers.

Contemporary Behavioral Science in Management   Munsterberg, Mayo, Maslow, McGregor, and others have made valuable contributions to management. Contemporary theorists, however, have noted that many assertions of the human relationists were simplistic and inadequate descriptions of work behavior. Current

human relations movement
Argued that workers respond primarily to the social context of the workplace

Theory X A pessimistic and negative view of workers consistent with the views of scientific management

Theory Y A positive view of workers, representing the assumptions that human relations advocates make

Table 1.1

Theory X and Theory Y

Douglas McGregor developed Theory X and Theory Y. He argued that Theory X best represented the views of scientific management and Theory Y represented the human relations approach. McGregor believed that Theory Y was the best philosophy for all managers.

Theory X Assumptions	1. People do not like work and try to avoid it. 2. People do not like work, so managers have to control, direct, coerce, and threaten employees to get them to work toward organizational goals. 3. People prefer to be directed, to avoid responsibility, and to want security; they have little ambition.
Theory Y Assumptions	1. People do not naturally dislike work; work is a natural part of their lives. 2. People are internally motivated to reach objectives to which they are committed. 3. People are committed to goals to the degree that they receive personal rewards when they reach their objectives. 4. People will both seek and accept responsibility under favorable conditions. 5. People have the capacity to be innovative in solving organizational problems. 6. People are bright, but under most organizational conditions their potential is underutilized.

Source: Douglas McGregor, *The Human Side of Enterprise,* pp. 33–34; 47–48, © 1960, reproduced with permission of The McGraw-Hill Companies.

organizational behavior Contemporary field focusing on behavioral perspectives on management

behavioral perspectives on management, best reflected by the field of **organizational behavior**, acknowledge that human behavior in organizations is much more complex than the human relationists realized. The field of organizational behavior draws from a broad, interdisciplinary base of psychology, sociology, anthropology, economics, and medicine.

Organizational behavior theory takes a holistic view of behavior and addresses individual, group, and organizational processes. These processes are major elements in contemporary management theory.[20] Important topics in this field include job satisfaction, stress, motivation, leadership, group dynamics, organizational politics, interpersonal conflict, and the structure and design of organizations.[21] A contingency orientation also characterizes the field (discussed more fully later in this chapter). Our discussions of organizing (Chapters 6–8) and leading (Chapters 9–13) are heavily influenced by the field of organizational behavior.

The Behavioral Perspective Today   The primary contributions of the behavioral perspective relate to ways in which this approach has changed managerial thinking. Managers are now more likely to recognize the importance of behavioral processes and to view employees as valuable resources instead of mere tools. On the other hand, organizational behavior theory is still imprecise in its ability to predict behavior. It is not always accepted or understood by practicing managers. Hence, the contributions of the behavioral school have yet to be fully realized.

The Quantitative Management Perspective

The third major school of management thought began to emerge during World War II. During the war, government officials and scientists in England and the United States worked to help the military deploy its resources more efficiently and effectively. These groups took some of the mathematical approaches to management developed decades earlier by Taylor and Gantt, and applied them to logistical problems during the war.[22] They learned that problems regarding troop, equipment, and submarine deployment, for example, could all be solved through mathematical analysis. After the war, companies such as Du Pont and General Electric began to use the same techniques for deploying employees, choosing plant locations, and planning warehouses. Basically, then, this perspective is concerned with applying quantitative techniques to management. More specifically, the **quantitative management perspective** focuses on decision making, economic effectiveness, mathematical models, and the use of computers. There are two branches of the quantitative approach: management science and operations management.

quantitative management perspective Applies quantitative techniques to management

Management Science   Unfortunately, the term *management science* appears to be related to scientific management, the approach developed by Taylor and others early in the twentieth century. But the two have little in common and should not be confused. **Management science** focuses specifically on the development of mathematical models. A mathematical model is a simplified representation of a system, process, or relationship.

management science Focuses specifically on the development of mathematical models

At its most basic level, management science focuses on models, equations, and similar representations of reality. For example, managers at Detroit Edison use mathematical models to determine how best to route repair crews during blackouts. The Bank of New England uses models to figure out how many tellers need to be on duty at each location at various times throughout the day. In recent years, paralleling the advent of the personal computer, management science techniques have become increasingly sophisticated. For example, automobile manufacturer DaimlerChrysler uses realistic computer simulations to study collision damage to cars. These simulations give them precise information and avoid the costs of crashing so many test cars.

Operations Management   Operations management is somewhat less mathematical and statistically sophisticated than management science and can be applied more directly to managerial situations. Indeed, we can think of **operations management** as a form of applied management science. Operations management techniques are generally concerned with helping the organization produce its products or services more efficiently and can be applied to a wide range of problems.

operations management Concerned with helping the organization more efficiently produce its products or services

For example, Rubbermaid and Home Depot use operations management techniques to manage their inventories. (Inventory management is concerned with specific inventory problems, such as balancing carrying costs and ordering costs, and determining the optimal order quantity.) Linear programming (which involves computing simultaneous solutions to a set of linear equations) helps United Air Lines to plan its flight schedules, Consolidated Freightways to develop its shipping routes, and General Instrument Corporation to plan what instruments to produce at various times. Other operations management techniques include queuing theory, breakeven analysis, and simulation. All of these techniques and procedures apply directly to operations, but they are also helpful in such areas as finance, marketing, and human resource management.

The Quantitative Perspective Today   Like the other management perspectives, the quantitative management perspective has made important contributions and has certain limitations. It has provided managers with an abundance of decision-making tools and techniques, and has increased understanding of overall organizational processes. It has been particularly useful in the areas of planning and controlling. On the other hand, mathematical models cannot fully account for individual behaviors and attitudes. Some believe that the time needed to develop competence in quantitative techniques retards the development of other managerial skills. Finally, mathematical models typically require a set of assumptions that may not be realistic.

Contemporary Management Thought

It is important to recognize that the classical, behavioral, and quantitative approaches to management are not necessarily contradictory or mutually exclusive. Even though each of the three perspectives makes very different assumptions and predictions, each can also complement the others. Indeed, a complete understanding of management requires an appreciation of all three perspectives. The systems and contingency perspectives can help us integrate the earlier approaches and enlarge our understanding of all three.

The Systems Perspective

The systems perspective is one important contemporary management theory. A **system** is an interrelated set of elements functioning as a whole.[23] As shown in Figure 1.4, by viewing an organization as a system, we can identify four basic elements: inputs, transformation processes, outputs, and feedback. First, inputs are the material, human, financial, and information resources the organization gets from its environment. Next, through technological and managerial processes, inputs are transformed into outputs. Outputs include products, services, or both (tangible and intangible); profits, losses, or both (even not-for-profit organizations

system An interrelated set of elements functioning as a whole

Figure 1.4

The Systems Perspective of Organizations

By viewing organizations as systems, managers can better understand the importance of their environment and the level of interdependence among subsystems within the organization. Managers must also understand how their decisions affect and are affected by other subsystems within the organization.

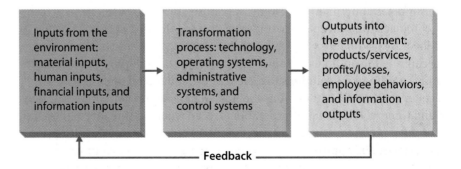

must operate within their budgets); employee behaviors; and information. Finally, the environment reacts to these outputs and provides feedback to the system.

Thinking of organizations as systems provides us with a variety of important viewpoints on organizations, such as the concepts of open systems, subsystems, synergy, and entropy. **Open systems** are systems that interact with their environment, whereas **closed systems** do not interact with their environment. Although organizations are open systems, some make the mistake of ignoring their environment and behaving as though their environment is not important.

The systems perspective also stresses the importance of **subsystems**—systems within a broader system. For example, the marketing, production, and finance functions within Mattel are systems in their own right but also subsystems within the overall organization. Because they are interdependent, a change in one subsystem can affect other subsystems as well. If the production department at Mattel lowers the quality of the toys being made (by buying lower-quality materials, for example), the effects are felt in finance (improved cash flow in the short run owing to lower costs) and marketing (decreased sales in the long run because of customer dissatisfaction). Managers must therefore remember that, although organizational subsystems can be managed with some degree of autonomy, their interdependence should not be overlooked.

Synergy suggests that organizational units (or subsystems) may often be more successful working together than working alone. The Walt Disney Company, for example, benefits greatly from synergy. The company's movies, theme parks, television programs, and merchandise licensing programs all benefit one another. Children who enjoy a Disney movie like *Tarzan* want to go to Disney World, see the Tarzan show there, and buy stuffed animals of the film's characters. Music from the film generates additional revenues for the firm, as do computer games and other licensing arrangements for lunchboxes, clothing, and so forth. Synergy is an important concept for managers because it emphasizes the importance of working together in a cooperative and coordinated fashion.

Finally, **entropy** is a normal process that leads to system decline. When an organization does not monitor feedback from its environment and make appropriate adjustments, it may fail. For example, witness the problems of Studebaker (an automobile manufacturer) and Montgomery Ward (a major retailer). Each of these organizations went bankrupt because it failed to revitalize itself and keep pace with changes in its environment. A primary objective of management, from a systems perspective, is to continually re-energize the organization to avoid entropy.

The Contingency Perspective

Another recent noteworthy addition to management thinking is the contingency perspective. The classical, behavioral, and quantitative approaches are considered **universal perspectives**, because they tried to identify the "one best way" to manage organizations. The **contingency perspective**, in contrast, suggests that universal theories cannot be applied to organizations, because each organization is unique. Instead, the contingency perspective suggests that appropriate managerial behavior in a given situation depends on, or is contingent on, unique elements in that situation.[24]

open system An organizational system that interacts with its environment

closed system An organizational system that does not interact with its environment

subsystem A system within another system

synergy Two or more subsystems working together to produce more than the total of what they might produce working alone

entropy A normal process leading to system decline

universal perspective An attempt to identify the "one best way" to do something

contingency perspective Suggests that appropriate managerial behavior in a given situation depends on, or is contingent on, a wide variety of elements

Stated differently, effective managerial behavior in one situation cannot always be generalized to other situations. Recall, for example, that Frederick Taylor assumed that all workers would generate the highest possible level of output to maximize their own personal economic gain. We can imagine some people being motivated primarily by money—but we can just as easily imagine other people being motivated by the desire for leisure time, status, social acceptance, or any combination of these (as Mayo found at the Hawthorne plant). This perspective relates perfectly to Leslie Wexner and The Limited, featured in the opening incident. His managerial style worked perfectly when his firm was small and rapidly growing but did not match as well when The Limited became a huge, mature enterprise. Thus Wexner had to alter his style at that point to better fit the changing needs of his business.

Contemporary Management Issues and Challenges

Managers today also face an imposing set of challenges as they guide and direct the fortunes of their companies. Coverage of each topic, introduced next, is thoroughly integrated throughout this book.

One of the most critical challenges facing managers in 1999 and 2000 was a labor shortage in the high-tech sector. This pattern manifests itself in several ways. First, companies in high-tech markets have found that they must offer lavish benefits and high salaries to attracted talented and motivated employees. And, even though they continue to provide an ever-growing array of benefits, many of these same employees still move on to other—and more lucrative—jobs more quickly than at any other time in recent memory. This trend has also trickled down to lower-skills jobs as well. Many hotels and restaurants, for example, are having difficulties in maintaining an adequate staff of house cleaners and dishwashers because of the abundance of more attractive jobs available today.[25] But the economic slowdown in 2001 decreased the demand for some workers and at least temporarily curtailed this management challenge.

A second important challenge today is the management of diversity. Diversity refers to differences among people. Although diversity may be reflected along numerous dimensions, most managers tend to focus on age, gender, ethnicity, and physical abilities or disabilities. The internationalization of businesses has also increased diversity in many organizations, carrying with it additional challenges as well as new opportunities.

Aside from demographic composition, the workforce today is also changing in other ways. It seems as if the values, goals, and ideals of each succeeding generation differ from those of their parents. Today's young workers, for example, are sometimes stereotyped as being less devoted to long-term career prospects and less willing to conform to a corporate mindset that stresses conformity and uniformity. Thus managers are increasingly faced with the challenge of first creating an environment that will be attractive to today's worker. And they must address the challenge of providing new and different incentives to keep people motivated and interested in their work. Finally, they must incorporate sufficient flexibility in the organization to accommodate an ever-changing set of lifestyles and preferences.

Another management challenge that managers must be prepared to address is change. Although organizations have always had to be concerned with managing change, the rapid and constant environmental change faced by businesses today has made change management even more critical. Simply put, an organization that fails to monitor its environment and to change to keep pace with that environment is doomed to failure. But more and more managers are seeing change as an opportunity, not as a cause for alarm. Indeed, some managers think that, if things get too calm in an organization and people start to become complacent, managers should shake things up to get everyone energized.

New technology, especially as it relates to information, also poses an increasingly important management challenge. The Internet and the increased use of e-mail and voice-mail systems are among the most recent technological changes in this area. Among the key issues associated with information technology are employee privacy, decision-making quality, and optimizing a firm's investments in new forms of technology as they continue to emerge. A related issue confronting managers has to do with the increased capabilities this technology provides for people to work at places other than their office. Finally, the appropriate role of the Internet in business strategy is also a complex arena for managers. That is, managers must make decisions regarding the role of the Internet throughout their operations, including purchasing, marketing, and human resources.

Another important management challenge today is the complex array of new ways of organizing which managers can consider. Many organizations are seeking greater flexibility and the ability to respond more quickly to their environment by adopting flat structures. These flat structures are characterized by few levels of management; broad, wide spans of management (the number of individuals reporting to a specific manager); and fewer rules and regulations. The increased use of work teams also goes hand in hand with this new approach to organizing.

Globalization is yet another significant contemporary challenge for managers.[26] Managing in a global economy poses many different challenges and opportunities. For example, at a macro level, property ownership arrangements vary widely. So does the availability of natural resources and components of the infrastructure, as well as the role of government in business. But, for our purposes, a very important consideration is how behavioral processes vary widely across cultural and national boundaries. For example, values, symbols, and beliefs differ sharply among cultures. Different work norms and the role work plays in a person's life, for example, influence patterns of both work-related behavior and attitudes toward work. They also affect the nature of supervisory relationships, decision-making styles and processes, and organizational configurations.

Another management challenge that has taken on renewed importance is the area of ethics and social responsibility. Unfortunately, business scandals have become almost commonplace today. From the social responsibility angle, increasing attention has been focused on pollution and business's obligation to help clean up our environment, business contributions to social causes, and so forth.

Quality also continues to pose an important management challenge today. Quality is an important issue for several reasons. First, more and more organizations are using quality as a basis for competition. Continental Airlines, for example, stresses its high rankings in the J. D. Powers survey of customer satisfaction with print advertising. Second, improving quality tends to increase productivity, because making higher-quality products generally results in less waste and rework. Third, enhancing quality lowers costs. Whistler Corporation once found that it was using 100 of its 250 employees to repair defective radar detectors that were built incorrectly the first time. Quality is also important because of its relationship to productivity.

Finally, the shift toward a service economy also continues to be important. Traditionally, most businesses were manufacturers—they used tangible resources like raw materials and machinery to create tangible products like automobiles and steel. In the last few decades, however, the service sector of the economy has become much more important. Indeed, services now account for well over half of the gross domestic product (GDP) in the United States and play a similarly important role in many other industrialized nations. Service technology involves the use of both tangible resources (such as machinery) and intangible resources (such as intellectual property) to create intangible services (such as a haircut, insurance protection, or transportation between two cities). Although there are obviously many similarities between managing in a manufacturing and in a service organization, there are also many fundamental differences.

Summary of Key Points

Management is a set of functions directed at achieving organizational goals in an efficient and effective manner. A manager is someone whose primary responsibility is to carry out the management process within an organization. Managers can be differentiated by level and by area. By level, we can identify top, middle, and first-line managers. Kinds of managers by area include marketing, financial, operations, human resource, administrative, and specialized managers.

The basic activities that comprise the management process are planning and decision making, organizing, leading, and controlling. These activities are not performed on a systematic and predictable schedule. Effective managers also tend to have technical, interpersonal, conceptual, diagnostic, communication, decision-making, and time management skills. The effective practice of management requires a synthesis of science and art; that is, a blend of rational objectivity and intuitive insight.

Theories are important as organizers of knowledge and as roadmaps for action. Understanding the historical context and precursors of management and organizations provides a sense of heritage and can also help managers avoid repeating the mistakes of others. Evidence

suggests that interest in management dates back thousands of years, but a scientific approach to management has emerged only in the last hundred years.

The classical management perspective had two major branches: scientific management and administrative management. Scientific management was concerned with improving efficiency and work methods for individual workers. Administrative management was more concerned with how organizations themselves should be structured and arranged for efficient operations. Both branches paid little attention to the role of the worker.

The behavioral management perspective, characterized by a concern for individual and group behavior, emerged primarily as a result of the Hawthorne studies. The human relations movement recognized the importance and potential of behavioral processes in organizations but made many overly simplistic assumptions about those processes. Organizational behavior, a more realistic outgrowth of the behavioral perspective, is of interest to many contemporary managers.

The quantitative management perspective and its two components, management science and operations management, attempt to apply quantitative techniques to decision making and problem solving. These areas are also of considerable importance to contemporary managers. The contributions of quantitative management have been facilitated by the tremendous increase in the use of personal computers and integrated information networks.

Two relatively recent additions to management theory, the systems and contingency perspectives, appear to have great potential both as approaches to management and as frameworks for integrating the other perspectives. Challenges facing managers today include a high-tech labor shortage, diversity and the new work force, change, information technology, new ways of organizing, globalization, ethics and social responsibility, the importance of quality, and the continued shift toward a service economy.

Discussion Questions

Questions for Review

1. What are the four basic functions that comprise the management process? How are they related to one another?
2. Identify different kinds of managers by both level and area in the organization.
3. Identify the different important skills that help managers succeed. Give an example of each.
4. Briefly summarize the classical and behavioral management perspectives and identify the most important contributors to each.
5. Describe the contingency perspective and outline its usefulness to the study and practice of management.

Questions for Analysis

6. The text notes that management is both a science and an art. Is one of these aspects more important than the other? Under what circumstances might one ingredient be more important than the other?
7. Recall a recent group project or task in which you have participated. Explain how the four basic management functions were performed.
8. Some people argue that CEOs in the United States are paid too much. Find out the pay for a CEO and discuss whether you think he or she is overpaid.
9. Explain how a manager can use tools and techniques from each major management perspective in a complementary fashion.
10. Which of the contemporary management challenges do you think will have the greatest impact on you and your career? Which will have the least?

BUILDING EFFECTIVE *technical* SKILLS

Exercise Overview

Technical skills refer to the manager's abilities to accomplish or understand work done in an organization. More and more managers today are realizing that having the technical ability to use the Internet is an important part of communication, decision making, and other facets of their work. This exercise introduces you to the Internet and provides some practice in using it.

Exercise Background

The so-called information highway, or the Internet, refers to an interconnected network of information and information-based resources using computers and computer systems. Whereas electronic mail was perhaps the first widespread application of the Internet, increasingly popular applications are based on home pages and search engines.

A *home page* is a file (or set of files) created by an individual, business, or other entity. It contains whatever information its creator chooses to include. For example, a company might create a home page for itself that includes its logo, its address and telephone number, information about its products and services, and so forth. An individual seeking employment might create a home page that includes a résumé and a statement of career interests. Home pages are indexed by key words chosen by their creators.

A *search engine* is a system through which an Internet user can search for home pages according to their indexed key words. For example, suppose an individual is interested in knowing more about art collecting. Key words that might logi-

cally be linked to home pages related to this interest include art, artists, galleries, and framing. A search engine will take these key words and provide a listing of all home pages that are indexed to them. The user can then browse each page to see what information they contain. Popular search engines include Yahoo!, Lycos, and Webcrawler.

Exercise Task

1. Visit your computer center and learn how to get access to the Internet.
2. Use a search engine to conduct a search for three or four terms related to general management (for example, management, organization, business).
3. Now select a more specific management topic and search for two or three topics (if you cannot think of any terms, scan the margin notes in this book).
4. Finally, select three or four companies and search for their home pages.

BUILDING EFFECTIVE *diagnostic* SKILLS

Exercise Overview

Diagnostic skills enable a manager to visualize the most appropriate response to a situation. This exercise encourages you to apply your diagnostic skills to a real business problem and to assess the possible consequences of various courses of action.

Exercise Background

For some time now, college textbook publishers have been struggling with a significant problem. The subject matter that constitutes a particular field, such as management, chemistry, or history, continues to increase in size, scope, and complexity. Thus authors feel compelled to add more and more information to new editions of their textbooks. Publishers have also sought to increase the visual sophistication of their texts by adding more color and photographs. At the same time, some instructors don't have time to

cover the material in longer textbooks. Moreover, longer and more attractive textbooks cost more money to produce, resulting in higher selling prices to students.

Publishers have considered a variety of options to confront this situation. One option is to work with authors to produce briefer and more economical books (such as this one). Another option is to cut back on the complimentary supplements that publishers provide to instructors (such as videos and color transparencies) as a way of lowering the overall cost of producing a book. Another option is to eliminate traditional publishing altogether and provide educational resources via CD-ROM, the Internet, or other new media.

Confounding the situation, of course, is cost. Profit margins in the industry are such that managers feel the need to be cautious and conservative. That is, they cannot do everything and must not risk alienating their users by taking too radical a step. Remember, too, that publishers must consider the concerns of three different sets of customers: the instructors who make adoption decisions, the bookstores that buy educational materials for resale (at a retail markup), and students who buy the books for classroom use and then often resell them back to the bookstore.

Exercise Task

With this background in mind, respond to the following:

1. Discuss the pros and cons of each option currently being considered by textbook publishers.
2. Identify the likely consequences of each option.
3. Can you think of other alternatives that publishers in the industry should consider?
4. What specific recommendations would you make to an executive in a publishing company regarding this set of issues?

BUILDING EFFECTIVE *communication & interpersonal* SKILLS

Exercise Overview

Communication skills refer to the manager's abilities both to effectively convey ideas and information to others and to effectively receive ideas and information from others. Interpersonal skills refer to the ability to communicate with, understand, and motivate individuals and groups. This exercise applies these skills from a contingency perspective in selecting modes of communication to convey various kinds of news.

Exercise Background

You are the regional branch manager for a large insurance company. For the last week, you have been so tied up in meetings that you have had little opportunity to communicate with any of your subordinates. You have now caught up on things, however, and have a lot of information to convey. Specifically, here are the things that people need to know or that you need to do:

1. Three people need to be told that they are getting a pay raise of 10 percent.
2. One person needs to be told that she has been placed on probation and will lose her job if her excessive absenteeism problem isn't corrected.

3. One person needs to be congratulated for receiving his master's degree.
4. Everyone needs to be informed about the schedule for the next cycle of performance reviews.
5. Two people need to be informed that their requests for transfers have been approved, whereas a third was denied. In addition, one other person is being transferred even though she did not submit a transfer request. You know that she will be unhappy.

You can convey this information via telephone calls during regular office hours, a cell phone call as you're driving home this evening, a formal written letter, a handwritten memo, a face-to-face meeting, or e-mail.

Exercise Task

With this background in mind, respond to the following:

1. Choose a communication mode for each message you need to convey.
2. What factors went into your decision about each situation?
3. What would be the least appropriate communication mode for each message?
4. What would be the likely consequences for each inappropriate choice?

SKILLS *self-assessment* INSTRUMENT

Self-Awareness

Introduction: Self-awareness is an important skill for effective management. This assessment is designed to help you evaluate your level of self-awareness.

Instructions: Please respond to the following statements by writing a number from the following rating scale in the column. Your answers should reflect your attitudes and behavior as they are *now,* not as you would *like* them to be. Be honest. This instrument is designed to help you discover how self-aware you are so that you can tailor your learning to your specific needs.

Rating Scale

6	Strongly agree	**3**	Slightly disagree
5	Agree	**2**	Disagree
4	Slightly agree	**1**	Strongly disagree

_____ 1. I seek information about my strengths and weaknesses from others as a basis for self-improvement.

_____ 2. When I receive negative feedback about myself from others, I do not get angry or defensive.

_____ 3. In order to improve, I am willing to be self-disclosing to others (that is, to share my beliefs and feelings).

_____ 4. I am very much aware of my personal style of gathering information and making decisions about it.

_____ 5. I am very much aware of my own interpersonal needs when it comes to forming relationships with other people.

_____ 6. I have a good sense of how I cope with situations that are ambiguous and uncertain.

_____ 7. I have a well-developed set of personal standards and principles that guide my behavior.

_____ 8. I feel very much in charge of what happens to me, good and bad.

_____ 9. I seldom, if ever, feel angry, depressed, or anxious without knowing why.

_____ 10. I am conscious of the areas in which conflict and friction most frequently arise in my interactions with others.

_____ 11. I have a close relationship with at least one other person in which I can share personal information and personal feelings.

For interpretation, see Interpretations of Skills Self-Assessment Instruments.

Source: *Developing Management Skills* by Whetton, Cameron, © 1991. Reprinted by permission of Pearson Education, Inc., Upper Saddle River, NJ.

EXPERIENTIAL EXERCISE

Johari Window

Purpose: This exercise has two purposes: to encourage you to analyze yourself more accurately and to start you working on small-group cohesiveness. This exercise encourages you to share data about yourself and then to assimilate and process feedback. Small groups are typically more trusting and work better together, as you will be able to see after this exercise has been completed. The Johari Window is a particularly good model for understanding the perceptual process in interpersonal relationships.

This skill builder focuses on the *human resources model* and will help you develop your *mentor role.* One of the skills of a mentor is self-awareness.

Introduction: Each individual has four sets of personality characteristics. One set, which includes such characteristics as working hard, is

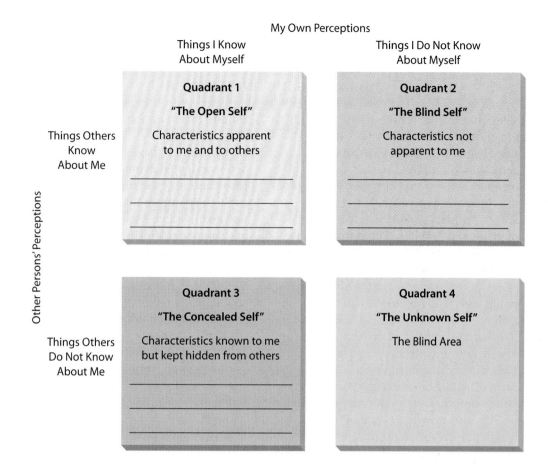

My Own Perceptions

	Things I Know About Myself	Things I Do Not Know About Myself
Things Others Know About Me	**Quadrant 1** "The Open Self" Characteristics apparent to me and to others	**Quadrant 2** "The Blind Self" Characteristics not apparent to me
Things Others Do Not Know About Me	**Quadrant 3** "The Concealed Self" Characteristics known to me but kept hidden from others	**Quadrant 4** "The Unknown Self" The Blind Area

Other Persons' Perceptions

well known to the individual and to others. A second set is unknown to the individual but obvious to others. For example, in a working situation, a peer might observe that your jumping in to get the group moving off dead center is appropriate. At other times, you jump in when the group is not really finished, and you seem to interrupt. A third set is known to the individual but not to others. These are situations that you have elected not to share, perhaps because of a lack of trust. Finally, there is a fourth set, which is not known to the individual or to others, such as why you are uncomfortable at office parties.

Instructions: Look at the Johari Window above. In quadrant 1, list three things that you know about yourself and that you think others know. List three things in quadrant 3 that others do not know about you. Finally, in quadrant 2, list three things that you did not know about yourself last semester that you learned from others.

Sources: Adapted from Joseph Luft, *Group Processes: An Introduction to Group Dynamics* (Palo Alto, CA: Mayfield, 1970), 10–11; William C. Morris and Marshall Sashkin, *Organizational Behavior in Action* (St. Paul, MN: West, 1976), 56.

MANAGING IN A WIRED WORLD

Although Amazon.com is not yet a decade old, it's already a case study in Internet success. Founded by Jeff Bezos in 1995 as an online bookstore, Seattle-based Amazon rings up more than $1.6 billion in e-commerce sales every year. First books, then music and videos, and now software, screwdrivers, and sofas—Amazon has grown into a virtual department store for its 17 million online customers worldwide. Even as successful chains such as Barnes & Noble and Wal-Mart try to grab a larger piece of the online retailing pie, CEO Bezos has maintained Amazon's market leadership and customer loyalty through constant innovation.

Nothing like Amazon existed when Bezos was researching software and the Internet for a New York City firm in 1994. He became intrigued by the business possibilities of selling books on the World Wide Web in much the same way that mail-order firms sell books by mail. This idea proved so compelling that Bezos quickly quit his job, raised money from family and friends, wrote a business plan, and moved out to Seattle to locate near a major book wholesaler. One year later, Amazon.com was open for business. In its first month, without advertising or public relations, the site attracted customers from every state in the Union and more than 40 other countries.

In those early days, the giant bookstore chains paid little attention to Amazon. Within two years, however, Amazon's discount prices, free e-mail book reviews, and easy search capabilities had attracted so many shoppers and so much media coverage that competitors started scrambling to open their own Internet bookstores. But Amazon's established reputation and loyal customer following were major hurdles for rivals to overcome. In fact, despite aggressive promotions and pricing, Barnesandnoble.com is still trying to catch up to Amazon's online sales and sizable customer base.

Meanwhile, Bezos has expanded into all kinds of products by buying stakes in e-commerce companies such as drugstore.com and pets.com. He's also set up an auction section on Amazon to tap the excitement generated by the success of eBay, the first Internet auction site. In addition, he made room on the Amazon site for zShops, an area where smaller businesses can, for a fee, sell products.

One reason for Amazon's success is founder Bezos's action-oriented management style. Although he carefully plans his company's future moves, he also wants to avoid the paralysis that can come from endless analysis and deliberation. As an e-commerce pioneer, Bezos is accustomed to making speedy decisions to take advantage of unexpected or fleeting opportunities. He encourages everyone at Amazon to do the same, even if that means an occasional misstep. Working on Internet time, Bezos would rather lead his troops into the unknown, and fix problems later, than slow down now.

To continue growing and innovating, Amazon must keep recruiting, training, and motivating good managers and employees. Bezos gets personally involved with hiring decisions about top managers, whom he trusts to hire the people who will work under them. Because he knows that a skilled workforce is critical to Amazon's success, Bezos asks probing questions about hiring techniques when he interviews top-management candidates.

Still, Bezos carves out precious time from his hectic management schedule to surf the Web, click around the Amazon site, and, on occasion, wander through shopping malls in search of new ideas. To stay in touch, he goes out of his way to thank specific employees for their efforts, and he reads e-mail messages from customers to find out what they like and don't like. About one-third of the CEO's time is devoted to visiting Amazon's national network of distribution centers, where he answers employee questions and reinforces the company's six "core values." These values include customer obsession, ownership, bias for action, frugality, high hiring bar, and innovation.

Every December, Bezos and his entire management team pitch in to meet the holiday rush. By wrapping packages for customer shipments or answering customer service phone calls, they all get a better sense of what Amazon's first-line managers and employees face—and what their customers want. This yearly tradition of hands-on experience also rekindles the managers' sense of purpose—no small consideration in an industry where change is the only constant.

Case Questions

1. Which managerial skills does Jeff Bezos appear to be emphasizing at Amazon?

2. How does Bezos carry out his interpersonal, informational, and decisional roles at Amazon?

3. Why are communication skills particularly vital for managers at a fast-growing firm like Amazon?

Case References

"Can Amazon Make It?" *Business Week*, July 11, 2000, pp. 38ff.; Miguel Helft, "Poster Boy Grows Up," *thestandard.com*, April 24, 2000, http://www.thestandard.com/article/display/0,1151,14264,00.html, June 2, 2000; George Anders, "Taming the Out-of-Control In-Box," *Wall Street Journal*, February 4, 2000, pp. B1, B4; Michael Krantz, "Cruising Inside Amazon," *Time*, December 27, 1999, pp. 68ff.; Joshua Cooper Ramo, "Jeffrey Preston Bezos: 1999 Person of the Year," *Time*, December 27, 1999, pp. 50ff.; and Joshua Quittner, "An Eye on the Future: Jeff Bezos Merely Wants Amazon.com to Be Earth's Biggest Seller of Everything," *Time*, December 27, 1999, pp. 56ff.

CHAPTER NOTES

1. "A Makeover That Began at the Top," *Wall Street Journal*, May 25, 2000, pp. B1, B4 (quote on p. B1); and *Hoover's Handbook of American Business 2001* (Austin, TX: Hoover's Business Press, 2001), pp. 870–871.

2. See "The Age of the $100 Million CEO," *Forbes*, April 3, 2000, pp. 122–129; and "Homes, Cars, Jets Among Perks Piling up for CEOs," *USA Today*, May 22, 2000, pp. 1B, 2B.

3. John P. Kotter, "What Effective General Managers Really Do," *Harvard Business Review*, March/April 1999, pp. 145–155.

4. See Robert L. Katz, "The Skills of an Effective Administrator," *Harvard Business Review*, September/October 1974, pp. 90–102, for a classic discussion of several of these skills.

5. Gary Hamel and C. K. Prahalad, "Competing for the Future," *Harvard Business Review*, July/August 1994, pp. 122–128.

6. Peter F. Drucker, "The Theory of the Business," *Harvard Business Review*, September/October 1994, pp. 95–104.

7. "Why Business History?" *Audacity*, Fall 1992, pp. 7–15. See also Alan L. Wilkins and Nigel J. Bristow, "For Successful Organization Culture, Honor Your Past," *Academy of Management Executive*, August 1987, pp. 221–227; and Andrea Gabor, *The Capitalist Philosophers* (New York: Times Business, 2000).

8. Daniel Wren, *The Evolution of Management Theory*, 4th ed. (New York: Wiley, 1994); and Page Smith, *The Rise of Industrial America* (New York: McGraw-Hill, 1984).

9. See Harriet Rubin, *The Princessa: Machiavelli for Women* (New York: Doubleday/Currency, 1997). See also Nanette Fondas, "Feminization Unveiled: Management Qualities in Contemporary Writings," *Academy of Management Review* (January 1997): 257–282.

10. Wren.

11. Frederick W. Taylor, *Principles of Scientific Management* (New York: Harper and Brothers, 1911).

12. Charles D. Wrege and Amedeo G. Perroni, "Taylor's Pig-Tale: A Historical Analysis of Frederick W. Taylor's Pig-Iron Experiment," *Academy of Management Journal* (March 1974): 6–27; and Charles D. Wrege and Ann Marie Stoka, "Cooke Creates a Classic: The Story Behind Taylor's Principles of Scientific Management," *Academy of Management Review* (October 1978): 736–749.

13. Robert Kanigel, *The One Best Way* (New York: Viking, 1997); and Oliver E. Allen, "This Great Mental Revolution," *Audacity*, Summer 1996, pp. 52–61.

14. Henri Fayol, *General and Industrial Management*, trans. J. A. Coubrough (Geneva: International Management Institute, 1930).

15. Max Weber, *Theory of Social and Economic Organizations*, trans. T. Parsons (New York: Free Press, 1947); and Richard M. Weis, "Weber on Bureaucracy: Management Consultant or Political Theorist?" *Academy of Management Review* (April 1983): 242–248.

16. Wren, pp. 255–264.

17. Elton Mayo, *The Human Problems of an Industrial Civilization* (New York: Macmillan, 1933); and Fritz J. Roethlisberger and William J. Dickson, *Management and the Worker* (Cambridge, MA: Harvard University Press, 1939).

18. Abraham Maslow, "A Theory of Human Motivation," *Psychological Review* (July 1943): 370–396.

19. Douglas McGregor, *The Human Side of Enterprise* (New York: McGraw-Hill, 1960).

20. Sara L. Rynes and Christine Quinn Trank, "Behavioral Science in the Business School Curriculum: Teaching in a Changing Institutional Environment," *Academy of Management Review* 24, no. 4 (1999): 808–824.

21. See Gregory Moorhead and Ricky W. Griffin, *Organizational Behavior*, 6th ed. (Boston: Houghton Mifflin, 2001), for a recent review of current developments in the field of organizational behavior.

22. Wren, chap. 21.

23. For more information on systems theory in general, see Ludwig von Bertalanffy, C. G. Hempel, R. E. Bass, and H. Jonas, "General Systems Theory: A New Approach to Unity of Science," I–VI, *Human Biology* 23 (1951): 302–361. For systems theory as applied to organizations, see Fremont E. Kast and James E. Rosenzweig, "General Systems Theory: Applications for Organizations and Management," *Academy of Management Journal* (December 1972): 447–465. For a recent update, see Donde P. Ashmos and George P. Huber, "The Systems Paradigm in Organization Theory: Correcting the Record and Suggesting the Future," *Academy of Management Review* (October 1987): 607–621.

24. Fremont E. Kast and James E. Rosenzweig, *Contingency Views of Organization and Management* (Chicago: Science Research Associates, 1973).

25. See Angelo S. DeNisi and Ricky W. Griffin, *Human Resource Management* (Boston: Houghton Mifflin, 2001), chap. 17.

26. See "Give Us This Day Our Global Bread," *Fast Company*, March 2001, pp. 158–169.

2 The Environment of Organizations and Managers

Most organizations operate within a complex network of environmental markets. A market is simply a mechanism for exchange between the buyers and sellers of a particular good or service. In earlier times, markets were actual physical settings where buyers and sellers would gather. Although such market settings are still used for products like fish, fruits and vegetables, and antiques and collectibles, many commercial markets today are fundamentally different, in that buyers and sellers are not at the same place—they arrange their exchange via mail order, telephone, fax, and so forth. And the growth of the Internet is serving to transform some markets to make it even easier for buyers and sellers to transact their business at a distance.

A good example of this trend is the recently announced partnership among some of the world's largest automobile manufacturers. It all started when various individual automobile makers began to create their own global purchasing web sites. Ford, for instance, was creating a site it called Auto-Xchange. The company intended to post all of its global procurement needs on the site, while also requesting that its suppliers post availability and prices for the parts and equipment they had to offer.

Concerns began to arise, however, when it quickly became apparent that other automobile companies were planning to do the same thing. Major suppliers to the auto industry, meanwhile, began to realize that they might soon be facing an unwieldy array of separate web sites for each car company, potentially driving their own costs up. So, a coalition of the largest suppli-

ers approached Ford and General Motors with a novel proposal—why not team up and create a single site that both firms could use?

Ford and GM executives quickly saw the wisdom of this idea and then convinced DaimlerChrysler to join them. Their plan is to create a single web site that will serve as a marketplace for all interested automobile manufacturers, suppliers, and dealers—essentially creating a

> "We brought in DaimlerChrysler to prevent Europe from creating a separate standard. We think we'll have the industry standard, and we see value in having that."
>
> —Harold Kutner, General Motors vice president responsible for purchasing

After studying this chapter, you should be able to

- Discuss the nature of organizational environments and identify the components of the general, task, and internal environments.

- Describe the ethical and social environment of management.

- Discuss the international environment of management.

- Describe the importance and determinants of an organization's culture.

global virtual market for all firms in the industry. Almost immediately, France's Renault and Japan's Nissan, which is controlled by Renault, indicated that they would join. Toyota also showed strong interest. In addition, both Ford and GM indicated that they would encourage their foreign affiliates and strategic partners as well. The three partners creating the web site also intend to establish it as a self-contained organization that will eventually offer shares to the public.

Experts also believe that the impact of this global electronic market will be tremendous. For example, it currently costs GM about $100 per transaction in ordering costs to buy parts or supplies the traditional way—with paper, over the telephone, and so on. But the firm estimates that its ordering costs will drop to less than $10 per transaction under the new system. Clearly, then, the automobile makers will realize substantial cost savings. The suppliers, too, will benefit in various ways. Besides having more information about what different companies need, they will be able to buy and sell among themselves.[1]

The Internet has become a major business tool for managers. Online auctions are just one of the myriad applications that managers can leverage for competitive advantage. And sometimes, as illustrated in the opening incident, it pays for competitors to work together. Indeed, the catalysts for cooperation among Ford, General Motors, and other competitors were their own suppliers, many of whom also compete with one another. Clearly, then, the environmental context of business today is changing in unprecedented ways.

The Organization's Environments

The **external environment** is everything outside an organization's boundaries that might affect it. There are actually two separate external environments: the **general environment** and the **task environment**. An organization's internal environment consists of conditions and forces within the organization.

The General Environment

Each of the following dimensions embodies conditions and events that have the potential to influence the organization in important ways.

The Economic Dimension   The **economic dimension** of an organization's general environment is the overall health and vitality of the economic system in which the organization operates.[2] Particularly important economic factors for business are general economic growth, inflation, interest rates, and unemployment. McDonald's U.S. operation has been functioning in an economy characterized by moderate growth, relatively low unemployment, and low inflation.[3] But economic strength sometimes has two sides. For example, low unemployment means that more people can eat out, but McDonald's also has to pay higher wages to attract new employees. Similarly, low inflation means that the prices McDonald's must pay for its supplies remain relatively constant, but it also is somewhat constrained from increasing the prices it charges consumers for a hamburger or milkshake. The economic dimension is important to non-business organizations as well. For example, during weak economic conditions, funding for state universities may drop, and charitable organizations like the Salvation Army are asked to provide greater assistance at the same time that their own incoming contributions dwindle. Similarly, hospitals are affected by the availability of government grants and the number of low-income patients they must treat free of charge.

The technological dimension of the general environment continues to evolve at breakneck speed. The pace of change and complexity involving computers and information technology is especially pronounced. Take this marketplace in Kampala, Uganda, for example. Buyers and sellers of fruits and vegetables have gathered here for centuries. But the presence of an Internet Service Provider is a new feature at the market, and one that has the potential to revolutionize how citizens of Africa live, work, and interact with the rest of the world.

The Technological Dimension The **technological dimension** of the general environment refers to the methods available for converting resources into products or services. Although technology is applied within the organization, the forms and availability of that technology come from the general environment. Computer-assisted manufacturing and design techniques, for example, allow Boeing to simulate the more than three miles of hydraulic tubing that run through a 777 aircraft. The results include decreased warehouse needs, higher-quality tube fittings, fewer employees, and major time savings. Although some people associate technology with manufacturing firms, it is also relevant in the service sector. For example, just as an automobile follows a predetermined pathway along an assembly line as it is built, a hamburger at McDonald's similarly follows a predefined path as the meat is cooked, the burger is assembled, and then the final product is wrapped and bagged for a customer. The rapid advancement of the Internet into all areas of business is also a reflection of the technological dimension. *Management InfoTech* discusses one unfortunate byproduct of the Internet.

external environment Everything outside an organization's boundaries that might affect it

general environment The set of broad dimensions and forces in an organization's surroundings that create its overall context

task environment Specific organizations or groups that affect the organization

economic dimension The overall health and vitality of the economic system in which the organization operates

technological dimension The methods available for converting resources into products or services

MANAGEMENT INFOTECH

VIRUSES CREATE MANAGEMENT NIGHTMARES

Who could resist opening an e-mail love letter? When computer users opened an e-mail with the subject line "I love you," they unleashed a computer virus that clogged electronic systems around the world in a matter of hours. Dubbed the "love bug," this virus infected computer networks at Ford, the U.S. Congress, the British Parliament, Nomura Securities in Japan, and nearly everywhere in between.

The virus lay hidden in an e-mail disguised as a love letter. Once a computer user opened the e-mail attachment, the virus launched itself and looked for the user's Microsoft Outlook mail program. Then it sent copies of its nasty attachment to every name in the user's online address book. These copies looked as though they actually came from the user, which is why recipients were tempted to open them. Some recipients maintained extensive online address books, so the virus spread quickly from user to user and organization to organization. The huge volume of messages crippled some corporate e-mail systems. Adding insult to injury, once the love bug was launched, it also damaged sound and graphics files on the recipient's hard drive.

The love bug virus demonstrated how computer problems are adding to the uncertainty of the organizational environment. First, no two viruses are exactly the same, so new viruses mean more change—and more scrambling to cope with the change. Second, managers never know what form a virus will take or when it will strike, yet they must plan in advance to prevent disasters.

The less destructive Melissa virus, which circulated a year before the love bug, was regarded as a wakeup call for organizations to strengthen their antivirus safeguards. However, months without any major virus attacks may have lulled computer users into a false sense of complacency. By the time the love bug emerged, people opened it without worrying about potential viruses. Now, while computer security firms develop new ways of detecting and disabling viruses, hackers are working on new types of viruses. The best antidote to this uncertainty remains prevention—training employees to leave suspicious e-mails (even love letters) alone.

> *All the technology in the world and they can't stop it from happening because people won't act responsibly.*
>
> —*Richard Power, Computer Security Institute**

References: Kevin Maney, "Tainted Love," *Wall Street Journal*, May 5, 2000, pp. 1B–2B (*quote on p. 2B).

political-legal dimension The government regulation of business and the general relationship between business and government

The Political-Legal Dimension The **political-legal dimension** of the general environment refers to government regulation of business and the relationship between business and government. It is important for three basic reasons. First, the legal system partially defines what an organization can and cannot do. Although the United States is basically a free market economy, there is still major regulation of business activity. McDonald's, for example, is subject to a variety of political and legal forces, including food preparation standards and local zoning requirements.

Second, pro- or antibusiness sentiment in government influences business activity. For example, during periods of probusiness sentiment, firms find it easier to compete and have fewer concerns about antitrust issues. On the other hand, during a period of antibusiness sentiment, firms may find their competitive strategies more restricted and may have fewer opportunities for mergers and acquisitions because of antitrust concerns. Among the most recent examples of the effects of the political-legal dimension were the court-ordered breakup of Microsoft in 2000 (subsequently overturned) and the Justice Department's efforts to block a proposed merger between WorldCom and Sprint that same year.[4]

Finally, political stability has ramifications for planning. No business wants to set up shop in another country unless trade relationships with that country are relatively well defined and stable. Hence, U.S. firms are more likely to do business with England, Mexico, and Canada than with Haiti and El Salvador. Similar issues are also relevant to assessments of local and state governments. A new mayor or governor can affect many organizations, especially small firms that do business in only one location and are susceptible to deed and zoning restrictions, property and school taxes, and the like.

The Task Environment

Because the impact of the general environment is often vague, imprecise, and long term, most organizations tend to focus their attention on their task environment. This environment includes competitors, customers, suppliers, regulators, and strategic allies. Although the task environment is also quite complex, it provides useful information more readily than does the general environment because the manager can identify environmental factors of specific interest to the organization rather than having to deal with the more abstract dimensions of the general environment.[5] Figure 2.1 depicts the task environment of McDonald's.

competitor An organization that competes with other organizations for resources

Competitors An organization's **competitors** are other organizations that compete with it for resources. The most obvious resources that competitors vie for are customer dollars. Reebok, Adidas, and Nike are competitors, as are Albertson's, Safeway, and Kroger. McDonald's competes with other fast-food operations like Burger King, Wendy's, Subway, and Dairy Queen. But competition also occurs between substitute products. Thus Ford competes with Yamaha (motorcycles) and Schwinn (bicycles) for your transportation dollars, and Walt Disney World, Club Med, and Carnival Cruise Lines compete for your vacation dollars. Nor is competition limited to business firms. Universities compete with trade schools, the military, other universities, and the external labor market to attract good students, and art galleries compete with each other to attract the best exhibits.

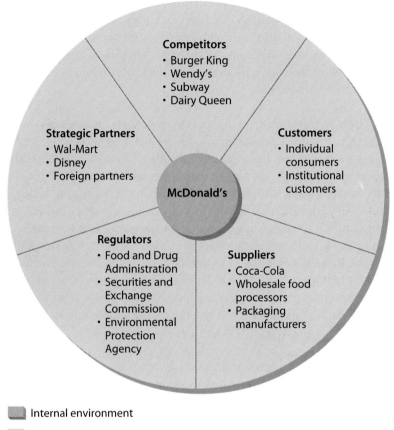

▨ Internal environment

▨ Task environment

Figure 2.1

McDonald's Task Environment

An organization's task environment includes its competitors, customers, suppliers, strategic partners, and regulators. This figure clearly highlights how managers at McDonald's can use this framework to better identify and understand their key constituents.

Customers   A second dimension of the task environment is **customers**, or whoever pays money to acquire an organization's products or services. Most of McDonald's customers are individuals who walk into a restaurant to buy food. But customers need not be individuals. Schools, hospitals, government agencies, wholesalers, retailers, and manufacturers are just a few of the many kinds of organizations that may be major customers of other organizations. Some institutional customers, such as schools, prisons, and hospitals, also buy food in bulk from restaurants like McDonald's.

Dealing with customers has become increasingly complex in recent years. New products and services, new methods of marketing, and more discriminating customers have all added uncertainty to how businesses relate to their customers, as has lower brand loyalty. A few years ago, McDonald's introduced a new sandwich called the Arch Deluxe, intended to appeal to adult customers. Unfortunately, the product failed because most adult customers preferred existing menu choices like the Quarter Pounder. Similarly, Tommy Hilfiger, a popular clothing designer, has fallen from favor in recent years in large part because it lost touch with its customers.[6]

Companies face especially critical differences among customers as they expand internationally. McDonald's sells beer in its German restaurants, for example,

customer Whoever pays money to acquire an organization's products or services

and wine in its French restaurants. Customers in those countries see those particular beverages as normal parts of a meal, much as customers in the United States routinely drink water, tea, or soft drinks with their meals. And the firm has even opened restaurants with no beef on the menu! Those restaurants are in India, where beef is not a popular menu option. Instead, the local McDonald's in that country use lamb in their sandwiches.

supplier An organization that provides resources for other organizations

Suppliers   **Suppliers** are organizations that provide resources for other organizations. McDonald's buys soft drink products from Coca-Cola, individually packaged servings of ketchup from Heinz, ingredients from wholesale food processors, and napkins, sacks, and wrappers from packaging manufacturers. Common wisdom in the United States used to be that a business should try to avoid depending exclusively on particular suppliers. A firm that buys all of a certain resource from one supplier may be crippled if the supplier goes out of business or is faced with a strike. This practice can also help maintain a competitive relationship among suppliers, keeping costs down. But firms eager to emulate successful Japanese firms have recently tried to change their approach. Japanese firms have a history of building major ties with only one or two major suppliers. This enables them to work together better for their mutual benefit and makes the supplier more responsive to the customer's needs.

regulator A unit that has the potential to control, legislate, or otherwise influence the organization's policies and practices

regulatory agency An agency created by the government to regulate business activities

Regulators   **Regulators** are elements of the task environment that have the potential to control, legislate, or influence an organization's policies and practices. There are two important kinds of regulators. The first, **regulatory agencies**, are created by the government to protect the public from certain business practices or to protect organizations from one another.

Powerful federal regulatory agencies include the Environmental Protection Agency (EPA), the Securities and Exchange Commission (SEC), the Food and Drug Administration (FDA), and the Equal Employment Opportunity Commission (EEOC). Many of these agencies play important roles in protecting the rights of individuals. The FDA, for example, helps ensure that the food we eat is free of contaminants and thus is an important regulator for McDonald's. At the same time, many managers complain that there is too much government regulation. Most large companies must devote thousands of labor hours and hundreds of thousands of dollars a year to comply with government regulations. To complicate the lives of managers even more, different regulatory agencies sometimes provide inconsistent—or even contradictory—mandates.

interest group A group formed by its own individual members to attempt to influence business

The other basic form of regulator is the interest group. An **interest group** is organized by its members to attempt to influence organizations. Prominent interest groups include the National Organization for Women (NOW), Mothers Against Drunk Drivers (MADD), the National Rifle Association (NRA), the League of Women Voters, the Sierra Club, Ralph Nader's Center for the Study of Responsive Law, Consumers Union, and industry self-regulation groups like the Council of Better Business Bureaus. Although interest groups lack the official power of government agencies, they can exert considerable influence by using the media to call attention to their positions. MADD, for example, puts considerable pressure on alcoholic beverage producers (to put warning labels on their products), automobile companies (to make it more difficult for intoxicated people to start their cars), local governments (to stiffen drinking ordinances), and bars and restaurants (to refuse to sell alcohol to people who are drinking too much).

Strategic Partners   A final dimension of the task environment is **strategic partners** (also called **strategic allies**)—two or more companies that work together in joint ventures or other partnerships. As shown in Figure 2.1, McDonald's has several strategic partners. For example, it has one arrangement with Wal-Mart whereby small McDonald's restaurants are built in many Wal-Mart stores. The firm also has a long-term deal with Disney; McDonald's will promote Disney movies in its stores, and Disney will build McDonald's restaurants or kiosks in its theme parks. And many of the firm's foreign stores are built in collaboration with local investors. Strategic partnerships help companies get from other companies the expertise they lack. They also help spread risk and open new market opportunities. Indeed, many strategic partnerships today involve international firms. For example, Ford has strategic partnerships with Volkswagen (sharing a distribution and service center in South America) and Nissan (building minivans in the United States).

> **strategic partner (strategic ally)**
> An organization working together with one or more other organizations in a joint venture or similar arrangement

The Internal Environment

Organizations also have an internal environment that consists of their owners, board of directors, employees, and the physical work environment. (Another especially important part of the internal environment is the organization's culture, discussed separately later in this chapter.)

Owners   The **owners** of a business are, of course, the people who have legal property rights to that business. Owners can be a single individual who establishes and runs a small business, partners who jointly own the business, individual investors who buy stock in a corporation, or other organizations. McDonald's has 700 million shares of stock, each of which represents one unit of ownership of the firm. The family of McDonald's founder Ray Kroc stills owns a large block of this stock, as do several large institutional investors. In addition, there are thousands of individuals each of whom owns just a few shares. McDonald's, in turn, also owns other businesses. For example, it owns several large regional bakeries that supply its restaurants with buns. Each of these is incorporated as a separate legal entity and managed as a wholly owned subsidiary by the parent company. McDonald's has also recently bought partial ownership of Chipolte Mexican Grill and Donatos Pizza chain.

> **owner** Whoever can claim property rights on an organization

Board of Directors   A corporate **board of directors** is elected by the stockholders and charged with overseeing the general management of the firm to ensure that it is being run in a way that best serves the stockholders' interests. Some boards are relatively passive. They perform a general oversight function but seldom get actively involved in how the company is really being run. But this trend is changing, as more and more boards are more carefully scrutinizing the firms they oversee and exerting more influence on how they are being managed.

> **board of directors** Governing body elected by a corporation's stockholders, charged with overseeing the general management of the firm to ensure that it is being run in a way that best serves the stockholders' interests

Employees   An organization's employees are also a major element of its internal environment. Of particular interest to managers today is the changing nature of the workforce as it becomes increasingly more diverse in terms of gender, ethnicity, age, and other dimensions. Workers are also calling for more job ownership—either partial ownership in the company or at least more say in how they perform their jobs. Another trend in many firms is the increased reliance on temporary workers—individuals hired for short periods of time with no expectation of permanent employment. Employers often prefer to use "temps" because they provide greater flexibility, earn lower wages, and often do not participate in benefits programs. But these managers also have to deal with what often amounts to a two-class workforce and a growing number of employees who have no loyalty to the organization where they work because they may be working for a different one tomorrow.

The permanent employees of many organizations are organized into labor unions, representing yet another layer of complexity for managers. The National Labor Relations Act of 1935 requires organizations to recognize and bargain with a union if that union has been legally established by the organization's employees. Presently, around 23 percent of the U.S. labor force is represented by unions. Some large firms, such as Ford, Exxon, and General Motors, have several different unions. Even when an organization's labor force is not unionized, its managers do not ignore unions. For example, Kmart, J. P. Stevens, Honda of America, and Delta Air Lines all actively work to avoid unionization. And even though people think primarily of blue-collar workers as union members, many white-collar workers, such as government employees and teachers, are also represented by unions.

Physical Work Environment   A final part of the internal environment is the actual physical environment of the organization and the work that people do. Some firms have their facilities in downtown skyscrapers, usually spread across several floors. Others locate in suburban or rural settings and may have facilities more closely resembling a college campus. Some facilities have long halls lined with traditional offices. Others have modular cubicles with partial walls and no doors. The top 100 managers at Mars, makers of Snickers and Milky Way, all work in a single vast room. Two copresidents are located in the very center of the room, whereas others are arrayed in concentric circles around them. Increasingly, newer facilities have an even more open arrangement, where people work in large rooms, moving between different tables to interact with different people on different projects. Freestanding computer workstations are available for those who need them, and a few small rooms might be off to the side for private business.[7]

The Ethical and Social Environment of Management

The ethical and social environment has become an especially important area for managers in the last few years. In this section we first explore the concept of individual ethics and then describe social responsibility.

Individual Ethics in Organizations

We define **ethics** as an individual's personal beliefs about whether a behavior, action, or decision is right or wrong.[8] Note that we define ethics in the context of the individual—people have ethics, organizations do not. Likewise, what constitutes ethical behavior varies from one person to another. For example, one person who finds a 20-dollar bill on the floor believes that it is okay to stick it in his pocket, whereas another feels compelled to turn it in to the lost-and-found department. Further, although **ethical behavior** is in the eye of the beholder, it usually refers to behavior that conforms to generally accepted social norms. **Unethical behavior**, then, is behavior that does not conform to generally accepted social norms.

Managerial Ethics **Managerial ethics** are the standards of behavior that guide individual managers in their work. One important area of managerial ethics is the treatment of employees by the organization. This area includes such areas as hiring and firing, wages and working conditions, and employee privacy and respect. Wages and working conditions, although tightly regulated, are also areas for potential controversy. For example, a manager paying an employee less than he deserves, simply because the manager knows the employee cannot afford to quit or risk losing his job by complaining, might be considered unethical. Finally, most observers would also agree that an organization is obligated to protect the privacy of its employees. A manager's spreading a rumor that an employee has AIDS or is having an affair with a coworker is generally seen as an unethical breach of privacy. Likewise, the manner in which an organization responds to and addresses issues associated with sexual harassment also involves employee privacy and related rights. The cartoon illustrates yet another perspective—if a manager feels pressure to get more work done, she or he may apply similar pressure on others to work extra hours, stay later in the evening, and so forth.

Numerous ethical issues also stem from how employees treat the organization, especially with regard to conflicts of interest, secrecy and confidentiality, and honesty. A conflict of interest occurs when a decision potentially benefits the individual

ethics An individual's personal beliefs regarding what is right and wrong or good and bad

ethical behavior Behavior that conforms to generally accepted social norms

unethical behavior Behavior that does not conform to generally accepted social norms

managerial ethics Standards of behavior that guide individual managers in their work

Managers should strive to be ethical in all their dealings with their employees. Sometimes the pressures and stresses they experience cause them to apply those same pressures and stresses to employees, often in inappropriate ways. For example, as illustrated here, managers sometimes go too far in their efforts to entice employees to work harder or to spend more time on the job. The result can be disgruntled employees and low morale.

Reprinted with special permission of King Features Syndicate.

to the possible detriment of the organization. To guard against such practices, most companies have policies that forbid their buyers from accepting gifts from suppliers. Divulging company secrets is also clearly unethical. Employees who work for businesses in highly competitive industries—electronics, software, and fashion apparel, for example—might be tempted to sell information about company plans to competitors. A third area of concern is honesty in general. Relatively common problems in this area include such behaviors as using a business telephone to make personal long distance calls, stealing supplies, and padding expense accounts. Although most employees are inherently honest, organizations must nevertheless be vigilant in order to avoid problems from behaviors like these.

Managerial ethics also come into play in the relationship between the firm and its employees with other economic agents. The primary agents of interest include customers, competitors, stockholders, suppliers, dealers, and unions. The behaviors between the organization and these agents that may be subject to ethical ambiguity include advertising and promotions, financial disclosures, ordering and purchasing, shipping and solicitation, bargaining and negotiation, and other business relationships. Sony recently admitted that it had created a fictitious film critic in order to ensure that it had a steady supply of glowing quotes to use in promoting its new movies. When challenged by the media, Sony acknowledged that it had deceived the public and promised to exercise more restraint in the future.[9]

Managing Ethical Behavior   Spurred partially by increased awareness of ethical scandals in business and partially by a sense of enhanced corporate consciousness about the importance of ethical and unethical behaviors, many organizations have reemphasized ethical behavior on the part of employees. This emphasis takes many forms, but any effort to enhance ethical behavior must begin with top management. It is top managers, for example, who establish the organization's culture and define what will and will not be acceptable behavior. Some companies have also started offering employees training in how to cope with ethical dilemmas. At Boeing, for example, line managers lead training sessions for other employees, and the company also has an ethics committee that reports directly to the board of directors. The training sessions involve discussions of different ethical dilemmas that employees might face and how managers might handle those dilemmas. Chemical Bank and Xerox also have ethics training programs for their managers.

Organizations are also going to greater lengths to formalize their ethical standards. Some, such as General Mills and Johnson & Johnson, have prepared guidelines that detail how employees are to treat suppliers, customers, competitors, and other constituents. Others, such as Whirlpool and Hewlett-Packard, have developed formal **codes of ethics**—written statements of the values and ethical standards that guide the firms' actions.

code of ethics A formal, written statement of the values and ethical standards that guide a firm's actions

Social Responsibility and Organizations

As we have seen, ethics relate to individuals and their decisions and behaviors. Organizations themselves do not have ethics but do relate to their environment in ways that often involve ethical dilemmas and decisions. These situations are gen-

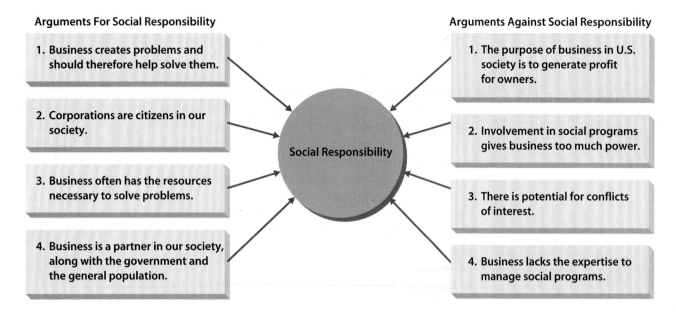

Arguments For Social Responsibility

1. Business creates problems and should therefore help solve them.

2. Corporations are citizens in our society.

3. Business often has the resources necessary to solve problems.

4. Business is a partner in our society, along with the government and the general population.

Social Responsibility

Arguments Against Social Responsibility

1. The purpose of business in U.S. society is to generate profit for owners.

2. Involvement in social programs gives business too much power.

3. There is potential for conflicts of interest.

4. Business lacks the expertise to manage social programs.

Figure 2.2

Arguments For and Against Social Responsibility

social responsibility The set of obligations an organization has to protect and enhance the societal context in which it functions

erally referred to within the context of the organization's social responsibility. Specifically, **social responsibility** is the set of obligations an organization has to protect and enhance the society in which it functions. Figure 2.2 summarizes common arguments for and against social responsibility.

Arguments for Social Responsibility   People who argue in favor of social responsibility claim that, because organizations create many of the problems that need to be addressed, such as air and water pollution and resource depletion, they should play a major role in solving them. They also argue that, because corporations are legally defined entities with most of the same privileges as private citizens, businesses should not try to avoid their obligations as citizens. Advocates of social responsibility point out that, whereas governmental organizations have stretched their budgets to the limit, many large businesses often have surplus revenues that could potentially be used to help solve social problems. For example, IBM routinely donates surplus computers to schools, and many restaurants give leftover food to homeless shelters.

Arguments Against Social Responsibility   Some people, however, including the famous economist Milton Friedman, argue that widening the interpretation of social responsibility will undermine the U.S. economy by detracting from the basic mission of business: to earn profits for owners. For example, money that Microsoft or General Electric contributes to social causes or charities is money that could otherwise be distributed to owners as a dividend. Ben & Jerry's Homemade Inc. has a very ambitious and widely touted social agenda. But some shareholders recently criticized the firm when it refused to accept a lucrative exporting deal to Japan simply because the Japanese distributor did not have a similar social agenda.[10]

Another objection to deepening the social responsibility of businesses points out that corporations already wield enormous power and that their activity in social programs gives them even more power. Another argument against social responsibility focuses on the potential for conflict of interest. Suppose, for example, that one manager is in charge of deciding which local social program or charity will receive a large grant from her business. The local civic opera company (a not-for-profit organization that relies on contributions for its existence) might offer her front-row tickets for the upcoming season in exchange for her support. If opera is her favorite form of music, she might be tempted to direct the money toward the local company, when it might actually be needed more in other areas.[11] Finally, critics argue that organizations lack the expertise to understand how to assess and make decisions about worthy social programs. How can a company truly know, they ask, which cause or program is most deserving of its support or how money might best be spent?

Managing Social Responsibility

The demands for social responsibility placed on contemporary organizations by an increasingly sophisticated and educated public are probably stronger than ever. As we have seen, there are pitfalls for managers who fail to adhere to high ethical standards and for companies that try to circumvent their legal obligations. Organizations therefore need to fashion an approach to social responsibility in the same way that they develop any other business strategy. In other words, they should view social responsibility as a major challenge that requires careful planning, decision making, consideration, and evaluation. They may accomplish this through both formal and informal dimensions of managing social responsibility.

Formal Organizational Dimensions   Some dimensions of managing social responsibility are a formal and planned activity on the part of the organization. Formal organizational dimensions that can help manage social responsibility are legal compliance, ethical compliance, and philanthropic giving.

legal compliance The extent to which an organization complies with local, state, federal, and international laws

    Legal compliance is the extent to which the organization conforms to local, state, federal, and international laws. The task of managing legal compliance is generally assigned to the appropriate functional managers. For example, the organization's top human resource executive is responsible for ensuring compliance with regulations concerning hiring, pay, and workplace safety and health. Likewise, the top finance executive generally oversees compliance with securities and banking regulations. The organization's legal department is also likely to contribute to this effort by providing general oversight and answering queries from managers about the appropriate interpretation of laws and regulations.

ethical compliance The extent to which an organization and its members follow basic ethical standards of behavior

    Ethical compliance is the extent to which the members of the organization follow basic ethical (and legal) standards of behavior. We noted earlier that organizations have increased their efforts in this area—providing training in ethics and developing guidelines and codes of conduct, for example. These activities serve as vehicles for enhancing ethical compliance. Many organizations also establish formal ethics committees, which may be asked to review proposals for new projects, help evaluate new hiring strategies, or assess a new environmental protection plan. They might also serve as a peer review panel to evaluate alleged ethical misconduct by an employee.[12]

Finally, **philanthropic giving** is the awarding of funds or gifts to charities or other social programs. Dayton-Hudson Corp. routinely gives 5 percent of its taxable income to charity and social programs. Giving across national boundaries is also becoming more common. For example, Alcoa gave $112,000 to a small town in Brazil to build a sewage treatment plant. And Japanese firms like Sony and Mitsubishi make contributions to a number of social programs in the United States. Unfortunately, in this age of cutbacks, many corporations have also had to limit their charitable gifts over the past several years as they continue to trim their own budgets. And many firms that continue to make contributions are increasingly targeting them toward programs or areas where the firm will get something in return. For example, firms today are more likely to give money to job training programs than to the arts than was the case just a few years ago. The logic is that they get more direct payoff from the former type of contribution—in this instance, a better-trained workforce from which to hire new employees.[13]

Informal Organizational Dimensions In addition to these formal dimensions for managing social responsibility, there are also informal ones. Leadership, organization culture, and how the organization responds to whistle blowers each helps shape and define people's perceptions of the organization's stance on social responsibility.

Leadership practices and organization culture can go a long way toward defining the social responsibility stance an organization and its members will adopt.[14] For example, Johnson & Johnson executives for years provided a consistent message to employees that customers, employees, and communities where the company did business and shareholders were all important—and primarily in that order. Thus, when packages of poisoned Tylenol showed up on store shelves in the 1980s, Johnson & Johnson employees didn't need to wait for orders from headquarters to know what to do: They immediately pulled all the packages from shelves before any other customers could buy them.[15]

Whistle blowing is the disclosure by an employee of illegal or unethical conduct on the part of others within the organization.[16] How an organization responds to this practice often indicates its stance on social responsibility. Whistle blowers may have to proceed through a number of channels to be heard, and they may even get fired for their efforts. Many organizations, however, welcome their contributions. A person who observes questionable behavior typically reports the incident first to his or her boss. If nothing is done, the whistle blower may then inform higher-level managers or an ethics committee, if one exists. Eventually, the person may have to go to a regulatory agency or even the media to be heard. For example, Charles W. Robinson, Jr., once worked as a director of a SmithKline lab in San Antonio. One day he noticed a suspicious billing pattern the firm was using to collect lab fees from Medicare that were considerably higher than the firm's normal charges for those same tests. He pointed the problem out to higher-level managers, but his concerns were ignored. He subsequently took his findings to

philanthropic giving Awarding funds or gifts to charities or worthy causes

whistle blowing The disclosure by an employee of illegal or unethical conduct on the part of others within the organization

the U.S. government, which sued SmithKline and eventually reached a settlement of $325 million.[17]

The International Environment of Management

Another important competitive issue for managers today is the international environment. After describing recent trends in international business, we examine levels of internationalization and the international context of business.

Trends in International Business

The stage for today's international business environment was set at the end of World War II. Businesses in war-torn countries like Germany and Japan had no choice but to rebuild from scratch. Because of this position, they essentially had to rethink every facet of their operations, including technology, production, finance, and marketing. Although it took many years for these countries to recover, they eventually did so, and their economic systems were subsequently poised for growth. During the same era, U.S. companies grew complacent. Their customer base was growing rapidly. Increased population spurred by the baby boom and increased affluence resulting from the postwar economic boom greatly raised the average person's standard of living and expectations. The U.S. public continually wanted new and better products and services. Many U.S. companies profited greatly from this pattern, but most were also perhaps guilty of taking it for granted.

Most international business experts see the People's Republic of China as the most important emerging marketplace in the world. Its vast population and growing interests in consumerism combine to offer tremendous potential for a wide array of products and services. This potential took a major step forward when the People's Republic was awarded the 2008 Olympic Games, since the Olympics will allow government leaders to further showcase their country to the rest of the world. These jubilant celebrants in Beijing have good reason to cheer this important public relations victory for their country.

But U.S. firms are no longer isolated from global competition or the global market. A few simple numbers help tell the full story of international trade and industry. First of all, the volume of international trade increased more than 3,000 percent from 1960 to 2000. Further, although 162 of the world's largest corporations are headquartered in the United States, there are also 126 in Japan, 42 in France, 41 in Germany, and 34 in Britain. Within certain industries, the preeminence of non-U.S. firms is even more striking. For example, only one of each of the world's ten largest banks and ten largest electronics companies is based in the United States. Only two of the ten largest chemical companies are U.S. firms. On the other hand, U.S. firms comprise six of the eight largest aerospace companies, four of the seven largest airlines, six of the nine largest computer companies, four of the five largest diversified financial companies, and six of the ten largest retailers.

U.S. firms are also finding that international operations are an increasingly important element of their sales and profits. For example, in 1999 Exxon Mobil Corporation realized 82 percent of its revenues and 68 percent of its profits abroad. For Avon, these percentages were 66 percent and 70 percent, respectively.[18] From any perspective, then, it is clear that we live in a truly global economy. Virtually all businesses today must be concerned with the competitive situations they face in lands far from home and with how companies from distant lands are competing in their homeland.

Levels of International Business Activity

Firms can choose various levels of international business activity as they seek to gain a competitive advantage in other countries. The general levels are exporting and importing, licensing, strategic alliances, and direct investment. Table 2.1 summarizes the advantages and disadvantages of each activity.

Exporting and Importing   Exporting or importing (or both) is usually the first type of international business in which a firm gets involved. **Exporting**, or making the product in the firm's domestic marketplace and selling it in another country, can involve both merchandise and services. **Importing** is bringing a good, service, or capital into the home country from abroad. For example, automobiles (Mazda, Ford, Volkswagen, Mercedes-Benz, Ferrari) and stereo equipment (Sony, Bang and Olufsen, Sanyo) are routinely exported by their manufacturers to other countries. Likewise, many wine distributors buy products from vineyards in France, Italy, or California and import them into their own countries for resale.

Licensing   A company may prefer to arrange for a foreign company to manufacture or market its products under a licensing agreement. Factors that may lead to this decision include excessive transportation costs, government regulations, and home production costs. **Licensing** is an arrangement whereby a firm allows another company to use its brand name, trademark, technology, patent, copyright,

exporting Making a product in the firm's domestic marketplace and selling it in another country

importing Bringing a good, service, or capital into the home country from abroad

licensing An arrangement whereby one company allows another company to use its brand name, trademark, technology, patent, copyright, or other assets in exchange for a royalty based on sales

Table 2.1

Advantages and Disadvantages of Various Approaches to Internationalization

When organizations decide to increase their level of internationalization, they can adopt several strategies. Each strategy is a matter of degree, as opposed to being a discrete and mutually exclusive category. And each has unique advantages and disadvantages that must be considered.

Approaches to Internationalization	Advantages	Disadvantages
Exporting or Importing	1. Small cash outlay 2. Little risk 3. No adaptation necessary	1. Tariffs and taxes 2. High transportation costs 3. Government restrictions
Licensing	1. Increased profitability 2. Extended profitability	1. Inflexibility 2. Helps competitors
Strategic alliances/ joint ventures	1. Quick market entry 2. Access to materials and technology	1. Shared ownership (limits control and profits)
Direct investment	1. Enhances control 2. Existing infrastructure	1. Complexity 2. Greater economic and political risk 3. Greater uncertainty

or other assets. In return, the licensee pays a royalty, usually based on sales. For example, Kirin Brewery, Japan's largest producer of beer, wanted to expand its international operations but feared that the time involved in shipping it from Japan would cause the beer to lose its freshness. Thus it has entered into a number of licensing arrangements with breweries in other markets. These brewers make beer according to strict guidelines provided by the Japanese firm and then package and market it as Kirin Beer. They then pay a royalty back to Kirin for each case sold. Molson produces Kirin in Canada under such an agreement, and the Charles Wells brewery does the same in England.[19]

strategic alliance A cooperative arrangement between two or more firms for mutual benefit

Strategic Alliances   In a **strategic alliance**, two or more firms jointly cooperate for mutual gain.[20] For example, Kodak and Fuji, along with three major Japanese camera manufacturers, collaborated on the development of a new film cartridge. This collaboration allowed Kodak and Fuji to share development costs, prevented an advertising war if the two firms had developed different cartridges, and made it easier for new cameras to be introduced at the same time as the new film cartridges. A **joint venture** is a special type of strategic alliance in which the partners actually share ownership of a new enterprise. Strategic alliances have enjoyed a tremendous upsurge in the past few years.

joint venture A special type of strategic alliance in which the partners share in the ownership of an operation on an equity basis

direct investment When a firm headquartered in one country builds or purchases operating facilities or subsidiaries in a foreign country

Direct Investment   Another level of commitment to internationalization is direct investment. **Direct investment** occurs when a firm headquartered in one country builds or purchases operating facilities or subsidiaries in a foreign country. The foreign operations then become wholly owned subsidiaries of the firm. Ford's acquisitions of Jaguar, Volvo, and Kia and British Petroleum's acquisition of Amoco were all major forms of direct investment. Similarly, Dell Computer's new factory in China is also a direct investment. A major reason why many firms make direct investments is to capitalize on lower labor costs; that is, the goal is often to transfer production to locations where labor is cheap. Japanese businesses have moved much of their production to Thailand because labor costs are much lower there than in Japan. Many U.S. firms are using maquiladoras for the same purpose. **Maquiladoras** are light assembly plants built in northern Mexico close to the U.S. border. The plants are given special tax breaks by the Mexican government, and the area is populated with workers willing to work for very low wages.

maquiladora Light assembly plant built in northern Mexico close to the U.S. border and given special tax breaks by the Mexican government

The Context of International Business

Managers involved in international business must also be aware of three areas of concern: controls on international business, the existence of economic communities, and cultural variations across national boundaries.

Controls on International Trade   To protect domestic business, governments may enact barriers to international trade. These barriers include tariffs, quotas, export restraint agreements, and "buy national" laws. A **tariff** is a tax collected on goods shipped across national boundaries. Tariffs can be collected by the exporting country, countries through which goods pass, and the importing country. Im-

tariff A tax collected on goods shipped across national boundaries port tariffs, which are the most common, can be levied to protect domestic companies by increasing the cost of foreign goods. Japan charges U.S. tobacco producers a tariff on cigarettes imported into Japan as a way to keep their prices higher than the prices charged by domestic firms. Tariffs can also be levied, usually by less-developed countries, to raise money for the government.

Quotas are the most common form of trade restriction. A quota is a limit on the number or value of goods that can be traded. The quota amount is typically designed to ensure that domestic competitors will be able to maintain a certain market share. Honda is allowed to import 425,000 autos each year into the United States. This quota is one reason why Honda opened manufacturing facilities here. The quota applies to cars imported into the United States, but the company can produce as many other cars within our borders as it wants, as they are not considered imports. **Export restraint agreements** are designed to convince other governments to voluntarily limit the volume or value of goods exported to a particular country. They are, in effect, export quotas. Japanese steel producers voluntarily limit the amount of steel they send to the United States each year.

"Buy national" legislation gives preference to domestic producers through content or price restrictions. Several countries have this type of legislation. Brazil requires that Brazilian companies purchase only Brazilian-made computers. The United States requires that the Department of Defense purchase only military uniforms manufactured in the United States, even though the price of foreign uniforms would be half as much. Mexico requires that 50 percent of the parts of cars sold in Mexico be manufactured in Mexico.

Economic Communities   Just as government policies can either increase or decrease the political risk facing international managers, trade relations between countries can either help or hinder international business. Relations dictated by quotas, tariffs, and so forth can hurt international trade. There is currently a strong movement around the world to reduce many of these barriers. This movement takes its most obvious form in international economic communities.

An international **economic community** is a set of countries that agree to markedly reduce or eliminate trade barriers among member nations. The first, and in many ways still the most important, of these economic communities is the **European Union (EU)**; the members of the EU are illustrated in Figure 2.3. The passage of the **North American Free Trade Agreement (NAFTA)** represents the first step toward the formation of a North American economic community. Other important economic communities include the Latin American Integration Association (Bolivia, Brazil, Colombia, Chile, Argentina, and other South American countries) and the Caribbean Common Market (the Bahamas, Belize, Jamaica, Antigua, Barbados, and 12 other countries).

The Cultural Environment   Another environmental challenge for the international manager is the cultural environment and how it affects business. Cultural values and beliefs are often unspoken; they may even be taken for granted by those who live in a particular country. Cultural factors do not necessarily cause problems for managers when the cultures of two countries are similar. Difficulties

quota A limit on the number or value of goods that can be traded

export restraint agreement Accord reached by governments in which countries voluntarily limit the volume or value of goods they export to and import from one another

economic community A set of countries that agree to markedly reduce or eliminate trade barriers among member nations (a formalized market system)

European Union (EU) The first and most important international market system

North American Free Trade Agreement (NAFTA) An agreement between the United States, Canada, and Mexico to promote trade with one another

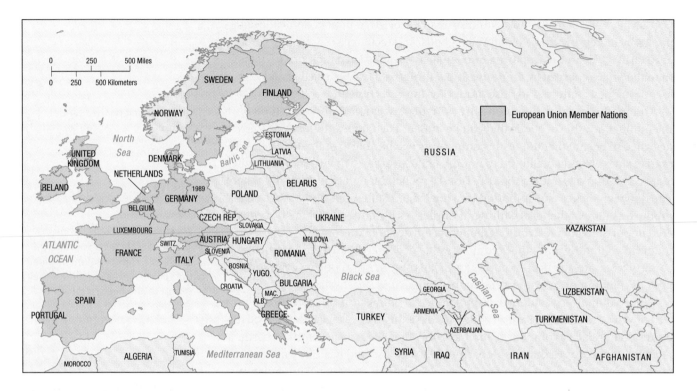

Figure 2.3

European Union Member Nations

can arise, however, when there is little overlap between the home culture of a manager and the culture of the country in which business is to be conducted. For example, most U.S. managers find the culture and traditions of England familiar. The people of both countries speak the same language and share strong historical roots, and there is a history of strong commerce between the two countries. When U.S. managers begin operations in Japan or the People's Republic of China, however, most of those commonalities disappear.

Cultural differences between countries can have a direct impact on business practice. For example, the religion of Islam teaches that people should not make a living by exploiting the misfortune of others and that making interest payments is immoral. This means that in Saudi Arabia there are few businesses that provide auto-wrecking services to tow stalled cars to the garage (because that would be capitalizing on misfortune), and in the Sudan banks cannot pay or charge interest. Given these cultural and religious constraints, those two businesses—automobile towing and banking—don't seem to hold great promise for international managers in those particular countries!

Some cultural differences between countries can be even more subtle and yet have a major impact on business activities. For example, in the United States most managers clearly agree about the value of time. Most U.S. managers schedule their activities very tightly and then adhere to their schedules. Other cultures don't put such a premium on time. In the Middle East, managers do not like to set appointments, and they rarely keep appointments set too far in the future. U.S. managers interacting with managers from the Middle East might misinterpret the late arrival of a potential business partner as a negotiation ploy or an insult, when it is rather a simple reflection of different views of time and its value.

Language itself can be an important factor. Beyond the obvious and clear barriers posed by people who speak different languages, subtle differences in meaning can also play a major role. For example, Imperial Oil of Canada markets gasoline under the brand name Esso. When the firm tried to sell its gasoline in Japan, it learned that Esso means "stalled car" in Japanese. The Chevrolet Nova was not selling well in Latin America, and General Motors executives couldn't understand why—until it was brought to their attention that, in Spanish, *no va* means "it doesn't go." The color green is used extensively in Muslim countries, but it signifies death in some other countries. The color associated with femininity in the United States is pink, but in many other countries yellow is the most feminine color.

The Organization's Culture

At its most general level, *culture* refers to the collection of values, beliefs, behaviors, customs, and attitudes that characterize a community of people. Culture is an amorphous concept that defies objective measurement or observation. Nevertheless, because it is the foundation of the organization's internal environment, **organization culture** plays a major role in shaping managerial behavior.

> **organization culture** The set of values, beliefs, behaviors, customs, and attitudes that helps an organization's members understand what it stands for, how it does things, and what it considers important

The Importance of Organization Culture

Executives at Ford Motor Company recently decided to move the firm's Lincoln Mercury division from Detroit to Southern California. Interestingly, though, this move had little to do with costs or any of the other reasons for most business relocations. Instead, they wanted to move Lincoln Mercury out of the corporate shadow of its dominating bigger corporate cousin, Ford itself. For years, Lincoln Mercury managers had complained that their business was always given short shrift and that most of the attention in Detroit's attention was focused on Ford. And, at least partially as a result, Mercury products all tended to look like clones of Ford products, and the division consistently failed to meet its goals or live up to its expectations. Finally, the company decided that the only way to turn the division around was to give it its own identity. And where better to start than by moving the whole operation—lock, stock, and barrel—to car-centric Southern California, where its managers could be freer to hire new creative talent and start carving out a new and unique business niche for themselves.[21] In short, they wanted to create a new culture.

Culture determines the "feel" of the organization. The stereotypic image of Microsoft, for example, is a workplace where people dress very casually and work very long hours. In contrast, the image of Bank of America for some observers is a formal setting with rigid work rules and people dressed in conservative business attire. And Texas Instruments likes to talk about its "shirtsleeve" culture, in which ties are avoided and few managers ever wear jackets. Southwest Airlines maintains a culture that stresses fun and excitement. The firm's CEO, Herb Kelleher, explains the company's emphasis on fun in an orientation video set to rap music. Of course, the same culture is not necessarily found throughout an entire organization. For example, the sales and marketing department may have a culture quite different from that of the operations and manufacturing department. Regardless of its nature, however, culture is a powerful force in organizations, one that can shape the firm's overall effectiveness and long-term success. Companies that can develop and maintain a strong culture, such as Hewlett-Packard and Procter & Gamble, tend to be more effective than companies that have trouble developing and maintaining a strong culture, such as Kmart.[22]

Determinants of Organization Culture

Where does an organization's culture come from? Typically it develops and blossoms over a long period of time. Its starting point is often the organization's founder. For example, James Cash Penney believed in treating employees and customers with respect and dignity. Employees at J. C. Penney are still called "associates" rather than "employees" (to reflect partnership), and customer satisfaction is of paramount importance. The impact of Sam Walton, Ross Perot, and Walt Disney is still felt in the organizations they founded.[23] As an organization grows, its culture is modified, shaped, and refined by symbols, stories, heroes, slogans, and ceremonies. For example, an important value at Hewlett-Packard is the avoidance of bank debt. A popular story still told at the company involves a new project being considered for several years. All objective criteria indicated that HP should borrow money from a bank to finance it, yet Bill Hewlett and David Packard rejected it out of hand simply because "HP avoids bank debt." This story, involving two corporate heroes and based on a slogan, dictates corporate culture today. And many decisions at Walt Disney Company today are still framed by asking, "What would Walt have done?"

Corporate success and shared experiences also shape culture. For example, Hallmark Cards has a strong culture derived from its years of success in the greeting card industry. Employees speak of the Hallmark family and care deeply about the company; many of them have worked at the company for decades. At Kmart, in contrast, the culture is quite weak, the management team changes rapidly, and few people sense any direction or purpose in the company. The differences in culture at Hallmark and Kmart are in part attributable to past successes and shared experiences.

Managing Organization Culture

How can managers deal with culture, given its clear importance but intangible nature? Essentially, the manager must understand the current culture and then decide if it should be maintained or changed. By understanding the organization's current culture, managers can take appropriate actions. At Hewlett-Packard, the values represented by "the HP way" still exist to guide and direct most important activities undertaken by the firm. Indeed, the firm's CEO, Carly Fiorina, launched her tenure at the firm with a series of television commercials focusing on the firm's Silicon Valley roots and the garage where it started. Culture can also be maintained by rewarding and promoting people whose behaviors are consistent with the existing culture and by articulating the culture through slogans, ceremonies, and so forth.

But managers must walk a fine line between maintaining a culture that still works effectively and changing a culture that has become dysfunctional. For example, many of the firms already noted, as well as numerous others, take pride in perpetuating their culture. Shell Oil Company, for example, has an elaborate display in the lobby of its Houston headquarters that tells the story of the firm's past. But other companies may face situations in which their culture is no longer a strength. For example, some critics feel that General Motors' culture places too much emphasis on product development and internal competition among divisions, and not enough on marketing and competition with other firms.

Culture problems sometimes arise from mergers or the growth of rival factions within an organization. For example, Wells Fargo and Company, which relies heavily on snazzy technology and automated banking services, acquired another large bank, First Interstate, which had focused more attention on personal services and customer satisfaction. Blending the two disparate organization cultures was difficult for the firm, as managers argued over how best to serve customers and operate the new enterprise.[24]

To change culture, managers must have a clear idea of what they want to create. Schwinn has tried to redefine itself to be more competitive and to break free of its old approaches to doing business. The firm's motto—"Established 1895. Reestablished 1994."—represents an effort to create a new culture that better reflects today's competitive environment in the bicycle market. Likewise, when Continental Airlines "reinvented" itself a few years ago, employees were taken outside the corporate headquarters building in Houston to watch the firm's old policies and procedures manuals set afire. The firm's new strategic direction is known throughout Continental as the "Go Forward" plan, intentionally named to avoid reminding people about the firm's troubled past and instead to focus on the future.

One major way to shape culture is by bringing outsiders into important managerial positions. The choice of a new CEO from outside the organization is often a clear signal that things will be changing. Indeed, new CEOs were the catalyst for the changes at Schwinn and Continental. Adopting new slogans, telling new stories, staging new ceremonies, and breaking with tradition can also alter culture.

Summary of Key Points

Managers need to have a thorough understanding of the environment in which they operate and compete. The general environment consists of economic, technological, and political-legal dimensions. The task environment consists of competitors, customers, suppliers, regulators, and strategic partners.

The internal environment consists of the organization's owners, board of directors, employees, and physical environment. Owners are those who have property rights claims on the organization. The board of directors, elected by stockholders, is responsible for overseeing a firm's top managers. Individual employees and the labor unions they sometimes join are other important parts of the internal environment. The physical environment, yet another part of the internal environment, varies greatly across organizations.

The ethical and social environment of management is also quite important. Understanding the differences between ethical and unethical behavior, as well as appreciating the special nature of managerial ethics, can guide effective decision making. Understanding the meaning of and arguments for and against social responsibility can help a manager effectively address both formal and informal dimensions of social responsibility.

The international environment of management is also very important. Current trends have resulted in the increasing globalization of markets, industries, and businesses. Organizations seeking to become more international can rely on importing, exporting, licensing, strategic alliances, and direct investment to do so. Controls on international trade, economic communities, and national culture combine to determine the context of international management.

The organization's culture is the set of values that helps its members understand what the organization stands for, how it does things, and what it considers important. Culture is a very important ingredient in organizational success. It is generally determined by factors such as the firm's founder, as well as symbols, slogans, stories, heroes, ceremonies, successes, and shared experiences. Culture can be managed, although changing it may be difficult.

Discussion Questions

Questions for Review

1. Identify and discuss each major dimension of the general environment and the task environment.
2. Do organizations have ethics? Why or why not?
3. What are the arguments for and against social responsibility?
4. Describe the four basic levels of international business activity. Do you think any organization will achieve the fourth level? Why or why not?
5. Describe various barriers to international trade.

Questions for Analysis

6. Can you think of dimensions of the task environment that are not discussed in the text? Indicate their linkage to those that are discussed.
7. What is the relationship between the law and ethical behavior? Can illegal behavior possibly be ethical?
8. How do you feel about whistle-blowing activity? If you were aware of a criminal activity taking place in your organization and if reporting it might cost you your job, what would you do?
9. What industries do you think will have the greatest impact on international business? Are any industries unlikely to be affected by the trend toward international business? If so, which ones? If not, explain why not.
10. What is the culture of your college or university? How clear is it? What are its most positive and negative characteristics?

BUILDING EFFECTIVE *time management* SKILLS

Exercise Overview

Time management skills refer to the manager's ability to prioritize work, to work efficiently, and to delegate appropriately. This exercise provides you with an opportunity to relate time management issues to environmental pressures and opportunities.

Exercise Background

As discussed in this chapter, managers and organizations must be sensitive to a variety of environmental dimensions and forces reflected in the general, task, and internal environments. The problem faced by managers is that time is a finite resource. There are only so many hours in a day and only so many things that can be done in a given period of time. Thus managers must constantly make choices about how they spend their time. Clearly, of course, they should try to use their time wisely and direct it toward the more important challenges and opportunities they face. Spending time on a trivial issue while an important issue gets neglected is a mistake.

Time management experts often suggest that managers begin each day by making a list of what they need to accomplish that day. After the list is compiled, the manager is then advised to sort these daily tasks into three groups: those that must be addressed that day, those that should be addressed that day but that could be postponed if necessary, and those that can easily be postponed. The manager is then advised to perform the tasks in order of priority.

Exercise Task

With the background information above as context, do the following:

1. Across the top of a sheet of paper, write the three priority levels noted above.
2. Down the left side of the same sheet of paper, write the various elements and dimensions of the task and internal environments of business.
3. At the intersection of each row and column, think of an appropriate example that a manager might face. For example, think of a higher-priority, a moderate-priority, and a low-priority situation involving a customer.
4. Form a small group with two or three classmates and discuss each person's examples. Focus on whether or not there is agreement as to the prioritization of each example.

BUILDING EFFECTIVE *decision-making* SKILLS

Exercise Overview

Decision-making skills refer to the manager's ability to correctly recognize and define problems and opportunities and to then select an appropriate course of action to solve problems and capitalize on opportunities. Many managerial decisions have an ethical component. This exercise demonstrates the potential role of ethics in making decisions.

Exercise Background

Read and reflect on each of the following scenarios:

1. You are the top manager of a major international oil company. Because of a recent oil spill by another firm, all the companies in the industry have been subjected to scrutiny regarding the safety of various work practices. Your safety manager has completed a review and informed you that your firm has one potential problem area. The manager estimates a 3 percent probability of a problem's occurring within the next five years. The cost of preventing the problem would be about $1.5 million. However, if you do nothing and a problem develops, the cost

will be $10 million, plus your firm will receive a lot of bad publicity.

2. You manage a small fast-food restaurant. The owner just told you to cut the payroll by 20 hours per week. You have two obvious choices. One candidate for layoff is a retired woman who works part time for you. She lives on a fixed income, is raising three grandchildren, and really needs the money she earns from this job. The other is a college student who also works part time. He is one year away from getting his degree and must work to pay his tuition and fees.

3. You have decided to donate $1,000 to a worthy cause in your neighborhood on behalf of the small business you own. Based on your own research, you have learned that the groups and charities most in need of funds are a local homeless shelter, a youth soccer league, an abortion clinic, and a tutoring program for illiterate adults.

Exercise Task

With the background information above as context, do the following:

1. Make a decision between the two courses of action for scenario 1.
2. Decide which employee to lay off in scenario 2.
3. Decide where to donate your money in scenario 3.
4. What role did your personal ethics play in making each decision?
5. Compare your decisions with those of a classmate and discuss any differences.

BUILDING EFFECTIVE *communication* SKILLS

Exercise Overview

Communication skills refer to the manager's ability to both effectively convey ideas and information to others and effectively receive ideas and information from others. International managers face additional communication challenges because of differences in language, time zones, and so forth. As a way to sharpen your communication skills, this exercise examines the impact of different time zones on business activities.

Exercise Background

Assume that you are a manager in a large multinational firm. Your office is in San Francisco. You need to arrange a conference call with several other managers to discuss an upcoming strategic change by your firm. The other managers are located in New York, London, Rome, Moscow, Tokyo, Singapore, and Sydney.

Exercise Task

Using the information above, do the following:

1. Determine the time differential in each city. For example, if it is 10 A.M. in San Francisco, what time is it in the other locations you need to call?
2. Assuming that people in each city have a "normal" workday of 8 A.M. to 5 P.M., determine the optimal time for your conference call; that is, what time can you place the call so as to minimize the number of people who are inconvenienced?
3. Now assume that you need to visit each office in person. You need to spend one full day in each city. Use the Internet to review airline schedules, take into account differences in time zones, and develop an itinerary.

SKILLS *self-assessment* INSTRUMENT

Global Awareness

Introduction: As we have noted, the environment of business is becoming more global. The following assessment is designed to help you understand your readiness to respond to managing in a global context.

Instructions: You will agree with some of the following statements and disagree with others. In some cases you may find it difficult to make a decision, but you should force a choice. Record your answers next to each statement according to the following scale:

4 Strongly agree   **2** Somewhat disagree

3 Somewhat agree   **1** Strongly disagree

_____ 1. Some areas of Switzerland are very much like Italy.

_____ 2. Although aspects of behavior such as motivation and attitudes within organizational settings remain quite diverse across cultures, organizations themselves appear to be increasingly similar in terms of design and technology.

_____ 3. Spain, France, Japan, Singapore, Mexico, Brazil, and Indonesia have cultures with a strong orientation toward authority.

_____ 4. Japan and Austria define male-female roles more rigidly and value qualities like forcefulness and achievement more than do Norway, Sweden, Denmark, and Finland.

_____ 5. Some areas of Switzerland are very much like France.

_____ 6. Australia, Great Britain, the Netherlands, Canada, and New Zealand have cultures that view people first as individuals and place a priority on their own interests and values, whereas Colombia, Pakistan, Taiwan, Peru, Singapore, Mexico, Greece, and Hong Kong have cultures in which the good of the group or society is considered the priority.

_____ 7. The United States, Israel, Austria, Denmark, Ireland, Norway, Germany, and New Zealand have cultures with a low orientation toward authority.

_____ 8. The same manager may behave differently in different cultural settings.

_____ 9. Denmark, Canada, Norway, Singapore, Hong Kong, and Australia have cultures in which employees tolerate a high degree of uncertainty, but such levels of uncertainty are not well tolerated in Israel, Austria, Japan, Italy, Argentina, Peru, France, and Belgium.

_____ 10. Some areas of Switzerland are very much like Germany.

For interpretation, see Interpretations of Skills Self-Assessment Instruments.

EXPERIENTIAL EXERCISE

Ethics of Employee Appraisal

Purpose: Many management activities occur within an ethical context. The appraisal of employee performance is one of those activities that can raise ethical issues. This skill builder focuses on the *human resources model*. It will help you develop the *mentor role* of the human resources model. One of the skills of the mentor is the ability to develop subordinates.

Introduction: Much attention has been given in recent years to ethics in business, yet one area often overlooked is ethical issues when hiring or appraising employees. Marian Kellogg developed a list of principles to keep in mind when recruiting or appraising.

How to Keep Your Appraisals Ethical: A Manager's Checklist
1. Don't appraise without knowing why the appraisal is required.
2. Appraise on the basis of **representative** information.
3. Appraise on the basis of **sufficient** information.
4. Appraise on the basis of **relevant** information.
5. Be honest in your assessment of all the facts you obtain.
6. Don't write one thing and say another.
7. In offering an appraisal, make it plain that this is only your personal opinion of the facts as you see them.
8. Pass appraisal information along only to those who have good reason to know it.
9. Don't imply the existence of an appraisal that hasn't been made.
10. Don't accept another's appraisal without knowing the basis on which it was made.

Instructions: Read each incident individually and decide which rule or rules it violates, marking the appropriate number on the right. In some cases, more than one rule is violated. In your group, go over each case and come to a consensus on which rules are violated.

Incidents:
1. Steve Wilson has applied for a transfer to Department O, headed by Marianne Kilbourn. As part of her fact finding, Marianne reads through the written evaluation, which is glowing, and then asks Steve's boss, Bill Hammond, for information on Steve's performance. Bill starts complaining about Steve because his last project was not up to par but does not mention that Steve's wife has been seriously ill for two months. Marianne then decides not to accept Steve's transfer.
   Rule violation # _____
2. Maury Nanner is a sales manager who is having lunch with several executives. One of them, Harvey Gant, asks Maury what he thinks of his subordinate George Williams, and Nanner gives a lengthy evaluation.
   Rule violation # _____
3. Phillip Randall is working on six-month evaluations of his subordinates. He decides to rate Elisa Donner less than average on initiative because he thinks she spends too much time, energy, and money making herself look attractive. He thinks it distracts the male employees.
   Rule violation # _____
4. Paul Trendant has received an application from an outstanding candidate, Jim Fischer. However, Paul decides not to hire Jim because he heard from someone that Jim only moved to town because his wife got a good job here. Trendant thinks Jim will quit whenever his wife gets transferred.
   Rule violation # _____
5. Susan Forman is on the fast track and tries to make herself look good to her boss, Peter Everly. This morning she has a meeting with Pete to discuss which person to promote. Just before the meeting, Pete's golf buddy, Harold, a coworker of Susan's, tells Susan

that Alice, Jerry, and Joe are favored by Pete. Susan had felt Darlene was the strongest candidate, but she goes into the meeting with Pete and suggests Alice, Jerry, and Joe as top candidates.

Rule violation # ____

6. Sandy is a new supervisor for seven people. After several months Sandy is certain that Linda is marginally competent and frequently cannot produce any useful work. Looking over past appraisals, Sandy sees that all of Linda's evaluations were positive, and she is told that Linda "has problems"

and not to be "too hard on her." Realizing this approach is not healthy, Sandy begins documenting Linda's inadequate performance. Several supervisors hint that she should "lighten up because we don't want Linda to feel hurt."

Rule violation # ____

Sources: Marian S. Kellogg, *What to Do About Performance Appraisal,* AMACOM, a division of the American Management Association, New York, 1975; Marian S. Kellogg, *Personnel,* July–August 1965, American Management Association, New York; and Dorothy Marcic, *Organizational Behavior: Experiences and Cases,* 3rd ed (Minneapolis, MN: West Publishing Company, 1992).

WAL-MART COURTS EUROPEAN SHOPPERS

With a beachhead of stores spread across England and Germany, Wal-Mart is bringing American-style retailing to European shoppers. Already the world's largest retail chain, with $165 billion in global sales, Wal-Mart entered the United Kingdom by buying the Asda chain, which operates more than 230 stores across the country. Wal-Mart wants its non–U.S. sales to bring in a larger chunk of its overall sales revenue, and Europe is an attractive region for a retailer that knows its business.

The Arkansas-based Wal-Mart began shaking up British retailing by cutting prices, highlighting selection, and promoting friendly service. Because British retailers are accustomed to higher profit margins, the Wal-Mart formula of low markup pricing has put pressure on rival chains such as Tesco and given smaller stores even bigger headaches. Wal-Mart has touched off price wars in food products and other categories, sending competitors scrambling to meet or beat its price tags. Through Asda@Home, the chain's first European Internet shopping site, Wal-Mart is expanding its brand of low-price retailing to reach shoppers in other countries.

In Germany, however, giant discounters are commonplace, so Wal-Mart is basing its competitive strategy there on service and selection. Many German stores have a much narrower merchandise selection than Wal-Mart. Small wonder that shoppers gawk at the huge quantities of food items, from fresh fruits and vegetables to specialty meats and cheeses in Wal-Mart outlets in Dortmund and other cities. As in the United States, the Wal-Mart stores in Germany also carry all sorts of toys, clothing, appliances, and assorted products for household and personal use. Customer service is as much a draw as selection, because service in German stores is much less friendly and personalized. The twin weaknesses of poor selection and poor service leave German retailing open to aggressive competitive attacks from Internet retailers as well as from Wal-Mart.

To enter the German market, Wal-Mart bought ninety-five stores from two struggling local chains and hung an American flag outside each to herald the change in management. Then it began a massive renovation project to enlarge and modernize each outlet. Renovations have proceeded slowly, however. Within three years of the acquisition, fewer than one-third of the stores had been renovated. The renovated stores are definitely more spacious and inviting, with wider aisles, brighter lights, and more accessible shelving loaded with merchandise—all of which is helping to boost sales. Few German stores allow credit payments, so Wal-Mart is successfully attracting shoppers by accepting major credit cards. German shoppers are also pleased at not having to bag their own purchases or pay for the plastic bags at Wal-Mart, amenities that U.S. shoppers take for granted.

Just as visible as the physical changes are the managerial changes. The managers in each Wal-Mart store hold a daily staff meeting to extol new products and motivate store personnel. For example, the comanager of the store in Dortmund, Germany, dressed in a sailor suit when announcing the introduction of a new line of nautical gifts. Knowing that customer service is spotlighted in the chain's television commercials, managers in the German stores encourage good service by praising good performance and keeping communication lines open. Still, even the best service will not make up for cramped stores, so Wal-Mart will have to speed up its renovations if it wants German shoppers to come back and buy—again and again.

Case Questions

1. On which of Hofstede's five dimensions are Wal-Mart's American roots and German operations fairly similar? How do these similarities affect the company's ability to manage its German stores?

2. Why would Wal-Mart choose to operate in Germany and Great Britain on the basis of direct investment rather than through a joint venture or strategic alliance?

3. If you were a retailer in Great Britain or Germany, what would you do to blunt Wal-Mart's competitive advantages?

Case References

Steven Komarow, "Wal-Mart Takes Slow Road in Germany," *USA Today*, May 9, 2000, p. 3B; Kerry Capell and Heidi Dawley, "Wal-Mart's Not-So-Secret British Weapon," *Business Week*, January 24, 2000, http://www.businessweek.com/2000/00_04/b3665095.htm (July 10, 2000).

CHAPTER NOTES

1. "Three Carmakers Create Link," *USA Today*, February 28, 2000, p. 8B; "Big Three Car Makers Plan Net Exchange," *Wall Street Journal*, February 28, 2000, pp. A3, A16 (quote on p. A16); and Shawn Tully, "The B2B Tool That Really *Is* Changing the World," *Fortune*, March 20, 2000, pp. 132–145.

2. See Jay B. Barney and William G. Ouchi, eds., *Organizational Economics* (San Francisco: Jossey-Bass, 1986), for a detailed analysis of linkages between economics and organizations.

3. "Long Live the New Economy," *Fast Company*, February 2001, pp. 96–109.

4. "A Breakup Primer for Microsoft?" *Wall Street Journal*, June 6, 2000, pp. B1, B4; and "WorldCom Takeover of Sprint Looks Dead as U.S. Sues to Halt It," *Wall Street Journal*, June 28, 2000, pp. A1, A6.

5. For example, see Susanne G. Scott and Vicki R. Lane, "A Stakeholder Approach to Organizational Identity," *Academy of Management Review* 25, no. 1 (2000): 43–62.

6. "Why Tommy Hilfiger Is So Like, Um, 1998," *Business Week*, April 24, 2000, p. 55.

7. "Curves Ahead," *Wall Street Journal*, March 10, 1999, pp. B1, B10.

8. See Norman Barry, *Business Ethics* (West Lafayette, IN: Purdue University Press, 1999).

9. "Sony 'Fires' Phony Movie Critic," *USA Today*, June 4, 2001, p. 1D.

10. "Is it Rainforest Crunch Time?" *Business Week*, July 15, 1996, pp. 70–71; and "Yo, Ben! Yo, Jerry! It's Just Ice Cream," *Fortune*, April 28, 1997, p. 374.

11. Andrew Singer, "Can a Company Be Too Ethical?" *Across the Board*, April 1993, pp. 17–22.

12. Lynn Sharp Paine, "Managing for Organizational Integrity," *Harvard Business Review*, March/April 1994, pp. 106–115.

13. "A New Way of Giving," *Time*, July 24, 2000, pp. 48–51.

14. David M. Messick and Max H. Bazerman, "Ethical Leadership and the Psychology of Decision Making," *Sloan Management Review*, Winter 1996, pp. 9–22.

15. "Unfuzzing Ethics for Managers," *Fortune*, November 23, 1987, pp. 229–234.

16. See Janet P. Near and Marcia P. Miceli, "Whistle-Blowing: Myth and Reality," *Journal of Management* 22, no. 3 (1996): 507–526, for a recent review of the literature on whistle blowing.

17. "Whistle-Blowers on Trial," *Business Week*, March 24, 1997, pp. 172–178. See also "How a Whistle-Blower Spurred Pricing Case Involving Drug Makers," *Wall Street Journal*, May 12, 2000, pp. A1, A8.

18. *Hoover's Handbook of American Business 2001* (Austin, TX: Hoover's Business Press, 2001), pp. 200–201, 576-577.

19. "Creating a Worldwide Yen for Japanese Beer," *Financial Times*, October 7, 1994, p. 20.

20. Kenichi Ohmae, "The Global Logic of Strategic Alliances," *Harvard Business Review*, March/April 1989, pp. 143–154.

21. Sue Zesinger, "Ford's Hip Transplant," *Fortune*, May 10, 1999, pp. 82–92.

22. Jay B. Barney, "Organizational Culture: Can It Be a Source of Sustained Competitive Advantage?" *Academy of Management Review* (July 1986): 656–665.

23. For example, see Carol J. Loomis, "Sam Would Be Proud," *Fortune*, April 17, 2000, pp. 131–144.

24. "Why Wells Fargo Is Circling the Wagons," *Wall Street Journal*, June 9, 1997, pp. 92–93.

Planning

3

Planning and Strategic Management

January 2000 brought with it global celebrations of the new millennium. It also marked one of the most significant mergers in the history of business—the joining of America Online (AOL) and Time Warner into a new enterprise that some observers predicted would rewrite the rules of business for years to come. AOL launched nationwide service in 1989 and went public in 1992. It grew rapidly over the rest of the decade, attracting millions of subscribers and swallowing rival CompuServe and premier Internet portal Netscape along the way.

Time Warner, on the other hand, is an old-line company tracing its roots back almost 100 years. Time, Inc., was founded in 1922 with the launch of its namesake magazine *Time*. Over the decades, Time also began publication of such periodicals as *Fortune, Sports Illustrated*,

and *People*, as well as creating the cable television network HBO. Warner Brothers was born alongside the Hollywood movie industry when it produced such classics as *Little Caesar* and *Casablanca*. Warner eventually grew to encompass a movie studio, television studios, cable television operations, and a publishing business headlined by such properties as *Superman* comics and *Mad* magazine. These two firms merged in 1989 to create Time Warner; the combined firm subsequently acquired TBS (consisting of CNN and other cable networks), launched numerous new magazines, and started a new broadcast television network.

As the 1990s drew to a close, managers at both AOL and Time Warner realized that their firms had some major strategic weaknesses. AOL, for example, lacked two key

competitive assets. For one thing, most of its services were carried by and delivered through telephone wire; many experts, though, were predicting that the future of this industry rested on so-called broadband technology, such as cable television. And for another, AOL itself had precious little "content" to deliver—it simply connected information sources with users who wanted access to that information.

Time Warner, meanwhile, had both of the things AOL desperately needed. Time Warner cable, for example, had over 13 million subscribers. And information content was the very thing Time Warner was based on—magazines, books,

"This is a merger of equals."

—*Stephen Case, CEO of AOL, and Gerald Levin, CEO of Time Warner* music, movies, and television programming. But the venerable media company itself, like so many of its old-line brethren, had failed to figure out for itself how to make the transformation to the e-world. At the time the merger was announced, Time Warner had already made a commitment of $500 million to develop a digital division, but most observers were unenthusiastic or downright skeptical about its ability to become a player.

The idea for a partnership was hatched in September 1999 at an international meeting of high-level CEOs in Paris; the players kept talking and met again two weeks later in Shanghai at a similar event. In October, a merger was formally proposed. Serious negotiations began in November. Two key AOL executives traveled to New York to meet with a senior vice president from Time Warner. The three managers locked themselves in a conference room and used poster-sized sheets of paper to sketch out how a combined firm might look. These sheets were then taken back to AOL headquarters for further examination. Finally, all the details were worked out, and a final accord was reached in January 2000. When the deal was announced, the business community was stunned. One observer went so far as to call it the most transformational event in his career. And indeed, the merger was so intriguing that many experts were simply at a loss to figure out what it truly meant.[1]

The actions taken by AOL and Time Warner reflect one of the most critical functions that managers perform for their businesses: strategy and strategic planning. Executives at each firm recognized that their firm had both significant strengths and worrisome weaknesses. They also saw that by combining their firms they could use the strengths of each firm to offset the weaknesses of the other. And they further recognized that a combined firm would be well positioned to capitalize on the emerging commercial potential of the Internet. Hence, the merger of the two firms represents a significant strategic decision by managers at the two firms.

This chapter is the first of three that explore the planning process in more detail. We begin by examining the nature of planning and organizational goals. We then discuss strategic management, including its components and alternatives, and describe the kinds of analyses needed for firms to formulate their strategies. Finally, we examine how strategies are implemented through tactical and operational planning.

Planning and Organizational Goals

The planning process itself can best be thought of as a generic activity. All organizations engage in planning activities, but no two organizations plan in exactly the same fashion. Figure 3.1 is a general representation of the planning process that many organizations attempt to follow. But, although most firms follow this general framework, each also has its own nuances and variations.

Figure 3.1

The Planning Process

The planning process takes place within an environmental context. Managers must develop a complete and thorough understanding of this context to determine the organization's mission and develop its strategic, tactical, and operational goals and plans.

As Figure 3.1 shows, all planning occurs within an environmental context. If managers do not understand this context, they are unable to develop effective plans. Thus understanding the environment is essentially the first step in planning. The previous chapter summarizes many of the basic environmental issues that affect organizations and how they plan. With this understanding as a foundation, managers must then establish the organization's mission. The mission outlines the organization's purpose, premises, values, and directions. Flowing from the mission are parallel streams of goals and plans. Directly following the mission are strategic goals. These goals and the mission help determine strategic plans. Strategic goals and plans are primary inputs for developing tactical goals. Tactical goals and the original strategic plans help shape tactical plans. Tactical plans, in turn, combine with the tactical goals to shape operational goals. These goals and the appropriate tactical plans determine operational plans. Finally, goals and plans at each level can also be used as input for future activities at all levels.

Organizational Goals

Goals are critical to organizational effectiveness, and they serve a number of purposes. Organizations can also have several different kinds of goals, all of which must be appropriately managed. And a number of different kinds of managers must be involved in setting goals.

Purposes of Goals

Goals serve four important purposes. First, they provide guidance and a unified direction for people in the organization. Goals can help everyone understand where the organization is going and why getting there is important.[2] Procter & Gamble (P&G) recently set a goal of doubling revenues by the year 2006; this goal helps everyone in the firm recognize the strong emphasis on growth and expansion that is driving the firm. Second, goal-setting practices strongly affect other aspects of planning. Effective goal setting promotes good planning, and good planning facilitates future goal setting. For example, the ambitious revenue goal set for P&G demonstrates how setting goals and developing plans to reach them should be seen as complementary activities. The strong growth goal should encourage managers to plan for expansion by looking for new market opportunities, for example. Similarly, they must also always be alert for competitive threats and new ideas that will help facilitate future expansion.

Third, goals can serve as a source of motivation to employees of the organization. Goals that are specific and moderately difficult can motivate people to work harder, especially if attaining the goal is likely to result in rewards.[3] The Italian furniture manufacturer Industrie Natuzzi SpA uses goals to motivate its workers. Each craftsperson has a goal for how long it should take to perform her or his job, such as sewing leather sheets together to make a sofa cushion or building wooden frames for chair arms. At the completion of assigned tasks, workers enter their ID number and job number into the firm's computer system. If they get a job done faster than their goal, a bonus is automatically added to their paycheck.[4] Finally, goals provide an effective mechanism for evaluation and control. This means that performance can be assessed in the future in terms of how successfully today's goals are accomplished.

Establishing goals and then working to achieve them play very important roles in organizational success. Some managers, however, have difficulty in setting meaningful goals. To enhance their abilities to set and achieve goals, some managers are starting to rely on executive coaches—essentially personal consultants who help them function more effectively. When Cheryl Weir started working with Charles Cleary at AT&T, she was unimpressed with his vague goal for his unit of "being number 1" or achieving what she saw as unambitious growth of 5 percent. She led him to set a growth goal of 16 percent and develop a plan for achieving it; and when they met this goal, Cleary's unit was among the top three in the company.

Kinds of Goals

Organizations establish many different kinds of goals. The four basic levels of goals are the mission and strategic, tactical, and operational goals. An organization's **mission** is a statement of its "fundamental, unique purpose that sets a business apart from other firms of its type and identifies the scope of the business's operations in product and market terms."[5] **Strategic goals** are goals set by and for top

mission A statement of an organization's fundamental purpose

strategic goal A goal set by and for top management of the organization

tactical goal A goal set by and for middle managers of the organization

operational goal A goal set by and for lower-level managers of the organization

management of the organization. They focus on broad, general issues. For example, Procter & Gamble's goal of doubling sales revenues is a strategic goal. **Tactical goals** are set by and for middle managers. Their focus is on how to operationalize actions necessary to achieve the strategic goals. Tactical goals at P&G might center around which new products to launch, which existing products to revise, and so forth. **Operational goals** are set by and for lower-level managers. Their concern is with shorter-term issues associated with the tactical goals. An operational goal for P&G might be a target number of new products to launch each of the next five years. (Some managers use the words *objective* and *goal* interchangeably. When they are differentiated, however, the term *objective* is usually used instead of *operational goal.*)

Kinds of Plans

Organizations establish many different kinds of plans. At a general level, these include strategic, tactical, and operational plans.

strategic plan A general plan outlining decisions of resource allocation, priorities, and action steps necessary to reach strategic goals

Strategic Plans   Strategic plans are the plans developed to achieve strategic goals. More precisely, a **strategic plan** is a general plan outlining decisions of resource allocation, priorities, and action steps necessary to reach strategic goals.[6] These plans are set by the board of directors and top management, generally have an extended time horizon, and address questions of scope, resource deployment, competitive advantage, and synergy. We discuss strategic planning further in the next major section.

tactical plan A plan aimed at achieving tactical goals and developed to implement parts of a strategic plan

Tactical Plans   A **tactical plan**, aimed at achieving tactical goals, is developed to implement specific parts of a strategic plan. Tactical plans typically involve upper and middle management and, compared with strategic plans, have a somewhat shorter time horizon and a more specific and concrete focus. Thus tactical plans are concerned more with actually getting things done than with deciding what to do. Tactical planning is covered after the discussion of strategic planning.

operational plan Focuses on carrying out tactical plans to achieve operational goals

Operational Plans   An **operational plan** focuses on carrying out tactical plans to achieve operational goals. Developed by middle and lower-level managers, operational plans have a short-term focus and are relatively narrow in scope. Each one deals with a fairly small set of activities. We cover operational planning in the last section of this chapter.

The Nature of Strategic Management

strategy A comprehensive plan for accomplishing an organization's goals

A **strategy** is a comprehensive plan for accomplishing an organization's goals. **Strategic management**, in turn, is a way of approaching business opportunities and challenges—it is a comprehensive and ongoing management process aimed at formulating and implementing effective strategies. Finally, **effective strategies** are those that promote a superior alignment between the organization and its environment and the achievement of strategic goals.[7]

The Components of Strategy

In general, a well-conceived strategy addresses three areas: distinctive competence, scope, and resource deployment. A **distinctive competence** is something the organization does exceptionally well. A distinctive competence of The Limited is speed in moving inventory. It tracks consumer preferences daily with point-of-sale computers, transmits orders to suppliers in Hong Kong electronically, charters 747s to fly products to the United States, and has products in stores 48 hours later. Because other retailers take weeks or sometimes months to accomplish the same things, The Limited relies on this distinctive competence to stay ahead of its competitors.[8]

The **scope** of a strategy specifies the range of markets in which an organization will compete. Hershey Foods has essentially restricted its scope to the confectionery business, with a few related activities in other food-processing areas. In contrast, its biggest competitor, Mars, has adopted a broader scope by competing in the pet food business and the electronics industry, among others. Some organizations, called *conglomerates*, compete in dozens or even hundreds of markets.

A strategy should also include an outline of the organization's projected **resource deployment**—how it will distribute its resources across the areas in which it competes. General Electric, for example, has been using profits from its highly successful U.S. operations to invest heavily in new businesses in Europe and Asia. Alternatively, the firm might instead have chosen to invest in different industries in its domestic market and/or to invest more heavily in Latin America. The choices it made as to where and how much to invest reflect issues of resource deployment.[9]

Types of Strategic Alternatives

Most businesses today also develop strategies at two distinct levels. These levels provide a rich combination of strategic alternatives for organizations. The two general levels are business and corporate strategies. **Business-level strategy** is the set of strategic alternatives from which an organization chooses as it conducts business in a particular industry or a particular market. Such alternatives help the organization focus its competitive efforts for each industry or market in a targeted and focused manner.

Corporate-level strategy is the set of strategic alternatives from which an organization chooses as it manages its operations simultaneously across several industries and several markets. As we discuss later, most large companies today compete in a variety of industries and markets. Thus, although they develop business-level strategies for each industry or market, they also develop an overall strategy that helps define the mix of industries and markets that are of interest to the firm.

Drawing a distinction between strategy formulation and strategy implementation is also instructive. **Strategy formulation** is the set of processes involved in creating or determining the strategies of the organization, whereas **strategy implementation** comprises the methods by which strategies are operationalized or executed within the organization. The primary distinction is along lines of content versus process: the formulation stage determines what the strategy is, and the implementation stage focuses on how the strategy is achieved.

strategic management A comprehensive and ongoing management process aimed at formulating and implementing effective strategies; a way of approaching business opportunities and challenges

effective strategy A strategy that promotes a superior alignment between the organization and its environment and the achievement of strategic goals

distinctive competence An organizational strength possessed by only a small number of competing firms

scope When applied to *strategy,* it specifies the range of markets in which an organization will compete

resource deployment How an organization distributes its resources across the areas in which it competes

business-level strategy The set of strategic alternatives from which an organization chooses as it conducts business in a particular industry or market

corporate-level strategy The set of strategic alternatives from which an organization chooses as it manages its operations simultaneously across several industries and several markets

strategy formulation The set of processes involved in creating or determining the strategies of the organization; focuses on the content of strategies

strategy implementation The methods by which strategies are operationalized or executed within the organization; focuses on the processes through which strategies are achieved

Using SWOT Analysis to Formulate Strategy

SWOT An acronym that stands for **s**trengths, **w**eaknesses, **o**pportunities, and **t**hreats

The starting point in formulating strategy is usually SWOT analysis. **SWOT** is an acronym that stands for **s**trengths, **w**eaknesses, **o**pportunities, and **t**hreats. As shown in Figure 3.2, SWOT analysis is a careful evaluation of an organization's internal strengths and weaknesses as well as its environmental opportunities and threats. In SWOT analysis, the best strategies accomplish an organization's mission by (1) exploiting an organization's opportunities and strengths while (2) neutralizing its threats and (3) avoiding (or correcting) its weaknesses.

Evaluating an Organization's Strengths

Organizational strengths are skills and capabilities that enable an organization to conceive of and implement its strategies. Sears, for example, has a nationwide network of trained service employees who repair Sears appliances. Jane Thompson, a Sears executive, conceived of a plan to consolidate repair and home improvement services nationwide under the well-known Sears brand name and to promote the plan as a general repair operation for all appliances, not just those purchased from Sears. Thus the firm is capitalizing on existing capabilities and the strength of its name to launch a new operation.[10] *Management InfoTech* explores how leading U.S. e-businesses are using their organizational strengths to expand aggressively into Europe.

A distinctive competence is a strength possessed by only a small number of competing firms. Distinctive competencies are rare among a set of competitors. George Lucas's Industrial Light and Magic (ILM), for example, has brought the cinematic art of special effects to new heights. Some of ILM's special effects can be produced by no other organization; these rare special effects are thus ILM's distinctive competencies. Organizations that exploit their distinctive competencies often obtain a competitive advantage and attain above-normal economic performance.[11]

Figure 3.2

SWOT Analysis

SWOT analysis is one of the most important steps in formulating strategy. Using the organization's mission as a context, managers assess internal strengths (distinctive competencies) and weaknesses as well as external opportunities and threats. The goal is to then develop good strategies that exploit opportunities and strengths, neutralize threats, and avoid weaknesses.

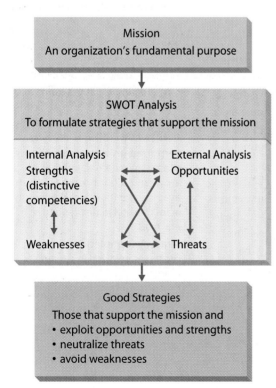

Evaluating an Organization's Weaknesses

Organizational weaknesses are skills and capabilities that do not enable an organization to choose and implement strategies that support its mission. An organization has essentially two ways of addressing weaknesses. First, it may need to make investments to obtain the strengths required to implement strategies that support its mission. Second, it may need to modify its mission so that it can be accomplished with the skills and capabilities that the organization already possesses.

U.S. E-Businesses Prospect for Growth in Europe

U.S. Internet innovators are seeking aggressive growth by building on their successful domestic strategies to enter global markets. Leading e-tailer Amazon .com, for example, used its innovative web technology to fuel an invasion of the British market. Much of the content on Amazon's British site (http://www.amazon.co.uk) is local—CDs by local artists, books by local authors—supported by the U.S. parent's online shopping technology and marketing expertise. The company used the same strategy to expand in France with a mix of local and global content supported by back-office technology imported from the U.S. parent. In addition, Amazon expanded by buying locally operated Internet bookstores. Despite competition from European e-businesses, Amazon's online cash registers have been ringing: Its European sales have already outdistanced those of Bertelsmann's BOL, its closest European rival, by 500 percent.

Online auction innovator eBay has also pursued growth by crossing the Atlantic to open country-specific web sites in Germany (http://www.ebay.de), Great Britain, and France. By initially concentrating on just three new markets, eBay sought to establish a strong customer base and build economies of scale for higher profitability and future expansion. Despite intense competition, eBay attracted far more users than QXL, its largest European rival, in less than a year.

Taking risks to support aggressive growth and ensure long-term viability is what helps U.S. e-businesses like Vaca-

tionSpot.com, which lists foreign vacation home rentals, compete more effectively against European rivals like Belgium's Rent-a-Holiday. Although Rent-a-Holiday had a nine-month head start, VacationSpot (http://vacationspot.com) went beyond merely listing rental properties, to allow customers to finalize and pay for rental arrangements online. VacationSpot also took financial risks, such as arranging expensive promotion deals with Expedia, Travelocity, and other popular travel web sites, to gain wider exposure and increase market share. Rent-a-Holiday soon sold out to VacationSpot, then the combined company merged with Expedia, gaining more financial backing and building the online clout to become an even more formidable force in the growing market for online home rentals.

> *You're not going to get scale by being number one in Norway.*
>
> —*Michael van Swaaij, European managing director for eBay**

References: William Echikson, "American E-Tailers Take Europe by Storm," *Business Week,* August 7, 2000, pp. 54–55 (*quote on p. 55); William Echikson, "Home Field Disadvantage," *Business Week,* December 13, 1999, pp. EB72–EB74; and "Rough Crossing for eBay," *Business Week,* February 7, 2000, p. EB48.

In practice, organizations have a difficult time focusing on weaknesses, in part because organization members are often reluctant to admit that they do not possess all the skills and capabilities needed. Evaluating weaknesses also calls into question the judgment of managers who chose the organization's mission in the first place and who failed to invest in the skills and capabilities needed to accomplish it. Organizations that fail to either recognize or overcome their weaknesses are likely to suffer from competitive disadvantages. An organization has a competitive disadvantage when it is not implementing valuable strategies that are being implemented by competing organizations. Organizations with a competitive disadvantage can expect to attain below-average levels of performance.

organizational strength A skill or capability that enables an organization to conceive of and implement its strategies

organizational weakness A skill or capability that does not enable an organization to choose and implement strategies that support its mission

organizational opportunity An area in the environment that, if exploited, may generate high performance

organizational threat An area in the environment that increases the difficulty of an organization's achieving high performance

Evaluating an Organization's Opportunities and Threats

Whereas evaluating strengths and weaknesses focuses attention on the internal workings of an organization, evaluating opportunities and threats requires analyzing an organization's environment. **Organizational opportunities** are areas that may generate higher performance. **Organizational threats** are areas that increase the difficulty of an organization's performing at a high level.

■ Formulating Business-Level Strategies

A number of frameworks have been developed for identifying the major strategic alternatives that organizations should consider when choosing their business-level strategies. Two important classification schemes are Porter's generic strategies and strategies based on the product life cycle.

Porter's Generic Strategies

According to Michael Porter, organizations may pursue a differentiation, overall cost leadership, or focus strategy at the business level.[12] An organization that pursues a **differentiation strategy** seeks to distinguish itself from competitors through the quality of its products or services. Firms that successfully implement a differentiation strategy are able to charge more than competitors because customers are willing to pay more to obtain the extra value they perceive. Rolex pursues a differentiation strategy. Rolex watches are handmade of gold and stainless steel and subjected to strenuous tests of quality and reliability. The firm's reputation enables it to charge thousands of dollars for its watches. Other firms that use differentiation strategies are Lexus, Nikon, Cross, and Ralph Lauren.

differentiation strategy A strategy in which an organization seeks to distinguish itself from competitors through the quality of its products or services

overall cost leadership strategy A strategy in which an organization attempts to gain a competitive advantage by reducing its costs below the costs of competing firms

An organization implementing an **overall cost leadership strategy** attempts to gain a competitive advantage by reducing its costs below the costs of competing firms. By keeping costs low, the organization is able to sell its products at low prices and still make a profit. Timex uses an overall cost leadership strategy. For decades, this firm has specialized in manufacturing relatively simple, low-cost watches for the mass market. The price of Timex watches, starting at around $39.95, is low because of the company's efficient, high-volume manufacturing capacity. Other firms that implement overall cost leadership strategies are Hyundai, Eastman Kodak, and Bic.

focus strategy A strategy in which an organization concentrates on a specific regional market, product line, or group of buyers

A firm pursuing a **focus strategy** concentrates on a specific regional market, product line, or group of buyers. This strategy may have either a differentiation focus, whereby the firm differentiates its products in the focus market, or an overall cost leadership focus, whereby the firm manufactures and sells its products at low cost in the focus market. In the watch industry, Tag Heuer follows a focus differentiation strategy by selling only rugged waterproof watches to active consumers. Fiat follows a focus cost leadership strategy by selling its automobiles only in Italy and in selected regions of Europe; Alpha Romeo uses focus differentiation to sell its high-performance cars in these same markets. Fisher-Price uses focus differentiation to sell electronic calculators with large, brightly colored buttons to the parents of preschoolers; stockbroker Edward Jones focuses on small-town settings. General Mills is focusing new product development on consumers who eat meals while driving—their watchword is "Can we make it 'one-handed'?" so that drivers can safely eat or drink it.[13]

Strategies Based on the Product Life Cycle

The **product life cycle** is a model that shows how sales volume changes over the life of products. Understanding the four stages in the product life cycle helps managers recognize that strategies need to evolve over time. As Figure 3.3 shows, the cycle begins when a new product or technology is first introduced. In this *introduction stage*, demand may be very high and sometimes outpaces the firm's ability to supply the product. At this stage, managers need to focus their efforts on "getting product out the door" without sacrificing quality. Managing growth by hiring new employees and managing inventories and cash flow are also concerns during this stage.

During the *growth stage,* more firms begin producing the product, and sales continue to grow. Important management issues include ensuring quality and delivery and beginning to differentiate an organization's product from competitors' products. Entry into the industry during the growth stage may threaten an organization's competitive advantages; thus strategies to slow the entry of competitors are important.

Firms can sometimes extend the life cycle of their products so as to continue to generate new revenues. Introducing existing products to new consumers, modernizing existing products, and reviving products from the past all can be effective ways for doing this. Because Volkswagen was so successful in re-launching its venerable Beetle, the firm is looking to duplicate its success by introducing a new version of its Microbus, which is currently in the design study phase. Once the vehicle of choice for counter-culture types, Volkswagen is hoping that today's consumers will see it as a fresh alternative to Sports Utility Vehicles.

product life cycle A model that portrays how sales volume for products changes over the life of products

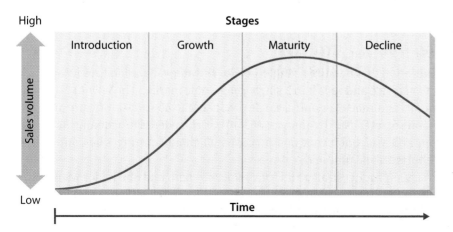

Figure 3.3

The Product Life Cycle
Managers can use the framework of the product life cycle—introduction, growth, maturity, and decline—to plot strategy. For example, management may decide on a differentiation strategy for a product in the introduction stage and cost leadership strategy for a product in the growth stage. By understanding this cycle and where a product falls within it, managers can develop more effective strategies for extending product life.

After a period of growth, products enter a third phase. During this *maturity stage,* overall demand growth for a product begins to slow down, and the number of new firms producing the product begins to decline. The number of established firms producing the product may also begin to decline. This period of maturity is essential if an organization is going to survive in the long run. Product differentiation concerns are still important during this stage, but keeping costs low and beginning the search for new products or services are also important strategic considerations.

In the *decline stage,* demand for the product or technology decreases, the number of organizations producing the product drops, and total sales drop. Demand often declines because all those who were interested in purchasing a particular product have already done so. Organizations that fail to anticipate the decline stage in earlier stages of the life cycle may go out of business. Those that differentiate their product, keep their costs low, or develop new products or services may do well during this stage.

■ *Formulating Corporate-Level Strategies*

strategic business unit (SBU) A single business or set of businesses within a larger organization

Most large organizations are engaged in several businesses, industries, and markets. Each business or set of businesses within such an organization is frequently referred to as a **strategic business unit**, or **SBU**. An organization such as General Electric Company operates hundreds of different businesses, making and selling products as diverse as jet engines, nuclear power plants, and light bulbs. GE organizes these businesses into approximately twenty SBUs. Even organizations that sell only one product may operate in several distinct markets.

diversification The number of different businesses that an organization is engaged in and the extent to which these businesses are related to one another

Decisions about which businesses, industries, and markets an organization will enter, and how to manage these different businesses, are based on an organization's corporate strategy. The most important strategic issue at the corporate level concerns the extent and nature of organizational diversification. **Diversification** describes the number of different businesses that an organization is engaged in and the extent to which these businesses are related to one another. There are three types of diversification strategies: single-product strategy, related diversification, and unrelated diversification.[14]

Single-Product Strategy

single-product strategy A strategy in which an organization manufactures just one product or service and sells it in a single geographic market

An organization that pursues a **single-product strategy** manufactures just one product or service and sells it in a single geographic market. The WD-40 Company, for example, manufactures only a single product, WD-40 spray lubricant, and sells it in just one market, North America. WD-40 has considered broadening its market to Europe and Asia, but it continues to center all manufacturing, sales, and marketing efforts on one product.

The single-product strategy has one major strength and one major weakness. By concentrating its efforts so completely on one product and market, a firm is likely to be very successful in manufacturing and marketing the product. Because it has staked its survival on a single product, the organization works very hard to make sure that the product is a success. Of course, if the product is not accepted by the market or is replaced by a new one, the firm will suffer. This happened to slide rule manufacturers when electronic calculators became widely available, and it happened to companies that manufactured only black-and-white televisions when low-priced color televisions were first mass-marketed. Similarly, Wrigley has long practiced what amounts to a single-product strategy with its line of chewing gums. But because younger consumers are buying less gum than earlier generations, Wrigley is facing declining revenues and lower profits.[15]

Related Diversification

Given the disadvantage of the single-product strategy, most large businesses today operate in several different businesses, industries, or markets. If the businesses are somehow linked, that organization is implementing a strategy of **related diversification**. Virtually all larger businesses in the United States use related diversification.

related diversification A strategy in which an organization operates in several businesses that are somehow linked with one another

Pursuing a strategy of related diversification has three primary advantages. First, it reduces an organization's dependence on any one of its business activities and thus reduces economic risk. Even if one or two of a firm's businesses lose money, the organization as a whole may still survive because the healthy businesses will generate enough cash to support the others. At The Limited, sales declines at Lerners of New York may be offset by sales increases at Express.

Second, by managing several businesses at the same time, an organization can reduce the overhead costs associated with managing any one business. In other words, if the normal administrative costs required to operate any business, such as legal services and accounting, can be spread over a large number of businesses, then the overhead costs *per business* will be lower than they would be if each business had to absorb all costs itself. Thus the overhead costs of businesses in a related diversified firm are usually lower than those of similar businesses that are not part of a larger corporation.

Third, related diversification allows an organization to exploit its strengths and capabilities in more than one business. When organizations do this successfully, they capitalize on synergies, which are complementary effects that exist among their businesses. **Synergy** exists among a set of businesses when the businesses' economic value together is greater than their economic value separately. McDonald's is using synergy as it diversifies into other restaurant and food businesses. For example, its McCafe premium coffee stands in some McDonald's restaurants and its acquisitions of Donatos Pizza, Chipotle Mexican Grill, and Boston Market allow the firm to create new revenue opportunities while utilizing the firm's existing strengths in food products purchasing and distribution.[16]

synergy Exists among a set of businesses when their economic value together is greater than the sum of their economic values separately

Unrelated Diversification

Firms that implement a strategy of **unrelated diversification** operate multiple businesses that are not logically associated with one another. At one time, for example, Quaker Oats owned clothing chains, toy companies, and a restaurant

unrelated diversification A strategy in which an organization operates in several businesses that are not related to one another

business. Unrelated diversification was a very popular strategy in the 1970s. During this time, several conglomerates, such as ITT and Transamerica, grew by acquiring literally hundreds of other organizations and then running these numerous businesses as independent entities. Even if there are important potential synergies among their different businesses, organizations implementing a strategy of unrelated diversification do not attempt to exploit them.

In theory, unrelated diversification has two advantages. First, a business that uses this strategy should have stable performance over time. During any given period, if some businesses owned by the organization are in a cycle of decline, others may be in a cycle of growth. Unrelated diversification is also thought to have resource allocation advantages. Every year, when a corporation allocates capital, people, and other resources among its various businesses, it must evaluate information about the future of those businesses so that it can place its resources where they have the highest return potential. Given that it owns the businesses in question and thus has full access to information about the future of those businesses, a firm implementing unrelated diversification should be able to allocate capital to maximize corporate performance.

Despite these presumed advantages, research suggests that unrelated diversification usually does not lead to high performance. First, corporate-level managers in such a company usually do not know enough about the unrelated businesses to provide helpful strategic guidance or to allocate capital appropriately. To make strategic decisions, managers must have complete and subtle understanding of a business and its environment. Because corporate managers often have difficulty fully evaluating the economic importance of investments for all the businesses under their wing, they tend to concentrate only on a business's current performance. This narrow attention at the expense of broader planning eventually hobbles the entire organization.

Second, because organizations that implement unrelated diversification fail to exploit important synergies, they are at a competitive disadvantage compared to organizations that use related diversification. Universal Studios has been at a competitive disadvantage relative to Disney because its theme parks, movie studios, and licensing divisions are less integrated and therefore achieve less synergy.

For these reasons, almost all organizations have abandoned unrelated diversification as a corporate-level strategy. Transamerica has sold off numerous businesses and now concentrates on a core set of related businesses and markets. Large corporations that have not concentrated on a core set of businesses eventually have been acquired by other companies and then broken up. Research suggests that these organizations are actually worth more when broken up into smaller pieces than they were when joined.

Managing Diversification

portfolio management technique A method that diversified organizations use to determine which businesses to engage in and how to manage these businesses to maximize corporate performance

However an organization implements diversification—whether through internal development, vertical integration, or mergers and acquisitions—it must monitor and manage its strategy. **Portfolio management techniques** are methods that diversified organizations use to make decisions about what businesses to engage in and how to manage these multiple businesses to maximize corporate performance. Two important portfolio management techniques are the BCG matrix and the GE Business Screen.

BCG Matrix   The **BCG** (Boston Consulting Group) **matrix** provides a framework for evaluating the relative performance of businesses in which a diversified organization operates. It also prescribes the preferred distribution of cash and other resources among these businesses. The BCG matrix uses two factors to evaluate an organization's set of businesses: the growth rate of a particular market and the organization's share of that market. The matrix suggests that fast-growing markets in which an organization has the highest market share are more attractive business opportunities than slow-growing markets in which an organization has small market share. Dividing market growth and market share into two categories (low and high) creates the simple matrix shown in Figure 3.4.

The matrix classifies the types of businesses that a diversified organization can engage in as dogs, cash cows, question marks, and stars. *Dogs* are businesses that have a very small share of a market that is not expected to grow. Because these businesses do not hold much economic promise, the BCG matrix suggests that organizations either should not invest in them or should consider selling them as soon as possible. *Cash cows* are businesses that have a large share of a market that is not expected to grow substantially. These businesses characteristically generate high profits that the organization should use to support question marks and stars. (Cash cows are "milked" for cash to support businesses in markets that have greater growth potential.) *Question marks* are businesses that have only a small share of a quickly growing market. The future performance of these businesses is uncertain. A question mark that is able to capture increasing amounts of this growing market may be very profitable. On the other hand, a question mark unable to keep up with market growth is likely to have low profits. The BCG matrix suggests that organizations should invest carefully in question marks. If their performance does not live up to expectations, question marks should be reclassified as dogs and divested. *Stars* are businesses that have the largest share of a rapidly growing market. Cash generated by cash cows should be invested in stars to ensure their preeminent position. For example, when BMW bought Rover a few years ago, experts thought that its products would help the German auto maker reach new consumers. But the company was not able to capitalize on this opportunity, so it ended up selling Rover's car business to a British firm and Land Rover to Ford.[17]

GE Business Screen   Because the BCG matrix is relatively narrow and overly simplistic, General Electric (GE) developed the **GE Business Screen**, a more sophisticated approach to managing diversified business units. The Business Screen is a portfolio management technique that can also be represented in the form of a matrix. Rather than focusing solely on market growth and market share, however, the GE Business Screen considers industry attractiveness and competitive position.

Figure 3.4
The BCG Matrix
The BCG matrix helps managers develop a better understanding of how different strategic business units contibute to the overall organization. By assessing each SBU on the basis of its market growth rate and relative market share, managers can make decisions about whether to commit further financial resources to the SBU or to sell or liquidate it.

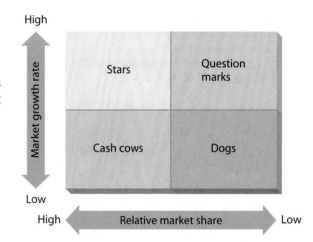

Source: From *Perspectives*, No. 66, "The Product Portfolio." Adapted by permission from The Boston Consulting Group. Inc., 1970.

BCG matrix A method of evaluating businesses relative to the growth rate of their market and the organization's share of the market

GE Business Screen A method of evaluating businesses along two dimensions: (1) industry attractiveness and (2) competitive position; in general, the more attractive the industry and the more competitive the position, the more an organization should invest in a business

Figure 3.5

The GE Business Screen

The GE Business Screen is a more sophisticated approach to portfolio management than the BCG matrix. As shown here, several factors combine to determine a business's competitive position and the attractiveness of its industry. These two dimensions, in turn, can be used to classify businesses as winners, question marks, average businesses, losers, or profit producers. Such a classification enables managers to more effectively allocate the organization's resources across various business opportunities.

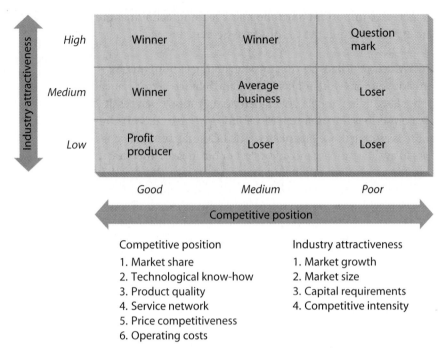

Competitive position
1. Market share
2. Technological know-how
3. Product quality
4. Service network
5. Price competitiveness
6. Operating costs

Industry attractiveness
1. Market growth
2. Market size
3. Capital requirements
4. Competitive intensity

Source: From Hofer, *Strategy Formulation: Analytical Concepts,* 5th ed., by Charles W. Hofer and Dan Schendel. Copyright © 1978. Reprinted with permission of South-Western College Publishing, a division of International Thomson Learning.

These two factors are divided into three categories, to make the nine-cell matrix shown in Figure 3.5. These cells, in turn, classify business units as winners, losers, question marks, average businesses, or profit producers.

As Figure 3.5 shows, both market growth and market share appear in a broad list of factors that determine the overall attractiveness of an industry and the overall quality of a firm's competitive position. In addition to market growth, other determinants of an industry's attractiveness include market size, capital requirements, and competitive intensity. In general, the greater the market growth, the larger the market, the smaller the capital requirements, and the less the competitive intensity, the more attractive an industry will be. Other determinants of an organization's competitive position in an industry (besides market share) include technological know-how, product quality, service network, price competitiveness, and operating costs. In general, businesses with large market share, technological know-how, high product quality, a quality service network, competitive prices, and low operating costs are in a favorable competitive position.

Think of the GE Business Screen as a way of applying SWOT analysis to the implementation and management of a diversification strategy. The determinants of industry attractiveness are similar to the environmental opportunities and threats in SWOT analysis, and the determinants of competitive position are similar to organizational strengths and weaknesses. By conducting this type of SWOT analysis across several businesses, a diversified organization can decide how to invest its resources to maximize corporate performance. In general, organizations should invest in winners and in question marks (where industry attractiveness and competitive position are both favorable); maintain the market position of average businesses and profit producers (where industry attractiveness and competitive position are average); and sell losers. For example, Unilever recently assessed its business portfolio using a similar framework and, as a result, decided to sell off several specialty chemical units that were not contributing to the firm's profitability as much as other businesses. The firm then used the revenues from these divestitures and bought more related businesses such as Ben & Jerry's Homemade and Slim-Fast.[18]

■ *Tactical Planning*

As we noted earlier, tactical plans are developed to implement specific parts of a strategic plan. You have probably heard the saying about winning the battle but losing the war. **Tactical plans** are to battles what strategy is to a war: an organized sequence of steps designed to execute strategic plans. Strategy focuses on resources, environment, and mission, whereas tactics focus primarily on people and action.

tactical plan A plan aimed at achieving tactical goals which is developed to implement parts of a strategic plan

Developing Tactical Plans

Although effective tactical planning depends on many factors that vary from one situation to another, we can identify some basic guidelines. First, the manager needs to recognize that tactical planning must address a number of tactical goals derived from a broader strategic goal. An occasional situation may call for a stand-alone tactical plan, but most tactical plans flow from and must be consistent with a strategic plan.

For example, a few years ago, top managers at Coca-Cola developed a strategic plan for maintaining the firm's dominance of the soft drink industry. As part of developing the plan, they identified a critical environmental threat—considerable unrest and uncertainty among the independent bottlers who packaged and distributed Coca-Cola's products. To simultaneously counter this threat and strengthen the company's position, Coca-Cola bought several large independent bottlers and combined them into one new organization called Coca-Cola Enterprises. Selling half of the new company's stock reaped millions in profits while still effectively keeping control of the enterprise in Coca-Cola's hands. Thus the creation of the new business was a tactical plan developed to contribute to the achievement of an overarching strategic goal.[19]

Second, although strategies are often stated in general terms, tactics must specify resources and time frames. A strategy can call for being number one in a particular market or industry, but a tactical plan must specify precisely what activities will be undertaken to achieve that goal. Consider the Coca-Cola example again. Another element of its strategic plan involves increased worldwide market share. To facilitate additional sales in Europe, managers developed tactical plans for building a new plant in the south of France to make soft drink concentrate and for building another canning plant in Dunkirk. Building these plants represents a concrete action involving measurable resources (funds to build the plants) and a clear time horizon (a target date for completion).

Finally, tactical planning requires the use of human resources. Managers involved in tactical planning spend a great deal of time working with other people.

They must be in a position to receive information from others in and outside of the organization, process that information in the most effective way, and then pass it on to others who might make use of it. Coca-Cola executives have been intensively involved in planning the new plants, setting up the new bottling venture noted earlier, and exploring a joint venture with Cadbury Schweppes in the United Kingdom. Each activity has required considerable time and effort from dozens of managers. One manager, for example, crossed the Atlantic 12 times while negotiating the Cadbury deal.

Executing Tactical Plans

Regardless of how well a tactical plan is formulated, its ultimate success depends on the way it is carried out. Successful implementation, in turn, depends on the astute use of resources, effective decision making, and insightful steps to ensure that the right things are done at the right time and in the right ways. A manager can see an absolutely brilliant idea fail because of improper execution.

Proper execution depends on a number of important factors. First, the manager needs to evaluate every possible course of action in light of the goal it is intended to reach. Next, he or she needs to make sure that each decision maker has the information and resources necessary to get the job done. Vertical and horizontal communication and integration of activities must be present to minimize conflict and inconsistent activities. And, finally, the manager must monitor ongoing activities derived from the plan to make sure they are achieving the desired results. This monitoring typically takes place within the context of the organization's ongoing control systems.

Operational Planning

Another critical element in effective organizational planning is the development and implementation of operational plans. Operational plans are derived from tactical plans and are aimed at achieving operational goals. Thus operational plans tend to be narrowly focused, have relatively short time horizons, and involve lower-level managers. The two most basic forms of operational plans and specific types of each are summarized in Table 3.1.

Single-Use Plans

single-use plan Developed to carry out a course of action that is not likely to be repeated in the future

A **single-use plan** is developed to carry out a course of action that is not likely to be repeated in the future. As Disney proceeds with its new theme park in Hong Kong, it will develop numerous single-use plans for individual rides, attractions, and hotels. The two most common forms of single-use plans are programs and projects.

program A single-use plan for a large set of activities

Programs   A **program** is a single-use plan for a large set of activities. It might consist of identifying procedures for introducing a new product line, opening a

Plan	Description
Single-use plan	Developed to carry out a course of action not likely to be carried out in the future
Program	Single-use plan for a large set of activities
Project	Single-use plan of less scope and complexity than a program
Standing plan	Developed for activities that recur regularly over a period of time
Policy	Standing plan specifying the organization's general response to a designated problem or situation
Standard operating procedure	Standing plan outlining steps to be followed in particular circumstances
Rules and regulations	Standing plans describing exactly how specific activities are to be carried out

Table 3.1

Types of Operational Plans
Organizations develop various operational plans to help achieve operational goals. In general, there are two types of single-use plans and three types of standing plans.

new facility, or changing the organization's mission. As part of its own strategic plans for growth, Black & Decker bought General Electric's small-appliance business. The deal involved the largest brand-name switch in history: 150 products were converted from the GE to the Black & Decker label. Each product was carefully studied, redesigned, and reintroduced with an extended warranty. A total of 140 steps were used for each product. It took three years to convert all 150 products over to Black & Decker. The total conversion of the product line was a program.

Projects A **project** is similar to a program but is generally of less scope and complexity. A project may be a part of a broader program, or it may be a self-contained single-use plan. For Black & Decker, the conversion of each of the 150 products was a separate project in its own right. Each product had its own manager, its own schedule, and so forth. Projects are also used to introduce a new product within an existing product line or to add a new benefit option to an existing salary package.

project A single-use plan of less scope and complexity than a program

Standing Plans

Whereas single-use plans are developed for nonrecurring situations, a **standing plan** is used for activities that recur regularly over a period of time. Standing plans can greatly enhance efficiency by making decision making routine. Policies, standard operating procedures, and rules and regulations are three kinds of standing plans.

standing plan Developed for activities that recur regularly over a period of time

Policies As a general guide for action, a policy is the most general form of standing plan. A **policy** specifies the organization's general response to a designated problem or situation. For example, McDonald's has a policy that it will not grant a franchise to an individual who already owns another fast-food restaurant. Similarly, Starbucks has a policy that it will not franchise at all, instead retaining ownership of all Starbucks' coffee shops. Likewise, a university admissions office

policy A standing plan that specifies the organization's general response to a designated problem or situation

Standard operating procedures, rules, and regulations can all be useful methods for saving time, improving efficiency and streamlining decision making and planning. But it is also helpful to periodically review SOPs, rules, and regulations to ensure that they remain useful. For example, as shown in this cartoon, an SOP for regularly ordering parts and supplies may become less effective if the demand for those parts and supplies changes.

standard operating procedure (SOP) A standing plan that outlines the steps to be followed in a particular circumstance

rules and regulations Describe exactly how specific activities are to be carried out

might establish a policy that admission will be granted only to applicants with a minimum SAT score of 1,000 and a ranking in the top quarter of their high school class. Admissions officers may routinely deny admission to applicants who fail to reach these minimums. A policy is also likely to describe how exceptions are to be handled. The university's policy statement, for example, might create an admissions appeals committee to evaluate applicants who do not meet minimum requirements but may warrant special consideration.

Standard Operating Procedures   Another type of standing plan is the **standard operating procedure**, or **SOP**. An SOP is more specific than a policy in that it outlines the steps to be followed in particular circumstances. The admissions clerk at the university, for example, might be told that, when an application is received, he or she should (1) set up a file for the applicant; (2) add test score records, transcripts, and letters of reference to the file as they are received; and (3) give the file to the appropriate admissions director when it is complete. Gallo Vineyards in California has a 300-page manual of standard operating procedures. This planning manual is credited with making Gallo one of the most efficient wine operations in the United States. McDonald's has SOPs explaining exactly how Big Macs are to be cooked, how long they can stay in the warming rack, and so forth.

Rules and Regulations   The narrowest of the standing plans, **rules and regulations,** describe exactly how specific activities are to be carried out. Rather than guiding decision making, rules and regulations actually take the place of decision making in various situations. Each McDonald's restaurant has a rule prohibiting customers from using its telephones, for example. The university admissions office might have a rule stipulating that, if an applicant's file is not complete two months before the beginning of a semester, the student cannot be admitted until the next semester. Of course, in most organizations a manager at a higher level can suspend or bend the rules. If the high school transcript of the child of a prominent university alumnus and donor arrives a few days late, the director of admissions might waive the two-month rule. Rules and regulations can become problematic if they are excessive or too rigidly enforced.

Rules and regulations and SOPs are similar in many ways. They are both relatively narrow in scope, and each can serve as a substitute for decision making. An SOP typically describes a sequence of activities, however, whereas rules and regulations focus on one activity. Recall our examples: The admissions desk SOP consisted of three activities, whereas the two-month rule related to one activity only. In an industrial setting, the SOP for orienting a new employee could involve enrolling the person in various benefit options, introducing him or her to coworkers and supervisors, and providing a tour of the facilities. A pertinent rule for the new employee might involve when to come to work each day.

Contingency Planning

Another important type of planning is **contingency planning**, or the determination of alternative courses of action to be taken if an intended plan of action is unexpectedly disrupted or rendered inappropriate. An excellent example of contingency planning is what was for a while called the Y2K problem. Concerns about the impact of technical glitches in computers stemming from their internal clocks' changing from 1999 to 2000 resulted in contingency planning for most organizations. Many banks and hospitals, for example, had extra staff available; some organizations created backup computer systems; and some even stockpiled inventory in case they couldn't purchase new products or materials.[20]

The mechanics of contingency planning are shown in Figure 3.6. In relation to an organization's other plans, contingency planning comes into play at four action points. At action point 1, management develops the basic plans of the organization. These may include strategic, tactical, and operational plans. As part of this development process, managers usually consider various contingency events.

contingency planning The determination of alternative courses of action to be taken if an intended plan is unexpectedly disrupted or rendered inappropriate

Figure 3.6

Contingency Planning

Most organizations develop contingency plans. These plans specify alternative courses of action to be taken if an intended plan is unexpectedly disrupted or rendered inappropriate.

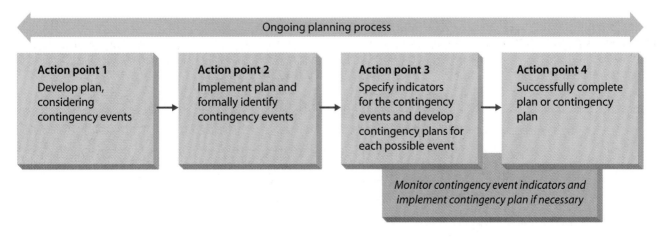

Some management groups even assign someone the role of devil's advocate to ask, "But what if . . ." about each course of action. A variety of contingencies are usually considered.

At action point 2, the plan that management chooses is put into effect. The most important contingency events are also defined. Only the events that are likely to occur and whose effects will have a substantial impact on the organization are used in the contingency-planning process. Next, at action point 3, the company specifies certain indicators or signs that suggest that a contingency event is about to take place. A bank might decide that a 2 percent drop in interest rates should be considered a contingency event. An indicator might be two consecutive months with a drop of 0.5 percent in each. As indicators of contingency events are being defined, the contingency plans themselves should also be developed. Examples of contingency plans for various situations are delaying plant construction, developing a new manufacturing process, and cutting prices.

After this stage, the managers of the organization monitor the indicators identified at action point 3. If the situation dictates, a contingency plan is implemented. Otherwise, the primary plan of action continues in force. Finally, action point 4 marks the successful completion of either the original or a contingency plan.

Contingency planning is becoming increasingly important for most organizations and especially for those operating in particularly complex or dynamic environments. Few managers have such an accurate view of the future that they can anticipate and plan for everything. Contingency planning is a useful technique for helping managers cope with uncertainty and change.

Indeed, one consequence of the September 11, 2001, terrorist attacks on the United States was a significant increase in contingency planning by virtually all organizations. Managers everywhere quickly began to develop contingency plans for how they would respond in the event of further terrorist attacks, including threats of bioterrorism and computer viruses.

Summary of Key Points

The planning process is the first basic managerial function that organizations must address. With an understanding of the environmental context, managers develop various types of goals and plans that serve different purposes. The major types of plans are strategic, tactical, and operational.

A strategy is a comprehensive plan for accomplishing the organization's goals. Strategic management is a comprehensive and ongoing process aimed at formulating and implementing effective strategies. Effective strategies address three organizational issues: distinctive competence, scope, and resource deployment. Most large companies have both business-level and corporate-level strategies.

SWOT analysis considers an organization's strengths, weaknesses, opportunities, and threats. Using SWOT analysis, an organization chooses strategies that support its mission and (1) exploit its opportunities and strengths, (2) neutralize its threats, and (3) avoid its weaknesses.

A business-level strategy is the plan an organization uses to conduct business in a particular industry or market. Porter suggests that, at this level, businesses may formulate a differentiation strategy, an overall cost leadership strategy, or a focus strategy. Business-level strategies may also take into account the stages in the product life cycle.

A corporate-level strategy is the plan an organization uses to manage its operations across several businesses. A firm that does not diversify is implementing a single-product strategy. An organization pursues a strategy of related diversification when it operates a set of businesses that are somehow linked. An organization pursues a strategy of unrelated diversification when it operates a set of businesses that are not logically associated with one another. Organizations usually manage diversification through portfolio management techniques. The BCG matrix classifies an organization's diversified businesses as dogs, cash cows, question marks, or stars according to market share and market growth rate. The GE Business Screen classifies businesses as winners, question marks, average businesses, losers, or profit producers according to industry attractiveness and competitive position.

After plans have been developed, the manager must address how they will be achieved. This step often involves tactical and operational plans. Tactical plans are at the middle of the organization, have an intermediate time horizon and moderate scope, and are developed to implement specific parts of a strategic plan. Tactical plans must flow from strategy, specify resource and time issues, commit human resources, and be executed effectively.

Operational plans are at the lower levels of the organization, have a shorter time horizon, and are narrower in scope. Operational plans are derived from a tactical plan and are aimed at achieving one or more operational goals. Two major types of operational plans are single-use and standing plans. Single-use plans carry out a course of action that is not likely to be repeated. Programs and projects are examples of single-use plans. Standing plans carry out a course of action that is likely to be repeated several times. Policies, standard operating procedures, and rules and regulations are all standing plans. Contingency planning is another important form of operational planning.

Discussion Questions

Questions for Review

1. Describe the purposes of organizational goals. Be certain to note how the purpose varies for different kinds of goals.
2. Identify and describe Porter's generic strategies.
3. What is the difference between a single-product strategy, a related diversification strategy, and an unrelated diversification strategy?
4. What is tactical planning? What is operational planning? What are the similarities and differences between them?
5. What is contingency planning? Is being flexible about your plans the same as contingency planning? Why or why not?

Questions for Analysis

6. Suppose that an organization does not have any distinctive competencies. If the organization is able to acquire some distinctive competencies, how long are these strengths likely to remain distinctive competencies? Why?

7. Suppose that an organization moves from a single-product strategy to a strategy of related diversification. How might the organization use SWOT analysis to select attributes of its current business to serve as bases of relatedness among its newly acquired businesses?
8. For decades now, Ivory Soap has advertised that it is 99 percent pure. Ivory has refused to add deodorants, facial creams, or colors to its soap. It also packages its soap in plain paper wrappers—no foil or fancy printing. Is Ivory implementing a product differentiation strategy, low-cost strategy, focus strategy, or some combination? Explain your answer.
9. Which kind of plan—tactical or operational—should an organization develop first? Why? Does the order of development really make a difference as long as plans of both types are made?
10. Identify examples of each type of operational plan you have used at work, in your school work, or even in your personal life.

BUILDING EFFECTIVE *communication* SKILLS

Exercise Overview

Communication skills refer to the manager's abilities to both effectively convey ideas and information to others and effectively receive ideas and information from others. Communicating goals is an important part of management and requires strong communication skills.

Exercise Background

Assume that you are the CEO of a large discount retailer. You have decided that your firm needs to change its strategy to survive. Specifically, you want the firm to move away from discount retailing and into specialty retailing.

To do so, you know that you will need to close 400 of your 1,200 discount stores within the next year. You also need to increase the expansion rate of your two existing specialty chains and to launch one new chain. Your tentative plans call for opening 300 new specialty stores in one business and 150 in the other next year. You also want the basic concept for the new chain to be finalized and to have 10 stores open next year as well. Finally, although you will be able to transfer some discount store employees to specialty retail jobs, a few hundred people will lose their jobs.

Exercise Task

With the background information above as context, do the following:

1. Develop a press release that outlines these goals.
2. Determine the best way to communicate the goals to your employees.
3. Develop a contingency plan for dealing with problems.

BUILDING EFFECTIVE *decision-making* SKILLS

Exercise Overview

Decision-making skills refer to the manager's ability to correctly recognize and define problems and opportunities and to then select an appropriate course of action to solve problems and capitalize on opportunities. As noted in this chapter, many organizations use SWOT analysis as part of the process of strategy formulation. This exercise will help you better understand how managers obtain the information they need to perform such an analysis and use it as a framework for making decisions.

Exercise Background

SWOT is an acronym for **s**trengths, **w**eaknesses, **o**pportunities, and **t**hreats. Good strategies exploit an organization's opportunities and strengths while neutralizing threats and avoiding or correcting weaknesses.

Assume that you have just been hired to run a medium-size manufacturing company. The firm has been manufacturing electric motors, circuit breakers, and similar electronic components for industrial use. In recent years the firm's financial performance has gradually eroded. You have been hired to turn things around.

Meetings with both current and former top managers of the firm have convinced you that a new strategy is necessary. In earlier times, the firm was successful in part because its products were of top quality. This allowed the company to charge premium prices. Recently, however, various cost-cutting measures have resulted in a decrease in quality. Moreover, competition has also increased. As a result, your firm no longer has a reputation for top-quality products, but your manufacturing costs are still relatively high. The next thing you want to do is to conduct a SWOT analysis.

Exercise Task

With the situation described above as context, do the following:

1. List the sources you will use to obtain information about the firm's strengths, weaknesses, opportunities, and threats.
2. Rate each source in terms of its probable reliability.
3. Rate each source in terms of how easy or difficult it will be to access.
4. How confident should you be in making decisions based on the information you obtained?

BUILDING EFFECTIVE *conceptual* SKILLS

Exercise Overview

Conceptual skills refer to the manager's ability to think in the abstract. This exercise gives you some experience in using your conceptual skills on real business opportunities and potential.

Exercise Background

Many successful managers have at one time or another had an idea for using an existing product for new purposes or in new markets. For example, Arm & Hammer Baking Soda (a food product used in cooking) is now also widely used to absorb odors in refrigerators. Commercials advise consumers to simply open a box of Arm & Hammer and place it in their refrigerator. This new approach has led to a big increase in sales of baking soda.

   In other situations, managers have extended the life cycles of products by moving them into new markets. The most common example today involves taking products that are becoming obsolete in more industrialized countries and introducing them in less industrialized countries.

Exercise Task

Apply your conceptual skills to the following exercise:

1. Make a list of ten simple products that have relatively straightforward purposes (for example, a pencil, which is used for writing).
2. Try to identify two or three alternative uses for each product (a pencil can be used as an emergency splint for a broken finger).
3. Evaluate the market potential for each alternative product use as high, moderate, or low (the market potential for pencils as splints is low).
4. Form small groups of two or three members and pool your ideas. Each group should choose two or three ideas to present to the class.

SKILLS *self-assessment* INSTRUMENT

Are You a Good Planner?

Introduction: Planning is an important skill for managers. The following assessment is designed to help you understand your planning skills. Instructions: Answer either yes or no to each of the following questions.

	Yes	No
1. My personal objectives are clearly spelled out in writing.	____	____
2. Most of my days are hectic and disorderly.	____	____
3. I seldom make any snap decisions and usually study a problem carefully before acting.	____	____
4. I keep a desk calendar or appointment book as an aid.	____	____
5. I make use of "Action" and "Deferred Action" files.	____	____
6. I generally establish starting dates and deadlines for all my projects.	____	____
7. I often ask others for advice.	____	____
8. I believe that all problems have to be solved immediately.	____	____

For interpretation, see Interpretations of Skills Self-Assessment Instruments.

Source: From Stephen P. Robbins, *Management*, 4th ed. Copyright © 1994 by National Research Bureau. Reprinted by permission of National Resource Bureau, P.O. Box 1, Burlington, Iowa 52601–0001.

EXPERIENTIAL EXERCISE

The SWOT Analysis

Purpose: SWOT analysis provides the manager with a cognitive model of the organization and its environmental forces. By developing this ability, the manager builds both process knowledge and a conceptual skill. This skill builder focuses on the *administrative management model*. It will help you develop the *coordinator role* of the administrative management model. One of the skills of the coordinator is the ability to plan.

Introduction: This exercise helps you understand the complex interrelationships between environmental opportunities and threats and organizational strengths and weaknesses.

Instructions:

Step 1: Study the exhibit that follows, "Strategy Formulation at Marriott," and the text materials concerning the matching of organizations with environments.

Step 2: The instructor will divide the class into small groups. Each group will conduct a SWOT (strengths, weaknesses, opportunities, threats) analysis for Marriott and prepare group responses to the discussion questions. Marriott has been successful in its hotel and food services businesses but less than successful in its cruise ship, travel agency, and theme park businesses.

Strategy formulation is facilitated by a SWOT analysis. First, the organization should study its internal operations in order to identify its strengths and weaknesses. Next, the organization should scan the environment to identify existing and future opportunities and threats. Then the organization should identify the relationships that exist among the strengths, weaknesses, opportunities, and threats. Finally, major business strategies usually result from matching an organization's strengths with appropriate opportunities or from matching threats with weaknesses. To facilitate the environmental analysis in search of opportunities and threats, it is helpful to divide the environment into its major components—international, economic, political-legal, sociocultural, and technological.

Step 3: One representative from each group may be asked to report on the group's SWOT analysis and to report the group's responses to the discussion questions.

Discussion Questions

1. What was the most difficult part of the SWOT analysis?
2. Why do most firms not develop major strategies for matches between threats and strengths?
3. Under what conditions might a firm develop a major strategy around a match between an opportunity and a weakness?

Source: Burton, Gene E., *Exercises in Management*, Fifth edition. Copyright © 1996 by Houghton Mifflin Company. Used with permission.

Strategy Formulation at Marriott

Opportunities
- High growth in market for low-cost lodging

Strengths
- Solid hotel business
- Solid food services business

Threats
- Low growth in market for high-cost lodging

Weaknesses
- Poor performance from cruise ship, travel agency, and theme park business
- Weak cash position

Relationships Between Opportunities and Strengths

1. _____

2. _____

3. _____

Relationships Between Opportunities and Weaknesses

1. _____

2. _____

3. _____

Relationships Between Threats and Strengths

1. _____

2. _____

3. _____

Relationships Between Threats and Weaknesses

1. _____

2. _____

3. _____

Major Strategies Matching Opportunities with Strengths

1. _____

2. _____

3. _____

Major Strategies Matching Threats with Weaknesses

1. _____

2. _____

3. _____

Marriott SWOT Analysis Sheet

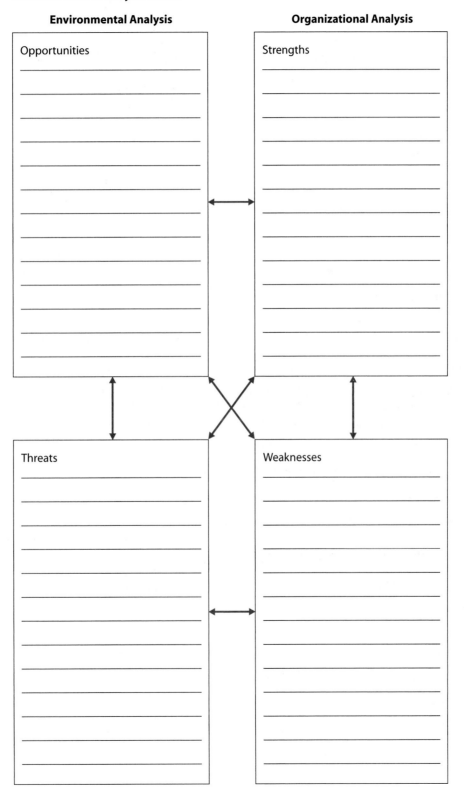

ROYAL CARIBBEAN LAUNCHES THE LARGEST LUXURY LINER

Top management at Royal Caribbean did not actually set out to create the largest passenger ship in the world. But by the time *Voyager of the Seas* set sail, it had become by far the largest ship in Royal Caribbean's 17-ship fleet—triple the size of the fabled *Titanic* and one-quarter larger than any competing ship. At a cost of $700 million, *Voyager* is not just another luxury liner—it represents a huge step toward the future by opening an entirely new portion of the vacation market. It also represents a long-term investment, because cruise ships generally stay in service for 25 years.

CEO Richard Fain and his managers started planning this ship more than three years before the anticipated launch. Their first step was establishing a challenging mission: to attract vacationers who had never taken a cruise. Because a mere 11 percent of U.S. vacationers have ever taken a cruise, this was a huge potential market as well as a huge gamble. But Fain and his team knew they were planning, not for the next year or two, but for the next decade, when lifestyles and vacations could be vastly different. For this reason, Royal Caribbean commissioned extensive research into consumer attitudes toward vacation activities. These attitudes became the basis for many of the special features built into *Voyager*, such as a state-of-the-art nightclub and a wedding chapel. Fain and his team also envisioned facilities for other activities not normally found on cruise ships, such as in-line skating, rock climbing, and ice skating.

With this broad outline of features in hand, Royal Caribbean managers began hiring companies to design and build everything, from the chandeliers above to the dance floors below. Rather than hire only architects and designers with experience working on cruise ships, Fain and his managers invited some proposals from talented designers who had never worked on ships. Although other cruise lines keep costs low and simplify the planning process by hiring the same designer for all ships, Royal Caribbean was more interested in innovation than in saving money. As a result, different parts of the ship were individually designed and often constructed in different parts of the world, then assembled in the shipyard in Turku, Finland. For example, the huge saltwater aquarium tanks were made in Colorado, whereas the fish came from Florida; the English pub was designed by a Rhode Island firm; and the Egyptian-theme dance lounge was designed by a British firm.

Planning and coordinating the construction of such a huge ship required careful attention to detail. So Fain created a steering committee of key managers to oversee the entire process. In regular one- to two-day sessions, the committee listened to progress reports and considered ideas for overcoming potential pitfalls. The CEO, known for his sharp memory, frequently asked hard questions that resulted in small and large changes, from moving some light fixtures (to improve the look of the room) to widening the ten-story atrium (to enhance the feeling of spaciousness). Fain and other committee members made numerous trips to Finland to examine the ship under construction and make on-the-spot decisions when necessary, knowing that details such as the noise level in the dining room can make or break the cruise experience for passengers.

Before the launch date, *Voyager* sailed a series of trial runs so managers could check that everything operated properly. Although nearly all of the 1,186 crew members were drawn from other Royal Caribbean ships, each received 92 hours of training about the intricacies of the ship and its equipment. By the time *Voyager* was officially launched, it was more than the world's largest and most expensive passenger ship—it was a major part of Royal Caribbean's future.

Case Questions

1. What was the underlying strategy in Royal Caribbean's decision to build *Voyager of the Seas*?

2. What kind of operational plan did Royal Caribbean create for the building of *Voyager*?

3. What kinds of problems might Royal Caribbean encounter when working on the design and construction of such a unique ship as *Voyager*? What role would contingency planning play in this situation?

Case References

Charles Fishman, "Fantastic Voyage," *Fast Company*, March 2000, pp. 170–200; and *Hoover's Handbook of American Business 2001* (Austin, TX: Hoover's Business Press, 2001), pp. 1218–1219.

CHAPTER NOTES

1. "Happily Ever After?" *Time*, January 24, 2000, pp. 38–43 (quote on p. 39); "Welcome to the 21st Century," *Business Week*, January 24, 2000, pp. 36–44; "You've Got Time Warner," *Wall Street Journal*, January 11, 2000, pp. B1, B12; and "Deal Ignites Tech, Media Stocks," *USA Today*, January 11, 2000, pp. 1B, 2B.

2. Jim Collins, "Turning Goals into Results: The Power of Catalytic Mechanisms," *Harvard Business Review*, July/August 1999, pp. 71–81.

3. Kenneth R. Thompson, Wayne A. Hochwarter, and Nicholas J. Mathys, "Stretch Targets: What Makes Them Effective?" *Academy of Management Executive* (August 1997): 48–58.

4. "A Methodical Man," *Forbes*, August 11, 1997, pp. 70–72.

5. John A. Pearce II and Fred David, "Corporate Mission Statements: The Bottom Line," *Academy of Management Executive* (May 1987): 109.

6. See Charles Hill and Gareth Jones, *Strategic Management*, 5th ed. (Boston: Houghton Mifflin, 2001).

7. For early discussions of strategic management, see Kenneth Andrews, *The Concept of Corporate Strategy*, rev. ed. (Homewood, IL: Dow Jones–Irwin, 1980); and Igor Ansoff, *Corporate Strategy* (New York: McGraw-Hill, 1965). For more recent perspectives, see Michael E. Porter, "What is Strategy?" *Harvard Business Review*, November/December 1996, pp. 61–78; and Kathleen M. Eisenhardt, "Strategy as Strategic Decision Making," *Sloan Management Review*, Spring 1999, pp. 65–74.

8. *Hoover's Handbook of American Business 2001* (Austin, TX: Hoover's Business Press, 2001), pp. 874–875.

9. Jim Rohwer, "GE Digs into Asia," *Fortune*, October 2, 2000, pp. 164–178.

10. "If It's on the Fritz, Take It to Jane," *Business Week*, January 27, 1997, pp. 74–75.

11. Jay Barney, "Firm Resources and Sustained Competitive Advantage," *Journal of Management* (June 1991): 99–120.

12. Michael Porter, *Competitive Strategy* (New York: Free Press, 1980). See also Colin Campbell-Hunt, "What Have We Learned About Generic Competitive Strategy? A Meta-Analysis," *Strategic Management Journal* 21 (2000): 127–154; and Keith Hammonds, "Michael Porter's Big Ideas," *Fast Company*, March 2001, pp. 150–156.

13. "General Mills Intends to Reshape Doughboy in Its Own Image," *Wall Street Journal*, July 18, 2000, pp. A1, A8.

14. Alfred Chandler, *Strategy and Structure: Chapters in the History of the American Industrial Enterprise* (Cambridge, MA: MIT Press, 1962); Richard Rumelt, *Strategy, Structure, and Economic Performance* (Cambridge, MA: Division of Research, Graduate School of Business Administration, Harvard University, 1974); and Oliver Williamson, *Markets and Hierarchies* (New York: Free Press, 1975).

15. "Not the Flavor of the Month," *Business Week*, March 20, 2000, p. 128.

16. "Did Somebody Say McBurrito?" *Business Week*, April 10, 2000, pp. 166–170.

17. "BMW: Unloading Rover May not Win the Race," *Business Week*, April 3, 2000, p. 59.

18. "Unilever to Sell Specialty-Chemical Unit to ICI of the U.K. for About $8 Billion," *Wall Street Journal*, May 7, 1997, pp. A3, A12; and "For Unilever, It's Sweetness and Light," *Wall Street Journal*, April 13, 2000, pp. B1, B4.

19. "Coca-Cola May Need to Slash Its Growth Targets," *Wall Street Journal*, January 28, 2000, p. B2.

20. "How the Fixers Fended off Big Disasters," *Wall Street Journal*, December 23, 1999, pp. B1, B4.

4 Managing Decision Making

Starbucks Corporation has arguably become the highest-profile and fastest-growing food and beverage company in the United States. Starbucks was started in Seattle in 1971 by three coffee aficionados. Their primary business at the time was buying premium coffee beans, roasting them, and then selling the coffee by the pound. The business performed modestly well and soon grew to nine stores, all in the Seattle area. The three partners sold Starbucks to a former employee, Howard Schultz, in 1987. Schultz promptly reoriented the business away from bulk coffee mail-order sales and emphasized retail coffee sales through the firm's coffee bars. Today, Starbucks is not only the largest coffee importer and roaster of specialty beans, but also the largest specialty coffee bean retailer in the United States. In addition, the firm is aggressively moving into several different foreign markets.

What is the key to Starbucks' phenomenal growth and success? One important ingredient is its well-conceived and well-implemented strategy. Although Starbucks is opening a new coffee shop somewhere almost every day, this growth is planned and coordinated each step of the way through careful site selection. And through its astute promotional campaigns and commitment to quality, the firm has elevated the coffee-drinking taste of millions of consumers and fueled a significant increase in demand. Another key to Starbucks' success is its near-fanatical emphasis on quality control. For example, milk must be at precise temperatures between 150 and 170 degrees, and every espresso shot must be pulled within 23 seconds or discarded. And no coffee is allowed to sit on a hot plate for more than 20 minutes. Schultz also refuses to franchise his Starbucks stores, fearing a loss of control and a potential deterioration of quality.

But even a firm as well managed as Starbucks can still make mistakes. Consider what happened, for example, when the firm opened its first store in New York City. Market research showed that New Yorkers strongly preferred drip coffees over the more exotic espresso-style coffees that were Starbucks mainstays in the west. Accordingly, the first Starbucks in New York was opened with more drip coffeemakers and fewer espresso machines than in other stores. But the drip coffees were largely ignored, and the line for espresso crept out the door and

> "Our management team is 100 percent focused on growing our core business without distraction or dilution from any other initiative."
>
> —Howard Schultz, CEO of Starbucks

After studying this chapter, you should be able to

▪ Define decision making and discuss types of decisions and decision-making conditions.

▪ Discuss rational perspectives on decision making, including the steps in decision making.

▪ Describe the behavioral nature of decision making.

▪ Discuss group and team decision making, including the advantages and disadvantages of group and team decision making and how it can be more effectively managed.

down the block. Thus a hasty renovation was necessary within the first month the store was open, so that it could provide more espresso and less drip coffee.

More recently, Starbucks stumbled again when Schultz announced to a group of investors that he and his management team were focusing their attention on diversification and were busily crafting a grand-scale Internet plan for Starbucks. According to Schultz, the plan would turn the company's web site into a "lifestyle portal" by partnering with various gourmet food vendors and home-decorating businesses. The investors, meanwhile, apparently decided that Schultz was getting too distracted by this plan and that he should remain focused on Starbucks' core businesses. They let him know their feelings by unloading the firm's stock so aggressively that its value plummeted by 28 percent the next day!

Of course, Schultz is a smart executive, and he quickly got the message. Although not totally abandoning his Internet strategy, he nevertheless began to refocus his attention on Star-

bucks' core business. For example, he stepped up expansion again, which had slowed, and began moving even more aggressively into foreign markets. He also began testing various new concepts for Starbucks shops, such as an expanded lunch menu and a wider assortment of products, such as CDs and chocolates. And how did the disgruntled investors take this about face? They sent the stock price back up by over 30 percent within just a few months.[1]

Managers at Starbucks make decisions every day, and most of these decisions are good ones. Because no one can be right all the time, however, even a skilled executive like Howard Schultz can occasionally make a mistake. But an important key to organizational effectiveness can be a manager's ability to recognize when a bad decision has been made and to respond quickly to mistakes.

Some experts believe that decision making is the most basic and fundamental of all managerial activities.[2] Thus we discuss it here in the context of the first management function, planning. Keep in mind, however, that, although decision making is perhaps most closely linked to the planning function, it is also part of organizing, leading, and controlling. We begin our discussion by exploring the nature of decision making. We then describe rational perspectives on decision making. Behavioral aspects of decision making are then introduced and described. We conclude with a discussion of group and team decision making.

The Nature of Decision Making

Managers at Ford recently made the decision to buy Land Rover from BMW for nearly $3 billion.[3] At about the same time, the general manager of the Ford dealership in Bryan, Texas, made a decision to sponsor a local youth soccer team for $200. Each of these examples includes a decision, but the decisions differ in many ways. Thus, as a starting point in understanding decision making, we must first explore the meaning of decision making as well as types of decisions and conditions under which decisions are made.[4]

Decision Making Defined

decision making The act of choosing one alternative from among a set of alternatives

decision-making process Recognizing and defining the nature of a decision situation, identifying alternatives, choosing the "best" alternative, and putting it into practice

Decision making can refer to either a specific act or a general process. **Decision making** per se is the act of choosing one alternative from among a set of alternatives. The decision-making process, however, is much more than this. One step of the process, for example, is that the person making the decision must recognize that a decision is necessary and identify the set of feasible alternatives before selecting one. Hence, the **decision-making process** includes recognizing and defining the nature of a decision situation, identifying alternatives, choosing the "best" alternative, and putting it into practice.

The word *best*, of course, implies effectiveness. Effective decision making requires that the decision maker understand the situation driving the decision. Most people would consider an effective decision to be one that optimizes some set of factors, such as profits, sales, employee welfare, and market share. In some situations, though, an effective decision may be one that minimizes loss, expenses, or employee turnover. It may even mean selecting the best method for going out of business, laying off employees, or terminating a contract.

We should also note that managers make decisions about both problems and opportunities. For example, making decisions about how to cut costs by 10 percent reflects a problem—an undesired situation that requires a solution. But decisions

Reprinted with special permission by King Features Syndicate, Inc.

Decision making is a pervasive part of most managerial activities. Virtually everything that happens in a company involves making a decision or implementing a decision that has been made. Although some decisions are grand and significant in scope, others, such as the ones shown in the center panel of this cartoon, involve more routine, day-to-day activities. And still others, illustrated in the right panel, deal with what to have for lunch or when to take a break. Regardless of their goals, however, the people making the decisions need to take them seriously and do what they believe to be best for the company.

are also necessary in situations of opportunity. Learning that the firm is earning higher-than-projected profits, for example, requires a subsequent decision. Should the extra funds be used to increase shareholder dividends, reinvested in current operations, or used to expand into new markets?

Of course, it may take a long time before a manager can know if the right decision was made. For example, when George Fisher took over as CEO of Kodak, he made several major decisions that will affect the company for decades. Among other things, for example, he sold off several chemical- and health-related businesses, reduced the firm's debt by $7 billion in the process, launched a major new line of advanced cameras and film called Advantix, and made major new investments in emerging technology, such as digital photography. But analysts believe that the payoffs from these decisions will not be known for at least ten years.[5]

Types of Decisions

Managers must make many different types of decisions. In general, however, most decisions fall into one of two categories: programmed or nonprogrammed.[6] A **programmed decision** is one that is fairly structured or recurs with some frequency (or both). Starbucks uses programmed decisions to purchase new supplies of coffee beans, cups, and napkins, and Starbucks employees are trained in exact procedures for brewing coffee. Likewise, the Bryan Ford dealer made a decision that he will sponsor a youth soccer team each year. Thus, when the soccer club president calls, the dealer already knows what he will do. Many decisions regarding basic operating systems and procedures, and standard organizational transactions are of this variety and can therefore be programmed.[7]

Nonprogrammed decisions, on the other hand, are relatively unstructured and occur much less often. Starbucks' decision to refocus its Internet strategy on lifestyles and then retreating from that plan are both nonprogrammed decisions. Likewise, Ford's decision to buy Land Rover was also a nonprogrammed decision. Managers faced with such decisions must treat each one as unique, investing enormous amounts of time, energy, and resources into exploring the situation from all perspectives. Intuition and experience are major factors in nonprogrammed decisions. Most of the decisions made by top managers involving

programmed decision A decision that is fairly structured or recurs with some frequency (or both)

nonprogrammed decision A decision that is relatively unstructured; occurs much less often than a programmed decision

strategy (including mergers, acquisitions, and takeovers) and organization design are nonprogrammed. So are decisions about new facilities, new products, labor contracts, and legal issues.

Decision-Making Conditions

Just as there are different kinds of decisions, there are also different conditions in which decisions must be made. Managers sometimes have an almost-perfect understanding of conditions surrounding a decision, but at other times, they have few clues about those conditions. In general, as shown in Figure 4.1, the circumstances that exist for the decision maker are conditions of certainty, risk, or uncertainty.[8]

state of certainty A condition in which the decision maker knows with reasonable certainty what the alternatives are and what conditions are associated with each alternative

state of risk A condition in which the availability of each alternative and its potential payoffs and costs are all associated with probability estimates

Decision Making Under Certainty   When the decision maker knows with reasonable certainty what the alternatives are and what conditions are associated with each alternative, a **state of certainty** exists. Suppose, for example, that managers at Singapore Airlines make a decision to buy five new jumbo jets. Their next decision is from whom to buy them. Because there are only two companies in the world that make jumbo jets, Boeing and Airbus, Singapore Airlines knows its options exactly. Each has proven products and will guarantee prices and delivery dates. The airline thus knows the alternative conditions associated with each. There is little ambiguity and relatively little chance of making a bad decision.

Few organizational decisions are made under conditions of true certainty. The complexity and turbulence of the contemporary business world make such situations rare. Even the airplane purchase decision we just considered has less certainty than it appears. The aircraft companies may not be able to really guarantee delivery dates, so they may write cost-increase or inflation clauses into contracts. Thus the airline may be only partially certain of the conditions surrounding each alternative.

Figure 4.1

Decision-Making Conditions

Most major decisions in organizations today are made under a state of uncertainty. Managers making decisions in these circumstances must be sure to learn as much as possible about the situation and approach the decision from a logical and rational perspective.

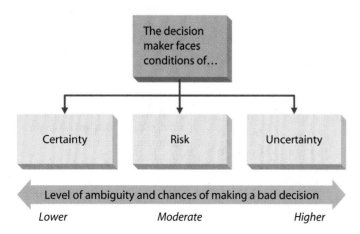

Decision Making Under Risk   A more common decision-making condition is a state of risk. Under a **state of risk**, the availability of each alternative and its potential payoffs and costs are all associated with probability estimates. Suppose, for example, that a labor contract negotiator for a company receives a "final" offer from the union right before a strike deadline. The negotiator has two alternatives: to accept or to reject the offer. The risk centers on whether the union representatives are bluffing. If the company negotiator accepts the offer, she avoids a strike but commits to a costly labor contract. If she rejects the contract, she may get a more favorable contract if the union is bluffing; she may provoke a strike if it is not.

On the basis of past experiences, relevant information, the advice of others, and her own judgment, she may conclude that there is about a 75 percent chance that union representatives are bluffing and about a 25 percent chance that they will back up their threats. Thus she can base a calculated decision on the two alternatives (accept or reject the contract demands) and the probable consequences of each. When making decisions under a state of risk, managers must accurately determine the probabilities associated with each alternative. For example, if the union negotiators are committed to a strike if their demands are not met, and the company negotiator rejects their demands because she guesses they will not strike, her miscalculation will prove costly. As indicated in Figure 4.1, decision making under conditions of risk is accompanied by moderate ambiguity and chances of a bad decision.[9] Ford's decision to buy Land Rover was made under a condition of risk.

Decision Making Under Uncertainty Most of the major decision making in contemporary organizations is done under a **state of uncertainty**. The decision maker does not know all the alternatives, the risks associated with each, or the likely consequences of each alternative. This uncertainty stems from the complexity and dynamism of contemporary organizations and their environments. Starbucks' initial decision to move more aggressively into lifestyle businesses was made under a state of uncertainty, as was its reversal of that decision. Indeed, the emergence of the Internet as a significant force in today's competitive environment has served to increase uncertainty for most managers.

To make effective decisions in these circumstances, managers must acquire as much relevant information as possible and approach the situation from a logical and rational perspective. Intuition, judgment, and experience always play major roles in the decision-making process under conditions of uncertainty. Even so, uncertainty is the most ambiguous condition for managers and the one most prone to error.[10] Indeed, many of the problems associated with the massive recall of tires by Firestone and Ford in 2000 were attributed to Firestone's apparent difficulties in responding to ambiguous and uncertain decision parameters regarding the firm's moral, ethical, and legal responsibilities.[11]

Managers generally attempt to follow a logical and rational approach to making decisions. This is especially true of individuals in positions like H. Carl McCall, the sole trustee of the Common Retirement Fund for the state of New York. McCall is responsible for managing a portfolio recently valued at $122 billion. The public trust vested in his position makes it especially important that he rationally consider various investment options and then select the ones that will provide the optimal blend of risk and return for the hundreds of thousands of retired state employees who depend on the fund.

state of uncertainty A condition in which the decision maker does not know all the alternatives, the risks associated with each, or the consequences each alternative is likely to have

Rational Perspectives on Decision Making

Most managers like to think of themselves as rational decision makers. And, indeed, many experts argue that managers should try to be as rational as possible in making decisions. [12]

The Classical Model of Decision Making

classical decision model A prescriptive approach to decision making that tells managers how they should make decisions; it assumes that managers are logical and rational and that their decisions will be in the best interests of the organization

The **classical decision model** is a prescriptive approach that tells managers how they should make decisions. It rests on the assumptions that managers are logical and rational and that they make decisions that are in the best interests of the organization. Figure 4.2 shows how the classical model views the decision-making process: (1) Decision makers have complete information about the decision situation and possible alternatives; (2) they can effectively eliminate uncertainty to achieve a decision condition of certainty; and (3) they evaluate all aspects of the decision situation logically and rationally. As we see later, these conditions rarely, if ever, actually exist.

Steps in Rational Decision Making

steps in rational decision making Recognize and define the decision situation; identify appropriate alternatives; evaluate each alternative in terms of its feasibility, satisfactoriness, and consequences; select the best alternative; implement the chosen alternative; follow up and evaluate the results of the chosen alternative

A manager who really wants to approach a decision rationally and logically should try to follow the **steps in rational decision making**, listed in Table 4.1. These steps in rational decision making help keep the decision maker focused on facts and logic, and help guard against inappropriate assumptions and pitfalls.

Recognizing and Defining the Decision Situation   The first step in rational decision making is recognizing that a decision is necessary—that is, there must be some stimulus or spark to initiate the process. For many decisions and problem situations, the stimulus may occur without any prior warning. When equipment malfunctions, the manager must decide whether to repair or replace it. Or when a major crisis erupts, the manager must quickly decide how to deal with it. As we already noted, the stimulus for a decision may be either positive or negative. A manager who must decide how to invest surplus funds, for example, faces a positive decision situation. A negative financial stimulus could involve having to trim budgets because of cost overruns. *Management InfoTech* illustrates how managers at SAP recently recognized and defined a decision situation.

Inherent in problem recognition is the need to define precisely what the problem is. The manager must develop a complete understanding of the problem, its causes, and its relationship to other factors. This understanding comes from care-

Figure 4.2

The Classical Model of Decision Making
The classical model of decision making assumes that managers are rational and logical. It attempts to prescribe how managers should approach decision situations.

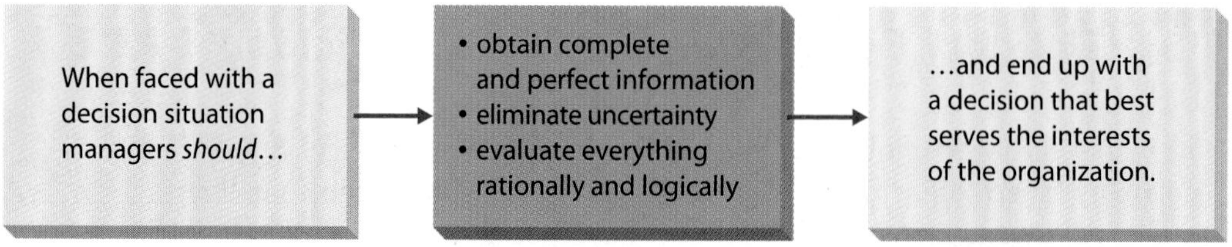

Table 4.1

Steps in the Rational Decision-Making Process

Although the presumptions of the classical decision model rarely exist, managers can approach decision making with rationality. By following the steps of rational decision making, managers ensure that they are learning as much as possible about the decision situation and its alternatives.

Step	Detail	Example
1. Recognizing and defining the decision situation	Some stimulus indicates that a decision must be made. The stimulus may be positive or negative.	A plant manager sees that employee turnover has increased by 5 percent.
2. Identifying alternatives	Both obvious and creative alternatives are desired. In general, the more important the decision, the more alternatives should be generated.	The plant manager can increase wages, increase benefits, or change hiring standards.
3. Evaluating alternatives	Each alternative is evaluated to determine its feasibility, its satisfactoriness, and its consequences.	Increasing benefits may not be feasible. Increasing wages and changing hiring standards may satisfy all conditions.
4. Selecting the best alternative	Consider all situational factors and choose the alternative that best fits the manager's situation.	Changing hiring standards will take an extended period of time to cut turnover, so increase wages.
5. Implementing the chosen alternative	The chosen alternative is implemented into the organizational system.	The plant manager may need permission of corporate headquarters. The human resource department establishes a new wage structure.
6. Following up and evaluating the results	At some time in the future, the manager should ascertain the extent to which the alternative chosen in step 4 and implemented in step 5 has worked.	The plant manager notes that, six months later, turnover dropped to its previous level.

ful analysis and thoughtful consideration of the situation. Consider the situation currently being faced in the air travel industry. Because of the growth of international travel related to business, education, and tourism, global carriers like Singapore Airlines, KLM, JAL, British Airways, American Airlines and others need to increase their capacity for international travel. Because most major international airports are already operating at or near capacity, adding a significant number of new flights to existing schedules is not feasible. As a result, the most logical alternative is to increase capacity on existing flights. Thus Boeing and Airbus, the world's only manufacturers of large commercial aircraft, have recognized an important opportunity and have defined their decision situation as how best to respond to the need for increased global travel capacity.[13]

Identifying Alternatives Once the decision situation has been recognized and defined, the second step is to identify alternative courses of effective action. Developing both obvious, standard alternatives and creative, innovative alternatives is generally useful. In general, the more important the decision, the more attention is

MANAGEMENT INFOTECH

SAP PLAYS CATCH-UP ON THE INTERNET

The Internet revolution started without SAP. This German software firm made its name developing sophisticated software for managing key operations such as purchasing, production, and customer transactions. But year after year of rapid sales growth during the 1990s gave way to slower growth and lower profits when SAP's top management failed to recognize how the Internet was changing the way companies do business.

Even as SAP continued to introduce complex stand-alone programs, its corporate customers were demanding software capable of web-based connections with customers and suppliers. Competitors such as Ariba and Siebel were already offering such software, but not SAP. From the vantage point of company headquarters in Walldorf, Germany, top managers were not in a hurry to adapt to the Internet and e-commerce. But when U.S. competitor Oracle began touting its e-commerce expertise in a high-profile advertising campaign, one of SAP's founders recognized that the firm needed an Internet strategy.

Two SAP programmers assigned to the task came up with the concept of enhancing the company's existing software with new programs designed to link suppliers and customers via the Internet. Dubbed mySAP.com, this enhancement worked only with SAP programs, a problem for businesses that use software purchased from different sources. Timing was also an issue. General Motors, for example, selected a rival's e-commerce software rather than risk delays in getting mySAP.com up and running.

SAP faced yet another Internet-related decision. While U.S. competitors were using stock options to attract, retain, and reward talented employees, SAP resisted requests by managers of SAP America for a similar plan. Finally, after SAP America's CEO and president left to join rival firms—amid dozens of other management defections from the United States and from international divisions—SAP devised a stock option plan.

Now mySAP .com is catching on with Hewlett-Packard and other major customers. To speed up software development and keep a closer eye on U.S. Internet trends, SAP has outsourced some work to a Boston-based firm (which was formerly based in Germany). The company has also decided to follow the lead of its U.S. rivals in more aggressively promoting new products and enhancements—even before they are introduced.

> *We made a decision two years ago and there has been a massive paradigm shift to the Internet.*
>
> —*Hasso Plattner, co-founder and co-CEO, SAP**

References: Neal E. Boudette, "How a Software Titan Missed the Internet Revolution," *Wall Street Journal*, January 18, 2000, pp. B1, B4 (*quote on p. B4).

---

directed to developing alternatives. If the decision involves a multimillion-dollar relocation, a great deal of time and expertise will be devoted to identifying the best locations. For instance, J.C. Penney Company spent two years searching before selecting the Dallas–Fort Worth area for its new corporate headquarters. If the problem is to choose a color for the company softball team uniforms, less time and expertise will be brought to bear.

Although managers should seek creative solutions, they must also recognize that various constraints often limit their alternatives. Common constraints include legal restrictions, moral and ethical norms, authority constraints, or constraints imposed by the power and authority of the manager, available technology, economic considerations, and unofficial social norms. Boeing and Airbus each identified three different alternatives to address the decision situation of increasing international airline travel capacity: They could independently develop new large planes, they could collaborate in a joint venture to create a single new large plane, or they could modify their largest existing planes to increase their capacity.

Evaluating Alternatives   The third step in the decision-making process is evaluating each of the alternatives. Figure 4.3 presents a decision tree that can be used to judge different alternatives. The figure suggests that each alternative be evaluated in terms of its *feasibility*, its *satisfactoriness*, and its *consequences*. The first question to ask is whether an alternative is feasible. Is it within the realm of probability and practicality? For a small, struggling firm, an alternative requiring a huge financial outlay is probably out of the question. Other alternatives may not be feasible because of legal barriers. And limited human, material, and information resources may make other alternatives impractical.

When an alternative has passed the test of feasibility, it must next be examined to see how well it satisfies the conditions of the decision situation. For example, a manager searching for ways to double production capacity might consider purchasing an existing plant from another company. If closer examination reveals that the new plant would increase production capacity by only 35 percent, this alternative may not be satisfactory. Finally, when an alternative has proven both feasible and satisfactory, its probable consequences must still be assessed. To what extent will a particular alternative influence other parts of the organization? What financial and nonfinancial costs will be associated with such influences? For example, a plan to boost sales by cutting prices may disrupt cash flows, require a new advertising program, and alter the behavior of sales representatives because it requires a different commission structure. The manager, then, must put "price tags" on the consequences of each alternative. Even an alternative that is both feasible and satisfactory must be eliminated if its consequences are too expensive for the total system. Airbus felt it would be at a disadvantage if it tried to simply enlarge its existing planes, because the Boeing 747 is already the largest aircraft being made and could be expanded to remain the largest. Boeing, meanwhile, was seriously concerned about the risk inherent in building a new and even larger plane, even if it shared the risk with Airbus as a joint venture.

Figure 4.3

Evaluating Alternatives in the Decision-Making Process

Managers must thoroughly evaluate all the alternatives, which increases the chances that the alternative finally chosen will be successful. Failure to evaluate an alternative's feasibility, satisfactoriness, and consequences can lead to a wrong decision.

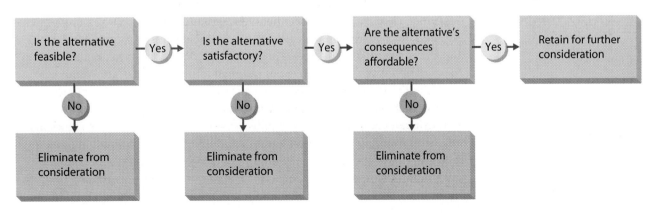

Selecting the Best Alternative   Even though many alternatives fail to pass the triple tests of feasibility, satisfactoriness, and affordable consequences, two or more alternatives may remain. Choosing the best of these is the real crux of decision making. One approach is to choose the alternative with the highest combined level of feasibility, satisfactoriness, and affordable consequences. Even though most situations do not lend themselves to objective, mathematical analysis, the manager can often develop subjective estimates and weights for choosing an alternative.

Optimization is also a frequent goal. Because a decision is likely to affect several individuals or units, any feasible alternative will probably not maximize all of the relevant goals. Suppose that the manager of the Kansas City Royals needs to select a new outfielder for the upcoming baseball season. Bill hits .350 but is barely able to catch a fly ball; Joe hits only .175 but is outstanding in the field; and Sam hits .290 and is a solid but not outstanding fielder. The manager would probably select Sam because of the optimal balance of hitting and fielding. Decision makers should also remember that finding multiple acceptable alternatives may be possible—selecting just one alternative and rejecting all the others might not be necessary. For example, the Royals' manager might decide that Sam will start each game, Bill will be retained as a pinch hitter, and Joe will be retained as a defensive substitute. In many hiring decisions, the candidates remaining after evaluation are ranked. If the top candidate rejects the offer, it may be automatically extended to the number two candidate, and, if necessary, to the remaining candidates in order. For the reasons noted earlier, Airbus proposed a joint venture with Boeing. Boeing, meanwhile, decided that its best course of action was to modify its existing 747 to increase its capacity. As a result, Airbus then decided to proceed on its own to develop and manufacture a new jumbo jet.

Implementing the Chosen Alternative   After an alternative has been selected, the manager must put it into effect. In some decision situations, implementation is fairly easy; in others, it is more difficult. In the case of an acquisition, for example, managers must decide how to integrate all the activities of the new business, including purchasing, human resource practices, and distribution, into an ongoing organizational framework. For example, when America Online and Time Warner announced their merger, they also acknowledged that it would take at least a year to integrate the two firms into a single one. Operational plans, which we discuss in Chapter 3, are useful in implementing alternatives.

Managers must also consider people's resistance to change when implementing decisions. The reasons for such resistance include insecurity, inconvenience, and fear of the unknown. When Penney's decided to move its headquarters from New York to Texas, many employees resigned rather than relocate. Managers should anticipate potential resistance at various stages of the implementation process. Managers should also recognize that, even when all alternatives have been evaluated as precisely as possible and the consequences of each alternative weighed, unanticipated consequences are still likely. Any number of things—unexpected cost increases, a less-than-perfect fit with existing organizational subsystems, or unpredicted effects on cash flow or operating expenses, for example—could develop after implementation has begun. Boeing has set its engineers to work expanding the capacity of its 747 from today's 416 passengers to as many as 520 passengers by adding 30 feet to the plane's body. Airbus engineers, meanwhile, are developing design concepts for a new jumbo jet, equipped with escalators and elevators, and capable of carrying 655 passengers. Airbus's development costs alone are estimated to be more than $12 billion.

Following Up and Evaluating the Results   The final step in the decision-making process requires that managers evaluate the effectiveness of their decision—that is, they should make sure that the chosen alternative has served its original purpose. If an implemented alternative appears not to be working, the manager can respond in several ways. Another previously identified alternative (the second or third choice) could be adopted. Or the manager might recognize that the situation was not correctly defined to start with and begin the process all over again. Finally, the manager might decide that the original alternative is in fact appropriate but has not yet had time to work or should be implemented in a different way.

Failure to evaluate decision effectiveness may have serious consequences. The Pentagon spent $1.8 billion and eight years developing the Sergeant York anti-aircraft gun. From the beginning, tests revealed major problems with the weapon system, but not until it was in its final stages, when it was demonstrated to be completely ineffective, was the project scrapped.[14] The examples in our opening incident illustrate a much more effective approach to evaluating decision effectiveness. When New Yorkers expressed their preferences for espresso over drip coffees, Starbucks quickly revamped its shops. And when investors let Howard Schultz know that they disapproved of his Internet strategy, he quickly changed it. Meanwhile, experts agree that it will be several years before the outcomes of decisions by Boeing and Airbus can be assessed.

Behavioral Aspects of Decision Making

If all decision situations were approached as logically as described in the previous section, more decisions would prove to be successful. Yet decisions are often made with little consideration for logic and rationality. Some experts have estimated that U.S. companies use rational decision-making techniques less than 20 percent of the time.[15] And even when organizations try to be logical, they sometimes fail. For example, Starbucks' original decision to emphasize drip over espresso coffee in New York was based on market research, taste tests, and rational deliberation—but the decision was still wrong. On the other hand, sometimes when a decision is made with little regard for logic, it can still turn out to be correct.[16] An important ingredient in how these forces work is the behavioral aspect of decision making. The administrative model better reflects these subjective considerations. Other behavioral aspects include political forces, intuition, escalation of commitment, risk propensity, and ethics.

The Administrative Model

Herbert A. Simon was one of the first experts to recognize that decisions are not always made with rationality and logic.[17] Simon was subsequently awarded the Nobel Prize in economics. Rather than prescribing how decisions should be made, his view of decision making, now called the **administrative model**, describes how decisions often actually are made. As illustrated in Figure 4.4, the model holds that managers (1) have incomplete and imperfect information, (2) are constrained by bounded rationality, and (3) tend to satisfice when making decisions.

administrative model A decision-making model that argues that decision makers (1) have incomplete and imperfect information, (2) are constrained by bounded rationality, and (3) tend to satisfice when making decisions

bounded rationality A concept suggesting that decision makers are limited by their values and unconscious reflexes, skills, and habits

Bounded rationality suggests that decision makers are limited by their values and unconscious reflexes, skills, and habits. They are also limited by less-than-complete information and knowledge. Bounded rationality partially explains how U.S. auto executives allowed Japanese automakers to get such a strong foothold in their domestic market. For years, executives at GM, Ford, and Chrysler compared their companies' performance only to one another's and ignored foreign imports. The foreign "threat" wasn't acknowledged until the domestic auto market had been changed forever. If managers had gathered complete information from the beginning, they might have been better able to thwart foreign competitors. Essentially, then, the concept of bounded rationality suggests that, although people try to be rational decision makers, their rationality has limits.

satisficing The tendency to search for alternatives only until one is found that meets some minimum standard of sufficiency

Another important part of the administrative model is **satisficing**. This concept suggests that, rather than conducting an exhaustive search for the best possible alternative, decision makers tend to search only until they identify an alternative that meets some minimum standard of sufficiency. A manager looking for a site for a new plant, for example, may select the first site she finds that meets basic requirements for transportation, utilities, and price, even though a further search might yield a better location. People satisfice for a variety of reasons. Managers may simply be unwilling to ignore their own motives (such as reluctance to spend time making a decision) and therefore not be able to continue searching after a minimally acceptable alternative is identified. The decision maker may be unable to weigh and evaluate large numbers of alternatives and criteria. Also, subjective and personal considerations often intervene in decision situations.

Figure 4.4

The Administrative Model of Decision Making

The administrative model is based on behavioral processes that affect how managers make decisions. Rather than prescribing how decisions should be made, it focuses more on describing how they are made.

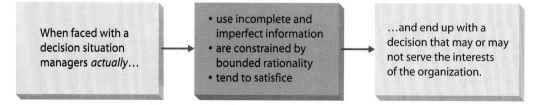

When faced with a decision situation managers *actually*...

- use incomplete and imperfect information
- are constrained by bounded rationality
- tend to satisfice

...and end up with a decision that may or may not serve the interests of the organization.

Because of the inherent imperfection of information, bounded rationality, and satisficing, the decisions made by a manager may or may not actually be in the best interests of the organization. A manager may choose a particular location for the new plant because it offers the lowest price and the best availability of utilities and transportation. Or she may choose the location because it is in a community in which she wants to live.

In summary, then, the classical and administrative models paint quite different pictures of decision making. Which is more correct? Actually, each can be used to better understand how managers make decisions. The classical model is prescriptive: It explains how managers can at least attempt to be more rational and logical in their approach to decisions. The administrative model can be used by managers to develop a better understanding of their inherent biases and limitations.[18] In the following sections, we describe more fully other behavioral forces that can influence decisions.

Political Forces in Decision Making

Political forces are another major element that contributes to the behavioral nature of decision making. Organizational politics is covered in Chapter 11, but one major element of politics, coalitions, is especially relevant to decision making. A **coalition** is an informal alliance of individuals or groups formed to achieve a common goal. This common goal is often a preferred decision alternative. For example, coalitions of stockholders frequently band together to force a board of directors to make a certain decision.

coalition An informal alliance of individuals or groups formed to achieve a common goal

Coalitions led to the formation of Unisys Corporation, a large computer firm. Sperry was once one of the United States' computer giants, but a series of poor decisions put the company on the edge of bankruptcy. Two major executives waged battle for three years over what to do. One wanted to get out of the computer business altogether, and the other wanted to stay in. Finally, the manager who wanted to remain in the computer business garnered enough support to earn promotion to the corporation's presidency. The other manager took early retirement. Shortly thereafter, Sperry agreed to be acquired by Burroughs Wellcome Company. The resulting combined company is called Unisys.

The impact of coalitions can be either positive or negative. They can help astute managers get the organization on a path toward effectiveness and profitability, or they can strangle well-conceived strategies and decisions. Managers must recognize when to use coalitions, how to assess whether coalitions are acting in the best interests of the organization, and how to constrain their dysfunctional effects.[19]

Intuition and Escalation of Commitment

Two other important decision processes that go beyond logic and rationality are intuition and escalation of commitment to a chosen course of action.

intuition An innate belief about something without conscious consideration

Intuition **Intuition** is an innate belief about something without conscious consideration. Managers sometimes decide to do something because it "feels right" or they have a hunch. This feeling is usually not arbitrary, however. Rather, it is based on years of experience and practice in making decisions in similar situations. An inner sense may help managers make an occasional decision without going through a full-blown rational sequence of steps. For example, a few years ago, the New York Yankees called three major sneaker manufacturers, Nike, Reebok, and Adidas, and informed them that they were looking to make a sponsorship deal. While Nike and Reebok were carefully and rationally assessing the possibilities, managers at Adidas quickly realized that a partnership with the Yankees made a lot of sense for them. They responded very quickly to the idea and ended up hammering out a contract while the competitors were still analyzing details.[20] Of course, all managers, but most especially inexperienced ones, should be careful not to rely on intuition too heavily. If rationality and logic are continually flaunted for what "feels right," the odds are that disaster will strike one day.

escalation of commitment A decision maker's staying with a decision even when it appears to be wrong

Escalation of Commitment Another important behavioral process that influences decision making is **escalation of commitment** to a chosen course of action. In particular, decision makers sometimes make decisions and then become so committed to the course of action suggested by that decision that they stay with it, even when it appears to have been wrong.[21] For example, when people buy stock in a company, they sometimes refuse to sell it even after repeated drops in price. They chose a course of action—buying the stock in anticipation of making a profit—and then stay with it even in the face of increasing losses.

For years Pan American World Airways ruled the skies and used its profits to diversify into real estate and other businesses. But with the advent of deregulation, Pan Am began to struggle and lose market share to other carriers. When Pan Am managers finally realized how ineffective the airline operations had become, experts today point out, the "rational" decision would have been to sell off the remaining airline operations and concentrate on the firm's more profitable businesses. But because they still saw the company as being first and foremost an airline, they instead began to slowly sell off the firm's profitable holdings to keep the airline flying. Eventually, the company was left with nothing but an ineffective and inefficient airline, and then had to sell off its more profitable routes before eventually being taken over by Delta. Had Pan Am managers made the more rational decision years earlier, chances are the firm could still be a profitable enterprise today, albeit one with no involvement in the airline industry.[22]

Thus decision makers must walk a fine line. On the one hand, they must guard against sticking with an incorrect decision for too long. To do so can bring about financial decline. On the other hand, managers should not bail out of a seemingly incorrect decision too soon, as did Adidas several years ago. Adidas once dominated the market for professional athletic shoes. It subsequently entered the market for amateur sports shoes and did well there also. But managers interpreted a sales slowdown as a sign that the boom in athletic shoes was over. They thought that they had made the wrong decision and ordered drastic cutbacks. The market took off again with Nike at the head of the pack, and Adidas never recovered. Fortunately, a new management team has changed the way Adidas makes decisions and, as illustrated earlier, the firm is again on its way to becoming a force in the athletic shoe and apparel markets.

Risk Propensity and Decision Making

The behavioral element of **risk propensity** is the extent to which a decision maker is willing to gamble when making a decision. Some managers are cautious about every decision they make. They try to adhere to the rational model and are extremely conservative in what they do. Such managers are more likely to avoid mistakes, and they infrequently make decisions that lead to big losses. Other managers are extremely aggressive in making decisions and are willing to take risks.[23] They rely heavily on intuition, reach decisions quickly, and often risk big investments on their decisions. As in gambling, these managers are more likely than their conservative counterparts to achieve big successes with their decisions; they are also more likely to incur greater losses.[24] The organization's culture is a prime ingredient in fostering different levels of risk propensity.

Ethics and Decision Making

As we introduced in Chapter 2, individual ethics are personal beliefs about right and wrong behavior. Ethics are clearly related to decision making in a number of ways. For example, suppose that, after careful analysis, a manager realizes that her company could save money by closing her department and subcontracting with a supplier for the same services. But to recommend this course of action would result in the loss of several jobs, including her own. Her own ethical standards will clearly shape how she proceeds.[25] Indeed, each component of managerial ethics (relationships of the firm to its employees, of employees to the firm, and of the firm to other economic agents) involves a wide variety of decisions, all of which are likely to have an ethical component. A manager must remember, then, that just as behavioral processes such as politics and risk propensity affect the decisions she makes, so, too, do her ethical beliefs.

risk propensity The extent to which a decision maker is willing to gamble in making a decision

Businesses frequently rely on groups and teams to make critical decisions. For example, a team of supply chain experts helped General Motors and Izusu plan and conduct an online auction to buy parts for use in the production of automobiles. The companies got a great buy on the parts they needed, plus saved 90 percent of their normal purchasing costs in doing so. More and more businesses are reporting similar success stories when they turn things over to teams.

■ *Group and Team Decision Making in Organizations*

In more and more organizations today, important decisions are made by groups and teams rather than by individuals. Examples include the executive committee of General Motors, product design teams at Texas Instruments, and marketing planning groups at Dell Computer. Managers can typically choose whether to have individuals or groups and teams make a particular decision. Thus knowing about forms of group and team decision making and their advantages and disadvantages is important.[26]

Forms of Group and Team Decision Making

The most common methods of group and team decision making are interacting groups, Delphi groups, and nominal groups. Increasingly, these methods of group decision making are being conducted online.

interacting group A decision-making group or team in which members openly discuss, argue about, and agree on the best alternative

Interacting Groups   **Interacting groups** and teams are the most common form of decision-making group. The format is simple—either an existing or a newly designated group or team is asked to make a decision. Existing groups or teams might be functional departments, regular work teams, or standing committees. Newly designated groups or teams can be ad hoc committees, task forces, or newly constituted work teams. The group or team members talk among themselves, argue, agree, argue some more, form internal coalitions, and so forth. Finally, after some period of deliberation, the group or team makes its decision. An advantage of this method is that the interaction among people often sparks new ideas and promotes understanding. A major disadvantage, though, is that political processes can play too big a role.

Delphi group A form of group decision making in which a group is used to achieve a consensus of expert opinion

Delphi Groups   A **Delphi group** is sometimes used for developing a consensus of expert opinion. Developed by the Rand Corporation, the Delphi procedure solicits input from a panel of experts who contribute individually. Their opinions are combined and, in effect, averaged. Assume, for example, that the problem is to establish an expected date for a major technological breakthrough in converting coal into usable energy. The first step in using the Delphi procedure is to obtain the cooperation of a panel of experts. For this situation, experts might include various research scientists, university researchers, and executives in a relevant energy industry. At first, the experts are asked to anonymously predict a time frame for the expected breakthrough. The persons coordinating the Delphi group collect the responses, average them, and ask the experts for another prediction. In this round, the experts who provided unusual or extreme predictions may be asked to justify them. These explanations may then be relayed to the other experts. When the predictions stabilize, the average prediction is taken to represent the decision of the "group" of experts. The time, expense, and logistics of the Delphi technique rule out its use for routine, everyday decisions, but it has been successfully used for forecasting technological breakthroughs at Boeing, market potential for new products at General Motors, research and development patterns at Eli Lilly, and future economic conditions for the U.S. government.[27]

Nominal Groups   Another useful group and team decision-making technique which is occasionally used is the **nominal group**. Unlike the Delphi method, in which group members do not see one another, nominal group members are brought together. The members represent a group in name only, however; they do not talk to one another freely like the members of interacting groups. Nominal groups are used most often to generate creative and innovative alternatives or ideas. To begin, the manager assembles a group of knowledgeable people and outlines the problem to them. The group members are then asked to individually write down as many alternatives as they can think of. The members then take turns stating their ideas, which are recorded on a flip chart or board at the front of the room. Discussion is limited to simple clarification. After all alternatives have been listed, more open discussion takes place. Group members then vote, usually by rank-ordering the various alternatives. The highest-ranking alternative represents the decision of the group. Of course, the manager in charge may retain the authority to accept or reject the group decision.

nominal group A structured technique used to generate creative and innovative alternatives or ideas

Advantages of Group and Team Decision Making

The advantages and disadvantages of group and team decision making relative to individual decision making are summarized in Table 4.2. One advantage is simply that more information is available in a group or team setting—as suggested by the old axiom "Two heads are better than one." A group or team represents a variety of education, experience, and perspective. Partly as a result of this increased information, groups and teams can typically identify and evaluate more alternatives than can one person.[28] The people involved in a group or team decision understand the

Advantages	Disadvantages
1. More information and knowledge are available.	1. The process takes longer than individual decision making, so it is costlier.
2. More alternatives are likely to be generated.	2. Compromise decisions resulting from indecisiveness may emerge.
3. More acceptance of the final decision is likely.	3. One person may dominate the group.
4. Enhanced communication of the decision may result.	4. Groupthink may occur.
5. Better decisions generally emerge.	

Table 4.2

Advantages and Disadvantages of Group and Team Decision Making
To increase the chances that a group or team decision will be successful, managers must learn how to manage the process of group and team decision making. Westinghouse, Federal Express, and IBM are increasingly using groups and teams in the decision-making process.

logic and rationale behind it, are more likely to accept it, and are equipped to communicate the decision to their work groups or departments.[29] Finally, research evidence suggests that groups may make better decisions than do individuals.[30]

Disadvantages of Group and Team Decision Making

Perhaps the biggest drawback of group and team decision making is the additional time and hence the greater expense entailed. The increased time stems from interaction and discussion among group or team members. If a given manager's time is worth $50 an hour, and if the manager spends two hours making a decision, the decision "costs" the organization $100. For the same decision, a group of five managers might require three hours of time. At the same $50-an-hour rate, the decision "costs" the organization $750. Assuming the group or team decision is better, the additional expense may be justified, but the fact remains that group and team decision making is more costly.

Group or team decisions may also represent undesirable compromises.[31] For example, hiring a compromise top manager may be a bad decision in the long run because he or she may not be able to respond adequately to various subunits in the organization nor have everyone's complete support. Sometimes one individual dominates the group process to the point where others cannot make a full contribution. This dominance may stem from a desire for power or from a naturally dominant personality. The problem is that what appears to emerge as a group decision may actually be the decision of one person.

Finally, a group or team may succumb to a phenomenon known as groupthink. **Groupthink** occurs when the desire for consensus and cohesiveness overwhelms the goal of reaching the best possible decision.[32] Under the influence of groupthink, the group may arrive at decisions that are not in the best interests of either the group or the organization, but rather avoid conflict among group members. One of the clearest documented examples of groupthink involved the space shuttle *Challenger* disaster. As NASA was preparing to launch the shuttle, numerous problems and questions arose. At each step of the way, however, decision makers argued that there was no reason to delay and that everything would be fine. Shortly after the launch in January 1986, the shuttle exploded, killing all seven crew members.

groupthink A situation that occurs when a group or team's desire for consensus and cohesiveness overwhelms its desire to reach the best possible decision

Managing Group and Team Decision-Making Processes

Managers can do several things to help promote the effectiveness of group and team decision making. One is simply being aware of the pros and cons of having a group or team make a decision to start with. Time and cost can be managed by setting a deadline by which the decision must be made final. Dominance can be at least partially avoided if a special group is formed just to make the decision. An astute manager, for example, should know who in the organization may try to dominate and can either avoid putting that person in the group or put several strong-willed people together.

To avoid groupthink, each member of the group or team should critically evaluate all alternatives. So that members present divergent viewpoints, the leader should not make his or her own position known too early. At least one member of the group or team might be assigned the role of devil's advocate. And, after reaching a preliminary decision, the group or team should hold a followup meeting in which divergent viewpoints can be raised again if any group members wish to do so.[33] Gould Paper Company used these methods by assigning managers to two different teams. The teams then spent an entire day in a structured debate presenting the pros and cons of each side of an issue to ensure the best possible decision. Sun Microsystems makes most of its major decisions using this same approach.

Summary of Key Points

Decisions are an integral part of all managerial activities, but they are perhaps most central to the planning process. Decision making is the act of choosing one alternative from among a set of alternatives. The decision-making process includes recognizing and defining the nature of a decision situation, identifying alternatives, choosing the best alternative, and putting it into practice. Two common types of decisions are programmed and nonprogrammed. Decisions may be made under states of certainty, risk, or uncertainty.

Rational perspectives on decision making rest on the classical model. This model assumes that managers have complete information and that they will behave rationally. The primary steps in rational decision making are (1) recognizing and defining the situation, (2) identifying alternatives, (3) evaluating alternatives, (4) selecting the best alternative, (5) implementing the chosen alternative, and (6) following up and evaluating the effectiveness of the alternative after it is implemented.

Behavioral aspects of decision making rely on the administrative model. This model recognizes that managers will have incomplete information and that they will not always behave rationally. The administrative model also recognizes the concepts of bounded rationality and satisficing. Political activities by coalitions, managerial intuition, and the tendency to become increasingly committed to a chosen course of action are all important. Risk propensity is also an important behavioral perspective on decision making. Finally, ethics also affect how managers make decisions.

To help enhance decision-making effectiveness, managers often use interacting, Delphi, or nominal groups or teams. Group and team decision making in general has several advantages as well as disadvantages relative to individual decision making. Managers can adopt a number of strategies to help groups and teams make better decisions.

Discussion Questions

Questions for Review

1. Describe the nature of decision making.
2. Identify and discuss the conditions under which most decisions are made.
3. What are the main features of the classical model of the decision-making process? What are the main features of the administrative model?
4. What are the steps in rational decision making? Which step do you think is the most difficult to carry out? Why?
5. Describe the behavioral nature of decision making. Be certain to provide some detail about political forces, risk propensity, ethics, and commitment in your description.

Questions for Analysis

6. Was your decision about which college or university to attend a rational decision? Did you go through each step in rational decision making? If not, why not?
7. Can any decision be purely rational, or are all decisions at least partially behavioral in nature? Defend your answer.
8. Think of an example for each condition for decision making. Then describe how conditions might change to alter the condition for each decision.
9. Is satisficing always a bad thing? Under what conditions, if any, might it be desirable?
10. Under what conditions would you expect group or team decision making to be preferable to individual decision making, and vice versa? Why?

BUILDING EFFECTIVE *decision-making & communication* SKILLS

Exercise Overview

Decision-making skills refer to the manager's ability to correctly recognize and define problems and opportunities and to then select an appropriate course of action to solve problems and capitalize on opportunities. Communication skills refer to the manager's abilities to both effectively convey ideas and information to others and to effectively receive ideas and information from others. Not surprisingly, these skills can be highly interrelated. This exercise gives you insights into some of those interrelations.

Exercise Background

Identify a decision that you will need to make sometime in the near future. If you work in a managerial position, you might select a real problem or issue to address. For example, you might use the selection or termination of an employee, the allocation of pay raises, or the selection of someone for a promotion.

If you do not work in a managerial position, you might instead select an upcoming decision related to your academic work. Example decisions might include what major to select, whether to attend summer school or to work, which job to select, or whether to live on or off campus next year. Be sure to select a decision that you have not yet made.

Exercise Task

Using the decision selected above, do the following:

1. On a sheet of paper, list the kinds of information that you will most likely use in making your decision. Beside each item, make notes as to where you can obtain the information, what form the information will be

presented in, the reliability of the information, and other characteristics of the information that you deem to be relevant.

2. Assume that you have used the information obtained above and have now made the decision. (It might be helpful at this point to select a hypothetical decision and choice to frame your answers. For instance, you might choose selecting a new plant location as the decision and St. Louis, Missouri, as the choice.) On the other side of the paper, list the various communication consequences that come with your decision. For example, if your choice involves an academic major, you may need to inform your advisor and your family. List as many consequences as you can. Beside each entry, make notes as to how you would communicate with each party, the timeliness of your communication, and other factors that seem to be relevant.

3. What behavioral forces might play a role in your decision?

BUILDING EFFECTIVE *interpersonal* SKILLS

Exercise Overview

Interpersonal skills refer to the manager's ability to understand and motivate individuals and groups. This exercise allows you to practice your interpersonal skills in a role-playing exercise.

Exercise Background

You supervise a group of six employees who work in an indoor facility in a relatively isolated location. The company you work for has recently adopted an ambiguous policy regarding smoking. Essentially, the policy states that all company work sites are to be smoke free unless the employees at a specific site choose differently and at the discretion of the site supervisor.

Four members of the work group you supervise are smokers. They have come to you with the argument that, because they constitute the majority, they should be allowed to smoke at work. The other two members of the group, both nonsmokers, have heard about this proposal and have also discussed the situation with you. They argue that the health-related consequences of secondary smoke should outweigh the preferences of the majority.

To compound the problem, your boss wrote the new policy and is quite defensive about it—numerous individuals have already criticized the policy. You know that your boss will get very angry with you if you also raise concerns about the policy. Finally, you are personally indifferent about the issue. You do not smoke yourself, but your spouse does smoke. Secondary smoke does not bother you, and you do not have strong opinions about it. Still, you have to make a decision. You see that your choices are to (1) mandate a smoke-free environment, (2) allow smoking in the facility, or (3) ask your boss to clarify the policy.

Exercise Task

Based on the background presented above, assume that you are the supervisor and do the following:

1. Assume that you have chosen option 1. Prepare an outline that you will use to announce your decision to the four smokers.
2. Assume that you have chosen option 2. Prepare an outline that you will use to announce your decision to the two nonsmokers.
3. Assume that you have chosen option 3. Prepare an outline that you will use when you meet with your boss.
4. Are there other alternatives?
5. What would you do if you were actually the group supervisor?

BUILDING EFFECTIVE *technical* SKILLS

Exercise Overview

Technical skills are the skills necessary to accomplish or understand the specific kind of work being done in an organization. This exercise enables you to practice technical skills using the Internet to obtain information for making a decision.

Exercise Background

Assume that you are a business owner seeking a location for a new factory. Your company makes products that are relatively "clean"—that is, they do not pollute the environment; in addition, your factory does not produce any dangerous waste products. Thus most communities would welcome your plant.

You are seeking a place that has a stable and well-educated workforce, good quality of life, good health care, and a good educational system. You have narrowed your choice to the following towns:

1. Columbia, Missouri
2. Madison, Wisconsin
3. Manhattan, Kansas
4. College Station, Texas
5. Baton Rouge, Louisiana
6. Athens, Georgia

Exercise Task

With the background information above as context, do the following:

1. Use the Internet to learn about these cities.
2. Rank-order each city on the basis of the criteria noted above.
3. Select the best city for your new factory.

SKILLS *self-assessment* INSTRUMENT

Decision-Making Styles

Introduction: Decision making is clearly important. However, individuals differ in their decision-making style, or the way they approach decisions. The following assessment is designed to help you understand your decision-making style.

Instructions: Respond to the following statements by indicating the extent to which they describe you. Circle the response that best represents your self-evaluation.

1. Overall, I'm _____ to act.
   1. quick   2. moderately fast   3. slow

2. I spend _____ amount of time making important decisions as/than I do making less important ones.
   1. about the same   2. a greater   3. a much greater

3. When making decisions, I _____ go with my first thought.
   1. usually   2. occasionally   3. rarely

4. When making decisions, I'm _____ concerned about making errors.
   1. rarely   2. occasionally   3. often

5. When making decisions, I _____ recheck my work more than once.
   1. rarely   2. occasionally   3. usually

6. When making decisions, I gather _____ information.
   1. little   2. some   3. lots of

7. When making decisions, I consider _____ alternatives.
   1. few   2. some   3. lots of

8. I usually make decisions _____ before the deadline.
   1. way   2. somewhat   3. just

9. After making a decision, I _____ look for other alternatives, wishing I had waited.
   1. rarely 2. occasionally 3. usually
10. I _____ regret having made a decision.
   1. rarely 2. occasionally 3. often

For interpretation, see Interpretations of Skills Self-Assessment Instruments.

Source: Adapted from Lussier, Robert N., *Supervision: A Skill-Building Approach*, Second Edition, pp. 122–123, copyright © 1994 by Richard D. Irwin, Inc. Reproduced with permission of The McGraw-Hill Companies.

EXPERIENTIAL EXERCISE

Programmed and Nonprogrammed Decision Making

Purpose: This exercise allows you to make decisions and helps you understand the difference between programmed and nonprogrammed decisions. You also learn how decision making by an individual differs from decision making by a group.

Introduction: You are asked to make decisions both individually and as a member of a group.

Instructions: Following is a list of typical organizational decisions. Your task is to determine whether they are programmed or nonprogrammed. Number your paper, and write P for programmed or N for nonprogrammed next to each number.

Next, your instructor will divide the class into groups of four to seven. All groups should have approximately the same number of members. Your task as a group is to make the decisions that you just made as individuals. In arriving at your decisions, do not use techniques such as voting or negotiating ("OK, I'll give in on this one if you'll give in on that one"). The group should discuss the difference between programmed and nonprogrammed decisions in each decision situation until all members at least partly agree with the decision.

Decision List:
1. Hiring a specialist for the research staff in a highly technical field
2. Assigning workers to daily tasks
3. Determining the size of the dividend to be paid to shareholders in the ninth consecutive year of strong earnings growth
4. Deciding whether to officially excuse an employee's absence for medical reasons
5. Selecting the location for another branch of a 150-branch bank in a large city
6. Approving the appointment of a new law school graduate to the corporate legal staff
7. Making the annual assignment of graduate assistants to the faculty
8. Approving the request of an employee to attend a local seminar in his or her special area of expertise
9. Selecting the appropriate outlets for print advertisements for a new college textbook
10. Determining the location for a new fast-food restaurant in a small but growing town on the major interstate highway between two very large metropolitan areas

Followup Questions:
1. To what extent did group members disagree about which decisions were programmed and which were nonprogrammed?
2. What primary factors did the group discuss in making each decision?
3. Were there any differences between the members' individual lists and the group lists? If so, discuss the reasons for the differences.

Source: From *Organizational Behavior*, Fourth edition, by Gregory Moorhead and Ricky Griffin. Copyright © 1994 by Houghton Mifflin Company. Reprinted by permission.

FIRST AID FOR AETNA

Aetna had been offering life insurance and property insurance for more than 140 years when Richard Huber became vice chairman and set in motion major decisions that took the company into an entirely new business. In 1996 Huber foresaw a rosy and profitable future for managed health care, in contrast to the increased competition and interest-rate pressures ahead for Aetna's financial services offerings. So he sold the company's U.S. property and life operations and plunked down $8 billion to buy U.S. Healthcare plus $2 billion to buy Prudential Health. With these purchases, Huber was able to say that Aetna insured one in every ten Americans who have insurance.

In retrospect, however, the price tag for entering the health care insurance field seems high. Aetna paid the equivalent of $2,800 per member for U.S. Healthcare, compared with a typical price of $600 per managed care member just four years after Aetna's purchase. The downward direction of these per-member prices reflects the downward direction of profits in the managed health care business during the late 1990s.

Once Aetna entered the ever-changing world of managed health care, it was subjected to risks and decisions it had never faced in the insurance industry. First, it was difficult to project the size of the medical bills that Aetna's health care units might have to pay on behalf of sick or injured members. Second, the units might be sued if they didn't pay for some medical treatments. Third, half of Aetna's health care members were in managed care plans. Such plans generally attract older, less healthy members, so costs were on the rise—but by how much was impossible to predict. As a result, Aetna's profit margins grew thinner and thinner. According to one analyst, the company's managed care profit margin was about 7.5 percent when it entered the business but had fallen to just 3.3 percent within four years.

In 1999 Aetna's stock price was battered by two pieces of bad news. The company disclosed that its Prudential health care unit was losing more money than analysts expected. Only days later, lawyers announced their intention to file charges against Aetna and other managed care companies over the issue of whether doctors were being forced to restrict member care. Still, Aetna had some strengths that Huber, now CEO, wanted to build on. But as Aetna's share price dropped to its lowest point in more than seven years, Huber submitted his resignation, and Bill Donaldson was brought in as CEO.

As one of the founders of investment bank Donaldson, Lufkin and Jenrette, Donaldson was a knowledgeable deal maker. He decided to sell off Aetna's insurance and financial units so the company could concentrate on turning around its health care operations, which now formed the core of the corporation. After several months of negotiation, Donaldson arranged for Internationale Nederlanden Groep, a Dutch banking and insurance company, to buy the insurance and financial units for $5 billion. Although this relieved some of the pressure, Donaldson was still looking for someone to take the top slot at the company's health care business, because that CEO had retired several months earlier. More tough decisions were ahead for Donaldson and Aetna.

Case Questions

1. How would you describe Richard Huber's risk propensity?

2. Under what conditions did Donaldson make the decision to sell off Aetna's insurance and financial units? Did Huber confront the same conditions when he decided to buy into the health care business?

3. Before deciding to sell the financial and insurance units, what other options do you think Donaldson considered? How would you evaluate those other options?

Case References

Bill Rigby, "Aetna's Donaldson Does Easy Part, Now Faces Tougher Task," *Reuters*, July 20, 2000, http://www.hoovers.com; and John Graham, "Train Wreck in Hartford," *Forbes*, March 6, 2000, pp. 70–71.

CHAPTER NOTES

1. "Now, Starbucks Uses Its Bean," *Business Week*, February 14, 2000, pp. 92–93 (quote on p. 92); Vijay Vishwanath and David Harding, "The Starbucks Effect," *Harvard Business Review*, March/April 2000, pp. 17–18; and *Hoover's Handbook of American Business 2001* (Austin, TX: Hoover's Business Press, 2001), pp. 1320–1321.

2. Richard Priem, "Executive Judgment, Organizational Congruence, and Firm Performance," *Organization Science*, August 1994, pp. 421–432.

3. "Ford Grabs Big Prize as Steep Losses Force BMW to Sell Rover," *Wall Street Journal*, March 17, 2000, pp. A1, A8.

4. Paul Nutt, "The Formulation Processes and Tactics Used in Organizational Decision Making," *Organization Science*, May 1993, pp. 226–240.

5. "Kodak Moment Came Early for CEO Fisher, Who Takes a Stumble," *Wall Street Journal*, July 25, 1997, pp. A1, A6.

6. George P. Huber, *Managerial Decision Making* (Glenview, IL: Scott, Foresman, 1980).

7. See Paul D. Collins, Lori V. Ryan, and Sharon F. Matusik, "Programmable Automation and the Locus of Decision-Making Power," *Journal of Management* 25 (1999): 29–53, for an example.

8. Huber. See also David W. Miller and Martin K. Starr, *The Structure of Human Decisions* (Englewood Cliffs, NJ: Prentice-Hall, 1976); and Alvar Elbing, *Behavioral Decisions in Organizations*, 2nd ed. (Glenview, IL: Scott, Foresman, 1978).

9. "Taking the Angst out of Taking a Gamble," *Business Week*, July 14, 1997, pp. 52–53.

10. Gerard P. Hodgkinson, Nicola J. Bown, A. John Maule, Keith W. Glaister, and Alan D. Pearman, "Breaking the Frame: An Analysis of Strategic Cognition and Decision Making Under Uncertainty," *Strategic Management Journal* 20 (1999): 977–985.

11. "Tension Between Ford and Firestone Mounts amid Recall Efforts," *Wall Street Journal*, August 28, 2000, pp. A1, A8; and "Bridgestone Boss Has Toughness, But Is That What Crisis Demands?" *Wall Street Journal*, September 12, 2000, pp. A1, A18.

12. Glen Whyte, "Decision Failures: Why They Occur and How to Prevent Them," *Academy of Management Executive*, August 1991, pp. 23–31.

13. Jerry Useem, "Boeing vs. Boeing," *Fortune*, October 2, 2000, pp. 148–160; and "Airbus Prepares to 'Bet the Company' as It Builds a Huge New Jet," *Wall Street Journal*, November 3, 1999, pp. A1, A10.

14. Kenneth Labich, "Coups and Catastrophes," *Fortune*, December 23, 1985, p. 125.

15. "The Wisdom of Solomon," *Newsweek*, August 17, 1987, pp. 62–63.

16. "Making Decisions in Real Time," *Fortune*, June 26, 2000, pp. 332–334.

17. Herbert A. Simon, *Administrative Behavior* (New York: Free Press, 1945). Simon's ideas have been refined and updated in Herbert A. Simon, *Administrative Behavior*, 3rd ed. (New York: Free Press, 1976); and Herbert A. Simon, "Making Management Decisions: The Role of Intuition and Emotion," *Academy of Management Executive*, February 1987, pp. 57–63.

18. Patricia Corner, Angelo Kinicki, and Barbara Keats, "Integrating Organizational and Individual Information Processing Perspectives on Choice," *Organization Science*, August 1994, pp. 294–302.

19. Kimberly D. Elsbach and Greg Elofson, "How the Packaging of Decision Explanations Affects Perceptions of Trustworthiness," *Academy of Management Journal* 43 (2000): 80–89.

20. Charles P. Wallace, "Adidas—Back in the Game," *Fortune*, August 18, 1997, pp. 176–182.

21. Barry M. Staw and Jerry Ross, "Good Money After Bad," *Psychology Today*, February 1988, pp. 30-33; and D. Ramona Bobocel and John Meyer, "Escalating Commitment to a Failing Course of Action: Separating the Roles of Choice and Justification," *Journal of Applied Psychology* 79 (1994): 360–363.

22. Mark Keil and Ramiro Montealegre, "Cutting Your Losses: Extricating Your Organization When a Big Project Goes Awry," *Sloan Management Review*, Spring 2000, pp. 55–64.

23. Gerry McNamara and Philip Bromiley, "Risk and Return in Organizational Decision Making," *Academy of Management Journal* 42 (1999): 330–339.

24. See Brian O'Reilly, "What It Takes to Start a Startup," *Fortune*, June 7, 1999, pp. 135–140, for an example.

25. Martha I. Finney, "The Catbert Dilemma—The Human Side of Tough Decisions," *HR Magazine*, February 1997, pp. 70–78.

26. Edwin A. Locke, David M. Schweiger, and Gary P. Latham, "Participation in Decision Making: When Should It Be Used?" *Organizational Dynamics*, Winter 1986, pp. 65–79; and Nicholas Baloff and Elizabeth M. Doherty, "Potential Pitfalls in Employee Participation," *Organizational Dynamics*, Winter 1989, pp. 51–62.

27. Andre L. Delbecq, Andrew H. Van de Ven, and David H. Gustafson, *Group Techniques for Program Planning* (Glenview, IL: Scott, Foresman, 1975); and Michael J. Prietula and Herbert A. Simon, "The Experts in Your Midst," *Harvard Business Review*, January/February 1989, pp. 120–124.

28. Norman P. R. Maier, "Assets and Liabilities in Group Problem Solving: The Need for an Integrative Function," in *Perspectives on Business in Organizations*, 2nd ed., eds . J. Richard Hackman, Edward E. Lawler III, and Lyman W. Porter (New York: McGraw-Hill, 1983), pp. 385–392.

29. Anthony L. Iaquinto and James W. Fredrickson, "Top Management Team Agreement About the Strategic Decision Process: A Test of Some of Its Determinants and Consequences," *Strategic Management Journal* 18 (1997): 63–75.

30. Tony Simons, Lisa Hope Pelled, and Ken A. Smith, "Making Use of Difference: Diversity, Debate, and Decision Comprehensiveness in Top Management Teams," *Academy of Management Journal* 42 (1999): 662–673.

31. Richard A. Cosier and Charles R. Schwenk, "Agreement and Thinking Alike: Ingredients for Poor Decisions," *Academy of Management Executive*, February 1990, pp. 69–78.

32. Irving L. Janis, *Groupthink*, 2nd ed. (Boston: Houghton Mifflin, 1982).

33. Ibid.

Entrepreneurship and New Venture Management

Just a few years ago, James Koch was a high-flying management consultant pulling in over $250,000 a year. To the surprise of his family and friends, however, he quit this job and invested his life's savings in starting a new business from scratch and going head to head with international competitors in a market that had not had a truly successful specialty product in decades. And, to their bigger surprise, he succeeded!

The company Koch founded is Boston Beer Company, and its flagship product is a premium beer called Samuel Adams. Koch's family had actually been brewing beer for generations, and he started with a recipe developed by his great-great-grandfather, who had sold the beer in St. Louis in the 1870s under the name Louis Koch Lager. To fund his operation, he used $100,000 in personal savings and another $300,000 invested by his friends.

He set up shop in an old warehouse in Boston, bought some surplus brewing equipment from a large brewery, and started operations. Because his beer used only the highest-quality ingredients, he needed to price it at about $1 more per case than such premium imports as Heineken. Boston-area distributors, meanwhile, doubted that consumers would pay $6 per six-pack for an American beer, and most refused to carry it. Thus Koch began selling the beer directly to retailers and bars himself.

But his big break came when he entered Samuel Adams Lager in the Great American Beer Festival, where it won the consumer preference poll—the industry's equivalent of the Oscar. Koch then started using this victory as his advertising mantra, proclaiming Samuel Adams as "The Best Beer in America." Sales began to take off, and national dis-

tributors began calling for the beer. In order to meet surging demand, Koch contracted part of the brewing to a near-deserted Stroh's brewery in Pittsburgh.

During the early 1990s, sales of Samuel Adams products grew at an annual rate of over 57 percent and today exceed $250 million per year. Boston Beer also exports Samuel Adams to Germany, where the beer has also become quite popular. Koch, meanwhile, has retained controlling interests in the business and still oversees the day-to-day brewing operations. Indeed, he claims that he has sampled at least one of the firm's products every day since the business started, primarily as a way of monitoring quality.

But Koch's success has not gone unnoticed, especially by industry gi-

> *"You don't create a whole new national market in the beer business by being frightened."*
>
> —James Koch, founder and owner, Boston Beer Company

After studying this chapter, you should be able to

- Discuss the nature of entrepreneurship.

- Describe the roles of entrepreneurs in society.

- Understand the major issues involved in choosing strategies for entrepreneurial firms and the role of international management in entrepreneurship.

- Discuss the structural challenges unique to entrepreneurial firms.

- Understand the determinants of the performance of entrepreneurial firms.

ant Anheuser Busch. Anheuser and other national brewers have recently seen their sales take a hit from so-called microbreweries, small regional or local companies that sell esoteric brews made in small quantities and deriving cachet from their very scarcity. The Boston Beer Company was the first of these to make it big, and most others are trying to follow in its footsteps. Obviously, therefore, Anheuser Busch has a vested interest in not letting these smaller startups gain too much market share, most of which would come at its own expense.

Recently, for example, Koch learned that Anheuser had made inquiries about buying the entire crop from a German hops farm that has an exclusive arrangement with Boston Beer. Had Anheuser succeeded, Koch says, he would have been put out of business. Anheuser has also complained that the labeling on Samuel Adams is misleading, hiding the fact that the beer made in Pittsburgh is actually being brewed under contract by

Stroh's, not Boston Beer. And the industry giant has even tried to convince wholesalers, who are highly dependent on Anheuser products like Budweiser, to stop selling specialty beers like Samuel Adams. Koch, meanwhile, simply sees all this attention as a clear sign that he has made it.[1]

Just like James Koch, thousands of people all over the world start new businesses each year. And like the Boston Beer Company, some of these businesses succeed whereas, unfortunately, many others fail. Some of the people who fail in a new business try again, and sometimes it takes two or more failures before a successful business gets under way. Henry Ford, for example, went bankrupt twice before succeeding with what is now the world's second-largest automobile company.

This process of starting a new business, sometimes failing and sometimes succeeding, is part of what is called *entrepreneurship*, the subject of this chapter. We begin by exploring the nature of entrepreneurship. We then examine the role of entrepreneurship in the business world and discuss strategies for entrepreneurial organizations. We then describe the structure and performance of entrepreneurial organizations.

The Nature of Entrepreneurship

entrepreneurship The process of planning, organizing, operating, and assuming the risk of a business venture

entrepreneur Someone who engages in entrepreneurship

Entrepreneurship is the process of planning, organizing, operating, and assuming the risk of a business venture. An **entrepreneur**, in turn, is someone who engages in entrepreneurship. James Koch, as highlighted in our opening incident, fits this description. He put his own resources on the line and took a personal stake in the success or failure of his budding enterprise. Business owners who hire professional managers to run their business and then turn their attention to other interests are not entrepreneurs. Although they are assuming the risk of the venture, they are not actively involved in organizing or operating it. Likewise, professional managers whose job is running someone else's business are not entrepreneurs, for they assume less-than-total personal risk for the success or failure of the business.

small business A business that is privately owned by one individual or a small group of individuals; it has sales and assets that are not large enough to influence its environment

Entrepreneurs start new businesses. We define a **small business** as one that is privately owned by one individual or a small group of individuals which has sales and assets that are not large enough to influence its environment. A small two-person software development company with annual sales of $100,000 would clearly be a small business, whereas Microsoft Corporation is just as clearly a large business. But the boundaries are not always this clear-cut. For example, a regional retailing chain with 20 stores and annual revenues of $30 million may sound large, but it is really very small when compared to such giants as Wal-Mart and Sears.

The Role of Entrepreneurship in Society

The history of entrepreneurship and of the development of new businesses is in many ways the history of great wealth and of great failure. Some entrepreneurs have been very successful and have accumulated vast fortunes from their entrepreneurial efforts. Many more entrepreneurs, however, have lost a great deal of money—especially during the "dot.com" crash in 2001. Research suggests that the majority of new businesses fail within the first few years of founding. Many that last longer do so only because the entrepreneurs themselves work long hours for very little income.

As Figure 5.1 shows, most U.S. businesses employ fewer than 100 people, and most U.S. workers are employed by small firms. For example, Figure 5.1(a) shows that 86.7 percent of all U.S. businesses employ 20 or fewer people; another 11 percent employ between 20 and 99 people. In contrast, only about one-tenth of 1 percent employ 1,000 or more workers. Figure 5.1(b) shows that 25.6 percent of all U.S. workers are employed by firms with fewer than 20 people; another 29.1 percent work in firms that employ between 20 and 99 people. The vast majority of these companies are owner operated.[2] Figure 5.1(b) also shows that 12.7 percent of U.S. workers are employed by firms with 1,000 or more total employees.

On the basis of numbers alone, then, small business is a strong presence in the economy, which is true in virtually all the world's mature economies. In Germany, for example, companies with fewer than 500 employees produce two-thirds of the nation's gross national product, train nine of ten apprentices, and employ four of every five workers. Small businesses also play major roles in the economies of Italy, France, and Brazil. In addition, experts agree that small businesses will be quite important in the emerging economies of Russia and Vietnam. The contribution of small business can be measured in terms of its effects on key aspects of an economic system. In the United States, these aspects include job creation, innovation, and importance to big business.

Figure 5.1

The Importance of Small Business in the United States

Over 86 percent of all U.S. businesses have no more than 20 employees. The total number of people employed by these small businesses is approximately one-fourth of the entire U.S. workforce. Another 29 percent work for companies with fewer than 100 employees.

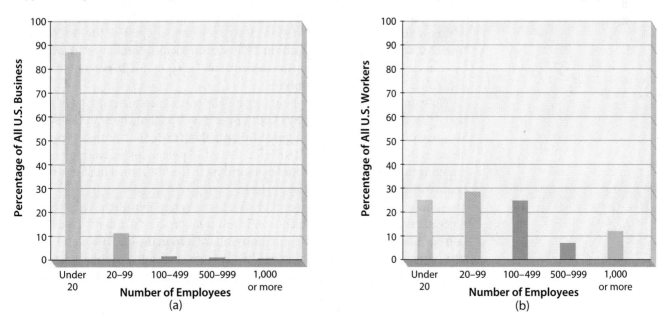

Source: U.S. Census Bureau, *Statistical Abstract of the United States: 2000* (120th Edition), Washington, D.C., 2000.

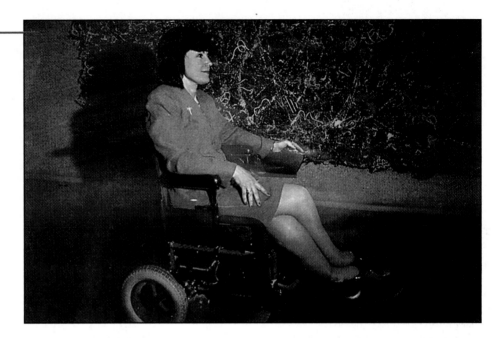

One important economic role played by small business startups is the creation of new jobs. For example, Susan Webb owns and manages Webb Transitions, a private employment agency that contracts with public agencies and private companies to help disabled employees return to work. Webb Transitions employs six people, and Ms. Webb forecasts a 10 percent annual revenue growth rate for each of the next several years. And as her business grows, she will continue to add new jobs as well.

Job Creation

In the early 1980s, a widely cited study proposed that small businesses create eight of every ten new jobs in the United States. This contention touched off considerable interest in the fostering of small business as a matter of public policy. As we will see, relative job growth among businesses of different sizes is not easy to determine. It is clear, however, that small business—especially in certain industries—is an important source of new (and often well-paid) jobs in this country. According to the Small Business Administration (SBA), for example, seven of the ten industries that added the most new jobs in 1998 were in sectors dominated by small businesses. Moreover, small businesses currently account for 38 percent of all jobs in high-tech sectors of the economy.[3]

Note that new jobs are also being created by small firms specializing in international business. For example, Bob Knosp operates a small business in Bellevue, Washington, that makes computerized sign-making systems. Knosp gets over half his sales from abroad and has dedicated almost 75 percent of his workforce to handling international sales. Indeed, according to the SBA, small businesses account for 96 percent of all U.S. exporters.[4]

Although small businesses certainly create many new jobs each year, the importance of entrepreneurial big businesses in job creation should also not be overlooked. Although big businesses cut thousands of jobs in the late 1980s and early 1990s, the booming U.S. economy resulted in large-scale job creation in many larger businesses beginning in the mid-1990s. Figure 5.2 details the changes in the number of jobs at 16 large U.S. companies during the ten-year period between 1990 and 1999. As you can see, General Motors eliminated 181,100 jobs, and General

Mills and Kmart eliminated over 86,000 jobs each. Wal-Mart alone, however, created 639,000 new jobs during the same period, and Dayton Hudson accounted for an additional 100,000.

But even these data have to be interpreted with care. PepsiCo, for example, "officially" eliminated 116,000 jobs. But most of those losses came in 1997, when the firm sold its restaurant chains (KFC, Pizza Hut, and Taco Bell) to Tricon. In reality, therefore, many of the jobs weren't actually eliminated but simply "transferred" to another employer. Likewise, although most of Wal-Mart's 639,000 new jobs are indeed "new," some came when the company acquired other businesses and were thus not net new jobs.

At least one message is clear: Entrepreneurial business success, more than business size, accounts for most new job creation. Whereas successful retailers, such as Wal-Mart and Dayton Hudson, have been growing and adding thousands of new jobs, struggling chains like Kmart have been eliminating thousands. At the same time, flourishing high-tech giants, such as Dell, Intel, and Microsoft, continue to add jobs at a constant pace. It is also essential to take a long-term view when analyzing job growth. Figure 5.2, for example, shows that IBM has eliminated 92,153 jobs, but the firm actually cut a total of 163,381 jobs between 1990 and 1994. Since 1995 it has created 71,228 new jobs as the company has recovered from an economic slump that caused the original job cuts to be so severe.

The reality, then, is that jobs are created by entrepreneurial companies of all sizes, all of which hire workers and all of which lay them off. Although small firms often hire at a faster rate than large ones, they are also likely to eliminate jobs at a far higher rate. Small firms are also the first to hire in times of economic recovery; large firms, the last. Conversely, however, big companies are also the last to lay off workers during economic downswings. In 1999, for instance, almost 35 percent of all small businesses had job openings, and almost 20 percent were planning to hire new employees. These trends had reversed themselves, however, by 2001.

Figure 5.2

Representative Jobs Created and Lost by Big Business, 1990–1999

All businesses create and eliminate jobs. Because of their size, the magnitude of job creation and elimination is especially pronounced in bigger businesses. This figure provides several representative examples of job creation and elimination at many big U.S. businesses during the 1990s. For example, while General Motors cut 181,100 jobs, Wal-Mart created 639,000 during the last decade.

JOB LOSSES

Toys "Я" Us	−3,400
Quaker Oats	−16,340
National Semi-Conductor	−21,100
Kmart	−86,475
General Mills	−86,578
IBM	−92,153
PepsiCo	−116,000
General Motors	−181,100

JOB GAINS

Wal-Mart	+ 639,000
Dayton Hudson	+100,000
Albertson's	+45,000
Circuit City	+36,270
Barnes and Noble	+29,000
Dell Corporation	+22,900
Conagra	+21,631
America Online	+12,100

Innovation

History has shown that major innovations are as likely to come from small businesses (or individuals) as from big businesses. For example, small firms and

THE FAR SIDE By GARY LARSON

PORKUPINE ON-A-STICK

Early business failures

The Far Side by Gary Larson © 1985 FarWorks, Inc. All rights reserved. Used by permission.

As noted in the text, successful entrepreneurs must choose an industry, emphasize their distinctive competencies, and develop an effective business plan. Unfortunately, entrepreneurs frequently misjudge or do not effectively implement one or more of these activities. As illustrated in this cartoon, for example, providing a product that people do not really want is almost certain to result in failure. Chocolate confections, sausages, and corn on the cob are often popular treats served on sticks at athletic events, fairs, festivals, and carnivals—but cucumbers, peaches, and porcupines are not as well received!

individuals invented the personal computer and the stainless-steel razorblade, the transistor radio and the photocopying machine, the jet engine and the self-developing photograph. They also gave us the helicopter and power steering, automatic transmissions and air conditioning, cellophane, and the 19-cent ballpoint pen. Today, says the SBA, small businesses supply 55 percent of all "innovations" introduced into the American marketplace.[5]

Not surprisingly, history is repeating itself infinitely more rapidly in the age of computers and high-tech communication. For example, much of today's most innovative software is being written at new startup companies such as Trilogy Software, Inc., an Austin-based company started by Stanford dropout Joe Liemandt. Trilogy's products help optimize and streamline complicated sales and marketing processes for big-business customers such as IBM and Whirlpool.[6] Yahoo! and Netscape brought the Internet into the average American living room, and online companies such as Amazon.com are using it to redefine our shopping habits. Each of these firms started out as a small business.

Importance to Large Business

Most of the products made by big manufacturers are sold to consumers by small businesses. For example, the majority of dealerships selling Fords, Chevrolets, Toyotas, and Volvos are independently owned and operated. Moreover, small businesses provide big businesses with many of the services, supplies, and raw materials they need. As we noted, for example, Trilogy Software has become an important supplier to big businesses. Likewise, Microsoft relies heavily on small businesses in the course of its routine business operations. For example, the software giant outsources much of its routine code-writing functions to hundreds of sole proprietorships and other small firms. It also outsources much of its packaging, delivery, and distribution to smaller companies. Dell Computer uses the same strategy, buying most of the parts and components used in its computers from small suppliers around the world.

Strategy for Entrepreneurial Organizations

One of the most basic challenges facing an entrepreneurial organization is choosing a strategy. The three strategic challenges facing small firms are choosing an industry in which to compete, emphasizing distinctive competencies, and writing a business plan.[7]

Choosing an Industry

Not surprisingly, small businesses are more common in some industries than in others. The major industry groups that include successful new ventures and small businesses are services, retailing, construction, financial and insurance, wholesaling, transportation, and manufacturing. Obviously, each group differs in its requirements for employees, money, materials, and machines. In general, the more resources an industry requires, the harder it is to start a business and the less likely the industry is dominated by small firms. Remember, too, that *small* is a relative term. The criteria (number of employees and total annual sales) differ from industry to industry and are often meaningful only when compared with businesses that are truly large. Figure 5.3 shows the distribution of all U.S. businesses employing fewer than 20 people across industry groups.

Services Primarily because they require few resources, service businesses are the fastest-growing segment of small business enterprise. In addition, no other industry group offers a higher return on time invested. Finally, services appeal to the talent for innovation typified by many small enterprises. As Figure 5.3 shows, 37.6 percent of all businesses with fewer than 20 employees are services. Small business services range from shoeshine parlors to car rental agencies, from marriage counseling to computer software, from accounting and management consulting to professional dog walking. In Dallas, for example, Jani-King has prospered by selling commercial cleaning services to local companies. In Virginia Beach, Virginia, Jackson Hewitt Tax Service has found a profitable niche in providing computerized tax preparation and electronic tax-filing services.

Retailing A retail business sells directly to consumers products manufactured by other firms. There are hundreds of different kinds of retailers, ranging from wig shops and frozen yogurt stands to automobile dealerships and department stores. Usually, however, people who start small businesses favor specialty shops—for example, big men's clothing or gourmet coffees—that let them focus limited resources on narrow market segments. Retailing accounts for 22.7 percent of all businesses with fewer than 20 employees. John Mackey, for example, launched Whole Foods out of his own frustration at being unable to find a full range of natural foods at other stores. He soon found, however, that he had tapped a lucrative market and started an ambitious expansion program. Today, with 90 outlets in 20 states and Washington, D.C., Whole Foods is the largest natural foods retailer in the United States, three times larger than its biggest competitor.[8] *Management InfoTech* discusses how the advent of the Internet has made it even easier for new businesses to enter the retailing arena.

Figure 5.3

Small Businesses (Businesses with Fewer Than Twenty Employees) by Industry

Small businesses are especially strong in certain industries, such as retailing and services. On the other hand, there are relatively fewer small businesses in industries such as transportation and manufacturing. The differences are affected primarily by factors such as the investment costs necessary to enter markets in these industries. For example, starting a new airline would require the purchase of large passenger aircraft and airport gates and hiring an expensive set of employees.

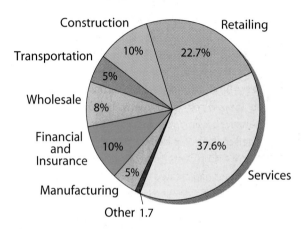

Source: U.S. Census Bureau, *Statistical Abstract of the United States: 2000* (120th Edition), Washington, D.C., 2000.

MANAGEMENT INFOTECH

ONLINE STARTUPS CHALLENGE STORE RETAILERS

Ever since Jeff Bezos pioneered the idea of an online bookstore by launching Amazon.com, the Internet has become a hotbed of entrepreneurial activity as more people open web sites to challenge traditional store retailers. According to Shop.org, a trade association, more than 30,000 web sites are devoted to online retailing. This number includes sites operated by traditional chains, such as Wal-Mart, as well as web-only giants like Amazon. Still, the vast majority of online retailers sell less than $500,000 worth of merchandise in a year, so traditional retailing is far from dead. But can the online start-ups successfully challenge their store counterparts?

With Amazon.com (http://www.amazon.com), Bezos seized the first-mover advantage in books. By the time the Barnes and Noble retail chain recognized the danger and opened its web site (http://www.bn.com), Amazon's discount pricing and user-friendly features had created a loyal and lucrative customer following. Although Barnes and Noble's site now ranks among the Internet's most visited, Amazon attracts many more visitors and completes more sales. Barnes and Noble continues to expand its chain and increase store sales, even though Amazon is siphoning off some of its overall market share.

In toys, web-only eToys (http://www.etoys.com) sought first-mover advantage over its counterparts in store retailing. During its first year-end holiday selling season, eToys' electronic wish lists and other novel features drew widespread media attention and helped the company ring up $20 million in sales. By the time eToys' second Christmas rolled around, however, the Toys 'R' Us chain had become a "clicks-and-mortar" retailer by opening a flashy web site (http://www.toysrus.com) amid much fanfare. Then the Toys 'R' Us site had difficulty handling the onslaught of visitors and fulfilling orders as promised, while eToys' sales soared. But mounting expenses, continuing losses, and intense online competition have given eToys headaches of its own and pushed its stock price down.

Given the high cost of sustaining their first-mover advantage, most online retailers are struggling with profitability. Well-established online pioneers like Amazon have the best chance of survival, but many smaller sites are headed for a shakeout as more entrepreneurs and more traditional retailers flock to the Internet.

> *It won't be about clicks versus mortar but coming up with a combination where a customer can do a transaction anytime, anywhere.*
>
> —*Elaine Rubin, chairman of Shop.org**

References: Herb Greenberg, "Dead Mall Walking," *Fortune,* May 1, 2000, p. 304; William Bulkeley and Jim Carlton, "Reality Bites: E-Tail Gets Derailed: How Web Upstarts Misjudged the Game," *Wall Street Journal*, April 5, 2000, pp. A1, A6 (*quote on p. A6); and Karl Taro Greenfeld, "Clicks and Bricks," *Time*, December 27, 1999, pp. 88ff.

Construction   About 10 percent of businesses with fewer than 20 employees are involved in construction. Because many construction jobs are relatively small, local projects, local construction firms are often ideally suited as contractors. Many such firms are begun by skilled craftspeople who start out working for someone else and subsequently decide to work for themselves. Common examples of small construction firms include home builders, wood finishers, roofers, painters, and plumbing, electrical, and roofing contractors. For example, Marek Brothers Construction in College Station, Texas, was started by two brothers, Pat and Joe Marek. They originally worked for other contractors but started their own partnership in 1980. Their only employee is a receptionist. They manage various construction projects, including new home construction and remodeling, subcontracting out the actual work to other businesses or individual craftspeople. Marek Brothers has an annual gross income of about $5 million.

Finance and Insurance   Financial and insurance businesses also comprise about 10 percent of all firms with fewer than 20 employees. In most cases, these businesses are either affiliates of or sell products provided by larger national firms. Although the deregulation of the banking industry has reduced the number of small local banks, other businesses in this sector are still doing quite well. Typically, for example, local State Farm Mutual offices are small businesses. State Farm itself is a major insurance company, but its local offices are run by 16,500 independent agents. In turn, agents hire their own staff, run their own office as an independent business, and so forth. They sell various State Farm insurance products and earn commissions from the premiums paid by their clients. Some local savings and loan operations, mortgage companies, and pawn shops also fall into this category.

Wholesaling   Small business owners often do very well in wholesaling, too; about 8 percent of businesses with fewer than 20 employees are wholesalers. A wholesale business buys products from manufacturers or other producers and then sells them to retailers. Wholesalers usually buy goods in bulk and store them in quantity at locations that are convenient for retailers. Wholesalers in the grocery industry, for instance, buy packaged food in bulk from companies like Del Monte and Campbell's and then sell it to both large grocery chains and smaller independent grocers. Luis Espinoza has found a promising niche for Inca Quality Foods, a midwestern wholesaler that imports and distributes Hispanic foods for consumers from Mexico, the Caribbean, and Central America. Partnered with Kroger, Espinoza's firm continues to grow steadily.[9]

Transportation   Some small firms—about 5 percent of all companies with fewer than 20 employees—do well in transportation and transportation-related businesses. Such firms include local taxi and limousine companies, charter airplane services, and tour operators. In addition, in many smaller markets, bus companies and regional airlines subcontract local equipment maintenance to small businesses. Consider, for example, some of the transportation-related small businesses at a ski resort like Steamboat Springs, Colorado. Most visitors fly to the town of Hayden, about 15 miles from Steamboat. Although some visitors rent vehicles, many others use the services of Alpine Taxi, a small local operation, to transport them to their destinations in Steamboat. While on vacation, they also rely on the local bus service, which is subcontracted by the town to another small business, to get to and from the ski slopes each day. Other small businesses offer van tours of the region, hot-air balloon rides, and helicopter lifts to remote areas for extreme skiers. Still others provide maintenance support at Hayden for Continental, American, and United aircraft that serve the area during ski season.

Manufacturing   More than any other industry, manufacturing lends itself to big business—and for good reason. Because of the investment normally required in equipment, energy, and raw materials, a good deal of money is usually needed to start a manufacturing business. Automobile manufacturing, for example, calls for billions of dollars of investment and thousands of workers before the first automobile rolls off the assembly line. Obviously, such requirements shut out most individuals. Although Henry Ford began with $28,000, it has been a long time since anyone started a new U.S. car company from scratch.

Research has shown that manufacturing costs often fall as the number of units produced by an organization increases. This relationship between cost and production is called an *economy of scale*.[10] Small organizations usually cannot compete effectively on the basis of economies of scale. As depicted in Figure 5.4(a), organizations with higher levels of production have a major cost advantage over those with lower levels of production. Given the cost positions of small and large firms when there are strong economies of scale in manufacturing, it is not surprising that small manufacturing organizations generally do not do as well as large ones.

Interestingly, when technology in an industry changes, it often shifts the economies-of-scale curve, thereby creating opportunities for smaller organizations. For example, steel manufacturing was historically dominated by a few large companies that owned several huge facilities. With the development of minimill technology, however, extracting economies of scale at a much smaller level of production became possible. This type of shift is depicted in Figure 5.4(b). Point A in this panel is the low-cost point with the original economies of scale. Point B is the low-cost point with the economies of scale brought on by the new technology. Notice that the number of units needed for low costs is considerably lower for the

Figure 5.4

Economies of Scale in Small Business Organizations

Small businesses sometimes find it difficult to compete in manufacturing-related industries because of the economies of scale associated with plant, equipment, and technology. As shown in (a), firms that produce a large number of units (that is, larger businesses) can do so at a lower per-unit cost. At the same time, however, new forms of technology occasionally cause the economies-of-scale curve to shift, as illustrated in (b). In this case, smaller firms may be able to compete more effectively with larger ones because of the drop in per-unit manufacturing cost.

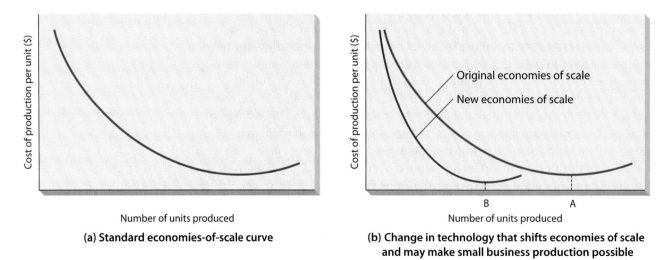

(a) Standard economies-of-scale curve

(b) Change in technology that shifts economies of scale and may make small business production possible

new technology. This has allowed the entry of numerous smaller firms into the steel industry. Such entry would not have been possible with the older technology.

This is also not to say that there are no small business owners who do well in manufacturing—about 5 percent of businesses with fewer than 20 employees are involved in some aspect of manufacturing. Indeed, it is not uncommon for small manufacturers to outperform big business in such innovation-driven industries as chemistry, electronics, toys, and computer software. Some small manufacturers prosper by locating profitable niches. For example, brothers Dave and Dan Hanlon and Dave's wife, Jennie, recently started a new motorcycle manufacturing business called Excelsior-Henderson. (Excelsior and Henderson are actually names of classic motorcycles from the early years of the twentieth century; the Hanlons acquired the rights to these brand names because of the images they evoke among motorcycle enthusiasts.) The Hanlons started by building 4,000 bikes in 1999 and expect to increase slowly to annual production of 20,000 per year. So far, Excelsior-Henderson motorcycles have been well received, and many Harley-Davidson dealers have started to sell them as a means of diversifying their product lines.[11]

Emphasizing Distinctive Competencies

As we define in Chapter 3, an organization's distinctive competencies are the aspects of business that the firm performs better than its competitors. The distinctive competencies of small business usually fall into three areas: the ability to identify new niches in established markets, the ability to identify new markets, and the ability to move quickly to take advantage of new opportunities.

Identifying Niches in Established Markets
An **established market** is one in which several large firms compete according to relatively well-defined criteria. For example, throughout the 1970s, several well-known computer manufacturing companies, including IBM, Digital Equipment, and Hewlett-Packard, competed according to three product criteria: computing power, service, and price. Over the years, the computing power and quality of service delivered by these firms continued to improve, while prices (especially relative to computing power) continued to drop.

Enter Apple Computer and the personal computer. For Apple, user-friendliness, not computing power, service, and price, was to be the basis of competition. Apple targeted every manager, every student, and every home as the owner of a personal computer. The major entrepreneurial act of Apple was not to invent a new technology (indeed, the first Apple computers used all standard parts taken from other computers) but to recognize a new kind of computer and a new way to compete in the computer industry.

Apple's approach to competition was to identify a new niche in an established market. A **niche** is simply a segment of a market that is not currently being exploited. In general, small entrepreneurial businesses are better at discovering these niches than are larger organizations. Large organizations usually have so many resources committed to older, established business practices that they may be unaware of new opportunities. Entrepreneurs can see these opportunities and move quickly to take advantage of them.[12]

established market A market in which several large firms compete according to relatively well-defined criteria

niche A segment of a market not currently being exploited

Would-be entrepreneurs can increase their chances for success by identifying a niche or potential market that no other business is serving. Consider, for instance, the success enjoyed by Boston entrepreneur Chris Murphy. He knew that some dog owners felt they faced the same day-care problems experienced by parents of small children. In response, he started The Common Dog, a service that picks dogs up on a school bus, takes them to a day-kennel while their owners work, and drops them off at the end of the day. The service costs the dog owners $325 a month. At the kennel, the dogs enjoy their own small swimming pool, several lounging couches, and frequent walks. They do, however, have to bring their own lunches!

first-mover advantage Any advantage that comes to a firm because it exploits an opportunity before any other firm does

Identifying New Markets   Successful entrepreneurs also excel at discovering whole new markets. Discovery can happen in at least two ways. First, an entrepreneur can transfer a product or service that is well established in one geographic market to a second market. This is what Marcel Bich did with ballpoint pens, which occupied a well-established market in Europe before Bich introduced them to this country. Bich's company, Bic Corporation, eventually came to dominate the U.S. market.

Second, entrepreneurs can sometimes create entire industries. Entrepreneurial inventions of the dry paper copying process and the semiconductor have created vast new industries. Not only have the first companies into these markets been very successful (Xerox and National Semiconductor, respectively), but their entrepreneurial activity has spawned the development of hundreds of thousands of other companies and hundreds of thousands of jobs. Again, because entrepreneurs are not encumbered with a history of doing business in a particular way, they are usually better at discovering new markets than are larger, more mature organizations.

First-Mover Advantages   A **first-mover advantage** is any advantage that comes to a firm because it exploits an opportunity before any other firm does. Sometimes large firms discover niches within existing markets or new markets at just about the same time as small entrepreneurial firms do but are not able to move as quickly as small companies to take advantage of these opportunities.

There are numerous reasons for this difference. For example, many large organizations make decisions slowly because each of their many layers of hierarchy has to approve an action before it can be implemented. Also, large organizations may sometimes put a great deal of their assets at risk when they take advantage of new opportunities. Every time Boeing decides to build a new model of a commercial jet, it is making a decision that could literally bankrupt the company if it does not turn out well. The size of the risk may make large organizations cautious. The dollar value of the assets at risk in a small organization, in contrast, is quite small. Managers may be willing to "bet the company" when the value of the company is only $100,000. They might be unwilling to "bet the company" when the value of the company is $1 billion.

Writing a Business Plan

Once an entrepreneur has chosen an industry to compete in and has determined which distinctive competencies to emphasize, these choices are usually included in a document called a business plan. In a **business plan,** the entrepreneur summarizes the business strategy and how that strategy is to be implemented. The very act of preparing a business plan forces prospective entrepreneurs to crystallize their thinking about what they must do to launch their business successfully and obliges them to develop their business on paper before investing time and money in it. The idea of a business plan is not new. What is new is the growing use of specialized business plans by entrepreneurs, mostly because creditors and investors demand them in deciding whether to help finance a small business.

business plan A document that summarizes the business strategy and structure

The plan should describe the match between the entrepreneur's abilities and the requirements for producing and marketing a particular product or service. It should define strategies for production and marketing, legal aspects and organization, and accounting and finance. In particular, it should answer three questions: (1) What are the entrepreneur's goals and objectives? (2) what strategies will the entrepreneur use to obtain these goals and objectives? and (3) how will the entrepreneur implement these strategies?

Business plans should also account for the sequential nature of much strategic decision making in small businesses. For example, entrepreneurs cannot forecast sales revenues without first researching markets. The sales forecast itself is one of the most important elements in the business plan. Without such a forecast, it is all but impossible to estimate intelligently the size of a plant, store, or office, or to determine how much inventory to carry or how many employees to hire.

Another important component of the overall business plan is financial planning, which translates all other activities into dollars. Generally, the financial plan is made up of a cash budget, an income statement, balance sheets, and a break-even chart. The most important of these statements is the cash budget, because it tells entrepreneurs how much money they need before they open for business and how much money they need to keep the business operating.

Entrepreneurship and International Management

Finally, although many people associate international management with big business, many smaller companies are also finding expansion and growth opportunities in foreign countries. For example, Fuci Metals, a small, but growing enterprise, buys metal from remote locations in areas such as Siberia and Africa and then sells it to big automakers like Ford and Toyota. Similarly, California-based Gold's Gym is expanding into foreign countries and has been especially successful in Russia.[13] Although such ventures are accompanied by considerable risk, they also give entrepreneurs new opportunities and can be a real catalyst for success.

■ *Structure of Entrepreneurial Organizations*

With a strategy in place and a business plan in hand, the entrepreneur can then proceed to devise a structure that turns the vision of the business plan into a reality. Many of the same concerns in structuring any business, which are described in the next five chapters of this book, are also relevant to small businesses. For example, entrepreneurs need to consider organization design and develop job descriptions, organization charts, and management control systems.

The Internet, of course, is rewriting virtually all of the rules for starting and operating a small business. Getting into business is easier and faster than ever before, there are many more potential opportunities than at any time in history, and the ability to gather and assimilate information is at an all-time high. Even so, however, would-be entrepreneurs must still make the right decisions when they start. They must decide, for example, precisely how to get into business. Should they buy an existing business or build from the ground up? In addition, would-be entrepreneurs must find appropriate sources of financing and decide when and how to seek the advice of experts.

Starting the New Business

An old Chinese proverb suggests that a journey of a thousand miles begins with a single step. This is also true of a new business. The first step is the individual's commitment to becoming a business owner. Next comes choosing the goods or services to be offered—a process that means investigating one's chosen industry and market. Making this choice also requires would-be entrepreneurs to assess not only industry trends but also their own skills. Like the managers of existing businesses, new business owners must also be sure that they understand the true nature of the enterprise in which they are engaged.

Buying an Existing Business   After choosing a product and making sure that the choice fits their own skills and interests, entrepreneurs must decide whether to buy an existing business or to start from scratch. Consultants often recommend the first approach. Quite simply, the odds are better: If successful, an existing business has already proved its ability to draw customers at a profit. It has also established working relationships with lenders, suppliers, and the community. Moreover, the track record of an existing business gives potential buyers a much clearer picture of what to expect than any estimate of a new business's prospects. Around 30 percent of the new businesses started in the past decade were bought from someone else. The McDonald's empire, for example, was started when Ray Kroc bought an existing hamburger business and then turned it into a global phenomenon. Likewise, Starbucks was a struggling mail-order business when Howard Schultz bought it and turned his attention to retail expansion.

Starting from Scratch   Some people, however, prefer the satisfaction that comes from planting an idea, nurturing it, and making it grow into a strong and sturdy business. There are also practical reasons to start a business from scratch. A new business does not suffer the ill effects of a prior owner's errors. The startup owner is also free to choose lenders, equipment, inventories, locations, suppliers, and workers, unbound by a predecessor's commitments and policies. Of the new businesses begun in the past decade, 64 percent were started from scratch.

Not surprisingly, though, the risks of starting a business from scratch are greater than those of buying an existing firm. Founders of new businesses can only make predictions and projections about their prospects. Success or failure thus depends heavily on identifying a genuine business opportunity—a product for which many customers will pay well but which is currently unavailable to them. To find openings, entrepreneurs must study markets and answer the following questions: (1) Who are my customers? (2) where are they? (3) at what price will they buy my product? (4) in what quantities will they buy? (5) who are my competitors? and (6) how will my product differ from those of my competitors?

Financing the New Business

Although the choice of how to start is obviously important, it is meaningless unless a new business owner can obtain the money to set up shop. Among the more common sources of funding are family and friends, personal savings, banks and similar lending institutions, investors, and governmental agencies. Lending institutions are more likely to help finance the purchase of an existing business than a new business because the risks are better understood. Individuals starting up new businesses, on the other hand, are more likely to have to rely on their personal resources.

Personal Resources   According to a study by the National Federation of Independent Business, an owner's personal resources, not loans, are the most important source of money. Including money borrowed from friends and relatives, personal resources account for over two-thirds of all money invested in new small businesses and one-half of that invested in the purchase of existing businesses. When Michael Dorf and his friends decided to launch a New York nightclub dubbed the Knitting Factory, he started with $30,000 of his own money. Within four months of opening, Dorf asked his father to co-sign the first of four consecutive Milwaukee bank loans (for $70,000, $200,000, $300,000, and, to move to a new facility, $500,000, respectively). Dorf and his partners also engaged in creative bartering, such as putting a sound system company's logo on all its advertising in exchange for free equipment. Finally, because the Knitting Factory has become so successful, other investors are now stepping forward to provide funds—$650,000 from one investor and $4.2 million from another.[14]

Strategic Alliances   Strategic alliances are also becoming a popular method for financing business growth. When Steven and Andrew Grundy decided to launch a CD-exchange Internet business called Spun.com, they had very little capital and thus made extensive use of alliances with other firms. They partnered, for example, with wholesaler Alliance Entertainment Corporation as a CD supplier. Orders to Spun.com actually go to Alliance, which ships products to customers and bills

Spun.com directly. This setup has allowed Spun.com to promote a vast inventory of labels without actually having to buy inventory. All told, the firm has created an alliance network that has provided the equivalent of $40 million in capital.[15]

Lenders Although banks, independent investors, and government loans all provide much smaller portions of startup funds than the personal resources of owners, they are important in many cases. Getting money from these sources, however, requires some extra effort. Banks and private investors usually want to see formal business plans—detailed outlines of proposed businesses and markets, owners' backgrounds, and other sources of funding. Government loans have strict eligibility guidelines.

venture capital company A company that actively seeks to invest in new businesses

Venture Capital Companies **Venture capital companies** are groups of small investors seeking to make profits on companies with rapid growth potential. Most of these firms do not lend money; they invest it, supplying capital in return for stock. The venture capital company may also demand a representative on the board of directors. In some cases, managers may even need approval from the venture capital company before making major decisions. Of all venture capital currently committed in the United States, 29 percent comes from true venture capital firms.[16]

Small Business Investment Companies Taking a more balanced approach in their choices than venture capital companies, small business investment companies (SBICs) seek profits by investing in companies with potential for rapid growth. Created by the Small Business Investment Act of 1958, SBICs are federally licensed to borrow money from the SBA and to invest it in or lend it to small businesses. They are themselves investments for their shareholders. Past beneficiaries of SBIC capital include Apple Computer, Intel, and Federal Express. In addition, the government has recently begun to sponsor minority enterprise small business investment companies (MESBICs). As the name suggests, MESBICs specialize in financing businesses that are owned and operated by minorities.

SBA Financial Programs Since its founding in 1953, the SBA has offered more than 20 financing programs to small businesses that meet standards in size and independence. Eligible firms must also be unable to get private financing at reasonable terms. Because of these and other restrictions, SBA loans have never been a major source of small business financing. In addition, budget cutbacks at the SBA have reduced the number of firms benefiting from loans. Nevertheless, several SBA programs currently offer funds to qualified applicants. For example, under the SBA's guaranteed loans program, small businesses can borrow from commercial lenders. The SBA guarantees to repay 75 to 85 percent of the loan amount, not to exceed $750,000. Under a related program, companies engaged in international trade can borrow up to $1.25 million. Such loans may be made for as long as 15 years. Most SBA lending activity flows through this program.

Sometimes, however, both the desired bank and SBA-guaranteed loans are unavailable (perhaps because the business cannot meet stringent requirements). In such cases, the SBA may help finance the entrepreneur through its immediate participation loans program. Under this arrangement, the SBA and the bank each puts up a share of the money, with the SBA's share not to exceed $150,000. Under the local development companies (LDCs) program, the SBA works with a corporation (either for-profit or nonprofit) founded by local citizens who want to boost the local economy. The SBA can lend up to $500,000 for each small business to be helped by an LDC. Spurred in large part by the boom in Internet businesses, both venture capital and loans are getting easier to get. Most small businesses, for example, report that it has generally gotten increasingly easier to obtain loans over the last ten years. Indeed, some technology companies are being offered so much venture capital that they are turning down part of it to keep from diluting their ownership unnecessarily.

Sources of Management Advice

Financing is not the only area in which small businesses need help. Until World War II, for example, the business world involved few regulations, few taxes, few records, few big competitors, and no computers. Since then, simplicity has given way to complexity. Today, few entrepreneurs are equipped with all the business skills they need to survive. Small business owners can no longer be their own troubleshooters, lawyers, bookkeepers, financiers, and tax experts. For these jobs, they rely on professional help. To survive and grow, however, small businesses also need advice regarding management. This advice is usually available from four sources: advisory boards, management consultants, the SBA, and a process called *networking*.

Advisory Boards   All companies, even those that do not legally need boards of directors, can benefit from the problem-solving abilities of advisory boards. Thus some small businesses create boards to provide advice and assistance. For example, an advisory board might help an entrepreneur determine the best way to finance a plant expansion or to start exporting products to foreign markets.

Management Consultants   Opinions vary widely about the value of management consultants—experts who charge fees to help managers solve problems. They often specialize in one area, such as international business, small business, or manufacturing. Thus they can bring an objective, trained outlook to problems and provide logical recommendations. They can be quite expensive, however, as some consultants charge $1,000 or more for a day of assistance. Indeed, like other professionals, consultants should be chosen with care. They can be found through major corporations who have used their services and who can provide references and reports on their work. Not surprisingly, they are most effective when the client helps (for instance, by providing schedules and written proposals for work to be done).

The Small Business Administration   Even more important than its financing role is the SBA's role in helping small business owners improve their management skills. It is easy for entrepreneurs to spend money; SBA programs are designed to show them how to spend it wisely. The SBA offers small businesses four major management counseling programs at virtually no cost.

A small business owner who needs help starting a new business can get it free through the Service Corps of Retired Executives (SCORE). All SCORE members are retired executives, and all are volunteers. Under this program, the SBA tries to match the expert to the need. For example, if a small business owner needs help putting together a marketing plan, the SBA will send a SCORE counselor with marketing expertise. Like SCORE, the Active Corps of Executives (ACE) program is designed to help small businesses that cannot afford consultants. The SBA recruits ACE volunteers from virtually every industry. All ACE volunteers are currently involved in successful activities, mostly as small business owners themselves. Together, SCORE and ACE have more than 12,000 counselors working out of 350 chapters throughout the United States. They provide assistance to some 140,000 small businesses each year.

The talents and skills of students and instructors at colleges and universities are fundamental to the Small Business Institute (SBI). Under the guidance of seasoned professors of business administration, students seeking advanced degrees work closely with small business owners to help solve specific problems, such as sagging sales or rising costs. Students earn credit toward their degree, with their grades depending on how well they handle a client's problems. Several hundred colleges and universities counsel thousands of small business owners through this program every year.

Finally, the newest of the SBA's management counseling projects is its Small Business Development Center (SBDC) program. Begun in 1976, SBDCs are designed to consolidate information from various disciplines and institutions, including technical and professional schools. Then they make this knowledge available to new and existing small businesses. In 1995 universities in 45 states took part in the program.

Networking   More and more, small business owners are discovering the value of networking—meeting regularly with one another to discuss common problems and opportunities and, perhaps most important, pool resources. Businesspeople have long joined organizations such as the local chamber of commerce and the National Federation of Independent Businesses (NFIB) to make such contacts.

Today, organizations are springing up all over the United States to facilitate small business networking. One such organization, the Council of Smaller Enterprises of Cleveland, boasts a total membership of more than 10,000 small business owners, the largest number in the country. This organization offers its members not only networking possibilities but also educational programs and services tailored to their needs. In a typical year, its 85 educational programs draw more than 8,500 small business owners.

In particular, women and minorities have found networking to be an effective problem-solving tool. The National Association of Women Business Owners (NAWBO; www.nawbo.org), for example, provides a variety of networking forums. NAWBO also has chapters in most major cities where its members can meet regularly. Increasingly, women are relying more on other women to help locate venture capital, establish relationships with customers, and provide such essential services as accounting and legal advice.

Franchising

As many would-be businesspeople have discovered, franchising agreements are an accessible doorway to entrepreneurship. A **franchise** is an arrangement that permits the franchisee (buyer) to sell the product of the franchiser (seller, or parent company). Franchisees can thus benefit from the selling corporation's experience and expertise. They can also consult the franchiser for managerial and financial help.

For example, the franchiser may supply financing. It may pick the store location, negotiate the lease, design the store, and purchase necessary equipment. It may train the first set of employees and managers, and provide standardized policies and procedures. Once the business is open, the franchiser may offer savings by allowing it to purchase from a central location. Marketing strategy (especially advertising) may also be handled by the franchiser. Finally, franchisees may benefit from continued management counseling. In short, franchisees receive—that is, invest in—not only their own ready-made businesses, but also expert help in running them.

Franchises offer many advantages to both sellers and buyers. For example, franchisers benefit from the ability to grow rapidly by using the investment money provided by franchisees. This strategy has enabled giant franchisers, such as McDonald's and Baskin-Robbins, to mushroom into billion-dollar concerns in a brief time.

For the franchisee, the arrangement combines the incentive of owning a business with the advantage of access to big-business management skills. Unlike the person who starts from scratch, the franchisee does not have to build a business step by step. Instead, the business is established virtually overnight. Moreover, because each franchise outlet is probably a carbon copy of every other outlet, the chances of failure are reduced. McDonald's, for example, is a model of consistency—Big Macs taste the same everywhere.

Of course, owning a franchise also involves certain disadvantages. Perhaps the most significant is the startup cost. Franchise prices vary widely. Fantastic Sam's (www.fantasticsams.com) hair salon franchise fees are $30,000, but a Gingiss Formalwear (www.gingiss.com) franchise can run as high as $125,000. Extremely profitable or hard-to-get franchises are even more expensive. A McDonald's franchise costs at least $650,000 to $750,000, and a professional sports team can cost several hundred million dollars. Franchisees may also have continued obligations to contribute percentages of sales to the parent corporation.

Buying a franchise also entails less tangible costs. For one thing, the small business owner sacrifices some independence. A McDonald's franchisee cannot change the way hamburgers or milkshakes are made. Nor can franchisees create an individual identity in their community; for all practical purposes, the McDonald's owner is anonymous. In addition, many franchise agreements are difficult to terminate.

Finally, although franchises minimize risks, they do not guarantee success. Many franchisees have seen their investments—and their dreams—disappear because of poor location, rising costs, or lack of continued franchiser commitment. Moreover, figures on failure rates are artificially low because they do not include

franchise An arrangement that permits the franchisee (the buyer) to sell the product of the franchiser (seller or parent company).

failing franchisees bought out by their franchising parent companies. An additional risk is that the chain itself could collapse. In any given year, dozens—sometimes hundreds—of franchisers close shop or stop selling franchises.

■ *The Performance of Entrepreneurial Organizations*

The formulation and implementation of an effective strategy plays a major role in determining the overall performance of an entrepreneurial organization. This section examines how entrepreneurial firms evolve over time and the attributes of these firms that enhance their chance for success. For every Henry Ford, Walt Disney, Mary Kay Ash, or Bill Gates—people who transformed small businesses into major corporations—there are many small business owners and entrepreneurs who fail.

Figure 5.5 illustrates recent trends in new business startup successes and failures. As you can see, over the last ten years new business startups have generally run between around 150,000 and 180,000 per year, with 155,141 new businesses being launched in 1998. Over this same period, business failures have generally run between 50,000 and 100,000, with a total of 71,857 failing in 1998. In this section, we look first at a few key trends in small business startups. Then we examine some of the main reasons for success and failure in small business undertakings.

Figure 5.5

Business Startup Successes and Failures

Over the most recent ten-year period for which data are available, new business startups numbered between 150,000 and 190,000 per year. Business failures during this same period, meanwhile, ranged from about 50,000 to nearly 100,000 per year.

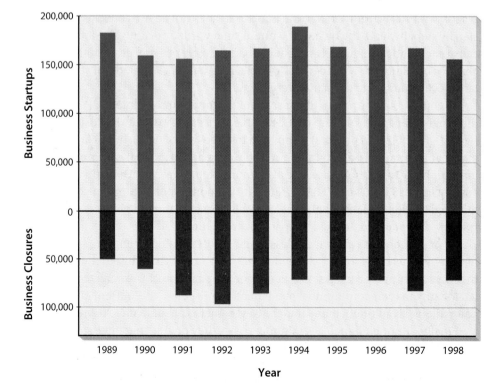

Source: U.S. Census Bureau, *Statistical Abstract of the United States: 2000* (120th Edition), Washington, D.C., 2000.

Trends in New Business Startups

Thousands of new businesses are started in the United States every year. Several factors account for this trend, and in this section we focus on four of them.

Emergence of E-Commerce Clearly, the most significant recent trend in small business startups is the rapid emergence of electronic commerce. Because the Internet has provided fundamentally new ways of doing business, savvy entrepreneurs have been able to create and expand new businesses faster and easier than ever before. Such leading-edge firms as America Online, Amazon.com, and eBay, for example, owe their very existence to the Internet. At the same time, the large number of dot.coms that folded in 2001 also clearly underscores that sound management practices are still necessary for survival.

Crossovers from Big Business It is interesting to note that increasingly more businesses are being started by people who have opted to leave big corporations and put their experience and know-how to work for themselves. In some cases, these individuals see great new ideas they want to develop. Often, they get burned out working for a big corporation. Sometimes they have lost their job, only to discover that working for themselves was a better idea anyway. Cisco Systems CEO John Chambers is acknowledged as one of the best entrepreneurs around. But he spent several years working first at IBM and then at Wang Laboratories before he set out on his own. Under his leadership, Cisco has become one of the largest and most important technology companies in the world. Indeed, for a few days in March 2000, Cisco had the world's highest market capitalization, and it remains one of the world's most valuable companies.[17]

Opportunities for Minorities and Women In addition to big-business expatriates, more small businesses are being started by minorities and women. For example, the number of African-American-owned businesses has increased by 46 percent during the most recent five-year period for which data are available and now totals about 620,000. Chicago's Gardner family is just one of thousands of examples illustrating this trend. The Gardners are the founders of Soft Sheen Products, Inc., a firm specializing in ethnic hair products. Soft Sheen attained sales of $80 million in the year before the Gardners sold it to France's L'Oréal S.A. for more than $160 million. The emergence of such opportunities is hardly surprising, either to African-American entrepreneurs or to the corporate marketers who have taken an interest in their companies. African-American purchasing power topped $530 billion in 1999. Up from just over $300 billion in 1990, that increase of 73 percent far outstrips the 57 percent increase experienced by all Americans.[18]

Hispanic-owned businesses have grown at an even faster rate of 76 percent and now number about 862,000. Other ethnic groups are also making their presence felt among U.S. business owners. Business ownership among Asian and Pacific Islanders has increased 56 percent, to over 600,000. Although the number of businesses owned by American Indians and Alaska Natives is still somewhat small, at slightly over 100,000, the total nevertheless represents a five-year increase of 93 percent.[19]

The number of women entrepreneurs is also growing rapidly. Celeste Johnson, for example, left a management position at Pitney Bowes to launch Obex, Inc., which makes gardening and landscaping products from mixed recycled plastics. Katrina Garnett gave up a lucrative job at Oracle to start her own software company, Crossworlds Software, Inc. Laila Rubenstein closed her management consulting practice to create Greeting Cards.com Inc., an Internet-based business selling customizable electronic greetings.

Likewise, the number of women-owned businesses is also growing rapidly. There are now 9.1 million businesses owned by women—about 40 percent of all businesses in the United States. Combined, they generate nearly $4 trillion in revenue a year—an increase of 132 percent since 1992. The number of people employed nationwide at women-owned businesses since 1992 has grown to around 27.5 million—an increase of 108 percent.[20] Figure 5.6 summarizes the corporate backgrounds of women entrepreneurs and provides some insight into what they like about running their own businesses. Corporate positions in general management (25 percent), sales (21 percent), and accounting and finance (18 percent) account for almost two-thirds of the women who start their own businesses. Once in charge of their own businesses, women also report that they like being their own boss, setting their own hours, controlling their own destiny, pleasing customers, making decisions, and achieving goals.

Better Survival Rates Finally, more people are encouraged to test their skills as entrepreneurs because the failure rate among small businesses has been declining in recent years. During the 1960s and 1970s, for example, less than half of all new startups survived more than 18 months; only one in five lasted 10 years. Now, however, new businesses have a better chance of surviving. Of new businesses started

Figure 5.6

Where Women Entrepreneurs Come from and What They Like About Their Work

Women entrepreneurs come from all sectors of large businesses, although management and sales are especially well represented. Women entrepreneurs indicate that they really like being their own boss, being independent, setting their own hours, and controlling their own destiny.

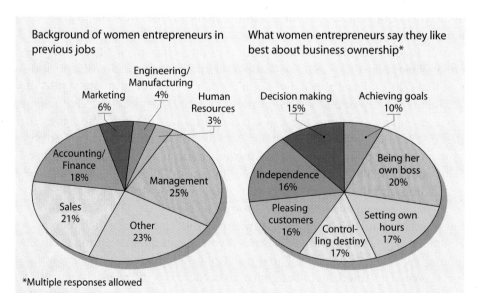

Background of women entrepreneurs in previous jobs

What women entrepreneurs say they like best about business ownership*

*Multiple responses allowed

Source: *Wall Street Journal*, Eastern Edition (Staff Produced Copy Only) by *Wall Street Journal*. Copyright 1999 by Dow Jones & Company, Inc. Reproduced with permission of Dow Jones & Company, Inc., in the format Textbook via Copyright Clearance Center.

in the 1980s, for instance, over 77 percent remained in operation for at least 3 years. Today, the SBA estimates that at least 40 percent of all new businesses can expect to survive for 6 years. For the reasons discussed in the next section, small businesses suffer a higher mortality rate than larger concerns. However, among those that manage to stay in business for 6 to 10 years, the survival rate levels off.

Reasons for Failure

Unfortunately, 63 percent of all new businesses will not celebrate a sixth anniversary. Why do some succeed and others fail? Although no set pattern has been established, four general factors contribute to new business failure. One factor is managerial incompetence or inexperience. Some would-be entrepreneurs assume that they can succeed through common sense, overestimate their own managerial acumen, or think that hard work alone will lead to success. But if managers do not know how to make basic business decisions or understand the basic concepts and principles of management, they are unlikely to be successful in the long run.

Neglect can also contribute to failure. Some entrepreneurs try either to launch their ventures in their spare time or to devote only a limited amount of time to a new business. But starting a new business requires an overwhelming time commitment. Entrepreneurs who are not willing to put in the time and effort that a business requires are unlikely to survive.

Third, weak control systems can lead to serious problems. Effective control systems are needed to keep a business on track and to help alert entrepreneurs to potential trouble. If control systems do not signal impending problems, managers may be in serious trouble before more visible difficulties alert them.

Finally, insufficient capital can contribute to new business failure. Some entrepreneurs are overly optimistic about how soon they will start earning profits. In most cases, however, it takes months or years before a business is likely to start turning a profit. Amazon.com, for example, has still not earned a profit. Most experts say that a new business should have enough capital to operate for at least six months without earning a profit; some recommend enough to last a year.[21]

Reasons for Success

Similarly, four basic factors are typically cited to explain new business success. One factor is hard work, drive, and dedication. New business owners must be committed to succeeding and be willing to put in the time and effort to make it happen. Gladys Edmunds, a single teenage mother in Pittsburgh, washed laundry, made chicken dinners to sell to cab drivers, and sold fire extinguishers and Bibles door to door to earn money to launch her own business. Today, Edmunds Travel Consultants employs eight people and earns about $6 million in annual revenue.[22]

Careful analysis of market conditions can help new business owners assess the probable reception of their products in the marketplace. This will provide insights about market demand for proposed products and services. Whereas attempts to expand local restaurants specializing in baked potatoes, muffins, and gelato have been largely unsuccessful, hamburger and pizza chains continue to have an easier time expanding into new markets.

Managerial competence also contributes to success. Successful new business owners may acquire competence through training or experience, or by using the expertise of others. Few successful entrepreneurs succeed alone or straight out of college. Most spend time working in successful companies or partner with others in order to bring more expertise to a new business.

Finally, luck also plays a role in the success of some firms. For example, after Alan McKim started Clean Harbors (www.cleanharbors.com), an environmental cleanup firm based in New England, he struggled to keep his business afloat. Then the U.S. government committed $1.6 billion to toxic waste cleanup—McKim's specialty. He was able to get several large government contracts and put his business on solid financial footing. Had the government fund not been created at just the right time, McKim may have had less success.

Summary of Key Points

Entrepreneurship is the process of planning, organizing, operating, and assuming the risk of a business venture. An entrepreneur is someone who engages in entrepreneurship. In general, entrepreneurs start small businesses. Small businesses are an important source of innovation, create numerous jobs, and contribute to the success of large businesses.

In choosing strategies, entrepreneurs have to consider the characteristics of the industry in which they are going to conduct business. A small business must also emphasize its distinctive competencies. Small businesses generally have several distinctive competencies that they should exploit in choosing their strategy. Small businesses are usually skilled at identifying niches in established markets, identifying new markets, and acting quickly to obtain first-mover advantages. Small businesses are usually not skilled at exploiting economies of scale. Once an entrepreneur has chosen a strategy, the strategy is normally written down in a business plan. Writing a business plan forces an entrepreneur to plan thoroughly and to anticipate problems that might occur.

With a strategy and business plan in place, entrepreneurs must choose a structure to implement them. All of the structural issues summarized in the next three chapters of this book are relevant to the entrepreneur. In addition, the entrepreneur has some unique structural choices to make. In determining ownership and financial structure, the entrepreneur can choose between a sole proprietorship, a partnership, a corporation, a master limited partnership, a subchapter S corporation, and a cooperative. In determining financial structure, an entrepreneur has to decide how much personal capital to invest in an organization, how much bank and government support to obtain, and whether to encourage venture capital firms to invest. Finally, entrepreneurs have to choose among the options of buying an existing business, starting a new business from scratch, or entering into a franchising agreement.

Most small businesses pass through a three-phase life cycle: acceptance, breakthrough, and maturity. Several factors explain why successful small businesses are able to move through all three of these stages of development: hard work, drive, and dedication; market demand for products or services provided; managerial competence; luck; strong control systems; and sufficient capitalization.

Discussion Questions

Questions for Review

1. Why are entrepreneurs and small businesses important to society?
2. In which types of industries do small firms often excel? In which types of industries do small firms struggle?
3. What are the basic questions that should be answered in a business plan?
4. What are the advantages and disadvantages of buying an existing business relative to starting a new one?
5. What are the elements of success for small businesses?

Questions for Analysis

6. Entrepreneurs and small businesses play a variety of important roles in society. If these roles are so important, do you think that the government should do more to encourage the development of small business? Why or why not?

7. Franchising agreements seem to be particularly popular ways of starting a new business in industries in which retail outlets are geographically widely spread and where the quality of goods or services purchased can be evaluated only after the purchase has occurred. For example, a hamburger may look tasty, but you know for sure that it is well made only after you buy it and eat it. By going to a McDonald's, you know exactly the kind and quality of hamburger you will receive, even before you walk in the door. What makes franchise arrangements so popular under these conditions?
8. If employing family members can cause problems in a small organization, why is this practice so common?
9. What steps might an entrepreneur take before deciding to expand into a foreign market?
10. Are there any obvious market niches in your town or city where an entrepreneur might succeed with a new venture?

BUILDING EFFECTIVE *communication* SKILLS

Exercise Overview

Communication skills refer to the manager's abilities to both effectively convey ideas and information to others and effectively receive ideas and information from others. Although communication skills are important to all organizations, some entrepreneurs argue that they are even more important in smaller organizations. This exercise helps you understand some of the complexities of communicating in smaller businesses.

Exercise Background

Assume that you are the owner-manager of a small retail chain. Your company sells moder-

ately priced apparel for professional men and women. You have ten stores located in the Midwest. Each store has a general manager responsible for the overall management of that specific store. Each store also has one assistant manager.

In addition, a human resource manager, an advertising specialist, and two buyers staff your corporate office. In the past, each store was managed at the total discretion of its local manager. As a result, each store had a different layout, a different culture, and different policies and procedures.

You want to begin opening more stores at a rapid pace. To expedite this process, you also want to standardize your stores. Unfortunately, however, you realize that many of your current managers will be unhappy with this decision. They will see standardization as a loss of authority and managerial discretion. Nevertheless, you believe that it is important to achieve standardization in all areas.

Your plans are to remodel all of your stores to fit a standard layout. You also intend to develop a policy and operations manual for each store. This manual will specify exactly how each store will be managed. You plan to inform your managers of this plan first in a memo and then in a followup meeting to discuss questions and concerns.

Exercise Task

With the information described above as context, please do the following:

1. Draft a memo that explains your intentions to the store managers.
2. Make a list of the primary objections you anticipate.
3. Outline an agenda for the meeting in which you plan to address the managers' questions and concerns.
4. Do you personally agree with this communication strategy? Why or why not?

BUILDING EFFECTIVE *technical* SKILLS

Exercise Overview

Technical skills are the skills necessary to accomplish or understand the specific work being done in an organization. This exercise allows you to gain insights into your own technical skills and the relative importance of technical skills in different kinds of organizations.

Exercise Background

Some entrepreneurs have the technical skills that they need to open and run their business successfully. For example, a hair stylist who opens a hair salon, an architect who starts a residential design firm, and a chef who launches a new restaurant have the technical skills needed to do the work of the organization (hair styling, blueprint rendering, and cooking, respectively).

In other cases, the entrepreneur who starts the organization may have general management skills but essentially "buys" required technical skills in the labor market. For example, an entrepreneur might start a new restaurant without knowing how to cook by hiring a professional chef to perform this function.

Exercise Task

With the background information provided above as a context, do the following:

1. Listed below are examples of ten small businesses that an individual entrepreneur might conceivably launch. Spend a few minutes thinking about each business. (Hint: Try to conceptualize an existing local business that might generally fit the description.)
2. Make notes about the specific technical skills required for each business.
3. For each business, decide whether it is especially important for the entrepreneur to actually possess the technical skills or whether it is feasible to consider hiring others who possess the skills instead.
4. What are some major factors that determine the viability of buying technical skills in the labor market?

New businesses:
a. Clothing retail store
b. Computer clone assembly business
c. Tavern
d. Sports card retail store
e. Aluminum recycling operation
f. Used compact disk retail store
g. Drop-in health care clinic
h. Gourmet coffee bean shop
i. Business services operation
j. Appliance repair shop

BUILDING EFFECTIVE *conceptual* SKILLS

Exercise Overview

Conceptual skills refer to the manager's ability to think in the abstract. This exercise helps you relate conceptual skills to entrepreneurship.

Exercise Background

Assume that you have made the decision to open a small business in the local business community when you graduate (the community where you are attending college, not your home). Assume that you have funds to start a business without having to worry about finding other investors.

Without regard for market potential, profitability, or similar considerations, list five businesses that you might want to open and operate based solely on your personal interests. For example, if you enjoy bicycling, you might enjoy opening a shop that caters to cyclists.

Next, without regard for personal attractiveness or interests, list five businesses that you might want to open and operate based solely on market opportunities. Evaluate the prospects for success of each of the ten businesses.

Exercise Task

With the background information above as context, do the following:

1. Form a small group with three or four classmates and discuss your respective lists. Look for instances of the same type of business appearing on either the same or alternative lists. Also look for cases where the same business appears with similar or dissimilar prospects for success.
2. How important is personal interest in small business success?
3. How important is market potential in small business success?

SKILLS *self-assessment* INSTRUMENT

An Entrepreneurial Quiz

Introduction: Entrepreneurs are starting ventures all the time. These new businesses are vital to the economy. The following assessment is designed to help you understand your readiness to start your own business—to be an entrepreneur.

Instructions: Place a checkmark or an X in the box next to the response that best represents your self-evaluation.

1. Are you a self-starter?
   - ☐ I do things on my own. Nobody has to tell me to get going.
   - ☐ If someone gets me started, I keep going all right.
   - ☐ Easy does it. I don't push myself until I have to.

2. How do you feel about other people?
   - ☐ I like people. I can get along with just about anybody.
   - ☐ I have plenty of friends—I don't need anybody else.
   - ☐ Most people irritate me.

3. Can you lead others?
   - ☐ I can get most people to go along when I start something.
   - ☐ I can give orders if someone tells me what we should do.
   - ☐ I let someone else get things moving. Then I go along if I feel like it.

4. Can you take responsibility?
  ☐ I like to take charge of things and see them through.
  ☐ I'll take over if I have to, but I'd rather let someone else be responsible.
  ☐ There are always eager beavers around wanting to show how smart they are. I let them.

5. How good an organizer are you?
  ☐ I like to have a plan before I start. I'm usually the one to get things lined up when the group wants to do something.
  ☐ I do all right unless things get too confused. Then I quit.
  ☐ You get all set and then something comes along and presents too many problems. So I just take things as they come.

6. How good a worker are you?
  ☐ I can keep going as long as I need to. I don't mind working hard for something I want.
  ☐ I'll work hard for a while, but when I've had enough, that's it.
  ☐ I can't see that hard work gets you anywhere.

7. Can you make decisions?
  ☐ I can make up my mind in a hurry if I have to. It usually turns out okay, too.
  ☐ I can if I have plenty of time. If I have to make up my mind fast, I think later I should have decided the other way.
  ☐ I don't like to be the one who has to decide things.

8. Can people trust what you say?
  ☐ You bet they can. I don't say things I don't mean.
  ☐ I try to be on the level most of the time, but sometimes I just say what's easiest.
  ☐ Why bother if the other person doesn't know the difference?

9. Can you stick with it?
  ☐ If I make up my mind to do something, I don't let *anything* stop me.
  ☐ I usually finish what I start—if it goes well.
  ☐ If it doesn't go well right away, I quit. Why beat your brains out?

10. How good is your health?
  ☐ I *never* run down!
  ☐ I have enough energy for most things I want to do.
  ☐ I run out of energy sooner than most of my friends.

Total the checks or Xs in each column here. _____

For interpretation, see Interpretations of Skills Self-Assessment Instruments.

Source: From *Business Startup Basics* by Donald Dible, pp. 9–10, © 1978. Adapted by permission of Prentice-Hall, Inc., Upper Saddle River, N.J.

EXPERIENTIAL EXERCISE

Negotiating a Franchise Agreement

Step 1: Assume that you are the owner of a rapidly growing restaurant chain. In order to continue your current level of growth, you are considering the option of selling franchises for new restaurants. Working alone, outline the major points of most concern to you that you would want to have in a franchising agreement. Also note the characteristics you would look for in potential franchisees.

Step 2: Assume that you are an individual investor looking to buy a franchise in a rapidly growing restaurant chain. Again working alone, outline the major factors that might determine which franchise you elect to buy. Also note the characteristics you would look for in a potential franchiser.

Step 3: Now form small groups of four. Randomly select one member of the group to play the role of the franchiser; the other three members will play the roles of potential franchisees. Role-play a negotiation meeting. The franchiser should stick as closely as possible to the major points developed in step 1. Similarly, the potential franchisees should do the same for points they developed in step 2.

Followup Questions

1. Did doing both step 1 and step 2 in advance help or hinder your negotiations?
2. Can a franchising agreement be so one-sided as to damage the interests of both parties? How so?

CHAPTER CLOSING CASE

CLEAR CHANNEL FOR ENTREPRENEURIAL SUCCESS

When L. Lowry Mays co-founded Clear Channel Communications in 1972, radio was already an old and unglamorous medium. Although he started with one money-losing country-western radio station in San Antonio, Texas, Mays was an entrepreneur with an eagerness to learn the business and a long-term plan. Watching and waiting, he was ready to act when federal regulations governing ownership of electronic media were relaxed in 1984. Then he began buying up small, weak radio stations and low-priced television stations. When the Fox network started looking for affiliates, Mays signed up his stations. That decision paid off as Fox's ratings climbed and it became a major network player in broadcast television.

Mays expanded his media empire in 1999 by acquiring AMFM, Inc. This $23.5 billion purchase positioned Clear Channel as the largest operator of radio stations in the United States, with 830 stations broadcasting to 96 million listeners in 187 markets. The nearest competitor, Infinity Broadcasting, had only 160 U.S. stations but reached 54 million listeners because its stations were in larger metropolitan areas. Because of duplication and federal oversight of the AMFM acquisition, Mays had to sell more than 100 radio stations, but radio still contributed more than three-quarters of Clear Channel's revenues, while television contributed less than 5 percent of revenues.

Billboards, another decidedly dowdy medium, provided the remainder of Clear Channel's revenues. Mays added this part of his business in the late 1990s. Now Clear Channel offered advertisers a choice of 425,000 billboards in 47 U.S. cities, as well as radio and television broadcast options for reaching audiences. In fact, the combination of billboards and radio was particularly attractive because television advertising was becoming more expensive and more fragmented as the number of channels multiplied. Mays reasoned that billboards would allow advertisers to reach a large audience and that radio would gave advertisers a way to repeat their messages over and over—a desirable combination for a reasonable fee.

Will the Internet, today's most glamorous and talked-about medium, threaten Clear Channel Communications? Decades ago, some observers believed that television would bury radio, but Mays—who clearly believes in the power of radio—does not see the Internet displacing the other electronic media. Instead, he has carved a profitable niche selling radio ad time and billboard space to dot.com businesses, many of which have only a shoestring budget on which to build their brands.

In addition, Clear Channel has teamed up with SamsDirect Internet to promote a new domain name alternative for individuals and businesses seeking new Internet addresses. The partners are encouraging people to register for online addresses that end in .cc rather than .com, which opens up new opportunities to claim unique or descriptive web addresses. Clear Channel radio stations and billboards in Houston were among the first to carry advertising for the .cc domain name registration service. In a dot.com address, the "com" stands

for "commercial," to distinguish businesses from non-profit organizations, which use the .org designation. In a .cc address, the "cc" stands for CoCos Islands, which are located near Australia, but Clear Channel and Sams-Direct see .cc as a good alternative for North American businesses that have missed the chance to use specific dot.com names. This is yet another example of how Mays has turned innovation to his advantage in the ever-changing world of media.

Case Questions

1. What distinctive competencies has Mays exploited to build Clear Channel Communications?

2. What role has economy of scale played in helping Mays build his business?

3. What else can Mays do to increase synergy among his various businesses?

Case References

Nancy Sarnoff, "New Domain Gives Local Market Second Shot at Filling in the Dots," *Houston Business Journal*, January 29, 2000, pp. 9–15; Brett Pulley, "America's Best Big Companies: Entertainment," *Forbes*, January 10, 2000, pp. 126–127; and Stephanie Anderson Forest, "The Biggest Media Mogul You Never Heard Of," *Business Week*, October 18, 1999, p. 56.

CHAPTER NOTES

1. Gary Hamel, "Driving Grassroots Growth," *Fortune*, September 4, 2000, pp. 173–187; "Fortune's 100 Fastest-Growing Companies," *Fortune*, September 4, 2000, pp. 142–160; and Ronald B. Lieber, "Beating the Odds," *Fortune*, March 31, 1997, pp. 82–90 (quote on p. 85).
2. U.S. Department of Commerce, *Statistical Abstract of the United States: 2000* (Washington, DC: Bureau of the Census, 2000).
3. "Small Business 'Vital Statistics,'" May 24, 2000, http://www.sba.gov/aboutsba/.
4. Ibid.
5. Ibid.
6. Chuck Salter, "Insanity, Inc.," *Fast Company*, January 1999, pp. 100–108.
7. Amar Bhide, "How Entrepreneurs Craft Strategies That Work," *Harvard Business Review*, March/April 1994, pp. 150–163.
8. *Hoover's Handbook of American Business 2001* (Austin, TX: Hoover's Business Press, 2001), pp. 1544–1545; and Wendy Zellner, "Peace, Love, and the Bottom Line," *Business Week*, December 7, 1998, pp. 79–82.
9. Nancy J. Lyons, "Moonlight over Indiana," *Inc.*, January 2000, pp. 71–74.
10. F. M. Scherer, *Industrial Market Structure and Economic Performance*, 2nd ed. (Boston: Houghton Mifflin, 1980).
11. "Three Biker-Entrepreneurs Take on Mighty Harley," *New York Times*, August 20, 1999, p. F1.
12. The importance of discovering niches is emphasized in Charles Hill and Gareth Jones, *Strategic Management: An Integrative Approach*, 5th ed. (Boston: Houghton Mifflin, 2001).

13. Gregory Patterson, "An American in . . . Siberia?" *Fortune,* August 4, 1997, p. 63; and "Crazy for Crunchies," *Newsweek,* April 28, 1997, p. 49.

14. Thea Singer, "Brandapalooza," *Inc. 500,* 1999, pp. 69–72.

15. "Cheap Tricks," *Forbes,* February 21, 2000, p. 116.

16. U.S. Department of Commerce.

17. Andy Serwer, "There's Something About Cisco," *Fortune,* May 15, 2000, pp. 114–138.

18. "The Courtship of Black Consumers," *New York Times,* August 16, 1998, pp. D1, D5.

19. See *The Wall Street Journal Almanac 1999,* pp. 179, 182.

20. "Women Increase Standing as Business Owners," *USA Today,* June 29, 1999, p. 1B.

21. Norman M. Scarborough and Thomas W. Zimmerer, *Effective Small Business Management: An Entrepreneurial Approach,* 6th ed. (Upper Saddle River, NJ: Prentice Hall, 2000), pp. 412–413.

22. "Expert Entrepreneur Got Her Show on the Road at an Early Age," *USA Today,* May 24, 2000, p. 5B.

Organizing

153

CHAPTER 6

Organization Structure and Design

Siemens AG, the large German conglomerate, can trace its roots back over 150 years to when its founder, Werner von Siemens, began making telegraph equipment. And since those early days, communication technology and equipment have been at the core of Siemens's global business enterprises. But as the firm grew, it also diversified into other businesses. By the beginning of the 1990s, Siemens was making everything from streetcars to satellites and from elevators to electron microscopes.

Siemens has always had engineering at the core of its operations—essentially it designed and made the best products possible but paid little attention to what other firms were doing. So focused on product quality were Siemens's engineers that the firm designed and made its own screws because they assumed that other manufacturers could not meet their exacting standards. At one time, television commercials for Siemens's telephones showed a harried user throwing the receiver against a wall, picking it up, and still having to listen to his boss yell at him. Lost on Siemens at the time, however, was the fact that, although the telephone featured in the commercials was tough, it was also heavy and unattractive. And this was just about the time that weight and appearance were becoming increasingly important to customers.

Thus perhaps it should not have really come as a surprise when Siemens began to struggle about ten years ago. Its biggest global competitors—firms like General Electric, Nokia, ABB, and Philips—had all taken steps to both more effectively integrate their various business operations and become more nimble and responsive to consumers. Siemens, meanwhile, had remained insular in its thinking and bureaucratic in its operations. But about that same time, a new CEO, Heinrich von Pierer, came on board and quickly recognized that he needed to get the lumbering behemoth back on track if it was to remain competitive.

Beginning in 1992, von Pierer cut Siemens's workforce by 17 percent and sold off several unrelated businesses for $2 billion. He also stripped out several layers of middle management and tried to change the firm's culture in order to better promote and reward innovation. And he began to move autonomous but related operations into the same business groups. By 1995 his changes started to pay off with increased revenues, lower operating costs, and increased share in several key markets. Unfortunately, however, the firm's

"In Germany, competition was like a wind. Now, it's like a storm. And it will become a hurricane. You have to move fast or lose."

—Heinrich von Pierer, CEO of Siemens

After studying this chapter, you should be able to

- Identify the basic elements of organizations.

- Describe the bureaucratic perspective on organization design.

- Identify and explain several situational influences on organization design.

- Describe the basic forms of organization design that characterize many organizations.

- Describe emerging issues in organization design.

turnaround stalled almost as quickly as it had started.

Closer analysis revealed to von Pierer that, although Siemens had indeed taken a big step in the right direction, its competitors had taken even bigger steps toward being agile and nimble players in the rapidly changing market for telecommunications technology and equipment. Undaunted, therefore, von Pierer redoubled his efforts to reinvent the firm. Among other actions, he decided to continue selling off business units that did not contribute to the firm's telecommunications core enterprises. He also went on an acquisition binge, buying up viable telecommunications businesses around the world. In addition, he totally overhauled the firm's structure by assigning all of its far-flung operations to one of 14 core business units. And he also decided to make it clear to the engineers running most Siemens operations that he expected them to perform better.

Now he holds quarterly meetings with the heads of Siemens's 14 business units and grills them on their performance. About 60 percent of the pay of those business unit heads is also now tied directly to their performance. He also reluctantly cut more jobs, including about one-fifth of all top management jobs in the company. And von Pierer continues to sell off businesses that are either underperforming or not central to telecommunications initiatives. So far, at least, his moves seem to be paying off. Siemens has once again established itself as a leader in its chosen markets, and investors have been pushing its valuation to an all-time high. Of course, it is also the case that in the volatile world of high technology the footing can be slippery, and one misstep can again lead to a big fall.[1]

One of the major ingredients in managing any business is the creation of an organization structure and design to link the various elements that comprise the organization. There is a wide array of alternatives that managers in any given organization might select for its design. Heinrich von Pierer and his executive team at Siemens are remaking one of the largest major corporations in the world. The basis for this makeover is the firm's organization design; the reasons behind the change involve the firm's environment and its strategy.

This chapter, the first of three devoted to organizing, discusses many of the critical elements of organization structure and design that managers can control. We first elaborate on the meaning of organization structure and design. Then we explore the basic elements that managers use to create an organization. We conclude by introducing several current issues in organizing.

The Nature of Organizing

organization structure and design The set of elements that can be used to configure an organization

The phrase **organization structure and design** refers to the overall set of structural elements and the relationships among those elements used to manage an organization. This section introduces and describes these elements.

Job Specialization

job specialization The degree to which the overall task of the organization is broken down and divided into smaller component parts

The first element of organization structure is job specialization. **Job specialization** is the degree to which the overall task of the organization is broken down and divided into smaller component parts. Job specialization is a normal extension of organizational growth. For example, when Walt Disney started his company, he did everything himself—wrote cartoons, drew them, and then marketed them to theaters. As the business grew, he eventually hired others to perform many of these same functions. As growth continued, so did specialization. As animation artists work on Disney movies today, they may specialize in drawing only a single character, such as Milo in *Atlantis*. And today, the Walt Disney Company has thousands of different specialized jobs. Clearly, no one person could perform them all.

Benefits and Limitations of Specialization   One benefit of job specialization is that workers performing small, simple tasks will become very proficient at those tasks. Another is that transfer time between tasks decreases. If employees perform several different tasks, some time is lost as they stop doing the first task and start doing the next. Third, the more narrowly defined a job is, the easier it is to develop specialized equipment to assist with that job. Fourth, when an employee who performs a highly specialized job is absent or resigns, the manager is able to train someone new at relatively low cost.

On the other hand, workers who perform highly specialized jobs may also become bored and dissatisfied. The job may be so specialized that it offers no challenge or stimulation. Boredom and monotony set in, absenteeism rises, and the quality of the work may suffer. Furthermore, the anticipated benefits of specialization do not always occur. For example, a study conducted at Maytag found that the time spent moving work in process from one worker to another was greater than the time needed for the same individual to change from job to job.[2] Thus, although some degree of specialization is necessary, it should not be carried to extremes because of the possible negative consequences. Managers must be sensitive to situations in which extreme specialization should be avoided. And indeed, several alternative approaches to designing jobs have been developed in recent years.

Alternatives to Specialization   To counter the problems associated with specialization, managers have sought other approaches to job design that achieve a better balance between organizational demands for efficiency and productivity, and individual needs for creativity and autonomy. Five alternative approaches are job rotation, job enlargement, job enrichment, the job characteristics approach, and work teams.

Designing jobs is a fundamental cornerstone of organizing. Most organizations today rely on a blend of job specialization and such alternatives to specialization as job enrichment and work teams. Take this Cessna factory in Independence, Kansas, for example. All of its assembly employees are expected to have a base specialization. But each is also expected to continuously learn new skills while simultaneously working as part of a team that has a lot to say about how its work gets done.

Job rotation involves systematically moving employees from one job to another. A worker in a warehouse might unload trucks on Monday, carry incoming inventory to storage on Tuesday, verify invoices on Wednesday, pull outgoing inventory from storage on Thursday, and load trucks on Friday. Thus the jobs do not change but, instead, workers move from job to job. Unfortunately, for this very reason, job rotation has not been very successful in enhancing employee motivation or satisfaction. Jobs that are amenable to rotation tend to be relatively standard and routine. Workers who are rotated to a "new" job may be more satisfied at first, but satisfaction soon wanes. Although many companies (among them Bethlehem Steel, Ford, Prudential Insurance, and IBM) have tried job rotation, it is most often used today as a training device to improve workers' skills and flexibility.

Job enlargement was developed to increase the total number of tasks workers perform. As a result, all workers perform a wide variety of tasks, which presumably reduces the level of job dissatisfaction. Many organizations have used job enlargement, including IBM, AT&T, and Maytag. At Maytag, for example, the assembly line for producing washing machine water pumps was systematically changed so that work that had originally been performed by six workers, who passed the work sequentially from one person to another, was performed by four workers, each of whom assembled a complete pump. Unfortunately, although job enlargement does have some positive consequences, training costs usually rise, unions argue that pay should increase because the worker is doing more tasks, and in many cases the work remains boring and routine even after job enlargement.

A more comprehensive approach, **job enrichment**, assumes that increasing the range and variety of tasks is not sufficient by itself to improve employee motivation.[3]

job rotation An alternative to job specialization that involves systematically moving employees from one job to another

job enlargement An alternative to job specialization that involves giving the employee more tasks to perform

job enrichment An alternative to job specialization that involves increasing both the number of tasks the worker does and the control the worker has over the job

Figure 6.1

The Job Characteristics Approach

The job characteristics approach to job de-sign provides a viable alternative to job specialization. Five core job dimensions may lead to critical psychological states that, in turn, may enhance motivation, performance, and satisfaction while also reducing absen-teeism and turnover.

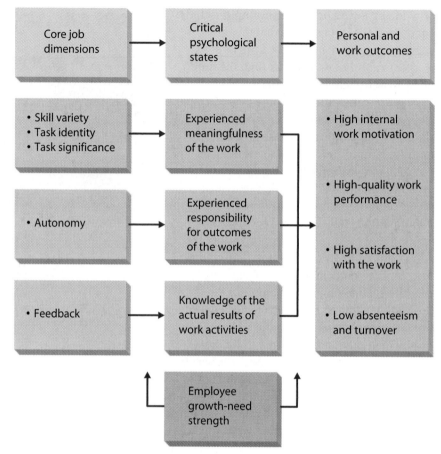

Source: From "Motivation Through the Design of Work: Test of a Theory," by J. R. Hackman and G. R. Oldham, in *Organizational Behavior and Human Performance*, Volume 16, pp. 250–279. Copyright © 1976 by Academic Press. Reproduced by permission of the publisher.

Thus job enrichment attempts to increase both the number of tasks a worker does and the control the worker has over the job. To implement job enrichment, managers remove some controls from the job, delegate more authority to employees, and structure the work in complete, natural units. These changes increase subordinates' sense of responsibility. Another part of job enrichment is to continually assign new and challenging tasks, thereby increasing employees' opportunity for growth and advancement. Texas Instruments, AT&T, IBM, and General Foods have all used job enrichment. This approach, however, also has disadvantages. For example, work systems should be analyzed before enrichment, but this seldom happens, and managers rarely ask for employee preferences when enriching jobs.

job characteristics approach An alternative to job specialization that suggests that jobs should be diagnosed and improved along five core dimensions, taking into account both the work system and employee preferences

The **job characteristics approach** is an alternative to job specialization that does take into account the work system and employee preferences.[4] As illustrated in Figure 6.1, the job characteristics approach suggests that jobs should be diagnosed and improved along the following five core dimensions:

1. *Skill variety*, the number of things a person does in a job
2. *Task identity*, the extent to which the worker does a complete or identifiable portion of the total job

3. *Task significance*, the perceived importance of the task
4. *Autonomy*, the degree of control the worker has over how the work is performed
5. *Feedback*, the extent to which the worker knows how well the job is being performed

Increasing the presence of these dimensions in a job presumably leads to high motivation, high-quality performance, high satisfaction, and low absenteeism and turnover. Numerous studies have tested the usefulness of the job characteristics approach. The Southwestern Division of Prudential Insurance, for example, used this approach in its claims division. Results included moderate declines in turnover and a small, but measurable improvement in work quality. Other research findings have not supported this approach as strongly. Thus, although the job characteristics approach is one of the most promising alternatives to job specialization, it is probably not the final answer.

Another alternative to job specialization is **work teams**. Under this arrangement, a group is given responsibility for designing the work system to be used in performing an interrelated set of jobs. In the typical assembly-line system, the work flows from one worker to the next, and each worker has a specified job to perform. In a work team, however, the group itself decides how jobs will be allocated. For example, the work team assigns specific tasks to members, monitors and controls its own performance, and has autonomy over work scheduling.[5]

work team An alternative to job specialization that allows an entire group to design the work system it will use to perform an interrelated set of tasks

Grouping Jobs: Departmentalization

The second building block of organization structure is the grouping of jobs according to some logical arrangement. This process is called **departmentalization**. When organizations are small, the owner-manager can personally oversee everyone who works there. As an organization grows, however, personally supervising all the employees becomes more and more difficult for the owner-manager. Consequently, new managerial positions are created to supervise the work of others. Employees are not assigned to particular managers randomly. Rather, jobs are grouped according to some plan. The logic embodied in such a plan is the basis for all departmentalization.

departmentalization The process of grouping jobs according to some logical arrangement

Functional Departmentalization   The most common base for departmentalization, especially among smaller organizations, is by function. **Functional departmentalization** groups together those jobs involving the same or similar activities. This approach, which is most common in smaller organizations, has three primary advantages. First, each department can be staffed by experts in that functional area. Marketing experts can be hired to run the marketing function, for example. Second, supervision is also facilitated because an individual manager needs to be familiar with only a relatively narrow set of skills. And, third, coordinating activities inside each department is easier.

On the other hand, as an organization begins to grow in size, several disadvantages of this approach may emerge. For one, decision making tends to become

functional departmentalization Grouping jobs involving the same or similar activities

slower and more bureaucratic. Employees may also begin to concentrate too narrowly on their own unit and lose sight of the total organizational system. Finally, accountability and performance become increasingly difficult to monitor. For example, determining whether a new product fails because of production deficiencies or a poor marketing campaign may not be possible.

product departmentalization
Grouping activities around products or product groups

Product Departmentalization   **Product departmentalization**, a second common approach, involves grouping and arranging activities around products or product groups. Most larger businesses adopt this form of departmentalization for grouping activities at the business or corporate level. Product departmentalization also has three major advantages. First, all activities associated with one product or product group can be easily integrated and coordinated. Second, the speed and effectiveness of decision making are enhanced. Third, the performance of individual products or product groups can be assessed more easily and objectively, thereby improving the accountability of departments for the results of their activities.

On the other hand, managers in each department may focus on their own product or product group to the exclusion of the rest of the organization. For instance, a marketing manager might see her or his primary duty as helping the group rather than helping the overall organization. In addition, administrative costs rise because each department must have its own functional specialists for tasks like marketing research and financial analysis.

customer departmentalization
Grouping activities to respond to and interact with specific customers or customer groups

Customer Departmentalization   Under **customer departmentalization**, the organization structures its activities to respond to and interact with specific customers or customer groups. The lending activities in most banks, for example, are usually tailored to meet the needs of different kinds of customers (business, consumer, mortgage, and agricultural loans). The basic advantage of this approach is that the organization is able to use skilled specialists to deal with unique customers or customer groups. It takes one set of skills to evaluate a balance sheet and lend a business $50,000 for operating capital, and a different set of skills to evaluate an individual's creditworthiness and lend $10,000 for a new car. However, a fairly large administrative staff is required to integrate the activities of the various departments. In banks, for example, coordination is necessary to make sure that the organization does not overcommit itself in any one area and to handle collections on delinquent accounts from a diverse set of customers.

location departmentalization
Grouping jobs on the basis of defined geographic sites or areas

Location Departmentalization   **Location departmentalization** groups jobs on the basis of defined geographic sites or areas. The defined sites or areas may range in size from a hemisphere to only a few blocks of a large city. Transportation companies, police departments (precincts represent geographic areas of a city), and the Federal Reserve Bank all use location departmentalization. The primary advantage of location departmentalization is that it enables the organization to respond easily to unique customer and environmental characteristics in the various regions. On the negative side, a larger administrative staff may be required if the organization must keep track of units in scattered locations.

Establishing Reporting Relationships

The third basic element of organizing is the establishment of reporting relationships among positions. The purpose of this activity is to clarify the chain of command and the span of management.

Chain of Command

Chain of command is an old concept, first popularized in the early years of the twentieth century. The chain of command actually has two components. The first, called *unity of command*, suggests that each person within an organization must have a clear reporting relationship to one and only one boss. The second, called the *scalar principle*, suggests that there must be a clear and unbroken line of authority that extends from the lowest to the highest position in the organization. The popular saying "The buck stops here" is derived from this idea—someone in the organization must ultimately be responsible for every decision.

chain of command A clear and distinct line of authority among the positions in an organization

Span of Management

Another part of establishing reporting relationships is determining how many people will report to each manager. This defines the **span of management** (sometimes called the *span of control*). For years, managers and researchers sought to determine the optimal span of management. For example, should it be relatively narrow (with few subordinates per manager) or relatively wide (with many subordinates)? Today, we recognize that the span of management is a crucial factor in structuring organizations but that there are no universal, cut-and-dried prescriptions for an ideal or optimal span.[6] Instead, managers have to carefully assess their situation and context when making decisions about determining the span best suited for their needs.

span of management The number of people who report to a particular manager

Tall Versus Flat Organizations

What difference does it make whether the organization is tall or flat? One early study at Sears Roebuck found that a flat structure led to higher levels of employee morale and productivity.[7] Researchers have also argued that a tall structure is more expensive (because of the larger number of managers involved) and that it fosters more communication problems (because of the increased number of people through whom information must pass). On the other hand, a wide span of management in a flat organization may result in a manager's having more administrative responsibility (because there are fewer managers) and more supervisory responsibility (because there are more subordinates reporting to each manager). If these additional responsibilities become excessive, the flat organization may suffer.[8]

Many experts agree that businesses can function effectively with fewer layers of organization than they currently have. The Franklin Mint, for example, reduced its number of management layers from 6 to 4. At the same time, CEO Stewart Resnick increased his span of management from 6 to 12. In similar fashion, IBM has eliminated several layers of management. One additional reason for this trend is that improved organizational communication networks allow managers to stay in touch with a larger number of subordinates than was possible even just a few years ago.[9]

Distributing Authority

Another important building block in structuring organizations is the determination of how authority is to be distributed among positions. **Authority** is power that has been legitimized by the organization. Two specific issues that managers must address when distributing authority are delegation and decentralization.

authority Power that has been legitimized by the organization

The Delegation Process   Delegation is the establishment of a pattern of authority between a superior and one or more subordinates. Specifically, **delegation** is the process by which managers assign a portion of their total workload to others. In theory, the delegation process involves three steps. First, the manager assigns responsibility or gives the subordinate a job to do. The assignment of responsibility might range from telling a subordinate to prepare a report to placing the person in charge of a task force. Along with the assignment, the individual is also given the authority to do the job. The manager may give the subordinate the power to requisition needed information from confidential files or to direct a group of other workers. Finally, the manager establishes the subordinate's accountability—that is, the subordinate accepts an obligation to carry out the task assigned by the manager.

delegation The process by which a manager assigns a portion of his or her total workload to others

Decentralization and Centralization   Just as authority can be delegated from one individual to another, organizations also develop patterns of authority across a wide variety of positions and departments. **Decentralization** is the process of systematically delegating power and authority throughout the organization to middle and lower-level managers. It is important to remember that decentralization is actually one end of a continuum anchored at the other end by **centralization**, the process of systematically retaining power and authority in the hands of higher-level managers. Hence, a decentralized organization is one in which decision-making power and authority are delegated as far down the chain of command as possible. Conversely, in a centralized organization, decision-making power and authority are retained at the higher levels of management. No organization is ever completely decentralized or completely centralized; some firms position themselves toward one end of the continuum, and some lean the other way.[10]

decentralization The process of systematically delegating power and authority throughout the organization to middle and lower-level managers

centralization The process of systematically retaining power and authority in the hands of higher-level managers

What factors determine an organization's position on the decentralization-centralization continuum? One common determinant is the organization's external environment. Usually, the greater the complexity and uncertainty of the environment, the greater is the tendency to decentralize. Another crucial factor is the history of the organization. Firms have a tendency to do what they have done in the past, so there is likely to be some relationship between what an organization did in its early history and what it chooses to do today in terms of centralization or decentralization. The nature of the decisions being made is also considered. The costlier and riskier the decision, the more pressure there is to centralize. Hence, a manager has no clear-cut guidelines to determine whether to centralize or decentralize. Many successful organizations, such as Sears and General Electric, are quite decentralized. Equally successful firms, such as McDonald's and Wal-Mart, have remained centralized.

Coordinating Activities

A fifth major element of organizing is coordination. As we discussed earlier, job specialization and departmentalization involve breaking jobs down into small units and then combining those jobs into departments. Once this has been accomplished, the activities of the departments must be linked—systems must be put in place to keep the activities of each department focused on the attainment of organizational goals. This is accomplished by **coordination**—the process of linking the activities of the various departments of the organization.

The Need for Coordination   The primary reason for coordination is that departments and work groups are interdependent—they depend on each other for information and resources to perform their respective activities. The greater the interdependence between departments, the more coordination the organization requires if departments are to be able to perform effectively.[11] **Pooled interdependence** represents the lowest level of interdependence. Units with pooled interdependence operate with little interaction—the output of the units is pooled at the organizational level. The Gap clothing stores operate with pooled interdependence. Each store is considered a department by the parent corporation. Each has its own operating budget, staff, and so forth. The profits or losses from each store are "added together" at the organizational level. The stores are interdependent to the extent that the final success or failure of one store affects the others, but they do not generally interact on a day-to-day basis.

In **sequential interdependence**, the output of one unit becomes the input for another in a sequential fashion. This creates a moderate level of interdependence. At Nissan, for example, one plant assembles engines and then ships them to a final assembly site at another plant, where the cars are completed. The plants are interdependent in that the final assembly plant must have the engines from engine assembly before it can perform its primary function of producing finished automobiles. But the level of interdependence is generally one way—the engine plant is not necessarily dependent on the final assembly plant.

Reciprocal interdependence exists when activities flow both ways between units. This form is clearly the most complex. Within a Marriott Hotel, for example, the reservations department, front desk checkin, and housekeeping are all reciprocally interdependent. Reservations has to provide front desk employees with information about how many guests to expect each day, and housekeeping needs to know which rooms require priority cleaning. If any of the three units does not do its job properly, all the others will be affected.

Structural Coordination Techniques   Because of the obvious coordination requirements that characterize most organizations, many techniques for achieving coordination have been developed. Organizations that use the *hierarchy* to achieve coordination place one manager in charge of interdependent departments or units. In Kmart distribution centers, major activities include receiving and unloading bulk shipments from railroad cars and loading other shipments onto trucks for distribution to retail outlets. The two groups (receiving and shipping) are interdependent in

coordination The process of linking the activities of the various departments of the organization

pooled interdependence When units operate with little interactions, their output is simply pooled

sequential interdependence When the output of one unit becomes the input of another in sequential fashion

reciprocal interdependence When activities flow both ways between units

that they share the loading docks and some equipment. To ensure coordination and minimize conflict, one manager is in charge of the whole operation.

Routine coordination activities can be handled via *rules and standard procedures*. In the Kmart distribution center, an outgoing truck shipment has priority over an incoming rail shipment. Thus, when trucks are to be loaded, the shipping unit is given access to all of the center's auxiliary forklifts. This priority is specifically stated in a rule. But, as useful as rules and procedures often are in routine situations, they are not particularly effective when coordination problems are complex or unusual.

As a device for coordination, a manager in a *liaison* role coordinates interdependent units by acting as a common point of contact. This individual may not have any formal authority over the groups but instead simply facilitates the flow of information between units. Two engineering groups working on component systems for a large project might interact through a liaison. The liaison maintains familiarity with each group as well as with the overall project. She can answer questions and otherwise serve to integrate the activities of all the groups.

A *task force* may be created when the need for coordination is acute. When interdependence is complex and several units are involved, a single liaison person may not be sufficient. Instead, a task force might be assembled by drawing one representative from each group. The coordination function is thus spread across several individuals, each of whom has special information about one of the groups involved. When the project is completed, task force members return to their original positions. For example, a college overhauling its degree requirements might establish a task force made up of representatives from each department affected by the change. Each person retains her or his regular departmental affiliation and duties but also serves on the special task force. After the new requirements are agreed on, the task force is dissolved.

Integrating departments are occasionally used for coordination. These are somewhat similar to task forces but more permanent. An integrating department generally has some permanent members as well as members who are assigned temporarily from units that are particularly in need of coordination. One study found that successful firms in the plastics industry, which is characterized by complex and dynamic environments, used integrating departments to maintain internal integration and coordination.[12] An integrating department usually has more authority than a task force and may even be given some budgetary control by the organization.

The Bureaucratic Model of Organization Design

bureaucracy A model of organization design based on a legitimate and formal system of authority

Max Weber, an influential German sociologist, was a pioneer of classical organization theory. At the core of Weber's writings was the bureaucratic model of organizations.[13] The Weberian perspective suggests that a **bureaucracy** is a model of organization design based on a legitimate and formal system of authority. Many people associate bureaucracy with "red tape," rigidity, and passing the buck. For example, how many times have you heard people refer disparagingly to the "federal bureaucracy"? And many U.S. managers believe that bureaucracy in the Japanese government is a major impediment to U.S. firms' ability to do business there.

Weber viewed the bureaucratic form of organization as logical, rational, and efficient. He offered the model as a framework to which all organizations should aspire, the "one best way" of doing things. According to Weber, the ideal bureaucracy exhibits five basic characteristics:

1. The organization should adopt a distinct division of labor, and each position should be filled by an expert.
2. The organization should develop a consistent set of rules to ensure that task performance is uniform.
3. The organization should establish a hierarchy of positions or offices that creates a chain of command from the top of the organization to the bottom.
4. Managers should conduct business in an impersonal way and maintain an appropriate social distance between themselves and their subordinates.
5. Employment and advancement in the organization should be based on technical expertise, and employees should be protected from arbitrary dismissal.

Perhaps the best examples of bureaucracies today are government agencies and universities. Consider, for example, the steps you must go through and the forms you must fill out to apply for admission to college, request housing, register each semester, change majors, submit a degree plan, substitute a course, and file for graduation. The reason these procedures are necessary is that universities deal with large numbers of people who must be treated equally and fairly. Hence, rules, regulations, and standard operating procedures are needed. Large labor unions are also usually organized as bureaucracies. Some bureaucracies, such as the U.S. Postal Service, are trying to portray themselves as less mechanistic and impersonal. The strategy of the Postal Service is to become more service oriented as a way to fight back against competitors like Federal Express and UPS.

A primary strength of the bureaucratic model is that several of its elements (such as reliance on rules and employment based on expertise) do, in fact, often improve efficiency. Bureaucracies also help prevent favoritism (because everyone must follow the rules) and make procedures and practices very clear to everyone. Unfortunately, however, this approach also has several disadvantages.

"YOU'RE OLD ENOUGH to KNOW THE RULES, HARLISS. NOW GET OUT THERE AND BREAK THEM!"

© Harley Schwadron

Bureaucratic organizations generally have myriad rules, regulations, and procedures. In today's fast-paced and rapidly changing world, many bureaucratic organizations are increasingly attempting to become more flexible and responsive to their environment. Making the necessary changes, however, is often more difficult than might be imagined. Some creative managers, therefore, have come up with innovative and unusual ways to promote new approaches to organizing. For example, sometimes simply eliminating rules can be a big help. And, although managers should be judicious in actually instructing people to break rules, as this manager is doing, this might sometimes be a good way to get started!

One major disadvantage is that the bureaucratic model results in inflexibility and rigidity. Once rules are created and put in place, making exceptions or changing them is often difficult. In addition, the bureaucracy often results in the neglect of human and social processes within the organization.

◼ *Situational Influences on Organization Design*

situational view of organization design Based on the assumption that the optimal design for any given organization depends on a set of relevant situational factors

The **situational view of organization design** is based on the assumption that the optimal design for any given organization depends on a set of relevant situational factors. In other words, situational factors play a role in determining the best organization design for any particular circumstance. Four basic situational factors—technology, environment, size, and organizational life cycle—are discussed here. *Management InfoTech* also illustrates how the Internet is affecting organization design.

MANAGEMENT INFOTECH

THE WEB'S INFLUENCE ON ORGANIZATION DESIGN

No organization design lasts forever, but e-businesses have to be especially attentive to design as they evolve and adapt to the dynamic Internet environment. The number of Internet users continues to rise every day, as does the number of companies opening web-based businesses. Because the Internet offers many choices and allows convenient comparisons between competing products and services, buyers have more power than ever before. As a result, e-businesses stand to lose customers if they fail to adjust to emerging needs and trends.

The web is also erasing geographic and time boundaries separating companies and consumers, business units and industrial suppliers. With a click of the mouse, customers can quickly find, price, and buy the best products for their requirements—regardless of location or time of day. These changes can spell disaster for bureaucratic organizations unprepared to respond quickly to shifts in customer buying patterns.

Charles Schwab, one of the largest U.S. discount brokerage firms, confronted these issues when management realized that the Internet was changing the way investors buy and sell stocks and bonds. At first, the company set up a separate e-business to offer basic brokerage services with lower fees for web-only transactions. Soon, its Internet customers were clamoring for the same service and choices as non-Internet customers. Meantime, non-Internet customers were asking for online trading privileges with the same low fees paid by Internet customers. In response, Schwab merged its Internet and non-Internet businesses to create one brokerage firm with multiple access choices for customers and the low fee structure offered by the Internet unit. Now, nearly 70 percent of all customer transactions move through the company's web site—making Schwab the leading broker on the Internet.

> *We used to reinvent the company about every 10 years. Now it seems like we have to reinvent our company every two years.*
>
> —*David P. Pottruck, president of Charles Schwab**

References: Fred Andrews, "Rock-Solid Values at Reinvention's Core," *New York Times,* April 30, 2000, sec. 3, p. 7 (*quote on p. 7); Megan Barnett, "Schwab's MVP," *Industry Standard,* May 1, 2000, p. 270; and Gary Hamel and Jeff Sampler, "The E-Corporation," *Fortune,* December 7, 1998, pp. 80–92.

Core Technology

Technology is the conversion processes used to transform inputs (such as materials or information) into outputs (such as products or services). Most organizations use multiple technologies, but an organization's most important one is called its *core technology*. Although most people visualize assembly lines and machinery when they think of technology, the term can also be applied to service organizations. For example, a brokerage firm like Merrill Lynch uses technology to transform investment dollars into income in much the same way that Union Carbide uses natural resources to manufacture chemical products.

The link between technology and organization design was first recognized by Joan Woodward.[14] Woodward studied 100 manufacturing firms in southern England. She collected information about such factors as the history of each organization, its manufacturing processes, its forms and procedures, and its financial performance. Woodward expected to find a relationship between the size of an organization and its design, but no such relationship emerged. As a result, she began to seek other explanations for differences. Close scrutiny of the firms in her sample led her to recognize a potential relationship between technology and organization design. This followup analysis led Woodward to first classify the organizations according to their technology. Three basic forms of technology were identified by Woodward:

1. *Unit or small-batch technology*. The product is custom-made to customer specifications or produced in small quantities. Organizations using this form of technology include a tailor shop like Brooks Brothers (custom suits), a printing shop like Kinko's (business cards, company stationery), and a photography studio.
2. *Large-batch or mass-production technology*. The product is manufactured in assembly-line fashion by combining component parts into another part or finished product. Examples include automobile manufacturers like Subaru, appliance makers like Whirlpool, and electronics firms like Philips.
3. *Continuous-process technology*. Raw materials are transformed to a finished product by a series of machine or process transformations. The composition of the materials themselves is changed. Examples include petroleum refineries like Exxon Mobil and Shell, and chemical refineries like Dow Chemical and Union Carbide.

These forms of technology are listed in order of their assumed levels of complexity. That is, unit or small-batch technology is presumed to be the least complex and continuous-process technology, the most complex. Woodward found that different configurations of organization design were associated with each technology.

Specifically, Woodward found that the two extremes (unit or small-batch and continuous-process) tended to be relatively organic—less rigid and formal—whereas the middle-range organizations (large-batch or mass-production) were much more like bureaucracies. The large-batch and mass-production organizations also had a higher level of specialization. Finally, she found that organizational success was related to the extent to which organizations followed the typical pattern. For example, successful continuous-process organizations tended to be more organic, whereas less-successful firms with the same technology were more bureaucratic.

technology Conversion processes used to transform inputs into outputs

Environment

Environmental elements and organization design also appear to be linked in a number of ways. The first widely recognized analysis of environment-organization design linkages was provided by Tom Burns and G. M. Stalker.[15] Like Woodward, Burns and Stalker worked in England. Their first step was identifying two extreme forms of organizational environment: stable (one that remains relatively constant over time) and unstable (subject to uncertainty and rapid change). Next, they studied the designs of organizations in each type of environment. Not surprisingly, they found that organizations in stable environments tended to have a different kind of design than did organizations in unstable environments. The two kinds of design that emerged were called mechanistic and organic organization.

A **mechanistic organization**, quite similar to the bureaucratic model, was most frequently found in stable environments. Free from uncertainty, organizations structured their activities in rather predictable ways by means of rules, specialized jobs, and centralized authority. Mechanistic organizations are also quite similar in nature to bureaucracies. Although no environment is completely stable, Kmart and Wendy's use mechanistic designs. Each Kmart store, for example, has pre-scribed methods for store design and merchandise-ordering processes. No deviations are allowed from these methods. An **organic organization**, on the other hand, was most often found in unstable and unpredictable environments, in which constant change and uncertainty usually dictate a much higher level of fluidity and flexibility. Motorola (facing rapid technological change) and The Limited (facing constant change in consumer tastes) each use organic designs. A manager at Motorola, for example, has considerable discretion over how work is performed and how problems can be solved.

These ideas were extended in the United States by Paul R. Lawrence and Jay W. Lorsch.[16] They agreed that environmental factors influence organization design but believed that this influence varies between different units of the same organization. In fact, they predicted that each organizational unit has its own unique environment and responds by developing unique attributes. Lawrence and Lorsch suggested that organizations could be characterized along two primary dimensions.

One of these dimensions, **differentiation**, is the extent to which the organization is broken down into subunits. A firm with many subunits is highly differentiated; one with few subunits has a low level of differentiation. The second dimension, **integration**, is the degree to which the various subunits must work together in a coordinated fashion. For example, if each unit competes in a different market and has its own production facilities, they may need little integration. Lawrence and Lorsch reasoned that the degree of differentiation and integration needed by an organization depends on the stability of the environments that its subunits face.

Organizational Size and Life Cycle

The size of an organization and its life cycle are other factors that affect its design.[17] Although several definitions of size exist, we define **organizational size** as the total

---

mechanistic organization Similar to the bureaucratic model, most frequently found in stable environments

organic organization Very flexible and informal model of organization design, most often found in unstable and unpredictable environments

differentiation Extent to which the organization is broken down into subunits

integration Degree to which the various subunits must work together in a coordinated fashion

organizational size Total number of full-time or full-time-equivalent employees

number of full-time or full-time-equivalent employees. A team of researchers at the University of Aston in Birmingham, England, believed that Woodward had failed to find a size-structure relationship (which was her original expectation) because almost all the organizations she studied were relatively small (three-fourths had fewer than 500 employees).[18] Thus they decided to undertake a study of a wider array of organizations to determine how size and technology both individually and jointly affect an organization's design.

Their primary finding was that technology did in fact influence structural variables in small firms, probably because all their activities tended to be centered around their core technology. In large firms, however, the strong technology-design link broke down, most likely because technology is not as central to ongoing activities in large organizations. The Aston studies yielded a number of basic generalizations: When compared to small organizations, large organizations tend to be characterized by higher levels of job specialization, more standard operating procedures, more rules, more regulations, and a greater degree of decentralization.

organizational life cycle Progression through which organizations evolve as they grow and mature

Of course, size is not constant. As we noted in Chapter 5, for example, some small businesses are formed but soon disappear. Others remain as small, independently operated enterprises as long as their owner-manager lives. A few, like Compaq Computer, Dell Computer, Liz Claiborne, and Reebok, skyrocket to become organizational giants. And occasionally large organizations reduce their size through layoffs or divestitures. For example, Navistar is today far smaller than was its previous incarnation as International Harvester Company.

Although no clear pattern explains changes in size, many organizations progress through a four-stage **organizational life cycle**.[19] The first stage is the *birth* of the organization. The second stage, *youth*, is characterized by growth and the expansion of organizational resources. *Midlife* is a period of gradual growth evolving eventually into stability. Finally, *maturity* is a period of stability, perhaps eventually evolving into decline. J. C. Penney is an example of a mature organization—it is experiencing little or no growth and appears to be falling behind the rest of the retailing industry today.

Managers must confront a number of organization design issues as the organization progresses through these stages. In general, as an organization passes from one stage to the next, it becomes bigger, more mechanistic, and more decentralized. It also becomes more specialized, devotes more attention to planning, and takes on an increasingly large staff component. Finally, coordination demands increase, formalization increases, organizational units become geographically more dispersed, and control systems become more extensive. Thus an organization's size and design are clearly linked, and this link is dynamic because of the organizational life cycle.

Organization design is a complex and an ever-changing process. Consider, for example, the organizational implications of hiring 3 million temporary workers! This is exactly the challenge faced by the U.S. Census Bureau as it began planning for the 2000 census. This man, for example, was hired to help conduct the census by going door-to-door in some neighborhoods. The organization itself had to create systems for hiring him, paying him, insuring that he did a good job, creating a reporting relationship between him and his boss, and ending his employment when the census was complete.

■ *Basic Forms of Organization Design*

Because so many factors can influence organization design, it should come as no surprise that organizations adopt many different kinds of designs. Most designs, however, fall into one of four basic categories. Others are hybrids based on one or more of the basic forms.

Functional (U-Form) Design

functional (U-form) design
Based on the functional approach to departmentalization

The **functional design** is an arrangement based on the functional approach to departmentalization. This design has also been termed **U-form** (for unitary).[20] Under the U-form arrangement, the members and units in the organization are grouped into functional departments such as marketing and production. For the organization to operate efficiently in this design, there must be considerable coordination across departments. Integration and coordination are most commonly the responsibility of the CEO and members of senior management. Figure 6.2 shows the U-form design as applied to the corporate level of a small manufacturing company. In a U-form organization, none of the functional areas can survive without the others. Marketing, for example, needs products from operations to sell and funds from finance to pay for advertising. The WD-40 Company, which makes a popular lubricating oil, and the McIlhenny Company, which makes Tabasco sauce, are both examples of firms that use the U-form design.

Figure 6.2

Functional U-Form Design for a Small Manufacturing Company
The U-form design is based on functional departmentalization. This small manufacturing firm uses managers at the vice presidential level to coordinate activities within each functional area of the organization. Note that each functional area is dependent on the others.

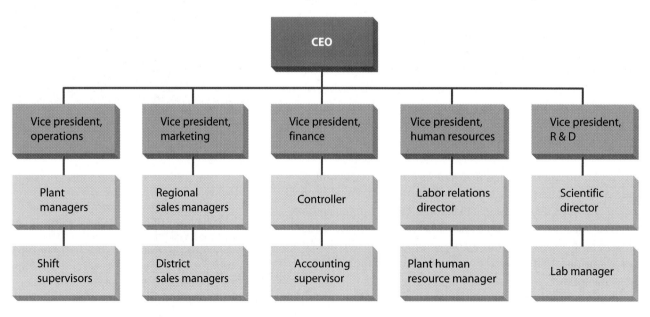

In general, this approach shares the basic advantages and disadvantages of functional departmentalization. Thus it allows the organization to staff all important positions with functional experts and facilitates coordination and integration. On the other hand, it also promotes a functional, rather than an organizational, focus and tends to promote centralization. And, as we noted earlier, functionally based designs are most commonly used in small organizations because an individual CEO can easily oversee and coordinate the entire organization. As an organization grows, the CEO finds staying on top of all functional areas increasingly difficult.

Conglomerate (H-Form) Design

Another common form of organization design is the **conglomerate,** or **H-form, design**.[21] The conglomerate design is used by an organization made up of a set of unrelated businesses. Thus the H-form design is essentially a holding company that results from unrelated diversification. (The *H* in this term stands for holding.) This approach is based loosely on the product form of departmentalization. Each business or set of businesses is operated by a general manager who is responsible for its profits or losses, and each general manager functions independently of the others. Pearson PLC, a British firm, uses the H-form design. As illustrated in Figure 6.3, Pearson consists of six business groups. Although its periodicals and publishing operations are related to one another, all of its other businesses are clearly unrelated. Other firms that use the H-form design include General Electric (aircraft engines, appliances, broadcasting, financial services, lighting products, plastics, and other unrelated businesses) and Tenneco (pipelines, auto parts, shipbuilding, financial services, and other unrelated businesses).

In an H-form organization, a corporate staff usually evaluates the performance of each business, allocates corporate resources across companies, and shapes decisions about buying and selling businesses. The basic shortcoming of the H-form design is the complexity associated with holding diverse and unrelated businesses.

conglomerate (H-form) design
Used by an organization made up of a set of unrelated businesses

Figure 6.3
Conglomerate (H-Form) Design at Pearson PLC
Pearson PLC, a British firm, uses the conglomerate form of organization design. This design, which results from a strategy of unrelated diversification, is complex to manage. Managers have trouble comparing and integrating activities among the dissimilar operations. Companies may abandon this design for another approach, such as the M-form design.

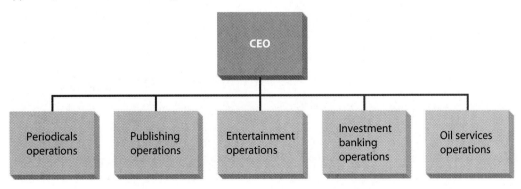

Managers usually find comparing and integrating activities across a large number of diverse operations difficult. Research suggests that many organizations following this approach achieve only average to weak financial performance.[22] Thus, although some U.S. firms are still using the H-form design, many have also abandoned it for other approaches.

Divisional (M-Form) Design

divisional (M-form) design
Based on multiple businesses in related areas operating within a larger organizational framework

In the divisional design, which is becoming increasingly popular, a product form of organization is also used; in contrast to the H-form, however, the divisions are related. Thus the **divisional design**, or **M-form** (for multidivisional), is based on multiple businesses in related areas operating within a larger organizational framework. This design results from a strategy of related diversification.

Some activities are extremely decentralized down to the divisional level; others are centralized at the corporate level.[23] For example, as shown in Figure 6.4, The Limited uses this approach. Each of its divisions is headed by a general manager and operates with reasonable autonomy, but the divisions also coordinate their activities as is appropriate. Other firms that use this approach are the Walt Disney Company (theme parks, movies, and merchandising units, all interrelated) and Hewlett-Packard (computers, printers, scanners, electronic medical equipment, and other electronic instrumentation).

The opportunities for coordination and shared resources represent one of the biggest advantages of the M-form design. The Limited's marketing research and purchasing departments are centralized. Thus a buyer can inspect a manufacturer's entire product line, buy some designs for The Limited chain, others for Express, and still others for Lerner New York. The M-form design's basic objective is to optimize internal competition and cooperation. Healthy competition among divisions for resources can enhance effectiveness, but cooperation should also be promoted. Research suggests that the M-form organization that can achieve and maintain this balance will outperform large U-form and all H-form organizations.[24]

Figure 6.4

Multidivisional (M-Form) Design at The Limited, Inc.

The Limited, Inc., uses the multidivisional approach to organization design. Although each unit operates with relative autonomy, all units function in the same general market. This design resulted from a strategy of related diversification. Other firms that use M-form designs include PepsiCo and Woolworth Corporation.

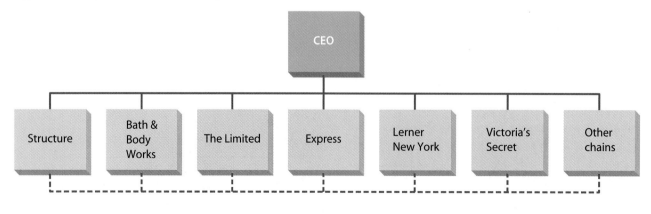

Matrix Design

The **matrix design**, another common approach to organization design, is based on two overlapping bases of departmentalization.[25] The foundation of a matrix is a set of functional departments. A set of product groups, or temporary departments, is then superimposed across the functional departments. Employees in a matrix are simultaneously members of a functional department (such as engineering) and of a project team.

Figure 6.5 shows a basic matrix design. At the top of the organization are functional units headed by vice presidents of engineering, production, finance, and marketing. Each of these managers has several subordinates. Along the side of the organization are a number of positions called *project manager.* Each project manager heads a project group composed of representatives or workers from the functional departments. Note from the figure that a matrix reflects a *multiple-command structure*—any given individual reports to both a functional superior and one or more project managers.

matrix design Based on two overlapping bases of departmentalization

Figure 6.5

A Matrix Organization

A matrix organization design is created by superimposing a product form of departmentalization onto an existing functional organization. Project managers coordinate teams of employees drawn from different functional departments. Thus a matrix relies on a multiple-command structure.

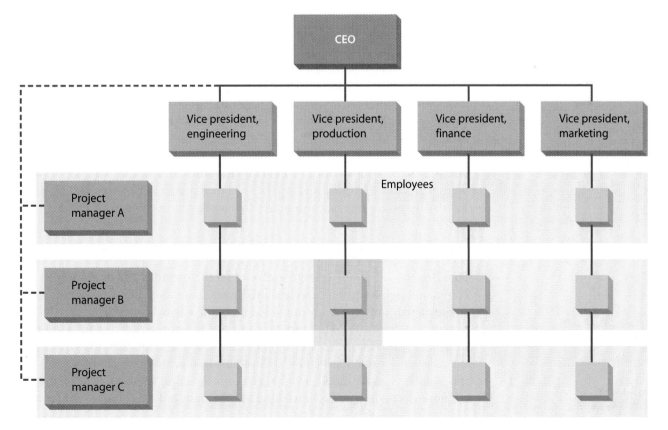

The project groups, or teams, are assigned to designated projects or programs. For example, the company might be developing a new product. Representatives are chosen from each functional area to work as a team on the new product. They also retain membership in the original functional group. At any given time, a person may be a member of several teams as well as a member of a functional group. Martha Stewart has created a matrix organization for her burgeoning lifestyle business. The company was first organized broadly into media and merchandising groups, each of which has specific products and product groups. Layered on top of this structure are teams of lifestyle experts organized into groups such as cooking, crafts, weddings, and so forth. Each of these groups is targeted toward specific customer needs, but each works as necessary across all of the product groups. For example, a wedding expert might contribute to an article on wedding planning for a Martha Stewart magazine, contribute a story idea for a cable television program, and supply content for a Martha Stewart web site. This same individual might also help select fabrics suitable for wedding gowns for retailing.[26]

The matrix design has several advantages. First, it enhances flexibility because teams can be created, redefined, and dissolved as needed. Second, because they assume a major role in decision making, team members are likely to be highly motivated and committed to the organization. Third, employees in a matrix organization have considerable opportunity to learn new skills. A fourth advantage of a matrix design is that it provides an efficient way for the organization to take full advantage of its human resources. Fifth, team members retain membership in their functional unit so that they can serve as a bridge between the functional unit and the team, enhancing cooperation. Sixth, the matrix design gives top management a useful vehicle for decentralization. Once the day-to-day operations have been delegated, top management can devote more attention to areas such as long-range planning.

On the other hand, the matrix design also has some major disadvantages. Employees may be uncertain about reporting relationships, especially if they are simultaneously assigned to a functional manager and to several project managers. To complicate matters, some managers see the matrix as a form of anarchy in which they have unlimited freedom. Another set of problems is associated with the dynamics of group behavior. Groups take longer than individuals to make decisions, may be dominated by one individual, and may compromise too much. They may also get bogged down in discussion and not focus on their primary objectives. Finally, in a matrix, more time may also be required for coordinating task-related activities.

Hybrid Designs

Some organizations use a design that represents a hybrid of two or more of the common forms of organization design. For example, an organization may have five related divisions and one unrelated division, making its design a cross between an M-form and an H-form. Indeed, few companies use a design in its pure form. Most firms have one basic organization design as a foundation to managing the business but maintain sufficient flexibility so that temporary or permanent modifications can be made for strategic purposes. Ford, for example, used the matrix approach to design the Taurus and the Mustang, but the company is basically a U-form organization showing signs of moving to an M-form design. As we noted earlier, any combination of factors may dictate the appropriate form of design for any particular company.

Emerging Issues in Organization Design

Finally, in today's complex and ever-changing environment, it should come as no surprise that managers continue to explore and experiment with new forms of organization design. This final section highlights some of the more important emerging issues.[27]

The Team Organization

Some organizations today are using the **team organization**, an approach to organization design that relies almost exclusively on project-type teams, with little or no underlying functional hierarchy. Within such an organization, people float from project to project as necessitated by their skills and the demands of those projects. At Cypress Semiconductor, T. J. Rodgers refuses to allow the organization to grow so large that it cannot function this way. Whenever a unit or group starts getting too large, he simply splits it into smaller units. Consequently, all units within the organization are small. This allows them to change direction, explore new ideas, and try new methods without dealing with a rigid bureaucratic organizational context. Although few organizations have actually reached this level of adaptability, Apple Computer and Xerox are among those moving toward it.[28]

team organization An approach to organization design that relies almost exclusively on project-type teams, with little or no underlying functional hierarchy.

The Virtual Organization

Closely related to the team organization is the virtual organization. A **virtual organization** is one that has little or no formal structure. Such an organization typically has only a handful of permanent employees and a very small staff and administrative headquarters facility. As the needs of the organization change, its managers bring in temporary workers, lease facilities, and outsource basic support services to meet the demands of each unique situation. As the situation changes, the temporary workforce changes in parallel, with some people leaving the organization and others entering. Facilities and the services subcontracted to others change as well. Thus the organization exists only in response to its needs. And, increasingly, virtual organizations are conducting most—if not all—of their business online.[29] For example, Global Research Consortium is a virtual organization. GRC offers research and consulting services to firms doing business in Asia. As clients request various services, GRC's staff of three permanent employees subcontracts the work to an appropriate set of several dozen independent consultants or researchers with whom it has relationships. At any given time, therefore, GRC may have several projects under way and 20 or 30 people working on projects. As the projects change, so, too, does the composition of the organization.

virtual organization One that has little or no formal structure

The Learning Organization

Another recent approach to organization design is the so-called learning organization. Organizations that adopt this approach work to integrate continuous improvement with continuous employee learning and development. Specifically, a **learning organization** is one that works to facilitate the lifelong learning and personal development of all of its employees while continually transforming itself to respond to changing demands and needs.[30]

Although managers might approach the concept of a learning organization from a variety of perspectives, improved quality, continuous improvement, and performance measurement are frequent goals. The idea is that the most consistent and logical strategy for achieving continuous improvement is by constantly upgrading employee talent, skill, and knowledge. For example, if each employee in an organization learns one new thing each day and can translate that knowledge into work-related practice, continuous improvement will logically follow. Indeed, organizations that wholeheartedly embrace this approach believe that only through constant learning by employees can continuous improvement really occur.

In recent years, many different organizations have implemented this approach. For example, the Shell Oil Company recently purchased an executive conference center north of its headquarters in Houston. The center boasts state-of-the-art classrooms and instructional technology, lodging facilities, a restaurant, and recreational amenities such as a golf course, swimming pool, and tennis courts. Line managers at the firm rotate through the Shell Learning Center, as the facility has been renamed, and serve as teaching faculty. Such teaching assignments last anywhere from a few days to several months. At the same time, all Shell employees routinely attend training programs, seminars, and related activities, all the while learning the latest information they need to contribute more effectively to the firm. Recent seminar topics have ranged from time management, to the implications of the Americans with Disabilities Act, to balancing work and family demands, to international trade theory.

learning organization One that works to facilitate the lifelong learning and personal development of all of its employees, while continually transforming itself to respond to changing demands and needs

Summary of Key Points

Organizations are made up of five basic elements. These elements are job specialization, departmentalization, reporting relationships, authority, and coordination.

One early universal model of organization design was the bureaucratic model. This model was based on the presumed need for rational and logical rules, regulations, and procedures.

The situational view of organization design is based on the assumption that the optimal organization design is a function of situational factors. Four important situational factors are technology, environment, size, and organizational life cycle. Each of these factors plays a role in determining how an organization should be designed.

Many organizations today adopt one of four basic organization designs: functional (U-form), conglomerate (H-form), divisional (M-form), or matrix. Other organizations use a hybrid design derived from two or more of these basic designs.

Three emerging issues in organization design are the team organization, the virtual organization, and the learning organization.

Discussion Questions

Questions for Review

1. What is job specialization? What are its advantages and disadvantages?
2. What is meant by *departmentalization*? Why and how is departmentalization carried out?
3. In what general ways can organizations be shaped? What are the implications of each approach with regard to the distribution of authority within the organization?
4. What are the basic situational factors that affect an organization's design?
5. Describe the basic forms of organization design. Outline the advantages and disadvantages of each.

Questions for Analysis

6. Seeing how specialization can be utilized in manufacturing organizations is easy. How can it be used by other types of organizations, such as hospitals, churches, schools, and restaurants? Should those organizations use specialization? Why or why not?
7. Try to develop a different way to departmentalize your college or university, a local fast-food restaurant, a manufacturing firm, or some other organization. What might be the advantages of your form of organization?
8. Can bureaucratic organizations avoid the problems usually associated with bureaucracies? If so, how? If not, why not? Do you think bureaucracies are still necessary? Why or why not? Is retaining the desirable aspects of bureaucracy and eliminating the undesirable ones possible? Why or why not?
9. The matrix organization design is complex and difficult to implement successfully. Why, then, do so many organizations use it?
10. Identify some problems in organization design that are common to both international and domestic businesses. Identify some problems that are unique to one or the other.

BUILDING EFFECTIVE *diagnostic* SKILLS

Exercise Overview

Diagnostic skills enable a manager to visualize the most appropriate response to a situation. This exercise enables you to develop your diagnostic skills as they relate to issues of centralization and decentralization in an organization.

Exercise Background

Managers often need to change the degree of centralization or decentralization in their organization. Begin this exercise by reflecting on two very different scenarios. In scenario A, assume that you are the top manager in a large organization. The organization has a long and well-known history of being very centralized. For valid reasons beyond the scope of this exercise, assume that you have made a decision to make the firm much more decentralized. For scenario B, assume the exact opposite situation. That is,

you are the top manager of a firm that has always used decentralization but has now decided to become much more centralized.

Exercise Task

With the background information above as context, do the following:

1. Make a list of the major barriers you see to implementing decentralization in scenario A.
2. Make a list of the major barriers you see to implementing centralization in scenario B.
3. Which scenario do you think would be easiest to actually implement? That is, is it likely to be easier to move from centralization to decentralization or from decentralization to centralization? Why?
4. Given a choice of starting your own career in a firm that is either highly centralized or highly decentralized, which do you think you would prefer? Why?

BUILDING EFFECTIVE *conceptual* SKILLS

Exercise Overview

Conceptual skills are a manager's ability to think in the abstract. This exercise encourages you to apply your conceptual skills to the concepts associated with the situational influences on organization design.

Exercise Background

As noted in this chapter, several factors affect the appropriate design of an organization. The key factors discussed in the text are core technology, the organization's environment, its size, and its life cycle. The chapter does not provide details, however, as to how the situational factors working together in different combinations might affect organization design. For example, how might a particular form of technology and certain environmental forces together influence organization design?

The text also notes several basic forms of organization design, such as the functional, con-glomerate, divisional, and matrix approaches. Some implications are also drawn as to how situational factors relate to each design.

Exercise Task

With these ideas in mind, do the following:
1. For each of the four basic forms of organization design, identify a firm that uses it. Assess the technology, environment, size, and life cycle of each firm.
2. Now relate each situational factor to the design used by each firm.
3. Form an opinion as to the actual relation between each factor and the design used by each firm. That is, do you think that each firm's design is directly determined by its environment, or are the relationships you observe coincidental?
4. Can you prioritize the relative importance of the situational factors across the firms? Does the rank-order importance of the factors vary in any systematic way?

BUILDING EFFECTIVE *decision-making* SKILLS

Exercise Overview

Decision-making skills refer to the manager's ability to correctly recognize and define problems and opportunities and to then select an appropriate course of action to solve problems and capitalize on opportunities. The purpose of this exercise is to give you insights into how managers must make decisions within the context of creating an organization design.

Exercise Background

Assume that you have decided to open a casual sportswear business in your local community. Your products will be athletic caps, shirts, shorts, and sweats emblazoned with the logos of your college and local high schools. You are a talented designer and have developed some ideas that will make your products unique and very popu-lar. You also have inherited enough money to get your business up and running, and to cover about one year of living expenses (that is, you do not need to pay yourself a salary).

You intend to buy sportswear in various sizes and styles from other suppliers. Your firm will then use silkscreen processes and add the logos and other decorative touches to the products. Local clothing store owners have seen samples of your products and have indicated a keen interest in selling them. You know, however, that you will still need to service accounts and keep your customers happy.

You are currently trying to determine how many people you need to get your business going and how to most effectively group them into an organization. You realize that you can start out quite small and then expand as sales warrant.

However, you also worry that confusion and inefficiency will result if you are continually adding people and rearranging your organization.

Exercise Task

Step 1: Under each of the following scenarios, decide how to best design your organization. Sketch a basic organization chart to show your thoughts.

Scenario 1—You will sell the products yourself, and you intend to start with a workforce of 5 people.

Scenario 2—You intend to oversee production yourself, and you intend to start with a workforce of 9 people.

Scenario 3—You do not intend to handle any one function yourself but will instead oversee the entire operation, and you intend to start with a workforce of 15 people.

Step 2: Form small groups of four to five people each. Compare your various organization charts, focusing on similarities and differences.

Step 3: Working in the same group, assume that five years have passed and that your business is a big success. You have a large plant for making your products and are shipping them to 15 states. You employ almost 500 people. Create an organization design that you think best fits this organization.

Followup Questions

1. How clear or ambiguous were the decisions about organization design?
2. What are your thoughts about starting out large enough to maintain stability as opposed to starting small and then growing?
3. What basic factors did you consider in choosing a design?

SKILLS *self-assessment* INSTRUMENT

How Is Your Organization Managed?

Introduction: Organizing is an important function of management. The following assessment helps you define how an organization is organized. This information enables you to determine whether this organization's design is consistent with the environmental forces it is facing.

Instructions: For this questionnaire, focus on either an organization for which you are currently working or one for which you have worked in the past. This organization could be a club, sorority, fraternity, or the university you are attending. Please circle the response on the scale indicating the degree to which you agree or disagree with each statement. There is no right or wrong answer. Respond on the following scale to how you see your organization being managed:

Strongly Agree (SA)	Agree (A)	Don't Know (DK)	Disagree (D)	Strongly Disagree (SD)

1. If people believe that they have the right approach to carrying out their job, they can usually go ahead without checking with their superior.   SA   A   DK   D   SD
2. People in this organization don't always have to wait for orders from their superior on important matters.   SA   A   DK   D   SD
3. People in this organization share ideas with their superior.   SA   A   DK   D   SD
4. Different individuals play important roles in making decisions.   SA   A   DK   D   SD

5. People in this organization are likely to express their feelings openly on important matters. SA A DK D SD
6. People in this organization are encouraged to speak their mind on important matters even if it means disagreeing with their superior. SA A DK D SD
7. Talking to other people about the problems someone might have in making decisions is an important part of the decision-making process. SA A DK D SD
8. Developing employees' talents and abilities is a major concern of this organization. SA A DK D SD
9. People are encouraged to make suggestions before decisions are made. SA A DK D SD
10. In this organization most people can have their point of view heard. SA A DK D SD
11. Superiors often seek advice from their subordinates before decisions are made. SA A DK D SD
12. Subordinates play an active role in running this organization. SA A DK D SD
13. For many decisions the rules and regulations are developed as we go along. SA A DK D SD
14. It is not always necessary to go through channels in dealing with important matters. SA A DK D SD
15. The same rules and regulations are not consistently followed by employees. SA A DK D SD
16. There are few rules and regulations for handling any kind of problem that may arise in making most decisions. SA A DK D SD
17. People from different departments are often put together in task forces to solve important problems. SA A DK D SD
18. For special problems we usually set up a temporary task force until we meet our objectives. SA A DK D SD
19. Jobs in this organization are not clearly defined. SA A DK D SD
20. In this organization adapting to changes in the environment is important. SA A DK D SD

Copy your responses to the following table and then total each column at the bottom. Now add across the Total Score row to get an overall score in the lower right corner.

Question	Strongly Agree (SA)	Agree (A)	Don't Know (DK)	Disagree (D)	Strongly Disagree (SD)
1.	5	4	3	2	1
2.	5	4	3	2	1
3.	5	4	3	2	1
4.	5	4	3	2	1
5.	5	4	3	2	1
6.	5	4	3	2	1
7.	5	4	3	2	1

8.	5	4	3	2	1
9.	5	4	3	2	1
10.	5	4	3	2	1
11.	5	4	3	2	1
12.	5	4	3	2	1
13.	5	4	3	2	1
14.	5	4	3	2	1
15.	5	4	3	2	1
16.	5	4	3	2	1
17.	5	4	3	2	1
18.	5	4	3	2	1
19.	5	4	3	2	1
20.	5	4	3	2	1

Total Score: __ + __ + __ + __ + __ = __

For interpretation, see Interpretations of Skills Self-Assessment Instruments.

Source: From *Type of Management System* by Robert T. Keller. Copyright © 1988. Used by permission of the author.

EXPERIENTIAL EXERCISE

Purpose: The purpose of this exercise is to help you better understand how new forms of technology can affect organization structure and design.

Introduction: Amazon.com, Inc., is generally held up as one of the first—and best—examples of a new business created solely to capitalize on the potential of the Internet. Amazon.com started in 1991 as a supplier of hard-to-find books. It rapidly grew and soon began selling all kinds of books, often at significant discounts. Sales grew from $511,000 in 1995 to almost $20 million in 1998. Amazon.com went public in May 1997.

Amazon.com essentially serves as a book distributor. The firm receives orders from customers and fills those orders from one of several different wholesalers with whom it works. As a result, Amazon.com has little warehouse space, low distribution costs, and modest sales costs. In recent times, the firm has started to branch out and now sells CDs, videos, DVDs, and electronic equipment as well.

Instructions:

Step 1: Working alone, draw an organization chart of how you think Amazon.com is likely to be structured.

Step 2: Still working alone, draw an organization chart of how a firm like Amazon.com might look if the Internet did not exist.

Step 3: Now form small groups with three or four classmates and discuss similarities and differences in the two organization charts each of you developed.

Followup Questions

1. Even though Amazon.com has yet to make a profit, it is a darling among investors. How do you explain this?
2. How might the Internet affect the organization structure and design of an existing business?
3. Research Amazon.com and see if you can locate what its organization chart actually looks like.

Managing the Golden Arches Around the World

From Boston to Beijing and beyond, the golden arches of McDonald's look out on highways and streets in nearly every country around the world. The Illinois-based fast-food chain is working toward higher sales and defending its market leadership in partnership with the 5,000 franchise owners who operate 27,000 restaurants in the United States and abroad. Although a variety of hamburgers and fish sandwiches built the chain into a powerhouse, McDonald's has not had a large-scale new-product hit for some years. Therefore, in addition to boosting sales in franchised restaurants, a good portion of McDonald's future growth may have to come from its stakes in nonburger chains, including Donatos Pizza, Chipotle Mexican Grill, and Boston Market.

For years, managers at McDonald's Illinois headquarters tightly controlled prices, product development, and other key functions to ensure chainwide consistency and quality. However, franchisees objected to some corporate decisions. For example, many U.S. franchisees refused to follow the corporation's strategy of cutting prices on Big Macs and breakfast items in 1997. Following that clash between franchisees and corporate management, McDonald's reversed course to decentralize pricing, among other operational details. Now the specially priced Happy Meal is the only discount that headquarters supports with national advertising, leaving other pricing to the discretion of local franchisees.

McDonald's has also divided its global business into five regional zones and has delegated decision-making authority to the managers overseeing each of these regions. This structure put the focus on each region's opportunities and challenges, to encourage faster and more responsive reaction to emerging changes and trends. On the local level, franchisees have the freedom to tailor their restaurants and menus to each local market. Customers at one McDonald's in Burleson, Texas, can play computer games while they sip their soft drinks; at a store in Plano, Texas, they sit on richly stained chairs beneath chandeliers. Halfway around the world, customers who visit McDonald's in Hong Kong can order tea and lounge around reading or bring their children to meet Uncle McDonald (the local counterpart of chain mascot Ronald McDonald).

Although the golden arches are clearly a symbol of American culture, franchisees carefully blend the corporation's efficient operating methods with locally influenced food and decor. They also follow McDonald's time-tested practice of promoting from within to build the ranks of local management. Behind the scenes, the fast-food giant searches out local suppliers for international restaurants rather than relying on long-distance shipments of potatoes and other ingredients from a few central suppliers. These details matter because McDonald's has all but saturated the U.S. market, so management is keenly interested in international expansion.

In more attention to detail, the company is improving its operational expertise by introducing a sophisticated cooking system to speed food preparation and keep menu items hot. Meanwhile, back in the kitchens at McDonald's Illinois headquarters, new-product experts are cooking up new offerings to supplement the chain's traditional menu selections. Did somebody say higher sales?

Case Questions

1. Which organization design is McDonald's using internationally? How is this an appropriate design for the company's international situation?

2. How does McDonald's working relationship with franchisees make it a learning organization?

3. Where in the organizational life cycle would you position McDonald's? How does this affect the company's organization design?

Case References

Hoover's Handbook of American Business 2001 (Austin, TX: Hoover's Business Press, 2001), pp. 938–939; Worth Wren, Jr., "McDonald's Reinvents Itself to Recoup Lost Market Share," *Fort Worth Star-Telegram*, July 27, 2000, pp. C1, C15; and James L. Watson, "China's Big Mac Attack," *Foreign Affairs*, May–June 2000, pp. 120–122.

CHAPTER NOTES

1. "Siemens Climbs Back," *Business Week*, June 5, 2000, pp. 79–82 (quote on p. 82); and *Hoover's Handbook of World Business 2001* (Austin, TX: Hoover's Business Press, 2001), pp. 544–545.
2. M. D. Kilbridge, "Reduced Costs Through Job Enlargement: A Case," *Journal of Business* 33 (1960): 357–362.
3. Frederick Herzberg, *Work and the Nature of Man* (Cleveland: World Press, 1966).
4. J. Richard Hackman and Greg R. Oldham, *Work Redesign* (Reading, MA: Addison-Wesley, 1980).
5. "Some Plants Tear out Long Assembly Lines, Switch to Craft Work," *Wall Street Journal*, October 24, 1994, pp. A1, A4.
6. David D. Van Fleet and Arthur G. Bedeian, "A History of the Span of Management," *Academy of Management Review*, 1977, pp. 356–372.
7. James C. Worthy, "Factors Influencing Employee Morale," *Harvard Business Review*, January 1950, pp. 61–73.
8. Dan R. Dalton, William D. Todor, Michael J. Spendolini, Gordon J. Fielding, and Lyman W. Porter, "Organization Structure and Performance: A Critical Review," *Academy of Management Review*, January 1980, pp. 49–64.
9. See Jerry Useem, "Welcome to the New Company Town," *Fortune*, January 10, 2000, pp. 62–70, for a related discussion.
10. "Remote Control," *HRMagazine*, August 1997, pp. 82–90.
11. James Thompson, *Organizations in Action* (New York: McGraw-Hill, 1967). For a recent discussion, see Bart Victor and Richard S. Blackburn, "Interdependence: An Alternative Conceptualization," *Academy of Management Review*, July 1987, pp. 486–498.
12. Paul R. Lawrence and Jay W. Lorsch, "Differentiation and Integration in Complex Organizations," *Administrative Science Quarterly*, March 1967, pp. 1–47.
13. Max Weber, *Theory of Social and Economic Organizations*, trans. T. Parsons (New York: Free Press, 1947).
14. Joan Woodward, *Industrial Organization: Theory and Practice* (London: Oxford University Press, 1965).
15. Tom Burns and G. M. Stalker, *The Management of Innovation* (London: Tavistock, 1961).
16. Paul R. Lawrence and Jay W. Lorsch, *Organization and Environment* (Homewood, IL: Irwin, 1967).
17. Edward E. Lawler III, "Rethinking Organization Size," *Organizational Dynamics*, Autumn 1997, pp. 24–33. See also Tom Brown, "How Big Is Too Big?" *Across the Board*, July–August 1999, pp. 14–20.
18. Derek S. Pugh and David J. Hickson, *Organization Structure in Its Context: The Aston Program I* (Lexington, MA: D. C. Heath, 1976).
19. Robert H. Miles and Associates, *The Organizational Life Cycle* (San Francisco: Jossey-Bass, 1980). See also "Is Your Company Too Big?" *Business Week*, March 27, 1989, pp. 84–94.
20. Oliver E. Williamson, *Markets and Hierarchies* (New York: Free Press, 1975).
21. Ibid.
22. Michael E. Porter, "From Competitive Advantage to Corporate Strategy," *Harvard Business Review*, May/June 1987, pp. 43–59.
23. Williamson.
24. Jay B. Barney and William G. Ouchi, eds., *Organizational Economics* (San Francisco: Jossey-Bass, 1986); and Robert E. Hoskisson, "Multidivisional Structure and Performance: The Contingency of Diversification Strategy," *Academy of Management Journal*, December 1987, pp. 625–644. See also Bruce Lamont, Robert Williams, and James Hoffman, "Performance During 'M-Form' Reorganization and Recovery Time: The Effects of Prior Strategy and Implementation Speed," *Academy of Management Journal* 37, no. 1 (1994): 153–166.
25. Stanley M. Davis and Paul R. Lawrence, *Matrix* (Reading, MA: Addison-Wesley, 1977).
26. "Martha, Inc.," *Business Week*, January 17, 2000, pp. 63–72.
27. Raymond E. Miles, Charles C. Snow, John A. Mathews, Grant Miles, and Henry J. Coleman, Jr., "Organizing in the Knowledge Age: Anticipating the Cellular Form," *Academy of Management Executive*, November 1997, pp. 7–24.
28. "The Horizontal Corporation," *Business Week*, December 20, 1993, pp. 76–81; and Shawn Tully, "The Modular Corporation," *Fortune*, February 8, 1993, pp. 106–114.
29. "Management by Web," *Business Week*, August 28, 2000, pp. 84–96.
30. Peter Senge, *The Fifth Discipline* (New York: Free Press, 1993). See also David Lei, John W. Slocum, and Robert A. Pitts, "Designing Organizations for Competitive Advantage: The Power of Unlearning and Learning," *Organizational Dynamics*, Winter 1999, pp. 24–35.

7 Organization Change and Innovation

Nike, of course, is the world's pre-eminent athletic shoe company. In 1996 Nike was earning about $4 billion a year from its footwear business and another $2 billion from sports apparel and equipment. That same year, the firm's founder and CEO, Philip Knight, stunned investors and competitors alike when he announced a goal of doubling the firm's annual revenues to a staggering $12 billion by the year 2001. But Nike has recently encountered a series of setbacks that have compelled Knight to embark on a major overhaul of the firm.

Things started coming apart for Nike in the late 1990s. For one thing, the retirement of Michael Jordan, Nike icon and arguably the world's best-known professional athlete, deprived the firm of its best spokesperson. For another, there was an unexpected major shift among teen-agers away from athletic shoes to hiking boots and casual leather shoes. Third, a series of reports involving substandard wages and working conditions at foreign Nike production facilities resulted in a public relations nightmare and caused some consumers to avoid the company's products. And, finally, Nike's brash, in-your-face reputation was beginning to get tiresome to many consumers. By 1998 Knight had been forced to back off from his bold forecasts of the recent past, and Nike was posting lower-than-expected earnings reports virtually every quarter.

This dramatic and unexpected series of events caused Knight to recognize that some big changes were necessary. And it didn't really take him too long to figure out what had happened—the brash upstart had turned into the very Establish-ment that Nike had long deplored. In other words, as it had grown, the firm had also been transformed from a nimble, free-form organization into a traditional bureaucratic behemoth. In addition, market conditions had also changed so completely that Nike's traditional way of doing business would simply no longer work.

Knight was quick to take up the challenge and has set about trying to restore the firm's lost luster. For one thing, he has totally revamped Nike's top management team, and today 9 of Nike's 41 vice presidents have been with the firm less than two years. He has also created a new sense of urgency about costs—in the old days, revenues grew so fast that

"I'm sure Nike's looking for fresh perspective, and newcomers bring a fresh perspective."

—Paul Heffernan, executive at Nike rival New Balance

After studying this chapter, you should be able to

- Describe the nature of organization change, including forces for change and planned versus reactive change.

- Discuss the steps in organization change, how to manage resistance to change, and major areas of organization change.

- Discuss the assumptions, techniques, and effectiveness of organization development.

- Describe the innovation process, forms of innovation, the failure to innovate, and how organizations can promote innovation.

costs almost didn't matter, but today they are continuously scrutinized. Knight also has Nike focusing on new, emerging, and growing markets, such as women's sports, extreme sports, and international markets. And he is paying much closer attention to foreign factories and production facilities.

Beyond these specific areas, however, Knight is also working to remake the very fabric of Nike. He wants to transform the company into one that incorporates the best of both worlds—an enterprise with the entrepreneurial spark and vision that fueled Nike in its early years combined with a more reasoned and structured business model. Toward this end, he has taken a more hands-on approach to business, spending more time at the company, being an active participant in key meetings, and voicing his opinion more strongly than he has in the past.

Knight has even acknowledged that Nike may have overdosed with its familiar "swoosh" logo by plastering it so prominently across all its various products and on so many different sporting venues. As a result, the swoosh emblem is being shrunk on some products. And other products are being launched with totally new logos. In a lot of ways, then, it seems that Nike is taking its own message to heart—the firm needed to "just do it," so it is![1]

Philip Knight has had to grapple with something all managers must eventually confront: the need for change. He first perceived that Nike needed to make certain changes because of its growth and because of changes in the marketplace. He then had to figure out how to actually make those changes. And now that most of them are completed, it will be some time before he and the rest of his managers know whether or not the changes they have made are having the intended effects.

Understanding when and how to implement change is a vital part of management. This chapter describes how organizations manage change. We first examine the nature of organization change and identify the basic issues of managing change. We then identify and describe major areas of change, including reengineering, a major type of change undertaken by many firms recently. We then examine organization development and conclude by discussing a related area: organizational innovation.

The Nature of Organization Change

organization change Any substantive modification to some part of the organization

Organization change is any substantive modification to some part of the organization.[2] Thus change can involve virtually any aspect of an organization: work schedules, bases for departmentalization, span of management, machinery, organization design, people themselves, and so on. It is important to keep in mind that any change in an organization may have effects extending beyond the actual area where the change is implemented. For example, when Northrup Grumman recently installed a new automated production system at one of its plants, employees were trained to operate new equipment, the compensation system was adjusted to reflect new skill levels, the span of management of supervisors was altered, and several related jobs were redesigned. Selection criteria for new employees were also changed, and a new quality control system was installed. In addition, it is quite common for multiple organization change activities to be going on simultaneously.[3]

Forces for Change

Why do organizations find change necessary? The basic reason is that something relevant to the organization either has changed or is going to change. The organization consequently has little choice but to change as well. Indeed, a primary reason for the problems that organizations often face is failure to anticipate or respond properly to changing circumstances. Forces for change may be external or internal to the organization.[4]

External Forces   External forces for change derive from the organization's general and task environments. For example, two energy crises, an aggressive Japanese automobile industry, floating currency exchange rates, and floating international interest rates—all manifestations of the international dimension of the general environment—profoundly influenced U.S. automobile companies. New rules of production and competition forced them to dramatically alter the way they do business. In the political area, new laws, court decisions, and regulations affect organizations. The technological dimension may yield new production techniques that the organization needs to explore. The economic dimension is affected by inflation, the cost of living, and money supplies. The sociocultural dimension, reflecting societal values, determines what kinds of products or services will be accepted in the market.

Because of its proximity to the organization, the task environment is an even more powerful force for change. Competitors influence an organization through their price structures and product lines. When Compaq lowers the prices it charges for computers, Dell and Gateway have little choice but to follow suit. Because customers determine what products can be sold at what prices, organizations must be concerned with consumer tastes and preferences. Suppliers affect organizations by raising or lowering prices or changing product lines. Regulators can have dramatic effects on an organization. For example, if OSHA rules that a particular production process is dangerous to workers, it can force a firm to close a plant until it meets higher safety standards. Unions can force change when they negotiate for higher wages or strike.[5]

Internal Forces A variety of forces inside the organization also may cause change. If top management revises the organization's strategy, organization change is likely to result. A decision by an electronics company to enter the home computer market or a decision to increase a ten-year product sales goal by 3 percent would occasion many organization changes. Other internal forces for change may be reflections of external forces. As sociocultural values shift, for example, workers' attitudes toward their jobs may also shift—and workers may demand a change in working hours or working conditions. In such a case, even though the force is rooted in the external environment, the organization must respond directly to the internal pressure it generates.

A variety of forces, some internal and some external, can be important forces for change. Energy trading companies, for example, have become very successful by looking for opportunities for change. In simple terms, these firms buy and sell gas, electricity, and other forms of energy and earn profits on the margin between what they pay and what they earn. These energy traders in Europe play a major role in determining Europe's energy production rates by influencing the prices that buyers will pay.

Planned Versus Reactive Change

Some change is planned well in advance; other change comes about as a reaction to unexpected events. **Planned change** is change that is designed and implemented in an orderly and timely fashion in anticipation of future events. **Reactive change** is a piecemeal response to events as they occur. Because reactive change may be hurried, the potential for poorly conceived and executed change is increased. Planned change is almost always preferable to reactive change.

Georgia-Pacific, a large forest products business, is an excellent example of a firm that went through a planned and well-managed change process. When A. D. Correll became CEO, he quickly became alarmed at the firm's high accident rate—9 serious injuries per 100 employees each year, and 26 deaths during the most recent five-year period. Although the forest products business is inherently

planned change Change that is designed and implemented in an orderly and timely fashion in anticipation of future events

reactive change A piecemeal response to circumstances as they develop

dangerous, Correll believed that the accident rate was far too high and set out on a major change effort to improve things. He and other top managers developed a multistage change program intended to educate workers about safety, improve safety equipment in the plant, and eliminate a long-standing part of the firm's culture that made injuries almost a badge of courage. And today, Georgia-Pacific has the best safety record in the industry, with relatively few injuries.[6]

On the other hand, a few years ago, Caterpillar was caught flatfooted by a worldwide recession in the construction industry, suffered enormous losses, and took several years to recover. Had managers at Caterpillar anticipated the need for change earlier, they might have been able to respond more quickly. Similarly, Kodak recently announced plans to cut 10,000 jobs, a reaction to sluggish sales and profits. Again, better anticipation might have forestalled these job cuts. The importance of approaching change from a planned perspective is reinforced by the frequency of organization change. Most companies or divisions of large companies implement some form of moderate change at least every year and one or more major changes every four to five years.[7] Managers who sit back and respond only when they have to are likely to spend a lot of time hastily changing and rechanging things. A more effective approach is to anticipate forces urging change and plan ahead to deal with them.[8]

Managing Change in Organizations

Organization change is a complex phenomenon. A manager cannot simply wave a wand and implement a planned change like magic. Instead, any change must be systematic and logical to have a realistic opportunity to succeed. To carry this off, the manager needs to understand the steps of effective change and how to counter with employee resistance to change.[9]

Steps in the Change Process

Over the years, researchers have developed a number of models or frameworks outlining steps for change. The Lewin model was one of the first, although a more comprehensive approach is usually more useful.

The Lewin Model Kurt Lewin, a noted organizational theorist, suggested that every change requires three steps.[10] The first step is *unfreezing*—individuals who will be affected by the impending change must be led to recognize why the change is necessary. Next, the *change itself* is implemented. Finally, *refreezing* involves reinforcing and supporting the change so that it becomes a part of the system. For example, one of the changes Caterpillar faced in response to the recession noted earlier involved a massive workforce reduction. The first step (unfreezing) was convincing the United Auto Workers to support the reduction because of its importance to long-term effectiveness. After this unfreezing was accomplished, 30,000 jobs were eliminated (implementation). Then Caterpillar worked to improve its damaged relationship with its workers (refreezing) by guaranteeing future pay hikes and promising no more cutbacks. As interesting as Lewin's model is, it unfortunately lacks operational specificity. Thus a more comprehensive perspective is often needed.

A Comprehensive Approach to Change The comprehensive approach to change takes a systems view and delineates a series of specific steps that often lead to successful change. This expanded model is illustrated in Figure 7.1. The first step is recognizing the need for change. Reactive change might be triggered by employee complaints, declines in productivity or turnover, court injunctions, sales slumps, or labor strikes. Recognition may simply be managers' awareness that change in a certain area is inevitable. For example, managers may be aware of the general frequency of organizational change undertaken by most organizations and recognize that their organization should probably follow the same pattern. The immediate stimulus might be the result of a forecast indicating new market potential, the accumulation of cash surplus for possible investment, or an opportunity to achieve and capitalize on a major technological breakthrough. Managers might also initiate change today because indicators suggest that it will be necessary in the near future.

Managers must next establish goals for the change. To increase market share, to enter new markets, to restore employee morale, to settle a strike, and to identify investment opportunities all might be goals for change. Third, managers must diagnose what brought on the need for change. Turnover, for example, might be caused by low pay, poor working conditions, poor supervisors, or employee dissatisfaction. Thus, although turnover may be the immediate stimulus for change, managers must understand its causes to make the right changes.

The next step is to select a change technique that will accomplish the intended goals. If turnover is caused by low pay, a new reward system may be needed. If the cause is poor supervision, interpersonal skills training may be called for. (Various change techniques are summarized later in this chapter.) After the appropriate technique has been chosen, its implementation must be planned. Issues to consider include the costs of the change, its effects on other areas of the organization, and the degree of employee participation appropriate for the situation. If the change is implemented as planned, the results should then be evaluated. If the change was intended to reduce turnover, managers must check turnover after the change has been in effect for a while. If turnover is still too high, other changes may be necessary.

Understanding Resistance to Change

Another element in the effective management of change is understanding the resistance that often accompanies change. Managers need to know why people resist change and what can be done about their resistance. When Westinghouse first provided all of its managers with personal computers, most people responded

Figure 7.1

Steps in the Change Process

Managers must understand how and why to implement change. A manager who, when implementing change, follows a logical and orderly sequence such as the one shown here is more likely to succeed than a manager whose change process is haphazard and poorly conceived.

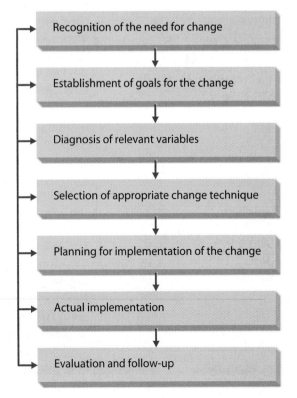

"As a newcomer to computer technology..."

© Nick Hobart

People in organizations resist change for a variety of different reasons, including uncertainty, threatened self-interests, different perceptions, and feelings of loss. And they occasionally may not even recognize that they are resisting a change. In this situation, for example, the manager is acknowledging his own lack of familiarity with computer technology but is not really making any adjustment at all. Instead, he is continuing to dictate to his assistant, who is actually using the new technology.

favorably. One manager, however, resisted the change to the point where he began leaving work every day at noon. It was some time before he began staying in the office all day again. This same phenomenon is illustrated in the cartoon. Such resistance is common for a variety of reasons.

Uncertainty Perhaps the biggest cause of employee resistance to change is uncertainty. In the face of impending change, employees may become anxious and nervous. They may worry about their ability to meet new job demands, they may think that their job security is threatened, or they may simply dislike ambiguity. Nabisco was once the target of an extended and confusing takeover battle, and during the entire time, employees were nervous about the impending change. The *Wall Street Journal* described them this way: "Many are angry at their leaders and fearful for their jobs. They are swapping rumors and spinning scenarios for the ultimate outcome of the battle for the tobacco and food giant. Headquarters staffers in Atlanta know so little about what's happening in New York that some call their office 'the mushroom complex,' where they are kept in the dark."[11]

Threatened Self-Interests Many impending changes threaten the self-interests of some managers within the organization. A change might potentially diminish their power or influence within the company, so they fight it. Managers at Sears, Roebuck and Company recently developed a plan calling for a new type of store. The new stores would be somewhat smaller than typical Sears stores and would not be located in large shopping malls. Instead, they would be located in smaller strip centers. They would carry clothes and other "soft goods," but not hardware, appliances, furniture, or automotive products. When executives in charge of the excluded product lines heard about the plan, they raised such strong objections that the plan was put on hold.

Different Perceptions A third reason why people resist change is different perceptions. A manager may make a decision and recommend a plan for change on the basis of her own assessment of a situation. Others in the organization may resist the change because they do not agree with the manager's assessment or may perceive the situation differently.[12] Executives at 7-Eleven are currently battling this problem as they attempt to enact a major organizational change. The corporation wants to take its convenience stores a bit "upscale" and begin selling fancy fresh foods to go, the newest hardcover novels, and some gourmet products. But many franchisees are balking because they see this move as taking the firm away from its core blue-collar customers.[13]

Feelings of Loss Many changes involve altering work arrangements in ways that disrupt existing social networks. Because social relationships are important, most people resist any change that might adversely affect those relationships. Other intangibles threatened by change include power, status, security, familiarity with existing procedures, and self-confidence.

Overcoming Resistance to Change

Of course, a manager should not give up in the face of resistance to change. Although there are no sure-fire cures, there are several techniques that at least have the potential to overcome resistance.[14]

Participation   Participation is often the most effective technique for overcoming resistance to change. Employees who participate in planning and implementing a change are better able to understand the reasons for the change. Uncertainty is reduced, and self-interests and social relationships are less threatened. Having had an opportunity to express their ideas and assume the perspectives of others, employees are more likely to accept the change gracefully. A classic study of participation monitored the introduction of a change in production methods among four groups in a Virginia pajama factory.[15] The two groups that were allowed to fully participate in planning and implementing the change improved their productivity and satisfaction significantly, relative to the two groups that did not participate. 3M Company recently attributed $10 million in cost savings to employee participation in several organization change activities.[16]

Education and Communication   Educating employees about the need for and expected results of an impending change should reduce their resistance. If open communication is established and maintained during the change process, uncertainty can be minimized. Caterpillar used these methods during many of its cutbacks to reduce resistance. First, it educated UAW representatives about the need for and potential value of the planned changes. Then management told all employees what was happening, when it would happen, and how it would affect them individually.

Facilitation   Several facilitation procedures are also advisable. For instance, making only necessary changes, announcing those changes well in advance, and allowing time for people to adjust to new ways of doing things can help reduce resistance to change.[17] One manager at a Prudential regional office spent several months systematically planning a change in work procedures and job design. He then became too hurried, coming in over the weekend with a work crew and rearranging the office layout. When employees walked in on Monday morning, they were hostile, anxious, and resentful. What had been a promising change became a disaster, and the manager had to scrap the entire plan.

Force-Field Analysis   Although force-field analysis may sound like something out of a Star Trek movie, it can help overcome resistance to change. In almost any change situation, forces are acting for and against the change. To facilitate the change, managers start by listing each set of forces and then try to tip the balance so that the forces facilitating the change outweigh those hindering the change.

Figure 7.2

Force-Field Analysis for Plant Closing at General Motors

A force-field analysis can help a manager facilitate change. A manager able to identify forces acting both for and against a change can see where to focus efforts to remove barriers to change (such as offering training and relocation to displaced workers). Removing the forces against the change can at least partially overcome resistance.

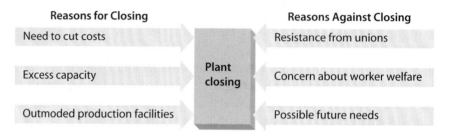

It is especially important to try to remove or at least minimize some of the forces acting against the change. Suppose, for example, that General Motors is considering a plant closing as part of a change. As shown in Figure 7.2, three factors are reinforcing the change: GM needs to cut costs, it has excess capacity, and the plant has outmoded production facilities. At the same time, there is resistance from the UAW, concern for workers being put out of their jobs, and a feeling that the plant might be needed again in the future. GM might start convincing the UAW that the closing is necessary by presenting profit and loss figures. It could then offer relocation and retraining to displaced workers. And it might shut down the plant and put it in "mothballs" so that it could be renovated later. The three major factors hindering the change are thus eliminated or reduced in importance.

Areas of Organization Change

We noted earlier that change can involve virtually any part of an organization. In general, however, most change interventions involve organization structure and design, technology and operations, or people.

Changing Structure and Design   Organization change might be focused on any of the basic components of organization structure or on the organization's overall design. Thus the organization might change the way it designs its jobs or its bases of departmentalization. Likewise, it might change reporting relationships or the distribution of authority. For example, we noted in Chapter 6 the trend toward flatter organizations. Coordination mechanisms and line-and-staff configurations are also subject to change. On a larger scale, the organization might change its overall design. For example, a growing business could decide to drop its functional design and adopt a divisional design. Or it might transform itself into a matrix. Finally, the organization might change any part of its human resource management system, such as its selection criteria, its performance appraisal methods, or its compensation package.[18] Toyota has been undergoing a significant series of changes in its organization structure and design intended to make it a flatter and more decentralized enterprise and thus more responsive to its external environment.[19]

Changing Technology and Operations   Technology is the conversion process used by an organization to transform inputs into outputs. Because of the rapid rate of all technological innovation, technological changes are becoming increasingly important to many organizations. One important area of change today revolves around information technology. The adoption and institutionalization of information technology innovations is almost constant in most firms today. Sun Microsystems, for example, has adopted a very short-range planning cycle in order to be best prepared for environmental changes.[20] Another important form of technological change involves equipment. To keep pace with competitors, firms periodically find that replacing existing machinery and equipment with newer models is necessary. And changes in work processes or work activities may be necessary if new equipment is introduced or new products are manufactured. Organizational control systems may also be targets of change.

Changing People   A third area of organization change has to do with human resources. For example, an organization might decide to change the skill level of its workforce. This change might be prompted by changes in technology or by a general desire to upgrade the quality of the workforce. Thus training programs and new selection criteria might be needed. The organization might also decide to improve its workers' performance levels. In this instance, a new incentive system or

Change can take place in a variety of areas in an organization. Technological change is an especially important area of change today. United Parcel Service, for example, is always on the alert for new technology that can improve its efficiency and effectiveness. One of its newest innovations is the wrist-mounted bar-code reader. Users can simply point their hand in the direction of a box, package, or other parcel and the bar-code reader registers the vital information needed to keep the shipment on-track. And users no longer have to stop and look for their reader, since it's strapped to their wrist!

performance-based training might be in order. Reader's Digest has been attempting to implement significant changes in its workforce. For example, the firm has eliminated 17 percent of its employees, reduced retirement benefits, and taken away many of the perks they once enjoyed. Part of the reason for the changes was to instill in the remaining employees a sense of urgency and the need to adopt a new perspective on how they did their jobs.[21] Perceptions and expectations are also a common focus of organization change.

Reengineering in Organizations

Many organizations today have also gone through a massive and comprehensive change program involving all aspects of organization design, technology, and people. Although various terms are used, the term currently in vogue for these changes is *reengineering*. Specifically, **reengineering** is the radical redesign of all aspects of a business to achieve major gains in cost, service, or time.[22] Corning, for example, has undergone a major reengineering over the last few years. Whereas the 150-year-old business once manufactured cookware and other durable consumer goods, it has transformed itself into a high-tech powerhouse making such products as the ultrathin screens used in items such as Palm Pilots and laptop computers.[23]

reengineering The radical redesign of all aspects of a business to achieve major gains in cost, service, or time

Figure 7.3

The Reengineering Process
Reengineering is a major redesign of all areas of an organization. To be successful, reengineering requires a systematic and comprehensive assessment of the entire organization. Goals, top management support, and a sense of urgency help the organization re-create itself and blend both top-down and bottom-up perspectives.

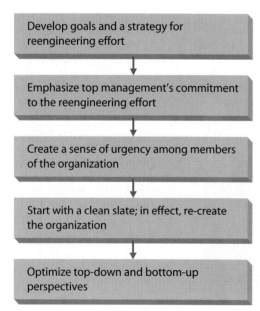

- Develop goals and a strategy for reengineering effort
- Emphasize top management's commitment to the reengineering effort
- Create a sense of urgency among members of the organization
- Start with a clean slate; in effect, re-create the organization
- Optimize top-down and bottom-up perspectives

The Need for Reengineering Why are so many organizations finding it necessary to reengineer themselves? We noted earlier that all systems, including organizations, are subject to entropy—a normal process leading to system decline. An organization is behaving most typically when it maintains the status quo, doesn't change in sync with its environment, and starts consuming its own resources to survive. In a sense, that is what happened to Kmart. In the early and mid-1970s Kmart was in such a high-flying growth mode that it passed first J. C. Penney and then Sears to become the world's largest retailer. But then the firm's managers grew complacent and assumed that the discount retailer's prosperity would continue and that they need not worry about environmental shifts, the growth of Wal-Mart, and so forth—and entropy set in. The key is to recognize the beginning of the decline and to immediately move toward reengineering. Major problems occur when managers either don't recognize the onset of entropy until it is well advanced or else are complacent in taking steps to correct it.

Approaches to Reengineering Figure 7.3 shows general steps in reengineering. The first step is setting goals and developing a strategy for reengineering. The organization must know in advance what reengineering is supposed to accomplish and how those accomplishments will be achieved. Next, top managers must begin and direct the reengineering effort. If a CEO simply announces that reengineering is to occur but does nothing else, the program is unlikely to be successful. But if the CEO is constantly involved in the process, underscoring its importance and taking the lead, reengineering stands a much better chance of success.

Most experts also agree that successful reengineering is usually accompanied by a sense of urgency. People in the organization must see the clear and present need for the changes being implemented and appreciate their importance. In addition, most successful reengineering efforts start with a new, clean slate. That is, rather than assuming that the existing organization is a starting point and then trying to modify it, reengineering usually starts by asking questions about how customers are best served and competitors best neutralized. New approaches and systems are then created and imposed in place of existing ones.

Finally, reengineering requires a careful blend of top-down and bottom-up involvement. On the one hand, strong leadership is necessary, but too much involvement by top management can make the changes seem autocratic. Similarly, employee participation is also important, but too little involvement by leaders can undermine the program's importance and create a sense that top managers don't care. Thus care must be taken to carefully balance these two countervailing forces.

Organization Development

We note in several places the importance of people and change. A special area of interest that focuses almost exclusively on people is organization development (OD).

OD Assumptions

Organization development is concerned with changing attitudes, perceptions, behaviors, and expectations. More precisely, **organization development** is a planned effort that is organizationwide and managed from the top, intended to increase organization effectiveness and health through planned interventions in the organization's "process," using behavioral science knowledge. The theory and practice of OD are based on several very important assumptions. The first is that employees have a desire to grow and develop. Another is that employees have a strong need to be accepted by others within the organization. Still another critical assumption of OD is that the total organization and the way it is designed will influence the way individuals and groups within the organization behave. Thus some form of collaboration between managers and their employees is necessary to (1) take advantage of the skills and abilities of the employees and (2) eliminate aspects of the organization that retard employee growth, development, and group acceptance. Because of the intensely personal nature of many OD activities, many large organizations rely on one or more OD consultants (either full-time employees assigned to this function or outside experts hired specifically for OD purposes) to implement and manage their OD program.[24]

organization development An effort that is planned, organization-wide, and managed from the top; it is intended to increase organization effectiveness and health through planned interventions in the organization's process, using behavioral science knowledge

OD Techniques

Several kinds of interventions or activities are generally considered to be part of organization development.[25] Some OD programs may use only one or a few of these; other programs use several of them at once.

Diagnostic Activities   Just as a physician examines patients to diagnose their current condition, an OD diagnosis analyzes the current condition of an organization. To carry out this diagnosis, managers use questionnaires, opinion or attitude surveys, interviews, archival data, and meetings to assess various characteristics of the organization. The results of this diagnosis may generate profiles of the organization's activities, which can then be used to identify problem areas in need of correction.

Team Building   Team-building activities are intended to enhance the effectiveness and satisfaction of individuals who work in groups or teams and to promote overall group effectiveness. Given the widespread use of teams today, these activities have taken on increased importance. An OD consultant might interview team members to determine how they feel about the group; then an off-site meeting could be held to discuss the issues that surfaced and to iron out any problem areas or member concerns. Caterpillar used team building as one method for changing the working relationships between workers and supervisors from confrontational to cooperative. An interesting new approach to team building involves having executive teams participate in group cooking classes to teach them the importance of interdependence and coordination.[26]

Survey Feedback   In survey feedback, each employee responds to a questionnaire intended to measure perceptions and attitudes (for example, satisfaction and supervisory style). Everyone involved, including the supervisor, receives the results of the survey. The aim of this approach is usually to change the behavior of supervisors by showing them how their subordinates view them. After the feedback has been provided, workshops may be conducted to evaluate results and suggest constructive changes.

Third-Party Peacemaking   Another approach to OD is through third-party peacemaking, which is most often used when substantial conflict exists within the organization. Third-party peacemaking can be appropriate on the individual, group, or organization level. The third party, usually an OD consultant, uses a variety of mediation or negotiation techniques to resolve any problems or conflicts between individuals or groups.

Technostructural Activities   Technostructural activities are concerned with the design of the organization, the technology of the organization, and the interrelationship of design and technology with people on the job. A structural change such as an increase in decentralization, a job design change such as an increase in the use of automation, and a technological change involving a modification in work flow all qualify as technostructural OD activities if their objective is to improve group and interpersonal relationships within the organization.

Process Consultation In process consultation, an OD consultant observes groups in the organization to develop an understanding of their communication patterns, decision-making and leadership processes, and methods of cooperation and conflict resolution. The consultant then provides feedback to the involved parties about the processes he or she has observed. The goal of this form of intervention is to improve the observed processes. A leader who is presented with feedback outlining deficiencies in his or her leadership style, for example, might be expected to change to overcome them.

Coaching and Counseling Coaching and counseling provide nonevaluative feedback to individuals. The purpose is to help people develop a better sense of how others see them and learn behaviors that will assist others in achieving their work-related goals. The focus is not on how the individual is performing today; instead, it is on how the person can perform better in the future.

Planning and Goal Setting More pragmatically oriented than many other interventions are activities designed to help managers improve their planning and goal setting. Emphasis still falls on the individual, however, because the intent is to help individuals and groups integrate themselves into the overall planning process. The OD consultant might use the same approach as in process consultation, but the focus is more technically oriented on the mechanics of planning and goal setting.

The Effectiveness of OD

Given the diversity of activities encompassed by OD, it is not surprising that managers report mixed results from various OD interventions. Organizations that actively practice some form of OD include American Airlines, Texas Instruments, Procter & Gamble, Polaroid, and B. F. Goodrich. Goodrich, for example, has trained 60 persons in OD processes and techniques. These trained experts have subsequently become internal OD consultants to assist other managers in applying the techniques. Many other managers, in contrast, report that they have tried OD but discarded it.

OD will probably remain an important part of management theory and practice. Of course, there are no sure things when dealing with social systems such as organizations, and the effectiveness of many OD techniques is difficult to evaluate. Because all organizations are open systems interacting with their environments, an improvement in an organization after an OD intervention may be attributable to the intervention, but it may also be attributable to changes in economic conditions, luck, or other factors.

Organizational Innovation

innovation The managed effort of an organization to develop new products or services or new uses for existing products or services

A final element of organization change that we address is innovation. **Innovation** is the managed effort of an organization to develop new products or services or new uses for existing products or services. Innovation is clearly important, because without new products or services, any organization will fall behind its competition.[27]

The Innovation Process

The organizational innovation process consists of developing, applying, launching, growing, and managing the maturity and decline of creative ideas. This process is depicted in Figure 7.4.

Innovation Development   Innovation development involves the evaluation, modification, and improvement of creative ideas. Innovation development can transform a product or service with only modest potential into a product or service with significant potential. Parker Brothers, for example, decided during innovation development not to market an indoor volleyball game but instead to sell separately the appealing little foam ball designed for the game. The firm will never know how well the volleyball game would have sold, but the Nerf ball and numerous related products generated millions of dollars in revenues for Parker Brothers.

Innovation Application   Innovation application is the stage in which an organization takes a developed idea and uses it in the design, manufacturing, or delivery of new products, services, or processes. At this point, the innovation emerges from the laboratory and is transformed into tangible goods or services. One example of innovation application is the use of radar-based focusing systems in Polaroid's in-

Figure 7.4

The Innovation Process

Organizations actively seek to manage the innovation process. These steps illustrate the general life cycle that characterizes most innovations. Of course, as with creativity, the innovation process will suffer if it is approached too mechanically and rigidly.

stant cameras. The idea of using radio waves to discover the location, speed, and direction of moving objects was first applied extensively by Allied forces during World War II. As radar technology developed during the following years, the electrical components needed became smaller and more streamlined. Researchers at Polaroid applied this well-developed technology in a new way.[28]

Application Launch   Application launch is the stage in which an organization introduces new products or services to the marketplace. The important question is not "Does the innovation work?" but "Will customers want to purchase the innovative product and service?" History is full of creative ideas that did not generate enough interest among customers to be successful. Some notable innovation failures include Sony's seat warmer, the Edsel automobile, and Polaroid's SX-70 instant camera (which cost $3 billion to develop but never sold more than 100,000 units in a year).[29] Thus, despite development and application, new products and services can still possibly fail at the launch phase.

Application Growth   Once an innovation has been successfully launched, it then enters the stage of application growth. This is a period of high economic performance for an organization, because demand for the product or service is often greater than supply. Organizations that fail to anticipate this stage may unintentionally limit their growth, as Gillette did by not anticipating demand for its Mach III razorblades. At the same time, overestimating demand for a new product can be just as detrimental to performance. Unsold products can sit in warehouses for years.

Innovation Maturity   After a period of growing demand, an innovative product or service often enters a period of maturity. Innovation maturity is the stage in which most organizations in an industry have access to an innovation and are applying it in approximately the same way. The technological application of an innovation during this stage of the innovation process can be very sophisticated. Because most firms have access to the innovation, however, as a result of either developing the innovation on their own or copying the innovation of others, it does not provide competitive advantage to any one of them. The time that elapses between innovation development and innovation maturity varies notably, depending on the particular product or service. Whenever an innovation involves the use of complex skills (such as a complicated manufacturing process or highly sophisticated teamwork), moving from the growth phase to the maturity phase will take longer. In addition, if the skills needed to implement these innovations are rare and difficult to imitate, then strategic imitation may be delayed, and the organization may enjoy a period of sustained competitive advantage.

Innovation Decline   Every successful innovation bears its own seeds of decline. Because an organization does not gain a competitive advantage from an innovation at maturity, it must encourage its creative scientists, engineers, and managers to begin looking for new innovations. This continued search for competitive advantage usually leads new products and services to move from the creative process through innovation maturity, and finally to innovation decline. Innovation decline is the stage during which demand for an innovation decreases and substitute innovations are developed and applied.

Forms of Innovation

Each creative idea an organization develops poses a different challenge for the innovation process. Innovations can be radical or incremental, technical or managerial, and product or process. *Management InfoTech* summarizes how Lucent is pursuing multiple forms of innovation simultaneously.

radical innovation A new product, service, or technology that completely replaces an existing one

incremental innovation A new product, service, or technology that modifies an existing one

Radical Versus Incremental Innovations **Radical innovations** are new products or technologies developed by an organization that completely replace the existing products or technologies in an industry.[30] **Incremental innovations** are new products or processes that modify existing ones. Firms that implement radical innovations fundamentally shift the nature of competition and the interaction of

---

MANAGEMENT INFOTECH

LUCENT'S BELL LABS RESEARCHERS LOOK AHEAD

Bell Labs is Lucent's secret weapon for innovation. With annual sales topping $40 billion, Lucent—spun off from AT&T in 1996—is the world's leading manufacturer of sophisticated telecommunications equipment, such as fiber-optic network switches. With the spin-off, Lucent gained Bell Labs, the world-renowned research center responsible for such radical innovations as the transistor (which replaced vacuum tubes in electronic equipment) and cellular telephone technology. Now, Bell Labs, which has nurtured 11 Nobel Prize winners and receives four patent approvals every business day, is continuing its quest under the Lucent banner for innovations of the future.

The largest group of researchers is investigating near-term product and process innovations, designed to be marketable within five years. This is a break from the past, when Bell Labs researchers pursued promising lines of scientific inquiry without having to consider the potential commercial implications. Researchers at today's Bell Labs are much more geared toward studies with real-world applications. From such research has come PathStar, a Lucent product for allowing voice signals to be transmitted along Internet networks, and the Lambda-Router, a large-scale all-optical switching device.

Despite the emphasis on products and processes that have more immediate commercial application, about 20 percent of Bell Labs researchers doing basic research are looking for breakthroughs that might lead to radical innovations in the distant future. In addition, Bell Labs maintains a venture capital unit to fund internal research into a variety of diverse projects, such as fingerprint identification technology. Even as product-oriented incremental research and development continues in other parts of Lucent, Bell Labs keeps its researchers pointed toward the innovations of tomorrow—and beyond.

> *The world's smartest people still work here, and everyone is expected to change the landscape.*
>
> —*David Bishop, head of micromechanics research, Bell Labs**

References: Stephanie N. Mehta, "Lucent's New Spin," *Fortune,* August 14, 2000, pp. 30–31; Neil Weinberg and Nikhil Hutheesing, "Wired and Restless," *Forbes,* February 7, 2000, pp. 90–96; and Nikhil Hutheesing, "Lucent's Labs," *Forbes,* February 7, 2000, p. 93 (*quote on p. 93).

firms within their environments. Firms that implement incremental innovations alter, but do not fundamentally change, competitive interaction in an industry.

Over the last several years, organizations have introduced many radical innovations. For example, compact disk technology has virtually replaced long-playing vinyl records in the recording industry, and high-definition television seems likely to replace regular television technology (both black-and-white and color) in the near future. Whereas radical innovations like these tend to be very visible and public, incremental innovations actually are more numerous. One example is Ford's sports utility vehicle, the Explorer. Although other companies had similar products, Ford more effectively combined the styling and engineering that resulted in increased demand for all sports utility vehicles.

Technical Versus Managerial Innovations   **Technical innovations** are changes in the physical appearance or performance of a product or service, or the physical processes through which a product or service is manufactured. Many of the most important innovations over the last 50 years have been technical. For example, the serial replacement of the vacuum tube with the transistor, the transistor with the integrated circuit, and the integrated circuit with the microchip has greatly enhanced the power, ease of use, and speed of operation of a wide variety of electronic products. Not all innovations developed by organizations are technical, however. **Managerial innovations** are changes in the management process by which products and services are conceived, built, and delivered to customers. Managerial innovations do not necessarily affect the physical appearance or performance of products or services directly. In effect, reengineering, as we discussed earlier, represents a managerial innovation.

> **technical innovation** A change in appearance or performance of products or services, or the physical processes through which a product or service passes

> **managerial innovation** A change in the management process in an organization

Product Versus Process Innovations   Perhaps the two most important types of technical innovations are product innovations and process innovations. **Product innovations** are changes in the physical characteristics or performance of existing products or services, or the creation of brand-new products or services. **Process innovations** are changes in the way products or services are manufactured, created, or distributed. Whereas managerial innovations generally affect the broader context of development, process innovations directly affect manufacturing.

Japanese organizations have often excelled at process innovation. The market for 35mm cameras was dominated by German and other European manufacturers when, in the early 1960s, Japanese organizations such as Canon and Nikon began making cameras. Some of these early Japanese products were not very successful, but these companies continued to invest in their process technology and eventually were able to increase quality and decrease manufacturing costs. Now these Japanese organizations dominate the worldwide market for 35mm cameras, and the German companies, because they were not able to maintain the same pace of process innovation, are struggling to maintain market share and profitability.

> **product innovation** A change in the physical characteristics of a product or service, or the creation of a new one

> **process innovation** A change in the way a product or service is manufactured, created, or distributed

The Failure to Innovate

To remain competitive in today's economy, organizations must be innovative. And yet, many organizations that should be innovative are not successful at bringing out new products or services, or do so only after innovations created by others are very mature. Organizations may fail to innovate for at least three reasons: lack of resources, failure to recognize opportunities, and resistance to change.

Lack of Resources Innovation is expensive in terms of dollars, time, and energy. If a firm does not have sufficient money to fund a program of innovation or does not currently employ the kinds of employees it needs to be innovative, it may lag behind in innovation. Even highly innovative organizations cannot become involved in every new product or service its employees think up. For example, numerous other commitments in the electronic instruments and computer industry forestalled Hewlett-Packard from investing in Steve Jobs's and Steve Wozniak's original idea for a personal computer. With infinite resources of money, time, and technical and managerial expertise, HP might have entered this market early. Because the firm did not have this flexibility, however, it had to make some difficult choices about which innovations to invest in.

Failure to Recognize Opportunities Because firms cannot pursue all innovations, they need to develop the capability to carefully evaluate innovations and to select the ones that hold the greatest potential. To obtain a competitive advantage, an organization usually must make investment decisions before the innovation process reaches the mature stage. The earlier the investment, however, the greater the risk. If organizations are not skilled at recognizing and evaluating opportunities, they may be overly cautious and fail to invest in innovations that turn out later to be successful for other firms.

Resistance to Change As we discussed earlier, many organizations tend to resist change. Innovation means giving up old products and old ways of doing things in favor of new products and new ways of doing things. These kinds of changes can be personally difficult for managers and other members of an organization. Thus resistance to change can slow the innovation process.

Promoting Innovation in Organizations

A wide variety of ideas for promoting innovation in organizations has been developed over the years. Three specific ways for promoting innovation are through the reward system, through the organizational culture, and through a process called "intrapreneurship."[31]

The Reward System A firm's reward system is the means by which it encourages and discourages certain behaviors by employees. Major components of the reward system include salaries, bonuses, and perquisites. Using the reward system to promote innovation is a fairly mechanical but nevertheless effective management technique. The idea is to provide financial and nonfinancial rewards to people and groups that develop innovative ideas. Once the members of an organization understand that they will be rewarded for such activities, they are more likely to work creatively. With this end in mind, Monsanto Company gives a $50,000 award each year to the scientist or group of scientists that develops the biggest commercial breakthrough.

It is important for organizations to reward creative behavior, but it is vital to avoid punishing creativity when it does not result in highly successful innovations. It is the nature of the creative and innovative processes that many new product ideas will simply not work out in the marketplace. Each process is fraught with too many uncertainties to generate positive results every time. An individual may have prepared herself to be creative, but an insight may not be forthcoming. Or managers may attempt to apply a developed innovation, only to recognize that it does not work. Indeed, some organizations operate according to the assumption that, if all their innovative efforts succeed, then they are probably not taking enough risks in research and development. At 3M, nearly 60 percent of the creative ideas suggested each year do not succeed in the marketplace.

Managers need to be very careful in responding to innovative failure. If innovative failure is due to incompetence, systematic errors, or managerial sloppiness, then a firm should respond appropriately—for example, by withholding raises or reducing promotion opportunities. People who act in good faith to develop an innovation that simply does not work out, however, should not be punished for failure. If they are, they will probably not be creative in the future. A punitive reward system will discourage people from taking risks and therefore reduce the organization's ability to obtain competitive advantages.

Organizational Culture   As we discussed in Chapter 2, an organization's culture is the set of values, beliefs, and symbols that help guide behavior. A strong, appropriately focused organizational culture can be used to support innovative activity. A well-managed culture can communicate a sense that innovation is valued and will be rewarded and that occasional failure in the pursuit of new ideas is not only acceptable but even expected. In addition to reward systems and intrapreneurial activities, firms such as 3M, Corning, Monsanto, Procter & Gamble, Texas Instruments, Johnson & Johnson, and Merck are all known to have strong, innovation-oriented cultures that value individual creativity, risk taking, and inventiveness.

Intrapreneurship in Larger Organizations   In recent years, many large businesses have realized that the entrepreneurial spirit that propelled their growth becomes stagnant after they transform themselves from a small but growing concern into a larger one. To help revitalize this spirit, some firms today encourage what they call "intrapreneurship." **Intrapreneurs** are similar to entrepreneurs except that they develop a new business in the context of a large organization. There are three intrapreneurial roles in large organizations.[32] To successfully use intrapreneurship to encourage creativity and innovation, the organization must find one or more individuals to perform these roles.

The *inventor* is the person who actually conceives of and develops the new idea, product, or service by means of the creative process. Because the inventor may lack the expertise or motivation to oversee the transformation of the product or service from an idea into a marketable entity, however, a second role comes into play. A *product champion* is usually a middle manager who learns about the project and becomes committed to it. He or she helps overcome organizational resistance and convinces others to take the innovation seriously. The product champion may have only

intrapreneurs Similar to entrepreneurs, except that they develop a new business in the context of a large organization

limited understanding of the technological aspects of the innovation. Nevertheless, product champions are skilled at knowing how the organization works, whose support is needed to push the project forward, and where to go to secure the resources necessary for successful development. A *sponsor* is a top-level manager who approves of and supports a project. This person may fight for the budget needed to develop an idea, overcome arguments against a project, and use organizational politics to ensure the project's survival. With a sponsor in place, the inventor's idea has a much better chance of being successfully developed.

Several firms have embraced intrapreneurship as a way to encourage creativity and innovation. Colgate-Palmolive has created a separate unit, Colgate Venture Company, staffed with intrapreneurs who develop new products. General Foods developed Culinova Group as a unit to which employees can take their ideas for possible development. S. C. Johnson & Sons established a $250,000 fund to support new product ideas, and Texas Instruments refuses to approve a new innovative project unless it has an acknowledged inventor, champion, and sponsor.

Summary of Key Points

Organization change is any substantive modification to some part of the organization. Change may be prompted by forces internal or external to the organization. In general, planned change is preferable to reactive change.

Managing the change process is very important. The Lewin model provides a general perspective on the steps involved in change, although a comprehensive model is usually more effective. People tend to resist change because of uncertainty, threatened self-interests, different perceptions, and feelings of loss. Participation, education and communication, facilitation, and force-field analysis are methods for overcoming this resistance.

Many change techniques or interventions are used. The most common ones involve changing organizational structure and design, technology, and people. There are several specific areas of change within each of these broad categories. Reengineering is the radical redesign of all aspects of a business to achieve major gains in cost, service, or time. It is occasionally needed to offset entropy. The basic steps are developing goals and strategies, conveying the involvement of top management, creating a sense of urgency, starting with a clean slate, and balancing top-down and bottom-up perspectives.

Organization development is concerned with changing attitudes, perceptions, behaviors, and expectations. Its effective use relies on an important set of assumptions. There are conflicting opinions about the effectiveness of several OD techniques.

The innovation process has six steps: development, application, launch, growth, maturity, and decline. Basic categories of innovation include radical, incremental, technical, managerial, product, and process innovations. Despite the importance of innovation, many organizations fail to innovate because they lack the required creative individuals or are committed to too many other creative activities, fail to recognize opportunities, or resist the change that innovation requires. Organizations can use a variety of tools to overcome these problems, including the reward system, organizational culture, and intrapreneurship.

Discussion Questions

Questions for Review

1. What forces or kinds of events lead to organization change? Identify each force or event as planned or reactive change.
2. How is each step in the process of organization change implemented? Are some of the steps more likely to meet with resistance than others? Why or why not?
3. What are the various areas of organization change? In what ways are they similar, and in what ways do they differ?
4. What are the basic techniques used for organization development?
5. What are the steps in the innovation process?

Questions for Analysis

6. Could reactive change of the type identified in question 1 have been planned for ahead of time? Why or why not? Should all organization change be planned? Why or why not?
7. A company has recently purchased equipment that, when installed, will do the work of 100 employees. The workforce of the company is very concerned and is threatening to take some kind of action. If you were the human resource manager, what would you try to do to satisfy all parties concerned? Why?
8. Think of several relatively new products or services that you use. What form of innovation was each?
9. Some people resist change, whereas others welcome change enthusiastically. To deal with the first group, one needs to overcome resistance to change; to deal with the second, one needs to overcome resistance to stability. What advice can you give a manager facing the latter situation?
10. Can a change made in one area of an organization—in technology, for instance—not lead to change in other areas? Why or why not?

BUILDING EFFECTIVE *time management* SKILLS

Exercise Overview

Time management skills refer to the manager's ability to prioritize work, to work efficiently, and to delegate appropriately. Using time management skills wisely can change how a person works.

Exercise Background

Almost every task we perform can theoretically be performed more efficiently. The next time you work on a particular task, such as studying for a test, writing a paper, or working on a project, take note of your work habits. You might even consider videotaping yourself while you work and reviewing the tape later.

Take special note of the things you do that do not seem to contribute to task performance. Examples might include going to the refrigerator and getting food, watching television while you are working, daydreaming, making an unnecessary telephone call, and so forth. Next, estimate how much of the total "work" time was actually spent on other activities.

Exercise Task

With the background information above as context, do the following:

1. Assess the extent to which each nonwork activity was wasted effort or actually contributed in some way to task performance.

2. Describe how the work might have been completed had you not done any of the nonwork activities.

3. Assuming that you want to change your work habits to use your time more efficiently, describe a change approach that you might use.

BUILDING EFFECTIVE *interpersonal* SKILLS

Exercise Overview

A manager's interpersonal skills are her or his ability to understand and motivate individuals and groups. These abilities are especially important during a period of change. This exercise helps you understand how to apply your interpersonal skills to a change situation.

Exercise Background

Assume that you are the manager of a retail store in a local shopping mall. Your staff consists of seven full-time and ten part-time employees. The full-time employees have worked together as a team for three years. The part-timers are all local college students; several of them have worked in the store for more than a year, but there tends to be a lot of turnover among this group.

Your boss, the regional manager, has just informed you that the national chain that owns your store is planning to open a second store in the same mall. She has also informed you that you must plan and implement the following changes:

1. You will serve as manager of both stores until the sales volume of the new store warrants its own full-time manager.
2. You are to designate one of the full-time employees in your present store as the assistant manager, because you will be in the store less often now.
3. To have experienced workers in the new store, you are to select three of your current full-time workers to move to the new store,

one of whom should also be appointed as assistant manager of that store.

4. You can hire three new people to replace those transferred from your present store and three new people to work at the new store.
5. You can decide for yourself how to deploy your part-timers, but you will need a total of ten in the present store and eight at the new store.

You realize that many of your employees will be unhappy with these changes. They know each other and work well together. However, the new store will be in a new section of the mall and will be a very nice place to work.

Exercise Task

With this background information in mind, do the following:

1. Determine the likely reasons for resistance to this change among your workers.
2. Determine how you will decide about promotions and transfers (make whatever assumptions you think are warranted).
3. Outline how you will inform your employees about the change.
4. An alternative strategy that could be adopted would involve keeping the existing staff intact and hiring all new employees for the new store. Outline a persuasion strategy for trying to convince your boss to adopt this alternative.

BUILDING EFFECTIVE *diagnostic* SKILLS

Exercise Overview

Diagnostic skills help a manager visualize the most appropriate response to a situation. Diagnostic skills are especially important during a period of organization change.

Exercise Background

Assume that you are the general manager of a hotel located on a tropical island. The hotel, situated along a beautiful stretch of beach, is one of six large resorts in the area. The hotel is owned by a group of foreign investors and is one of the oldest on the island. For several years the hotel has been operated as a franchise unit of a large international hotel chain, as are all of the others on the island.

For the last few years, the hotel's owners have been taking most of the profits for themselves and putting relatively little back into the hotel. They also have let you know that their business is not in good financial health; the money earned from your hotel is being used to offset losses the owners are incurring elsewhere. Most of the neighboring hotels have recently been refurbished, and plans have just been announced to build two new hotels in the near future.

A team of executives from franchise headquarters has just visited your hotel. They expressed considerable disappointment in the property. They feel that it has not kept pace with the other resorts on the island. They also informed you that if the property is not brought up to their standards, the franchise agreement, up for review in a year, will be revoked. You see

this as potentially disastrous, because you would lose the franchise's "brand name," access to its reservation system, and so forth.

Sitting alone in your office, you have identified a variety of alternatives that seem viable:

1. Try to convince the owners to remodel the hotel. You estimate that it will take $10 million to meet the franchiser's minimum standards and another $10 million to bring the hotel up to the standards of the top resort on the island.
2. Try to convince the franchiser to give you more time and more options to upgrade the facility.
3. Allow the franchise agreement to terminate and try to succeed as an independent hotel.
4. Assume that the hotel is going to fail and start looking for another job. You have a good reputation, although you might have to start at a lower level with another firm (perhaps as an assistant manager).

Exercise Task

With the background information presented above, do the following:

1. Rank-order the four alternatives in terms of their potential success (make assumptions as appropriate).
2. Identify other alternatives not noted above.
3. Can any alternatives be pursued simultaneously?
4. Develop an overall strategy for trying to save the hotel while also protecting yourself.

SKILLS *self-assessment* INSTRUMENT

Innovative Attitude Scale

Introduction: Change and innovation are important to organizations. The following assessment surveys your readiness to accept and participate in innovation.

Instructions: Indicate the extent to which each of the following statements is true of either your *actual* behavior or your *intentions* at work. That is, describe the way you are or the way you intend to be on the job. Use this scale for your responses:

Almost always true = 5
Often true = 4
Not applicable = 3
Seldom true = 2
Almost never true = 1

_____ 1. I openly discuss with my boss how to get ahead.

_____ 2. I try new ideas and approaches to problems.

_____ 3. I take things or situations apart to find out how they work.

_____ 4. I welcome uncertainty and unusual circumstances related to my tasks.

_____ 5. I negotiate my salary openly with my supervisor.

_____ 6. I can be counted on to find a new use for existing methods or equipment.

_____ 7. Among my colleagues and coworkers, I will be the first or nearly the first to try out a new idea or method.

_____ 8. I take the opportunity to translate communications from other departments for my work group.

_____ 9. I demonstrate originality.

_____ 10. I will work on a problem that has caused others great difficulty.

_____ 11. I provide critical input toward a new solution.

_____ 12. I provide written evaluations of proposed ideas.

_____ 13. I develop contacts with experts outside my firm.

_____ 14. I use personal contacts to maneuver myself into choice work assignments.

_____ 15. I make time to pursue my own pet ideas or projects.

_____ 16. I set aside resources for the pursuit of a risky project.

_____ 17. I tolerate people who depart from organizational routine.

_____ 18. I speak out in staff meetings.

_____ 19. I work in teams to try to solve complex problems.

_____ 20. If my coworkers are asked, they will say I am a wit.

For interpretation, see Interpretations of Skills Self-Assessment Instruments.

Source: From J. E. Ettlie and R. D. O'Keefe, "Innovative Attitudes, Values, and Intentions in Organizations," *Journal of Management Studies* 19, p. 176. Copyright © 1982 by Blackwell Publishers Ltd. Reprinted by permission of Blackwell Publishing Ltd.

Innovation in Action: Egg Drop

Purpose: Managers are continuously improving the work flow, the product, and the packaging of products. This is what total quality management is all about. To do this means thinking creatively and acting innovatively. This skill builder focuses on the *open systems model*. It helps you develop the *innovator role*. One of the skills of the innovator is thinking creatively and acting innovatively.

Introduction: This activity is a practical and entertaining demonstration of creativity and innovation in action. The "Egg Drop" exercise provides practice in identifying, defining, or refining a problem or opportunity; developing options and alternatives; choosing the best option or alternative; actually launching the alternative into reality; and verifying the results within a specified time period. Your instructor will provide you with further instructions.

Source: Reproduced with permission from "Metaphorically Speaking," from *50 Activities on Creativity and Problem Solving* by Geof Cox, Chuck DuFault, and Walt Hopkins, Gower, Aldershot, 1992.

CHAPTER CLOSING CASE

GENERAL ELECTRIC'S GLOBAL CULTURE OF CHANGE

Jack Welch, the long-time CEO of General Electric, was well aware that large organizations can be unwieldy and complacent, even though they need to be streamlined and speedy. This is why Welch and his successor worked out a variety of strategies for managing change and innovation to take advantage of GE's size rather than being tripped up by it. Over the years, GE has been successfully transformed from a largely U.S.-focused company into a truly global, boundaryless business—one of the world's most profitable.

General Electric has long had a few joint ventures in Europe, but for years its main international business activity was exporting. This changed in 1987, when the company exchanged its consumer electronics business for ownership of a French-based medical equipment manufacturer. Within two years, GE made another European acquisition, this time buying a Hungarian lighting manufacturer. Since then, GE has bought more than 133 European firms in industries ranging from insurance to energy equipment, swelling its European payroll to 90,000 and generating more than $20 billion in annual revenue from the area.

After so many years, GE has worked out a pattern for effectively managing change during and after the acquisition. Even before management has finished negotiating a deal, experts from finance and human resources are drafting a plan to set change in motion immediately after the contract is signed. The first change that occurs after a deal has been completed is that GE's finance expert shows up and starts converting the firm's financial systems to the accepted GE format. GE also sends in an integration manager to supervise the unification effort, while the overall manager of the acquired company concentrates on operations and profitability issues.

Within 100 days or less, GE has the basic change plan well under way, covering activities ranging from cost-cutting measures to plans for switching from matrix or geographic departmentalization (where it exists) to a functional organization. By this time, GE's experts will have identified and taken steps to remove people who seem to be blocking change within the acquired firm. They will also have identified which personnel should be retained; these people are offered key roles within the integrated organization.

Next, GE introduces its special brand of management tools, including highly effective quality management programs and other best-practices tools that have proven to significantly boost profit margins in other acquired firms. One tool, known as Work-Out, encourages employees to get together and come up with a plan for solving any problem in the business, then present it to management for immediate approval or rejection. This seemingly informal, no-nonsense team tool brings about needed change more quickly and with more grassroots support than the traditional method of passing the problem up and down the hierarchy in the course of debating and making a decision. Teams, in fact, are commonplace in every GE unit around the world, moving information through the organization at lightning speed and allowing employees to get the job done without intense management supervision.

The Internet is a powerful catalyst for overall change within GE, because top management sees the web as redefining relationships with customers, employees, and suppliers. To get the corporation ready to take advantage of emerging web-related opportunities, management called for a three-month Work-Out procedure held entirely online. Participants shared ideas for breaking down bureaucratic blocks and moving more quickly

to implement e-commerce strategies that represent GE's future. GE has also invited web-savvy executives, such as Sun Microsystem's Scott McNealy, to join its board of directors and prod management about key technology issues. GE knows that, with the advent of the Internet, no country is isolated, so it plans to continue its winning ways by bringing systematic change to every unit around the world.

Case Questions

1. Does Work-Out represent planned or reactive change? Explain your answer.

2. Identify some of the most important internal and external forces for change affecting GE.

3. In what areas does GE intervene to make change after an acquisition? Why does GE concentrate on these areas?

Case References

Brent Schlender, "The Odd Couple," *Fortune*, May 1, 2000, pp. 106–126; Thomas A. Stewart, "See Jack Run. See Jack Run Europe," *Fortune*, September 27, 1999, pp. 124–136; and Jack Welch, *Jack: Straight from the Gut* (New York: Warren Books), 2001.

CHAPTER NOTES

1. "Can Nike Still Do It?" *Business Week*, February 21, 2000, pp. 120–128 (quote on p. 122); and *Hoover's Handbook of American Business 2001* (Austin, TX: Hoover's Business Press, 2001), pp. 1032–1033.

2. For an excellent review of this area, see Achilles A. Armenakis and Arthur G. Bedeian, "Organizational Change: A Review of Theory and Research in the 1990s," *Journal of Management* 25, no. 3 (1999): 293–315.

3. Joel Cutcher-Gershenfeld, Ellen Ernst Kossek, and Heidi Sandling, "Managing Concurrent Change Initiatives," *Organizational Dynamics*, Winter 1997, pp. 21–38.

4. Michael A. Hitt, "The New Frontier: Transformation of Management for the New Millennium," *Organizational Dynamics*, Winter 2000, pp. 7–15. See also Michael Beer and Nitin Nohria, "Cracking the Code of Change," *Harvard Business Review*, May/June 2000, pp. 133–144.

5. See Warren Boeker, "Strategic Change: The Influence of Managerial Characteristics and Organizational Growth," *Academy of Management Journal* 40, no. 1 (1997): 152–170.

6. Anne Fisher, "Danger Zone," *Fortune*, September 8, 1997, pp. 165–167.

7. John P. Kotter and Leonard A. Schlesinger, "Choosing Strategies for Change," *Harvard Business Review*, March/April 1979, p. 106.

8. Clayton M. Christensen and Michael Overdorf, "Meeting the Challenge of Disruptive Change," *Harvard Business Review*, March/April 2000, pp. 67–77.

9. See Eric Abrahamson, "Change Without Pain," *Harvard Business Review*, July/August 2000, pp. 75–85. See also Gib Akin and Ian Palmer, "Putting Metaphors to Work for Change in Organizations," *Organizational Dynamics*, Winter 2000, pp. 67–76.

10. Kurt Lewin, "Frontiers in Group Dynamics: Concept, Method, and Reality in Social Science," *Human Relations*, June 1947, pp. 5–41.

11. "RJR Employees Fight Distraction amid Buy-out Talks," *Wall Street Journal*, November 1, 1988, p. A8.

12. Arnon E. Reichers, John P. Wanous, and James T. Austin, "Understanding and Managing Cynicism About Organizational Change," *Academy of Management Executive*, February 1997, pp. 48–59.

13. "How Classy Can 7-Eleven Get?" *Business Week*, September 1, 1997, pp. 74–75.

14. See Paul R. Lawrence, "How to Deal with Resistance to Change," *Harvard Business Review*, January/February 1969, pp. 4–12, 166–176, for a classic discussion.

15. Lester Coch and John R. P. French, Jr., "Overcoming Resistance to Change," *Human Relations*, August 1948, pp. 512–532.

16. Eric von Hippel, Stefan Thomke, and Mary Sonnack, "Creating Breakthroughs at 3M," *Harvard Business Review*, September/October 1999, pp. 47–54.

17. Benjamin Schneider, Arthur P. Brief, and Richard A. Guzzo, "Creating a Climate and Culture for Sustainable Organizational Change," *Organizational Dynamics*, Spring 1996, pp. 7–19.

18. Paul Bate, Raza Khan, and Annie Pye, "Towards a Culturally Sensitive Approach to Organization Structuring: Where Organization Design Meets Organization Development," *Organization Science*, March–April 2000, pp. 197–211.

19. "Founding Clan Vies with Outside 'Radical' for the Soul of Toyota," *Wall Street Journal*, May 5, 2000, pp. A1, A12.

20. David Kirkpatrick, "The New Player," *Fortune*, April 17, 2000, pp. 162–168.

21. "Mr. Ryder Rewrites the Musty Old Book at Reader's Digest," *Wall Street Journal*, April 18, 2000, pp. A1, A10.

22. Thomas A. Stewart, "Reengineering—The Hot New Managing Tool," *Fortune*, August 23, 1993, pp. 41–48.

23. "Old Company Learns New Tricks," *USA Today*, April 10, 2000, pp. 1B, 2B.

24. W. Warner Burke, "The New Agenda for Organization Development," *Organizational Dynamics*, Summer 1997, pp. 7–20.

25. Wendell L. French and Cecil H. Bell, Jr., *Organization Development: Behavioral Science Interventions for Organization Improvement*, 2nd ed. (Englewood Cliffs, NJ: Prentice-Hall, 1978).

26. "Memo to the Team: This Needs Salt!" *Wall Street Journal*, April 4, 2000, pp. B1, B14.

27. Constantinos Markides, "Strategic Innovation," *Sloan Management Review*, Spring 1997, pp. 9–24. See also James Brian Quinn, "Outsourcing Innovation: The New Engine of Growth," *Sloan Management Review*, Summer 2000, pp. 13–21.

28. See Alan Patz, "Managing Innovation in High Technology Industries," *New Management*, September 1986, pp. 54–59.

29. "Flops," *Business Week*, August 16, 1993, pp. 76–82.

30. See Willow A. Sheremata, "Centrifugal and Centripetal Forces in Radical New Product Development Under Time Pressure," *Academy of Management Review* 25, no. 2 (2000): 389–408.

31. Dorothy Leonard and Jeffrey F. Rayport, "Spark Innovation Through Empathic Design," *Harvard Business Review*, November/December 1997, pp. 102–115.

32. See Gifford Pinchot III, *Intrapreneuring* (New York: Harper & Row, 1985).

8 Managing Human Resources

S AS Institute, Inc., based in rural North Carolina, is perhaps the least well-known major software company in the world today. SAS creates software that helps big companies better manage and analyze especially large quantities of data and information. For example, Marriott Hotels uses SAS software to manage its frequent-visitor program; the U.S. government uses SAS software to compute the Consumer Price Index and other complex measures; and pharmaceutical companies like Pfizer and Merck use SAS software to compare nearly infinite combinations of elements as they develop new drugs.

Because SAS is a private firm, the general public knows little about its revenues and profits. A few details are illuminating, however. For one thing, the firm's founder and leader, Jim Goodnight, with a net worth of $3 billion, is listed by *Forbes* as the

43rd richest individual in the United States. (This is based on his two-thirds ownership of the company; the other third is owned by senior vice president John Sall, who still spends much of his time writing code.) And, for another, SAS hires several hundred new employees each year, a clear indicator that the firm is consistently growing at a strong pace. And the firm also continues to invest in impressive—and clearly expensive—buildings and related facilities.

But SAS is even more impressive under the surface. For example, even though it pays salaries that are merely competitive for the industry, the firm's employees are almost fanatical in their devotion to SAS in general and to Jim Goodnight in particular. As a result, annual turnover at SAS is less than 4 percent, far below that of other firms in the industry, and employees are constantly

coming up with new and better ways of doing things for the company. And both insiders and outside experts agree that the key to all this is how Goodnight treats his employees.

For example, all SAS employees get unlimited sick days, and they can use sick days to stay home to care for ill family members. In order to keep work from interfering with employees' families, SAS operates the largest childcare facility in the state. And company cafeterias have baby seats and highchairs so that employees can eat with their children. SAS has also adopted a seven-hour workday; the company switchboard shuts down at 5:00 each day, and the front gate is locked at 6:00. Unlike many high-tech firms

> "Jim's idea is that if you hire adults and treat them like adults, then they'll behave like adults."
>
> —David Russo, head of human resources at SAS

LEARNING OBJECTIVES

After studying this chapter, you should be able to

- Describe the environmental context of human resource management, including its strategic importance and its relationship with legal factors.

- Discuss how organizations attract human resources, including human resource planning, recruiting, and selecting.

- Describe how organizations develop human resources, including training and development, performance appraisal, and performance feedback.

- Discuss how organizations maintain human resources, including the determination of compensation and benefits.

- Discuss the nature of diversity, including its meaning, associated trends, impact, and management.

- Discuss labor relations, including how employees form unions and the mechanics of collective bargaining.

in other parts of the country, Goodnight doesn't want his employees to work late or to come back to the office on the weekend.

If they want, however, they can come in early—to work out in a lavish 36,000 square foot gym and health center. The center also offers massages several times a week, as well as classes in golf, tennis, tai chi, and African dance. And center staff even launder dirty workout clothes at the end of the day and return them clean and neatly folded. SAS provides unlimited free soda, coffee, tea, and juice, and has live piano

music in the cafeteria. The company shuts down for the week between Christmas and New Year's Day each year, but everyone still gets paid. An on-site health clinic has two full-time physicians and six nurses; health insurance is free for everyone. And all this comes from Jim Goodnight's most fundamental philosophy: If you treat people with dignity and respect, and reward them for their contributions, they will treat you the same in return. And when this relationship can be established and maintained within the context of a business, everyone can win.[1]

SAS is one of the most successful businesses around these days. And human resources are clearly an integral part of its success. From the company's earliest days, Jim Goodnight made a strategic commitment to identify, hire, and retain the best and brightest people available. Moreover, the firm has been able to maintain this strategy and today is still the employer of choice for many talented people in a highly volatile industry.

This chapter is about how organizations manage the people who comprise them. This set of processes is called human resource management, or HRM. We start by describing the environmental context of HRM. We then discuss how organizations attract human resources. Next we describe how organizations seek to further develop the capacities of their human resources. We also examine how high-quality human resources are maintained by organizations. Diversity in organizations is discussed next, then we conclude by discussing labor relations.

The Environmental Context of Human Resource Management

human resource management (HRM) The set of organizational activities directed at attracting, developing, and maintaining an effective workforce

Human resource management (HRM) is the set of organizational activities directed at attracting, developing, and maintaining an effective workforce.[2] Human resource management takes place within a complex and ever-changing environmental context.

The Strategic Importance of HRM

Human resources are critical for effective organizational functioning. HRM (or personnel, as it is sometimes called) was once relegated to second-class status in many organizations, but its importance has grown dramatically in the last two decades. Its new importance stems from increased legal complexities, the recognition that human resources are a valuable means for improving productivity, and the awareness today of the costs associated with poor human resource management.[3]

Indeed, managers now realize that the effectiveness of their HR function has a substantial impact on the bottom-line performance of the firm. Poor human resource planning can result in spurts of hiring followed by layoffs—costly in terms of unemployment compensation payments, training expenses, and morale. Haphazard compensation systems do not attract, keep, and motivate good employees, and outmoded recruitment practices can expose the firm to expensive and embarrassing discrimination lawsuits. Consequently, the chief human resource executive of most large businesses is a vice president directly accountable to the CEO, and many firms are developing strategic HR plans and integrating those plans with other strategic planning activities.

Even organizations with as few as 200 employees usually have a human resource manager and a human resource department charged with overseeing these activities. Responsibility for HR activities, however, is shared between the HR department and line managers. The HR department may recruit and initially screen candidates, but the final selection is usually made by managers in the department where the new employee will work. Similarly, although the HR department may establish performance appraisal policies and procedures, the actual evaluating and coaching of employees is done by their immediate superiors.

The Legal Environment of HRM

A number of laws regulate various aspects of employee-employer relations, especially in the areas of equal employment opportunity, compensation and benefits, labor relations, and occupational safety and health. Several major ones are summarized in Table 8.1.

Table 8.1

The Legal Environment of Human Resource Management

As much as any area of management, HRM is subject to wide-ranging laws and court decisions. These laws and decisions affect the human resource function in many areas. For example, AT&T was once fined several million dollars for violating Title VII of the Civil Rights Act of 1964.

Equal Employment Opportunity

Title VII of the Civil Rights Act of 1964 (as amended by the *Equal Employment Opportunity Act of 1972*): forbids discrimination in all areas of the employment relationship

Age Discrimination in Employment Act: outlaws discrimination against people older than 40 years

Various executive orders, especially *Executive Order 11246* in 1965: requires employers with government contracts to engage in affirmative action

Pregnancy Discrimination Act: specifically outlaws discrimination on the basis of pregnancy

Vietnam Era Veterans Readjustment Assistance Act: extends affirmative action mandate to military veterans who served during the Vietnam War

Americans with Disabilities Act: specifically outlaws discrimination against disabled persons

Civil Rights Act of 1991: makes it easier for employees to sue an organization for discrimination but limits punitive damage awards if they win

Compensation and Benefits

Fair Labor Standards Act: establishes minimum wage and mandated overtime pay for work in excess of 40 hours per week

Equal Pay Act of 1963: requires that men and women be paid the same amount for doing the same jobs

Employee Retirement Income Security Act of 1974: regulates how organizations manage their pension funds

Family and Medical Leave Act of 1993: requires employers to provide up to 12 weeks of unpaid leave for family and medical emergencies

Labor Relations

National Labor Relations Act: spells out procedures by which employees can establish labor unions and requires organizations to bargain collectively with legally formed unions; also known as the *Wagner Act*

Labor-Management Relations Act: limits union power and specifies management rights during a union organizing campaign; also known as the *Taft-Hartley Act*

Health and Safety

Occupational Safety and Health Act of 1970: mandates the provision of safe working conditions

Title VII of the Civil Rights Act of 1964 Forbids discrimination on the basis of sex, race, color, religion, or national origin in all areas of the employment relationship

adverse impact When minority group members pass a selection standard at a rate less than 80 percent of the pass rate of majority group members

Equal Employment Opportunity Commission (EEOC) Charged with enforcing Title VII of the Civil Rights act of 1964

Age Discrimination in Employment Act Outlaws discrimination against people older than 40 years; passed in 1967, amended in 1978 and 1986

affirmative action Intentionally seeking and hiring qualified or qualifiable employees from racial, sexual, and ethnic groups that are underrepresented in the organization

Americans with Disabilities Act Prohibits discrimination against people with disabilities

Civil Rights Act of 1991 Amends the original Civil Rights Act, making it easier to bring discrimination lawsuits while also limiting punitive damages

Fair Labor Standards Act Sets a minimum wage and requires overtime pay for work in excess of 40 hours per week; passed in 1938 and amended frequently since then

Equal Pay Act of 1963 Requires that men and women be paid the same amount for doing the same jobs

Equal Employment Opportunity   **Title VII of the Civil Rights Act of 1964** forbids discrimination in all areas of the employment relationship. The intent of Title VII is to ensure that employment decisions are made on the basis of an individual's qualifications rather than according to personal biases. The law has reduced direct forms of discrimination (refusing to promote blacks into management, failing to hire men as flight attendants, refusing to hire women as construction workers) as well as indirect forms of discrimination (using employment tests that whites pass at a higher rate than blacks).

Employment requirements such as test scores and other qualifications are legally defined as having an **adverse impact** on minorities and women when such individuals meet or pass the requirement at a rate less than 80 percent of the rate of majority group members. Criteria that have an adverse impact on protected groups can be used only when there is solid evidence that they effectively identify individuals who are better able than others to do the job. The **Equal Employment Opportunity Commission (EEOC)** is charged with enforcing Title VII as well as several other employment-related laws.

The **Age Discrimination in Employment Act**, passed in 1967, amended in 1978, and amended again in 1986, is an attempt to prevent organizations from discriminating against older workers. In its current form, it outlaws discrimination against people older than 40 years. Both the Age Discrimination Act and Title VII require passive nondiscrimination, or equal employment opportunity. Employers are not required to seek out and hire minorities, but they must treat fairly all who apply.

Several executive orders, however, require that employers holding government contracts engage in **affirmative action**—intentionally seeking and hiring employees from groups that are underrepresented in the organization. These organizations must have a written affirmative action plan that spells out employment goals for underutilized groups and how those goals will be met. These employers are also required to act affirmatively in hiring Vietnam-era veterans and qualified handicapped individuals.

In 1990 Congress passed the **Americans with Disabilities Act**, which forbids discrimination on the basis of disabilities and requires employers to provide reasonable accommodations for disabled employees. More recently, the **Civil Rights Act of 1991** amended the original Civil Rights Act, as well as other related laws, by both making it easier to bring discrimination lawsuits (which partially explains the aforementioned backlog of cases) while simultaneously limiting the amount of punitive damages that can be awarded in those lawsuits.

Compensation and Benefits   Laws also regulate compensation and benefits. The **Fair Labor Standards Act**, passed in 1938 and amended frequently since then, sets a minimum wage and requires the payment of overtime rates for work in excess of 40 hours per week. Salaried professional, executive, and administrative employees are exempt from the minimum hourly wage and overtime provisions. The **Equal Pay Act of 1963** requires that men and women be paid the same amount for doing the same jobs. Attempts to circumvent the law by having different job titles and pay rates for men and women who perform the same work are also illegal. Basing an employee's pay on seniority or performance is legal, however, even if it means that a man and woman are paid different amounts for doing the same job.

The provision of benefits is also regulated in some ways by state and federal laws. Certain benefits are mandatory—for example, workers' compensation insurance for employees who are injured on the job. Employers who provide a pension plan for their employees are regulated by the **Employee Retirement Income Security Act of 1974 (ERISA)**. The purpose of this act is to help ensure the financial security of pension funds by regulating how they can be invested. The **Family and Medical Leave Act of 1993** requires employers to provide up to 12 weeks of unpaid leave for family and medical emergencies.

Labor Relations Union activities and management's behavior toward unions constitute another heavily regulated area. The **National Labor Relations Act** (also known as the Wagner Act), passed in 1935, sets up a procedure for employees of a firm to vote on whether to have a union. If they vote for a union, management is required to bargain collectively with the union. The **National Labor Relations Board (NLRB)** was established by the Wagner Act to enforce its provisions. Following a series of severe strikes in 1946, the **Labor-Management Relations Act** (also known as the Taft-Hartley Act) was passed in 1947 to limit union power. The law increases management's rights during an organizing campaign. The Taft-Hartley Act also contains the National Emergency Strike provision, which allows the president of the United States to prevent or end a strike that endangers national security. Taken together, those laws balance union and management power. Employees can be represented by a legally created and managed union, but the business can make nonemployee-related business decisions without interference.

Health and Safety The **Occupational Safety and Health Act of 1970 (OSHA)** directly mandates the provision of safe working conditions. It requires that employers (1) provide a place of employment that is free from hazards that may cause death or serious physical harm and (2) obey the safety and health standards established by the Department of Labor. Safety standards are intended to prevent accidents, whereas occupational health standards are concerned with preventing occupational disease. For example, standards limit the concentration of cotton dust in the air, because this contaminant has been associated with lung disease in textile workers. The standards are enforced by OSHA inspections, which are conducted when an employee files a complaint of unsafe conditions or when a serious accident occurs. Spot inspections of plants in especially hazardous industries, such as mining and chemicals, are also made. Employers who fail to meet OSHA standards may be fined.

Employee Retirement Income Security Act of 1974 (ERISA) Sets standards for pension plan management and provides federal insurance if pension funds go bankrupt

Family and Medical Leave Act of 1993 Requires employers to provide up to 12 weeks of unpaid leave for family and medical emergencies

National Labor Relations Act Passed in 1935 to set up procedures for employees to vote whether to have a union; also known as the Wagner Act

National Labor Relations Board (NLRB) Established by the Wagner Act to enforce its provisions

Labor-Management Relations Act Passed in 1947 to limit union power; also known as the Taft-Hartley Act

Occupational Safety and Health Act of 1970 (OSHA) Directly mandates the provision of safe working conditions

Attracting Human Resources

With an understanding of the environmental context of human resource management as a foundation, we are now ready to address its first substantive concern—attracting qualified people who are interested in employment with the organization.

Human Resource Planning

The starting point in attracting qualified human resources is planning. HR planning, in turn, involves job analysis and forecasting the demand and supply of labor.

job analysis A systematized procedure for collecting and recording information about jobs

Job Analysis   **Job analysis** is a systematic analysis of jobs within an organization. A job analysis is made up of two parts. The *job description* lists the duties of a job, the job's working conditions, and the tools, materials, and equipment used to perform it. The *job specification* lists the skills, abilities, and other credentials needed to do the job. Job analysis information is used in many human resource activities. For instance, knowing about job content and job requirements is necessary to develop appropriate selection methods and job-relevant performance appraisal systems, and to set equitable compensation rates.

Forecasting Human Resource Demand and Supply   After managers fully understand the jobs to be performed within the organization, they can start planning for the organization's future human resource needs. Figure 8.1 summarizes the steps most often followed. The manager starts by assessing trends in past human resources usage, future organizational plans, and general economic trends. A good sales forecast is often the foundation, especially for smaller organizations. Historical ratios can then be used to predict demand for employees such as operating employees and sales representatives. Of course, large organi-

Figure 8.1

Human Resource Planning
Attracting human resources cannot be left to chance if an organization expects to function at peak efficiency. Human resource planning involves assessing trends, forecasting supply and demand of labor, and then developing appropriate strategies for addressing any differences.

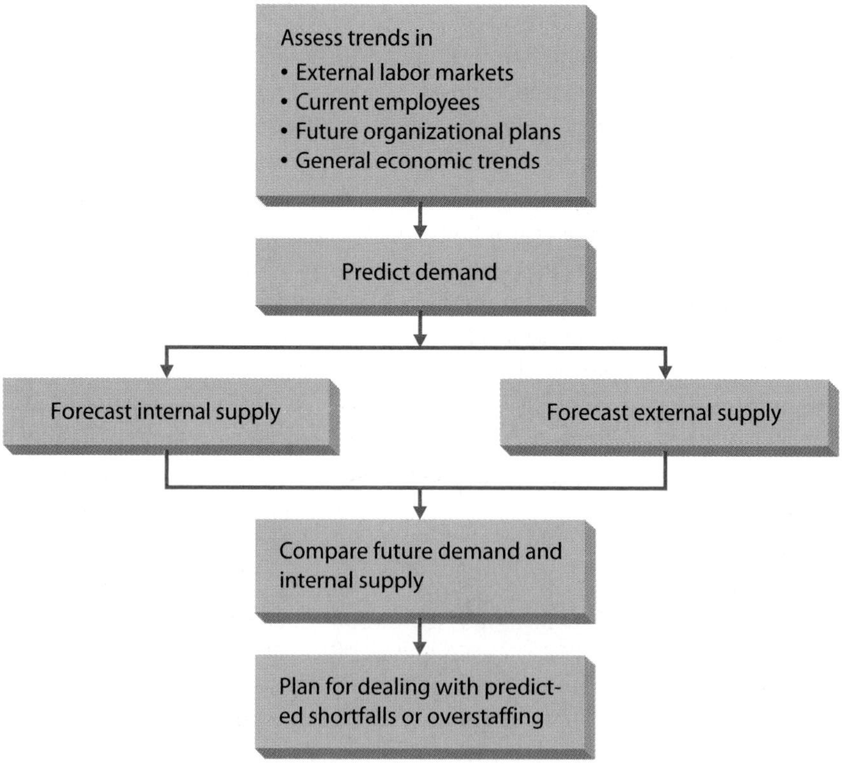

zations use much more complicated models to predict their future human resource needs.

Forecasting the supply of labor is really two tasks: forecasting the internal supply (the number and type of employees who will be in the firm at some future date) and forecasting the external supply (the number and type of people who will be available for hiring in the labor market at large). The simplest approach merely adjusts present staffing levels for anticipated turnover and promotions. Again, though, large organizations use extremely sophisticated models to make these forecasts. Union Oil Company of California, for example, has a complex forecasting system for keeping track of the present and future distributions of professionals and managers. The Union Oil system can spot areas where there will eventually be too many qualified professionals competing for too few promotions or, conversely, too few good people available to fill important positions.[4]

At higher levels of the organization, managers plan for specific people and positions. The technique most commonly used is the **replacement chart**, which lists each important managerial position, who occupies it, how long he or she will probably stay in it before moving on, and who (by name) is now qualified or soon will be qualified to move into the position. This technique allows ample time to plan developmental experiences for persons identified as potential successors to critical managerial jobs. Charles Knight, CEO of Emerson Electric Company, has an entire room dedicated to posting the credentials of his top 700 executives.[5]

To facilitate both planning and identifying persons for current transfer or promotion, some organizations also have an **employee information system**, or **skills inventory**. Such systems are usually computerized and contain information on each employee's education, skills, work experience, and career aspirations. Such a system can quickly locate all the employees in the organization who are qualified to fill a position requiring, for instance, a degree in chemical engineering, three years of experience in an oil refinery, or fluency in Spanish.

Forecasting the external supply of labor is a different problem altogether. How does a manager, for example, predict how many electrical engineers will be seeking work in Georgia three years from now? To get an idea of the future availability of labor, planners must rely on information from such outside sources as state employment commissions, government reports, and figures supplied by colleges on the number of students in major fields.

Matching Human Resource Supply and Demand   After comparing future demand and internal supply, managers can make plans to manage predicted shortfalls or overstaffing. If a shortfall is predicted, new employees can be hired, present employees can be retrained and transferred into the understaffed area, individuals approaching retirement can be convinced to stay on, or labor-saving or productivity-enhancing systems can be installed. If the organization needs to hire, the external labor supply forecast helps managers plan how to recruit based on whether the type of person needed is readily available or scarce in the labor market. If overstaffing is expected to be a problem, the main options are transferring the extra employees, not replacing individuals who quit, encouraging early retirement, and laying people off.

replacement chart Lists each important managerial position in the organization, who occupies it, how long he or she will probably remain in the position, and who is or will be a qualified replacement

employee information system (skills inventory) Contains information on each employee's education, skills, experience, and career aspirations; usually computerized

Bertha Freeman was Detroit's first black female tool-and-die maker. A die is a form carved out of a block of steel to create a reverse version of, say, a car door. It's then installed in a machine that stamps out thousands of car doors. Ms. Freeman got her opportunity when General Motors first opened its apprenticeship program to women in the early 1970s. At the time, GM was doing a lot of internal recruiting; Ms. Freeman was working on one of the company's assembly lines, but was looking for better opportunities. She took the required tests and was the only woman to pass. After a rigorous four-year apprenticeship, she emerged as one of the company's top tool-and-die makers. Today she is with Focus: HOPE, a private nonprofit organization that trains mostly black inner-city kids to become precision machinists.

recruiting The process of attracting individuals to apply for jobs that are open

internal recruiting Considering current employees as applicants for higher-level jobs in the organization

external recruiting Getting people from outside the organization to apply for jobs

realistic job preview (RJP) Provides the applicant with a real picture of what performing the job the organization is trying to fill would be like

Recruiting Human Resources

Once an organization has an idea of its future human resource needs, the next phase is usually recruiting new employees. **Recruiting** is the process of attracting qualified persons to apply for the jobs that are open. Where do recruits come from? Some recruits are found internally; others come from outside the organization. *Management InfoTech* describes how some firms are using the Internet to recruit new employees.

Internal recruiting means considering present employees as candidates for openings. Promotion from within can help build morale and keep high-quality employees from leaving the firm. In unionized firms, the procedures for notifying employees of internal job change opportunities are usually spelled out in the union contract. For higher-level positions, a skills inventory system may be used to identify internal candidates, or managers may be asked to recommend individuals who should be considered. One disadvantage of internal recruiting is its "ripple effect." When an employee moves to a different job, someone else must be found to take his or her old job. In one organization, 454 job movements were necessary as a result of filling 195 initial openings!

External recruiting involves attracting persons outside the organization to apply for jobs. External recruiting methods include advertising, campus interviews, employment agencies or executive search firms, union hiring halls, referrals by present employees, and hiring "walk-ins" or "gate hires" (people who show up without being solicited). Of course, a manager must select the most appropriate methods, using the state employment service to find maintenance workers but not a nuclear physicist, for example. Private employment agencies can be a good source of clerical and technical employees, and executive search firms specialize in locating top-management talent. Newspaper ads are often used because they reach a wide audience and thus allow minorities "equal opportunity" to find out about and apply for job openings. One generally successful method for facilitating effective external recruiting is through the so-called **realistic job preview (RJP)**. As the term suggests, the RJP involves providing the applicant with a real picture of what performing the job that the organization is trying to fill would be like.[6]

Selecting Human Resources

Once the recruiting process has attracted a pool of applicants, the next step is to select whom to hire. The intent of the selection process is to gather from applicants information that will predict their job success and then to hire the

ATTRACTING APPLICANTS WITH HIGH-TECH TOOLS

DVCi Technologies, which specializes in e-commerce, is one of a growing number of organizations boosting their recruiting efforts by giving job seekers a high-tech, behind-the-scenes view of the work environment. DVCi aims cameras at employees working in its New York office and posts the images on its web site, so that potential applicants can get a sense of the workplace and the daily rhythm of activities. This virtual realistic job preview sets DVCi apart from other Internet firms that are recruiting for similar jobs, and it is a proven recruiting tool: Marta Sant, now senior art director, applied for the job after she spent time looking at the images on the DVCi site.

The U.S. Army takes another approach to online recruiting by offering a virtual visit to a typical barracks facility. Potential enlistees can click their way through views of the sleeping quarters, laundry rooms, and other areas. They can also use online chat mode to converse with army recruiters or click to download a video clip of a tank. In this way, military recruiters can attract web-savvy recruits who might otherwise have little knowledge of army living arrangements and career opportunities.

Telecommunications giant Sprint invites e-mail inquiries about job openings from people who browse its web site. If no appropriate positions are open, the company retains the inquiries and, through an automated system, e-mails the applicants when suitable jobs become available. Sprint's human resources experts see e-mail as a good way to build relationships with job seekers and encourage them to keep the company in mind as a potential employer.

Cisco Systems, which makes systems that power Internet activities, also uses e-mail in its recruiting process. Knowing that applicants are keenly interested in an insider's view of the company, Cisco offers to have employees answer questions by e-mail. This program, dubbed "Make Friends at Cisco," helps job seekers learn more about actual working conditions from the people who are in the best position to know. At the same time, it ensures that newly hired employees know at least one colleague when they join Cisco.

> *Every company is looking at ways to maximize the Internet as a recruiting tool.*
>
> —*Sonja Ambur, national staffing director for Sprint**

References: Stephanie Armour, "Companies Put Web to Work as Recruiter," *USA Today*, January 25, 2000, p. 1B (*quote on p. 1B).

---

candidates likely to be most successful. Of course, the organization can only gather information about factors that are predictive of future performance. The process of determining the predictive value of information is called **validation**.

Application Blanks The first step in selection is usually asking the candidate to fill out an application blank. Application blanks are an efficient method of gathering information about the applicant's previous work history, educational background, and other job-related demographic data. They should not contain questions about areas not related to the job, such as gender, religion, or national origin. Application blank data are generally used informally to decide whether a candidate merits further evaluation, and interviewers use application blanks to familiarize themselves with candidates before interviewing them.

Tests Tests of ability, skill, aptitude, or knowledge that is relevant to the particular job are usually the best predictors of job success, although tests of general

validation Determining the extent to which a selection device is really predictive of future job performance

intelligence or personality are occasionally useful as well. In addition to being validated, tests should be administered and scored consistently. All candidates should be given the same directions, should be allowed the same amount of time, and should experience the same testing environment (temperature, lighting, distractions).[7]

Interviews   Although a popular selection device, interviews are sometimes poor predictors of job success. For example, biases inherent in the way people perceive and judge others on first meeting affect subsequent evaluations by the interviewer. Interview validity can be improved by training interviewers to be aware of potential biases and by increasing the structure of the interview. In a structured interview, questions are written in advance, and all interviewers follow the same question list with each candidate they interview. This procedure introduces consistency into the interview procedure and allows the organization to validate the content of the questions to be asked.

For interviewing managerial or professional candidates, a somewhat less structured approach can be used. Question areas and information-gathering objectives are still planned in advance, but the specific questions vary with the candidates' backgrounds. Trammell Crow Real Estate Investors uses a novel approach in hiring managers. Each applicant is interviewed not only by two or three other managers but also by a secretary or young leasing agent. This provides information about how the prospective manager relates to nonmanagers.

Assessment Centers   Assessment centers are a popular method used to select managers and are particularly good for selecting current employees for promotion. The assessment center is a content-valid simulation of major parts of the managerial job. A typical center lasts two to three days, with groups of 6 to 12 persons participating in a variety of managerial exercises. Centers may also include interviews, public speaking, and standardized ability tests. Candidates are assessed by several trained observers, usually managers several levels above the job for which the candidates are being considered. Assessment centers are quite valid if properly designed and are fair to members of minority groups and women.[8] For some firms, the assessment center is a permanent facility created for these activities. For other firms, the assessment activities are performed in a multipurpose location such as a conference room. AT&T pioneered the assessment center concept. For years the firm has used assessment centers to make virtually all of its selection decisions for management positions.

Other Techniques   Organizations also use other selection techniques depending on the circumstances. Polygraph tests, once popular, are declining in popularity. On the other hand, more and more organizations are requiring that applicants take physical exams after they have been offered employment. Organizations are also increasingly using drug tests, especially in situations in which drug-related performance problems could create serious safety hazards. For example, applicants for jobs in a nuclear power plant would likely be tested for drug use. And some organizations today even run credit checks on prospective employees.

Developing Human Resources

Regardless of how effective a selection system is, however, most employees need additional training if they are to grow and develop in their job. Evaluating their performance and providing feedback are also necessary.

Training and Development

In HRM, **training** usually refers to teaching operational or technical employees how to do the job for which they were hired. **Development** refers to teaching managers and professionals the skills needed for both present and future jobs. Most organizations provide regular training and development programs for managers and employees. For example, IBM spends more than $700 million annually on programs and has a vice president in charge of employee education. U.S. businesses spend more than $30 billion annually on training and development programs away from the workplace. And this figure does not include wages and benefits paid to employees while they are participating in such programs.

Assessing Training Needs The first step in developing a training plan is to determine what needs exist. For example, if employees do not know how to operate the machinery necessary to do their job, a training program on how to operate the machinery is clearly needed. On the other hand, when a group of office workers is performing poorly, training may not be the answer. The problem could be motivation, aging equipment, poor supervision, inefficient work design, or a deficiency of skills and knowledge. Only the last could be remedied by training. As training programs are being developed, the manager should set specific and measurable goals specifying what participants are to learn. Managers should also plan to evaluate the training program after employees complete it.

Common Training Methods Many different training and development methods are available. The selection of methods depends on many considerations, but perhaps the most important is training content. When the training content is factual material (such as company rules or explanations of how to fill out forms), assigned reading, programmed learning, and lecture methods work well. When the content is interpersonal relations or group decision making, however, firms must use a method that allows interpersonal contact, such as role-playing or case discussion groups. When employees must learn a physical skill, methods allowing practice and the actual use of tools and material are needed, as

training Teaching operational or technical employees how to do the job for which they were hired

development Teaching managers and professionals the skills needed for both present and future jobs

Training and developing people is an important part of human resource management. Craig Tysdal, president and CEO of NetSolve, makes this function a central part of his job. Every employee at the firm must go through a three-day training program on employee service, whether or not they will ever speak to a customer. And to underscore the importance he places on customer service, Tysdal himself teaches most of the program.

in on-the-job training or vestibule training. (Vestibule training enables participants to focus on safety, learning, and feedback rather than on productivity.) CD-ROM and Internet-based training are also becoming popular. Xerox, Massachusetts Mutual Life Insurance, and Ford have all reported tremendous success with these methods. In addition, most training programs actually rely on a mix of methods. Boeing, for example, sends managers to an intensive two-week training seminar involving tests, simulations, role-playing exercises, and CD-ROM flight simulation exercises.[9]

Evaluation of Training   Training and development programs should always be evaluated. Typical evaluation approaches include measuring one or more relevant criteria (such as attitudes or performance) before and after the training, and determining whether the criteria changed. Evaluation measures collected at the end of training are easy to get, but actual performance measures collected when the trainee is on the job are more important. Trainees may say that they enjoyed the training and learned a lot, but the true test is whether their job performance improves after their training.

Performance Appraisal

performance appraisal
A formal assessment of how well an employee is doing his or her job

When employees are trained and settled into their jobs, one of management's next concerns is performance appraisal. **Performance appraisal** is a formal assessment of how well employees are doing their job. Employees' performance should be evaluated regularly for many reasons. One reason is that performance appraisal may be necessary for validating selection devices or assessing the impact of training programs. A second reason is administrative—to aid in making decisions about pay raises, promotions, and training. Still another reason is to provide feedback to employees to help them improve their present performance and plan future careers. Because performance evaluations often help determine wages and promotions, they must be fair and nondiscriminatory.

Common Appraisal Methods   Two basic categories of appraisal methods commonly used in organizations are objective methods and judgmental methods. Objective measures of performance include actual output (that is, number of units produced), scrap rate, dollar volume of sales, and number of claims processed. Objective performance measures may be contaminated by "opportunity bias" if some persons have a better chance to perform than others. For example, a sales representative selling snow blowers in Michigan has a greater opportunity than does a colleague selling the same product in Arkansas. Fortunately, adjusting raw performance figures for the effect of opportunity bias and thereby arriving at figures that accurately represent each individual's performance is often possible.

Another type of objective measure, the special performance test, is a method in which each employee is assessed under standardized conditions. This kind of appraisal also eliminates opportunity bias. For example, Verizon Southwest, a large telephone company, has a series of prerecorded calls that operators in a test booth answer. The operators are graded on speed, accuracy, and courtesy in handling the calls. Performance tests measure ability but do not measure the extent to which one is motivated to use that ability on a daily basis. (A high-ability person may be a lazy performer except when being tested.) Special performance tests must therefore be supplemented by other appraisal methods to provide a complete picture of performance.

Judgmental methods, including ranking and rating techniques, are the most common way to measure performance. Ranking compares employees directly with each other and rank orders them from best to worst. Ranking has a number of drawbacks. Ranking is difficult for large groups because the persons in the middle of the distribution may be hard to distinguish from one another accurately. Comparisons of people in different work groups are also difficult. For example, an employee ranked third in a strong group may be more valuable than an employee ranked first in a weak group. Another criticism of ranking is that the manager must rank people on the basis of overall performance, although each person likely has both strengths and weaknesses. Furthermore, rankings do not provide useful information for feedback. To be told that one is ranked third is not nearly as helpful as to be told that the quality of one's work is outstanding, its quantity is satisfactory, one's punctuality could use improvement, or one's paperwork is seriously deficient.

Rating differs from ranking in that it compares each employee with a fixed standard rather than with other employees. A rating scale provides the standard. Figure 8.2 gives examples of three graphic rating scales for a bank teller. Each consists of

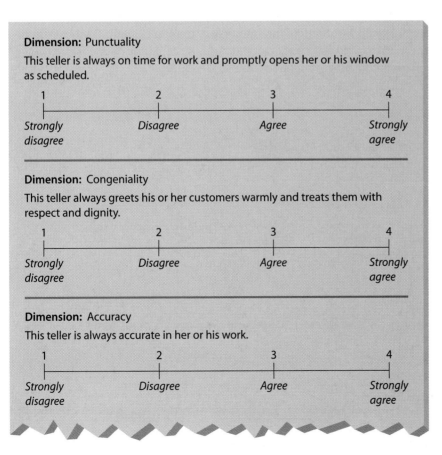

Figure 8.2

Graphic Rating Scales for a Bank Teller

Graphic rating scales are a very common method for evaluating employee performance. The manager who is doing the rating circles the point on each scale that best reflects her or his assessment of the employee on that scale. Graphic rating scales are widely used for many different kinds of jobs.

a performance dimension to be rated (punctuality, congeniality, and accuracy) followed by a scale on which to make the rating. In constructing graphic rating scales, performance dimensions that are relevant to job performance must be selected. In particular, they should focus on job behaviors and results rather than on personality traits or attitudes.

Behaviorally Anchored Rating Scale (BARS) A sophisticated rating method in which supervisors construct a rating scale associated with behavioral anchors

The **Behaviorally Anchored Rating Scale (BARS)** is a sophisticated and useful rating method. Supervisors construct rating scales with associated behavioral anchors. They first identify relevant performance dimensions and then generate anchors—specific, observable behaviors typical of each performance level. Figure 8.3 shows an example of a behaviorally anchored rating scale for the dimension "inventory control."

Errors in Performance Appraisal   Errors or biases can occur in any kind of rating or ranking system. One common problem is recency error—the tendency to base judgments on the subordinate's most recent performance because it is most easily recalled. Often, a rating or ranking is intended to evaluate performance over an entire time period, such as six months or a year, so the recency error does introduce error into the judgment. Other errors include overuse of one part of the scale—being too lenient, being too severe, or giving everyone a rating of "average." Halo error is allowing the assessment of an employee on one dimension to "spread" to ratings of that employee on other dimensions. For instance, if an employee is outstanding on quality of output, a rater might tend to give her or him higher marks than deserved on other dimensions. Errors can also occur because of race, sex, or age discrimination, intentionally or unintentionally. The best way to offset these errors is to ensure that a valid rating system is developed at the outset and then to train managers in how to use it.

Figure 8.3

Behaviorally Anchored Rating Scale

Behaviorally Anchored Rating Scales help overcome some of the limitations of standard rating scales. Each point on the scale is accompanied by a behavioral anchor—a summary of employee behavior that fits that spot on the scale.

Job: Specialty store manager
Dimension: Inventory control

7 Always orders in the right quantities and at the right time

6 Almost always orders at the right time but occasionally orders too much or too little of a particular item

5 Usually orders at the right time and almost always in the right quantities

4 Often orders in the right quantities and at the right time

3 Occasionally orders at the right time but usually not in the right quantities

2 Occasionally orders in the right quantities but usually not at the right time

1 Never orders in the right quantities or at the right time

©2000 by King Features Syndicate, Inc. World rights reserved.

Reprinted with special permission of King Features Syndicate.

Performance Feedback

The last step in most performance appraisal systems is giving feedback to subordinates about their performance. This is usually done in a private meeting between the person being evaluated and his or her boss. The discussion should generally be focused on the facts—the assessed level of performance, how and why that assessment was made, and how it can be improved in the future. Feedback interviews are not easy to conduct. Many managers are uncomfortable with the task, especially if feedback is negative and subordinates are disappointed by what they hear. These points are amplified in the cartoon. Properly training managers, however, can help them conduct more effective feedback interviews.

A recent innovation in performance appraisal used in many organizations today is called "360 degree" feedback: Managers are evaluated by everyone around them—their boss, their peers, and their subordinates. Such a complete and thorough approach provides people with a far richer array of information about their performance than does a conventional appraisal given just by the boss. Of course, such a system also takes considerable time and must be handled so as not to breed fear and mistrust in the workplace.[10]

Providing performance feedback is a difficult process for many managers. For example, they may have a hard time giving negative feedback or simply feel uncomfortable with the process. And in some cases, as illustrated here, a manager may feel that it is only his or her opinion that counts. The employee, of course, is likely to figure out what is going on, and thus the information value of the performance feedback process can be completely lost.

■ Maintaining Human Resources

After organizations have attracted and developed an effective workforce, they must also make every effort to maintain that workforce. To do so requires effective compensation and benefits as well as career planning.

Determining Compensation

Compensation is the financial remuneration given by the organization to its employees in exchange for their work. There are three basic forms of compensation. *Wages* are the hourly compensation paid to operating employees. The minimum

compensation The financial remuneration given by the organization to its employees in exchange for their work

hourly wage paid in the United States today is $5.15. *Salary* refers to compensation paid for total contributions, as opposed to being based on hours worked. For example, managers earn an annual salary, usually paid monthly. They receive the salary regardless of the number of hours they work. Some firms have started paying all their employees a salary instead of hourly wages. For example, all employees at Chaparral Steel Company earn a salary, starting at $20,000 a year for entry-level operating employees. Finally, *incentives* represent special compensation opportunities that are usually tied to performance. Sales commissions and bonuses are among the most common incentives. A good compensation system can help attract qualified applicants, retain present employees, and stimulate high performance at a cost reasonable for one's industry and geographic area. To set up a successful system, management must make decisions about wage levels, the wage structure, and the individual wage determination system.

Wage-Level Decision   The wage-level decision is a management policy decision about whether the firm wants to pay above, at, or below the going rate for labor in the industry or the geographic area. Most firms choose to pay near the average, whereas those that cannot afford more pay below average. Large, successful firms may like to cultivate the image of being "wage leaders" by intentionally paying more than average and thus attracting and keeping high-quality employees. IBM, for example, pays top dollar to get the new employees it wants. McDonald's, on the other hand, often pays close to the minimum wage. The level of unemployment in the labor force also affects wage levels. Pay declines when labor is plentiful and increases when labor is scarce. Once managers make the wage-level decision, they need information to help set actual wage rates. Managers need to know what the maximum, minimum, and average wages are for particular jobs in the appropriate labor market. This information is collected by means of a wage survey. Area wage surveys can be conducted by individual firms or by local HR or business associations. Professional and industry associations often conduct surveys and make the results available to employers.

Wage-Structure Decision   Wage structures are usually set up through a procedure called **job evaluation**—an attempt to assess the worth of each job relative to other jobs. The simplest method for creating a wage structure is to rank jobs from those that should be paid the most (for example, the president) to those that should be paid the least (for example, a mail clerk or a janitor). In a smaller firm with few jobs, this method is quick and practical, but larger firms with many job titles require more sophisticated methods. The next step is setting actual wage rates on the basis of a combination of survey data and the wage structure that results from job evaluation. Jobs of equal value are often grouped into wage grades for ease of administration.

job evaluation An attempt to assess the worth of each job relative to other jobs

Individual Wage Decisions   After wage-level and wage-structure decisions are made, the individual wage decision must be addressed. This decision concerns how much to pay each employee in a particular job. Although the easiest decision is to pay a single rate for each job, more typically, a range of pay rates is associated with each job. For example, the pay range for an individual job might be $7 to $9 per hour, with different employees earning different rates within the range. A system is then needed for setting individual rates. This may be done on the basis of seniority (enter the job at $7, for example, and increase 25 cents per hour every six months on the job), on initial qualifications (inexperienced people start at $7, more experienced start at a higher rate), or merit (raises above the entering rate are given for good performance). Combinations of these bases may also be used.

Determining Benefits

Benefits are things of value other than compensation that the organization provides to its workers. The average company spends an amount equal to more than one-third of its cash payroll on employee benefits. Thus an average employee who is paid $18,000 per year averages about $6,588 more per year in benefits. Benefits come in several forms. Pay for time not worked includes sick leave, vacation, holidays, and unemployment compensation. Insurance benefits often include life and health insurance for employees and their dependents. Workers' compensation is a legally required insurance benefit that provides medical care and disability income for employees injured on the job. Social security is a government pension plan to which both employers and employees contribute. Many employers also provide a private pension plan to which they and their employees contribute. Employee service benefits include such options as tuition reimbursement and recreational opportunities.

> **benefits** Things of value other than compensation that an organization provides to its workers

Some organizations have instituted "cafeteria benefit plans," whereby basic coverage is provided for all employees, but employees are then allowed to choose which additional benefits they want (up to a cost limit based on salary). An employee with five children might choose medical and dental coverage for dependents, a single employee might prefer more vacation time, and an older employee might elect increased pension benefits. Flexible systems are expected to encourage people to stay in the organization and even help the company attract new employees.[11]

■ Managing Workforce Diversity

Workforce diversity has become a very important issue in many organizations. The management of diversity is often seen as a key human resource function.

The Meaning of Diversity

Diversity exists in a community of people when its members differ from one another along one or more important dimensions. Especially important dimensions of diversity include gender, age, and ethnicity. For example, the average age of the U.S. workforce is gradually increasing and will continue to do so for the next

> **diversity** Exists in a group or organization when its members differ from one another along one or more important dimensions

several years. Similarly, as more females have entered the workforce, organizations have experienced changes in the relative proportions of male and female employees. And within the United States, more organizations reflect varying degrees of ethnicity, with workforces comprising whites, African Americans, Hispanics, and Asians. Other groups, such as single parents, dual-career couples, same-sex couples, and the physically challenged, are also important.

The Impact of Diversity

There is no question that organizations are becoming ever more diverse. But how does this affect organizations? Diversity provides both opportunities and challenges for organizations.

Diversity as a Competitive Advantage   Many organizations have found that diversity can be a source of competitive advantage in the marketplace. For example, businesses that manage diversity effectively will generally have higher levels of productivity and lower levels of turnover and absenteeism, thus lowering costs. Ortho Pharmaceutical Corporation estimates that it has saved $500,000 by lowering turnover among women and ethnic minorities. In addition, organizations that manage diversity effectively become known among women and minorities as good places to work. These organizations are thus better able to attract qualified employees from among these groups. Moreover, organizations with diverse workforces are better able to understand different market segments. For example, a cosmetics firm like Avon, which wants to sell its products to women and African Americans, can better understand how to create such products and effectively market them if female and African-American managers are available to provide inputs into product development, design, packaging, advertising, and so forth.[12] Finally, organizations with a diverse workforce are generally more creative and innovative than other organizations in which the workforce is less diverse.

Diversity as a Source of Conflict   Unfortunately, diversity in an organization can also create conflict. This conflict can arise for a variety of reasons.[13] One potential avenue for conflict is when an individual thinks that someone has been hired, promoted, or fired because of her or his diversity status. Another source of conflict stemming from diversity is through misunderstood, misinterpreted, or inappropriate interactions between people of different groups. Conflict may also arise as a result of fear, distrust, or individual prejudice. Members of the dominant group in an organization may worry that newcomers from other groups pose a personal threat to their own position in the organization. For example, when U.S. firms have been taken over by Japanese firms, U.S. managers have sometimes been resentful of or hostile toward Japanese managers assigned to work with them. People may also be unwilling to accept people who are different from themselves. And personal bias and prejudices are still very real among some people today and can lead to potentially harmful conflict.

Managing Diversity in Organizations

Because of the tremendous potential that diversity holds for competitive advantage, as well as the possible consequences of associated conflict, much attention has been focused in recent years on how individuals and organizations can better manage diversity.

Individual Strategies   One important element of managing diversity in an organization consists of things that individuals themselves can do. Understanding, of course, is the starting point. Although people need to be treated fairly and equitably, managers must understand that differences among people do, in fact, exist. People in an organization should try to understand the perspective of others. Tolerance is important. Even though managers learn to understand diversity and even though they may try to empathize with others, the fact remains that they may still not accept or enjoy some aspect of their behavior. Communication is also important. Problems often get magnified over diversity issues because people are afraid or otherwise unwilling to openly discuss issues that relate to diversity. For example, suppose a younger employee has a habit of making jokes about the age of an elderly colleague. Perhaps the younger colleague means no harm and is just engaging in what she sees as good-natured kidding. But the older employee may find the jokes offensive. If there is no communication between the two, the jokes will continue, and the resentment will grow. Eventually, what started as a minor problem may erupt into a much bigger one.

Organizational Approaches to Managing Diversity   Whereas individuals are important in managing diversity, the organization itself must play a fundamental role. The starting point in managing diversity is the policies that an organization adopts that directly or indirectly affect how people are treated. Another aspect of organizational policies that affect diversity is how the organization addresses and responds to problems arising from differences among people. For example, consider the example of a manager charged with sexual harassment. If the organization's policies put an excessive burden of proof on the individual being harassed and invoke only minor sanctions against the guilty party, it is sending a clear signal about the importance of such matters. But the organization that has a balanced set of policies for addressing questions like sexual harassment sends its employees a message that diversity and individual rights and privileges are important.

Organizations can also help manage diversity through a variety of ongoing practices and procedures. Avon's creation of networks for various groups represents one example of an organizational practice that fosters diversity. In general, the idea is that, because diversity is characterized by differences among people, organizations can more effectively manage that diversity by following practices and procedures that are based on flexibility rather than rigidity. Many organizations are finding that diversity training is an effective means of managing diversity and minimizing its associated conflict. More specifically, diversity training is specifically designed to better enable members of an organization to function in a diverse workplace. The ultimate test of an organization's commitment to managing diversity, as discussed earlier in this book, is its culture. Regardless of what managers say or put in writing, unless there is a basic and fundamental belief that diversity is valued, it can never become truly an integral part of an organization.

Managing Labor Relations

labor relations The process of dealing with employees when they are represented by a union

Labor relations is the process of dealing with employees who are represented by a union.[14] Managing labor relations is an important part of HRM.

How Employees Form Unions

For employees to form a new local union, several things must occur. First, employees must become interested in having a union. Nonemployees who are professional organizers employed by a national union (such as the Teamsters or the United Auto Workers) may generate interest by making speeches and distributing literature outside the workplace. Inside, employees who want a union try to convince other workers of the benefits of a union.

The second step is to collect employees' signatures on authorization cards. These cards state that the signer wishes to vote to determine whether the union will represent him or her. Thirty percent of the employees in the potential bargaining unit must sign these cards to show the National Labor Relations Board that interest is sufficient to justify holding an election. Before an election can be held, however, the bargaining unit must be defined. The bargaining unit consists of all employees who will be eligible to vote in the election and to join and be represented by the union if one is formed.

The election is supervised by an NLRB representative (or, if both parties agree, by the American Arbitration Association—a professional association of arbitrators) and is conducted by secret ballot. If a simple majority of those voting (not of all those eligible to vote) votes for the union, then the union becomes certified as the official representative of the bargaining unit.[15] The new union then organizes itself by officially signing up members and electing officers; it will soon be ready to negotiate the first contract. The union organizing process is diagrammed in Figure 8.4. If workers become disgruntled with their union or if management presents strong evidence that the union is not representing workers appropriately, the NLRB can arrange a decertification election. The results of such an election determine whether the union remains certified.

Organizations usually prefer that employees not be unionized, because unions limit management's freedom in many areas. Management may thus wage its own campaign to convince employees to vote against the union. "Unfair labor practices" are often committed at this point. For instance, it is an unfair labor practice for management to promise to give employees a raise (or any other benefit) if the union is defeated. Experts agree that the best way to avoid unionization is to practice good employee relations all the time—not just when threatened by a union election. Providing absolutely fair treatment with clear standards in the areas of

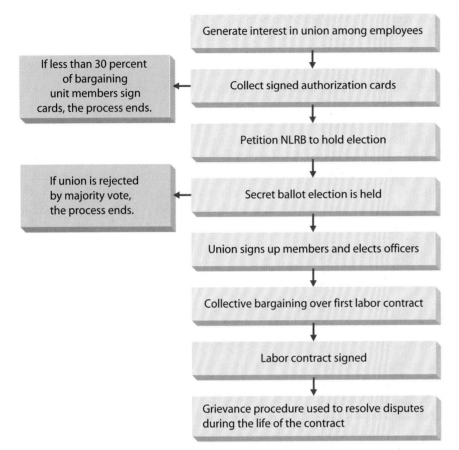

Figure 8.4

The Union Organizing Process
If employees of an organization want to form a union, the law prescribes a specific set of procedures that both employees and the organization must follow. Assuming that these procedures are followed and the union is approved, the organization must engage in collective bargaining with the new union.

pay, promotion, layoff, and discipline; having a complaint or appeal system for persons who feel unfairly treated; and avoiding any kind of favoritism will help make employees feel that a union is unnecessary.

Collective Bargaining

The intent of **collective bargaining** is to agree on a labor contract between management and the union which is satisfactory to both parties. The contract contains agreements such as wages, hours, about conditions of employment promotion, layoff, discipline, benefits, methods of allocating overtime, vacations, rest periods, and the grievance procedure. The process of bargaining may go on for weeks, months, or longer, with representatives of management and the union meeting to make proposals and counterproposals. The resulting agreement must be ratified by the union membership. If it is not approved, the union may strike to put pressure on management, or it may choose not to strike and simply continue negotiating until a more acceptable agreement is reached.

The **grievance procedure** is the means by which the contract is enforced. Most of what is in a contract concerns how management will treat employees. When

collective bargaining The process of agreeing on a satisfactory labor contract between management and a union

grievance procedure The means by which a labor contract is enforced

employees feel that they have not been treated fairly under the contract, they file a grievance to correct the problem. The first step in a grievance procedure is for the aggrieved employee to discuss the alleged contract violation with his or her immediate superior. Often the grievance is resolved at this stage. If the employee still believes that he or she is being mistreated, however, the grievance can be appealed to the next level. A union official can help an aggrieved employee present his or her case. If the manager's decision is also unsatisfactory to the employee, additional appeals to successively higher levels are made, until finally all in-company steps are exhausted. The final step is to submit the grievance to binding arbitration. An arbitrator is a labor law expert who is paid jointly by the union and management. The arbitrator studies the contract, hears both sides of the case, and renders a decision that both parties must obey. The grievance system for resolving disputes about contract enforcement prevents any need to strike during the term of the contract.

Summary of Key Points

Human resource management is concerned with attracting, developing, and maintaining the human resources an organization needs. Its environmental context consists of its strategic importance and the legal environment that affects human resource management.

Attracting human resources is an important part of the HRM function. Human resource planning starts with job analysis and then focuses on forecasting the organization's future need for employees, forecasting the availability of employees both within and outside the organization, and planning programs to ensure that the proper number and type of employees are available when needed. Recruitment and selection are the processes by which job applicants are attracted, assessed, and hired. Methods for selecting applicants include application blanks, tests, interviews, and assessment centers. Any method used for selection should be properly validated.

Organizations must also work to develop their human resources. Training and development enable employees to perform their present jobs effectively and to prepare for future jobs. Performance appraisals are important for validating selection devices, assessing the impact of training programs, deciding pay raises

and promotions, and determining training needs. Both objective and judgmental methods of appraisal can be applied, and a good system usually includes several methods. The validity of appraisal information is always a concern, because it is difficult to accurately evaluate the many aspects of a person's job performance.

Maintaining human resources is also important. Compensation rates must be fair compared with rates for other jobs within the organization and with rates for the same or similar jobs in other organizations in the labor market. Properly designed incentive or merit pay systems can encourage high performance, and a good benefits program can help attract and retain employees. Career planning is also a major aspect of human resource management.

Diversity exists in a community of people when its members differ from one another along one or more important dimensions. There are several important dimensions of diversity, including age, gender, and ethnicity. Diversity can affect an organization in a number of different ways. Managing diversity in organizations can be done by both individuals and the organization itself.

If a majority of a company's nonmanagement employees so desire, they have the right to be represented by a union. Management must engage in collective bargaining with the union in an effort to agree on a contract. While the contract is in effect, the grievance system is used to settle disputes with management.

Discussion Questions

Questions for Review

1. Describe recruiting and selection. What are the major sources for recruits? What are the common selection methods?
2. What is the role of compensation and benefits in organizations? How should the amount of compensation and benefits be determined?
3. Identify the major dimensions of diversity and discuss recent trends for each.
4. Summarize the basic impact of diversity on organizations.
5. What are the basic steps that employees can follow if they wish to unionize?

Questions for Analysis

6. What are the advantages and disadvantages of internal and external recruiting? Which do you feel is best in the long term? Why? Be sure to think about this issue from the standpoint of both the organization and individuals (whether inside or outside of the organization) who might be considered for positions.
7. How do you know if a selection device is valid? What are the possible consequences of using invalid selection methods? How can an organization ensure that its selection methods are valid?
8. Are benefits more important than compensation to an organization? to an individual? Why?
9. The text outlines many different advantages of diversity in organizations. Can you think of any disadvantages?
10. When you finish school and begin your career, what should you be prepared to do to succeed in a diverse workforce?

BUILDING EFFECTIVE *communication* SKILLS

Exercise Overview

All managers must be able to effectively communicate with others in the organization. Communication is especially important in the human resource area, because people are the domain of HRM.

Exercise Background

Many companies provide various benefits to their workers. These benefits may include such options as pay for time not worked, insurance coverage, pension plans, and so forth. These benefits are often very costly to the organization. As noted in the text, for example, benefits often equal around one-third of what employees are paid in wages and salaries. In some countries, such as Germany, the figures are even higher.

Yet many employees often fail to appreciate the actual value of the benefits their employers provide. For example, employees frequently underestimate the dollar value of their benefits. And, when comparing their income to that of others or when comparing alternative job offers, many people focus almost entirely on direct compensation—wages and salaries paid directly to the individual.

For example, consider a college graduate who has two offers. One job offer is for $20,000 a year, and the other is for $22,000. The individual is likely to see the second offer as being more attractive even if the first offer has sufficiently more attractive benefits to make the total compensation packages equivalent to one another.

Exercise Task

With this information as context, respond to the following:

1. Why do you think most people focus on pay when assessing their compensation?

2. If you were the human resource manager for a firm, how would you go about communicating the value of benefits to your employees?

3. Suppose an employee comes to you and says that he is thinking about leaving for a "better job." You then learn that he is defining "better" only in terms of higher pay. How might you help him compare total compensation (including benefits)?

4. Some firms today are cutting their benefits. How would you communicate a benefit cut to your employees?

BUILDING EFFECTIVE *technical* SKILLS

Exercise Overview

Technical skills refer to the manager's abilities to accomplish or understand work done in an organization. Many managers must have technical skills to hire appropriate people to work in the organization. This exercise helps you use technical skills as part of the selection process.

Exercise Background

Variation 1: If you currently work full time, or have worked full time in the past, select two jobs with which you have some familiarity. One job should be relatively low in skill level, responsibility, required education, and pay; the other should be relatively high in skill level, responsibility, required education, and pay. The exercise will be more useful to you if you use real jobs that you can relate to at a personal level.

Variation 2: If you have never worked full time or if you are not personally familiar with an array of jobs, assume that you are a manager for a small manufacturing facility. You need to hire individuals to fill two jobs. One job is for the po-

sition of plant custodian. This individual will sweep floors, clean bathrooms, empty trashcans, and so forth. The other person will be office manager. This individual will supervise a staff of three clerks and secretaries, administer the plant payroll, and coordinate the administrative operations of the plant.

Exercise Task

With the information above as background, do the following:

1. Identify the most basic skills that you think are necessary for someone to perform each job effectively.

2. Identify the general indicators or predictors of whether or not a given individual can perform each job.

3. Develop a brief set of interview questions which you might use to determine whether or not an applicant has the qualifications to perform each job.

4. How important is it for a manager hiring employees to perform a job to have the technical skills to do that job him- or herself?

BUILDING EFFECTIVE *decision-making* SKILLS

Exercise Overview

Decision-making skills include the manager's ability to correctly recognize and define problems and opportunities and to then select an appropriate course of action to solve problems and capitalize on opportunities. This exercise helps you develop decision-making skills by applying them to a human resource problem. Managers must frequently select one or more employees from a pool of employees for termination, layoff, special recognition, training, or promotion. Each such selection represents a decision.

Exercise Task

Your company recently developed a plan to identify and train top hourly employees for promotion to first-line supervisor. As part of this program, your boss has requested a ranking of the six hourly employees who report to you with respect to their promotion potential. Given their biographical data, rank them in the order in which you would select them for promotion to first-line supervisor; that is, the person ranked number one would be first in line for promotion. Repeat this process in a group with three or four of your classmates.

Biographical Data

1. *Sam Nelson:* White male, age 45, married, with four children. Sam has been with the company for five years, and his performance evaluations have been average to above average. He is well liked by the other employees in the department. He devotes his spare time to farming and plans to farm after retirement.

2. *Ruth Hornsby:* White female, age 32, married, with no children. Her husband has a management-level job with a power company. Ruth has been with the company for two years and has received above-average performance evaluations. She is very quiet and keeps to herself at work. She says she is working to save for a down payment on a new house.

3. *Joe Washington:* Black male, age 26, single. Joe has been with the company for three years and has received high performance evaluations. He is always willing to take on new assignments and to work overtime. He is attending college in the evenings and someday wants to start his own business. He is well liked by the other employees in the department.

4. *Ronald Smith:* White male, age 35, recently divorced, with one child, age four. Ronald has received excellent performance evaluations during his two years with the company. He seems to like his present job but has removed himself from the line of progression. He seems to have personality conflicts with some of the employees in the department.

5. *Betty Norris:* Black female, age 44, married, with one grown child. Betty has been with the company for ten years and is well liked by fellow employees. Her performance evaluations have been average to below average, and her advancement has been limited by a lack of formal education. She has participated in a number of technical training programs conducted by the company.

6. *Roy Davis:* White male, age 36, married, with two teen-age children. Roy has been with the company for ten years and has received excellent performance evaluations until last year. His most recent evaluation was average. He is friendly and well liked by his fellow employees. One of his children has had a serious illness for over a year, resulting in a number of large medical expenses. Roy is working a second job on weekends to help with these expenses. He has expressed a serious interest in promotion to first-line supervisor.

Source: From *Supervisory Management: The Art of Working With* and Through People, 3rd edition by Donald C. Mosley, L. C. Megginson, and P. H. Pietri, pp. 90–91. ©1993. Reprinted with permission of South-Western College Publishing, a division of International Thomson Publishing. Fax 800-730-2215.

SKILLS *self-assessment* INSTRUMENT

Diagnosing Poor Performance and Enhancing Motivation

Introduction: Formal performance appraisal and feedback are part of assuring proper performance in an organization. The following assessment is designed to help you understand how to detect poor performance and overcome it.

Instructions: Please respond to these statements by entering a number from the following rating scale. Your answers should reflect your attitudes and behaviors as they are *now*.

Rating Scale

6 Strongly agree	**3** Slightly disagree
5 Agree	**2** Disagree
4 Slightly agree	**1** Strongly disagree

When another person needs to be motivated,

_____ 1. I always approach a performance problem by first establishing whether it is caused by a lack of motivation or ability.

_____ 2. I always establish a clear standard of expected performance.

_____ 3. I always offer to provide training and information, without offering to do the task myself.

_____ 4. I am honest and straightforward in providing feedback on performance and assessing advancement opportunities.

_____ 5. I use a variety of rewards to reinforce exceptional performances.

_____ 6. When discipline is required, I identify the problem, describe its consequences, and explain how it should be corrected.

_____ 7. I design task assignments to make them interesting and challenging.

_____ 8. I determine what rewards are valued by the person and strive to make those available.

_____ 9. I make sure that the person feels fairly and equitably treated.

_____ 10. I make sure that the person gets timely feedback from those affected by task performance.

_____ 11. I carefully diagnose the causes of poor performance before taking any remedial or disciplinary actions.

_____ 12. I always help the person establish performance goals that are challenging, specific, and time bound.

_____ 13. Only as a last resort do I attempt to reassign or release a poorly performing individual.

_____ 14. Whenever possible I make sure that valued rewards are linked to high performance.

_____ 15. I consistently discipline when effort is below expectations and capabilities.

_____ 16. I try to combine or rotate assignments so that the person can use a variety of skills.

_____ 17. I try to arrange for the person to work with others in a team, for the mutual support of all.

_____ 18. I make sure that the person is using realistic standards for measuring fairness.

_____ 19. I provide immediate compliments and other forms of recognition for meaningful accomplishments.

_____ 20. I always determine whether the person has the necessary resources and support to succeed in the task.

For interpretation, see Interpretations of Skills Self-Assessment Instruments.

Source: *Developing Management Skills* by Whetton, Cameron. © 1991. Reprinted by permission of Pearson Education, Inc., Upper Saddle River, NJ.

EXPERIENTIAL EXERCISE

Choosing a Compensation Strategy

Purpose: This exercise helps you better understand how internal and external market forces affect compensation strategies.

Introduction: Assume that you are the head of a large academic department in a major research university. Your salaries are a bit below external market salaries. For example, your assistant professors make between $45,000 and $55,000 a year; your associate professors make between $57,000 and $65,000 a year; and your full professors make between $67,000 and $75,000 a year.

Faculty who have been in your department for a long time enjoy the work environment and appreciate the low cost of living in the area. They know that they are somewhat underpaid but offset this against the advantages of being in your department. Recently, however, external market forces have caused salaries for people in your field to escalate rapidly. Unfortunately, although your university acknowledges this problem, you have also been told that no additional resources can be made available to your department.

You currently have four vacant positions that need to be filled. One of these is at the rank of associate professor, and the other three are at the rank of assistant professor. You have surveyed other departments in similar universities, and realize that, to hire the best new assistant professors, you will need to offer at least $58,000 a year, and to get a qualified associate professor, you will need to pay at least $70,000. You have been given the budget to hire new employees at more competitive salaries but cannot do anything to raise the salaries of faculty currently in your department. You have identified the following options:

1. You can hire new faculty from lower-quality schools that pay salaries below market rate.
2. You can hire the best people available, pay market salaries, and deal with internal inequities later.
3. You can hire fewer new faculty, use the extra money to boost the salaries of your current faculty, and cut class offerings in the future.

Instructions

Step 1: Working alone, decide how you will proceed.

Step 2: Form small groups with your classmates and compare solutions.

Step 3: Identify the strengths and weaknesses of each option.

Followup Questions

1. Are there other options that might be pursued?
2. Assume that you chose option 2. How would you go about dealing with the internal equity problems?
3. Discuss with your instructor the extent to which this problem exists at your school.

HOW THE MOST ADMIRED COMPANIES MANAGE HUMAN RESOURCES

The most admired companies in America have at least one thing in common: They all pay careful attention to the management of that most precious asset, their employees. General Electric, which appears at the top of many "best-managed" lists, has made training and development one of its top priorities. Through ongoing training, assignment rotation, and performance evaluation, GE gives promising managers the skills and seasoning they need to move up and handle increased responsibilities. The company has also created a unique mentoring program which pairs tech-savvy younger employees with tech-wary senior managers. As the younger employees teach the senior managers how to navigate the Internet, both benefit from the sharing of ideas and expertise. Given GE's intense focus on human resources, it is not surprising that the company attracts 20 applicants for every job opening.

Another company widely admired for its management of human resources is Southwest Airlines. Consistently profitable in a notoriously competitive industry, Southwest hires a mere 4 percent of the 90,000 people who apply for jobs every year. The airline uses personality tests to identify applicants with the right mix of can-do attitude, communication skills, decision-making skills, and team spirit. New hires are immersed in intensive training at the company's University for People before they start their job. When internal conflicts occasionally erupt between employees who handle different jobs, Southwest has the employees switch jobs for a day so they can see things from the other side—a tactic that generally diffuses the tension.

Wal-Mart, a perennial on most-admired lists, calls its human resources management group the People Division, as a reflection of the firm's no-nonsense approach. Wal-Mart, like other retailing firms, has been plagued by turnover that can run as high as 70 percent among hourly store workers. As many as 400,000 employees leave and must be replaced every year. Factoring in new store openings, Wal-Mart winds up hiring some 550,000 employees annually. Now the company is aiming to slash this turnover rate by being more selective in hiring, training and communicating more effectively, and offering recognition and pay for performance. The effort is already paying off: Turnover is dropping, which means that Wal-Mart is well on its way toward saving a huge chunk of its recruiting and training budget. The retailer is also known for promoting from within, which attracts ambitious people looking for opportunity who are willing to be held accountable for their decisions—another Wal-Mart hallmark.

Chip maker Intel, much admired for its management excellence, is always on the lookout for new employees with potential. Competition for applicants with high-tech skills is so fierce that Intel has set up an internship program to attract college students before they are in the market for full-time jobs. Every year, 1,000 college interns rotate through different departments, moving from service operations to procurement and other groups to get hands-on, practical experience in the work world. The interns also get immersed in Intel's culture and form relationships that come in handy if they continue working at Intel after graduation—which 70 percent do. Intel invites interns to participate in benefits such as the stock purchase plan and counts their internship period toward vacation time once they sign on as full-time employees. These college internships help Intel tap a fresh pool of talented employees every year.

Case Questions

1. What recruiting techniques are being used by these companies? Why are these techniques effective?

2. Why would Southwest and other companies go beyond the use of applications and interviews when selecting new employees?

3. How do training and development programs help companies reduce turnover?

Case References

Brent Schlender, "The Odd Couple," *Fortune,* May 1, 2000, pp. 106–110; "Can the House That Jack Built Stand When He Goes? Sure, Welch Says," *Wall Street Journal,* April 13, 2000, pp. A1, A10; Carol J. Loomis, "Sam Would Be Proud," *Fortune,* April 17, 2000, pp. 130–144; Katrina Brooker, "Can Anyone Replace Herb?" *Fortune,* April 17, 2000, pp. 186–192; "Raising the Bar," *Fortune,* February 21, 2000, pp. 115–116; and Geoffrey Colvin, "America's Most Admired Companies," *Fortune,* February 21, 2000, pp. 108–135.

CHAPTER NOTES

1. "Dr. Goodnight's Company Town," *Business Week*, June 19, 2000, pp. 192–202; Charles Fishman, "Sanity Inc.," *Fast Company*, January 1999, pp. 84–96 (quote on p. 89); and Jerry Useem, "Welcome to the New Company Town," *Fortune*, January 10, 2000, pp. 62–70.

2. For a complete review of human resource management, see Angelo S. DeNisi and Ricky W. Griffin, *Human Resource Management* (Boston: Houghton Mifflin, 2001).

3. Patrick Wright and Gary McMahan, "Strategic Human Resources Management: A Review of the Literature," *Journal of Management*, June 1992, pp. 280–319.

4. "The New Workforce," *Business Week*, March 20, 2000, pp. 64–70.

5. John Beeson, "Succession Planning," *Across the Board*, February 2000, pp. 38–41.

6. James A. Breaugh and Mary Starke, "Research on Employee Recruiting: So Many Studies, So Many Remaining Questions," *Journal of Management* 26, no. 3 (2000): 405–434.

7. Frank L. Schmidt and John E. Hunter, "Employment Testing: Old Theories and New Research Findings," *American Psychologist*, October 1981, 1128–1137.

8 Paul R. Sackett, "Assessment Centers and Content Validity: Some Neglected Issues," *Personnel Psychology* 40 (1987): 13–25.

9. "'Boeing U': Flying by the Book," *USA Today*, October 6, 1997, pp. 1B, 2B.

10. See Angelo S. DeNisi and Avraham N. Kluger, "Feedback Effectiveness: Can 360 Degree Appraisals Be Improved?" *Academy of Management Executive* 14, no. 1 (2000): 129–139.

11. "To Each According to His Needs: Flexible Benefits Plans Gain Favor," *Wall Street Journal*, September 16, 1986, p. 29.

12. For an example, see "A Female Executive Tells Furniture Maker What Women Want," *Wall Street Journal*, June 25, 1999, pp. A1, A11.

13. Patricia L. Nemetz and Sandra L. Christensen, "The Challenge of Cultural Diversity: Harnessing a Diversity of Views to Understand Multiculturalism," *Academy of Management Review* 21, no. 2 (1996): 434–462. See also "Generational Warfare," *Forbes*, March 22, 1999, pp. 62–66.

14. Barbara Presley Nobel, "Reinventing Labor," *Harvard Business Review*, July/August 1993, pp. 115–125.

15. John A. Fossum, "Labor Relations: Research and Practice in Transition," *Journal of Management*, Summer 1987, pp. 281–300.

PART FOUR

Leading

CHAPTER

9

Managing Individual Behavior

Levi Strauss & Company and the ubiquitous denim blue jeans it sells around the world have been icons for as long as baby boomers can remember. Levi's real growth started in the late 1950s when its denim jeans became a uniform for the youth of the United States. The momentum continued into the 1960s as denim took its place alongside incense, tie-dyed T-shirts, peace signs, and long hair as symbols of a rebellious youth. And as the baby boomers of the 1950s and 1960s grew into adulthood, Levi's jeans became a fashion staple. Indeed, even the name Levi's became almost synonymous with blue jeans. During the 1970s through the 1990s, Levi's also expanded rapidly overseas and today sells its products in more than 70 countries.

Over a period of decades, Levi's also forged an innovative relationship with its employees. High levels of job security, an innovative reward structure, and an open and participative approach to management created a loyal and dedicated workforce that helped keep the organization at the top of its industry. Indeed, when experts first began ranking "best places to work," Levi Strauss was always near the top of the list. Many employees spent their entire careers at Levi, seeing it almost like family and defending it against any and all critics.

But as the decade of the nineties drew to a close, Levi Strauss seemed to hit a wall. As a result, the firm found it necessary to reexamine every aspect of its business operations while simultaneously redefining its relationship with its workforce. The catalyst for change was a relatively sudden drop in market share. For example, in 1990 Levi held about one-third of the jeans market in the United States. But by the end of the decade that figure had been cut in half. Especially disturb-

ing was the fact that today's young consumers in particular had seemed to lose interest in Levi's products.

As a result of this alarming trend, company executives faced an intense and detailed period of introspection to find out what was happening to the company. Their conclusion was that they had been so successful with their core baby-boomer consumers that they had essentially neglected younger consumers. As a result, top-end designers like Tommy Hilfiger and Ralph Lauren, and discounted store brands sold at Sears and J. C. Penney had seized significant market share from Levi's. In addition, the firm's cost structure was out of line with those of other clothing manu-

> *"You can stretch denim over a wide butt, but you can't stretch it over too many generations. The problem is, your parents wore Levi's, and kids want to wear something different."*
>
> —Al Ries, Atlanta-based marketing consultant*

After studying this chapter, you should be able to

- Explain the nature of the individual-organization relationship.

  Define personality and describe personality attributes that affect behavior in organizations.

- Discuss individual attitudes in organizations and how they affect behavior.

- Describe basic perceptual processes and the role of attributions in organizations.

- Discuss the causes and consequences of stress, and describe how it can be managed.

- Describe creativity and its role in organizations.

  Explain how workplace behaviors can directly or indirectly influence organizational effectiveness.

facturers, who had already moved most of their production to lower-cost facilities in other countries. In contrast, Levi's had tried to maintain most of its production inside the United States, even though labor costs in this country are higher than at many other locations.

Once they saw their problem, Levi's managers took quick action along a number of fronts. Most painfully, in 1997 the firm announced that it was closing 11 U.S. factories and laying off one-third of its North American workforce—its first layoff in history. In 1999 another 22 plants were shuttered and almost 6,000 more workers released. Needless to say, these steps dramatically and inalterably changed the firm's relationship with its workforce. Its previously loyal workers quickly became disenchanted and embittered, for example, and went from being the company's staunchest defenders to its biggest critics.

The company also acknowledged that it needed to alter the composition of its executive team to boost creativity and market knowledge. Too many company officials, executives said, had come up through the ranks and knew only one way of doing things—the old, tried-and-true Levi's way. Thus one goal now is to fill 30 percent of all new management jobs with outsiders. Experts agree that it will take the firm a while to get its act together again, but they also acknowledge that the changes seem to fit the situation as well as a pair of the firm's jeans fit after a long day at the office.[1]

Levi Strauss and Company and its employees are in the process of redefining their relationship with one another. To do so, they are having to each assess how well their respective needs and capabilities now match the other's. And a variety of different and unique characteristics that reside in each and every employee affect how they feel about these changes, how they will alter their future attitudes about the firm, and how they perform their jobs. These characteristics reflect the basic elements of individual behavior in organizations.

This chapter describes several of these basic elements and is the first of several chapters designed to develop a more complete perspective on the leading function of management. In the next section, we investigate the psychological nature of individuals in organizations. The following section introduces the concept of personality and discusses several important personality attributes that can influence behavior in organizations. We then examine individual attitudes and their role in organizations. The role of stress in the workplace is then discussed, followed by a discussion of individual creativity. Finally, we describe a number of basic individual behaviors that are important to organizations.

Understanding Individuals in Organizations

As a starting point in understanding human behavior in the workplace, we must consider the basic nature of the relationship between individuals and organizations. We must also gain an appreciation of the nature of individual differences.

psychological contract The overall set of expectations held by an individual with respect to what he or she will contribute to the organization and what the organization will provide to the individual

The Psychological Contract

Most people have a basic understanding of a contract. Whenever we buy a car or sell a house, for example, both buyer and seller sign a contract that specifies the terms of the agreement. A psychological contract is similar in some ways to a standard legal contract, but it is less formal and well defined. In particular, a **psychological contract** is the overall set of expectations held by an individual with respect to what he or she will contribute to the organization and what the organization will provide in return. Thus a psychological contract is not written on paper, nor are all of its terms explicitly negotiated.

The essential nature of a psychological contract is illustrated in Figure 9.1. The individual makes a variety of **contributions** to the organization—effort, skills, ability, time, loyalty, and so forth. These contributions presumably satisfy various needs and requirements of the organization. That is, because the organization may have hired the person because of her skills, it is reasonable for the organization to expect that she will subsequently display those skills in the performance of her job.

Figure 9.1

The Psychological Contract

Psychological contracts are the basic assumptions that individuals have about their relationships with their organization. Such contracts are defined in terms of contributions by the individual relative to inducements from the organization.

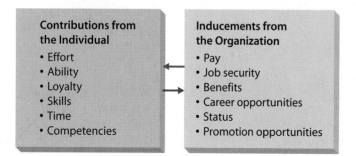

Contributions from the Individual	Inducements from the Organization
• Effort	• Pay
• Ability	• Job security
• Loyalty	• Benefits
• Skills	• Career opportunities
• Time	• Status
• Competencies	• Promotion opportunities

In return for these contributions, the organization provides **inducements** to the individual. Some inducements, like pay and career opportunities, are tangible rewards. Others, like job security and status, are more intangible. Just as the contributions from the individual must satisfy the needs of the organization, the inducements offered by the organization must serve the needs of the individual. That is, if a person accepts employment with an organization because he thinks he will earn an attractive salary and have an opportunity to advance, he will subsequently expect that those rewards will actually be forthcoming.

If both the individual and the organization perceive that the psychological contract is fair and equitable, they will be satisfied with the relationship and will likely continue it. On the other hand, if either party sees an imbalance or inequity in the contract, it may initiate a change. For example, the individual may request a pay raise or promotion, decrease her contributed effort, or look for a better job elsewhere. The organization can also initiate change by requesting that the individual improve his skills through training, transfer the person to another job, or terminate the person's employment altogether.

A basic challenge faced by the organization, then, is to manage psychological contracts. The organization must ensure that it is getting value from its employees. At the same time, it must also be sure that it is providing employees with appropriate inducements. If the organization is underpaying its employees for their contributions, for example, they may perform poorly or leave for better jobs elsewhere. On the other hand, if they are being overpaid relative to their contributions, the organization is incurring unnecessary costs.[2]

contributions What the individual provides to the organization

inducements What the organization provides to the individual

person-job fit The extent to which the contributions made by the individual match the inducements offered by the organization

The Person-Job Fit

One specific aspect of managing psychological contracts is managing the person-job fit. **Person-job fit** is the extent to which the contributions made by the individual match the inducements offered by the organization. In theory, each employee has a specific set of needs that he wants fulfilled and a set of job-related behaviors and abilities to contribute. Thus, if the organization can take perfect advantage of those behaviors and abilities and exactly fulfill his needs, it will have achieved a perfect person-job fit. *Management InfoTech* explains how some organizations are using technology in an effort to improve person-job fit.

Of course, such a precise level of person-job fit is seldom achieved. There are several reasons for this. For one thing, organizational selection procedures are imperfect. Organizations can make

"I'M PUTTING YOU ON THE CHINA SHOP ACCOUNT. DO YOU THINK YOU CAN HANDLE IT?"

P.C. Vey

Person-job fit is a very important construction in organizations. A good person-job fit benefits both the employee and the organization. But a poor person-job fit can result in a dissatisfied and low-performing employee. In the example portrayed here, for example, the manager is literally picking a "bull" to work in a "china shop." And the result is likely to be chaos!

MANAGEMENT INFOTECH

USING TECHNOLOGY TO GET THE RIGHT PERSON-JOB FIT

In today's high-speed, highly competitive business environment, knowledge is power. Opportunities and challenges can pop up without warning, so companies need people with the right mix of expertise and skills for each situation. The ability to effectively tap employee knowledge is particularly important when companies organize work activities as a series of cross-functional or problem-solving projects rather than as ongoing functional tasks. In this dynamic work environment, how can companies be sure that the right people are working on the right tasks?

The answer, for a growing number of firms, is to use technology to systematically identify and catalogue the talents and capabilities of each employee. For example, KPMG, a multinational accounting and consulting firm, uses software from Tacit Knowledge Systems to examine employees' e-mail messages. Based on the content of these messages, the system builds a profile of each employee's areas of expertise. After the employee reviews and edits the personal profile, it is stored in a database. Then, when a KPMG employee needs help with a specific problem or project, he or she queries the system. The software searches the database to identify the expert with the right set of skills and, with the expert's permission, makes the connection with the employee who needs

help. This system is only part of the $100 million worth of tech projects KPMG has mounted to capture and share its employees' knowledge.

At Monitor Group, a Boston-based consulting firm, a chief knowledge officer (CKO) is responsible for sharing information about employees' expertise and removing organizational barriers that can slow access to knowledge and experts. Monitor uses the Internet, among other tech tools, to match the right person to the right job—again and again. Jobs, titles, and tasks are constantly in flux as the firm groups and regroups people into teams to tackle a wide variety of projects for clients. And, once a project is over, that team's experts are ready to put their knowledge to work on new assignments.

> *Like nomads, we pitch tents and fight battles, then fold up the tents and move on.*
>
> —*Alan Kantrow, chief knowledge officer, Monitor Group**

References: Neil Gross, "Mining a Company's Mother Lode of Talent," *Business Week,* August 28, 2000, pp. 135, 137 (*quote on p.137).

approximations of employee skill levels when making hiring decisions and can improve them through training. But even simple performance dimensions are hard to measure objectively and validly. The cartoon provides a humorous example of poor "person"-job fit.

Another reason for imprecise person-job fits is that both people and organizations change. An individual who finds a new job stimulating and exciting may find the same job boring and monotonous after a few years of performing it. And when the organization adopts new technology, it has changed the skills it needs from its employees. Still another reason for imprecision in the person-job fit is that each individual is unique. Measuring skills and performance is difficult enough. Assessing needs, attitudes, and personality is far more complex. Each of these individual differences serves to make matching individuals with jobs a difficult and complex process.

The Nature of Individual Differences

Individual differences are personal attributes that vary from one person to another. Individual differences may be physical, psychological, and emotional. Taken together, all of the individual differences that characterize any specific person serve to make that individual unique from everyone else. Much of the remainder of this chapter is devoted to individual differences. Before proceeding, however, we must also note the importance of the situation in assessing the behavior of individuals.

Are specific differences that characterize a given individual good or bad? Do they contribute to or detract from performance? The answer, of course, is that it depends on the circumstances. One person may be very dissatisfied, withdrawn, and negative in one job setting but very satisfied, outgoing, and positive in another. Working conditions, coworkers, and leadership are all important ingredients.

Thus, whenever an organization attempts to assess or account for individual differences among its employees, it must also be sure to consider the situation in which behavior occurs. Individuals who are satisfied or productive workers in one context may prove to be dissatisfied or unproductive workers in another context. Attempting to consider both individual differences and contributions in relation to inducements and contexts, then, is a major challenge for organizations as they attempt to establish effective psychological contracts with their employees and achieve optimal fits between people and jobs.

individual differences Personal attributes that vary from one person to another

Personality and Individual Behavior

Personality traits represent some of the most fundamental sets of individual differences in organizations. **Personality** is the relatively stable set of psychological attributes that distinguish one person from another.[3] Managers should strive to understand basic personality attributes and the ways they can affect people's behavior in organizational situations, not to mention their perceptions of and attitudes toward the organization.

personality The relatively permanent set of psychological and behavioral attributes that distinguish one person from another

The "Big Five" Personality Traits

Psychologists have identified literally thousands of personality traits and dimensions that differentiate one person from another. But, in recent years, researchers have identified five fundamental personality traits that are especially relevant to organizations. Because these five traits are so important and because they are currently the subject of so much attention, they are commonly referred to now as the **"big five" personality traits**.[4] Figure 9.2 illustrates the "big five" traits.

Agreeableness refers to a person's ability to get along with others. Agreeableness causes some people to be gentle, cooperative, forgiving, understanding, and good-natured in their dealings with others. But it results in others being irritable,

"big five" personality traits A popular personality framework based on five key traits

agreeableness A person's ability to get along with others

Figure 9.2

The "Big Five" Model of Personality

The "big five" personality model represents an increasingly accepted framework for understanding personality traits in organizational settings. In general, experts tend to agree that personality traits toward the left end of each dimension, as illustrated in this figure, are more positive in organizational settings, whereas traits closer to the right are less positive.

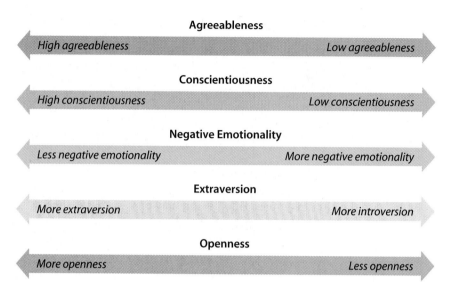

Agreeableness

High agreeableness — Low agreeableness

Conscientiousness

High conscientiousness — Low conscientiousness

Negative Emotionality

Less negative emotionality — More negative emotionality

Extraversion

More extraversion — More introversion

Openness

More openness — Less openness

conscientiousness The number of goals on which a person focuses

negative emotionality Extent to which a person is poised, calm, resilient and secure

extraversion a person's comfort level with relationships

short-tempered, uncooperative, and generally antagonistic toward other people. Although research has not yet fully investigated the effects of agreeableness, it would seem likely that highly agreeable people will be better able to develop good working relationships with coworkers, subordinates, and higher-level managers, whereas less agreeable people will not have particularly good working relationships. This same pattern might also extend to relationships with customers, suppliers, and other key organizational constituents.

Conscientiousness refers to the number of goals on which a person focuses. People who focus on relatively few goals at one time are likely to be organized, systematic, careful, thorough, responsible, and self-disciplined as they work to pursue those goals. Others, however, tend to take on a wider array of goals and, as a result, to be more disorganized, careless, and irresponsible, as well as less thorough and self-disciplined. Research has found that more conscientious people tend to be higher performers than less conscientious people across a variety of different jobs. This pattern seems logical, of course, because more conscientious people will take their jobs seriously and will approach the performance of their jobs in a highly responsible fashion.

The third of the "big five" personality dimensions is **negative emotionality**. People with less negative emotionality will be relatively poised, calm, resilient, and secure. But people with more negative emotionality will be more excitable, insecure, reactive, and subject to extreme mood swings. People with less negative emotionality might be expected to better handle job stress, pressure, and tension. Their stability might also lead them to be seen as being more reliable than their less stable counterparts.

Extraversion refers to a person's comfort level with relationships. People who are called extraverts are sociable, talkative, assertive, and open to establishing new relationships. But introverts are much less sociable, talkative, assertive, and less open to establishing new relationships. Research suggests that extraverts tend to be higher overall job performers than introverts and that they are also more likely to be attracted to jobs based on personal relationships, such as sales and marketing positions.

Finally, **openness** refers to a person's rigidity of beliefs and range of interests. People with high levels of openness are willing to listen to new ideas and to change their own ideas, beliefs, and attitudes as a result of new information. They also tend to have broad interests and to be curious, imaginative, and creative. On the other hand, people with low levels of openness tend to be less receptive to new ideas and less willing to change their minds. Further, they tend to have fewer and narrower interests and to be less curious and creative. People with more openness might be expected to be better performers, owing to their flexibility and the likelihood that they will be better accepted by others in the organization. Openness may also encompass an individual's willingness to accept change. For example, people with high levels of openness may be more receptive to change, whereas people with low levels of openness may be more likely to resist change.

openness A person's rigidity of beliefs and range of interests

The "big five" framework continues to attract the attention of both researchers and managers. The potential value of this framework is that it encompasses an integrated set of traits that appear to be valid predictors of certain behaviors in certain situations. Thus managers who can develop both an understanding of the framework and the ability to assess these traits in their employees will be in a good position to understand how and why they behave as they do.[5] On the other hand, managers must also be careful not to overestimate their ability to assess the "big five" traits in others. Even assessment using the most rigorous and valid measures, for instance, is still likely to be somewhat imprecise. Another limitation of the "big five" framework is that it is based primarily on research conducted in the United States. Thus there are unanswered questions as to its generalizability to other cultures. And, even within the United States, a variety of other factors and traits are also likely to affect behavior in organizations.

locus of control The degree to which an individual believes that behavior has a direct impact on the consequences of that behavior

Other Personality Traits at Work

Besides the "big five", there are several other personality traits that influence behavior in organizations. Among the most important are locus of control, self-efficacy, authoritarianism, Machiavellianism, self-esteem, and risk propensity.

Locus of control is the extent to which people believe that their behavior has a real effect on what happens to them.[6] Some people, for example, believe that if they work hard they will succeed. They also may believe that people who fail do so because they lack ability or motivation. People who believe that individuals are in control of their lives are said to have an *internal locus of control*. Other people think that fate, chance, luck, or other people's behavior determines what happens to them. For example, an employee who fails to get a promotion may attribute that failure to a politically motivated boss or just bad luck, rather than to her or his own lack of skills or poor performance record. People who think that forces beyond their control dictate what happens to them are said to have an *external locus of control*.

Locus of control is the degree to which an individual believes that behavior has a direct impact on the consequences of that behavior. Most professional athletes, for instance, are very self-confident and assume that they can defeat their opponent. Venus Williams, for instance, shown here winning the Wimbledon title, expects to win every time she steps on the tennis court. Thus, she clearly has an internal locus of control.

self-efficacy An individual's beliefs about her or his capabilities to perform a task

Self-efficacy is a related but subtly different personality characteristic. Self-efficacy is a person's beliefs about his or her capabilities to perform a task. People with high self-efficacy believe that they can perform well on a specific task, whereas people with low self-efficacy tend to doubt their ability to perform a specific task. Although self-assessments of ability contribute to self-efficacy, so, too, does the individual's personality. Some people simply have more self-confidence than others. This belief in their ability to perform a task effectively results in their being more self-assured and more able to focus their attention on performance.

authoritarianism The extent to which an individual believes that power and status differences are appropriate within hierarchical social systems like organizations

Another important personality characteristic is **authoritarianism**, the extent to which an individual believes that power and status differences are appropriate within hierarchical social systems like organizations.[7] For example, a person who is highly authoritarian may accept directives or orders from someone with more authority purely because the other person is "the boss." On the other hand, although a person who is not highly authoritarian may still carry out appropriate and reasonable directives from the boss, he or she is also more likely to question things, express disagreement with the boss, and even refuse to carry out orders if they are for some reason objectionable. A highly authoritarian manager may be autocratic and demanding, and highly authoritarian subordinates will be more likely to accept this behavior from their leader. On the other hand, a less authoritarian manager may allow subordinates a bigger role in making decisions, and less authoritarian subordinates will respond positively to this behavior.

Machiavellianism Behavior directed at gaining power and controlling the behavior of others

Machiavellianism is another important personality trait. This concept is named after Niccolo Machiavelli, a sixteenth-century author. In his book *The Prince*, Machiavelli explained how the nobility could more easily gain and use power. Machiavellianism is now used to describe behavior directed at gaining power and controlling the behavior of others. Research suggests that Machiavellianism is a personality trait that varies from person to person. More Machiavellian individuals tend to be rational and nonemotional, may be willing to lie to attain their personal goals, put little weight on loyalty and friendship, and enjoy manipulating others' behavior. Less Machiavellian individuals are more emotional, less willing to lie to succeed, value loyalty and friendship highly, and get little personal pleasure from manipulating others.

self-esteem The extent to which a person believes that he or she is a worthwhile and deserving individual

Self-esteem is the extent to which a person believes that she is a worthwhile and deserving individual. A person with high self-esteem is more likely to seek higher-status jobs, be more confident in his ability to achieve higher levels of performance, and derive greater intrinsic satisfaction from his accomplishments. In contrast, a person with less self-esteem may be more content to remain in a lower-level job, be less confident of her ability, and focus more on extrinsic rewards. Among the major personality dimensions, self-esteem is the one that has been most widely studied in other countries. Although more research is clearly needed, the published evidence does suggest that self-esteem as a personality trait does indeed exist in a variety of countries and that its role in organizations is reasonably important across different cultures.[8]

risk propensity The degree to which an individual is willing to take chances and make risky decisions

Risk propensity is the degree to which an individual is willing to take chances and make risky decisions. A manager with a high risk propensity, for example, might be expected to experiment with new ideas and gamble on new products.

She might also lead the organization in new and different directions. This manager might also be a catalyst for innovation. On the other hand, the same individual might also jeopardize the continued well-being of the organization if the risky decisions prove to be bad ones. A manager with low risk propensity might lead to a stagnant and overly conservative organization or help the organization successfully weather turbulent and unpredictable times by maintaining stability and calm. Thus the potential consequences of risk propensity to an organization are heavily dependent on that organization's environment.

■ *Attitudes and Individual Behavior*

Another important element of individual behavior in organizations is attitudes. **Attitudes** are complexes of beliefs and feelings that people have about specific ideas, situations, or other people. Attitudes are important because they are the mechanism through which most people express their feelings. An employee's statement that he feels underpaid by the organization reflects his feelings about his pay. Similarly, when a manager says that she likes the new advertising campaign, she is expressing her feelings about the organization's marketing efforts.

attitudes Complexes of beliefs and feelings that people have about specific ideas, situations, or other people

Attitudes have three components. The *affective component* of an attitude reflects feelings and emotions an individual has toward a situation. The *cognitive component* of an attitude is derived from knowledge an individual has about a situation. It is important to note that cognition is subject to individual perceptions (something we discuss more fully later). Thus one person might "know" that a certain political candidate is better than another, whereas someone else may "know" just the opposite. Finally, the *intentional component* of an attitude reflects how an individual expects to behave toward or in a situation.

To illustrate these three components, consider the case of a manager who places an order for some supplies for his organization from a new office supply firm. Suppose many of the items he orders are out of stock, others are overpriced, and still others arrive damaged. When he calls someone at the supply firm for assistance, he is treated rudely and gets disconnected before his claim is resolved. When asked how he feels about the new office supply firm, he might respond, "I don't like that company (affective component). They are the worst office supply firm I've ever dealt with (cognitive component). I'll never do business with them again (intentional component)."

People try to maintain consistency among the three components of their attitudes as well as among all their attitudes. However, circumstances sometimes arise that lead to conflicts. The conflict that individuals may experience among their own attitudes is called **cognitive dissonance**.[9] Say, for example, an individual who has vowed never to work for a big, impersonal corporation intends instead to open her own business and be her own boss. Unfortunately, a series of financial setbacks leads her to have no choice but to take a job with a large company and work for someone else. Cognitive dissonance occurs: The affective and cognitive components of the individual's attitude conflict with intended behavior. In order to

cognitive dissonance Caused when an individual has conflicting attitudes

reduce cognitive dissonance, which is usually an uncomfortable experience for most people, the individual might tell herself that the situation is only temporary and that she can go back out on her own in the near future. Or she might revise her cognitions and decide that working for a large company is more pleasant than she had ever expected.

Work-Related Attitudes

People in organizations form attitudes about many different things. For example, employees are likely to have attitudes about their salary, promotion possibilities, boss, employee benefits, the food in the company cafeteria, and the color of the company softball team uniforms. Of course, some of these attitudes are more important than others. Especially important attitudes are job satisfaction or dissatisfaction and organizational commitment.[10]

job satisfaction or dissatisfaction An attitude that reflects the extent to which an individual is gratified by or fulfilled in his or her work

Job Satisfaction or Dissatisfaction   **Job satisfaction or dissatisfaction** is an attitude that reflects the extent to which an individual is gratified by or fulfilled in his or her work. Extensive research conducted on job satisfaction has indicated that personal factors, such as an individual's needs and aspirations, determine this attitude, along with group and organizational factors, such as relationships with coworkers and supervisors and working conditions, work policies, and compensation.[11]

A satisfied employee also tends to be absent less often, make positive contributions, and stay with the organization.[12] In contrast, a dissatisfied employee may be absent more often, experience stress that disrupts coworkers, and be continually looking for another job. Contrary to what many managers believe, however, high levels of job satisfaction do not necessarily lead to higher levels of performance. One survey has also indicated that, contrary to popular opinion, Japanese workers are less satisfied with their jobs than are their counterparts in the United States.[13]

organizational commitment An attitude that reflects an individual's identification with and attachment to the organization itself

Organizational Commitment   **Organizational commitment** is an attitude that reflects an individual's identification with and attachment to the organization itself. A person with a high level of commitment is likely to see herself as a true member of the organization (for example, referring to the organization in personal terms, like "we make high-quality products"), to overlook minor sources of dissatisfaction with the organization, and to see herself remaining a member of the organization. In contrast, a person with less organizational commitment is more likely to see himself as an outsider (for example, referring to the organization in less personal terms, like "They don't pay their employees very well"), to express more dissatisfaction about things, and not to see himself as a long-term member of the organization. Research suggests that Japanese workers may be more committed to their organizations than are American workers.[14]

As indicated by research, commitment strengthens with an individual's age, years with the organization, sense of job security, and participation in decision making. Employees who feel committed to an organization have highly reliable habits, plan a long tenure with the organization, and muster more effort in performance. Although there are few definitive things that organizations can do to create and promote commitment, there are a few specific guidelines available. For one thing, if the organization treats its employees fairly and provides reasonable rewards and job security, those employees will more likely be satisfied and committed. Allowing employees to have a say in how things are done can also promote all three attitudes.

Affect and Mood in Organizations

Researchers have recently started to focus renewed interest on the affective component of attitudes. Recall from our discussion above that the affect component of an attitude reflects our feelings and emotions. Although managers once believed that emotion and feelings varied among people from day to day, research now suggests that, though some short-term fluctuation does indeed occur, there are also underlying stable predispositions toward fairly constant and predictable moods and emotional states.[15]

Some people, for example, tend to have a higher degree of *positive affectivity*. This means that they are relatively upbeat and optimistic, that they have an overall sense of well-being, and that they usually see things in a positive light. Thus they always seem to be in a good mood. Other people, those with more *negative affectivity*, are just the opposite. They are generally downbeat and pessimistic, and they usually see things in a negative way. They seem to be in a bad mood most of the time.

Of course, as noted above, there can be short-term variations among even the most extreme types. People with a lot of positive affectivity, for example, may still be in a bad mood if they have just received some bad news—being passed over for a promotion, getting extremely negative performance feedback, or being laid off or fired, for instance. Similarly, those with negative affectivity may still be in a good mood—at least for a short time—if they have just been promoted, received very positive performance feedback, or had other good things befall them. After the initial impact of these events wears off, however, those with positive affectivity will generally return to their normal positive mood, whereas those with negative affectivity will gravitate back to their normal bad mood.

■ Perception and Individual Behavior

As noted earlier, an important element of an attitude is the individual's perception of the object about which the attitude is formed. Because perception plays a role in a variety of other workplace behaviors, managers need to have a general understanding of basic perceptual processes.[16] The role of attributions is also important.

Basic Perceptual Processes

Perception is the set of processes through which an individual becomes aware of and interprets information about the environment. As shown in Figure 9.3, basic perceptual processes that are particularly relevant to organizations are selective perception and stereotyping.

perception The set of processes through which an individual becomes aware of and interprets information about the environment

Figure 9.3

Perceptual Processes

Two of the most basic perceptual processes are selective perception and stereotyping. As shown here, selective perception occurs when we screen out information (represented by the – symbols) that causes us discomfort or that contradicts our beliefs. Stereotyping occurs when we categorize or label people on the basis of a single attribute, illustrated here by color.

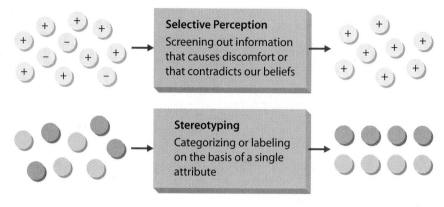

selective perception The process of screening out information that we are uncomfortable with or which contradicts our beliefs

Selective Perception   **Selective perception** is the process of screening out information that we are uncomfortable with or which contradicts our beliefs. For example, suppose a manager is exceptionally fond of a particular worker. The manager has a very positive attitude about the worker and thinks he is a top performer. One day the manager notices that the worker seems to be goofing off. Selective perception may cause the manager to quickly forget what he observed. Similarly, suppose a manager has formed a very negative image of a particular worker. She thinks this worker is a poor performer and never does a good job. When she happens to observe an example of high performance from the worker, she, too, may not remember it for very long. In one sense, selective perception is beneficial because it allows us to disregard minor bits of information. Of course, this only holds true if our basic perception is accurate. If selective perception causes us to ignore important information, however, it can become quite detrimental.

stereotyping The process of categorizing or labeling people on the basis of a single attribute

Stereotyping   **Stereotyping** is the process of categorizing or labeling people on the basis of a single attribute. Common attributes from which people often stereotype are race and gender. Of course, stereotypes along these lines are inaccurate and can be harmful. For example, suppose a manager forms the stereotype that women can perform only certain tasks and that men are best suited for other tasks. To the extent that this affects the manager's hiring practices, the manager is (1) costing the organization valuable talent for both sets of jobs, (2) violating federal law, and (3) behaving unethically. On the other hand, certain forms of stereotyping can be useful and efficient. Suppose, for example, that a manager believes that communication skills are important for a particular job and that speech communication majors tend to have exceptionally good communication skills. As a result, whenever he interviews candidates for jobs, he pays especially close attention to speech communication majors. To the extent that communication skills truly predict job performance and that majoring in speech communication does indeed provide those skills, this form of stereotyping can be beneficial.

Perception and Attribution

Perception is also closely linked with another process called attribution. **Attribution** is a mechanism through which we observe behavior and then attribute causes to it.[17] The behavior that is observed may be our own or that of others. For example, suppose someone realizes one day that she is working fewer hours than before, that she talks less about her work, and that she calls in sick more frequently. She might conclude from this that she must have become disenchanted with her job and subsequently decide to quit. Thus she observed her own behavior, attributed a cause to it, and developed what she thought was a consistent response.

More common is attributing cause to the behavior of others. For example, if the manager of the individual described above has observed the same behavior, he might form exactly the same attribution. On the other hand, he might instead decide that she has a serious illness, that he is driving her too hard, that she is experiencing too much stress, that she has a drug problem, or that she is having family problems.

The basic framework around which we form attributions is *consensus* (the extent to which other people in the same situation behave the same way), *consistency* (the extent to which the same person behaves in the same way at different times), and *distinctiveness* (the extent to which the same person behaves in the same way in other situations). For example, suppose a manager observes that an employee is late for a meeting. The manager might further realize that he is the only one who is late (low consensus), recall that he is often late for other meetings (high consistency), and subsequently realize that the same employee is sometimes late for work and returning from lunch (low distinctiveness). This pattern of attributions might cause the manager to decide that the individual's behavior is something that should be changed. As a result, the manager might meet with the subordinate and establish some punitive consequences for future tardiness.

attribution The process of observing behavior and attributing causes to it

■ Stress and Individual Behavior

Another important element of behavior in organizations is stress. **Stress** is an individual's response to a strong stimulus. This stimulus is called a **stressor**. Stress generally follows a cycle referred to as the **general adaptation syndrome (GAS)**,[18] shown in Figure 9.4. According to this view, when an individual first encounters a stressor, the GAS is initiated, and the first stage, alarm, is activated. He may feel panic, may wonder how to cope, and may feel helpless. For example, suppose a manager is told to prepare a detailed evaluation of a plan by his firm to buy one of its competitors. His first reaction may be, "How will I ever get this done by tomorrow?"

If the stressor is too intense, the individual may feel unable to cope and never really try to respond to its demands. In most cases, however, after a short period of alarm, the individual gathers some strength and starts to resist the negative effects of the stressor. For example, the manager with the evaluation to write may calm down, call home to say he's working late, role up his sleeves, order out for coffee,

stress An individual's response to a strong stimulus, which is called a **stressor**

general adaptation syndrome (GAS) General cycle of the stress process

Figure 9.4

The General Adaptation Syndrome

The general adaptation syndrome represents the normal process by which we react to stressful events. At stage 1—alarm—we feel panic and alarm and our level of resistance to stress drops. Stage 2—resistance—represents our efforts to confront and control the stressful circumstance. If we fail, we may eventually reach stage 3—exhaustion—and just give up or quit.

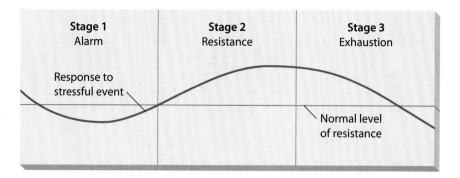

and get to work. Thus, at stage 2 of the GAS, the person is resisting the effects of the stressor.

In many cases, the resistance phase may end the GAS. If the manager is able to complete the evaluation earlier than expected, he may drop it in his briefcase, smile to himself, and head home tired but satisfied. On the other hand, prolonged exposure to a stressor without resolution may bring on stage 3 of the GAS—exhaustion. At this stage, the individual literally gives up and can no longer resist the stressor. The manager, for example, might fall asleep at his desk at 3:00 A.M. and never finish the evaluation.

We should note that stress is not all bad. In the absence of stress, we may experience lethargy and stagnation. An optimal level of stress, on the other hand, can result in motivation and excitement. Too much stress, however, can have negative consequences. It is also important to understand that stress can be caused by "good" as well as "bad" things. Excessive pressure, unreasonable demands on our time, and bad news can all cause stress. But even receiving a bonus and then having to decide what to do with the money can be stressful. So, too, can receiving a promotion, gaining recognition, and similar "good" things.

One important line of thinking about stress focuses on **Type A** and **Type B** personalities.[19] Type A individuals are extremely competitive, are very devoted to work, and have a strong sense of time urgency. They are likely to be aggressive, impatient, and very work oriented. They have a lot of drive and want to accomplish as much as possible as quickly as possible. Type B individuals are less competitive, are less devoted to work, and have a weaker sense of time urgency. Such individuals are less likely to experience conflict with other people and more likely to have a balanced, relaxed approach to life. They are able to work at a constant pace without time urgency. Type B people are not necessarily more or less successful than are Type A people. But they are less likely to experience stress.

Type A Individuals who are extremely competitive, very devoted to work, and have a strong sense of time urgency

Type B Individuals who are less competitive, less devoted to work, and have a weaker sense of time urgency

Causes and Consequences of Stress

Stress is obviously not a simple phenomenon. As noted in Figure 9.5, several different things can cause stress. Note that this list includes only work-related conditions. We should keep in mind that stress can be the result of personal circumstances as well.

Figure 9.5

Causes of Work Stress

There are several causes of work stress in organizations. Four general sets of organizational stressors are task demands, physical demands, role demands, and interpersonal demands.

Causes of Stress   Work-related stressors fall into one of four categories—task, physical, role, and interpersonal demands. *Task demands* are associated with the task itself. Some occupations are inherently more stressful than others. Having to make fast decisions, decisions with less than complete information, or decisions that have relatively serious consequences are some of the things that can make some jobs stressful. The jobs of surgeon, airline pilot, and stockbroker are relatively more stressful than the jobs of general practitioner, airplane baggage loader, and office receptionist. Although a general practitioner makes important decisions, he is also likely to have time to make a considered diagnosis and fully explore a number of different treatments. But during surgery, the surgeon must make decisions quickly while realizing that the wrong one may endanger her patient's life.

Physical demands are stressors associated with the job setting. Working outdoors in extremely hot or cold temperatures, or even in an improperly heated or cooled office, can lead to stress. A poorly designed office, which makes it difficult for people to have privacy or promotes too little social interaction, can result in stress, as can poor lighting and inadequate work surfaces. Even more severe are actual threats to health. Examples include jobs like coal mining, poultry processing, and toxic waste handling.

Role demands can also cause stress. (Roles are discussed more fully in Chapter 13.) A role is a set of expected behaviors associated with a position in a group or organization. Stress can result from either role ambiguity or role conflict which people can experience in groups. For example, an employee who is feeling pressure from her boss to work longer hours or to travel more while also being asked by her family for more time at home will almost certainly experience stress.[20] Similarly, a new employee experiencing role ambiguity because of poor orientation and training practices by the organization will also suffer from stress.

Interpersonal demands are stressors associated with relationships that confront people in organizations. For example, group pressures regarding restriction of output and norm conformity can lead to stress. Leadership style may also cause stress. An employee who feels a strong need to participate in decision making may feel stress if his boss refuses to allow participation. And individuals with conflicting personalities may experience stress if required to work too closely together. A person with an internal locus of control might be frustrated when working with someone who prefers to wait and just let things happen.

Consequences of Stress   As noted earlier, the results of stress may be positive or negative. The negative consequences may be behavioral, psychological, or medical. Behaviorally, for example, stress may lead to detrimental or harmful actions, such as smoking, alcoholism, overeating, and drug abuse. Other stress-induced behaviors are accident proneness, violence toward self or others, and appetite disorders.

Psychological consequences of stress interfere with an individual's mental health and well-being. These outcomes include sleep disturbances, depression, family problems, and sexual dysfunction. Managers are especially prone to sleep disturbances when they experience stress at work.[21] Medical consequences of stress affect an individual's physiological well-being. Heart disease and stroke have been linked to stress, as have headaches, backaches, ulcers and related disorders, and skin conditions such as acne and hives.

Individual stress also has direct consequences for businesses. For an operating employee, stress may translate into poor-quality work and lower productivity. For a manager, it may mean faulty decision making and disruptions in working relationships. Withdrawal behaviors can also result from stress. People who are having difficulties with stress in their jobs are more likely to call in sick or to leave the organization. More subtle forms of withdrawal may also occur. A manager may start missing deadlines, for example, or taking longer lunch breaks. Employees may also withdraw by developing feelings of indifference. The irritation displayed by people under great stress can make them difficult to get along with. Job satisfaction, morale, and commitment can all suffer as a result of excessive levels of stress. So, too, can motivation to perform.

Another consequence of stress is **burnout**—a feeling of exhaustion that may develop when someone experiences too much stress for an extended period of time. Burnout results in constant fatigue, frustration, and helplessness. Increased rigidity follows, as does a loss of self-confidence and psychological withdrawal. The individual dreads going to work, often puts in longer hours but get less accomplished than before, and exhibits mental and physical exhaustion. Because of the damaging effects of burnout, some firms are taking steps to help avoid it. For example, British Airways provides all of its employees with training designed to help them recognize the symptoms of burnout and develop strategies for avoiding it.

burnout A feeling of exhaustion that may develop when someone experiences too much stress for an extended period of time

Managing Stress

Given the potential consequences of stress, it follows that both people and organizations should be concerned about how to limit its more damaging effects. Numerous ideas and approaches have been developed to help manage stress. Some are strategies for individuals; others are strategies for organizations.[22]

One way people manage stress is through exercise. People who exercise regularly feel less tension and stress, are more self-confident, and feel more optimistic. Their better physical condition also makes them less susceptible to many common illnesses. People who do not exercise regularly, on the other hand, tend to feel more stress and are more likely to be depressed. They are also more likely to have heart attacks. And because of their physical condition they are more likely to contract illnesses.

Another method people use to manage stress is relaxation. Relaxation allows individuals to adapt to, and therefore better deal with, their stress. Relaxation comes in many forms, such as taking regular vacations. A recent study found that people's attitudes toward a variety of workplace characteristics improved significantly following a vacation. People can also learn to relax while on their jobs. For example, some experts recommend that people take regular rest breaks during their normal workday.

People can also use time management to control stress. The idea behind time management is that many daily pressures can be reduced or eliminated if individuals do a better job of managing time. One approach to time management is to make a list every morning of the things to be done that day. The items on the list are then grouped into three categories: critical activities that must be performed, important activities that should be performed, and optional or trivial things that can be delegated or postponed. The individual performs the items on the list in their order of importance.

Finally, people can manage stress through support groups. A support group can be as simple as a group of family members or friends to enjoy leisure time with. Going out after work with a couple of coworkers to a basketball game or a movie, for example, can help relieve stress built up during the day. Family and friends can help people cope with stress on an ongoing basis and during times of crisis. For example, an employee who has just learned that she did not get the promotion she has been working toward for months may find it helpful to have a good friend to lean on, talk to, or yell at. People also may make use of more elaborate and formal support groups. Community centers or churches, for example, may sponsor support groups for people who have recently gone through a divorce, the death of a loved one, or some other tragedy.

Organizations are also beginning to realize that they should be involved in helping employees cope with stress. One argument for this is that, because the business is at least partially responsible for stress, it should also help relieve it. Another is that stress-related insurance claims by employees can cost the organization considerable sums of money. Still another is that workers experiencing lower levels of detrimental stress will be able to function more effectively. AT&T has initiated a series of seminars and workshops to help its employees cope with the stress they face in their jobs. The firm was prompted to develop these seminars for all three of the reasons noted above.

A wellness stress program is a special part of the organization specifically created to help deal with stress. Organizations have adopted stress management programs, health promotion programs, and other kinds of programs for this purpose. The AT&T seminar program noted earlier is similar to this idea, but true wellness programs are ongoing activities that have a number of different components. They commonly include exercise-related activities as well as classroom instruction programs dealing with smoking cessation, weight reduction, and general stress management.

Some companies are developing their own programs or using existing programs of this type. Johns-Manville, for example, has a gym at its corporate headquarters.

Other firms negotiate discounted health club membership rates with local establishments. For the instructional part of the program, the organization can again either sponsor its own training or perhaps jointly sponsor seminars with a local YMCA, civic organization, or church. Organization-based fitness programs facilitate employee exercise, a very positive consideration, but such programs are also quite costly. Still, more and more companies are developing fitness programs for employees.

Creativity in Organizations

creativity The ability of an individual to generate new ideas or to conceive of new perspectives on existing ideas

Creativity is yet another important component of individual behavior in organizations. **Creativity** is the ability of an individual to generate new ideas or to conceive of new perspectives on existing ideas. What makes a person creative? How do people become creative? How does the creative process work? Although psychologists have not yet discovered complete answers to these questions, examining a few general patterns can help us understand the sources of individual creativity within organizations.[23]

Organizations frequently look for new ways to make their employees more creative and to promote innovation and entrepreneurial activity. Second City, the improvisational comedy troupe that launched the careers of Bill Murray and John Belushi, has developed a lucrative business by using comedy to help businesses promote creativity. Rob Nickerson, a Canadian comic working for Second City, is helping this room full of Nortel accountants think more creatively. People who attend the sessions swear by them; Second City, meanwhile, charges between $2,500 and $8,500 for a day-long program.

The Creative Individual

Numerous researchers have focused their efforts on attempting to describe the common attributes of creative individuals. These attributes generally fall into three categories: background experiences, personal traits, and cognitive abilities.

Background Experiences and Creativity

Researchers have observed that many creative individuals were raised in an environment in which creativity was nurtured. Mozart was raised in a family of musicians and began composing and performing music at age six. Pierre and Marie Curie, great scientists in their own right, also raised a daughter, Irene, who won the Nobel Prize in chemistry. Thomas Edison's creativity was nurtured by his mother. However, people with background experiences very different from theirs have also been creative. The African-American abolitionist and writer Frederick Douglass was born into slavery in Tuckahoe, Maryland, and had very limited opportunities for education. Nonetheless, his powerful oratory and creative thinking helped lead to the Emancipation Proclamation, which outlawed slavery in the United States.

Personal Traits and Creativity   Certain personal traits have also been linked to creativity in individuals. The traits shared by most creative people are openness, an attraction to complexity, high levels of energy, independence and autonomy, strong self-confidence, and a strong belief that one is, in fact, creative. Individuals who possess these traits are more likely to be creative than are those who do not have them.

Cognitive Abilities and Creativity   Cognitive abilities are an individual's power to think intelligently and to analyze situations and data effectively. Intelligence may be a precondition for individual creativity—although most creative people are highly intelligent, not all intelligent people are necessarily creative. Creativity is also linked with the ability to think divergently and convergently. *Divergent thinking* is a skill that allows people to see differences among situations, phenomena, or events. *Convergent thinking* is a skill that allows people to see similarities among situations, phenomena, or events. Creative people are generally very skilled at both divergent and convergent thinking.

Interestingly, Japanese managers have recently questioned their own creative ability. The concern is that their emphasis on group harmony has perhaps stifled individual initiative and hampered the development of individual creativity. As a result, many Japanese firms, including Omron Corporation, Fuji Photo, and Shimizu Corporation, have launched employee training programs intended to boost creativity.[24]

The Creative Process

Although creative people often report that ideas seem to come to them "in a flash," individual creative activity actually tends to progress through a series of stages. Not all creative activity has to follow these four stages, but much of it does.

Preparation   The creative process normally begins with a period of *preparation*. Formal education and training are usually the most efficient ways of becoming familiar with this vast amount of research and knowledge. To make a creative contribution to business management or business services, individuals must usually receive formal training and education in business. This is one reason for the strong demand for undergraduate and master's-level business education. Formal business education can be an effective way for an individual to get "up to speed" and begin making creative contributions quickly. Experiences that managers have on the job after their formal training has finished can also contribute to the creative process. In an important sense, the education and training of creative people never really ends. It continues as long as they remain interested in the world and curious about the way things work.

Incubation   The second phase of the creative process is *incubation*—a period of less intense conscious concentration during which the knowledge and ideas acquired during preparation mature and develop. A curious aspect of incubation is that it is often helped along by pauses in concentrated rational thought. Some creative people rely on physical activity such as jogging or swimming to provide a "break" from thinking. Others may read or listen to music. Sometimes sleep may even supply the needed pause.

Insight   Usually occurring after preparation and incubation, *insight* is a spontaneous breakthrough in which the creative person achieves a new understanding of some problem or situation. Insight represents a coming together of all the scattered thoughts and ideas that were maturing during incubation. It may occur suddenly or develop slowly over time. Insight can be triggered by some external event, such as a new experience or an encounter with new data that forces the individual to think about old issues and problems in new ways, or it can be a completely internal event in which patterns of thought finally coalesce in ways that generate new understanding. One manager's key insight led to a complete restructuring of Citibank's back room operations. "Back room operations" refers to the enormous avalanche of paperwork that a bank must process in order to serve its customers— listing checks and deposits, updating accounts, and preparing bank statements. Historically, back room operations at Citibank had been managed as if they were part of the regular banking operation. But a new executive realized that back room operations had less to do with banking and more to do with manufacturing. The insight, then, was that back room operations could be managed like a paper-manufacturing process. On the basis of this insight, he hired former manufacturing managers from Ford and other automobile companies. By reconceptualizing the nature of back room operations, the executive was able to substantially reduce the costs of these operations for Citibank.

Verification   Once an insight has occurred, *verification* determines the validity or truthfulness of the insight. For many creative ideas, verification includes scientific experiments to determine whether or not the insight actually leads to the results expected. Verification may also include the development of a product or service prototype. A prototype is one (or a very small number) of products built just to see if the ideas behind this new product actually work. Product prototypes are rarely sold to the public but are very valuable in verifying the insights developed in the creative process. Once the new product or service is developed, verification in the marketplace is the ultimate test of the creative idea behind it.

Enhancing Creativity in Organizations

Managers who wish to enhance and promote creativity in their organizations can do so in a variety of ways.[25] One important method for enhancing creativity is to make it a part of the organization's culture, often through explicit goals. Firms that truly want to stress creativity, like 3M and Rubbermaid, for example, state goals that some percent of future revenues are to be gained from new products. This clearly communicates that creativity and innovation are valued.

Another important part of enhancing creativity is to reward creative successes, while being careful not to punish creative failures. Many ideas that seem worthwhile on paper fail to pan out in reality. If the first person to come up with an idea that fails is fired or otherwise punished, others in the organization will become more cautious in their own work. And, as a result, fewer creative ideas will emerge.

Types of Workplace Behavior

Now that we have looked closely at how individual differences can influence behavior in organizations, let's turn our attention to what we mean by workplace behavior. **Workplace behavior** is a pattern of action by the members of an organization that directly or indirectly influences organizational effectiveness. Important workplace behaviors include performance and productivity, absenteeism and turnover, and organizational citizenship.

workplace behavior A pattern of action by the members of an organization that directly or indirectly influences organizational effectiveness

Performance Behaviors

Performance behaviors are the total set of work-related behaviors that the organization expects the individual to display. Thus they derive from the psychological contract. For some jobs, performance behaviors can be narrowly defined and easily measured. For example, an assembly-line worker who sits by a moving conveyor and attaches parts to a product as it passes by has relatively few performance behaviors. He or she is expected to remain at the workstation and correctly attach the parts. Performance can often be assessed quantitatively by counting the percentage of parts correctly attached.

performance behaviors The total set of work-related behaviors that the organization expects the individual to display

For many other jobs, however, performance behaviors are more diverse and much more difficult to assess. For example, consider the case of a research and development scientist at Merck. The scientist works in a lab trying to find new scientific breakthroughs that have commercial potential. The scientist must apply knowledge learned in graduate school with experience gained from previous research. Intuition and creativity are also important elements. And the desired breakthrough may take months or even years to accomplish. As we discussed in Chapter 8, organizations rely on a number of different methods for evaluating performance. The key, of course, is to match the evaluation mechanism with the job being performed.

Withdrawal Behaviors

Another important type of work-related behavior is that which results in withdrawal—absenteeism and turnover. **Absenteeism** occurs when an individual does not show up for work. The cause may be legitimate (illness, jury duty, death in the family) or feigned (reported as legitimate but actually just an excuse to stay home). When an employee is absent, her or his work does not get done at all, or a substitute must be hired to do it. In either case, the quantity or quality of actual output is likely to suffer. Obviously, some absenteeism is expected. The key concern of organizations is to minimize feigned absenteeism and reduce legitimate absences as much as possible. High absenteeism may be a symptom of other problems as well, such as job dissatisfaction and low morale.

absenteeism When an individual does not show up for work

turnover When people quit their job

Turnover occurs when people quit their job. An organization usually incurs costs in replacing individuals who have quit, but if turnover involves especially productive people, it is even more costly. Turnover seems to result from a number of factors, including aspects of the job, the organization, the individual, the labor market, and family influences. In general, a poor person-job fit is also a likely cause of turnover.

Efforts to directly manage turnover are frequently fraught with difficulty, even in organizations that concentrate on rewarding good performers. Of course, some turnover is inevitable, and in some cases it may even be desirable. For example, if the organization is trying to cut costs by reducing its staff, having people voluntarily choose to leave is preferable to having to terminate them. And if the people who choose to leave are low performers or express high levels of job dissatisfaction, the organization may also benefit from turnover.

Organizational Citizenship

organizational citizenship The behavior of individuals that makes a positive overall contribution to the organization

Organizational citizenship refers to the behavior of individuals that makes a positive overall contribution to the organization.[26] Consider, for example, an employee who does work that is acceptable in terms of both quantity and quality. However, she refuses to work overtime, she won't help newcomers learn the ropes, and she is generally unwilling to make any contribution to the organization beyond the strict performance of her job. Although this person may be seen as a good performer, she is not likely to be seen as a good organizational citizen.

Another employee may exhibit a comparable level of performance. In addition, however, he will always work late when the boss asks him to, he takes time to help newcomers learn their way around, and he is perceived as being helpful and committed to the organization's success. Although his level of performance may be seen as equal to that of the first worker, he is also likely to be seen as a better organizational citizen.

The determinant of organizational citizenship behaviors is likely to be a complex mosaic of individual, social, and organizational variables. For example, the personality, attitudes, and needs of the individual will have to be consistent with citizenship behaviors. Similarly, the social context, or work group, in which the individual works will need to facilitate and promote such behaviors (we discuss group dynamics in Chapter 13). And the organization itself, especially its culture, must be capable of promoting, recognizing, and rewarding these types of behaviors if they are to be maintained. Although the study of organizational citizenship is still in its infancy, preliminary research suggests that it may play a powerful role in organizational effectiveness.[27]

Summary of Key Points

Understanding individuals in organizations is an important consideration for all managers. A basic framework that can be used to facilitate this understanding is the psychological contract—the set of expectations held by people with respect to what they will contribute to the organization and what they expect to get in return. Organizations strive to achieve an optimal person-job fit, but this process is complicated by the existence of individual differences.

Personality is the relatively stable set of psychological and behavioral attributes that distinguish one person from another. The "big five" personality traits are agreeableness, conscientiousness, negative emotionality, extraversion, and openness. Other important traits are locus of control, self-efficacy, authoritarianism, Machiavellianism, self-esteem, and risk propensity.

Attitudes are based on emotion, knowledge, and intended behavior. Whereas personality is relatively stable, some attitudes can be formed and changed easily. Others are more constant. Job satisfaction or dissatisfaction and organizational commitment are important work-related attitudes.

Perception is the set of processes through which an individual becomes aware of and interprets information about the environment.

Basic perceptual processes include selective perception and stereotyping. Perception and attribution are also closely related.

Stress is an individual's response to a strong stimulus. The general adaptation syndrome (GAS) outlines the basic stress process. Stress can be caused by task, physical, role, and interpersonal demands. Consequences of stress include organizational and individual outcomes, as well as burnout. Several things can be done to manage stress.

Creativity is the capacity to generate new ideas. Creative people tend to have certain profiles of background experiences, personal traits, and cognitive abilities. The creative process itself includes preparation, incubation, insight, and verification.

Workplace behavior is a pattern of action by the members of an organization that directly or indirectly influences organizational effectiveness. Performance behaviors are the set of work-related behaviors the organization expects the individual to display in order to fulfill the psychological contract. Basic withdrawal behaviors are absenteeism and turnover. Organizational citizenship refers to behavior that makes a positive overall contribution to the organization.

Discussion Questions

Questions for Review

1. What is a psychological contract? Why is it important?
2. Identify and describe five basic personality attributes.
3. What are the basic causes and consequences of stress in organizations?
4. Identify and discuss the steps in the creative process.
5. Identify and describe several important workplace behaviors.

Questions for Analysis

6. An individual was heard to describe someone else as having "no personality." What is

wrong with this statement? What did the individual actually mean?
7. Describe a circumstance in which you formed a new attitude about something.
8. Identify the basic causes of stress in your life. How might you go about reducing or eliminating them?
9. Identify a person whom you consider to be especially creative. What evidence can you cite to support your choice? What factors do you think most clearly led to this person's being so creative?
10. As a manager, how would you go about trying to make someone a better organizational citizen?

BUILDING EFFECTIVE *diagnostic & conceptual* SKILLS

Exercise Overview

Conceptual skills refer to a manager's ability to think in the abstract, and diagnostic skills focus on responses to situations. These skills must frequently be used together to better understand the behavior of others in the organization, as illustrated by this exercise.

Exercise Background

Human behavior is a complex phenomenon in any setting, but especially so in organizations. Understanding how and why people choose particular behaviors can be difficult and frustrating, but quite important. Consider, for example, the following scenario.

Sandra Buckley has worked in your department for several years. Until recently, she has been a model employee. She was always on time or early for work and stayed late whenever necessary to get her work done. She was upbeat, cheerful, and worked very hard. She frequently said that the company was the best place she had ever worked and that you were the perfect boss.

About six months ago, however, you began to see changes in Sandra's behavior. She began to occasionally come in late, and you cannot remember the last time she agreed to work past 5:00. She also complains a lot. Other workers have started to avoid her because she is so negative all the time. You also suspect that she may be looking for a new job.

Exercise Task

Using the scenario described above as background, do the following:

1. Assume that you have done some background work to find out what has happened. Write a brief case with more information that explains why Sandra's behavior has changed (for example, your case might note that you recently promoted someone else when Sandra might have expected to get the job). Make the case as descriptive as possible.
2. Relate elements of your case to the various behavioral concepts discussed in this chapter.

3. Decide whether or not you might be about to resolve things with Sandra to overcome whatever issues have arisen.

4. Which behavioral process or concept discussed in this chapter is easiest to change? Which is the most difficult to change?

BUILDING EFFECTIVE *time management* SKILLS

Exercise Overview

Time management skills help people prioritize work, work more efficiently, and delegate appropriately. Poor time management, in turn, may result in stress. This exercise helps you relate time management skills to stress reduction.

Exercise Background

Make a list of several major causes of stress for you. Stressors might involve school (hard classes, too many exams, and so on), work (financial pressures or a demanding work schedule, for example), or personal circumstances (friends, romance, family, and so on). Try to be as specific as possible. Also try to identify at least ten different stressors.

Exercise Task

Using the list developed above, do each of the following:

1. Evaluate the extent to which poor time management on your part plays a role in how each stressor affects you. For example, do exams cause stress because you delay studying?
2. Develop a strategy for using time more efficiently in relation to each stressor that relates to time.
3. Note interrelationships among different kinds of stressors and time. For example, financial pressures may cause you to work, but work may interfere with school. Can any of these interrelationships be more effectively managed vis-à-vis time?
4. How do you manage the stress in your life? Is it possible to manage stress in a more time-effective manner?

BUILDING EFFECTIVE *interpersonal* SKILLS

Exercise Overview

Interpersonal skills refer to the ability to communicate with, understand, and motivate individuals and groups. Implicit in this definition is the notion that a manager should try to understand important characteristics of others, including their personalities. This exercise gives you insights into the importance of personality in the workplace as well as some of the difficulties associated with assessing personality traits.

Exercise Background

You will first try to determine which personality traits are most relevant for different jobs. You

will then write a series of questions that you think may help assess or measure those traits in prospective employees. First, read the following job descriptions:

Sales representative: This position involves calling on existing customers to ensure that they continue to be happy with your firm's products. It also requires the sales representative to try to get those customers to buy more of your products, as well as to attract new customers. A sales representative should be aggressive but not pushy.

Office manager: The office manager oversees the work of a staff of 20 secretaries, receptionists, and clerks. The manager hires them, trains them, evaluates their performance, and sets their pay. The manager also schedules working hours and, when necessary, disciplines or fires workers.

Warehouse worker: Warehouse workers unload trucks and carry shipments to shelves for storage. They also pull orders for customers from shelves and take products for packing. The job requires workers to follow orders precisely and has little room for autonomy or interaction with others during work.

Exercise Task

Working alone, identify a single personality trait that you think is especially important for a person to effectively perform each job. Next, write five questions which, when answered by a job applicant, will help you assess how that applicant scores on that particular trait. These ques-

tions should be of the type that can be answered on a five-point scale (for example, strongly agree, agree, neither agree or disagree, disagree, strongly disagree).

Exchange questions with a classmate. Then pretend you are a job applicant. Provide honest and truthful answers to each question. Next, discuss the traits each of you identified for each position and how well you think the questions actually measure those traits.

Conclude by considering the following questions:

1. How easy is it to measure personality?
2. How important do you believe it is for organizations to consider personality in hiring decisions?
3. Do perception and attitudes affect how people answer personality questions?

SKILLS *self-assessment* INSTRUMENT

Assessing Your Mental Abilities

Introduction: Mental abilities are important to job performance, especially in this information age. The following assessment surveys your judgments about your personal mental abilities.

Instructions: Judge how accurately each of the following statements describes you. In some cases, making a decision may be difficult, but you should force a choice. Record your answers next to each statement according to the following scale:

Rating Scale

5 Very descriptive of me	**2** Not very descriptive of me
4 Fairly descriptive of me	**1** Not descriptive of me at all
3 Somewhat descriptive of me	

_____ 1. I am at ease learning visually. I readily take in and hold in mind visual precepts.

_____ 2. I can produce remotely associated, clever, or uncommon responses to statements or situations.

_____ 3. I can formulate and test hypotheses directed at finding a principle of relationships among elements of a case or problem.

_____ 4. I am able to remember bits of unrelated material and can recall parts of such material.

_____ 5. I can recall perfectly for immediate reproduction a series of items after only one presentation of the series.

_____ 6. I can manipulate numbers in arithmetic operations rapidly.

_____ 7. I am fast in finding figures, making comparisons, and carrying out other very simple tasks involving visual perception.

_____ 8. I can reason from stated premises to their necessary conclusion.

_____ 9. I can perceive spatial patterns or maintain orientation with respect to objects in space. I can manipulate or transform the image of spatial patterns into other visual arrangements.

_____ 10. I have a large knowledge of words and their meanings and am able to apply this knowledge in understanding connected discourse.

For interpretation, see Interpretations of Skills Self-Assessment Instruments.

Source: Adapted from M. D. Dunnette, "Aptitudes, Abilities, and Skills," in M. D. Dunnette (ed.), *Handbook of Industrial and Organizational Psychology,* Rand McNally, pp. 481–483. © 1976 by Rand McNally. Reprinted by permission of the author.

EXPERIENTIAL EXERCISE

Assumptions That Color Perceptions

Purpose: Perceptions rule the world. In fact, everything we know or think we know is filtered through our perceptions. Our perceptions are rooted in past experiences and socialization by significant others in our life. This exercise is designed to help you become aware of how much our assumptions influence our perceptions and evaluations of others. It also illustrates how we compare our perceptions with others to find similarities and differences.

Instructions

1. Read the descriptions of the four individuals provided in the personal descriptions below.
2. Decide which occupation is most likely for each person and place the name by the corresponding occupation in the occupations list. Each person is in a different occupation, and no two people hold the same one.

Personal Descriptions

R. B. Red is a trim, attractive woman in her early thirties. She holds an undergraduate degree from an eastern woman's college and is active in several professional organizations. She is an officer (on the national level) of Toastmistress International. Her hobbies include classical music, opera, and jazz. She is an avid traveler who is planning a sojourn to China next year.

W. C. White is a quiet, meticulous person. W. C. is tall and thin with blond hair and wire-framed glasses. Family, friends, and church are very important, and W. C. devotes any free time to community activities. W. C. is a wizard with figures but can rarely be persuaded to demonstrate this ability to do mental calculations.

G. A. Green grew up on a small farm in rural Indiana. He is an avid hunter and fisherman. In fact, he and his wife joke about their "deer-hunting honeymoon" in Colorado. One of his primary goals is to "get back to the land," and he hopes to be able to buy a small farm before he is 50. He drives a pickup truck and owns several dogs.

B. E. Brown is the child of wealthy professionals who reside on Long Island. B. E.'s father is a "self-made" financial analyst who made it a point to stress the importance of financial security as B. E. grew up. B. E. values the ability to structure one's use of time and can often be found on the golf course on Wednesday afternoons. B. E. dresses in a conservative upper-class manner and professes to be "allergic to polyester."

Occupations: Choose the occupations that seem most appropriate for each person described. Place the correct names in the spaces next to the corresponding occupations.

_____ Banker
_____ Labor negotiator
_____ Production manager
_____ Travel agent
_____ Accountant
_____ Teacher
_____ Clerk
_____ Army general
_____ Salesperson
_____ Truck driver
_____ Physician
_____ Financial analyst
_____ Computer operations manager

Source: Jerri L. Frantzve, *Behaving in Organizations* (Boston: Allyn & Bacon, 1983), pp. 63–65.

THE RISE OF FREE AGENTS

The sports tradition of free agents is taking hold in the business world. Free agents—self-employed individuals who contract for organizational work on a project basis—already account for more than one-quarter of the U.S. workforce. Within a decade, as many as four in ten workers are likely to be free agents, flitting from project to project and company to company as their talents are needed.

Several factors are fueling this trend. First, companies that downsized in earlier years find they sometimes need specialists with particular skills to handle certain projects, technologies, or clients. Second, companies can avoid the expense and hassles of constant hiring-and-firing cycles by selectively contracting with free agents to supplement their full-time, permanent workforce during peak sales, planning, or production periods. And, third, companies now have the technology to transcend organizational and geographical boundaries by connecting free agents outside the organization with employees inside for effective teamwork and collaboration.

For their part, free agents gain more flexibility in choosing among clients and projects, learning and applying new skills, managing time and other resources, balancing work and family obligations, and negotiating compensation. Free agents can work solo or come together as needed for specific projects. For example, web site designer Andrew Keeler often establishes temporary teams to work with him on projects for Adobe Systems, Hewlett-Packard, and other clients. Keeler has had face-to-face contact with only a few of his free-agent colleagues; in most cases, he uses e-mail to assemble a team, coordinate all work, and complete the project—quickly.

Keeler's experience illustrates one of the downsides to being a free agent: lack of personal interaction. E-mailing a joke adorned with a smiley face just isn't the same as sharing a laugh with a colleague while standing around the proverbial water cooler. Also, free agents can't always find as much work as they'd like, nor do they always get paid on time. Still, free agents in high-demand fields such as e-commerce technology can earn significantly more as independents than as employees, even though they have to arrange for their own health insurance and fund their own retirement account instead of receiving those as corporate benefits.

Companies are increasingly using free agents to keep their organizations flat and lean. When the Finnish telecommunications giant Nokia began selling computer displays in the United States, it hired only five permanent employees to staff the new office. The company relied on a network of free agents and outside suppliers to manage a wide range of activities, from marketing and sales to shipping and technical support.

But how do companies and free agents find each other? In addition to word-of-mouth communication, more matches are being made on the Internet. Monster Talent Market (http://www.talentmarket.monster.com) allows free agents to post information about their skills, schedules, and prices, so that companies can bid for their services. FreeAgent.com (http://www.freeagent.com) stores free agents' résumés for review by prospective clients and lists projects open for free agents' bids; similarly, eLance (http://www.elance.com) displays résumés and projects for which companies are seeking free agents. Free agents in search of community can visit Guru.com (http://www.guru.com), a site that goes beyond project and free-agent listings to offer articles and advice about working independently. Watch for even more matchmaking web sites as the free-agent movement gathers momentum outside high-tech industries.

Case Questions

1. How is the free-agent movement likely to influence workplace behaviors?

2. What work-related attitudes are more important for employees than for free agents?

3. Which personality traits do free agents need to be effective?

Case References

Michelle Conlin, "And Now, the Just-in-Time Employee," *Business Week*, August 28, 2000, pp. 169–170; and Katherine Mieszkowski, "Report from the Future: The E-Lance Economy," *Fast Company*, November 1999, pp. 66–68.

CHAPTER NOTES

1. "Company Cuts Jobs, Closes Plants as Sales Shrink, Popularity Fades," *USA Today*, February 23, 1999, pp. 1B, 2B (*quote on p. 2B); "Its Share Shrinking, Levi Strauss Lays Off 6,395," *Wall Street Journal*, November 4, 1997, pp. B1, B8; and *Hoover's Handbook of American Business 2001* (Austin, TX: Hoover's Business Press, 2001), pp. 862–863.

2. Elizabeth Wolfe Morrison and Sandra L. Robinson, "When Employees Feel Betrayed: A Model of How Psychological Contract Violation Develops," *Academy of Management Review*, January 1997, pp. 226–256.

3. Lawrence Pervin, "Personality," in *Annual Review of Psychology*, vol. 36, ed. Mark Rosenzweig and Lyman Porter (Palo Alto, CA: Annual Reviews, 1985), pp. 83–114; and S. R. Maddi, *Personality Theories: A Comparative Analysis*, 4th ed. (Homewood, IL: Dorsey, 1980).

4. L. R. Goldberg, "An Alternative 'Description of Personality': The Big Five Factor Structure," *Journal of Personality and Social Psychology* 59 (1990): 1216–1229.

5. Michael K. Mount, Murray R. Barrick, and J. Perkins Strauss, "Validity of Observer Ratings of the Big Five Personality Factors," *Journal of Applied Psychology* 79, no. 2 (1994): 272–280; and Timothy A. Judge, Joseph J. Martocchio, and Carl J. Thoreson, "Five-Factor Model of Personality and Employee Absence," *Journal of Applied Psychology* 82, no. 5 (1997): 745–755.

6. J. B. Rotter, "Generalized Expectancies for Internal vs. External Control of Reinforcement," *Psychological Monographs* 80 (1966): 1–28. See also Simon S. K. Lam and John Schaubroeck, "The Role of Locus of Control in Reactions to Being Promoted and to Being Passed Over: A Quasi Experiment," *Academy of Management Journal* 43, no.1 (2000): 66–78.

7. T. W. Adorno, E. Frenkel-Brunswick, D. J. Levinson, and R. N. Sanford, *The Authoritarian Personality* (New York: Harper & Row, 1950).

8. Michael Harris Bond and Peter B. Smith, "Cross-Cultural Social and Organizational Psychology," in *Annual Review of Psychology*, vol. 47, ed. Janet Spence (Palo Alto, CA: Annual Reviews, 1996), pp. 205–235.

9. Leon Festinger, *A Theory of Cognitive Dissonance* (Palo Alto, CA: Stanford University Press, 1957).

10. See John J. Clancy, "Is Loyalty Really Dead?" *Across the Board*, June 1999, pp. 15–19.

11. Patricia C. Smith, L. M. Kendall, and Charles Hulin, *The Measurement of Satisfaction in Work and Behavior* (Chicago: Rand-McNally, 1969).

12. "Companies Are Finding Real Payoffs in Aiding Employee Satisfaction," *Wall Street Journal*, October 11, 2000, p. B1.

13. James R. Lincoln, "Employee Work Attitudes and Management Practice in the U.S. and Japan: Evidence from a Large Comparative Study," *California Management Review*, Fall 1989, pp. 89–106.

14. Ibid.

15. For research work in this area, see Jennifer M. George and Gareth R. Jones, "The Experience of Mood and Turnover Intentions: Interactive Effects of Value Attainment, Job Satisfaction, and Positive Mood," *Journal of Applied Psychology* 81, no. 3 (1996): 318–325; and Larry J. Williams, Mark B. Gavin, and Margaret Williams, "Measurement and Nonmeasurement Processes with Negative Affectivity and Employee Attitudes," *Journal of Applied Psychology* 81, no. 1 (1996): 88–101.

16. Kathleen Sutcliffe, "What Executives Notice: Accurate Perceptions in Top Management Teams," *Academy of Management Journal* 37, no. 5 (1994): 1360–1378.

17. See H. H. Kelley, *Attribution in Social Interaction* (Morristown, NJ: General Learning Press, 1971), for a classic treatment of attribution.

18. Hans Selye, *The Stress of Life* (New York: McGraw-Hill, 1976).

19. M. Friedman and R. H. Rosenman, *Type A Behavior and Your Heart* (New York: Alfred A. Knopf, 1974).

20. Richard S. DeFrank, Robert Konopaske, and John M. Ivancevich, "Executive Travel Stress: Perils of the Road Warrior," *Academy of Management Executive* 14, no. 2 (2000): 58–67.

21. "Breaking Point," *Newsweek*, March 6, 1995, pp. 56–62.

22. John M. Kelly, "Get a Grip on Stress," *HRMagazine*, February 1997, pp. 51–58.

23. See Richard W. Woodman, John E. Sawyer, and Ricky W. Griffin, "Toward a Theory of Organizational Creaticity," *Academy of Management Review*, April 1993, pp. 293–321.

24. Emily Thornton, "Japan's Struggle to Be Creative," *Fortune*, April 19, 1993, pp. 129–134.

25. Christina E. Shalley, Lucy L. Gilson, and Terry C. Blum, "Matching Creativity Requirements and the Work Environment: Effects on Satisfaction and Intentions to Leave," *Academy of Management Journal* 43, no. 2 (2000): 215–223. See also Filiz Tabak, "Employee Creative Performance: What Makes It Happen?" *Academy of Management Executive* 11, no. 1 (1997): 119–122.

26. See Philip M. Podsakoff, Scott B. MacKenzie, Julie Beth Paine, and Daniel G. G. Bacharah, "Organizational Citizenship Behaviors: A Critical Review of the Theoretical and Empirical Literature and Suggestions for Future Research," *Journal of Management* 26, no. 3 (2000): 513–563, for recent findings regarding this behavior.

27. Dennis W. Organ, "Personality and Organizational Citizenship Behavior," *Journal of Management* 20, no. 2 (1994): 465–478; and Mary Konovsky and S. Douglas Pugh, "Citizenship Behavior and Social Exchange," *Academy of Management Journal* 37, no. 3 (1994): 656–669.

Motivating Employee Performance

For years, Continental Airlines was a company going nowhere. The firm was wallowing in red ink and had perhaps the poorest reputation of any carrier in the airline industry. For example, the company lost $2.4 billion in 1990 alone, and many business travelers routinely refused to fly Continental. The airline also went through two bankruptcies and a succession of ineffective senior leaders. Continental's pilots and rank-and-file workers endured layoffs, wage cuts, poor benefits, and broken promises by management. Indeed, many were frequently embarrassed to tell people where they worked, and few were motivated to work any harder than was necessary.

But in late 1994 things began to change. The key to what would eventually become one of the biggest turnarounds in the history of U.S. business was the appointment of a new CEO, Gordon Bethune. Bethune, a former fighter pilot in the navy and chief engineer at Boeing, had a repu-

tation for making tough but effective decisions. He was also known to be fair and open with employees. The board of directors told him to do whatever needed to be done to make Continental competitive again.

One area that needed immediate attention was operations. Bethune frantically cut unprofitable routes and added new and more profitable ones in their place. He also overhauled the firm's ticketing and baggage-handling operations, improved marketing, and updated the firm's aging fleet of aircraft. He also overhauled Continental's cash management system. But Bethune knew that operations alone were not the only problem areas—he also knew that employee motivation was at the root of many of the company's problems.

One of the biggest problems Bethune had to overcome was the legacy of his predecessors. Employees at Continental had endured ten CEOs in 15 years. Many of these CEOs, in turn, had been perceived as

being ineffective at best and as exhibiting little concern for the company's employees. As a result, many of those same employees had developed a deep-seeded distrust of top managers, and few were motivated to follow their lead.

One thing Bethune noticed immediately was that the primary variable-pay component in how the firm paid its pilots was based on fuel-cost savings. This arrangement, in turn, caused pilots to fly at relatively slower speeds and to be unwilling to increase air speed to make up for lost ground time. As soon as he changed this system to instead pay for on-time performance, Continental quickly moved from last in the industry in on-time performance to the middle of the industry.

"I've never heard of a successful company that didn't have people who liked working there."

—*Gordon Bethune, CEO of Continental Airlines**

LEARNING OBJECTIVES

After studying this chapter, you should be able to

- Characterize the nature of motivation, including its importance and basic historical perspectives.

  Identify and describe the major content perspectives on motivation.

- Identify and describe the major process perspectives on motivation.

- Describe reinforcement perspectives on motivation.

- Identify and describe popular motivational strategies.

- Describe the role of organizational reward systems in motivation.

Bethune then calculated that this increase in performance was saving the firm millions of dollars, because when planes are late, an airline must often pay for passengers' meals and hotel rooms and for rebooking them onto other airlines. He divided the total savings by the number of employees and sent each of them a check for that amount—$65 per employee. Although not a big sum, this served as an important demonstration that he was willing to share success with everyone. He also announced that henceforth each employee would receive a check for $65 every month that Continental was in the top five in on-time performance and a check for $100 when it was in the top three.

Bethune also wanted to improve communication throughout Continental. He set up a toll-free number for employees to call with complaints and problems. And he created a committee to respond to every call within 48 hours. He also gave employees his own personal voice-mail number and returns many of these calls himself. And today, he is careful to refer to Continental's employees as his "coworkers."

Bethune also began to restore wages to employees which had previously been cut. And, again, Continental's employees have responded in dramatic fashion. Once the joke of the airline industry, Continental is now among the most profitable carriers in the world, and its reputation among business travelers has soared near the top of the ratings. Indeed, the firm won the J. D. Powers customer satisfaction award as the best long-haul carrier in the United States several times in the last few years, and Continental was recently listed as one of the 100 best companies to work for by *Fortune* magazine.[1]

everal different factors have contributed to the remarkable turnaround at Continental. Enhanced employee motivation, moreover, is clearly one of the most significant. Virtually any organization is capable of developing and maintaining a motivated workforce. The trick is figuring out how to create a system in which employees can receive rewards that they genuinely want by performing in ways that fit the organization's goals and objectives.

In most settings, people can choose how hard they work and how much effort they expend. Thus managers need to understand how and why employees make different choices regarding their own performance. The key ingredient behind this choice is motivation, the subject of this chapter. We first examine the nature of employee motivation and then explore the major perspectives on motivation. Newly emerging approaches are then discussed. We conclude with a description of rewards and their role in motivation.

The Nature of Motivation

motivation The set of forces that cause people to behave in certain ways

Motivation is the set of forces that cause people to behave in certain ways.[2] On any given day, an employee may choose to work as hard as possible at a job, to work just hard enough to avoid a reprimand, or to do as little as possible. The goal for the manager is to maximize the likelihood of the first behavior and minimize the likelihood of the last one. This goal becomes all the more important when we understand how important motivation is in the workplace.

Individual performance is generally determined by three things: motivation (the desire to do the job), ability (the capability to do the job), and the work environment (the resources needed to do the job). If an employee lacks ability, the manager can provide training or replace the worker. If there is a resource problem, the manager can correct it. But if motivation is the problem, the task for the manager is more challenging. Individual behavior is a complex phenomenon, and the manager may be hard pressed to figure out the precise nature of the problem and how to solve it. Thus motivation is important because of its significance as a determinant of performance and because of its intangible character.[3]

The motivation framework in Figure 10.1 is a good starting point for understanding how motivated behavior occurs. The motivation process begins with a need or deficiency. For example, when a worker feels that she is underpaid, she experiences a need for more income. In response, the worker searches for ways to satisfy the need, such as working harder to try to earn a raise or seeking a new job. Next, she chooses an option to pursue. After carrying out the chosen option—working harder and putting in more hours for a reasonable period of time, for example—she then evaluates her success. If her hard work resulted in a pay raise, she probably feels good about things and will continue to work hard. But if no raise has been provided, she is likely to try another option.

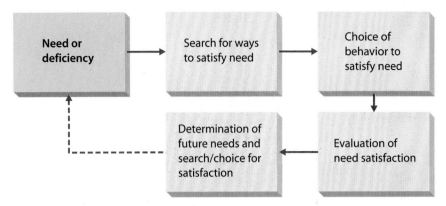

Figure 10.1

The Motivation Framework
The motivation process progresses through a series of discrete steps. Content, process, and reinforcement perspectives on motivation address different parts of this process.

Content Perspectives on Motivation

Content perspectives on motivation deal with the first part of the motivation process—needs and need deficiencies. More specially, **content perspectives** address the question: What factors in the workplace motivate people? Labor leaders often argue that workers can be motivated by more pay, shorter working hours, and improved working conditions. Meanwhile, some experts suggest that motivation can be more effectively enhanced by providing employees with more autonomy and greater responsibility.[4] Both of these views represent content views of motivation. The former asserts that motivation is a function of pay, working hours, and working conditions; the latter suggests that autonomy and responsibility are the causes of motivation. Two widely known content perspectives on motivation are the need hierarchy and the two-factor theory.

The Need Hierarchy Approach

Need hierarchies assume that people have different needs that can be arranged in a hierarchy of importance. The best-known need hierarchy was advanced by Abraham Maslow, who argued that people are motivated to satisfy five need levels.[5] **Maslow's hierarchy of needs** is shown in Figure 10.2. At the bottom of the hierarchy are the *physiological needs*—needs for food, sex, and air, which represent basic issues of survival and biological function. In organizations, these needs are generally satisfied by adequate wages and the work environment itself, which provides restrooms, adequate lighting, comfortable temperatures, and ventilation.

Next are the *security needs* for a secure physical and emotional environment. Examples include the desire for housing and clothing, and the need to be free from worry about money and job security. These needs can be satisfied in the workplace by job continuity (no layoffs), a grievance system (to protect against arbitrary supervisory actions), and an adequate insurance and retirement benefit package (for security against illness and provision of income in later life). Even today, however,

content perspectives Approaches to motivation that try to answer the question: What factor or factors motivate people?

Maslow's hierarchy of needs Suggests that people must satisfy five groups of needs in order—physiological, security, belongingness, esteem, and self-actualization

Figure 10.2

Maslow's Hierarchy of Needs

Maslow's hierarchy suggests that human needs can be classified into five categories and that these categories can be arranged in a hierarchy of importance. A manager should understand that an employee may not be satisfied with only a salary and benefits; he or she may also need challenging job opportunities to experience self-growth and satisfaction.

NEEDS

General Examples — Organizational Examples

General Examples		Organizational Examples
Achievement	Self-actualization	Challenging job
Status	Esteem	Job title
Friendship	Belongingness	Friends at work
Stability	Security	Pension plan
Food	Physiology	Base salary

Source: Adapted from Abraham H. Maslow, "A Theory of Human Motivation," *Psychological Review,* Vol. 50, 1943, pp. 370–396.

depressed industries and economic decline can put people out of work and restore the primacy of security needs.

Belongingness needs relate to social processes. They include the need for love and affection, and the need to be accepted by one's peers. These needs are satisfied for most people by family and community relationships outside of work and by friendships on the job. A manager can help satisfy these needs by allowing social interaction and by making employees feel like part of a team or work group.

Esteem needs actually comprise two different sets of needs: the need for a positive self-image and self-respect, and the need for recognition and respect from others. A manager can help address these needs by providing a variety of extrinsic symbols of accomplishment, such as job titles, nice offices, and similar rewards as appropriate. At a more intrinsic level, the manager can provide challenging job assignments and opportunities for the employee to feel a sense of accomplishment.

At the top of the hierarchy are *self-actualization needs.* These involve realizing one's potential for continued growth and individual development. The self-actualization needs are perhaps the most difficult for a manager to address. In fact, it can be argued that these needs must be met entirely from within the individual. But a manager can help by promoting a culture wherein self-actualization is possible. For instance, a manager could give employees a chance to participate in making decisions about their work and the opportunity to learn new things.

Maslow suggests that the five need categories constitute a hierarchy. An individual is motivated first and foremost to satisfy physiological needs. As long as they remain unsatisfied, the individual is motivated to fulfill only them. When satisfaction of physiological needs is achieved, they cease to act as primary motivational factors, and the individual moves "up" the hierarchy and becomes concerned with security needs. This process continues until the individual reaches the self-actualization level. Maslow's concept of the need hierarchy has a certain intuitive logic and has been accepted by many managers. But research has revealed certain shortcomings and defects in the theory. Some research has found that five levels of need are not always present and that the order of the levels is not always the same as postulated by Maslow.[6] In addition, people from different cultures are likely to have different need categories and hierarchies.

The Two-Factor Theory

Another popular content perspective is the **two-factor theory of motivation**.[7] Frederick Herzberg developed his theory by interviewing 200 accountants and engineers. He asked them to recall occasions when they had been satisfied and motivated, and occasions when they had been dissatisfied and unmotivated. Surprisingly, he found that different sets of factors were associated with satisfaction and with dissatisfaction; that is, a person might identify "low pay" as causing dissatisfaction but would not necessarily mention "high pay" as a cause of satisfaction. Instead, different factors—such as recognition or accomplishment—were cited as causing satisfaction and motivation.

This finding led Herzberg to conclude that the traditional view of job satisfaction was incomplete. That view assumed that satisfaction and dissatisfaction are at opposite ends of a single continuum. People might be satisfied, dissatisfied, or somewhere in between. But Herzberg's interviews had identified two different dimensions altogether: one ranging from satisfaction to no satisfaction and the other ranging from dissatisfaction to no dissatisfaction. This perspective, along with several examples of factors that affect each continuum, is shown in Figure 10.3. Note that the factors influencing the satisfaction continuum—called *motivation factors*—are related specifically to work content. The factors presumed to cause dissatisfaction—called *hygiene factors*—are related to the work environment.

Based on these findings, Herzberg argued that there are two stages in the process of motivating employees. First, managers must ensure that the hygiene factors are not deficient. Pay and security must be appropriate, working conditions must be

two-factor theory of motivation
Suggests that people's satisfaction and dissatisfaction are influenced by two independent sets of factors—motivation factors and hygiene factors

Figure 10.3

The Two-Factor Theory of Motivation

The two-factor theory suggests that job satisfaction has two dimensions. A manager who tries to motivate an employee using only hygiene factors such as pay and good working conditions will likely not succeed. To motivate employees and produce a high level of satisfaction, managers must also offer factors such as responsibility and the opportunity for advancement (motivation factors).

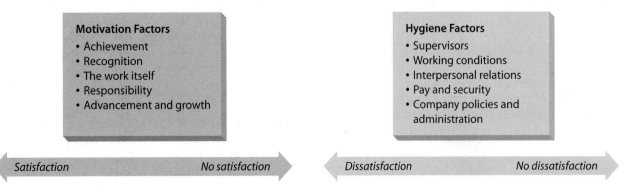

safe, technical supervision must be acceptable, and so on. By providing hygiene factors at an appropriate level, managers do not stimulate motivation but merely ensure that employees are "not dissatisfied." Employees whom managers attempt to "satisfy" through hygiene factors alone will usually do just enough to get by. Thus managers should proceed to stage 2—giving employees the opportunity to experience motivation factors such as achievement and recognition. The result is predicted to be a high level of satisfaction and motivation. Herzberg also goes a step further than most theorists and describes exactly how to use the two-factor theory in the workplace. Specifically, he recommends job enrichment, as discussed in Chapter 6. He argues that jobs should be redesigned to provide higher levels of the motivation factors.

Although widely accepted by many managers, Herzberg's two-factor theory is not without its critics. One criticism is that the findings in Herzberg's initial interviews are subject to different explanations. Another charge is that his sample was not representative of the general population and that subsequent research often failed to uphold the theory.[8] At the present time, Herzberg's theory is not held in high esteem by researchers in the field. The theory has had a major impact on managers, however, and has played a key role in increasing their awareness of motivation and its importance in the workplace.

need for achievement The desire to accomplish a goal or task more effectively than in the past

need for affiliation The desire for human companionship and acceptance

People have a variety of individual needs, including the needs for achievement and for affiliation. This group of women, for example, clearly reflects both needs. The women are successful venture capitalists in California's Silicon Valley. Their individual needs for achievement have no doubt played a significant roll in their climb to success. But while each has attained a high degree of personal success, they still feel a need to spend time with others. As a result, they have started a weekly poker match just to get together and have fun.

Individual Human Needs

In addition to these theories, research has also focused on specific individual human needs that are important in organizations. The three most important individual needs are achievement, affiliation, and power.[9]

The **need for achievement**, the best known of the three, is the desire to accomplish a goal or task more effectively than in the past. People with a high need for achievement have a desire to assume personal responsibility, a tendency to set moderately difficult goals, a desire for specific and immediate feedback, and a preoccupation with their task. David C. McClelland, the psychologist who first identified this need, argues that only about 10 percent of the U.S. population has a high need for achievement. In contrast, almost one-quarter of the workers in Japan have a high need for achievement.

The **need for affiliation** is less well understood. Like Maslow's belongingness need, the need for affiliation is a desire for human companionship and acceptance. People with a strong need for affiliation are likely to prefer (and perform better in) a job that entails a lot of social interaction and offers opportunities to make friends. The need for power has also received considerable attention as an important ingredient in managerial success.

The **need for power** is the desire to be influential in a group and to control one's environment. Research has shown that people with a strong need for power are likely to be superior performers, have good attendance records, and occupy supervisory positions. One study found that managers as a group tend to have a stronger power motive than the general population and that successful managers tend to have stronger power motives than less successful managers.[10]

need for power The desire to be influential in a group and to control one's environment

■ *Process Perspectives on Motivation*

Process perspectives are concerned with how motivation occurs. Rather than attempting to identify motivational stimuli, **process perspectives** focus on why people choose certain behavioral options to satisfy their needs and how they evaluate their satisfaction after they have attained these goals. Three useful process perspectives on motivation are the expectancy, equity, and goal-setting theories.

process perspectives Approaches to motivation that focus on why people choose certain behavioral options to fulfill their needs and how they evaluate their satisfaction after they have attained these goals

Expectancy Theory

Expectancy theory suggests that motivation depends on two things—how much we want something and how likely we think we are to get it.[11] Assume that you are approaching graduation and looking for a job. You see in the want ads that General Motors is seeking a new vice president with a starting salary of $500,000 per year. Even though you might want the job, you will not apply because you realize that you have little chance of getting it. The next ad you see is for someone to scrape bubble gum from underneath theater seats for a starting salary of $6 an hour. Even though you could probably get this job, you do not apply because you do not want it. Then you see an ad for a management trainee for a big company, with a starting salary of $35,000. You will probably apply for this job because you want it and because you think you have a reasonable chance of getting it.

expectancy theory Suggests that motivation depends on two things—how much we want something and how likely we think we are to get it

Expectancy theory rests on four basic assumptions. First, it assumes that behavior is determined by a combination of forces in the individual and in the environment. Second, it assumes that people make decisions about their own behavior in organizations. Third, it assumes that different people have different types of needs, desires, and goals. Fourth, it assumes that people make choices from among alternative plans of behavior based on their perceptions of the extent to which a given behavior will lead to desired outcomes.

Figure 10.4 summarizes the basic expectancy model. The model suggests that motivation leads to effort and that effort, combined with employee ability and environmental factors, results in performance. Performance, in turn, leads to various outcomes, each of which has an associated value called its valence. The most important parts of the expectancy model cannot be shown in the figure, however. These are the individual's expectation that effort will lead to high performance, that performance will lead to outcomes, and that each outcome will have some kind of value.

Effort-to-Performance Expectancy The **effort-to-performance expectancy** is the individual's perception of the probability that effort will lead to high

effort-to-performance expectancy The individual's perception of the probability that his or her effort will lead to high performance

Figure 10.4

The Expectancy Model of Motivation

The expectancy model of motivation is a complex but relatively accurate portrayal of how motivation occurs. According to this model, a manager must understand what employees want (such as pay, promotions, or status) to begin to motivate them.

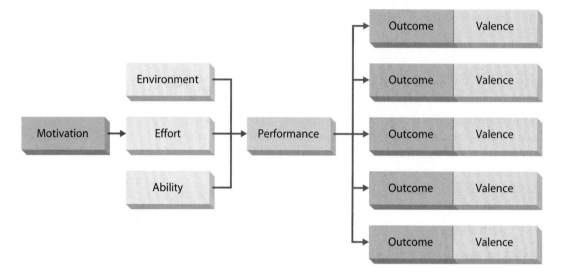

performance. When the individual believes that effort will lead directly to high performance, expectancy will be quite strong (close to 1.00). When the individual believes that effort and performance are unrelated, the effort-to-performance expectancy is very weak (close to 0). The belief that effort is somewhat but not strongly related to performance carries with it a moderate expectancy (somewhere between 0 and 1.00).

performance-to-outcome expectancy The individual's perception that her or his performance will lead to a specific outcome

Performance-to-Outcome Expectancy   The **performance-to-outcome expectancy** is the individual's perception that performance will lead to a specific outcome. For example, if the individual believes that high performance will result in a pay raise, the performance-to-outcome expectancy is high (approaching 1.00). The individual who believes that high performance may lead to a pay raise has a moderate expectancy (between 1.00 and 0). The individual who believes that performance has no relationship to rewards has a low performance-to-outcome expectancy (close to 0).

outcomes Consequences of behaviors in an organizational setting; usually rewards

valence An index of how much an individual desires a particular outcome; the attractiveness of the outcome to the individual

Outcomes and Valences   Expectancy theory recognizes that an individual's behavior results in a variety of **outcomes**, or consequences, in an organizational setting. A high performer, for example, may get bigger pay raises, faster promotions, and more praise from the boss. On the other hand, he or she may also be subject to more stress and incur resentment from coworkers. Each of these outcomes also has an associated value, or **valence**—an index of how much an individual values a particular outcome. If the individual wants the outcome, its valence is positive; if the individual does not want the outcome, its valence is negative; and if the individual is indifferent to the outcome, its valence is zero.

It is this part of expectancy theory that goes beyond the content perspectives on motivation. Different people have different needs, and they will try to satisfy these needs in different ways. For an employee who has a high need for achievement and a low need for affiliation, the pay raise and promotions cited above as outcomes of high performance might have positive valences, the praise and resentment zero valences, and the stress a negative valence. For a different employee, with a low need for achievement and a high need for affiliation, the pay raise, promotions, and praise might all have positive valences, whereas both resentment and stress could have negative valences.

For motivated behavior to occur, three conditions must be met. First, the effort-to-performance expectancy must be greater than zero (the individual must believe that, if effort is expended, high performance will result). The performance-to-outcome expectancy must also be greater than zero (the individual must believe that, if high performance is achieved, certain outcomes will follow). And the sum of the valences for the outcomes must be greater than zero. (One or more outcomes may have negative valences if they are more than offset by the positive valences of other outcomes. For example, the attractiveness of a pay raise, a promotion, and praise from the boss may outweigh the unattractiveness of more stress and resentment from coworkers.) Expectancy theory suggests that when these conditions are met, the individual is motivated to expend effort.

Starbucks credits its unique stock ownership program with maintaining a dedicated and motivated workforce. Based on the fundamental concepts of expectancy theory, Starbucks employees earn stock as a function of their seniority and performance. Thus their hard work helps them earn shares of ownership in the company.[12]

The Porter-Lawler Extension An interesting extension of expectancy theory has been proposed by Porter and Lawler.[13] Recall from Chapter 1 that the human relationists assumed that employee satisfaction causes good performance. We also noted that research has not supported such a relationship. Porter and Lawler suggest that there may indeed be a relationship between satisfaction and performance but that it goes in the opposite direction—that is, high performance may lead to high satisfaction. Figure 10.5 summarizes Porter and Lawler's logic. Performance results

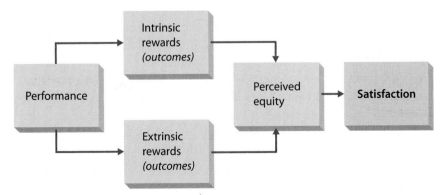

Figure 10.5

The Porter-Lawler Extension of Expectancy Theory

The Porter-Lawler extension of expectancy theory suggests that, if performance results in equitable rewards, people will be more satisfied. Thus performance can lead to satisfaction. Managers must therefore be sure that any system of motivation includes rewards that are fair, or equitable, for all.

Source: Edward E. Lawler III and Lyman W. Porter, "The Effect of Performance on Job Satisfaction," *Industrial Relations*, October 1967, p. 23. Permission granted courtesy of Blackwell Publishers, Inc.

in rewards for an individual. Some of these are extrinsic (such as pay and promotions); others are intrinsic (such as self-esteem and accomplishment). The individual evaluates the equity, or fairness, of the rewards relative to the effort expended and the level of performance attained. If the rewards are perceived to be equitable, the individual is satisfied.

Equity Theory

equity theory Suggests that people are motivated to seek social equity in the rewards they receive for performance

After needs have stimulated the motivation process and the individual has chosen an action that is expected to satisfy those needs, the individual assesses the fairness, or equity, of the resultant outcome. **Equity theory** contends that people are motivated to seek social equity in the rewards they receive for performance.[14] Equity is an individual's belief that the treatment he or she is receiving is fair relative to the treatment received by others. According to equity theory, outcomes from a job include pay, recognition, promotions, social relationships, and intrinsic rewards. To get these rewards, the individual makes inputs to the job, such as time, experience, effort, education, and loyalty. The theory suggests that people view their outcomes and inputs as a ratio and then compare it to the ratio of someone else. This other "person" may be someone in the work group or some sort of group average or composite. The process of comparison looks like this:

$$\frac{\text{Outcomes (self)}}{\text{Inputs (self)}} = \frac{\text{Outcomes (other)}}{\text{Inputs (other)}}$$

Both the formulation of the ratios and comparisons between them are very subjective and based on individual perceptions. As a result of comparisons, three conditions may result: the individual may feel equitably rewarded, underrewarded, or overrewarded. A feeling of equity will result when the two ratios are equal. This may occur even though the other person's outcomes are greater than the individual's own outcomes—provided that the other's inputs are also proportionately greater. Suppose that Mark has a high school education and earns $30,000. He may still feel equitably treated relative to Susan, who earns $35,000, because she has a college degree.

People who feel underrewarded try to reduce the inequity. Such an individual might decrease her inputs by exerting less effort, increase her outcomes by asking for a raise, distort the original ratios by rationalizing, try to get the other person to change her or his outcomes or inputs, leave the situation, or change the object of comparison. An individual may also feel overrewarded relative to another person. This is not likely to be terribly disturbing to most people, but research suggests that some people who experience inequity under these conditions are somewhat motivated to reduce it. Under such a circumstance, the person might increase his inputs by exerting more effort, reduce his outcomes by producing fewer units (if paid on a per-unit basis), distort the original ratios by rationalizing, or try to reduce the inputs or increase the outcomes of the other person.

Goal-Setting Theory

goal-setting theory Assumes that behavior is a result of conscious goals and intentions

The **goal-setting theory** of motivation assumes that behavior is a result of conscious goals and intentions.[15] Therefore, by setting goals for people in the organization, a manager should be able to influence their behavior. Given this premise, the challenge is to develop a thorough understanding of the processes by which people set goals and then work to reach them. In the original version of goal-setting theory, two specific goal characteristics—goal difficulty and goal specificity—were expected to shape performance.

Goal Difficulty   *Goal difficulty* is the extent to which a goal is challenging and requires effort. If people work to achieve goals, it is reasonable to assume they will work harder to achieve more difficult goals. But a goal must not be so difficult that it is unattainable. If a new manager asks her sales force to increase sales by 300 percent, the group may become disillusioned. A more realistic but still difficult goal—perhaps a 30 percent increase— would be a better incentive. A substantial body of research supports the importance of goal difficulty. In one study, for example, managers at Weyerhauser set difficult goals for truck drivers hauling loads of timber from cutting sites to wood yards. Over a nine-month period, the drivers increased the quantity of wood they delivered by an amount that would have required $250,000 worth of new trucks at the previous per-truck average load.[16]

Goal Specificity   *Goal specificity* is the clarity and precision of the goal. A goal of "increasing productivity" is not very specific; a goal of "increasing productivity by 3 percent in the next six months" is quite specific. Some goals, such as those involving costs, output, profitability, and growth are readily amenable to specificity. Other goals, however, such as improving employee job satisfaction, morale, company image and reputation, ethics, and socially responsible behavior, may be much harder to state in specific terms. Like difficulty, specificity has also been shown to be consistently related to performance. The study of timber truck drivers mentioned above, for example, also examined goal specificity. The initial loads the truck drivers were carrying were found to be 60 percent of the maximum weight each truck could haul. The managers set a new goal for drivers of 94 percent, which the drivers were soon able to reach. Thus the goal was both specific and difficult.

Because the theory attracted so much widespread interest and research support from researchers and managers alike, an expanded model of the goal-setting process was eventually proposed. The expanded model, shown in Figure 10.6, attempts to capture more fully the complexities of goal setting in organizations.

The expanded theory argues that goal-directed effort is a function of four goal attributes: difficulty and specificity, as already discussed, and acceptance and commitment. *Goal acceptance* is the extent to which a person accepts a goal as his or her own. *Goal commitment* is the extent to which she or he is personally interested in reaching the goal. The manager who vows to take whatever steps are necessary to cut costs by 10 percent has made a commitment to achieve the goal. Factors that can foster goal acceptance and commitment include participating in the goal-setting process, making goals challenging but realistic, and believing that goal achievement will lead to valued rewards.

The interaction of goal-directed effort, organizational support, and individual abilities and traits determines actual performance. Organizational support is whatever the organization does to help or hinder performance. Positive support might mean making available adequate personnel and a sufficient supply of raw materials;

286   PART FOUR | *Leading*

Figure 10.6

The Expanded Goal-Setting Theory of Motivation

One of the most important process theories of motivation is goal-setting theory. This theory suggests that goal difficulty, specificity, acceptance, and commitment combine to determine an individual's goal-directed effort. This effort, when complemented by appropriate organizational support and individual abilities and traits, results in performance. Finally, performance is seen as leading to intrinsic and extrinsic rewards, which in turn result in employee satisfaction.

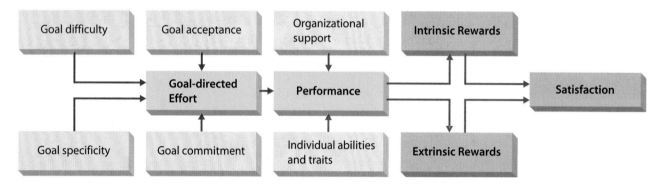

Source: Reprinted from *Organizational Dynamics*, Autumn 1979, Gary P. Latham and Edwin A. Locke, "A Motivational Technique That Works." p. 79. Copyright © 1979 with permission from Elsevier Science.

negative support might mean failing to fix damaged equipment. Individual abilities and traits are the skills and other personal characteristics necessary for doing a job. As a result of performance, a person receives various intrinsic and extrinsic rewards, which in turn influence satisfaction. Note that the latter stages of this model are quite similar to those in the Porter and Lawler expectancy model discussed earlier.

Reinforcement Perspectives on Motivation

A third element of the motivational process addresses why some behaviors are maintained over time and why other behaviors change. As we have seen, content perspectives deal with needs, whereas process perspectives explain why people choose various behaviors to satisfy needs and how they evaluate the equity of the rewards they get for those behaviors. Reinforcement perspectives explain the role of those rewards as they cause behavior to change or remain the same over time. Specifically, **reinforcement theory** argues that behavior that results in rewarding consequences is likely to be repeated, whereas behavior that results in punishing consequences is less likely to be repeated.[17]

reinforcement theory Approach to motivation that explains the role of rewards as they cause behavior to change or remain the same over time

Kinds of Reinforcement in Organizations

There are four basic kinds of reinforcement that can result from behavior—positive reinforcement, avoidance, punishment, and extinction.[18] Two kinds of reinforcement strengthen or maintain behavior, whereas the other two weaken or decrease behavior.

Positive reinforcement, a method of strengthening behavior, is a reward or a positive outcome after a desired behavior is performed. When a manager observes an employee doing an especially good job and offers praise, the praise serves to positively reinforce the behavior of good work. Other positive reinforcers in organizations include pay raises, promotions, and awards. Employees who work at General Electric's customer service center receive clothing, sporting goods, and even trips to Disney World as rewards for outstanding performance. The other method of strengthening desired behavior is through **avoidance**. An employee may come to work on time to avoid a reprimand. In this instance, the employee is motivated to perform the behavior of punctuality to avoid an unpleasant consequence that is likely to follow tardiness.

Punishment is used by some managers to weaken undesired behaviors. When an employee is loafing, coming to work late, doing poor work, or interfering with the work of others, the manager might resort to reprimands, discipline, or fines. The logic is that the unpleasant consequence will reduce the likelihood that the employee will choose that particular behavior again. Given the counterproductive side effects of punishment (such as resentment and hostility), it is often advisable to use the other kinds of reinforcement if at all possible.

Extinction can also be used to weaken behavior, especially behavior that has previously been rewarded. When an employee tells an off-color joke and the boss laughs, the laughter reinforces the behavior, and the employee may continue to tell off-color jokes. By simply ignoring this behavior and not reinforcing it, the boss can cause the behavior to subside and eventually become "extinct."

positive reinforcement A method of strengthening behavior with rewards or positive outcomes after a desired behavior is performed

avoidance Used to strengthen behavior by avoiding unpleasant consequences that would result if the behavior were not performed

punishment Used to weaken undesired behaviors by using negative outcomes or unpleasant consequences when the behavior is performed

extinction Used to weaken undesired behaviors by simply ignoring or not reinforcing that behavior

Providing Reinforcement in Organizations

Not only is the kind of reinforcement important, but so is when or how often it occurs. Various strategies are possible for providing reinforcement. The **fixed-interval schedule** provides reinforcement at fixed intervals of time, regardless of behavior. A good example of this schedule is the weekly or monthly paycheck. This method provides the least incentive for good work, because employees know they will be paid regularly, regardless of their effort. A **variable-interval schedule** also uses time as the basis for reinforcement, but the time interval varies from one reinforcement to the next. This schedule is appropriate for praise or other rewards based on visits or inspections. When employees do not know when the boss is going to drop by, they tend to maintain a reasonably high level of effort all the time.

A **fixed-ratio schedule** gives reinforcement after a fixed number of behaviors, regardless of the time that elapses between behaviors. This results in an even higher level of effort. For example, when Sears is recruiting new credit card customers, salespersons get a small bonus for every fifth application returned from their department. Under this arrangement, motivation will be high, because each application gets the person closer to the next bonus. The **variable-ratio schedule**, the most powerful schedule in terms of maintaining desired behaviors, varies the number of behaviors needed for each reinforcement. A supervisor who praises an employee for her second order, the seventh order after that, the ninth after that, then the fifth, and then the third is using a variable-ratio schedule. The

fixed-interval schedule Provides reinforcement at fixed intervals of time, such as regular weekly paychecks

variable-interval schedule Provides reinforcement at varying intervals of time, such as occasional visits by the supervisor

fixed-ratio schedule Provides reinforcement after a fixed number of behaviors regardless of the time interval involved, such as a bonus for every fifth sale

variable-ratio schedule Provides reinforcement after varying numbers of behaviors are performed, such as the use of complements by a supervisor on an irregular basis

employee is motivated to increase the frequency of the desired behavior, because each performance increases the probability of receiving a reward. Of course, a variable-ratio schedule is difficult (if not impossible) to use for formal rewards such as pay because it would be too complicated to keep track of who was rewarded when.

Managers wanting to explicitly use reinforcement theory to motivate their employees generally do so with a technique call **behavior modification**, or **OB mod**.[19] An OB mod program starts by specifying behaviors that are to be increased (such as producing more units) or decreased (such as coming to work late). These target behaviors are then tied to specific forms of reinforcement. Although many organizations (such as Procter & Gamble and Ford) have used OB mod, the best-known application was at Emery Air Freight. Management felt that the containers used to consolidate small shipments into fewer, larger shipments were not being packed efficiently. Through a system of self-monitored feedback and rewards, Emery increased container usage from 45 percent to 95 percent and saved over $3 million during the first three years of the program.[20]

behavior modification (OB mod) A reinforcement program that starts by specifying behaviors that are to be increased or decreased, then ties these target behaviors to specific forms of reinforcement

Popular Motivational Strategies

Although these theories provide a solid explanation for motivation, managers must use various techniques and strategies to actually apply them. Among the most popular motivational strategies today are empowerment and participation, and alternative forms of working arrangements.

Empowerment and Participation

Empowerment and participation represent important methods that managers can use to enhance employee motivation. **Empowerment** is the process of enabling workers to set their own work goals, make decisions, and solve problems within their sphere of responsibility and authority. **Participation** is the process of giving employees a voice in making decisions about their own work. Thus empowerment is a somewhat broader concept which promotes participation in a wide variety of areas, including but not limited to the work itself, work context, and work environment.[21]

The role of participation and empowerment in motivation can be expressed in terms of both content perspectives and expectancy theory. Employees who participate in decision making may be more committed to executing decisions properly. Furthermore, the successful process of making a decision, executing it, and then seeing the positive consequences can help satisfy one's need for achievement, provide recognition and responsibility, and enhance self-esteem. Simply being asked to participate in organizational decision making also may enhance an employee's self-esteem. In addition, participation should help clarify expectancies; that is, by participating in decision making, employees may better understand the linkage between their performance and the rewards they want most.

empowerment The process of enabling workers to set their own work goals, make decisions, and solve problems within their sphere of responsibility and authority

participation The process of giving employees a voice in making decisions about their own work

New Forms of Working Arrangements

Many organizations today are also experimenting with a variety of alternative work arrangements. These alternative arrangements are generally intended to enhance employee motivation and performance by providing them with greater flexibility in how and when they work. Among the more popular alternative work arrangements are compressed work schedules, flexible work schedules, job sharing, and telecommuting.[22]

Compressed work schedules generally involve working a full 40-hour week in fewer than the traditional five days.[23] One approach involves working 10 hours a day for four days, leaving an extra day off. Another alternative is for employees to work slightly less than 10 hours a day but to complete the 40 hours by lunchtime on Friday. And a few firms have tried having employees work 12 hours a day for three days, followed by four days off. Organizations that have used these forms of compressed workweeks include John Hancock, BP Amoco, and Philip Morris. One problem with this schedule is that, when employees put in too much time in a single day, they tend to get tired and perform at a lower level later in the day.

A schedule that some organizations today are beginning to use is what they call a "9-80" schedule. Under this arrangement, an employee works a traditional schedule one week and a compressed schedule the next, getting every other Friday off. That is, they work 80 hours (the equivalent of two weeks of full-time work) in nine days. By alternating the regular and compressed schedules across half of its workforce, the organization can be fully staffed at all times, while still giving employees two full days off each month. Shell Oil and Amoco Chemicals are two of the firms that currently use this schedule.

Another popular alternative work arrangement is **flexible work schedules**, sometimes called **flextime**. Flextime gives employees more personal control over the times they work. The workday is broken down into two categories, flexible time and core time. All employees must be at their workstations during core time, but they can choose their own schedules during flexible time. Thus one employee may choose to start work early in the morning and leave in mid-afternoon, another to start in the late morning and work until late afternoon, and still another to start early in the morning, take a long lunch break, and work until late afternoon. Organizations that have used the flexible work schedule method for arranging work include Hewlett-Packard, Compaq Computer, Microsoft, and Texas Instruments.

Yet another potentially useful alternative work arrangement is job sharing. In **job sharing**, two part-time employees share one full-time job. One person may perform the job from 8:00 A.M. to noon and the other from 1:00 P.M. to 5:00 P.M. Job sharing may be desirable for people who want to work only part time or when job markets are tight. For its part, the organization can accommodate the preferences of a broader range of employees and may benefit from the talents of more people.

A relatively new approach to alternative work arrangements is **telecommuting**—allowing employees to spend part of their time working off site, usually at home. By using e-mail, the Internet, and other forms of information technology, many employees can maintain close contact with their organization and still get just as much work done at home as if they were in their office. The increased

compressed work schedule
Working a full 40-hour week in fewer than the traditional five days

flexible work schedules (flextime) Allowing employees to select, within broad parameters, the hours they work

job sharing When two part-time employees share one full-time job.

telecommuting Allowing employees to spend part of their time working off site, usually at home

power and sophistication of modern communication technology is making telecommuting easier and easier.

Using Reward Systems to Motivate Performance

reward system The formal and informal mechanisms by which employee performance is defined, evaluated, and rewarded

Aside from these types of motivational strategies, an organization's reward system is its most basic tool for managing employee motivation. An organizational **reward system** is the formal and informal mechanisms by which employee performance is defined, evaluated, and rewarded. *Management InfoTech* discusses how managers today can use the Internet to learn more about rewards their peers are making around the world.

Managers sometimes resort to unusual rewards as a way to retain valuable employees. Mercer Management, a consulting firm, was having trouble holding on to its best consultants, who were beginning to feel a bit restless. Mercer found that some of them were leaving to help implement strategies they had developed for Mercer clients. So, the firm now allows its consultants to take a leave of absence for up to one year to work for other companies. Mercer consultant Gregg Dixon, for example, helped Binney & Smith develop a new strategy for its popular Crayola crayons. He then went to work for Binney & Smith to help implement the strategy. After he has finished, he will return to his old job at Mercer Management.

Effects of Organizational Rewards

Organizational rewards can affect attitudes, behaviors, and motivation. Thus it is important for managers to clearly understand and appreciate their importance.[24]

Effect of Rewards on Attitudes   Although employee attitudes such as satisfaction are not a major determinant of job performance, they are nonetheless important. They contribute to (or discourage) absenteeism and affect turnover, and they help establish the culture of the organization. We can draw four major generalizations about employee attitudes and rewards.[25] First, employee satisfaction is influenced by how much is received and how much the individual thinks should be received. Second, employee satisfaction is affected by comparisons with what happens to others. Third, employees often misperceive the rewards of others. When an employee believes that someone else is making more money than that person really makes, the potential for dissatisfaction increases. Fourth, overall job satisfaction is affected by how satisfied employees are with both the extrinsic and the intrinsic rewards they derive from their jobs. Drawing from the content theories and expectancy theory, this conclusion suggests that a variety of needs may cause behavior and that behavior may be channeled toward a variety of goals.

Effect of Rewards on Behaviors   An organization's primary purpose in giving rewards is to influence employee behavior. Extrinsic rewards affect employee satisfaction, which in turn plays a major role in determining whether an employee will remain on the job or seek a new job. Reward systems also influence patterns

SEARCHING OUT SALARIES AROUND THE WORLD

How can job seekers, employees, and human resource professionals find the general salary range for a particular position in Harrisburg or Hong Kong? More and more salary information is migrating to the Internet, where it is available to anyone, anywhere in the world. With just a few keystrokes, employees and job candidates can read advice about negotiating salaries and see how pay packages in e-businesses compare with pay packages in traditional industries. Meanwhile, managers can log on and scroll through local, national, and international surveys of salaries in different fields.

Salary.com (http://www.salary.com), for example, presents news about salary trends, offers expert advice about pay and promotion, and allows users to look up salary ranges for job categories in dozens of U.S. metropolitan areas. Monster.com (http://www.monster.com) offers salary comparison data, negotiating tips, and other information on its various country-specific sites. Visitors to the U.K. Monster site (http://salary .monster.co.uk/salary.monster.co.uk) can click to see what a particular position typically pays (in euros, pounds, and other currencies) in different European countries.

Other sites display the results of salary surveys in specific functional areas. *Industry Week* (http://www.industryweek.com),

for instance, regularly reports on national and international salary trends in manufacturing positions. Similarly, *Advertising Age* (http://www.adage.com) displays the results of its salary surveys among marketing and advertising specialists.

Easy Internet availability of salary data is helping job candidates negotiate better starting salaries. It is also helping employees support requests for raises at review time. On the company side, online salary data help managers stay abreast of the latest salary trends for all business locations, so that they can offer competitive pay packages to attract and retain skilled employees. Now managers, applicants, and employees in nearly any country can back up discussions about salary issues with objective, up-to-date information gleaned from online sources.

> *The information age is so real time, and [employees] keep an eye on where everyone is.*
>
> — *Mike Caggiano, president of FutureNext**

References: Stephanie Armour, "Show Me the Money, More Workers Say," *USA Today*, June 6, 2000, p. 1B (*quote on p. 1B).

---

of attendance and absenteeism and if rewards are based on actual performance, employees tend to work harder to earn those rewards.

Effect of Rewards on Motivation   Reward systems are clearly related to the expectancy theory of motivation. The effort-to-performance expectancy is strongly influenced by the performance appraisal that is often a part of the reward system. An employee is likely to put forth extra effort if he or she knows that performance will be measured, evaluated, and rewarded. The performance-to-outcome expectancy is affected by the extent to which the employee believes that performance will be followed by rewards. Finally, as expectancy theory predicts, each reward or potential reward has a somewhat different value for each individual. One person may want a promotion more than benefits; someone else may want just the opposite.

"I think I should warn you that the flip side of our generous bonus-incentive program is capital punishment."

© The New Yorker Collection 1994 Robert Mankoff from the cartoonbank.com. All rights reserved.

Organizations provide rewards and incentives that can serve as positive reinforcement to desired behavior. Similarly, most also have various forms of punishment that can be used to weaken or eliminate undesired behaviors. Although not as extreme as the humorous example shown here, positive reinforcement and punishment that are clearly linked to desired and undesired behaviors, respectively, can play a major role in boosting employee performance and organizational effectiveness.

merit system A reward system whereby people get different pay raises at the end of the year, depending on their overall job performance

incentive system A reward system whereby people get different pay amounts at each pay period in proportion to what they do

Designing Effective Reward Systems

What are the elements of an effective reward system? Experts agree that they have four major characteristics.[26] First, the reward system must meet the individual's needs for basic necessities. Next, the rewards should compare favorably with those offered by other organizations. Unfavorable comparisons with people in other settings could result in feelings of inequity. Third, the distribution of rewards within the organization must be equitable. And, fourth, the reward system must recognize that different people have different needs and choose different paths to satisfy those needs. Both content theories and expectancy theory contribute to this conclusion. Insofar as possible, a variety of rewards and a variety of methods for achieving them should be made available to employees.

Popular Approaches to Rewarding Employees

Organizational reward systems have traditionally been one of two kinds: a fixed hourly or monthly rate, or an incentive system. Fixed-rate systems are familiar to most people. Hourly employees are paid a specific wage (based on job demands, experience, or other factors) for each hour they work. Salaried employees receive a fixed sum of money on a weekly or monthly basis. Although some reductions may be made for absences, the amount is usually the same regardless of whether the individual works less than or more than a normal amount of time.[27]

From a motivational perspective, such rewards can be tied more directly to performance through merit pay raises. A **merit system** is one whereby people get different pay raises at the end of the year, depending on their overall job performance.[28] When the organization's performance appraisal system is appropriately designed, merit pay is a good system for maintaining long-term performance. Increasingly, however, organizations are experimenting with various kinds of incentive systems. **Incentive systems** attempt to reward employees in proportion to what they do. A piece-rate pay plan is a good example of an incentive system. In a factory manufacturing luggage, for example, each worker may be paid 50 cents for each handle and set of locks installed on a piece of luggage. Hence, there is incentive for the employee to work hard: The more units produced, the higher the pay. Four increasingly popular incentive systems are profit sharing, gain sharing, lump-sum bonuses, and pay-for-knowledge.

Profit sharing provides a varying annual bonus to employees based on corporate profits. This system unites workers and management toward the same goal— higher profits. Ford, Continental Airlines, USX, and Alcoa all have profit-sharing plans. Gain sharing is a group-based incentive system in which group members all get bonuses when predetermined performance levels are exceeded. The lump-sum bonus plan gives each employee a one-time cash bonus, rather than a base salary increase. Finally, pay-for-knowledge systems focus on paying the individual rather than the job.

Summary of Key Points

Motivation is the set of forces that cause people to behave in certain ways. Motivation is an important consideration for managers because it, along with ability and environmental factors, determines individual performance.

Content perspectives on motivation are concerned with what factor or factors cause motivation. Popular content theories include Maslow's need hierarchy and Herzberg's two-factor theory. Other important needs are the needs for achievement, affiliation, and power.

Process perspectives on motivation deal with how motivation occurs. Expectancy theory suggests that people are motivated to perform if they believe that their effort will result in high performance, that this performance will lead to rewards, and that the positive aspects of the outcomes outweigh the negative aspects. Equity theory is based on the premise that people are motivated to achieve and maintain social equity. Goal-setting theory helps to put both expectancy and equity theory into operation.

The reinforcement perspective focuses on how motivation is maintained. Its basic assumption is that behavior that results in rewarding consequences is likely to be repeated, whereas behavior resulting in negative consequences is less likely to be repeated. Reinforcement contingencies can be arranged in the form of positive reinforcement, avoidance, punishment, and extinction, and they can be provided on fixed-interval, variable-interval, fixed-ratio, or variable-ratio schedules.

Among the most popular motivational strategies today are empowerment and participation, and alternative forms of work arrangements.

Organizational reward systems are the primary mechanisms managers have for managing motivation. Properly designed systems can improve attitudes, motivation, and behaviors. Effective reward systems must provide sufficient rewards on an equitable basis at the individual level. Contemporary reward systems include merit systems and various kinds of incentive systems.

Discussion Questions

Questions for Review

1. Summarize the basic motivation process.
2. What are the differences between the motivation and hygiene factors in the two-factor theory?

3. Compare and contrast content, process, and reinforcement perspectives on motivation.
4. In what ways do empowerment, participation, and alternative forms of work arrangements rely on the content, process, and reinforcement perspectives?

5. What are the similarities and differences among the motivational strategies described in this chapter?

Questions for Analysis

6. Compare and contrast the different content theories. Can you think of any ways in which the theories are contradictory?
7. Expectancy theory seems to make a great deal of sense, but it is complicated. Some people argue that its complexity reduces its value to practicing managers. Do you agree or disagree?
8. Under what circumstances might a famous athlete earning $3 million a year feel underpaid?
9. Offer examples other than those from this chapter to illustrate positive reinforcement, avoidance, punishment, and extinction.
10. Think of examples of when you have been motivated by the various theories in this chapter.

BUILDING EFFECTIVE *interpersonal* SKILLS

Exercise Overview

Interpersonal skills—the ability to understand and motivate individuals and groups—are especially critical when managers attempt to deal with issues associated with equity and justice in the workplace. This exercise provides you with insights into how these skills may be used.

Exercise Background

You are the manager of a group of professional employees in the electronics industry. One of your employees, David Brown, has asked to meet with you. You think you know what David wants to discuss, and you are unsure as to how to proceed.

You hired David about ten years ago. During his time in your group, he has been a solid, but not outstanding, employee. His performance, for example, has been satisfactory in every respect, but seldom outstanding. As a result, he has consistently received average performance evaluations, pay increases, and so forth. Indeed, he actually makes somewhat less today than do a couple of people with less tenure in the group but with stronger performance records.

The company has just announced an opening for a team leader position in your group, and you know that David wants the job. He believes that he has earned the opportunity to have the job on the basis of his consistent efforts. Unfortunately, you see things a bit differently. You really want to appoint another individual, Becky Thomas, to the job. Becky has worked for the firm for only six years but is your top performer. You want to reward her performance and think that she will do an excellent job. On the other hand, you do not want to lose David, because he is a solid member of the group.

Exercise Task

Using the information above, respond to the following:

1. Using equity theory as a framework, how are David and Becky likely to see the situation?
2. Outline a conversation with David in which you will convey your decision to him.
3. What advice might you offer Becky, in her new job, about interacting with David?
4. What other rewards might you offer David to keep him motivated?

BUILDING EFFECTIVE *decision-making* SKILLS

Exercise Overview

Decision-making skills include the manager's ability to correctly recognize and define situations and to select courses of action. This exercise allows you to use expectancy theory as part of a hypothetical decision-making situation.

Exercise Background

Assume that you are about to graduate from college and have received three job offers, as summarized below.

1. Offer number 1 is an entry-level position in a large company. The salary offer is for $25,000, and you will begin work in a very attractive location. However, you also see promotion prospects as being relatively limited, and you know that you are likely to have to move frequently.

2. Offer number 2 is a position with a new startup company. The salary offer is $22,000. You know that you will have to work especially long hours. If the company survives for a year, however, opportunities there are unlimited. You may need to move occasionally, but not for a few years.

3. Offer number 3 is a position in a business owned by your family. The salary is $28,000, and you start as a middle manager. You know that you can control your own transfers, but you also know that some people in the company may resent you because of your family ties.

Exercise Task

Using the three job offers as a framework, do the following:

1. Use expectancy theory as a framework to assess your own personal valence for each outcome in selecting a job.

2. Evaluate the three jobs in terms of their outcomes and associated valences.

3. Decide which of the three jobs you would select.

4. Determine what other outcomes will be important to you in selecting a job.

BUILDING EFFECTIVE *conceptual* SKILLS

Exercise Overview

Conceptual skills refer to the manager's ability to think in the abstract. This exercise enables you to develop your conceptual skills by relating theory to reality in a personal way.

Exercise Background

First, you will develop a list of things you want from life. Then you will categorize them according to one of the theories in the chapter. Next, you will discuss your results with a small group of classmates.

Exercise Task

1. Prepare a list of approximately 15 things you want from life. These can be very specific (such as a new car) or very general (such as a feeling of accomplishment in school). Try to include some things you want right now and other things you want later in life. Next, choose the one motivational theory discussed in this chapter that best fits your set of needs. Classify each item from your "wish list" in terms of the need or needs it might satisfy.

2. Your instructor will then divide the class into groups of three. Spend a few minutes in the group discussing each person's list and its classification according to needs.

3. After the small-group discussions, your instructor will reconvene the entire class. Discussion should center on the extent to

which each theory can serve as a useful framework for classifying individual needs. Students who found that their needs could be neatly categorized or those who found little correlation between their needs and the theories are especially encouraged to share their results.

4. As a result of this exercise, do you now place more or less trust in the need theories as viable management tools?
5. Could a manager use some form of this exercise in an organizational setting to enhance employee motivation?

SKILLS *self-assessment* INSTRUMENT

Assessing Your Needs

Introduction: Needs are one factor that influences motivation. The following assessment surveys your judgments about your personal needs that might be partially shaping your motivation.

Instructions: Judge how descriptively accurate each of the following statements is about you. You may find making a decision difficult in some cases, but you should force a choice. Record your answers next to each statement according to the following scale:

Rating Scale

5 Very descriptive of me   **2** Not very descriptive of me

4 Fairly descriptive of me   **1** Not descriptive of me at all

3 Somewhat descriptive of me

_____ 1. I aspire to accomplish difficult tasks and maintain high standards and am willing to work toward distant goals.
_____ 2. I enjoy being with friends and people in general and accept people readily.
_____ 3. I am easily annoyed and am sometimes willing to hurt people to get my way.
_____ 4. I try to break away from restraints or restrictions of any kind.
_____ 5. I want to be the center of attention and enjoy having an audience.
_____ 6. I speak freely and tend to act on the spur of the moment.
_____ 7. I assist others whenever possible, giving sympathy and comfort to those in need.
_____ 8. I believe in the saying that "there is a place for everything and everything should be in its place." I dislike clutter.
_____ 9. I express my opinions forcefully, enjoy the role of leader, and try to control my environment as much as I can.
_____10. I want to understand many areas of knowledge and value synthesizing ideas and generalization.

For interpretation, see Interpretations of Skills Self-Assessment Instruments.

EXPERIENTIAL EXERCISE

An Exercise in Thematic Apperception

Purpose: All people have needs, and those needs make people pursue different goals. This exercise introduces one of the tools by which managers can identify both their own needs and those of their employees.

Introduction: Over the last 30 years, behaviorists have researched the relationship between a person's fantasies and his or her motivation. One popular instrument used to establish this relationship is the Thematic Apperception Test (TAT).

Instructions

Step 1:
1. Examine each of six pictures (provided by your instructor) for about one minute. Then cover the picture.
2. Using the picture as a guide, write a story that could be used in a TV soap opera. Make your story continuous, dramatic, and interesting. Do not just answer the questions. Try to complete the story in less than ten minutes.
3. Do not be concerned about obtaining negative results from this instrument. There are no right or wrong stories.
4. After finishing one story, repeat the same procedure until all six stories are completed.

Step 2: Conduct a story interpretation in groups of three persons each. Taking turns reading one story at a time, each person will read a story out loud to the other two people in the group. Then all three will examine the story for statements that fall into one of the following three categories:

- Category AC—Statements that refer to
    High standards of excellence
    A desire to win, do well, succeed
    Unique accomplishments
    Long-term goals
    Careers

- Category PO—Statements that refer to
    Influencing others
    Controlling others
    The desire to instruct others
    The desire to dominate others
    The concern over weakness, failure, or humiliation
    Superior-subordinate relationships or status relationship

- Category AF—Statements that refer to
    Concern over establishing positive emotional relationships
    Warm friendships or their loss
    A desire to be liked
    One person's liking another
    Parties, reunions, or visits
    Relaxed small talk
    Concern for others when not required by social custom

To assist in the interpretation of the test results, assign ten points to each story. Divide the ten points among the three categories based on the frequency of statements that refer to AC, PO, and AF behaviors in the story. Once the allocation of the ten points is determined, record the results in the following scoring table.

Divide ten points among the following categories:

Number of Story Scored	AC	PO	AF	TOTAL
1	___ +	___ +	___ =	_10_
2	___ +	___ +	___ =	_10_
3	___ +	___ +	___ =	_10_
4	___ +	___ +	___ =	_10_
5	___ +	___ +	___ =	_10_
6	___ +	___ +	___ =	_10_
TOTAL	___ +	___ +	___ =	_60_

Divide totals by ten times number of stories scored ___ + ___ + ___

Category percentages ___ % ___ % ___ % = _100%_

Your Thematic Apperception Test values of AC, PO, and AF indicate your mix of needs for achievement (AC), power (PO), and affiliation (AF), respectively. Due to the circumstances under which this exercise was conducted, your values should be considered as only rough estimates. If you feel uncomfortable with your results, it is suggested that you consult with your instructor.

Step 3: In small groups, discuss the following questions:

Do you agree with your TAT results?

Can you cite specific behaviors to substantiate your opinions?

Do other members of your group perceive you as having the needs indicated by your TAT results?

Can they cite specific behaviors to substantiate their opinions?

What interpersonal problems might exist between a manager and an employee who had different need mixes?

In what type of job would you place an employee with a high need for achievement? a high need for power? a high need for affiliation?

Source: From *Motives in Fantasy, Action and Society: Methods of Assessment and Study*, John W. Atkinson, ed. (Princeton, NJ: D. Van Nostrand Co.,Inc.,1958.) Copyright© 1958. Used with permission of John W. Atkinson, copyright 1986.

A LEGEND IN ITS OWN TIME

Living up to its name, Legend Holdings has become the most successful computer maker in China. A group of engineers from the Chinese Academy of Sciences founded Legend in 1984 as a computer-trading firm. Originally, the company sold Hewlett-Packard printers and other computer-related products, and assembled PCs for a U.S. company. Over time, however, the company evolved into a manufacturer. First, the company developed a new computer system to accommodate Chinese characters; then it was ready to design and produce PCs specifically for the Chinese market.

Thanks to a combination of low labor costs, local sources for parts, a just-in-time manufacturing system, and economies of scale, Legend eventually reduced its production costs and passed the savings on to customers in the form of lower prices. With PCs priced as much as 25 percent below competing models, Legend saw its sales soar in the late 1990s. The sales momentum has made Legend the top-selling PC maker in China, easily surpassing global computer powerhouses like IBM.

Sales to government agencies and businesses account for a large chunk of Legend's revenues. For example, journalists in the Beijing bureau of Reuters use Legend computers to file their news reports. But the company has also built a solid regional reputation selling and servicing PCs for home use. One of its most popular consumer products is the Conet, a snazzy PC featuring one-button access to the Internet. Another promising product, developed in conjunction with Microsoft, is a set-top device that plugs into a television to enable viewers to browse the Internet.

Behind the scenes, Legend's successful performance has been driven by the vision of chairman Liu Chuanzhi and the hard work of a motivated group of managers and employees. Legend is a publicly traded company listed on the Hong Kong stock exchange, and its reward structure is unusual for China. More than two dozen of the founding employees, including the chairman, have been given shares in the company; their combined stakes are worth more than $800 million. The company offers generous pay packages and grants stock options. Small wonder that managers act like owners when making decisions. The availability of options also helps Legend recruit and retain skilled employees, an especially difficult challenge now that China's economy is expanding at a rapid pace and foreign firms entering the market want to hire local talent.

However, financial rewards are not Liu's only motivation. Consider his reaction to a comment made by a local computer executive in Taiwan. Showing off a new palm-sized PC, the executive told Liu that Legend could not create such a product without outside help. The chairman quickly rose to the challenge. On his return to Beijing, the chairman rallied a team of Legend engineers to work together toward the goal of developing a world-class palm-sized PC. Within four months, Legend launched the Tianji as the first palm-sized PC made by a Chinese manufacturer for the Chinese market—and its less-expensive, full-featured version became an instant hit. Sales were so strong that Legend formed an alliance with a foreign company to adapt the Tianji for the European market.

With demand for PCs swelling throughout China and Asia, Legend wants to expand into other computer-related products and other markets. It is already acquiring other computer firms and developing new Internet access products for home and business use. This expansion is part of Liu's plan to reach an aggressive goal of $10 billion in annual sales by 2005. The chairman believes his managers and employees have the attitudes, behaviors, and motivation to make that goal a reality.

Case Questions

1. Which theory or theories seem to explain Liu Chuanzhi's motivation?

2. Under equity theory, how would you expect employees at other Chinese computer companies to react to Legend's stock option and pay packages?

3. How is Liu Chuanzhi applying goal-setting theory at Legend?

Case References

Justin Doebele, "Who Needs an M.B.A.?" *Forbes*, January 24, 2000, p. 80; "Earnings Double for China PC Maker," *CNet News.com*, July 25, 2000, http://news.cnet.com/news/0-1006-200-2344281.html?tag=st.ne.1002.srchres.ni (September 13, 2000); and Lynne Curry, "Legend in the Making," *CFO Asia*, May 1999, http://www.cfoasia.com/archives/9905-22.htm (September 13, 2000).

CHAPTER NOTES

1. "Fliers Give Continental Sky-High Marks," *USA Today*, May 10, 2000, p. 3B; "Continental Delivers Goods," *USA Today*, May 10, 2000, p. 3B; Brian O'Reilly, "The Mechanic Who Fixed Continental," *Fortune*, December 20, 1999, pp. 176–186; and Sheila Puffer, interviewer, "Continental Airlines' CEO Gordon Bethune on Teams and New Product Development," *Academy of Management Executive* 13, no. 3 (August 1999): 28–35 (*quote on 32).

2. Richard M. Steers, Gregory A. Bigley, and Lyman W. Porter, *Motivation and Leadership at Work*, 6th ed. (New York: McGraw-Hill, 1996). See also Maureen L. Ambrose and Carol T. Kulik, "Old Friends, New Faces: Motivation Research in the 1990s," *Journal of Management* 25, no. 3 (1999): 231–292.

3. See Jeffrey Pfeffer, *The Human Equation* (Boston: Harvard Business School Press, 1998).

4. See Eryn Brown, "So Rich So Young—But Are They Really Happy?" *Fortune*, September 18, 2000, pp. 99–110, for a recent discussion of these questions.

5. Abraham H. Maslow, "A Theory of Human Motivation," *Psychological Review* 50 (1943): 370–396; and Abraham H. Maslow, *Motivation and Personality* (New York: Harper & Row, 1954). Maslow's most recent work is Abraham H. Maslow and Richard Lowry, *Toward a Psychology of Being* (New York: Wiley, 1999).

6. For a review, see Craig Pinder, *Work Motivation in Organizational Behavior* (Upper Saddle River, NJ: Prentice-Hall, 1998).

7. Frederick Herzberg, Bernard Mausner, and Barbara Snyderman, *The Motivation to Work* (New York: Wiley, 1959); and Frederick Herzberg, "One More Time: How Do You Motivate Employees?" *Harvard Business Review*, January/February 1987, pp. 109–120.

8. Robert J. House and Lawrence A. Wigdor, "Herzberg's Dual-Factor Theory of Job Satisfaction and Motivation: A Review of the Evidence and a Criticism," *Personnel Psychology*, Winter 1967, pp. 369–389; and Victor H. Vroom, *Work and Motivation* (New York: Wiley, 1964). See also Pinder.

9. David C. McClelland, *The Achieving Society* (Princeton, NJ: Van Nostrand, 1961); and David C. McClelland, *Power: The Inner Experience* (New York: Irvington, 1975).

10. David McClelland and David H. Burnham, "Power Is the Great Motivator," *Harvard Business Review*, March/April 1976, pp. 100–110.

11. Victor H. Vroom, *Work and Motivation* (New York: Wiley, 1964).

12. "Starbucks' Secret Weapon," *Fortune*, September 29, 1997, p. 268.

13. Lyman W. Porter and Edward E. Lawler III, *Managerial Attitudes and Performance* (Homewood, IL: Dorsey Press, 1968).

14. J. Stacy Adams, "Towards an Understanding of Inequity," *Journal of Abnormal and Social Psychology*, November 1963, pp. 422–436.

15. See Edwin A. Locke, "Toward a Theory of Task Performance and Incentives," *Organizational Behavior and Human Performance* 3 (1968): 157–189.

16. Gary P. Latham and J. J. Baldes, "The Practical Significance of Locke's Theory of Goal Setting," *Journal of Applied Psychology* 60 (1975): 187–191.

17. B. F. Skinner, *Beyond Freedom and Dignity* (New York: Knopf, 1971).

18. Fred Luthans and Robert Kreitner, *Organizational Behavior Modification and Beyond: An Operant and Social Learning Approach* (Glenview, IL: Scott, Foresman, 1985).

19. Ibid.; and W. Clay Hamner and Ellen P. Hamner, "Behavior Modification on the Bottom Line," *Organizational Dynamics*, Spring 1976, pp. 2–21.

20. "At Emery Air Freight: Positive Reinforcement Boosts Performance," *Organizational Dynamics*, Winter 1973, pp. 41–50. For a recent update, see Alexander D. Stajkovic and Fred Luthans, "A Meta-Analysis of the Effects of Organizational Behavior Modification on Task Performance, 1975–95," *Academy of Management Journal* 40, no. 5 (1997): 1122–1149.

21. David J. Glew, Anne M. O'Leary-Kelly, Ricky W. Griffin, and David D. Van Fleet, "Participation in Organizations: A Preview of the Issues and Proposed Framework for Future Analysis," *Journal of Management* 21, no. 3 (1995): 395–421.

22. Baxter W. Graham, "The Business Argument for Flexibility," *HRMagazine*, May 1996, pp. 104–110.

23. A. R. Cohen and H. Gadon, *Alternative Work Schedules: Integrating Individual and Organizational Needs* (Reading, MA: Addison-Wesley, 1978).

24. Michelle Neely Martinez, "Rewards Given the Right Way," *HRMagazine*, May 1997, pp. 109–118. See also Angelo S. DeNisi and Ricky W. Griffin, *Human Resource Management* (Boston: Houghton Mifflin, 2001).

25. Edward E. Lawler III, *Pay and Organizational Development* (Reading, MA: Addison-Wesley, 1981). See also Edward E. Lawler III, *Pay and Organizational Effectiveness: A Psychological View* (New York: McGraw-Hill, 1971).

26. Lawler.

27. Bill Leonard, "New Ways to Pay Employees," *HRMagazine*, February 1994, pp. 61–69.

28. "Grading 'Merit Pay,'" *Newsweek*, November 14, 1988, pp. 45–46; and Frederick S. Hills, K. Dow Scott, Steven E. Markham, and Michael J. Vest, "Merit Pay: Just or Unjust Desserts," *Personnel Administrator*, September 1987, pp. 53–59. See also DeNisi and Griffin.

11 Leadership and Influence Processes

When Daimler Benz and Chrysler merged in 1998, it was hailed as a great corporate marriage, one that would allow two disparate firms to use their respective strengths to offset weaknesses inherent in the other. For example, experts agreed that Chrysler's U.S. distribution network and low-cost production expertise would blend perfectly with Daimler's engineering expertise and global presence.

But DaimlerChrysler, as the merged firm was named, proved to be a disaster, at least at first. A worldwide drop in demand for automobiles, coupled with unanticipated weaknesses embedded within each firm, quickly led to plummeting profits and a precipitous drop in share prices. DaimlerChrysler's top management team, comprised almost exclusively of German executives, pointed most of the blame at Chrysler but agreed to allow its American managers time to turn things around. Meanwhile, Jurgen Schrempp, DaimlerChrysler's CEO, came under increased fire from shareholders and other critics, but managed to hold onto his job.

Finally, in late 2000, Schrempp had seen enough. He fired James Holden, the American running Chrysler, and installed a senior Daimler executive, Dieter Zetsche, in his place. Almost immediately, this decision came under fire in the U.S. business press. Basically, critics were concerned that a German leader would disrupt what had been allowed to remain essentially an American company.

What's the difference between an American and a German leader? At the risk of being overly simplistic, American leaders and their followers are generally open, are accustomed to a decentralized approach to management, and place a premium on the human element at work. Germans, in contrast, tend to be somewhat more closed in their communication style, are generally more centralized in their approach to management, and focus more on financial indicators of business performance. Skeptics also assumed that Zetsche would move quickly to replace all of Chrysler's senior management team with his German colleagues.

And as if to validate their fears, one of Zetsche's first actions was to announce 26,000 job cuts. But to the surprise of many observers, that's about the only harsh step he has taken thus far. Indeed, he seems to have gone out of his way to become more of an American-style leader

"It is a non-issue."

—*Dieter Zetsche, President of Chrysler, talking about his German heritage and how it works in a U.S. firm*

After studying this chapter, you should be able to

- Describe the nature of leadership and distinguish leadership from management.

- Discuss and evaluate the trait approach to leadership.

- Discuss and evaluate models of leadership focusing on behaviors.

- Identify and describe the major situational approaches to leadership.

- Identify and describe three related perspectives on leadership.

- Discuss political behavior in organizations and how it can be managed.

than trying to transform Chrysler into a German-style firm. For example, when asked how many Germans he would be bringing with him, he answered four—his wife and their three children.

Zetsche has integrated himself into the local community and made required changes with sensitivity, winning kudos from others in the firm. He also has maintained the same degree of openness and decentralization as his predecessors, and he has even gone a step further—he usually abandons his reserved seat in Chrysler's executive dining room and instead chooses to eat in the same cafeteria as the hourly workers. He has worked hard at developing a good relationship with the United Auto Workers. White it's far too soon to know whether or not he will succeed, he does seem to be on the right track.[1]

303

This chapter examines people like Dieter Zetsche more carefully by focusing on leadership and its role in management. We characterize the nature of leadership and trace the three major approaches to studying leadership—traits, behaviors, and situations. After examining other perspectives on leadership, we conclude by describing another approach to influencing others—political behavior in organizations.

The Nature of Leadership

In Chapter 10, we described various models and perspectives on employee motivation. From the manager's standpoint, trying to motivate people is an attempt to influence their behavior. In many ways, leadership, too, is an attempt to influence the behavior of others. In this section, we first define leadership, then differentiate it from management, and conclude by relating it to power.

The Meaning of Leadership

leadership As a process, the use of noncoercive influence to shape the group's or organization's goals, motivate behavior toward the achievement of those goals, and help define group or organization culture; as a property, the set of characteristics attributed to individuals who are perceived to be leaders

leader One who can influence the behaviors of others without having to rely on force; one accepted by others as a leader

Leadership is both a process and a property.[2] As a process—focusing on what leaders actually do—leadership is the use of noncoercive influence to shape the group or organization's goals, motivate behavior toward the achievement of those goals, and help define group or organization culture.[3] As a property, leadership is the set of characteristics attributed to individuals who are perceived to be leaders. Thus **leaders** are people who can influence the behaviors of others without having to rely on force; leaders are people whom others accept as leaders.

Leadership Versus Management

From these definitions, it should be clear that leadership and management are related, but they are not the same. A person can be a manager, a leader, both, or neither[4] Some of the basic distinctions between the two are summarized in Table 11.1. At the left side of the table are four elements that differentiate leadership from management. The two columns show how each element differs when considered from a management and from a leadership point of view. For example, when executing plans, managers focus on monitoring results, comparing them with goals, and correcting deviations. In contrast, the leader focuses on energizing people to overcome bureaucratic hurdles to reach goals. Thus, when Dieter Zetsche monitors the performance of his employees, he is playing the role of manager. But when he inspires them to work harder at achieving their goals, he is a leader.

Organizations need both management and leadership if they are to be effective. Leadership is necessary to create change, and management is necessary to achieve orderly results. Management in conjunction with leadership can produce orderly change, and leadership in conjunction with management can keep the organization properly aligned with its environment. *Management InfoTech* describes Selina Lo, an individual who is clearly both a manager and a leader.

Table 11.1

Distinctions Between Management and Leadership

Management and leadership are related, but distinct, constructs. Managers and leaders differ in how they go about creating an agenda, developing a rationale for achieving the agenda, and executing plans, as well as in the types of outcomes they achieve.

Activity	Management	Leadership
Creating an agenda	**Planning and budgeting.** Establishing detailed steps and timetables for achieving needed results; allocating the resources necessary to make those needed results happen	**Establishing direction.** Developing a vision of the future, often the distant future, and strategies for producing the changes needed to achieve that vision
Developing a human network for achieving the agenda	**Organizing and staffing.** Establishing some structure for accomplishing plan requirements, staffing that structure with individuals, delegating responsibility and authority for carrying out the plan, providing policies and procedures to help guide people, and creating methods or systems to monitor implementation	**Aligning people.** Communicating the direction by words and deeds to everyone whose cooperation may be needed to influence the creation of teams and coalitions that understand the vision and strategies and accept their validity
Executing plans	**Controlling and problem solving.** Monitoring results versus planning in some detail, identifying deviations, and then planning and organizing to solve these problems	**Motivating and inspiring.** Energizing people to overcome major political, bureaucratic, and resource barriers by satisfying very basic, but often unfulfilled, human needs
Outcomes	Produces a degree of predictability and order and has the potential to consistently produce major results expected by various stakeholders (for example, for customers, always being on time; for stockholders, being on budget)	Produces change, often to a dramatic degree, and has the potential to produce extremely useful change (for example, new products that customers want and new approaches to labor relations that help make a firm more competitive)

Source: Reprinted with the permission of The Free Press, a Division of Simon & Schuster, Inc., from *A Force for Change: How Leadership Differs from Management* by John P. Kotter. Copyright © 1990 by John P. Kotter, Inc.

Power and Leadership

To fully understand leadership, it is necessary to understand power. **Power** is the ability to affect the behavior of others. One can have power without actually using it. For example, a football coach has the power to bench a player who is not performing up to par. The coach seldom has to use this power, because players recognize that the power exists and work hard to keep their starting positions. In organizational settings, there are usually five kinds of power: legitimate, reward, coercive, referent, and expert power.[5]

power The ability to affect the behavior of others

Legitimate Power **Legitimate power** is power granted through the organizational hierarchy; it is the power accorded people occupying a particular position as defined by the organization. A manager can assign tasks to a subordinate, and a subordinate who refuses to do them can be reprimanded or even fired. Such outcomes stem from the manager's legitimate power as defined and vested in her or him by the organization. Legitimate power, then, is authority. All managers have legitimate power over their subordinates. The mere possession of legitimate power, however, does not by itself make someone a leader. Some subordinates follow only orders that are strictly within the letter of organizational rules and policies. If asked

legitimate power Power granted through the organizational hierarchy; the power defined by the organization that is to be accorded people occupying particular positions

MANAGEMENT INFOTECH

HARD-DRIVING MANAGEMENT IN THE HIGH-TECH ARENA

Managers in high-tech industries have to race the clock as well as the competition, as Selina Y. Lo well knows. Lo is the vice president of product management and marketing for Alteon WebSystems, a young, fast-growing company that makes sophisticated networking systems for web-based businesses such as Ticketmaster Online and Yahoo! Competing against well-established, fleet-footed rivals such as Cisco Systems, Lo uses her considerable power to speed product innovation, spur higher performance, and meet customers' needs.

One reason the CEO of Alteon hired Lo was for her keen sense of cutting-edge technology and her understanding of customer needs, developed during a rising-star background in a series of well-regarded information technology firms. She started with Hewlett-Packard after college, moved to Network Equipment Technologies, and then cofounded Centillion Networks, where she was part of the team that invented an innovative new data-switching device. Small wonder that employees and customers alike respect Lo's judgment and pay close attention when she talks about products and features.

Lo supervises product development for Alteon, a critical function in an industry where a product's life can be measured in months. She spends most of her day in the field, sniffing out customer problems. When she comes back to the office to hammer out design changes with development engineers, her aggressive management style—sometimes pounding the table, sometimes raising her voice—makes it hard for engineers to say no. Although Lo is known as a tough manager, she is also known for her habit of giving away trips and other valuable rewards to recognize performance. After 15 years in the networking industry, Lo is anything but shy about using her hard-driving approach to overpower the competition and push Alteon to the top of a crowded but lucrative market.

> *I've left a few dead bodies behind me.*
>
> —*Selina Y. Lo, vice president of marketing for Alteon WebSystems**

References: Andy Reinhardt, "'I've Left a Few Dead Bodies,'" *Business Week,* January 31, 2000, pp. 69–70 (*quote on p. 69).

---

to do something not in their job description, they refuse or do a poor job. The manager of such employees is exercising authority but not leadership.

reward power The power to give or withhold rewards, such as salary increases, bonuses, promotions, praise, recognition, and interesting job assignments

Reward Power   **Reward power** is the power to give or withhold rewards. Rewards that a manager may control include salary increases, bonuses, promotion recommendations, praise, recognition, and interesting job assignments. In general, the more rewards a manager controls and the more important the rewards are to subordinates, the greater is the manager's reward power. If the subordinate sees as valuable only the formal organizational rewards provided by the manager, then he or she is not a leader. If the subordinate also wants and appreciates the manager's informal rewards, such as praise, gratitude, and recognition, however, then the manager is also exercising leadership.

coercive power The power to force compliance by means of psychological, emotional, or physical threat

Coercive Power   **Coercive power** is the power to force compliance by means of psychological, emotional, or physical threat. In the past, physical coercion in organizations was relatively common. In most organizations today, however, coercion is limited to verbal reprimands, written reprimands, disciplinary layoffs, fines, demotion, and termination. Some managers occasionally go so far as to use verbal abuse, humiliation, and psychological coercion in an attempt to manipulate subordinates. (Of course, most people would agree that these are not appropriate managerial behaviors.) James Dutt, former CEO of Beatrice Company, once told a subordinate that, if his wife and family got in the way of his working a 24-hour day seven days a week, he should get rid of them.[6] The more punitive the elements under a manager's control and the more important they are to subordinates, the more coercive power the manager possesses. On the other hand, the more a manager uses coercive power, the more likely he is to provoke resentment and hostility, and the less likely he is to be seen as a leader.[7]

Referent Power   Compared with legitimate, reward, and coercive power, which are relatively concrete and grounded in objective facets of organizational life, **referent power** is abstract. It is based on identification, imitation, loyalty, or charisma. Followers may react favorably because they identify in some way with a leader, who may be like them in personality, background, or attitudes. In other situations, followers might choose to imitate a leader with referent power by wearing the same kinds of clothes, working the same hours, or espousing the same management philosophy. Referent power may also take the form of charisma, an intangible attribute of the leader that inspires loyalty and enthusiasm. Thus a manager might have referent power, but it is more likely to be associated with leadership.

referent power The personal power that accrues to someone based on identification, imitation, loyalty, or charisma

Expert Power   **Expert power** is derived from information or expertise. A manager who knows how to interact with an eccentric but important customer, a scientist who is capable of achieving an important technical breakthrough that no other company has dreamed of, and a secretary who knows how to unravel bureaucratic red tape all have expert power over anyone who needs that information. The more important the information and the fewer the people who have access to it, the greater is the degree of expert power possessed by any one individual. In general, people who are both leaders and managers tend to have a lot of expert power.

expert power The personal power that accrues to someone based on the information or expertise that they possess

The Search for Leadership Traits

The first organized approach to studying leadership analyzed the personal, psychological, and physical traits of strong leaders. The trait approach assumed that some basic trait or set of traits existed that differentiated leaders from nonleaders. If those traits could be defined, potential leaders could be identified. Researchers thought that leadership traits might include intelligence, assertiveness, above-average height, good vocabulary, attractiveness, self-confidence, and similar attributes.[8]

During the first several decades of the twentieth century, hundreds of studies were conducted in an attempt to identify important leadership traits. For the most part, the results of the studies were disappointing. For every set of leaders who possessed a common trait, a long list of exceptions was also found, and the list of suggested traits soon grew so long that it had little practical value. Alternative explanations usually existed even for relationships between traits and leadership that initially appeared valid. For example, it was observed that many leaders have good communication skills and are assertive. Rather than those traits' being the cause of leadership, however, successful leaders may begin to display those traits after they have achieved leadership positions.

Although most researchers gave up trying to identify traits as predictors of leadership ability, many people still explicitly or implicitly adopt a trait orientation.[9] For example, politicians are all too often elected on the basis of personal appearance, speaking ability, or an aura of self-confidence. In addition, traits like honesty and integrity may very well be fundamental leadership traits that do serve an important purpose.

Leadership Behaviors

Spurred on by their lack of success in identifying useful leadership traits, researchers soon began to investigate other variables, especially the behaviors or actions of leaders. The new hypothesis was that effective leaders somehow behaved differently than less-effective leaders. Thus the goal was to develop a fuller understanding of leadership behaviors.

job-centered leader behavior
The behavior of leaders who pay close attention to the job and work procedures involved with that job

employee-centered leader behavior The behavior of leaders who develop cohesive work groups and ensure employee satisfaction

Michigan Studies

Researchers at the University of Michigan, led by Rensis Likert, began studying leadership in the late 1940s.[10] Based on extensive interviews with both leaders (managers) and followers (subordinates), this research identified two basic forms of leader behavior: job centered and employee centered. Managers using **job-centered leader behavior** pay close attention to subordinates' work, explain work procedures, and are keenly interested in performance. Managers using **employee-**

Most effective leaders demonstrate sincere interest in the personal welfare of their followers. This interest can extend to concern about their families and personal lives as well. When the interest is real, employees may feel more valued and appreciated by their leader and develop stronger job satisfaction and dedication. But if the leader's interest is superficial and is an obvious ploy to show interest, employees will likely see what's going on and come to resent and to lose respect for the leader.

DILBERT by Scott Adams reprinted by permission of United Feature Syndicate, Inc.

centered leader behavior are interested in developing a cohesive work group and ensuring that employees are satisfied with their jobs. Their primary concern is the welfare of subordinates. The two styles of leader behavior were presumed to be at the ends of a single continuum. Although this suggests that leaders may be extremely job centered, extremely employee centered, or somewhere in between, Likert studied only the two end styles for contrast. He argued that employee-centered leader behavior generally tended to be more effective.

Ohio State Studies

At about the same time that Likert was beginning his leadership studies at the University of Michigan, a group of researchers at Ohio State University also began studying leadership.[11] The extensive questionnaire surveys conducted during the Ohio State studies also suggested that there are two basic leader behaviors or styles: initiating-structure behavior and consideration behavior. When using **initiating-structure behavior**, the leader clearly defines the leader-subordinate role so that everyone knows what is expected, establishes formal lines of communication, and determines how tasks will be performed. Leaders using **consideration behavior** show concern for subordinates and attempt to establish a friendly and supportive climate. The behaviors identified at Ohio State are similar to those described at Michigan, but there are important differences. One major difference is that the Ohio State researchers did not interpret leader behavior as being one dimensional: Each behavior was assumed to be independent of the

Two common leader behaviors are those that focus on the job and those that focus on people. Take Nobuyuki Idei, CEO of Sony, for example. Mr. Idei is totally focused on insuring that Sony retains its preeminence among the world's consumer products giants. To help keep the firm on track, he is constantly setting new goals, developing new strategies, and pushing the firm into new markets. But at the same time, his colleagues report that he is a sensitive and caring leader who is always concerned for the well-being of others.

other. Presumably, then, a leader could exhibit varying levels of initiating structure and at the same time varying levels of consideration.

At first, the Ohio State researchers thought that leaders who exhibit high levels of both behaviors would tend to be more effective than other leaders. A study at International Harvester Company (now Navistar International Corporation), however, suggested a more complicated pattern.[12] The researchers found that employees of supervisors who ranked high on initiating structure were high performers but expressed low levels of satisfaction and had a higher absence rate. Conversely, employees of supervisors who ranked high on consideration had low performance ratings but high levels of satisfaction and few absences from work. Later research isolated other variables that make consistent prediction difficult and determined that situational influences also occurred. (This body of research is discussed in the section on situational approaches to leadership.)

initiating-structure behavior The behavior of leaders who define the leader-subordinate role so that everyone knows what is expected, establishes formal lines of communication, and determines how tasks will be performed

consideration behavior The behavior of leaders who show concern for subordinates and attempt to establish a warm, friendly, and supportive climate

Leadership Grid®

Yet another behavioral approach to leadership is the Leadership Grid.[13] The Leadership Grid provides a means for evaluating leadership styles and then training managers to move toward an ideal style of behavior. The Leadership Grid is shown in Figure 11.1. The horizontal axis represents **concern for production** (similar to job-centered and initiating-structure behaviors), and the vertical axis represents **concern for people** (similar to employee-centered and consideration behavior). Note the five extremes of managerial behavior: the 1,1 manager (impoverished management), who exhibits minimal concern for both production and people; the 9,1 manager (authority-compliance), who is highly concerned about production but exhibits little concern for people; the 1,9 manager (country club management), who has the exact opposite concerns from the 9,1 manager; the 5,5 manager (middle-of-the-road management), who maintains adequate concern for both people and production; and the 9,9 manager (team management), who exhibits maximum concern for both people and production.

concern for production The part of the Leadership Grid that deals with the job and task aspects of leader behavior

concern for people The part of the Leadership Grid that deals with the human aspects of leader behavior

Figure 11.1

The Leadership Grid®
The Leadership Grid® is a method of evaluating leadership styles. The overall objective of an organization using the Grid is to train its managers using OD techniques so that they are simultaneously more concerned for both people and production (9, 9 style on the Grid).

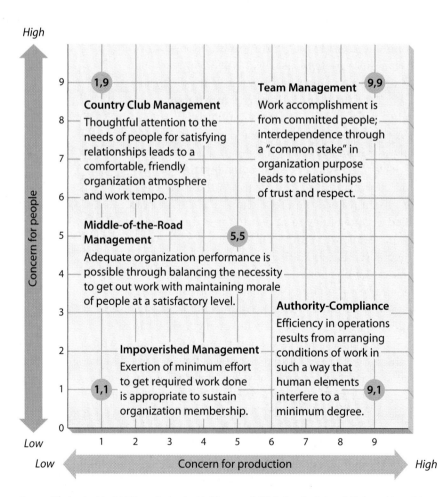

Source: The Leadership Grid Figure for *Leadership Dilemmas-Grid Solutions*, by Robert R. Blake and Anne Adams McCanse. (Formerly the Managerial Grid by Robert R. Blake and Jane S. Mouton.) Houston: Gulf Publishing Company, p. 29. Copyright © 1997 by Grid International, Inc. Reproduced with permission of the owners.

According to this approach, the ideal style of leadership behavior is 9,9. Thus there is a six-phase program to assist managers in achieving this style of behavior. A.G. Edwards, Westinghouse, FAA, Equicor, and other companies have used the Leadership Grid with reasonable success. However, there is little published scientific evidence regarding its true effectiveness.

The leader-behavior theories have played an important role in the development of contemporary thinking about leadership. In particular, they urge us not to be preoccupied with what leaders are (the trait approach) but to concentrate on what leaders do (their behaviors). Unfortunately, these theories also make universal prescriptions about what constitutes effective leadership. When we are dealing with complex social systems composed of complex individuals, few if any relationships are consistently predictable, and certainly no formulas for success are infallible. Yet the behavior theorists tried to identify consistent relationships between leader behaviors and employee responses in the hope of finding a dependable prescription for effective leadership. As we might expect, they often failed. Other approaches to understanding leadership were therefore needed. The catalyst for these new approaches was the realization that, although interpersonal and task-oriented dimensions might be useful to describe the behavior of leaders, they were not useful for predicting or prescribing it. The next step in the evolution of leadership theory was the creation of situational models.

■ *Situational Approaches to Leadership*

Situational models assume that appropriate leader behavior varies from one situation to another. The goal of a situational theory, then, is to identify key situational factors and to specify how they interact to determine appropriate leader behavior. In the following sections, we describe four of the most important and widely accepted situational theories of leadership: the LPC theory, the path-goal theory, Vroom's decision tree approach, and the leader-member exchange (LMX) approach.

LPC Theory

The **LPC theory**, developed by Fred Fiedler, was the first true situational theory of leadership.[14] As we will discuss later, LPC stands for "least-preferred coworker." Beginning with a combined trait and behavior approach, Fiedler identified two styles of leadership: task oriented (analogous to job-centered and initiating-structure behavior) and relationship oriented (similar to employee-centered and consideration behavior). He went beyond the earlier behavioral approaches by arguing that the style of behavior is a reflection of the leader's personality and that most personalities fall into one of his two categories, task oriented or relationship oriented by nature. Fiedler measures leader style by means of a controversial questionnaire called the **least-preferred coworker** (**LPC**) measure. To use the measure, a manager or leader is asked to describe the specific person with whom he or she is able

LPC theory A theory of leadership that suggests that the appropriate style of leadership varies with situational favorableness

least-preferred coworker (LPC) The measuring scale that asks leaders to describe the person with whom he or she is able to work least well to work least well—the LPC—by filling in a set of 16 scales anchored at each end by a positive or negative adjective. For example, 3 of the 16 scales are

Helpful __ __ __ __ __ __ __ __ Frustrating
         8 7 6 5 4 3 2 1

Tense   __ __ __ __ __ __ __ __ Relaxed
         1 2 3 4 5 6 7 8

Boring   __ __ __ __ __ __ __ __ Interesting
         1 2 3 4 5 6 7 8

The leader's LPC score is then calculated by adding up the numbers below the line checked on each scale. Note in these three examples that the higher numbers are associated with the positive qualities (helpful, relaxed, and interesting), whereas the negative qualities (frustrating, tense, and boring) have low point values. A high total score is assumed to reflect a relationship orientation and a low score, a task orientation on the part of the leader. The LPC measure is controversial because researchers disagree about its validity. Some question exactly what an LPC measure reflects and whether the score is an index of behavior, personality, or some other factor.[15]

Favorableness of the Situation   The underlying assumption of situational models of leadership is that appropriate leader behavior varies from one situation to another. According to Fiedler, the key situational factor is the favorableness of the situation from the leader's point of view. This factor is determined by leader-member relations, task structure, and position power. *Leader-member relations* refer to the nature of the relationship between the leader and the work group. If the leader and the group have a high degree of mutual trust, respect, and confidence, and if they like one another, relations are assumed to be good. If there is little trust, respect, or confidence, and if they do not like each other, relations are poor. Naturally, good relations are more favorable.

Task structure is the degree to which the group's task is well defined. The task is structured when it is routine, easily understood, and unambiguous, and when the group has standard procedures and precedents to rely on. An unstructured task is nonroutine, ambiguous, complex, with no standard procedures or precedents. You can see that high structure is more favorable for the leader, whereas low structure is less favorable. For example, if the task is unstructured, the group will not know what to do, and the leader will have to play a major role in guiding and directing its activities. If the task is structured, the leader will not have to get so involved and can devote time to nonsupervisory activities.

Position power is the power vested in the leader's position. If the leader has the power to assign work and to reward and punish employees, position power is assumed to be strong. But if the leader must get job assignments approved by someone else and does not administer rewards and punishment, position power is weak, and it is more difficult to accomplish goals. From the leader's point of view, strong position power is clearly preferable to weak position. However, position power is not as important as task structure and leader-member relations.

Favorableness and Leader Style Fiedler and his associates conducted numerous studies linking the favorableness of various situations to leader style and the effectiveness of the group.[16] The results of these studies—and the overall framework of the theory—are shown in Figure 11.2. To interpret the model, look first at the situational factors at the top of the figure: good or bad leader-member relations, high or low task structure, and strong or weak leader position power can be combined to yield eight unique situations. For example, good leader-member relations, high task structure, and strong leader position power (at the far left) are presumed to define the most favorable situation; bad leader-member relations, low task structure, and weak leader position power (at the far right) are the least favorable. The other combinations reflect intermediate levels of favorableness.

Below each set of situations are shown the degree of favorableness and the form of leader behavior found to be most strongly associated with effective group performance for those situations. When the situation is most and least favorable, Fiedler has found that a task-oriented leader is most effective. When the situation is only moderately favorable, however, a relationship-oriented leader is predicted to be most effective.

Flexibility of Leader Style Fiedler argued that, for any given individual, leader style is essentially fixed and cannot be changed: leaders cannot change their behavior to fit a particular situation, because it is linked to their particular personality traits. Thus, when a leader's style and the situation do not match, Fiedler argued that the

Figure 11.2

The Least-Preferred Coworker Theory of Leadership

Fiedler's LPC theory of leadership suggests that appropriate leader behavior varies as a function of the favorableness of the situation. Favorableness, in turn, is defined by task structure, leader-member relations, and the leader's position power. According to LPC theory, the most and least favorable situations call for task-oriented leadership, whereas moderately favorable situations suggest the need for relationship-oriented leadership.

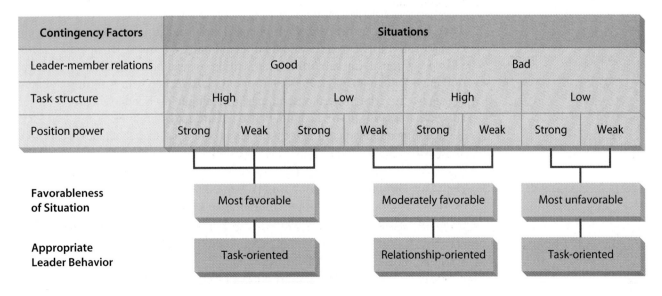

situation should be changed to fit the leader's style. When leader-member relations are good, task structure low, and position power weak, the leader style most likely to be effective is relationship oriented. If the leader is task oriented, a mismatch exists. According to Fiedler, the leader can make the elements of the situation more congruent by structuring the task (by developing guidelines and procedures, for instance) and increasing power (by requesting additional authority or by other means).

Fiedler's contingency theory has been attacked on the grounds that it is not always supported by research, that his findings are subject to other interpretations, that the LPC measure lacks validity, and that his assumptions about the inflexibility of leader behavior are unrealistic. However, Fiedler's theory was one of the first to adopt a situational perspective on leadership. It has helped many managers recognize the important situational factors they must contend with, and it has fostered additional thinking about the situational nature of leadership. Moreover, in recent years, Fiedler has attempted to address some of the concerns about his theory by revising it and adding such elements as cognitive resources.

Path-Goal Theory

path-goal theory A theory of leadership suggesting that the primary functions of a leader are to make valued or desired rewards available in the workplace and to clarify for the subordinate the kinds of behavior that will lead to those rewards

The path-goal theory of leadership—associated most closely with Martin Evans and Robert House—is a direct extension of the expectancy theory of motivation discussed in Chapter 10.[17] Recall that the primary components of expectancy theory included the likelihood of attaining various outcomes and the value associated with those outcomes. The **path-goal theory** of leadership suggests that the primary functions of a leader are to make valued or desired rewards available in the workplace and to clarify for the subordinate the kinds of behavior that will lead to goal accomplishment and valued rewards—that is, the leader should clarify the paths to goal attainment.

Leader Behavior   The most fully developed version of path-goal theory identifies four kinds of leader behavior. *Directive leader behavior* is letting subordinates know what is expected of them, giving guidance and direction, and scheduling work. *Supportive leader behavior* is being friendly and approachable, showing concern for subordinate welfare, and treating members as equals. *Participative leader behavior* is consulting subordinates, soliciting suggestions, and allowing participation in decision making. *Achievement-oriented leader* behavior is setting challenging goals, expecting subordinates to perform at high levels, encouraging subordinates, and showing confidence in subordinates' abilities.

In contrast to Fiedler's theory, path-goal theory assumes that leaders can change their style or behavior to meet the demands of a particular situation. For example, when encountering a new group of subordinates and a new project, the leader may be directive in establishing work procedures and in outlining what needs to be done. Next, the leader may adopt supportive behavior to foster group cohesiveness and a positive climate. As the group becomes familiar with the task and as new problems are encountered, the leader may exhibit participative behavior to enhance group members' motivation. Finally, achievement-oriented behavior may be used to encourage continued high performance.

Situational Factors   Like other situational theories of leadership, path-goal theory suggests that appropriate leader style depends on situational factors. Path-goal theory focuses on the situational factors of the personal characteristics of subordinates and environmental characteristics of the workplace.

Important personal characteristics include the subordinates' perception of their own ability and their locus of control. If people perceive that they are lacking in ability, they may prefer directive leadership to help them better understand path-goal relationships. If they perceive themselves to have a lot of ability, however, employees may resent directive leadership. Locus of control is a personality trait. People who have an internal locus of control believe that what happens to them is a function of their own efforts and behavior. Those who have an external locus of control assume that fate, luck, or "the system" determines what happens to them. A person with an internal locus of control may prefer participative leadership, whereas a person with an external locus of control may prefer directive leadership. Managers can do little or nothing to influence the personal characteristics of subordinates, but they can shape the environment to take advantage of these personal characteristics by providing rewards and structuring tasks, for example.

Environmental characteristics include factors outside the subordinate's control. Task structure is one such factor. When structure is high, directive leadership is less effective than when structure is low. Subordinates do not usually need their boss to continually tell them how to do an extremely routine job. The formal authority system is another important environmental characteristic. Again, the higher the degree of formality, the less directive is the leader behavior that will be accepted by subordinates. The nature of the work group also affects appropriate leader behavior. When the work group provides the employee with social support and satisfaction, supportive leader behavior is less critical. When social support and satisfaction cannot be derived from the group, the worker may look to the leader for this support.

The basic path-goal framework, as illustrated in Figure 11.3, shows that different leader behaviors affect subordinates' motivation to perform. Personal and environmental characteristics are seen as defining which behaviors lead to which outcomes. The path-goal theory of leadership is a dynamic and incomplete

Figure 11.3

The Path-Goal Framework
The path-goal theory of leadership suggests that managers can use four types of leader behavior to clarify subordinates' paths to goal attainment. Both personal characteristics of the subordinate and environmental characteristics within the organization must be taken into account when determining which style of leadership will work best for a particular situation.

model. The original intent was to state the theory in general terms so that future research could explore a variety of interrelationships and modify the theory. Research that has been done suggests that the path-goal theory is a reasonably good description of the leadership process and that future investigations along these lines should enable us to discover more about the link between leadership and motivation.[18]

Vroom's Decision Tree Approach

Vroom's decision tree approach
Predicts what kinds of situations call for what degrees of group participation

The third major contemporary approach to leadership is **Vroom's decision tree approach**. The earliest version of this model was proposed by Victor Vroom and Philip Yetton and later revised and expanded by Vroom and Arthur Jago.[19] Most recently, Vroom has developed yet another refinement of the original model.[20] Like the path-goal theory, this approach attempts to prescribe a leadership style appropriate to a given situation. It also assumes that the same leader may display different leadership styles. But Vroom's approach concerns itself with only a single aspect of leader behavior: subordinate participation in decision making.

Basic Premises   Vroom's decision tree approach assumes that the degree to which subordinates should be encouraged to participate in decision making depends on the characteristics of the situation. In other words, no one decision-making process is best for all situations. After evaluating a variety of problem attributes (characteristics of the problem or decision), the leader determines an appropriate decision style that specifies the amount of subordinate participation.

Vroom's current formulation suggests that managers use one of two different decision trees.[21] To do so, the manager first assesses the situation in terms of several factors. This assessment involves determining whether the given factor is "high" or "low" for the decision that is to be made. For instance, the first factor is decision significance. If the decision is extremely important and may have a major impact on the organization (such as choosing a location for a new plant), its significance is high. But if the decision is routine and its consequences not terribly important (such as selecting a color for the firm's softball team uniforms), its significance is low. This assessment guides the manager through the paths of the decision tree to a recommended course of action. One decision tree is to be used when the manager is interested primarily in making the decision on the most timely basis possible; the other is to be used when time is less critical and the manager is interested in helping subordinates to improve and develop their own decision-making skills.

The two decision trees are shown in Figures 11.4 and 11.5. The problem attributes (situational factors) are arranged along the top of the decision tree. To use the model, the decision maker starts at the left side of the diagram and assesses the first problem attribute (decision significance). The answer determines the path to the second node on the decision tree, where the next attribute (importance of commitment) is assessed. This process continues until a terminal node is reached. In this way, the manager identifies an effective decision-making style for the situation.

Problem Statement	Decision Significance	Importance of Commitment	Leader Expertise	Likelihood of Commitment	Group Support	Group Expertise	Team Competence	Recommended Process
P R O B L E M S T A T E M E N T	H	H	H	H	—	—	—	Decide
				L	H	H	H	Delegate
							L	Consult (group)
						L	—	Consult (group)
					L	—	—	Consult (group)
			L	H	H	H	H	Facilitate
							L	Consult (individually)
						L	—	Consult (individually)
					L	—	—	Consult (individually)
				L	H	H	H	Facilitate
							L	Consult (group)
						L	—	Consult (group)
					L	—	—	Consult (group)
		L	H	—	—	—	—	Decide
			L	—	H	H	H	Facilitate
							L	Consult (individually)
						L	—	Consult (individually)
					L	—	—	Consult (individually)
	L	H	—	H	—	—	—	Decide
				L	—	—	H	Delegate
							L	Facilitate
		L	—	—	—	—	—	Decide

Source: Adapted and reprinted from *Leadership and Decision-Making,* by Victor H. Vroom and Philip W. Yetton, by permission of the University of Pittsburgh Press. © 1973 by University of Pittsburgh Press.

Figure 11.4

Vroom's Time-driven Decision Tree

This matrix is recommended for situations in which time is of the highest importance in making a decision. The matrix operates like a funnel. You start at the left with a specific decision problem in mind. The column headings denote situational factors that may or may not be present in that problem. You progress by selecting High or Low (H or L) for each relevant situational factor. Proceed across the funnel, judging only those situational factors for which a judgment is called for, until you reach the recommended process.

Decision-Making Styles   The various decision styles reflected at the ends of the tree branches represent different levels of subordinate participation that the manager should attempt to adopt in a given situation. The five styles are defined as follows:

Decide: The manager makes the decision alone and then announces or "sells" it to the group.

Consult (individually): The manager presents the program to group members individually, obtains their suggestions, and then makes the decision.

Consult (group): The manager presents the problem to group members at a meeting, gets their suggestions, and then makes the decision.

Facilitate: The manager presents the problem to the group at a meeting, defines the problem and its boundaries, and then facilitates group member discussion as they make the decision.

Delegate: The manager allows the group to define for itself the exact nature and parameters of the problem and then to develop a solution.

Figure 11.5

Vroom's Development-driven Decision Tree

This matrix is to be used when the leader is interested more in developing employees than in making the decision as quickly as possible. Just as with the time-driven tree shown in Figure 11.4, the leader assesses up to seven situational factors. These factors, in turn, funnel the leader to a recommended process for making the decision.

	Decision Significance	Importance of Commitment	Leader Expertise	Likelihood of Commitment	Group Support	Group Expertise	Team Competence	
P R O B L E M S T A T E M E N T	H	H	—	H	H	H	H	Decide
							L	Facilitate
						L	—	Consult (group)
					L	—	—	
				L	H	H	H	Delegate
						L	L	Facilitate
							—	
					L	—	—	Consult (group)
		L	—	—	H	H	H	Delegate
						L	L	Facilitate
							—	
					L	—	—	Consult (group)
	L	H	—	H	—	—	—	Decide
				L	—	—	—	Delegate
		L	—	—	—	—	—	Decide

Source: Adapted and reprinted from *Leadership and Decision-Making,* by Victor H. Vroom and Philip W. Yetton, by permission of the University of Pittsburgh Press. © 1973 by University of Pittsburgh Press.

Vroom's decision tree approach represents a very focused but quite complex perspective on leadership. To compensate for this difficulty, Vroom has developed elaborate expert system software to help managers assess a situation accurately and quickly, and then to make an appropriate decision regarding employee participation.[22] Many firms, including Halliburton Company, Litton Industries, and Borland International, have provided their managers with training in how to use the various versions of this model.

Evaluation Because Vroom's current approach is relatively new, it has not been fully scientifically tested. The original model and its subsequent refinement, however, attracted a great deal of attention and were generally supported by research.[23] For example, there is some support for the idea that individuals who make decisions consistent with the predictions of the model are more effective than those who make decisions inconsistent with it. The model therefore appears to be a tool that managers can apply with some confidence in deciding how much subordinates should participate in the decision-making process.

The Leader-Member Exchange Approach

leader-member exchange (LMX) model Stresses that leaders have different kinds of relationships with different subordinates

Because leadership is such an important area, managers and researchers continue to study it. As a result, new ideas, theories, and perspectives are continuously being developed. The **leader-member exchange** (**LMX**) **model** of leadership, conceived by George Graen and Fred Dansereau, stresses the importance of variable relationships

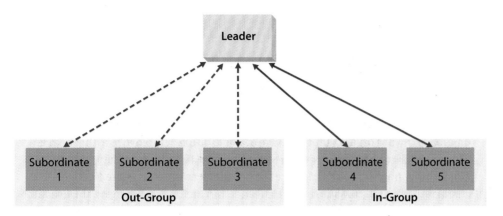

Figure 11.6

The Leader-Member Exchange (LMX) Model
The LMX model suggests that leaders form unique independent relationships with each of their subordinates. As illustrated here, a key factor in the nature of this relationship is whether the individual subordinate is in the leader's out-group or in-group.

between supervisors and each of their subordinates.[24] Each superior-subordinate pair is referred to as a "vertical dyad." The model differs from earlier approaches in that it focuses on the differential relationships leaders often establish with different subordinates. Figure 11.6 shows the basic concepts of the leader-member exchange theory.

The model suggests that supervisors establish a special relationship with a small number of trusted subordinates referred to as the in-group. The in-group usually receives special duties requiring responsibility and autonomy; they may also receive special privileges. Subordinates who are not a part of this group are called the out-group, and they receive less of the supervisor's time and attention. Note in the figure that the leader has a dyadic, or one-to-one, relationship with each of the five subordinates.

Early in his or her interaction with a given subordinate, the supervisor initiates either an in-group or an out-group relationship. It is not clear how a leader selects members of the in-group, but the decision may be based on personal compatibility and subordinates' competence. Research has confirmed the existence of in-groups and out-groups. In addition, studies generally have found that in-group members have a higher level of performance and satisfaction than out-group members.[25]

Related Perspectives on Leadership

Because of its importance to organizational effectiveness, leadership continues to be the focus of a great deal of research and theory building. New approaches that have attracted much attention are the concepts of substitutes for leadership, charismatic leadership, and transformational leadership.

Substitutes for Leadership

The concept of **substitutes for leadership** was developed because existing leadership models and theories do not account for situations in which leadership is not needed.[26] They simply try to specify what kind of leader behavior is appropriate. The substitute concepts, however, identify situations in which leader behaviors are

substitutes for leadership A concept that identifies situations in which leader behaviors are neutralized or replaced by characteristics of subordinates, the task, or the organization

neutralized or replaced by characteristics of the subordinate, the task, or the organization. For example, when a patient is delivered to a hospital emergency room, the professionals on duty do not wait to be told what to do by a leader. Nurses, doctors, and attendants all go into action without waiting for directive or supportive leader behavior from the emergency room supervisor.

Characteristics of the subordinate that may serve to neutralize leader behavior include ability, experience, need for independence, professional orientation, and indifference toward organizational rewards. For example, employees with a high level of ability and experience may not need to be told what to do. Similarly, a subordinate's strong need for independence may render leader behavior ineffective. Task characteristics that may substitute for leadership include routineness, the availability of feedback, and intrinsic satisfaction. When the job is routine and simple, the subordinate may not need direction. When the task is challenging and intrinsically satisfying, the subordinate may not need or want social support from a leader.

Organizational characteristics that may substitute for leadership include formalization, group cohesion, inflexibility, and a rigid reward structure. Leadership may not be necessary when policies and practices are formal and inflexible, for example. Similarly, a rigid reward system may rob the leader of reward power and thereby decrease the importance of the role. Preliminary research has provided support for the concept of substitutes for leadership.[27]

Charismatic Leadership

charismatic leadership Assumes that charisma is an individual characteristic of the leader

charisma A form of interpersonal attraction that inspires support and acceptance

The concept of **charismatic leadership**, like trait theories, assumes that charisma is an individual characteristic of the leader. **Charisma** is a form of interpersonal attraction that inspires support and acceptance. All else equal, then, someone with charisma is more likely to be able to influence others than is someone without

Phil Jackson is considered to be one of the top coaches in the National Basketball Association, having won world championships first with the Chicago Bulls and more recently with the Los Angeles Lakers. One key to his success is his personal charisma. Jackson is able to simultaneously command both the respect and the affection of his players. This rare combination allows him to channel and direct the energies of players toward the singular goal of winning basketball games, putting aside personal goals and petty differences of opinion.

charisma. For example, a highly charismatic supervisor will be more successful in influencing subordinate behavior than a supervisor who lacks charisma. Thus influence is again a fundamental element of this perspective.

Robert House first proposed a theory of charismatic leadership in 1977, based on research findings from a variety of social science disciplines.[28] His theory suggests that charismatic leaders are likely to have a lot of self-confidence, a firm conviction in their beliefs and ideals, and a strong need to influence people. They also tend to communicate high expectations about follower performance and express confidence in followers. Donald Trump is an excellent example of a charismatic leader. Even though he has made his share of mistakes and generally is perceived as only an "average" manager, many people view him as larger than life.

There are three elements of charismatic leadership in organizations that most experts acknowledge today.[29] First, the leader needs to be able to envision the future, to set high expectations, and to model behaviors consistent with meeting those expectations. Next, the charismatic leader must be able to energize others through a demonstration of personal excitement, personal confidence, and patterns of success. And, finally, the charismatic leader enables others by supporting them, empathizing with them, and expressing confidence in them.

Charismatic leadership ideas are quite popular among managers today and are the subject of numerous books and articles. Unfortunately, few studies have specifically attempted to test the meaning and impact of charismatic leadership. There are also lingering ethical issues about charismatic leadership, however, that trouble some people.

Transformational Leadership

Another new perspective on leadership has been called by a number of labels: charismatic leadership, inspirational leadership, symbolic leadership, and transformational leadership. We use the term **transformational leadership** and define it as leadership that goes beyond ordinary expectations by transmitting a sense of mission, stimulating learning experiences, and inspiring new ways of thinking.[30] Because of rapid change and turbulent environments, transformational leaders are increasingly being seen as vital to the success of business.

transformational leadership
Leadership that goes beyond ordinary expectations by transmitting a sense of mission, stimulating learning experiences, and inspiring new ways of thinking

A recent popular-press article identified seven keys to successful leadership: trusting one's subordinates, developing a vision, keeping cool, encouraging risk, being an expert, inviting dissent, and simplifying things. Although this list was the result of a simplistic survey of the leadership literature, it is nevertheless consistent with the premises underlying transformational leadership. So, too, are recent examples cited as effective leadership. Take, for example, the case of General Electric. When Jack Welch assumed the position of CEO, GE was a lethargic behemoth composed of more than 100 businesses. Decision making was slow, and bureaucracy stifled individual initiative. Welch stripped away the bureaucracy, streamlined the entire organization, sold dozens of businesses, and bought many new ones. He literally re-created the organization, and today GE is one of the most admired and profitable firms in the world. Indeed, Welch's most recent change at GE was his acquisition of Honeywell in late 2000 for $44 billion.[31] Transformational leadership was the basis for all of Welch's changes.

Political Behavior in Organizations

political behavior The activities carried out for the specific purpose of acquiring, developing, and using power and other resources to obtain one's preferred outcomes

Another common influence on behavior is politics and political behavior. **Political behavior** describes activities carried out for the specific purpose of acquiring, developing, and using power and other resources to obtain one's preferred outcomes.[32] Political behavior may be undertaken by managers dealing with their subordinates, subordinates dealing with their managers, and managers and subordinates dealing with others at the same level. In other words, it may be directed upward, downward, or laterally. Decisions ranging from where to locate a manufacturing plant to where to put the company coffee maker are subject to political action. In any situation, individuals may engage in political behavior to further their own ends, to protect themselves from others, to further goals they sincerely believe to be in the organization's best interest, or to simply acquire and exercise power. And power may be sought by individuals, by groups of individuals, or by groups of groups.[33]

Although political behavior is difficult to study because of its sensitive nature, one early survey found that many managers believed that politics influenced salary and hiring decisions in their firms. Many also believed that the incidence of political behavior was greater at the upper levels of their organizations and less at the lower levels. More than half of the respondents felt that organizational politics was bad, unfair, unhealthy, and irrational, but most suggested that successful executives have to be good politicians and be political to "get ahead."[34]

Common Political Behaviors

Research has identified four basic forms of political behavior widely practiced in organizations.[35] One form is *inducement*, which occurs when a manager offers to give something to someone else in return for that individual's support. For example, a product manager might suggest to another product manager that she will put in a good word with his boss if he supports a new marketing plan that she has developed. A second tactic is *persuasion*, which relies on both emotion and logic. An operations manager wanting to construct a new plant on a certain site might persuade others to support his goal on grounds that are objective and logical (it is less expensive, taxes are lower) as well as subjective and personal.

A third political behavior involves the *creation of an obligation*. For example, one manager might support a recommendation made by another manager for a new advertising campaign. Although he may really have no opinion on the new campaign, he may think that by going along he is incurring a debt from the other manager and will be able to "call in" that debt when he wants to get something done and needs additional support. *Coercion* is the use of force to get one's way. For example, a manager may threaten to withhold support, rewards, or other resources as a way to influence someone else.

impression management A direct and intentional effort by someone to enhance his or her image in the eyes of others

Impression management is a subtle form of political behavior that deserves special mention. **Impression management** is a direct and intentional effort by someone to enhance his or her image in the eyes of others. People engage in impression management for a variety of reasons. For one thing, they may do so in order to further their own career. By making themselves look good, they think they are more likely to receive rewards, to be given attractive job assignments, or to receive promotions. They may also engage in impression management in order to boost their own self-esteem. When people have a solid image in an organization, others make them aware of it through compliments, respect, and so forth. Still another reason why people use impression management is in an effort to acquire more power and hence more control.

People attempt to manage how others perceive them through a variety of mechanisms. Appearance is one of the first things people think of. Hence, a person motivated by impression management will pay close attention to choice of attire, selection of language, and the use of manners and body posture. People interested in impression management are also likely to jockey to be associated only with successful projects. By being assigned to high-profile projects led by highly successful managers, a person can begin to link their own name with such projects in the minds of others.

Sometimes people too strongly motivated by impression management become obsessed by it and may resort to dishonest or unethical means. For example, some people have been known to take credit for others' work in an effort to make themselves look better. People have also been known to exaggerate or even falsify their personal accomplishments in an effort to build an enhanced image.[36]

Managing Political Behavior

By its very nature, political behavior is tricky to approach in a rational and systematic way. But managers can handle political behavior so that it does not do excessive damage. First, managers should be aware that, even if their actions are not politically motivated, others may assume that they are. Second, by providing subordinates with autonomy, responsibility, challenge, and feedback, managers reduce the likelihood of political behavior by subordinates. Third, managers should avoid using power if they want to avoid charges of political motivation. Fourth, managers should get disagreements out in the open so that subordinates will have less opportunity for political behavior, using conflict for their own purposes. Finally, managers should avoid covert activities. Behind-the-scenes activities give the impression of political intent even if none really exists.[37] Other guidelines include clearly communicating the bases and processes for performance evaluations, tying rewards directly to performance, and minimizing competition among managers for resources.[38]

Of course, those guidelines are a lot easier to list than they are to implement. The well-informed manager should not assume that political behavior does not exist or, worse yet, attempt to eliminate it by issuing orders or commands. Instead, the manager must recognize that political behavior exists in virtually all organizations and that it cannot be ignored or stamped out. It can, however, be managed in such a way that it will seldom inflict serious damage on the organization. It may even play a useful role in some situations.[39] For example, a manager may be able to use his or her political influence to stimulate a greater sense of social responsibility or to heighten awareness of the ethical implications of a decision.

Summary of Key Points

As a process, leadership is the use of noncoercive influence to shape the group's or organization's goals, motivate behavior toward the achievement of those goals, and help define group or organization culture. As a property, leadership is the set of characteristics attributed to those who are perceived to be leaders. Leadership and management are often related but are also different. Managers and leaders use legitimate, reward, coercive, referent, and expert power.

The trait approach to leadership assumed that some basic trait or set of traits differentiates leaders from nonleaders. The leadership-behavior approach to leadership assumed that the behavior of effective leaders was somehow different from the behavior of nonleaders. Research at the University of Michigan and Ohio State identified two basic forms of leadership behavior—one concentrating on work and performance and the other concentrating on employee welfare and support. The Leadership Grid attempts to train managers to exhibit high levels of both forms of behavior.

Situational approaches to leadership recognize that appropriate forms of leadership behavior are not universally applicable and attempt to specify situations in which various behaviors are appropriate. The LPC theory suggests that a leader's behaviors should be either task oriented or relationship oriented depending on the favorableness of the situation. The path-goal theory suggests that directive, supportive, participative, or achievement-oriented leader behaviors may be appropriate, depending on the personal characteristics of subordinates and the environment. Vroom's decision tree approach maintains that leaders should vary the extent to which they allow subordinates to participate in making decisions as a function of problem attributes. The leader-member exchange (LMX) model focuses on individual relationships between leaders and followers and in-group versus out-group considerations.

Related leadership perspectives are the concepts of substitutes for leadership, charismatic leadership, and transformational leadership in organizations.

Political behavior is another influence process frequently used in organizations. Impression management, one especially important form of political behavior, is a direct and intentional effort by someone to enhance his or her image in the eyes of others. Managers can take steps to limit the effects of political behavior.

Discussion Questions

Questions for Review

1. Could someone be a manager but not a leader? a leader but not a manager? both a leader and a manager? Explain.
2. What were the major findings of the Michigan and Ohio State studies of leadership behaviors? Briefly describe each group of studies and compare and contrast their findings.
3. What are the situational approaches to leadership? Briefly describe each and compare and contrast their findings.
4. Describe charismatic and transformation perspectives on leadership. How can they be integrated with existing approaches to leadership?
5. What are the most common forms of political behavior in organizations? How can political behavior be managed?

Questions for Analysis

6. What traits best seem to describe student leaders? military leaders? business leaders? political leaders? religious leaders? What might account for the similarities and differences in your lists of traits?

7. How is it possible for a leader to be both task oriented and employee oriented at the same time? Can you think of other forms of leader behavior that would be important to a manager? If so, share your thoughts with your class.

8. Think about a decision that would affect you as a student. Use Vroom's model to decide whether the administrator making that decision should involve students in the decision. Which parts of the model seem most important in making that decision? Why?

9. When all or most of the leadership substitutes are present, does the follower no longer need a leader? Why or why not?

10. Why should members of an organization be aware that political behavior may be going on within the organization? What might occur if they were not aware?

BUILDING EFFECTIVE *diagnostic* SKILLS

Exercise Overview

Diagnostic skills help a manager visualize appropriate responses to a situation. One situation managers often face is whether to use power to solve a problem. This exercise helps you develop your diagnostic skills as they relate to using different types of power in different situations.

Exercise Background

Several methods have been identified for using power. These include

1. *Legitimate request*—The manager requests that the subordinate comply because the subordinate recognizes that the organization has given the manager the right to make the request. Most day-to-day interactions between manager and subordinate are of this type.

2. *Instrumental compliance*—In this form of exchange, a subordinate complies to get the reward the manager controls. Suppose that a manager asks a subordinate to do something outside the range of the subordinate's normal duties, such as working extra hours on the weekend, terminating a relationship with a long-standing buyer, or delivering bad news. The subordinate complies and, as a direct result, reaps praise and a bonus from the manager. The next time the subordinate is asked to perform a similar activity, that subordinate will recognize that compliance will be instrumental in her getting more rewards. Hence, the basis of instrumental compliance is clarifying important performance-reward contingencies.

3. *Coercion*—This form of power is used when the manager suggests or implies that the subordinate will be punished, fired, or reprimanded if he does not do something.

4. *Rational persuasion*—This form of power is used when the manager can convince the subordinate that compliance is in the subordinate's best interest. For example, a manager might argue that the subordinate should accept a transfer because it would be good for the subordinate's career. In some ways, rational persuasion is like reward power, except that the manager does not really control the reward.

5. *Personal identification*—This use of power occurs when a manager who recognizes that she has referent power over a subordinate can shape the behavior of that

subordinate by engaging in desired behaviors. The manager consciously becomes a model for the subordinate and exploits personal identification.

6. *Inspirational appeal*—This use of power occurs when a manager can induce a subordinate to do something consistent with a set of higher ideals or values through inspirational appeal. For example, a plea for loyalty represents an inspirational appeal.

Exercise Task

With these ideas in mind, do the following:
1. Relate each use of power listed above to the five types of power identified in the chapter.

That is, indicate which types of power are most closely associated with each use of power, which types may be related to each use of power, and which types are unrelated to each use of power.
2. Consider whether a manager is more likely to be using multiple forms of power at the same time or a single type of power.
3. Identify other methods and approaches to using power.
4. Describe some of the dangers and pitfalls associated with using power.

BUILDING EFFECTIVE *decision-making* SKILLS

Exercise Overview

Vroom's decision tree approach to leadership is an effective method for determining how much participation a manager might allow his or her subordinates in making a decision. This exercise enables you to refine your decision-making skills by applying Vroom's approach to a hypothetical situation.

Exercise Background

Assume that you are the branch manager of the West Coast region of the United States for an international manufacturing and sales company. The company is making a major effort to control costs and boost efficiency. As part of this effort, the firm recently installed a networked computer system linking sales representatives, customer service employees, and other sales support staff. The goal of this network was to increase sales while cutting sales expenses.

Unfortunately, just the opposite has resulted—sales are down slightly, whereas expenses are increasing. You have looked into this problem and believe that, although the computer hardware in use is fine, the software is flawed. It is too hard to use and provides less-than-complete information.

Your employees disagree with your assessment, however. They believe that the entire system is fine. They attribute the problems to poor training in how to use the system and a lack of incentive for using it to solve many problems that they already know how to handle using other methods. Some employees also think that their colleagues are just resisting change.

Your boss has just called and instructed you to "solve the problem." She indicated that she has complete faith in your ability to do so, will let you decide how you proceed, and wants a report suggesting a course of action in five days.

Exercise Task

Using the information presented above, do the following:
1. Using your own personal preferences and intuition, describe how you think you would proceed.
2. Now use Vroom's decision tree approach to determine a course of action.
3. Compare and contrast your initial approach and the approach suggested by Vroom's approach.

BUILDING EFFECTIVE *conceptual* SKILLS

Exercise Overview

Conceptual skills refer to the manager's ability to think in the abstract. This exercise enables you to apply your conceptual skills to the identification of leadership qualities in others.

Exercise Task

1. Working alone, list the names of ten people you think of as leaders. Note that the names should not necessarily be confined to "good" leaders but instead should identify "strong" leaders.

2. Form small groups with three or four classmates and compare lists. Focus on common and unique examples, as well as the kinds of individuals listed (for example, male versus female, contemporary versus historical, business versus nonbusiness).

3. From all the lists, choose two leaders whom most people in the group consider to be the most successful and the least successful.

4. Identify similarities and differences between the two successful leaders and the two less successful leaders.

5. Relate the successes and failures to at least one theory or perspective discussed in the chapter.

6. Select one group member to report your findings to the rest of the class.

SKILLS *self-assessment* INSTRUMENT

Managerial Leader Behavior Questionnaire

Introduction: Leadership is now recognized as being an important set of characteristics for everyone in an organization to develop. The following assessment surveys your leadership practices or beliefs in a management role, that is, managerial leadership.

Instructions: The following statements refer to the possible ways you might behave in a managerial leadership role. Indicate how you do behave or how you think you would behave for each statement. Describing yourself may be difficult in some cases, but you should force a selection. Record your answers next to each statement according to the following scale:

Rating Scale

5	Very descriptive of me	**2**	Not very descriptive of me
4	Fairly descriptive of me	**1**	Not descriptive of me at all
3	Somewhat descriptive of me		

_____ 1. I emphasize the importance of performance and encourage everyone to make a maximum effort.

_____ 2. I am friendly, supportive, and considerate toward others.

_____ 3. I offer helpful advice to others on how to advance their careers and encourage them to develop their skills.

_____ 4. I stimulate enthusiasm for the work of the group and say things to build the group's confidence.

_____ 5. I provide appropriate praise and recognition for effective performance and show appreciation for special efforts and contributions.

_____ 6. I reward effective performance with tangible benefits.

_____ 7. I inform people about their duties and responsibilities, clarify rules and policies, and let people know what is expected of them.

_____ 8. Either alone or jointly with others, I set specific and challenging but realistic performance goals.

_____ 9. I provide any necessary training and coaching or arrange for others to do it.

_____ 10. I keep everyone informed about decisions, events, and developments that affect their work.

_____ 11. I consult with others before making work-related decisions.

_____ 12. I delegate responsibility and authority to others and allow them discretion in determining how to do their work.

_____ 13. I plan in advance how to efficiently organize and schedule the work.

_____ 14. I look for new opportunities for the group to exploit, propose new undertakings, and offer innovative ideas.

_____ 15. I take prompt and decisive action to deal with serious work-related problems and disturbances.

_____ 16. I provide subordinates with the supplies, equipment, support services, and other resources necessary to work effectively.

_____ 17. I keep informed about the activities of the group and check on its performance.

_____ 18. I keep informed about outside events that have important implications for the group.

_____ 19. I promote and defend the interests of the group and take appropriate action to obtain necessary resources for the group.

_____ 20. I emphasize teamwork and try to promote cooperation, cohesiveness, and identification with the group.

_____ 21. I discourage unnecessary fighting and bickering within the group and help settle conflicts and disagreements in a constructive manner.

_____ 22. I criticize specific acts that are unacceptable, find positive things to say, and provide an opportunity for people to offer explanations.

_____ 23. I take appropriate disciplinary action to deal with anyone who violates a rule, disobeys an order, or has consistently poor performance.

For interpretation, see Interpretations of Skills Self-Assessment Instruments.

Source: Reprinted from *Military Leadership: An Organizational Behavior Perspective*, pp. 38–39, David D. Van Fleet and Gary A. Yukl. Copyright 1986 with permission from Elsevier Science.

EXPERIENTIAL EXERCISE

The Leadership/Management Interview Experiment

Purpose: Leadership and management are in some ways the same, but more often they are different. This exercise allows you to develop a conceptual framework for leadership and management.

Introduction: Because most management behaviors and leadership behaviors are a product of individual work experience, each leader/manager tends to have a unique leadership/management style. An analysis of leadership/management styles and a comparison of such styles with different organizational experiences are often rewarding experiences in learning.

Instructions: *Fact-finding and Execution of the Experiment*

1. Develop a list of questions relating to issues studied in this chapter that you want to ask a practicing manager and leader during a face-to-face interview. Prior to the actual interview, submit your list of questions to your instructor for approval.

2. Arrange to interview a practicing manager and a practicing leader. For purposes of this assignment, a manager or leader is a person

whose job priority involves supervising the work of other people. The leader/manager may work in a business or in a public or private agency.

3. Interview at least one manager and one leader, using the questions you developed. Take good notes on their comments and on your own observations. Do not take more than one hour of each leader's/manager's time.

Oral Report

Prepare an oral report using the questions here and your interview information. Complete the following report after the interview. (Attach a copy of your interview questions.)

The Leadership/Management Interview Experiment Report

1. How did you locate the leaders/managers you interviewed? Describe your initial contacts.

2. Describe the level and responsibilities of your leaders/managers. Do not supply names—their responses should be anonymous.

3. Describe the interview settings. How long did the interview last?

4. In what ways were the leaders/managers similar or in agreement about issues?

5. What were some of the major differences between the leaders/managers and the ways in which they approached their jobs?

6. In what ways would the managers agree or disagree with ideas presented in this course?

7. Describe and evaluate your own interviewing style and skills.

8. How did your managers feel about having been interviewed? How do you know that?

CHAPTER CLOSING CASE

How Southwest Airlines Soars

Southwest Airlines has been profitable since 1973—an enviable record that no other U.S. airline can match, let alone beat. Much of the credit for the airline's enduring success goes to CEO Herb Kelleher, an affable, hard-driving leader whose fun-loving personality pervades the entire organization, top to bottom. After all, how many airlines have the ticker symbol LUV or paint Seaworld's Shamu the Whale on a jetliner?

The history of Southwest reflects its CEO's tenacity. Kelleher had a law practice in San Antonio when a client suggested starting a discount airline to link three Texas cities. After five years of legal battles due to competitors' objections—this was before deregulation opened the skies to anything-goes competition and pricing—Southwest finally got off the ground in 1971. To keep airfares low, the startup avoided such extras as meal service and got planes in and out of the gate in 20 minutes or less. The airline now serves dozens of cities across the United States, using the original formula of low prices, low costs, and high productivity to keep profits high; in fact, Southwest's operating margins are now three times higher than the industry average.

Kelleher knows that other airlines can buy the same planes and fly the same routes, even set the same prices. However, what they cannot imitate, he pointedly notes, is Southwest's legendary team spirit. The workforce of 30,000 is fiercely loyal to Kelleher and the company, pitching in to get things done on time and within budget. Consider the reaction when Kelleher wrote a memo warning employees that rising fuel prices threatened the airline's profitability and asking every employee to find a way to save $5 per day. Within six weeks, employees had dreamed up enough cost-cutting measures to save more than $2 million—and ideas were still coming in.

Under Kelleher, Southwest has made flying fun for employees and passengers alike. Flight attendants set the tone by weaving in humorous remarks along with their regular in-flight announcements; gate agents lighten up by wearing offbeat hats and bantering with passengers getting on and off planes. Southwest employees really let loose on Halloween, wearing wacky costumes, decorating gate areas, and munching on trick-or-treat snacks.

Keeping this spirit alive as the airline expands is a major challenge. Southwest uses personality testing to identify job applicants who will fit in with the airline's unique approach to business because they are cheerful and optimistic, able to make decisions, team oriented, good communicators, and able to take initiative. New hires are then sent to the airline's University for People to hone their interpersonal and technical skills and to learn about the airline's traditions. Out in the field, local culture committees are charged with perpetuating the culture at each airport and outpost through meetings, games, and parties.

When trouble erupts within the organization, the solution generally comes out of Southwest's own culture. For example, flight attendants once complained about the work schedules devised by the scheduling department; the schedulers, meanwhile, said the flight attendants were uncooperative. In typical Southwest style, management successfully defused the situation by having the two groups switch jobs to learn firsthand about the pressures each group faced.

What would Southwest be like under another CEO? Management is already thinking ahead to the time, not so long from now, when Kelleher steps down and a new CEO takes over. Although Kelleher is always ready with a funny line, even on formal occasions, he turns serious when speaking about leaving a legacy that will keep Southwest soaring for the long term. Until he relinquishes the CEO position, however, Kelleher will keep pushing to bring the Southwest spirit to new destinations, keep costs down, keep profits high, and—above all—put the fun back in flying.

Case Questions

1. What leadership theories and concepts have contributed to Herb Kelleher's success at Southwest?

2. Do you consider Kelleher to be a manager, a leader, or both? Why?

3. What should Southwest look for in a CEO to succeed Kelleher?

Case References

Katrina Brooker, "Can Anyone Replace Herb?" *Fortune,* April 17, 2000, pp. 186–192; and *Hoover's Handbook of American Business 2001* (Austin, Texas: Hoover's Business Press, 2001), pp. 872–873.

CHAPTER NOTES

1. "Schrempp Survives Shares Slump But Unions Shown the Door," *Financial Times,* September 28, 2001, p. 18; "CEO Wants Leaner, Meaner Chrysler," *USA Today,* December 20, 2000, p. B1 (*quote on p. B1); "DaimlerChrysler Workers Have a Pal With Connections to the Home Office," *The Detroit News,* March 6, 2001, p. C1; "Can This Man Save Chrysler?" *Business Week,* September 17, 2001, pp. 34–37.

2. See Ronald A. Heifetz and Donald L. Laurie, "The Work of Leadership," *Harvard Business Review,* January/February 1997, pp. 124–134. See also Arthur G. Jago, "Leadership: Perspectives in Theory and Research," *Management Science,* March 1982, pp. 315–336, and "The New Leadership," *Business Week,* August 28, 2000, pp. 100–187.

3. Gary A. Yukl, *Leadership in Organizations,* 3rd ed. (Englewood Cliffs, NJ: Prentice-Hall, 1994), p. 5. See also Gregory G. Dess and Joseph C. Picken, "Changing Roles: Leadership in the 21st Century," *Organizational Dynamics,* Winter 2000, pp. 18–28.

4. John P. Kotter, "What Leaders Really Do," *Harvard Business Review,* May/June 1990, pp. 103–111. See also Daniel Goleman, "Leadership That Gets Results," *Harvard Business Review,* March/April 2000, pp. 78–88; and Keith Grints, *The Arts of Leadership* (Oxford, UK: Oxford University Press, 2000).

5. John R. P. French and Bertram Raven, "The Bases of Social Power," in *Studies in Social Power,* ed. Dorwin Cartwright (Ann Arbor: University of Michigan Press, 1959), pp. 150–167.

6. Hugh D. Menzies, "The Ten Toughest Bosses," *Fortune,* April 21, 1980, pp. 62–73.

7. Bennett J. Tepper, "Consequences of Abusive Supervision," *Academy of Management Journal* 43, no. 2 (2000): 178–190.

8. Bernard M. Bass, *Bass & Stogdill's Handbook of Leadership,* 3rd. ed. (Riverside, NJ: Free Press, 1990).

9. Shelley A. Kirkpatrick and Edwin A. Locke, "Leadership: Do Traits Matter?" *Academy of Management Executive,* May 1991, pp. 48–60. See also Robert J. Sternberg, "Managerial Intelligence: Why IQ Isn't Enough," *Journal of Management* 23, no. 3 (1997): 475–493.

10. Rensis Likert, *New Patterns of Management* (New York: McGraw-Hill, 1961), and *The Human Organization* (New York: McGraw-Hill, 1967).

11. The Ohio State studies stimulated many articles, monographs, and books. A good overall reference is Ralph M. Stogdill and A. E. Coons, eds., *Leader Behavior: Its Description and Measurement* (Columbus: Bureau of Business Research, Ohio State University, 1957).

12. Edwin A. Fleishman, E. F. Harris, and H. E. Burt, *Leadership and Supervision in Industry* (Columbus: Bureau of Business Research, Ohio State University, 1955).

13. Robert R. Blake and Jane S. Mouton, *The Managerial Grid* (Houston, TX: Gulf Publishing, 1964), and *The Versatile Manager: A Grid Profile* (Homewood, IL: Dow Jones–Irwin, 1981).

14. Fred E. Fiedler, *A Theory of Leadership Effectiveness* (New York: McGraw-Hill, 1967).

15. Chester A. Schriesheim, Bennett J. Tepper, and Linda A. Tetrault, "Least Preferred Co-Worker Score, Situational Control, and Leadership Effectiveness: A Meta-Analysis of Contingency Model Performance Predictions," *Journal of Applied Psychology* 79, no. 4 (1994): 561–573.

16. Fiedler; and Fred E. Fiedler and M. M. Chemers, *Leadership and Effective Management* (Glenview, IL: Scott, Foresman, 1974).

17. Martin G. Evans, "The Effects of Supervisory Behavior on the Path-Goal Relationship," *Organizational Behavior and Human Performance*, May 1970, pp. 277–298; and Robert J. House and Terence R. Mitchell, "Path-Goal Theory of Leadership," *Journal of Contemporary Business*, Autumn 1974, pp. 81-98. See also Yukl.

18. For a recent review, see J. C. Wofford and Laurie Z. Liska, "Path-Goal Theories of Leadership: A Meta-Analysis," *Journal of Management* 19, no. 4 (1993): 857–876.

19. See Victor H. Vroom and Philip H. Yetton, *Leadership and Decision Making* (Pittsburgh: University of Pittsburgh Press, 1973); and Victor H. Vroom and Arthur G. Jago, *The New Leadership* (Englewood Cliffs, NJ: Prentice-Hall, 1988).

20. Victor Vroom, "Leadership and the Decision-Making Process," *Organizational Dynamics* 28, no. 4 (2000): 82–94.

21. Vroom and Jago.

22. Ibid.

23. See Madeline E. Heilman, Harvey A. Hornstein, Jack H. Cage, and Judith K. Herschlag, "Reaction to Prescribed Leader Behavior as a Function of Role Perspective: The Case of the Vroom-Yetton Model," *Journal of Applied Psychology*, February 1984, pp. 50–60; and R. H. George Field, "A Test of the Vroom-Yetton Normative Model of Leadership," *Journal of Applied Psychology*, February 1982, pp. 523–532.

24. George Graen and J. F. Cashman, "A Role-Making Model of Leadership in Formal Organizations: A Developmental Approach," in *Leadership Frontiers*, ed. J. G. Hunt and L. L. Larson (Kent, OH: Kent State University Press, 1975), pp. 143–165; and Fred Dansereau, George Graen, and W. J. Haga, "A Vertical Dyad Linkage Approach to Leadership Within Formal Organizations: A Longitudinal Investigation of the Role-Making Process," *Organizational Behavior and Human Performance* 15 (1975): 46–78.

25. See Charlotte R. Gerstner and David V. Day, "Meta-Analytic Review of Leader-Member Exchange Theory: Correlates and Construct Issues," *Journal of Applied Psychology* 82, no. 6 (1997): 827–844; and Chester A. Schriesheim, Linda L. Neider, and Terri A. Scandura, "Delegation and Leader-Member Exchange: Main Effects, Moderators, and Measurement Issues," *Academy of Management Journal* 41, no. 3 (1999): 298–318.

26. Steven Kerr and John M. Jermier, "Substitutes for Leadership: Their Meaning and Measurement," *Organizational Behavior and Human Performance*, December 1978, pp. 375–403.

27. See Charles C. Manz and Henry P. Sims, Jr., "Leading Workers to Lead Themselves: The External Leadership of Self-managing Work Teams," *Administrative Science Quarterly*, March 1987, pp. 106–129. See also "Living Without a Leader," *Fortune*, March 20, 2000, pp. 218–219.

28. See Robert J. House, "A 1976 Theory of Charismatic Leadership," in *Leadership: The Cutting Edge*, ed. J. G. Hunt and L. L. Larson (Carbondale, IL: Southern Illinois University Press, 1977), pp. 189–207. See also Jay A. Conger and Rabindra N. Kanungo, "Toward a Behavioral Theory of Charismatic Leadership in Organizational Settings," *Academy of Management Review*, October 1987, pp. 637–647.

29. David A. Nadler and Michael L. Tushman, "Beyond the Charismatic Leader: Leadership and Organizational Change," *California Management Review*, Winter 1990, pp. 77–97.

30. James MacGregor Burns, *Leadership* (New York: Harper & Row, 1978). See also Rajnandini Pillai, Chester A. Schriesheim, and Eric J. Williams, "Fairness Perceptions and Trust as Mediators for Transformational and Transactional Leadership: A Two-Sample Study," *Journal of Management* 25, no. 6 (1999): 897–933.

31. "On Eve of Retirement, Jack Welch Decides to Stick Around a Bit," *Wall Street Journal*, October 23, 2000, pp. A1, A32.

32. Jeffrey Pfeffer, *Power in Organizations* (Marshfield, MA: Pitman Publishing, 1981), p. 7.

33. Timothy Judge and Robert Bretz, "Political Influence Behavior and Career Success," *Journal of Management* 20, no. 1 (1994): 43–65.

34. Victor Murray and Jeffrey Gandz, "Games Executives Play: Politics at Work," *Business Horizons*, December 1980, pp. 11–23; and Jeffrey Gandz and Victor Murray, "The Experience of Workplace Politics," *Academy of Management Journal*, June 1980, pp. 237–251.

35. Don R. Beeman and Thomas W. Sharkey, "The Use and Abuse of Corporate Power," *Business Horizons*, March–April 1987, pp. 26–30.

36. See William L. Gardner, "Lessons in Organizational Dramaturgy: The Art of Impression Management," *Organizational Dynamics*, Summer 1992, pp. 51–63; and Elizabeth Wolf Morrison and Robert J. Bies, "Impression Management in the Feedback-Seeking Process: A Literature Review and Research Agenda," *Academy of Management Review*, July 1991, pp. 522–541.

37. Murray and Gandz.

38. Beeman and Sharkey.

39. Stefanie Ann Lenway and Kathleen Rehbein, "Leaders, Followers, and Free Riders: An Empirical Test of Variation in Corporate Political Involvement," *Academy of Management Journal*, December 1991, pp. 893–905.

12 Communication in Organizations

Although few people may have heard of Chaparral Steel Corporation, the company enjoys a strong reputation as one of the most effective firms in the steel industry. Chaparral was founded as a subsidiary of Texas Industries about 30 years ago and today enjoys annual sales of over $800 million. In earlier times, most steel companies were large, bureaucratic operations like U.S. Steel (now USX) and Bethlehem Steel. However, increased competition from low-cost foreign steel firms—especially those in Japan and Korea—caused major problems for these manufacturers with their high overhead costs and inflexible modes of operation.

These competitive pressures, in turn, led to the formation of so-called minimills like Chaparral and Nucor. Because of their size, technology, and flexibility, these firms are able to maintain much lower production costs and to respond more quickly to customer requests. And today, Chaparral is recognized as one of the best of this new breed of steel companies. For example, whereas most mills produce an average of one ton of steel with three to five labor-hours, Chaparral produces a ton with less than 1.2 labor-hours.

Since its inception, Chaparral has been led by Gordon Forward. Forward knew that if Chaparral was going to succeed it would need to be managed in new and different ways. One of the first things he decided to do was to break down the traditional barriers that often exist between management and labor. Thus he mandated that there would be no reserved parking spaces nor a separate dining area for managers. He also insisted that all employees be paid on a salary basis—no time clocks or time sheets for anyone. He also pioneered a concept called "open-book management"—any employee can access any document, record, or other piece of information at any time.

Moreover, Forward himself maintains an open-door policy. Any employee can drop by his office at any time, with or without an appointment, and discuss issues or ask questions about what is going on in the company. Forward also believes in trusting everyone in the organization. When the firm recently needed a new rolling mill lathe, it budgeted $1 million for its purchase, then put the purchase decision in the hands of an operating machinist. That machinist in turn investigated various options, visited

> "We encourage people at all organizational levels to have face-to-face dialogues."
>
> —Dennis Beach,
> Chaparral executive vice president

After studying this chapter, you should be able to

- Describe the role and importance of communication in the manager's job.

- Identify the basic forms of communication in organizations.

- Describe electronic communication in organizations.

- Discuss informal communication, including its various forms and types.

- Describe how the communication process can be managed so as to recognize and overcome barriers.

other mills in Japan and Europe, and then recommended an alternative piece of machinery costing less than half the budgeted amount.

Forward also recognizes the importance of investing in and rewarding people. Continuous education is an integral part of Chaparral's culture, with a variety of classes being offered all the time. Everyone also participates in the good—and bad—times. For example, workers have a guaranteed base salary that is adequate, but below the standard market rate. In addition, however, each employee gets a pay-for-performance bonus based on his or her individual achievements. Finally, there are also companywide bonuses paid to everyone on a quarterly basis. These bonuses are tied to overall company performance.[1]

Gordon Forward seems to have what is a surprisingly rare combination of communication skills and managerial acumen. Communication is a vital part of managerial work. Indeed, managers around the world agree that communication is one of their most important tasks. It is important for them to communicate with others in order to convey their vision and goals for the organization. And it is important for others to communicate with them so that they will better understand what is going on in their environment and how they and their organizations can become more effective.

This chapter discusses communication, one of the most basic forms of interaction among people. We begin by examining communication in the context of the manager's job. We then identify and discuss forms of interpersonal, group, and organizational communication. Next, we discuss electronic communication in organizations. After discussing informal communication, we describe how organizational communication can be effectively managed.

Communication and the Manager's Job

A typical day for a manager includes attending scheduled meetings, placing and receiving telephone calls, reading and sending electronic messages, reading and answering paper correspondence, and attending unscheduled meetings and tours.[2] Most of these activities involve communication. In fact, managers usually spend over half of their time on some form of communication. Communication always involves two or more people, so other behavioral processes, such as motivation, leadership, and group and team processes, all come into play. Top executives must handle communication effectively if they are to be true leaders.

A Definition of Communication

Imagine three managers working in an office building. The first is all alone but is nevertheless yelling for a subordinate to come help. No one appears, but he continues to yell. The second is talking on the telephone to a subordinate, but static on the line causes the subordinate to misunderstand some important numbers being provided by the manager. As a result, the subordinate sends 1,500 crates of eggs to 150 Fifth Street, when he should have sent 150 crates of eggs to 1500 Fifteenth Street. The third manager is talking in her office with a subordinate who clearly hears and understands what is being said. Each of these managers is attempting to communicate, but with different results.

communication The process of transmitting information from one person to another

effective communication The process of sending a message in such a way that the message received is as close in meaning as possible to the message intended

Communication is the process of transmitting information from one person to another. Did any of our three managers communicate? The last did, and the first did not. How about the second? In fact, she did communicate. She transmitted information, and information was received. The problem was that the message transmitted and the message received were not the same. The words spoken by the manager were distorted by static and noise. **Effective communication**, then, is the process of sending a message in such a way that the message received is as close in meaning as possible to the message intended. Although the second manager engaged in communication, it was not effective.

A key element in effective communication is the distinction between data and information. **Data** are raw figures and facts reflecting a single aspect of reality. The facts that a plant has 35 machines, that each machine is capable of producing 1,000 units of output per day, that current and projected future demand for the units is 30,000 per day, and that workers sufficiently skilled to run the machines make $15 per hour are data. **Information** is data presented in a way or form that has meaning. Thus summarizing the preceding four pieces of data provides information—the plant has excess capacity and is therefore incurring unnecessary costs. Information has meaning to a manager and provides a basis for action. The plant manager might use the information and decide to sell four machines (keeping one as a backup) and transfer five operators to other jobs.

data Raw figures and facts reflecting a single aspect of reality

information Data presented in a way or form that has meaning

Characteristics of Useful Information

What factors differentiate information that is useful and information that is not useful? In general, information is useful if it is accurate, timely, complete, and relevant.

Accurate   For information to be of real value to a manager, it must be accurate. Accuracy means that the information must provide a valid and reliable reflection of reality. A Japanese construction company once bought information from a consulting firm about a possible building site in London. The Japanese were told that the land, which would be sold in a sealed bid auction, would attract bids of close to $250 million. They were also told that the land currently held an old building that could easily be demolished. Thus the Japanese bid $255 million—which ended up being $90 million more than the next-highest bid. And, to make matters worse, a few days later the British government declared the building historic, pre-empting any thought of demolition. Clearly, the Japanese acted on information that was less than accurate.

Timely   Information also needs to be timely. Timeliness does not necessarily mean speediness; it means only that information needs to be available in time for appropriate managerial action. What constitutes timeliness is a function of the situation facing the manager. When Marriott was gathering information for its Fairfield Inn project, managers projected a six-month window for data collection. They felt this would give them an opportunity to do a good job of getting the information they needed while not delaying things too much. In contrast, Marriott's computerized reservation and accounting system can provide a manager today with last night's occupancy level at any Marriott facility.[3]

Complete   Information must tell a complete story for it to be useful to a manager. If it is less than complete, the manager is likely to get an inaccurate or distorted picture of reality. For example, managers at Kroger used to think that house-brand products were more profitable than national brands because they yielded higher unit profits. On the basis of this information, they gave house brands a lot of shelf space and centered a lot of promotional activities on them. As Kroger's managers became more sophisticated in understanding their information, however, they realized that national brands were actually more profitable over time, because they sold many more units than house brands during any given period of time. Hence, although a store might sell 10 cans of Kroger coffee in a day with a profit of 50 cents per can (total profit of $5), it would also sell 15 cans of Maxwell House with a profit of 40 cents per can (total profit of $6) and 10 vacuum bags of Starbucks coffee with a profit of $1 per bag (total profit of $10). With this more complete picture, managers can do a better job of selecting the right mix of Kroger, Maxwell House, and Starbucks coffee to display and promote.

Relevant   Finally, information must be relevant if it is to be useful to managers. Relevance, like timeliness, is defined according to the needs and circumstances of a particular manager. Operations managers need information on costs and productivity; human resource managers need information on hiring needs and turnover rates; and marketing managers need information on sales projections and advertising rates. As Wal-Mart contemplates countries for possible expansion opportunities, it gathers information about local regulations, customs, and so forth. But the information about any given country is not really relevant until the decision is made to enter that market.

The Communication Process

Figure 12.1 illustrates how communication generally takes place between people. The process of communication begins when one person (the sender) wants to transmit a fact, idea, opinion, or other information to someone else (the receiver). This fact, idea, or opinion has meaning to the sender, whether it be simple and concrete or complex and abstract. The next step is to encode the meaning into a form appropriate to the situation. The encoding might take the form of words, facial expressions, gestures, or even artistic expressions and physical actions.

After the message has been encoded, it is transmitted through the appropriate channel or medium. The channel through which the present encoded message is being transmitted to you is the printed page. Common channels in organizations include meetings, e-mail, memos, letters, reports, and telephone calls. After the message is received, it is decoded back into a form that has meaning for the receiver. In many cases, the meaning prompts a response, and the cycle is continued when a new message is sent by the same steps back to the original sender. The manager might have called the sales representative to offer congratulations, written her a personal note of praise, offered praise in an e-mail, or sent a formal letter of acknowledgment.

"Noise" may disrupt communication anywhere along the way. Noise can be the sound of someone coughing, a truck driving by, or two people talking close at hand. It can also include such disruptions as a letter being lost in the mail, a telephone line going dead, an e-mail getting misrouted or infected with a virus, or one of the participants in a conversation being called away before the communication process is completed.

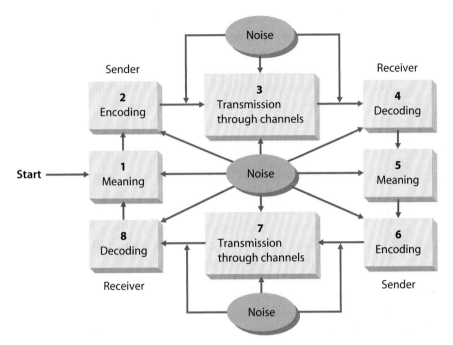

Figure 12.1

The Communication Process

As the figure shows, noise can disrupt the communication process at any step. Managers must therefore understand that a conversation in the next office, a fax machine out of paper, and the receiver's worries may all thwart the manager's best attempts to communicate.

The numbers indicate the sequence in which steps take place.

Forms of Communication in Organizations

Managers need to understand several kinds of communication that are common in organizations today. These include interpersonal communication, communication in networks and teams, organizational communication, and electronic communication, which we discuss in a separate section.

Interpersonal Communication

Interpersonal communication generally takes one of two forms: oral or written. As we will see, each has clear strengths and weaknesses.

Oral Communication   **Oral communication** takes place in conversations, group discussions, telephone calls, and other situations in which the spoken word is used to express meaning. Henry Mintzberg demonstrated the importance of oral communication when he found that most managers spend between 50 and 90 percent of their time talking to people.[4] Oral communication is so prevalent for several reasons. The primary advantage of oral communication is that it promotes prompt feedback and interchange in the form of verbal questions or agreement, facial expressions, and gestures. Oral communication is also easy (all the sender needs to do is talk), and it can be done with little preparation (though careful

oral communication Face-to-face conversation, group discussions, telephone calls, and other circumstances in which the spoken word is used to transmit meaning

Communication in networks and work teams is an increasingly important issue in most organizations. Because much of its work is done by teams, Merill Lynch, the big brokerage firm, is keenly interested in further enhancing how its employees communicate with one another. These agents, for example, are linked to members of their team via the Internet; the technology employed by the firm makes it possible for them to talk to one another in real time while they send and receive information from computer to computer.

written communication Memos, letters, reports, notes, and other circumstances in which the written word is used to transmit meaning

preparation is advisable in certain situations). The sender does not need pencil and paper, keyboard, or other equipment. In one survey, 55 percent of the executives sampled felt that their own written communication skills were fair or poor, so they chose oral communication to avoid embarrassment![5]

However, oral communication also has drawbacks. It may suffer from problems of inaccuracy if the speaker chooses the wrong words to convey meaning or leaves out pertinent details, if noise disrupts the process, or if the receiver forgets part of the message. In a two-way discussion, there is seldom time for a thoughtful, considered response or for introducing many new facts, and there is no permanent record of what has been said. In addition, although most managers are comfortable talking to people individually or in small groups, fewer enjoy speaking to larger audiences.[6]

Written Communication   "Putting it in writing" in a letter, report, memorandum, handwritten note, or e-mail can solve many of the problems inherent in oral communication. Nevertheless, and perhaps surprisingly, **written communication** is not as common as one might imagine, nor is it a mode of communication much respected by managers. One sample of managers indicated that only 13 percent of the mail they received was of immediate use to them.[7] Over 80 percent of the managers who responded to another survey indicated that the written communication they received was of fair or poor quality.[8]

The biggest single drawback of traditional forms of written communication is that it inhibits feedback and interchange. When one manager sends another manager a letter, it must be written or dictated, typed, mailed, received, routed, opened, and read. If there is a misunderstanding, it may take several days for it to be recognized, let alone rectified. Although the use of e-mail is, of course, much faster, both sender and receiver must still have access to a computer, and the receiver must open and read the message in order for it to actually be received. A phone call could settle the whole matter in just a few minutes. Thus written communication often inhibits feedback and interchange and is usually more difficult and time consuming than oral communication.

Of course, written communication offers some advantages. It is often quite accurate and provides a permanent record of the exchange. The sender can take the time to collect and assimilate the information, and draft and revise it before it is transmitted. The receiver can take the time to read it carefully and refer to it repeatedly, as needed. For these reasons, written communication is generally preferable when important details are involved. At times it is important to one or both parties to have a written record available as evidence of exactly what took place. Julie Regan, founder of Toucan-Do, an importing company based in Honolulu, relies heavily on formal business letters in establishing contacts and buying merchandise from vendors in Southeast Asia. She believes that such letters give her an opportunity to carefully think through what she wants to say, tailor her message to each individual, and avoid misunderstandings later.

Choosing the Right Form   Which form of interpersonal communication should the manager use? The best medium will be determined by the situation. Oral communication or e-mail is often preferred when the message is personal, nonroutine, and brief. More formal written communication is usually best when the message is more impersonal, routine, and longer. The manager can also combine media to capitalize on the advantages of each. For example, a quick telephone call to set up a meeting is easy and gets an immediate response. Following up the call with a reminder e-mail or handwritten note helps ensure that the recipient will remember the meeting, and it provides a record of the meeting's having been called. Electronic communication, discussed more fully later, blurs the differences between oral and written communication and can help each be more effective.

Communication in Networks and Teams

Although communication among team members in an organization is clearly interpersonal in nature, substantial research also exists focusing specifically on how people in networks and work teams communicate with one another. A **communication network** is the pattern through which the members of a group or team communicate. Researchers studying group dynamics have discovered several typical networks in groups and teams consisting of three, four, and five members. Representative networks among members of five-member teams are shown in Figure 12.2.[9]

In the wheel pattern, all communication flows through one central person, who is probably the group's leader. In a sense, the wheel is the most centralized network, because one person receives and disseminates all information. The Y

communication network The pattern through which the members of a group communicate

Figure 12.2

Types of Communication Networks
Research on communication networks has identified five basic networks for five-person groups. These vary in terms of information flow, position of the leader, and effectiveness for different types of tasks. Managers might strive to create centralized networks when group tasks are simple and routine. Alternatively, managers can foster decentralized groups when group tasks are complex and nonroutine.

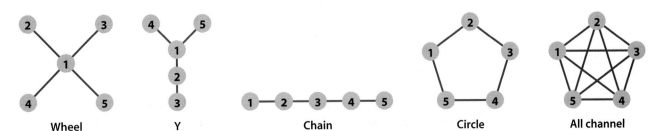

pattern is slightly less centralized—two persons are close to the center. The chain offers a more even flow of information among members, although two people (the ones at each end) interact with only one other person. This path is closed in the circle pattern. Finally, the all-channel network, the most decentralized, allows a free flow of information among all group members. Everyone participates equally, and the group's leader, if there is one, is not likely to have excessive power.

Research conducted on networks suggests some interesting connections between the type of network and group performance. For example, when the group's task is relatively simple and routine, centralized networks tend to perform with greatest efficiency and accuracy. The dominant leader facilitates performance by coordinating the flow of information. When a group of accounting clerks is logging incoming invoices and distributing them for payment, for example, one centralized leader can coordinate things efficiently. When the task is complex and nonroutine, such as making a major decision about organizational strategy, decentralized networks tend to be most effective, because open channels of communication permit more interaction and a more efficient sharing of relevant information. Managers should recognize the effects of communication networks on group and organizational performance and should try to structure networks appropriately.

Organizational Communication

Still other forms of communication in organizations are those that flow among and between organizational units or groups. Each of these involves oral or written communication, but each also extends to broad patterns of communication across the organization. As shown in Figure 12.3, two of these forms of communication follow vertical and horizontal linkages in the organization.

Figure 12.3

Formal Communication in Organizations

Formal communication in organizations follows official reporting relationships and/or prescribed channels. For example, vertical communication, shown here with solid lines, flows between levels in the organization and involves subordinates and their managers. Horizontal communication flows between people at the same level and is usually used to facilitate coordination.

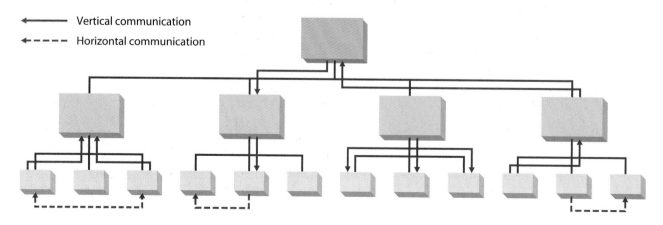

DILBERT by Scott Adams reprinted by permission of United Feature Syndicate, Inc.

Vertical Communication

Vertical communication is communication that flows both up and down the organization, usually along formal reporting lines—that is, it is the communication that takes place between managers and their superiors and subordinates. Vertical communication may involve only two people, or it may flow through several different organizational levels. A common perspective on vertical communication that exists in some organizations is illustrated in the cartoon.

Upward communication consists of messages from subordinates to superiors. This flow is usually from subordinates to their direct superior, then to that person's direct superior, and so on up the hierarchy. Occasionally, a message might bypass a particular superior. The typical content of upward communication is requests, information that the lower-level manager thinks is of importance to the higher-level manager, responses to requests from the higher-level manager, suggestions, complaints, and financial information. Research has shown that upward communication is more subject to distortion than is downward communication. Subordinates are likely to withhold or distort information that makes them look bad. The greater the degree of difference in status between superior and subordinate and the greater the degree of distrust, the more likely the subordinate is to suppress or distort information.[10] For example, subordinates might choose to withhold information about problems from their boss if they thought the news would make him angry and if they thought they could solve the problem themselves without his ever knowing about it.

Downward communication occurs when information flows down the hierarchy from superiors to subordinates. The typical content of these messages is directives on how something is to be done, the assignment of new responsibilities, performance feedback, and general information that the higher-level manager thinks will be of value to the lower-level manager. Vertical communication can, and usually should, be two-way in nature. That is, give-and-take communication with active feedback is generally likely to be more effective than one-way communication.[11]

Horizontal Communication

Whereas vertical communication involves a superior and a subordinate, **horizontal communication** involves colleagues and peers at the same level of the organization. For example, an operations manager might communicate to a marketing manager that inventory levels are running

Vertical communication is communication that flows up and down the organizational hierarchy, usually along formal reporting channels involving supervisors and subordinates. In some organizational settings, generally those characterized by trust and openness, anyone can feel free to talk to others several levels higher or lower in the organization. But in other cases, such as the one shown here, individuals who bypass the formal chain of command can create serious problems for themselves. This result usually relates to a feeling of insecurity or strong needs for power and control on the part of those who may feel bypassed.

vertical communication Communication that flows up and down the organization, usually along formal reporting lines; it takes place between managers and their subordinates and may involve several different levels of the organization

horizontal communication Communication that flows laterally within the organization; it involves colleagues and peers at the same level of the organization and may involve individuals from several different organizational units

low and that projected delivery dates should be extended by two weeks. Horizontal communication probably occurs more among managers than among nonmanagers.

This type of communication serves a number of purposes.[12] It facilitates coordination among interdependent units. For example, a manager at Motorola was once researching the strategies of Japanese semiconductor firms in Europe. He found a great deal of information that was relevant to his assignment. He also uncovered some additional information that was potentially important to another department; so he passed it along to a colleague in that department, who used it to improve his own operations. Horizontal communication can also be used for joint problem solving, as when two plant managers at Northrup Grumman got together to work out a new method to improve productivity. Finally, horizontal communication plays a major role in work teams with members drawn from several departments.

Electronic Communication

information technology (IT) Refers to the resources used by an organization to manage information that it needs to carry out its mission

An increasingly important form of organization communication relies on electronic communication technology. **Information technology**, or **IT**, refers to the resources used by an organization to manage information that it needs to carry out its mission. IT may consist of computers, computer networks, telephones, facsimile machines, and other pieces of hardware. In addition, IT involves software that facilitates the system's abilities to manage information in a way that is useful for managers.[13] Both formal information systems and personal informational technology have reshaped how managers communicate with one another.

Formal Information Systems

Organizations can use various kinds of information systems. The six most general kinds of information systems are transaction processing systems, basic management information systems, decision support systems, executive support systems, intranets, and expert systems.

transaction processing systems (TPS) Applications of information processing for basic day-to-day business transactions

Transaction Processing Systems   **Transaction processing systems (TPS)** are applications of information processing for basic day-to-day business transactions. Customer order taking by online retailers, approval of claims at insurance companies, receiving and confirming reservations by airlines, payroll processing, and bill payment at almost every company—all are routine business processes. Typically, the TPS for first-level (operational) activities is well defined, with predetermined data requirements, and follows the same steps to complete all transactions in the system.

management information systems (MIS) Support an organization's managers by providing daily reports, schedules, plans, and budgets

Management Information Systems   **Management information systems (MIS)** support an organization's managers by providing daily reports, schedules, plans, and budgets. Each manager's information activities vary according to his or her functional area (say, accounting or marketing) and management level. Whereas midlevel managers focus mostly on internal activities and information, higher-level managers are also engaged in external activities. Middle managers, the largest MIS user group, need networked information to plan such upcoming activities as personnel training, materials movements, and cash flows. They also need to know the current status of the jobs and projects being carried out in their departments: What stage is it at now? When will it be finished? Is there an opening so we can start the next job? Many of a firm's management information systems—cash flow, sales, production scheduling, shipping—are indispensable for helping managers find answers to such questions.

Electronic communication technology is profoundly changing the way people work. Anny Wong, for example, is a sales representative for Caterpillar. Her cell phone makes it possible for her to quickly get new information from corporate headquarters that clients need in order to keep their equipment moving. She is shown here expediting an order for new parts from a U.S. distribution center to be shipped by courier to a construction site in the People's Republic of China.

Decision Support Systems   Middle and top-level managers receive decision-making assistance from a **decision support system (DSS),** an interactive system that locates and presents information needed to support the decision-making process. Whereas some DSSs are devoted to specific problems, others serve more general purposes, allowing managers to analyze different types of problems. Thus a firm that often faces decisions on plant capacity, for example, may have a capacity DSS: The manager inputs data on anticipated levels of sales, working capital, and customer delivery requirements. Then the DSS's built-in transaction processors manipulate the data and make recommendations on the best levels of plant capacity for each future time period. In contrast, a general-purpose system, such as a marketing DSS, might respond to a variety of marketing-related problems. It may be programmed to handle "what-if" questions, such as "When is the best time to introduce a new product if my main competitor introduces one in three months, our new product has an 18-month expected life, demand is seasonal with a peak in the autumn, and my goal is to gain the largest possible market share?" The DSS can assist in decisions for which predetermined solutions are unknown by using sophisticated modeling tools and data analysis.

decision support system (DSS)
An interactive system that locates and presents information needed to support the decision-making process in an organization

Executive Support Systems   An **executive support system (ESS)** is a quick-reference, easy-access application of information systems specially designed for instant access by upper-level managers. ESSs are designed to assist with executive-level decisions and problems, ranging from "What lines of business should we be in five years from now?" to "Based on forecasted developments in electronic technologies, to what extent should our firm be globalized in five years? in ten years?" The ESS also uses a wide range of both internal information and external sources, such

executive support system (ESS)
A quick-reference, easy-access application of information systems specially designed for instant access by upper-level managers

as industry reports, global economic forecasts, and reports on competitors' capabilities. Because senior-level managers do not usually possess advanced computer skills, they prefer systems that are easily accessible and adaptable. Accordingly, ESSs are not designed to address only specific, predetermined problems. Instead, they allow the user some flexibility in attacking a variety of problem situations. They are easily accessible by means of simple keyboard strokes or even voice commands.

intranet A private network that functions much like the Internet

Intranets The success of the Internet has led some companies to extend the Net's technology internally, for browsing internal web sites containing information throughout the firm. These private networks, or **intranets**, are accessible only to employees via entry through electronic firewalls. Security barriers called *firewalls* are used to limit access to an intranet. At Compaq Computer, the intranet allows employees to shuffle their retirement savings among various investment funds. Ford's intranet connects 120,000 workstations in Asia, Europe, and the United States to thousands of Ford web sites containing private information on Ford activities in production, engineering, distribution, and marketing. Sharing such information has helped reduce the lead time for getting models into production from 36 to 24 months. Ford's latest project in improving customer service through internal information sharing is called "manufacturing on demand." Now, for example, the Mustang that required 50 days' delivery time in 1996 is available in less than two weeks. The savings to Ford, of course, will be billions of dollars in inventory and fixed costs.[14]

expert system An information system designed to imitate the thought processes of human experts in a particular field

Expert Systems Expert systems are also becoming more and more practical. An **expert system** is an information system designed to imitate the thought processes of human experts in a particular field. Expert systems incorporate the rules that an expert applies to specific types of problems, such as the judgments that a physician makes for diagnosing illnesses. In effect, expert systems supply everyday users with "instant expertise." General Electric's Socrates Quick Quote, for example, imitates the decisions of a real estate expert and then places a package of recommendations about real estate transactions at the fingertips of real estate dealers on GE's private computer network. A system called MOCA (for Maintenance Operations Center Advisor), by imitating the thought processes of a maintenance manager, schedules routine maintenance for American Airlines' entire fleet.

Personal Electronic Technology

The nature of organizational communication continues to change dramatically, mainly because of breakthroughs in personal electronic communication technology, and the future promises even more change. Electronic typewriters and photocopying machines were early breakthroughs. The photocopier, for example, enables a manager to distribute a typed report to many people in an extremely short time. Personal computers have accelerated the process even more. E-mail systems, the Internet, and corporate intranets promise to carry communication technology even further in the years to come.

It is now possible to have teleconferences in which managers stay at their own locations (such as offices in different cities) but are seen on television or computer monitors as they "meet." A manager in New York can keyboard a letter or memorandum at her personal computer, point and click with a mouse, and have it delivered to hundreds or even thousands of colleagues around the world in a matter of seconds. Highly detailed information can be retrieved with ease from large electronic databanks. This has given rise to a new version of an old work arrangement—telecommuting is the label given to a new electronic cottage industry. In a cottage industry, people work at home (in their "cottages") and periodically bring the product of their labor in to the company. In telecommuting, people work at home on their computers and transmit their work to the company by means of telephone or cable modems.

Cellular telephones and facsimile machines have made it even easier for managers to communicate with one another. Many now use cellular phones to make calls while commuting to and from work, and carry them in briefcases so they can receive calls while at lunch. Facsimile machines make it easy for people to use written communication media and get rapid feedback. And new personal computing devices (called PDAs, or personal digital assistants) such as Palm Pilots are further revolutionizing how people communicate with one another.

Psychologists, however, are beginning to associate some problems with these communication advances. For one thing, managers who are seldom in their "real" offices are likely to fall behind in their fields and to be victimized by organizational politics because they are not present to keep in touch with what's going on and to protect themselves. They drop out of the organizational grapevine and miss out on much of the informal communication that takes place. Moreover, the use of electronic communication at the expense of face-to-face meetings and conversations makes it hard to build a strong culture, develop solid working relationships, and create a mutually supportive atmosphere of trust and cooperativeness.[15] Finally, electronic communication is also opening up new avenues for dysfunctional employee behavior, such as the passing of lewd or offensive materials to others. For example, the New York Times recently fired almost 10 percent of its workers at one of its branch offices for sending inappropriate e-mails at work.[16]

Informal Communication in Organizations

The aforementioned forms of organizational communication all represent planned, formal communication mechanisms. However, in many cases, much of the communication that takes place in an organization transcends these formal channels and instead follows any of several informal methods. Figure 12.4 illustrates numerous examples of informal communication. Common forms of informal communication in organizations include the grapevine, management by wandering around, and nonverbal communication.

Figure 12.4

Informal Communication in Organizations

Informal communication in organizations may or may not follow official reporting relationships and/or prescribed channels. It may cross different levels and different departments or work units, and may or may not have anything to do with official organizational business.

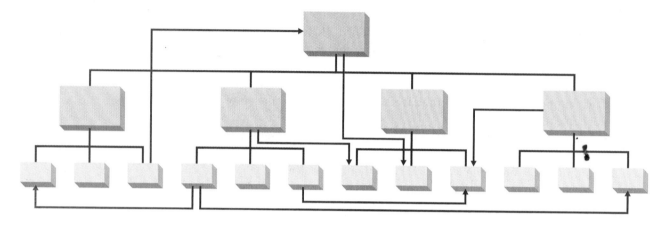

The Grapevine

grapevine An informal communication network among people in an organization

The **grapevine** is an informal communication network that can permeate an entire organization. Grapevines are found in all organizations except the very smallest, but they do not always follow the same patterns as, nor do they necessarily coincide with, formal channels of authority and communication. There is some disagreement about how accurate the information carried by the grapevine is, but research is increasingly finding it to be fairly accurate, especially when the information is based on fact rather than speculation. One study found that the grapevine may be between 75 percent and 95 percent accurate.[17] That same study also found that informal communication is increasing in many organizations for two basic reasons. One contributing factor is the recent increase in merger, acquisition, and takeover activity. Because such activity can greatly affect the people within an organization, it follows that they may spend more time talking about it.[18] The second contributing factor is that, as more and more corporations move facilities from inner cities to suburbs, employees tend to talk less and less to others outside the organization and more and more to each other.

Attempts to eliminate the grapevine are fruitless, but fortunately the manager does have some control over it. By maintaining open channels of communication and responding vigorously to inaccurate information, the manager can minimize the damage the grapevine can do. The grapevine can actually be an asset. By learning who the key people in the grapevine are, for example, the manager can partially control the information they receive and use the grapevine to sound out employee reactions to new ideas, such as a change in human resource policies or benefit packages. The manager can also get valuable information from the grapevine and use it to improve decision making.[19]

Management by Wandering Around

Another popular form of informal communication is called **management by wandering around**.[20] The basic idea is that some managers keep in touch with what's going on by wandering around and talking with people—immediate subordinates, subordinates far down the organizational hierarchy, delivery people, customers, or anyone else who is involved with the company in some way. Bill Marriott, for example, frequently visits the kitchens, loading docks, and custodial work areas whenever he tours a Marriott hotel. He claims that, by talking with employees throughout the hotel, he gets new ideas and has a better feel for the entire company.

A related form of organizational communication that really has no specific term is the informal interchange that takes place outside the normal work setting. Employees attending the company picnic, playing on the company softball team, or taking fishing trips together will almost always spend part of their time talking about work. For example, Texas Instruments engineers at TI's Lewisville, Texas, facility often frequent a local bar in town after work. On any given evening, they talk about the Dallas Cowboys, the newest government contract received by the company, the weather, their boss, the company's stock price, local politics, and problems at work. There is no set agenda, and the key topics of discussion vary from group to group and from day to day. Still, the social gatherings serve an important role. They promote a strong culture and enhance understanding of how the organization works.

Nonverbal Communication

Nonverbal communication is a communication exchange that does not use words or that uses words to carry more meaning than the strict definition of the words themselves. Nonverbal communication is a powerful but little-understood form of communication in organizations. It often relies on facial expression, body movements, physical contact, and gestures. One study found that as much as 55 percent of the content of a message is transmitted by facial expression and body posture and that another 38 percent derives from inflection and tone. Words themselves account for only 7 percent of the content of the message.[21]

Research has identified three kinds of nonverbal communication practiced by managers: images, settings, and body language.[22] In this context, images are the kinds of words people elect to use. "Damn the torpedoes, full speed ahead" and "Even though there are some potential hazards, we should proceed with this course of action" may convey the same meaning. Yet the person who uses the first expression may be perceived as a maverick, a courageous hero, an individualist, or a reckless and foolhardy adventurer. The person who uses the second might be described as aggressive, forceful, diligent, or narrow-minded and resistant to change. In short, our choice of words conveys much more than just the strict meaning of the words themselves.

The setting for communication also plays a major role in nonverbal communication. Boundaries, familiarity, the home turf, and other elements of the setting

management by wandering around An approach to communication that involves the manager's literally wandering around and having spontaneous conversations with others

nonverbal communication Any communication exchange that does not use words or that uses words to carry more meaning than the strict definition of the words themselves

are all important. Much has been written about the symbols of power in organizations. The size and location of an office, the kinds of furniture in the office, and the accessibility of the person in the office all communicate useful information. For example, H. Ross Perot positions his desk so that it is always between him and a visitor. This keeps him in charge. When he wants a less formal dialogue, he moves around to the front of the desk and sits beside his visitor. Michael Dell of Dell Computers has his desk facing a side window, so that when he turns around to greet a visitor there is never anything between them.

A third form of nonverbal communication is body language.[23] The distance we stand from someone as we speak has meaning. In the United States, standing very close to someone to whom you are talking generally signals either familiarity or aggression. The English and Germans stand farther apart than Americans when talking, whereas the Arabs, Japanese, and Mexicans stand closer together.[24] Eye contact is another effective means of nonverbal communication. For example, prolonged eye contact might suggest either hostility or romantic interest. Other kinds of body language include body and arm movement, pauses in speech, and mode of dress.

The manager should be aware of the importance of nonverbal communication and recognize its potential impact. Giving an employee good news about a reward with the wrong nonverbal cues can destroy the reinforcement value of the reward. Likewise, reprimanding an employee but providing inconsistent nonverbal cues can limit the effectiveness of the sanctions. The tone of the message, where and how the message is delivered, facial expressions, and gestures can all amplify or weaken the message, or change the message altogether.

Managing Organizational Communication

In view of the importance and pervasiveness of communication in organizations, it is vital for managers to understand how to manage the communication process. Managers should understand how to maximize the potential benefits of communication and minimize the potential problems. We begin our discussion of communication management by considering the factors that might disrupt effective communication and how to deal with them.

Barriers to Communication

Several factors may disrupt the communication process or serve as barriers to effective communication.[25] *Management InfoTech* illustrates how technology itself can be a barrier to effective communication. As shown in Table 12.1, these may be divided into two classes: individual barriers and organizational barriers.

Individual Barriers   Several individual barriers may disrupt effective communication. One common problem is conflicting or inconsistent signals. A manager is sending conflicting signals when she says on Monday that things should be done one way, but then prescribes an entirely different procedure on Wednesday. Incon-

TONE DOWN THE TECHNOLOGY—AND THAT'S AN ORDER!

The U.S. military is going back to communication basics. The chairman of the Joint Chiefs of Staff has ordered military personnel to tone down the technology in their electronic slide presentations, because the razzle-dazzle is detracting from the message. From noisy sound effects to eye-popping animation and convoluted diagrams, military presentations are so laden with flashy extras that listeners sometimes have difficulty distilling the main ideas.

Formal slide presentations have a long tradition within the U.S. military, where they have been used to update commanders about troop movements. Now, jazzy electronic slide presentations have taken the place of static overheads as up-and-coming officers try to impress their superiors by cramming every possible detail into their presentations. Too often, these presentations wind up as a war of graphics, with presenters adding more electronic bells and whistles so that they will stand out.

Listeners complain that these electronic slide shows can be endless and mind numbing—the last reaction a presenter wants when discussing sensitive defense issues or asking for increased funding. In fact, Navy Secretary Richard Danzig wants his briefings submitted in writing so that he won't have to sit through presentation after presentation with electronic slide accompaniment.

Because electronic slides are easy and inexpensive to create, military personnel in other countries are starting to use the technology to enliven presentations to their commanders. Meanwhile, electronic slide shows are not disappearing from military briefings throughout the Pentagon, although they are becoming somewhat simpler in response to the growing backlash from the top. And organizations that work with the U.S. military have adopted electronic slide presentations to show they can speak the same graphics language as their audience.

> *People are not listening to us, because they are spending so much time trying to understand these incredibly complex slides.*
>
> —*Louis Caldera, U.S. Secretary of the Army**

References: Greg Jaffe, "What's Your Point, Lieutenant? Just Cut to the Pie Charts," *Wall Street Journal*, April 26, 2000, pp. A1, A6 (*quote on p. A1).

---

sistent signals are being sent by a manager who says that he has an "open-door" policy and wants his subordinates to drop by, but keeps his door closed and becomes irritated whenever someone stops in.

Another barrier is lack of credibility. Credibility problems arise when the sender is not considered a reliable source of information. He may not be trusted or may not be perceived as knowledgeable about the subject at hand. When a

Individual Barriers	Organizational Barriers
Conflicting or inconsistent signals	Semantics
Lack of credibility	Status or power differences
Reluctance to communicate	Different perceptions
Poor listening habits	Noise
Predispositions about the subject	Overload
	Language differences

Table 12.1

Barriers to Effective Communication
Numerous barriers can disrupt effective communication. Some of these barriers involve individual characteristics and processes. Others are a function of the organizational context in which communication is taking place.

politician is caught withholding information or when a manager makes a series of bad decisions, the extent to which they will be listened to and believed thereafter diminishes. In extreme cases, people may talk about something they obviously know little or nothing about.

Some people are simply reluctant to initiate a communication exchange. This reluctance may occur for a variety of reasons. A manager may be reluctant to tell subordinates about an impending budget cut because he knows they will be unhappy about it. Likewise, a subordinate may be reluctant to transmit information upward for fear of reprisal or because it is felt that such an effort would be futile.

Poor listening habits can be a major barrier to effective communication. Some people are simply poor listeners. When someone is talking to them, they may be daydreaming, looking around, reading, or listening to another conversation. Because they are not concentrating on what is being said, they may not comprehend part of the message. They may even think that they really are paying attention, only to realize later that they cannot remember parts of the conversation.

Receivers may also bring certain predispositions to the communication process. They may already have their minds made up, firmly set in a certain way. For example, a manager may have heard that his new boss is unpleasant and hard to work with. When she calls him in for an introductory meeting, he may go into that meeting predisposed to dislike her and discount what she has to say.

Organizational Barriers   Other barriers to effective communication involve the organizational context in which the communication occurs. Semantics problems arise when words have different meanings for different people. Words and phrases such as *profit*, *increased output*, and *return on investment* may have positive meanings for managers but less positive meanings for labor.

Communication problems may also arise when people of different power or status try to communicate with each other. The company president may discount a suggestion from an operating employee, thinking, "How can someone at that level help me run my business?" Or, when the president goes out to inspect a new plant, workers may be reluctant to offer suggestions because of their lower status. The marketing vice president may have more power than the human resource vice president and consequently may not pay much attention to a staffing report submitted by the human resource department.

If people perceive a situation differently, they may have difficulty communicating with one another. When two managers observe that a third manager has not spent much time in her office lately, one may believe that she has been to several important meetings, whereas the other may think she is "hiding out." If they need to talk about her in some official capacity, problems may arise because one has a positive impression and the other, a negative impression.

Environmental factors may also disrupt effective communication. As mentioned earlier, noise may affect communication in many ways. Similarly, overload may be a problem when the receiver is being sent more information than he or she can effectively handle. As e-mail becomes increasingly common, many managers report getting so many messages each day as to sometimes feel overwhelmed.[26] And, when the manager gives a subordinate many jobs on which to work and at the same time the subordinate is being told by family and friends to do other things, overload may result, and communication effectiveness diminishes.

Finally, as businesses become more and more global, different languages can create problems. To counter this problem, some firms are adopting an "official language." For example, when the German chemical firm Hoechst merged with the French firm Rhone-Poulenc, the new company adopted English as its official language. Indeed, English is increasingly becoming the standard business language around the world.[27]

Improving Communication Effectiveness

Considering how many factors can disrupt communication, it is fortunate that managers can resort to several techniques for improving communication effectiveness. As shown in Table 12.2, these techniques include both individual and organizational skills.

Individual Skills   The single most important individual skill for improving communication effectiveness is being a good listener.[28] Being a good listener requires that the individual be prepared to listen, not interrupt the speaker, concentrate on both the words and the meaning being conveyed, be patient, and ask questions as appropriate.[29] So important are good listening skills that companies like Delta, IBM, and Boeing conduct programs to train their managers to be better listeners. Figure 12.5 illustrates the characteristics of poor listeners versus good listeners.

In addition to being a good listener, several other individual skills can also promote effective communication. Feedback, one of the most important, is facilitated by two-way communication. Two-way communication allows the receiver to ask questions, request clarification, and express opinions that let the sender know whether he or she has been understood. In general, the more complicated the message, the more useful two-way communication is. In addition, the sender should be aware of the meanings that different receivers might attach to various words. For example, when addressing stockholders, a manager might use the word *profits* often. When addressing labor leaders, however, she may choose to use *profits* less often.

Individual Skills	Organizational Skills
Develop good listening skills	Follow up
Encourage two-way communication	Regulate information flows
Be aware of language and meaning	Understand the richness of media
Maintain credibility	
Be sensitive to receiver's perspective	
Be sensitive to sender's perspective	

Table 12.2

Overcoming Barriers to Communication
Because communication is so important, managers have developed a number of methods for overcoming barriers to effective communication. Some of these methods involve individual skills, whereas others are based on organizational skills.

Figure 12.5

More and Less Effective Listening Skills

Effective listening skills are a vital part of communication in organizations. There are several barriers that can contribute to poor listening skills by individuals in organizations. Fortunately, there are also several practices for improving listening skills.

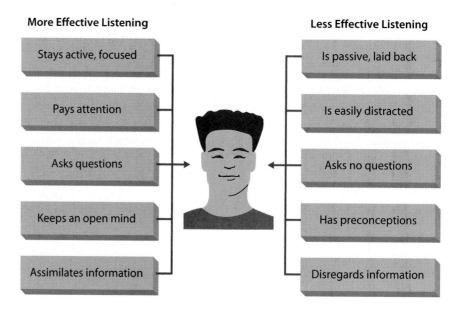

Furthermore, the sender should try to maintain credibility. This can be accomplished by not pretending to be an expert when one is not, by "doing one's homework" and checking facts, and by otherwise being as accurate and honest as possible. The sender should also try to be sensitive to the receiver's perspective. A manager who must tell a subordinate that she has not been recommended for a promotion should recognize that the subordinate will be frustrated and unhappy. The content of the message and its method of delivery should be chosen accordingly. The manager should be primed to accept a reasonable degree of hostility and bitterness without getting angry in return. Finally, the receiver should also try to be sensitive to the sender's point of view. Suppose that a manager has just received some bad news—for example, that his position is being eliminated next year. Others should understand that he may be disappointed, angry, or even depressed for a while. Thus they might make a special effort not to take too much offense if he snaps at them, and they might look for signals that he needs someone to talk to.

Organizational Skills   Three useful organizational skills can also enhance communication effectiveness for both the sender and the receiver—following up, regulating information flows, and understanding the richness of different media. Following up simply involves checking at a later time to be sure that a message has been received and understood. After a manager mails a report to a colleague, she might call a few days later to make sure the report has arrived. If it has, the manager might ask whether the colleague has any questions about it. Regulating information flows means that the sender or receiver takes steps to ensure that overload does not occur.

For the sender, this could mean not passing too much information through the system at one time. For the receiver, it might mean calling attention to the fact that he is being asked to do too many things at once. Many managers limit the influx of information by periodically weeding out the list of journals and routine reports they receive, or they train a secretary to screen phone calls and visitors. Both parties should also understand the richness associated with different media. When a manager is going to lay off a subordinate temporarily, the message should be delivered in person. A face-to-face channel of communication gives the manager an opportunity to explain the situation and answer questions. When the purpose of the message is to grant a pay increase, written communication may be appropriate because it can be more objective and precise. The manager could then follow up the written notice with personal congratulations.

Summary of Key Points

Communication is the process of transmitting information from one person to another. Effective communication is the process of sending a message in such a way that the message received is as close in meaning as possible to the message intended.

Communication is a pervasive and important part of the manager's world. The communication process consists of a sender's encoding meaning and transmitting it to one or more receivers, who receive the message and decode it into meaning. In two-way communication, the process continues with the roles reversed. Noise can disrupt any part of the overall process.

Several forms of organizational communication exist. Interpersonal communication focuses on communication among a small number of people. Two important forms of interpersonal communication, oral and written, both offer unique advantages and disadvantages. Thus the manager should weigh the pros and cons of each when choosing a medium for communication. Communication networks are recurring patterns of communication among members of a group or work team. Vertical communication between superiors and subordinates may flow upward or downward. Horizontal communication involves peers and colleagues at the same level in the organization.

Electronic communication is having a profound effect on managerial and organizational communication. The kinds of information systems are transaction processing systems, basic management information systems, decision support systems, executive support systems, intranets, and expert systems. Each provides certain types of information and is most valuable for specific types of managers.

There is also a great deal of informal communication in organizations. The grapevine is the informal communication network among people in an organization. Management by wandering around is also a popular informal method of communication. Nonverbal communication includes facial expressions, body movement, physical contact, gestures, and inflection and tone.

Managing the communication process necessitates recognizing the barriers to effective communication and understanding how to overcome them. Barriers can be identified at both the individual and the organizational level. Likewise, both individual and organizational skills can be used to overcome these barriers.

Discussion Questions

Questions for Review

1. Define communication. What are the components of the communication process?

2. Which form of interpersonal communication is best for long-term retention? Why? Which form is best for getting across subtle nuances of meaning? Why?

3. Describe three different communication networks. Which type of network seems to most accurately describe the grapevine? Why?

4. Identify and describe the basic kinds of information systems commonly used in organizations today.

5. What are the informal methods of communication? Identify five examples of nonverbal communication that you have recently observed.

Questions for Analysis

6. Is it possible for an organization to function without communication? Why or why not?

7. At what points in the communication process can problems occur? Give examples of communication problems and indicate how they might be prevented or alleviated.

8. How are electronic communication devices likely to affect the communication process in the future? Why?

9. Do you participate in one or more grapevines? Would you say they are relatively accurate?

10. In terms of the barriers most likely to be encountered, what are the differences between horizontal and vertical communication in an organization? How might a formal information system be designed to reduce such barriers?

BUILDING EFFECTIVE *technical* SKILLS

Exercise Overview

Technical skills are the skills necessary to perform the work of the organization. This exercise helps you develop and apply technical skills involving the Internet and its potential for gathering information relevant to making important decisions.

Exercise Background

Assume that you are a manager for a large national retailer. You have been assigned the responsibility for identifying potential locations for the construction of a warehouse and distribution center. The idea behind such a center is that the firm can use its enormous purchasing power to buy many products in large bulk quantities at relatively low prices. Individual stores can then order specific quantities they need from the warehouse.

The location will need an abundance of land. The warehouse itself, for example, will occupy more than four square acres of land. In addition, the location needs to be close to railroads and major highways; shipments will be arriving by both rail and trucks, although outbound shipments will be exclusively by truck. Other important variables are that land prices and the cost of living should be relatively low and that weather conditions should be mild (to minimize disruptions to shipments).

The firm's general experience is that small to midsize communities work best. Moreover, warehouses are already in place in the western and eastern parts of the United States, so this new one will most likely be in the central or south-central area. Your boss has asked you to identify three or four potential sites.

Exercise Task

With the information above as a framework, do the following:

1. Use the Internet to identify up to ten possible locations.
2. Use additional information from the Internet to narrow the set of possible locations to three or four.
3. Finally, use the Internet to find out as much as possible about the potential locations.

BUILDING EFFECTIVE *communication* SKILLS

Exercise Overview

Communication skills refer to a manager's ability to both effectively convey ideas and information to others and to effectively receive ideas and information from others. This exercise focuses on communication skills as they involve deciding on the best way to convey information.

Exercise Background

Assume that you are a middle manager for a large electronics firm. People in your organization generally use one of three means for communicating with one another. The most common way is verbal communication, either face to face or by telephone. E-mail is also widely used. Finally, a surprisingly large amount of communication is still paper based, such as memos, reports, and letters.

On a typical day, you receive and send a variety of messages and other communication, and you generally use some combination of all of the communication methods noted above. Here are some of the communication tasks on your to-do list for today:

1. You need to schedule a meeting with five subordinates.
2. You need to congratulate a coworker who just had a baby.
3. You need to reprimand a staff assistant who has been coming in to work late for the last several days.
4. You need to inform the warehouse staff that several customers have recently complained because their shipments were not packed properly.
5. You need to schedule a meeting with your boss.
6. You need to announce two promotions.
7. You need to fire someone who has been performing poorly for some time.
8. You need to inform several individuals about a set of new government regulations that will soon affect them.
9. You need to inform a supplier that your company will soon be cutting back on its purchases because a competing supplier has lowered its prices, and you plan to shift more of your business to that supplier.
10. You need to resolve a disagreement between two subordinates who want to take their vacation at the same time.

Exercise Task

Using the information presented above, do the following:

1. Indicate which methods of communication would be appropriate for each situation.
2. Rank-order the methods for each communication situation from best to worst.
3. Compare your rankings with those of a classmate and discuss any differences.

BUILDING EFFECTIVE *time management* SKILLS

Exercise Overview

Time management skills refer to the manager's ability to prioritize work, to work efficiently, and to delegate appropriately. This exercise helps you develop your time management skills as they relate to communication.

Exercise Background

Communication is a vital and necessary part not only of management but also of our daily lives. We benefit when communication takes place in effective ways. But ineffective communication can be a major source of wasted time and energy.

Exercise Task

With this idea as context, do the following:

1. Reflect back on your communication for one day. Recall whom you talked to, when, for how long, and about what subjects.
2. Do the same for mail you received and mail you sent.
3. Evaluate each communication exchange as being more valuable or less valuable.
4. Estimate how much time you spent on less-valuable communication.
5. Decide how you could have either avoided those less-valuable communication exchanges or made them more valuable.
6. Consider how much control we really have over our communication.

SKILLS *self-assessment* INSTRUMENT

Sex Talk Quiz

Introduction: As more women enter the workforce, communication between men and women will increase. Research shows that men and women frequently have difficulty in communicating effectively with one another because of differences in their beliefs and values about each sex. The following assessment surveys your beliefs and values about each sex.

Instructions: Mark each statement as either true or false. In some cases, you may find making a decision difficult, but you should force a choice.

	True	False
1. Women are more intuitive than men. They have a sixth sense, which is typically called "women's intuition."	[ ]	[ ]
2. At business meetings, coworkers are more likely to listen to men than they are to women.	[ ]	[ ]
3. Women are the "talkers." They talk much more than men in group conversations.	[ ]	[ ]
4. Men are the "fast talkers." They talk much more quickly than women.	[ ]	[ ]
5. Men are more outwardly open than women. They use more eye contact and exhibit more friendliness when first meeting someone than do women.	[ ]	[ ]
6. Women are more complimentary and give more praise than men.	[ ]	[ ]
7. Men interrupt more than women and will answer a question even when it is not addressed to them.	[ ]	[ ]
8. Women give more orders and are more demanding in the way they communicate than are men.	[ ]	[ ]

9. In general, men and women laugh at the same things. [] []

10. When making love, both men and women want to hear the same things from their partner. [] []

11. Men ask for assistance less often than do women. [] []

12. Men are harder on themselves and blame themselves more often than do women. [] []

13. Through their body language, women make themselves less confrontational than men. [] []

14. Men tend to explain things in greater detail when discussing an incident than do women. [] []

15. Women tend to touch others more often than men. [] []

16. Men appear to be more attentive than women when they are listening. [] []

17. Women and men are equally emotional when they speak. [] []

18. Men are more likely than women to discuss personal issues. [] []

19. Men bring up more topics of conversation than do women. [] []

20. Today we tend to raise our male children the same way we do our female children. [] []

21. Women tend to confront problems more directly and are likely to bring up the problem first. [] []

22. Men are livelier speakers who use more body language and facial animation than do women. [] []

23. Men ask more questions than women. [] []

24. In general, men and women enjoy talking about similar things. [] []

25. When asking whether their partner has had an AIDS test or when discussing safe sex, a woman will likely bring up the topic before a man. [] []

For interpretation, see Interpretations of Skills Self-Assessment Instruments.

Source: "Sex Talk Quiz," from *He Says, She Says* by Lillian Glass, Ph.D. Copyright © 1992 by Lillian Glass, Ph.D. Used by permission of G. P. Putnam's Sons, a division of Penguin Putnam Inc.

EXPERIENTIAL EXERCISE

Developing Communication Skills

Purpose: Some ways of giving instructions to people are quicker or more accurate than others. Some generate more satisfaction in or greater compliance by the recipient. It is important for you to recognize different communication models with their resulting costs and benefits. This exercise identifies the types of behaviors that assist or interfere with effective transmission of instructions. It also illustrates forms of communication and investigates the differing outcomes as well as the processes resulting from these means of communication. The exercise allows you to explore possible techniques for dealing with dysfunctional communication behaviors.

Instructions: Your instructor will provide further instructions.

Source: From Ritchie, *Organization and People: Readings, Cases, and Exercises in Organizational Behavior,* Third edition, pp. 259–261, by J. B. Ritchie and Paul Thompson. © 1984. Reprinted with permission of South-Western College Publishing, a division of International Thomson Publishing. Fax: 1-800-730-2215.

COMMUNICATION IS THE REAL THING FOR COCA-COLA

Coca-Cola was in trouble when Douglas Daft became CEO following the brief tenure of M. Douglas Ivester. The previous year, European Union regulators had raided the European offices of Coca-Cola and its bottlers, and leveled serious anticompetitive charges against the venerable soft-drink marketer. That same year, the company was hurt by negative publicity when hundreds of people in Belgium complained of headaches and nausea after drinking Coca-Cola beverages. Ultimately, Coca-Cola's products were found to have posed no health threat, but top management's slow response to the scare contributed to the firm's reputation for aggressive, arrogant behavior. This so disturbed some company executives that they departed from tradition and submitted a confidential memo criticizing Coca-Cola's actions. To complicate matters, worldwide sales were slowing due to economic woes in some countries, employee morale was lower, and the stock price was lagging.

Clearly, the company had a lot of relationships to repair by the time Daft became CEO. Daft opened a new chapter in Coca-Cola's history by taking a more conciliatory tone in his internal and external communications. Stronger stakeholder relationships, in the CEO's view, would go a long way toward helping polish Coca-Cola's image and protect its 51 percent share of the global market for fizzy soft drinks.

So Daft set out on a goodwill tour designed to improve communication around the world. In Belgium, the CEO met with the regulator who had pursued antitrust charges against Coca-Cola the year before. Daft listened intently as the regulator explained his reasoning and spoke against the company's highly aggressive behavior. Afterward, Daft said that the company had to stop arguing and start listening when competing in other countries. By strengthening relationships with regulators, Daft hoped to get a better understanding of local rules and at the same time to put Coca-Cola in a better light.

Daft also met with Italy's top antitrust regulator, who had presided over an investigation that resulted in Coca-Cola's paying a $16 million fine for anticompetitive practices. Again, the CEO sought to rebuild relations by asking what the company had done wrong and paying close attention as the regulator spoke his mind. Daft also directed the top Coca-Cola executive in Europe to find ways of working more closely with regulators, smoothing the way for business practices that fit both the company's goals and the European Union's competitive guidelines.

The goodwill tour included meetings and meals with local Coca-Cola managers, offering opportunities to talk informally about Daft's vision for the company and his strategies for building bridges to numerous constituencies. The CEO also met with the U.S. ambassador to France, several CEOs of French firms, and numerous Coca-Cola executives around Europe. Back home, Daft made it a point to stay in touch with members of the board and the bottlers who make and distribute Coca-Cola's products. By making contact with so many people inside and outside the organization, Daft was developing a more rounded picture of Coca-Cola's strengths and weaknesses.

Since his initial goodwill tour, Daft has returned to Europe a number of times to meet with managers, bottlers, and regulators. He has also brought some of his senior U.S. and European managers together in Europe to hear reports on regional results and initiatives. In line with Daft's preference for direct communication, oral presentations are shorter, more to the point, and heavier on recommendations. The CEO is also speeding up decision making, allowing Coca-Cola to bring new products to new and existing markets much faster than before. Knowing that 80 percent of the company's profits are derived from sales outside the United States, Daft is stressing decentralization rather than concentrating functions and power in Coca-Cola's Atlanta headquarters. At the same time, he is signaling his determination to keep the lines of communication open so that Coca-Cola will gain a new reputation for cooperation throughout the world.

Case Questions

1. Where in the communication process would you recommend that Daft concentrate on making changes?

2. Why would Daft bring U.S. and European executives together to make oral presentations about regional results, rather than asking them to share written reports?

3. Which barriers to communication did Daft seem to be addressing during his goodwill tour?

Case References

Betsy McKay, "New Formula to Fix Coca-Cola, Daft Sets out to Get Relationships Right," *Wall Street Journal*, June 23, 2000, p. A1, A12; and *Hoover's Handbook of American Business 2001* (Austin, TX: Hoover's Business Press, 2001), pp. 386–387.

CHAPTER NOTES

1. *Hoover's Handbook of American Business 2001* (Austin, TX: Hoover's Business Press, 2001), pp. 1054–1055; John Case, "Opening the Books," *Harvard Business Review*, March/April 1997, pp. 118–129; and Brian Dumaine, "Chaparral Steel: Unleash Workers and Cut Costs," *Fortune*, May 18, 1992, pp. 88.
2. Henry Mintzberg, *The Nature of Managerial Work* (New York: Harper & Row, 1973).
3. Edward W. Desmond, "How Your Data May Soon Seek You Out," *Fortune*, September 1997, pp. 149–154.
4. Mintzberg.
5. Reid Buckley, "When You Have to Put It to Them," *Across the Board*, October 1999, pp. 44–48.
6. "Executives Who Dread Public Speaking Learn to Keep Their Cool in the Spotlight," *Wall Street Journal*, May 4, 1990, pp. B1, B6.
7. Mintzberg.
8. Buckley.
9. A. Vavelas, "Communication Patterns in Task-oriented Groups," *Journal of the Accoustical Society of America* 22 (1950): 725–730; and Jerry Wofford, Edwin Gerloff, and Robert Cummins, *Organizational Communication* (New York: McGraw-Hill, 1977).
10. Walter Kiechel III, "Breaking Bad News to the Boss," *Fortune*, April 9, 1990, pp. 111–112.
11. Mary Young and James Post, "How Leading Companies Communicate with Employees," *Organizational Dynamics*, Summer 1993, pp. 31–43.
12. For one example, see Kimberly D. Elsbach and Greg Elofson, "How the Packaging of Decision Explanations Affects Perceptions of Trustworthiness," *Academy of Management Journal* 43, no. 1 (2000): 80–89.
13. Donald A. Marchand, William J. Kettinger, and John D. Rollins, "Information Orientation: People, Technology, and the Bottom Line," *Sloan Management Review*, Summer 2000, pp. 69–79.
14. Mary Cronin, "Ford's Intranet Success," *Fortune*, March 30, 1998, p. 158.
15. Walter Kiechel III, "Hold for the Communicaholic Manager," *Fortune*, January 2, 1989, pp. 107–108.
16. "Those Bawdy E-Mails Were Good for a Laugh—Until the Ax Fell," *Wall Street Journal*, February 4, 2000, pp. A1, A8.
17. "Spread the Word: Gossip Is Good," *Wall Street Journal*, October 4, 1988, p. B1.
18. See David M. Schweiger and Angelo S. DeNisi, "Communication with Employees Following a Merger: A Longitudinal Field Experiment," *Academy of Management Journal*, March 1991, pp. 110–135.
19. Nancy B. Kurland and Lisa Hope Pelled, "Passing the Word: Toward a Model of Gossip and Power in the Workplace," *Academy of Management Review* 25, no. 2 (2000): 428–438.
20. See Tom Peters and Nancy Austin, *A Passion for Excellence* (New York: Random House, 1985).
21. Albert Mehrabian, *Non-verbal Communication* (Chicago: Aldine, 1972).
22. Michael B. McCaskey, "The Hidden Messages Managers Send," *Harvard Business Review*, November/December 1979, pp. 135–148.
23. David Givens, "What Body Language Can Tell You That Words Cannot," *U.S. News & World Report*, November 19, 1984, p. 100.
24. Edward J. Hall, *The Hidden Dimension* (New York: Doubleday, 1966).
25. See Otis W. Baskin and Craig E. Aronoff, *Interpersonal Communication in Organizations* (Glenview, IL: Scott, Foresman, 1980).
26. See "You Have (Too Much) E-Mail," *USA Today*, March 12, 1999, p. 3B.
27. Justin Fox, "The Triumph of English," *Fortune*, September 18, 2000, pp. 209–212.
28. See "Making Silence Your Ally," *Across the Board*, October 1999, p. 11.
29. Boyd A. Vander Houwen, "Less Talking, More Listening," *HRMagazine*, April 1997, pp. 53–58.

CHAPTER

13

Managing Groups and Teams

Few people have ever heard of a small company called Fastener Supply. The 23-year-old, 18-employee company based in Reading, Massachusetts, distributes 18,000 different types of metal, rubber, and nylon fasteners—devices used to hold together the parts that comprise everything from automobiles to personal computers to bug zappers. Motorola, Polaroid, and Lucent Technologies are among the company's biggest 350 or so customers.

No one at Fastener Supply believed that the firm had a quality problem. At the same time, however, John Jenkins, the company president, was aware of recent trends and concerns in quality management and knew that his firm needed to be ahead of the industry, not behind it. A small firm like Fastener Supply can really suffer from the loss of only one big customer, so Jenkins de-cided to be proactive with regard to quality.

An initial quality audit revealed no significant customer complaints. And on a percentage basis, things seemed to be fine. For example, less than 1 percent of the firm's fasteners failed to meet customer standards. But in absolute terms, the numbers didn't look quite so good. Because the firm ships over 70 million products a year, that meant that about 112,000 fasteners were returned each year due to a quality problem. Jenkins decided to cut that rate to 500 per million.

To tackle this problem, Jenkins created a team of three employees, one each from purchasing, sales, and quality control. The group was named the Continuous Improvement Team, or CIT, and given the charge of reducing the customer rejection rate by 50 percent. The team members were initially concerned about meeting such an ambitious goal but quickly set to work.

They decided to focus their efforts on three areas: supplier quality, customer feedback, and training. Fastener Supply doesn't actually make fasteners at all, but instead buys them from a variety of fastener manufacturers. The CIT instructed each of the firm's suppliers to improve their own quality for production and delivery or risk losing business. Some suppliers did indeed balk, and 37 were dropped from Fastener Supply's supplier network. The remaining 250 or so did meet the new standards and continue to have a strong relationship with the firm.

The CIT also sought feedback about areas where customers were not unhappy but where there was still room for improvement. Almost

"Staying still wasn't going to cut it anymore."

—John Jenkins,
president of Fastener Supply*

After studying this chapter, you should be able to

- Define and identify types of groups and teams in organizations, discuss reasons people join groups and teams, and the stages of group and team development.

- Identify and discuss four essential characteristics of groups and teams.

- Discuss interpersonal and intergroup conflict in organizations.

- Describe how organizations manage conflict.

40 useful suggestions were received and implemented. For example, one suggestion was that a Fastener Supply representative inform customers in advance when a shipment was going to be delayed for even a day or two. Although the firm had been doing this for extended delays, it was easy enough to begin doing it routinely. Finally, the CIT also suggested that all employees at Fastener Supply receive more training in every phase of the operation, ranging from packing and loading boxes to logging inventory in computers. As a result, virtually all phases of the firm's operations improved as well. For example, the year after shipping employees received better training, only 2 of the 7,000 boxes shipped were returned with parts damaged from bad packing.

By virtually any measure, the CIT has been a big success for Fastener Supply. It actually beat its lofty quality improvement goal by driving defects down to only 216 per million, a phenom-

enally low level. In addition, the firm's business has been increasing at a rapid pace, as word of its quality spreads throughout the industry. But neither the firm nor the CIT are finished. Indeed, the mantra heard throughout Fastener Supply today is achieving the ultimate goal—zero defects. Although this ideal may never truly be reached, Fastener Supply's CIT vows to keep working toward it.[1]

John Jenkins at Fastener Supply recognized and took advantage of what many experts are increasingly seeing as a tremendous resource for all organizations—the power of groups and teams. When he needed some changes made at his firm, Jenkins could have just mandated them himself. Or he could have hired an outside consulting firm to tell his employees how to improve. Instead, he created a team of employees and allowed them to figure it out themselves.

This chapter is about processes that lead to and follow from activities like those at Fastener Supply. We first introduce and discuss basic concepts of group and team dynamics. Subsequent sections explain the characteristics of groups and teams in organizations. We then describe interpersonal and intergroup conflict. Finally, we conclude with a discussion of how conflict can be managed.

Groups and Teams in Organizations

group Consists of two or more people who interact regularly to accomplish a common purpose or goal

Groups are a ubiquitous part of organizational life. They are the basis for much of the work that gets done, and they evolve both inside and outside the normal structural boundaries of the organization. We will define a **group** as two or more people who interact regularly to accomplish a common purpose or goal.[2] The purpose of a group or team may range from preparing a new advertising campaign, to informally sharing information, to making important decisions, or to fulfilling social needs.

Types of Groups and Teams

In general, three basic kinds of groups are found in organizations—functional groups, informal or interest groups, and task groups and teams.[3] These are illustrated in Figure 13.1.

Task groups are created by the organization to accomplish a relatively narrow range of purposes within a stated or implied time horizon. Take this group of software engineers, for example. They work for Trilogy Software, a high-tech firm based in Austin, Texas. The group is working on the development of a new software application program. Once the program is finished, the task group members will return to their previous responsibilities.

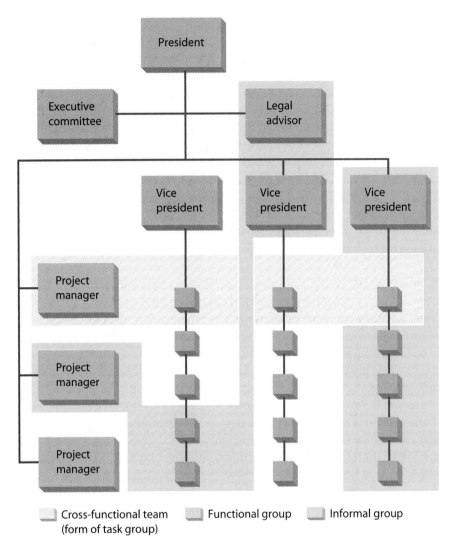

Figure 13.1

Types of Groups in Organizations
Every organization has many different types of groups. In this hypothetical organization, a functional group is shown within the blue area, a cross-functional group within the yellow area, and an informal group within the green area.

President

Executive committee

Legal advisor

Vice president

Vice president

Vice president

Project manager

Project manager

Project manager

Cross-functional team (form of task group)   Functional group   Informal group

Functional Groups A **functional group** is a permanent group created by the organization to accomplish a number of organizational purposes with an unspecified time horizon. The advertising department at Kmart, the management department at the University of North Texas, and the nursing staff at the Mayo Clinic are functional groups. The advertising department at Kmart, for example, seeks to plan effective advertising campaigns, increase sales, run in-store promotions, and develop a unique identity for the company. It is assumed that the functional group will remain in existence after it attains its current objectives; those objectives will be replaced by new ones.

Informal or Interest Groups An **informal or interest group** is created by its own members for purposes that may or may not be relevant to organizational goals. It also has an unspecified time horizon. A group of employees who lunch

functional group A group created by the organization to accomplish a number of organizational purposes with an indefinite time horizon

informal or interest group Created by its members for purposes that may or may not be relevant to those of the organization

together every day may be discussing how to improve productivity, how to embezzle money, or local politics and sports. As long as the group members enjoy eating together, they will probably continue to do so. When lunches cease to be pleasant, they will seek other company or a different activity.

Informal groups can be a powerful force that managers cannot ignore. One writer described how a group of employees at a furniture factory subverted their boss's efforts to increase production. They tacitly agreed to produce a reasonable amount of work but not to work too hard. One man kept a stockpile of completed work hidden as a backup in case he got too far behind. In another example, auto workers described how they left out gaskets and seals and put soft-drink bottles inside doors.[4] Of course, informal groups can also be a positive force, as demonstrated recently when Continental Airlines' employees worked together to buy a new motorcycle for Gordon Bethune, the company's CEO, to show their support and gratitude for his excellent leadership.

task group   A group created by the organization to accomplish a relatively narrow range of purposes within a stated or implied time horizon

Task Groups   A **task group** is a group created by the organization to accomplish a relatively narrow range of purposes within a stated or implied time horizon. Most committees and task forces are task groups. The organization specifies group membership and assigns a relatively narrow set of goals, such as developing a new product or evaluating a proposed grievance procedure. The time horizon for accomplishing these purposes is either specified (a committee may be asked to make a recommendation within 60 days) or implied (the project team will disband when the new product is developed). *Management InfoTech* describes how organizations can use intranets to create task groups in new and innovative ways.

team   A group of workers that functions as a unit, often with little or no supervision, to carry out work-related tasks, functions, and activities

Teams are a special form of task group that have become increasingly popular.[5] In the sense used here, a **team** is a group of workers that functions as a unit, often with little or no supervision, to carry out work-related tasks, functions, and activities. Table 13.1 lists and defines some of the various types of teams that are being used today. Earlier forms of teams included autonomous work groups and quality circles. Today, teams are also sometimes called *self-managed teams, cross-functional teams,* or *high-performance teams.* Many firms today are routinely using teams to carry out most of their daily operations.[6]

Table 13.1
Types of Teams

> **Problem-solving team**   Most popular type of team; comprises knowledge workers who gather to solve a specific problem and then disband
>
> **Management team**   Consists mainly of managers from various functions like sales and production; coordinates work among other teams
>
> **Work team**   An increasingly popular type of team, work teams are responsible for the daily work of the organization; when empowered, they are self-managed teams
>
> **Virtual team**   A new type of work team that interacts by computer; members enter and leave the network as needed and may take turns serving as leader
>
> **Quality circle**   Declining in popularity, quality circles, comprising workers and supervisors, meet intermittently to discuss workplace problems

Source: Reprinted by permission from Brian Dumaine, "The Trouble with Teams," *Fortune,* September 5, 1994, page 87. Copyright © 1994 Time Inc. All rights reserved.

SHARING THE WORKLOAD WITH COLLEAGUES IN OTHER COUNTRIES

When employees in Caltex Petroleum's Singapore headquarters work with colleagues in accounting or web site management, they have to stop and think whether to call Manila, where the accounting department is located, or South Africa, where web development is located. Caltex, a joint venture between Texaco and Chevron, operates a chain of gasoline stations across Southeast Asia, Africa, and countries in between. The company was once based in Dallas but moved the main office to Singapore to be closer to its main markets. Thanks to telecommunications technology, Caltex can open an office wherever it finds an expert workforce and keep employees linked horizontally and vertically by phone, fax, and—most frequently—e-mail.

Caltex is in the vanguard of a movement to move selected positions out of higher-cost countries (such as the United States and some European countries) and into lower-cost nations (such as Ireland, Jamaica, India, and the Philippines). By hiring skilled, English-speaking employees for software development, customer service support, clerical activities, and other jobs, employers can save 30 percent or more on labor costs, gain access to a larger labor pool, and take advantage of time differences to keep work flowing virtually around the clock. And they can still expect those individuals to interact effectively on group projects.

Citigroup and Microsoft are just two of a growing number of global firms that have opened software outposts in Ireland;

Motorola and Bell Labs both operate research centers in Bangalore; and General Electric Capital has a customer service call center in India employing 1,000 representatives. General Electric is so happy with the integration of this workforce that it is opening more offices in India to handle payroll and other functions.

In this Internet age, countries must have a strong telecommunications infrastructure to attract the interest of multinational companies. U.S.-based companies such as Brigade are flocking to ready-wired high-tech office parks in India, where they can set up shop quickly and hire computer-savvy locals to work on customer service projects for Compaq and other clients. As these firms recognize, e-mail shrinks the time and distance between employees in far-flung offices while facilitating communication in every direction.

> *As technology and communication improve, we are scattering centers of excellence around the world.*
>
> —*William Pfluger, general manager of Caltex's accounting division in Manila**

References: Mark Clifford and Manjeet Kripalani, "Different Countries, Adjoining Cubicles," *Business Week,* August 28, 2000, pp. 182–184 (*quote on p.182).

Organizations create teams for a variety of reasons. For one thing, they give more responsibility for task performance to the workers who are actually performing the tasks. They also empower workers by giving them greater authority and decision-making freedom. In addition, they allow the organization to capitalize on the knowledge and motivation of their workers. Finally, they enable the organization to shed its bureaucracy and to promote flexibility and responsiveness. Ford used a team to design its new Thunderbird. Similarly, General Motors also used a team to develop the newest model of the Chevrolet Blazer.

When an organization decides to use teams, it is essentially implementing a major form of organization change, as discussed in Chapter 7. Thus it is important to follow a logical and systematic approach to planning and implementing teams within an existing organization design. It is also important to recognize that resistance may be encountered. This resistance is most likely from first-line managers, who will be giving up much of their authority to the team. Many organizations find that they must change the whole management philosophy of such managers away from being a supervisor to being a coach or facilitator.[7]

After teams are in place, managers should continue to monitor their contributions and how effectively they are functioning. In the best circumstance, teams will become very cohesive groups with high performance norms. To achieve this state, the manager can use any or all of the techniques described later in this chapter for enhancing cohesiveness. If implemented properly, and with the support of the workers themselves, performance norms will likely be relatively high. That is, if the change is properly implemented, the team participants will understand the value and potential of teams and the rewards they may expect to get as a result of their contributions. On the other hand, poorly designed and implemented teams will do a less effective job and may detract from organizational effectiveness.[8]

Why People Join Groups and Teams

People join groups and teams for a variety of reasons. They join functional groups simply by virtue of joining organizations. People accept employment to earn money or to practice their chosen profession. Once inside the organization, they are assigned to jobs and roles and thus become members of functional groups. People in existing functional groups are told, are asked, or volunteer to serve on committees, task forces, and teams. People join informal or interest groups for a variety of reasons, most of them quite complex.[9] Indeed, the need to be a team player has grown so strong today that many organizations will actively resist hiring someone who does not want to work with others.[10]

Interpersonal Attraction   One reason people choose to form informal or interest groups is that they are attracted to one another. Many different factors contribute to interpersonal attraction. When people see a lot of each other, pure proximity increases the likelihood that interpersonal attraction will develop. Attraction is increased when people have similar attitudes, personalities, or economic standing.

Group Activities   Individuals may also be motivated to join a group because the activities of the group appeal to them. Jogging, playing bridge, bowling, discussing poetry, playing war games, and flying model airplanes are all activities that some people enjoy. Many of them are more enjoyable to participate in as a member of a group, and most require more than one person. Many large firms, like Shell Oil and Apple Computer, have a league of football, softball, or bowling teams. A person may join a bowling team not because of any noticeable attraction to other group members but simply because being a member of the group allows that person to participate in a pleasant activity. Of course, if the level of interpersonal attraction of the group is very low, a person may choose to forego the activity rather than join the group.

Group Goals　The goals of a group may also motivate people to join. The Sierra Club, which is dedicated to environmental conservation, is a good example of this kind of interest group. Various fund-raising groups are another illustration. Members may or may not be personally attracted to the other fundraisers, and they probably do not enjoy the activity of knocking on doors asking for money, but they join the group because they subscribe to its goal. Workers join unions like the United Auto Workers because they support its goals.

Need Satisfaction　Still another reason for joining a group is to satisfy the need for affiliation. New residents in a community may join the Newcomers Club partially as a way to meet new people and partially just to be around other people. Likewise, newly divorced individuals often join support groups as a way to have companionship.

Instrumental Benefits　A final reason people join groups is that membership is sometimes seen as instrumental in providing other benefits to the individual. For example, it is fairly common for college students entering their senior year to join several professional clubs or associations because listing such memberships on a résumé is thought to enhance the chances of getting a good job. Similarly, a manager might join a certain racquet club not because she is attracted to its members (although she might be) and not because of the opportunity to play tennis (although she may enjoy it). The club's goals are not relevant, and her affiliation needs may be satisfied in other ways. However, she may feel that being a member of this club will lead to important and useful business contacts. The racquet club membership is instrumental in establishing those contacts. Membership in civic groups such as the Junior League and Rotary may be solicited for similar reasons.

Stages of Group and Team Development

Imagine the differences between a collection of five people who have just been brought together to form a group or team and a group or team that has functioned like a well-oiled machine for years. Members of a new group or team are unfamiliar with how they will function together and are tentative in their interactions. In a group or team with considerable experience, members are familiar with one another's strengths and weaknesses, and are more secure in their role in the group. The former group or team is generally considered to be immature; the latter, mature. To progress from the immature phase to the mature phase, a group or team must go through certain stages of development, as shown in Figure 13.2.[11]

The first stage of development is called *forming*. The members of the group or team get acquainted and begin to test which interpersonal behaviors are acceptable and which are unacceptable to the other members. The members are very dependent on others at this point to provide cues about what is acceptable. The basic ground rules for the group or team are established, and a tentative group structure may emerge. At Reebok, for example, a merchandising team was created to handle its sportswear business. The team leader and his members were barely acquainted and had to spend a few weeks getting to know one another.

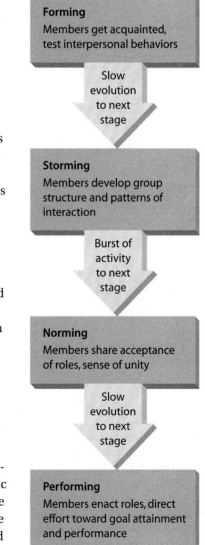

Figure 13.2
Stages of Group Development

As groups mature, they tend to evolve through four distinct stages of development. Managers must understand that group members need time to become acquainted, accept each other, develop a group structure, and become comfortable with their roles in the group before they can begin to work directly to accomplish goals.

Forming
Members get acquainted, test interpersonal behaviors

Slow evolution to next stage

Storming
Members develop group structure and patterns of interaction

Burst of activity to next stage

Norming
Members share acceptance of roles, sense of unity

Slow evolution to next stage

Performing
Members enact roles, direct effort toward goal attainment and performance

The second stage of development, often slow to emerge, is *storming*. During this stage, there may be a general lack of unity and uneven interaction patterns. At the same time, some members of the group or team may begin to exert themselves to become recognized as the group leader or at least to play a major role in shaping the group's agenda. In Reebok's team, some members advocated a rapid expansion into the marketplace; others argued for a slower entry. The first faction won, with disastrous results. Because of the rush, product quality was poor, and deliveries were late. As a result, the team leader was fired and a new manager placed in charge.

The third stage of development, called *norming*, usually begins with a burst of activity. During this stage, each person begins to recognize and accept her or his role and to understand the roles of others. Members also begin to accept one another and to develop a sense of unity. There may also be temporary regressions to the previous stage. For example, the group or team might begin to accept one particular member as the leader. If this person later violates important norms or otherwise jeopardizes his or her claim to leadership, conflict might reemerge as the group rejects this leader and searches for another. Reebok's new leader transferred several people away from the team and set up a new system and structure for managing things. The remaining employees accepted his new approach and settled into doing their jobs.

Performing, the final stage of group or team development, is again slow to develop. The team really begins to focus on the problem at hand. The members enact the roles they have accepted, interaction occurs, and the efforts of the group are directed toward goal attainment. The basic structure of the group or team is no longer an issue, but has become a mechanism for accomplishing the purpose of the group. Reebok's sportswear business is now growing consistently and has successfully avoided the problems that plagued it at first.

Characteristics of Teams

As groups and teams mature and pass through the four basic stages of development, they begin to take on four important characteristics—a role structure, norms, cohesiveness, and informal leadership.

Role Structures

role The part an individual plays in a group in helping the group reach its goals

role structure The set of defined roles and interrelationships among those roles that group members define and accept

Each individual in a team has a part—or **role**—to play, in helping the group reach its goals. Some people are leaders, some do the work, some interface with other teams, and so on. Indeed, a person may take on a *task-specialist role* (concentrating on getting the group's task accomplished) or a *socioemotional role* (providing social and emotional support to others on the team). A few people, usually the leaders, perform both roles; a few others may do neither. The group's **role structure** is the set of defined roles and interrelationships among those roles that the group or team members define and accept. Each of us belongs to many

Figure 13.3

The Development of a Role

Roles and role structures within a group generally evolve through a series of role episodes. The first two stages of role development are group processes, as the group members let individuals know what is expected of them. The other two parts are individual processes, as the new group members perceive and enact their roles.

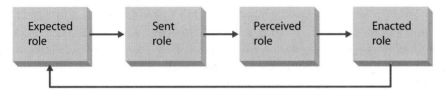

groups and therefore plays multiple roles—in work groups, classes, families, and social organizations.

Role structures emerge as a result of role episodes, as shown in Figure 13.3. The process begins with the expected role—what other members of the team expect the individual to do. The expected role gets translated into the sent role—the messages and cues that team members use to communicate the expected role to the individual. The perceived role is what the individual perceives the sent role to mean. Finally, the enacted role is what the individual actually does in the role. The enacted role, in turn, influences future expectations of the team. Of course, role episodes seldom unfold this easily. When major disruptions occur, individuals may experience role ambiguity, conflict, or overload.[12]

Role Ambiguity   **Role ambiguity** arises when the sent role is unclear. If your instructor tells you to write a term paper but refuses to provide more information, you will probably experience role ambiguity. You do not know what the topic is, how long the paper should be, what format to use, or when the paper is due. In work settings, role ambiguity can stem from poor job descriptions, vague instructions from a supervisor, or unclear cues from coworkers. The result is likely to be a subordinate who does not know what to do. Role ambiguity can be a significant problem for both the individual who must contend with it and the organization that expects the employee to perform.

role ambiguity Arises when the sent role is unclear and the individual does not know what is expected of him or her

Role Conflict   **Role conflict** occurs when the messages and cues composing the sent role are clear but contradictory or mutually exclusive.[13] One common form is *interrole conflict*—conflict between roles. For example, if a person's boss says that to get ahead one must work overtime and on weekends, and the same person's spouse says that more time is needed at home with the family, conflict may result. In a matrix organization, interrole conflict often arises between the roles one plays in different teams as well as between team roles and one's permanent role in a functional group.

Intrarole conflict may occur when the person gets conflicting demands from different sources within the context of the same role. A manager's boss may tell her

role conflict Occurs when the messages and cues comprising the sent role are clear but contradictory or mutually exclusive

that she needs to put more pressure on subordinates to follow new work rules. At the same time, her subordinates may indicate that they expect her to get the rules changed. Thus the cues are in conflict, and the manager may be unsure about which course to follow. *Intrasender conflict* occurs when a single source sends clear but contradictory messages. This might arise if the boss says one morning that there can be no more overtime for the next month, but after lunch tells someone to work late that same evening. *Person-role conflict* results from a discrepancy between the role requirements and the individual's personal values, attitudes, and needs. If a person is told to do something unethical or illegal, or if the work is distasteful (for example, firing a close friend), person-role conflict is likely. Role conflict of all varieties is of particular concern to managers. Research has shown that conflict may occur in a variety of situations and lead to a variety of adverse consequences, including stress, poor performance, and rapid turnover.

role overload Occurs when expectations for the role exceed the individual's capabilities to perform

Role Overload   A final consequence of a weak role structure is **role overload**, which occurs when expectations for the role exceed the individual's capabilities. When a manager gives an employee several major assignments at once while increasing the person's regular workload, the employee will probably experience role overload. Role overload may also result when an individual takes on too many roles at one time. For example, a person trying to work extra hard at work, run for election to the school board, serve on a committee at church, coach Little League baseball, maintain an active exercise program, and be a contributing member to her or his family will probably encounter role overload.

Implications   In a functional group or team, the manager can take steps to avoid role ambiguity, conflict, and overload. Having clear and reasonable expectations and sending clear and straightforward cues go a long way toward eliminating role ambiguity. Consistent expectations that take into account the employee's other roles and personal value system may minimize role conflict. Role overload can be avoided simply by recognizing the individual's capabilities and limits. In friendship and interest groups, role structures are likely to be less formal; hence, the possibility of role ambiguity, conflict, or overload may not be so great. However, if one or more of these problems does occur, they may be difficult to handle. Because roles in friendship and interest groups are less likely to be partially defined by a formal authority structure or written job descriptions, the individual cannot turn to these sources to clarify a role.

Behavioral Norms

norm Standard of behavior that the group accepts and expects of its members

Norms are standards of behavior that the group or team accepts for its members. Most committees, for example, develop norms governing their discussions. A person who talks too much is perceived as doing so to make a good impression or to get his or her own way. Other members may not talk much to this person, may not sit nearby, may glare at the person, and may otherwise "punish" the individual for violating the norm. Norms, then, define the boundaries between acceptable and unacceptable behavior.[14] Some groups develop norms that limit the upper bounds of behavior to "make life easier" for the group. In general, these norms are counter-productive—don't make more than two comments in a committee discussion or don't produce any more than you have to. Other groups may develop norms that limit the lower bounds of behavior. These norms tend to reflect motivation, commitment, and high performance—don't come to meetings unless you've read the reports to be discussed or produce as much as you can. Managers can sometimes use norms for the betterment of the organization. For example, Kodak has successfully used group norms to reduce injuries in some of its plants.[15]

Norm Generalization The norms of one group cannot always be generalized to another group. Some academic departments, for example, have a norm that suggests that faculty members dress up on teaching days. People who fail to observe this norm are "punished" by sarcastic remarks or even formal reprimands. In other departments, the norm may be casual clothes, and the person unfortunate enough to wear dress clothes may be punished just as vehemently. Even within the same work area, similar groups or teams can develop different norms. One team may strive always to produce above its assigned quota; another may maintain productivity just below its quota. The norm of one team may be to be friendly and cordial to its supervisor; that of another team may be to remain aloof and distant. Some differences are due primarily to the composition of the teams.

Norm Variation In some cases, there can also be norm variation within a group or team. A common norm is that the least-senior member of a group is expected to perform unpleasant or trivial tasks for the rest of the group. These tasks might be to wait on customers who are known to be small tippers (in a restaurant), to deal with complaining customers (in a department store), or to handle the low-commission line of merchandise (in a sales department). Another example is when certain individuals, especially informal leaders, may violate some norms. If the team is going to meet at 8 o'clock, anyone arriving late will be chastised for holding things up. Occasionally, however, the informal leader may arrive

THE FAR SIDE   By GARY LARSON

The Far Side by Gary Larson © 1987 FarWorks, Inc. All rights reserved. Used with permission.

Groups and teams are powerful forces in many organizations. People working together in a coordinated and integrated way can often accomplish far more than they could working alone. One problem that can arise, however, is called "free riding." Free riding occurs when someone in a group or team fails to carry out his or her responsibilities and lets others do all the work. As illustrated in this cartoon, the Viking in the back of the boat is neglecting his work and letting the rest of the group carry his weight. Thus he is a free rider!

a few minutes late. As long as this does not happen too often, the group will probably not do anything.

Norm Conformity   Four sets of factors contribute to norm conformity. First, factors associated with the group are important. For example, some groups or teams may exert more pressure for conformity than others. Second, the initial stimulus that prompts behavior can affect conformity. The more ambiguous the stimulus (for example, news that the team is going to be transferred to a new unit), the more pressure there is to conform. Third, individual traits determine the individual's propensity to conform (for example, more intelligent people are often less susceptible to pressure to conform). Finally, situational factors such as team size and unanimity influence conformity. As an individual learns the group's norms, he can do several different things. The most obvious is to adopt the norms. For example, the new male professor who notices that all the other men in the department dress up to teach can also start wearing a suit. A variation is to try to obey the "spirit" of the norm while retaining individuality. The professor may recognize that the norm is actually to wear a tie; thus he might succeed by wearing a tie with his sport shirt, jeans, and sneakers.

The individual may also ignore the norm. When a person does not conform, several things can happen. At first the group may increase its communication with the deviant individual to try to bring her back into line. If this does not work, communication may decline. Over time, the group may begin to exclude the individual from its activities and, in effect, to ostracize the person. Finally, we need to briefly consider another aspect of norm conformity—socialization. **Socialization** is generalized norm conformity that occurs as a person makes the transition from being an outsider to being an insider. A newcomer to an organization, for example, gradually begins to learn the norms about such things as dress, working hours, and interpersonal relations. As the newcomer adopts these norms, she is being socialized into the organizational culture. Some organizations, like Texas Instruments, work to actively manage the socialization process; others leave it to happenstance.

socialization   Generalized norm conformity that occurs as a person makes the transition from being an outsider to being an insider in the organization

cohesiveness   The extent to which members are loyal and committed to the group; the degree of mutual attractiveness within the group

Cohesive teams can be highly effective contributors to the success of any organization. In the wake of the terrorist attacks on the United States on September 11, 2001, New York Mayor Rudy Giuliani and other key leaders had to work together to restore order and rebuild public confidence. While these individuals already had a history of working together effectively, the crisis served to coalesce them into an even more effective team.

Cohesiveness

A third important team characteristic is cohesiveness. **Cohesiveness** is the extent to which members are loyal and committed to the group. In a highly cohesive team, the members work well together, support and trust one another, and are generally effective at achieving their chosen goal.[16] In contrast, a team that lacks cohesiveness is not very coordi-

Factors That Increase Cohesiveness	Factors That Reduce Cohesiveness
Intergroup competition	Group size
Personal attraction	Disagreement on goals
Favorable evaluation	Intragroup competition
Agreement on goals	Domination
Interaction	Unpleasant experiences

Table 13.2

Factors That Influence Group Cohesiveness
Several different factors can potentially influence the cohesiveness of a group. For example, a manager can establish intergroup competition, assign compatible members to the group, create opportunities for success, establish acceptable goals, and foster interaction to increase cohesiveness. Other factors can be used to decrease cohesiveness.

nated, and its members do not necessarily support one another fully and may have a difficult time reaching goals. Of particular interest are the factors that increase and reduce cohesiveness and the consequences of team cohesiveness. These are listed in Table 13.2.

Factors That Increase Cohesiveness   Five factors can increase the level of cohesiveness in a group or team. One of the strongest is intergroup competition. When two or more groups are in direct competition (for example, three sales groups competing for top sales honors or two football teams competing for a conference championship), each group is likely to become more cohesive. Second, just as personal attraction plays a role in causing a group to form, so, too, does attraction seem to enhance cohesiveness. Third, favorable evaluation of the entire group by outsiders can increase cohesiveness. Thus a group's winning a sales contest or a conference title, or receiving recognition and praise from a superior will tend to increase cohesiveness.

Similarly, if all the members of the group or team agree on their goals, cohesiveness is likely to increase. And the more frequently members of the group interact with one another, the more likely the group is to become cohesive. A manager who wants to foster a high level of cohesiveness in a team might do well to establish some form of intergroup competition, assign members to the group who are likely to be attracted to one another, provide opportunities for success, establish goals that all members are likely to accept, and allow ample opportunity for interaction.

Factors That Reduce Cohesiveness   There are also five factors that are known to reduce team cohesiveness. First of all, cohesiveness tends to decline as a group increases in size. Second, when members of a team disagree on what the goals of the group should be, cohesiveness may decrease. For example, when some members believe the group should maximize output and others think output should be restricted, cohesiveness declines. Third, intragroup competition reduces cohesiveness. When members are competing among themselves, they focus more on their own actions and behaviors than on those of the group.

Fourth, domination by one or more persons in the group or team may cause overall cohesiveness to decline. Other members may feel that they are not being given an opportunity to interact and contribute, and they may become less

Figure 13.4

The Interaction Between Cohesiveness and Performance Norms

Group cohesiveness and performance norms interact to determine group performance. From the manager's perspective, high cohesiveness combined with high performance norms is the best situation, and high cohesiveness with low performance norms is the worst situation. Managers who can influence the level of cohesiveness and performance norms can greatly improve the effectiveness of a work group.

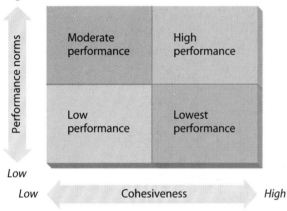

attracted to the group as a consequence. Finally, unpleasant experiences that result from group membership may reduce cohesiveness. A sales group that comes in last in a sales contest, an athletic team that sustains a long losing streak, and a work group reprimanded for poor-quality work may all become less cohesive as a result of their unpleasant experience.

Consequences of Cohesiveness   In general, as teams become more cohesive, their members tend to interact more frequently, conform more to norms, and become more satisfied with the team. Cohesiveness may also influence team performance. However, performance is also influenced by the team's performance norms. Figure 13.4 shows how cohesiveness and performance norms interact to help shape team performance.

When both cohesiveness and performance norms are high, high performance should result, because the team wants to perform at a high level (norms) and its members are working together toward that end (cohesiveness). When norms are high and cohesiveness is low, performance will be moderate. Although the team wants to perform at a high level, its members are not necessarily working well together. When norms are low, performance will be low, regardless of whether group cohesiveness is high or low. The least desirable situation occurs when low performance norms are combined with high cohesiveness. In this case, all team members embrace the standard of restricting performance (owing to the low performance norm), and the group is united in its efforts to maintain that standard (owing to the high cohesiveness). If cohesiveness were low, the manager might be able to raise performance norms by establishing high goals and rewarding goal attainment or by bringing in new group members who are high performers. But a highly cohesive group is likely to resist these interventions.

Formal and Informal Leadership

Most functional groups and teams have a formal leader—that is, one appointed by the organization or chosen or elected by the members of the group. Because friendship and interest groups are formed by the members themselves, however, any formal leader must be elected or designated by the members. Although some groups do designate such a leader (a softball team may elect a captain, for example), many do not. Moreover, even when a formal leader is designated, the group or team may also look to others for leadership. An **informal leader** is a person who engages in leadership activities but whose right to do so has not been formally recognized. The formal and the informal leader in any group or team may be the

informal leader   A person who engages in leadership activities but whose right to do so has not been formally recognized by the organization or group

same person, or they may be different people. We noted earlier the distinction between the task-specialist and socioemotional roles within groups. An informal leader is likely to be a person capable of carrying out both roles effectively. If the formal leader can fulfill one role but not the other, an informal leader often emerges to supplement the formal leader's functions. If the formal leader cannot fill either role, one or more informal leaders may emerge to carry out both sets of functions.

Is informal leadership desirable? In many cases, informal leaders are quite powerful because they draw from referent or expert power. When they are working in the best interest of the organization, they can be a tremendous asset. Notable athletes, such as Brett Favre and Mia Hamm, are classic examples of informal leaders. However, when informal leaders work counter to the goals of the organization, they can cause significant difficulties. Such leaders may lower performance norms, instigate walkouts or wildcat strikes, or otherwise disrupt the organization.

Interpersonal and Intergroup Conflict

Of course, when people work together in an organization, things do not always go smoothly. Indeed, conflict is an inevitable element of interpersonal relationships in organizations. In this section we will look at how conflict affects overall performance. We also explore the causes of conflict between individuals, between groups, and between an organization and its environment.

The Nature of Conflict

Conflict is a disagreement among two or more individuals, groups, or organizations. This disagreement may be relatively superficial or very strong. It may be short-lived or exist for months or even years, and it may be work related or personal. Conflict may manifest itself in a variety of ways. People may compete with one another, glare at one another, shout, or withdraw. Groups may band together to protect popular members or oust unpopular members. Organizations may seek legal remedy.

Most people assume that conflict is something to be avoided, because it connotes antagonism, hostility, unpleasantness, and dissension. Indeed, managers and management theorists have traditionally viewed conflict as a problem to be avoided.[17] In recent years, however, we have come to recognize that, although conflict can be a major problem, certain kinds of conflict may also be beneficial.[18] For example, when two members of a site selection committee disagree over the best location for a new plant, each may be forced to more thoroughly study and defend his or her preferred alternative. As a result of more systematic analysis and discussion, the committee may make a better decision and be better prepared to justify it

conflict A disagreement between two or more individuals or groups

Figure 13.5

The Nature of Organizational Conflict

Either too much or too little conflict can be dysfunctional for an organization. In either case performance may be low. However, an optimal level of conflict that sparks motivation, creativity, innovation, and initiative can result in higher levels of performance. T. J. Rodgers, CEO of Cypress Semiconductor, maintains a moderate level of conflict in his organization as a way of keeping people energized and motivated.

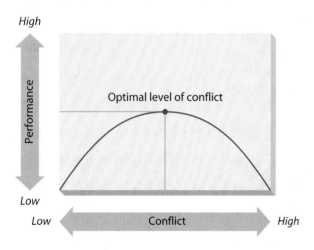

to others than if everyone had agreed from the outset and accepted an alternative that was perhaps less well analyzed.

As long as conflict is being handled in a cordial and constructive manner, it is probably serving a useful purpose in the organization. On the other hand, when working relationships are being disrupted and the conflict has reached destructive levels, it has likely become dysfunctional and needs to be addressed. We discuss ways of dealing with such conflict later in this chapter.

Figure 13.5 depicts the general relationship between conflict and performance for a group or organization. If there is absolutely no conflict in the group or organization, its members may become complacent and apathetic. As a result, group or organizational performance and innovation may subsequently begin to suffer. A moderate level of conflict among group or organizational members, on the other hand, can spark motivation, creativity, innovation, and initiative, and raise performance. Too much conflict, though, can produce such undesirable results as hostility and lack of cooperation, which lower performance. The key for managers is to find and maintain the optimal amount of conflict that fosters performance. Of course, what constitutes optimal conflict varies with both situation and the people involved.[19]

Causes of Conflict

Conflict may arise in both interpersonal and intergroup relationships. Occasionally, conflict between individuals and groups may be caused by particular organizational strategies and practices. A third arena for conflict is between an organization and its environment.

Interpersonal Conflict   Conflict between two or more individuals is almost certain to occur in any organization, given the great variety in perceptions, goals, attitudes, and so forth among its members. William Gates, founder and CEO of Microsoft, and Kazuhiko Nishi, a former business associate from Japan, ended a long-term business relationship because of interpersonal conflict. Nishi accused Gates of becoming too political, while Gates charged that Nishi became too unpredictable and erratic in his behavior.[20]

A frequent source of interpersonal conflict in organizations is what many people call a "personality clash"—when two people distrust each other's motives, dislike each other, or for some other reason simply cannot get along. Conflict also may arise between people who have different beliefs or perceptions about some aspect of their work or their organization. For example, one manager may want the organization to require that all employees use Microsoft Office software to promote standardization. Another manager may believe that a variety of software packages should be allowed in order to recognize individuality. Similarly, a male manager may disagree with his female colleague over whether the organization is guilty of discriminating against women in promotion decisions.

Conflict can also result from excessive competitiveness among individuals. Two people vying for the same job, for example, may resort to political behavior in an effort to gain an advantage. If either competitor sees the other's behavior as inappropriate, accusations are likely to result. Even after the "winner" of the job is determined, such conflict may continue to undermine interpersonal relationships, especially if the reasons given in selecting one candidate are ambiguous or open to alternative explanation. Robert Allen resigned as CEO of Delta Airlines because he disagreed with other key executives over how best to reduce the carrier's costs. After he began looking for a replacement for one of his rivals without the approval of the firm's board of directors, the resultant conflict and controversy left him no choice but to leave.[21]

Intergroup Conflict   Conflict between two or more organizational groups is also quite common. For example, the members of a firm's marketing group may disagree with the production group over product quality and delivery schedules. Two sales groups may disagree over how to meet sales goals, and two groups of managers may have different ideas about how best to allocate organizational resources.

Many intergroup conflicts arise more from organizational causes than from interpersonal causes. In Chapter 6, we described three forms of group interdependence—pooled, sequential, and reciprocal. Just as increased interdependence makes coordination more difficult, it also increases the potential for conflict. For example, recall that, in sequential interdependence, work is passed from one unit to another. Intergroup conflict may arise if the first group turns out too much work (the second group will fall behind), too little work (the second group will not meet its own goals), or poor-quality work.

At a J. C. Penney's department store, conflict recently arose between stockroom employees and sales associates. The sales associates claimed that the stockroom employees were slow in delivering merchandise to the sales floor so that it could be priced and shelved. The stockroom employees, in turn, claimed that the sales associates were not giving them enough lead time to get the merchandise delivered and failed to understand that they had additional duties besides carrying merchandise to the sales floor.

Just like people, different departments often have different goals. Further, these goals may often be incompatible. A marketing goal of maximizing sales, achieved partially by offering many products in a wide variety of sizes, shapes, colors, and models, probably conflicts with a production goal of minimizing costs, achieved partially by long production runs of a few items. Reebok recently confronted this very situation. One group of managers wanted to introduce a new sportswear line as quickly as possible, whereas other managers wanted to expand more deliberately and cautiously. Because the two groups were not able to reconcile their differences effectively, conflict between the two factions led to quality problems and delivery delays that plagued the firm for months.

Competition for scarce resources can also lead to intergroup conflict. Most organizations—especially universities, hospitals, government agencies, and businesses in depressed industries—have limited resources. In one New England town, for example, the public works department and the library recently battled over funds from a federal construction grant. The Oldsmobile, Pontiac, and Chevrolet divisions of General Motors have frequently fought over the rights to manufacture various new products developed by the company.

Conflict Between Organization and Environment   Conflict that arises between one organization and another is called interorganizational conflict. A moderate amount of interorganizational conflict resulting from business competition is, of course, expected, but sometimes conflict becomes more extreme. For example, the owners of Jordache Enterprises, Inc., and Guess? Inc., battled in court for years over ownership of the Guess label, allegations of design theft, and several other issues.[22] Similarly, General Motors and Volkswagen went to court to resolve a bitter conflict that spanned more than four years. It all started when a key GM executive, Jose Ignacio Lopez de Arriortua, left for a position at Volkswagen. GM claimed that he took with him key secrets that could benefit its German competitor. After the messy departure, dozens of charges and countercharges were made by the two firms, and only a court settlement was able to put the conflict to an end.[23]

Conflict can also arise between an organization and other elements of its environment. For example, an organization may conflict with a consumer group over claims it makes about its products. McDonald's faced this problem a few years ago when it published nutritional information about its products that omitted details about fat content. A manufacturer might conflict with a governmental agency such as OSHA. For example, the firm's management may believe it is in compliance with OSHA regulations, whereas officials from the agency itself may feel the firm is not in compliance. Or a firm might conflict with a supplier over the quality of raw materials. The firm may think the supplier is providing inferior materials, whereas the supplier thinks the materials are adequate. Finally, individual managers may obviously have disagreements with groups of workers. For example, a manager may think her workers are doing poor-quality work and that they are unmotivated. The workers, on the other hand, may believe they are doing a good job and that the manager is doing a poor job of leading them.

Managing Conflict in Organizations

How do managers cope with all this potential conflict? Fortunately, as Table 13.3 shows, there are ways to stimulate conflict for constructive ends, to control conflict before it gets out of hand, and to resolve it if it does. Below we look at ways of managing conflict.

Stimulating Conflict

In some situations, an organization may stimulate conflict by placing individual employees or groups in competitive situations. Managers can establish sales contests, incentive plans, bonuses, or other competitive stimuli to spark competition.

Stimulating conflict
    Increase competition among individuals and teams
    Hire outsiders to shape things up
    Change established procedures
Controlling conflict
    Expand resource base
    Enhance coordination of interdependence
    Set supraordinate goals
    Match personalities and work habits of employees
Resolving and eliminating conflict
    Avoid conflict
    Convince conflicting parties to compromise
    Bring conflicting parties together to confront and negotiate conflict

Table 13.3

Methods for Managing Conflict
Conflict is a powerful force in organizations and has both negative and positive consequences. Managers can draw on several techniques to stimulate, control, resolve, or eliminate conflict, depending on their unique circumstances.

As long as the ground rules are equitable and all participants perceive the contest as fair, the conflict created by the competition is likely to be constructive, because each participant will work hard to win (thereby enhancing some aspect of organizational performance).

Another useful method for stimulating conflict is to bring in one or more outsiders who will shake things up and present a new perspective on organizational practices. Outsiders may be new employees, current employees assigned to an existing work group, or consultants or advisers hired on a temporary basis. Of course, this action can also provoke resentment from insiders who feel they were qualified for the position. The Beecham Group, a British company, once hired an executive from the United States for its CEO position, expressly to change how the company did business. His arrival brought with it new ways of doing things and a new enthusiasm for competitiveness. Unfortunately, some valued employees also chose to leave Beecham because they resented some of the changes that were made.

Changing established procedures, especially procedures that have outlived their usefulness, can also stimulate conflict. Such actions cause people to reassess how they perform their jobs and whether they perform them correctly. For example, one university president announced that all vacant staff positions could be filled only after written justification had received his approval. Conflict arose between the president and the department heads, who felt they were having to do more paperwork than was necessary. Most requests were approved, but because department heads now had to think through their staffing needs, a few unnecessary positions were appropriately eliminated.

Controlling Conflict

One method of controlling conflict is to expand the resource base. Suppose a top manager receives two budget requests for $100,000 each. If she has only $180,000 to distribute, the stage is set for conflict, because each group will feel its proposal is worth funding and will be unhappy if it is not fully funded. If both proposals are indeed worthwhile, it may be possible for her to come up with the extra $20,000 from some other source and thereby avoid difficulty.

As noted earlier, pooled, sequential, and reciprocal interdependence can all result in conflict. If managers use an appropriate technique for enhancing coordination, they can reduce the probability that conflict will arise. Techniques for coordination (described in Chapter 6) include making use of the managerial hierarchy, relying on rules and procedures, enlisting liaison persons, forming task forces, and integrating departments. At the J. C. Penney store mentioned earlier, the conflict was addressed by providing salespeople with clearer forms on which to specify the merchandise they needed and in what sequence. If one coordination technique does not have the desired effect, a manager might shift to another one.

Competing goals can also be a potential source of conflict among individuals and groups. Managers can sometimes focus employee attention on higher-level, or supraordinate, goals as a way of eliminating lower-level conflict. When labor unions such as the United Auto Workers make wage concessions to ensure survival of the automobile industry, they are responding to a superordinate goal. Their immediate goal may be higher wages for members, but they realize that, without the automobile industry, their members would not even have jobs.

Finally, managers should try to match the personalities and work habits of employees so as to avoid conflict between individuals. For instance, two valuable subordinates, one a chain smoker and the other a vehement antismoker, should probably not be required to work together in an enclosed space. If conflict does arise between incompatible individuals, a manager might seek an equitable transfer for one or both of them to other units.

Resolving and Eliminating Conflict

Despite everyone's best intentions, conflict will sometimes flare up. If it is disrupting the workplace, creating too much hostility and tension, or otherwise harming the organization, attempts must be made to resolve it. Some managers who are uncomfortable dealing with conflict choose to avoid the conflict and hope it will go away. Avoidance may sometimes be effective in the short run for some kinds of interpersonal disagreements, but it does little to resolve long-run or chronic conflict. Even more unadvisable, though, is "smoothing"—minimizing the conflict and telling everyone that things will "get better." Often the conflict will only worsen as people continue to brood over it.

Compromise is striking a middle-range position between two extremes. This approach can work if it is used with care, but in most compromise situations, someone wins and someone loses. Budget problems are one of the few areas amenable to compromise because of their objective nature. Assume, for example, that additional resources are not available to the manager mentioned earlier. She has $180,000 to divide, and each of two groups claims to need $100,000. If the manager believes that both projects warrant funding, she can allocate $90,000 to each. The fact that the two groups have at least been treated equally may minimize the potential conflict.

The confrontation approach to conflict resolution—also called *interpersonal problem solving*—consists of bringing the parties together to confront the conflict. The parties discuss the nature of their conflict and attempt to reach an agreement or a solution. Confrontation requires a reasonable degree of maturity on the part of the participants, and the manager must structure the situation carefully. If handled well, this approach can be an effective means of resolving conflict. In recent years, many organizations have experimented with a technique called *alternative dispute resolution,* using a team of employees to arbitrate conflict in this way.[24]

Regardless of the approach, organizations and their managers must realize that conflict must be addressed if it is to serve constructive purposes and be prevented from bringing about destructive consequences. Conflict is inevitable in organizations, but its effects can be constrained with proper attention. For example, Union Carbide once sent 200 of its managers to a three-day workshop on conflict management. The managers engaged in a variety of exercises and discussions to learn with whom they were most likely to come into conflict and how they should try to resolve it. As a result, managers at the firm later reported that hostility and resentment in the organization had been greatly diminished and that people in the firm reported more pleasant working relationships.

Summary of Key Points

A group is two or more people who interact regularly to accomplish a common purpose or goal. General kinds of groups in organizations are functional groups, task groups and teams, and informal or interest groups. A team is a group of workers that functions as a unit, often with little or no supervision, to carry out organizational functions.

People join functional groups and teams to pursue a career. Their reasons for joining informal or interest groups include interpersonal attraction, group activities, group goals, need satisfaction, and potential instrumental benefits. The stages of team development include testing and dependence (forming), intragroup conflict and hostility (storming), development of group cohesion (norming), and focusing on the problem at hand (performing).

Four important characteristics of teams are role structures, behavioral norms, cohesiveness, and informal leadership. Role structures define task-specialist and socioemotional specialists and may be victimized by role ambiguity, role conflict, or role overload. Norms are standards of behavior for group members. Cohesiveness is the extent to which members are loyal and committed to the team and to one another. Several factors can increase or reduce team cohesiveness. The relationship between performance norms and cohesiveness is especially important. Informal leaders are those leaders whom the group members themselves choose to follow.

Conflict is a disagreement between two or more people, groups, or organizations. Too little or too much conflict may hurt performance, but an optimal level of conflict may improve performance. Interpersonal and intergroup conflict in organizations may be caused by personality differences or by particular organizational strategies and practices.

Organizations may encounter conflict with one another and with various elements of the environment. Three methods of managing conflict are to stimulate it, control it, or resolve and eliminate it.

Discussion Questions

Questions for Review

1. What is a group? Describe the several different types of groups and indicate the similarities and differences between them.
2. Why do people join groups? Do all teams develop through all the stages discussed in this chapter? Why or why not?
3. Describe the characteristics of teams. How might the management of a mature team differ from the management of teams that are not yet mature?
4. Identify and summarize the causes and consequences of group cohesiveness.
5. Describe the nature and causes of conflict in organizations. Is conflict always bad? Why or why not?

Questions for Analysis

6. Is it possible for a group to be of more than one type at a time? If so, under what circumstances? If not, why not?
7. Think of several groups of which you have been a member. Why did you join each? Did each group progress through the stages of development discussed in this chapter? If not, why not?
8. Do you think teams are a valuable new management technique that will endure, or are they just a fad that will be replaced with something else in the near future?
9. Suppose you were the manager of a highly cohesive group with low performance norms. What would you do?
10. Would a manager ever want to stimulate conflict in his or her organization? Why or why not?

BUILDING EFFECTIVE *interpersonal* SKILLS

Exercise Overview

A manager's interpersonal skills refer to her or his ability to understand and motivate individuals and groups. Clearly, then, interpersonal skills play a major role in determining how well a manager can interact with others in a group setting. This exercise allows you to practice your interpersonal skills in relation to just such a setting.

Exercise Background

You have just been transferred to a new position supervising a group of five employees. The small business you work for has few rules and regulations. Unfortunately, the lack of rules and regulations is creating a problem that you must now address.

Specifically, two of the group members are nonsmokers. They are becoming increasingly vocal about the fact that two other members of the group smoke at work. The nonsmokers believe that the secondary smoke in the workplace is endangering their health and want to establish a no-smoking policy like that of many large businesses today.

The two smokers, however, argue that, because the firm did not have such a policy when they started working there, it would be unfair to impose such a policy on them now. One of them in particular says that he turned down an attractive job with another company because he wanted to work in a place where he could smoke.

The fifth worker is also a nonsmoker but says that she doesn't care if others smoke. Her husband smokes at home anyway, and she says she is used to being around smokers. You suspect that if the two vocal nonsmokers are not appeased, they may leave. At the same time, you also think that the two smokers will leave if you mandate a no-smoking policy. All five workers do good work, and you do not want any of them to leave. [Note: Several states and many cities regulate smoking in public places to varying degrees. For purposes of this exercise, assume that no such regulations exist for your location.]

Exercise Task

With this information as context, do the following:

1. Explain the nature of the conflict that exists in this work group.
2. Develop a course of action for dealing with the situation.

BUILDING EFFECTIVE *conceptual* SKILLS

Exercise Overview

Groups and teams are becoming ever more important in organizations. This exercise allows you to practice your conceptual skills as they apply to work teams in organizations.

Exercise Background

Many highly effective groups exist outside the boundaries of typical business organizations, as described in the preceding case study. For example, each of the following represents a team:

1. A basketball team
2. An elite military squadron
3. A government policy group such as the presidential cabinet
4. A student planning committee

Exercise Task

1. Identify an example of a real team, such as one of the above. Choose one that (a) is not part of a normal business, (b) you can argue is highly effective, and (c) was not discussed in the case study.
2. Determine the reasons for the team's effectiveness.
3. Determine how a manager can learn from this particular team and use its success determinants in a business setting.

BUILDING EFFECTIVE *time management* SKILLS

Exercise Overview

Time management skills refer to the manager's ability to prioritize work, to work efficiently, and to delegate appropriately. This exercise enables you to develop time management skills as they relate to running team meetings.

Exercise Background

Although teams and team meetings are becoming more and more common, some managers worry that they waste too much time. Listed below are several suggestions that experts have made for being more efficient in a meeting.

1. Have an agenda.
2. Meet only when there is a reason.
3. Set clear starting and ending times.
4. Put a clock in front of everyone.
5. Take away all the chairs and make people stand.
6. Lock the door at starting time to "punish" latecomers.

7. Give everyone a role in the meeting.

8. Use visual aids.

9. Have a recording secretary to document what transpires.

10. Have a one-day-a-week meeting "holiday"—a day on which no one can schedule a meeting.

Exercise Task

With the information above as context, do the following:

1. Evaluate the likely effectiveness of each of these suggestions.

2. Rank-order the suggestions in terms of their likely value.

3. Identify at least three other suggestions that you think might improve the efficiency of a team meeting.

SKILLS *self-assessment* INSTRUMENT

Using Teams

Introduction: The use of groups and teams is becoming more common in organizations throughout the world. The following assessment surveys your beliefs about the effective use of teams in work organizations.

Instructions: You will agree with some of the statements and disagree with others. In some cases you may find making a decision difficult, but you should force a choice. Record your answers next to each statement according to the following scale:

Rating Scale

4 Strongly agree   **2** Somewhat disagree

3 Somewhat agree   **1** Strongly disagree

_____ 1. Each individual in a work team should have a clear assignment so that individual accountability can be maintained.

_____ 2. For a team to function effectively, the team must be given complete authority over all aspects of the task.

_____ 3. One way to get teams to work is to simply assemble a group of people, tell them in general what needs to be done, and let them work out the details.

_____ 4. Once a team gets going, management can turn its attention to other matters.

_____ 5. To ensure that a team develops into a cohesive working unit, managers should be especially careful not to intervene in any way during the initial startup period.

_____ 6. Training is not critical to a team because the team will develop any needed skills on its own.

_____ 7. It's easy to provide teams with the support they need because they are basically self-motivating.

_____ 8. Teams need little or no structure to function effectively.

_____ 9. Teams should set their own direction with managers determining the means to the selected end.

_____ 10. Teams can be used in any organization.

For interpretation, see Interpretations of Skills Self-Assessment Instruments.

Source: Test: adapted from J. Richard Hackman (ed.), *Groups That Work (and Those That Don't)*, San Francisco: Jossey-Bass Publishers, 1990, pp. 493–504.

EXPERIENTIAL EXERCISE

Individual Versus Group Performance

Purpose: This exercise demonstrates the benefits a group can bring to accomplishing a task.

Introduction: You will be asked to do the same task both individually and as part of a group.

Instructions: Part 1: You will need a pen or pencil and an 8 ½" × 11" sheet of paper. Working alone, do the following:

1. Write the letters of the alphabet in a vertical column down the left side of the paper: A–Z.
2. Your instructor will randomly select a sentence from any written document and read out loud the first 26 letters in that sentence. Write these letters in a vertical column immediately to the right of the alphabet column. Everyone should have identical sets of 26 two-letter combinations.
3. Working alone, think of a famous person whose initials correspond to each pair of letters and write the name next to the letters; for example, "MT Mark Twain." You will have ten minutes. Only one name per set is allowed. One point is awarded for each legitimate name, so the maximum score is 26 points.
4. After time expires, exchange your paper with another member of the class and score each other's work. The instructor will settle disputes about the legitimacy of names. Keep your score for use later in the exercise.

Part 2: Your instructor will divide the class into groups of five to ten. All groups should have approximately the same number of members. Each group now follows the procedure given in part 1. Again write the letters of the alphabet down the left side of the sheet of paper, this time in reverse order: Z–A. Your instructor will dictate a new set of letters for the second column. The time limit and scoring procedure are the same. The only difference is that the groups will generate the names.

Part 3: Each team identifies the group member who came up with the most names. The instructor places these "best" students into one group. Then all groups repeat part 2, but this time the letters from the reading will be in the first column, and the alphabet letters will be in the second column.

Part 4: Each team calculates the average individual score of its members on part one and compares it with the team score from parts 2 and 3. Your instructor will put the average individual score and team scores for each group on the board.

Followup Questions

1. Do the average individual scores and the team scores differ? What are the reasons for the difference, if any?
2. Although the team scores in this exercise usually are higher than the average individual scores, under what conditions might individual averages exceed group scores?

Source: Adapted from *The 1979 Annual Handbook for Group Facilitators* by John E. Jones and J. W. Pfeiffer (eds.), pp. 19–20. Copyright © 1979 by Pfeiffer, an imprint of Jossey-Bass Inc., Publishers, San Francisco, CA. This material is used by permission of John Wiley & Sons, Inc.

TOTAL TEAMWORK SPARKS IMAGINATION

Run more like a circus than like a traditional company, Imagination Ltd., a London-based design firm, relies on high-performance teams to create museum exhibits, design cruise ship lighting, develop product packaging, and much more. Its 350 employees are experts in 26 wide-ranging disciplines, including architecture, lighting, graphics, web design, and choreography. Despite this diversity, Imagination is anything but hierarchical: Only four employees have official titles such as creative director. How does anything get done? Imagination's answer is total teamwork.

When a client consults with Imagination, the company quickly assembles a cross-functional team of in-house experts to help define the project and determine the goals. Once the client and Imagination agree on the scope of the project, the team members come up with a specific goal statement which they use to guide their work. For example, when Imagination was hired to create a pleasant waiting area for people lining up for the Skyscape attraction inside London's Millennium Dome, the goal statement called for creating a climate of "uncomplicated joy." The team for this project started with an architect, lighting expert, graphic expert, and film director, then expanded to include a choreographer. As in other Imagination projects, the Skyscape team met weekly to brainstorm, flesh out the best ideas, and then adjourn to bring the ideas to life. Clients do not attend these meetings, but their views are well represented, and their feedback is incorporated into team decisions.

Because personnel in other parts of the company are often affected by team actions, everyone is invited to attend each team's weekly project meetings. This tradition keeps the entire workforce informed of problems and progress and allows nonteam members to plan ahead for a later role, such as arranging for printing or transportation at the end of the project. In effect, the entire company functions as a team, with employees monitoring projects and staying up to speed so they are ready to get involved when their expertise is needed.

Many organizations assemble teams of free agents who are hired to work on particular projects and then leave after their work is complete. However, one of Imagination's strengths is that its experts are all employees, so their talents are available to any team at any time. Another strength is that Imagination's teams have no formal leadership. Instead, every member accepts responsibility for the project's success and acts accordingly, providing input and tackling tasks that bring the entire team closer to its goal.

Imagination's team members have earned reputations as experts in their fields and have developed respect for each other through the course of multiple team experiences. As a result, they are open to each other's ideas and listen carefully when colleagues make suggestions. Such interaction crosses disciplines as well, with writers offering advice to lighting specialists, for example. The diversity of the team and the free flow of ideas and information stimulate creativity and enhance the team's effectiveness. Nonetheless, team meetings can be noisy and difficult on occasion, as members staunchly defend their creative ideas and argue over different approaches.

Since Imagination was established in 1978, its talented teams have tackled a wide range of design challenges. One team created the lighting design for Disney cruise ships; another created a dinosaur exhibit for the Natural History Museum in London; yet another designed the Millennium Dome Journey Zone building and exhibit content for corporate sponsor Ford Motor. The company has even worked with clients to train the personnel who staff the places it has designed, to ensure that the entire experience lives up to the goals set at the start of the project. Thanks to total teamwork, Imagination continues to build on its rich internal resources to meet clients' goals in new and exciting ways.

Case Questions

1. What role does conflict play in stimulating creativity at Imagination?

2. Why do Imagination's teams function well without formal leadership?

3. What factors appear to be increasing the cohesiveness of Imagination's teams?

Case References

Charles Fishman, "Total Teamwork: Imagination Ltd.," *Fast Company*, April 2000, pp. 156–168.

CHAPTER NOTES

1. Bradley L. Kirkman and Benson Rosen, "Powering up Teams," *Organizational Dynamics*, Winter 2000, pp. 48–58; and "Fastener's 3-Prong Plan Yields Perfection," *USA Today*, May 2, 1997, p. 9B (*quote on p. 9B).

2. See Gregory Moorhead and Ricky W. Griffin, *Organizational Behavior*, 6th ed. (Boston: Houghton Mifflin, 2001), for a review of definitions of groups.

3. Dorwin Cartwright and Alvin Zander, eds., *Group Dynamics: Research and Theory*, 3rd ed. (New York: Harper & Row, 1968).

4. Robert Schrank, *Ten Thousand Working Days* (Cambridge, Mass.: MIT Press, 1978); and Bill Watson, "Counter Planning on the Shop Floor," in *Organizational Reality*, 2nd ed., ed. Peter Frost, Vance Mitchell, and Walter Nord (Glenview, IL: Scott, Foresman, 1982), pp. 286–294.

5. Kirkman and Rosen.

6. Brian Dumaine, "Payoff from the New Management," *Fortune*, December 13, 1993, pp. 103–110.

7. "Why Teams Fail," *USA Today*, February 25, 1997, pp. 1B, 2B.

8. Brian Dumaine, "The Trouble with Teams," *Fortune*, September 5, 1994, pp. 86–92. See also Susan G. Cohen and Diane E. Bailey, "What Makes Teams Work: Group Effectiveness Research from the Shop Floor to the Executive Suite," *Journal of Management* 23, no. 3 (1997): 239–290.

9. Marvin E. Shaw, *Group Dynamics—The Psychology of Small Group Behavior*, 4th ed. (New York: McGraw-Hill, 1985).

10. "How to Avoid Hiring the Prima Donnas Who Hate Teamwork," *Wall Street Journal*, February 15, 2000, p. B1.

11. See Connie Gersick, "Marking Time: Predictable Transitions in Task Groups," *Academy of Management Journal*, June 1989, pp. 274–309. See also Avan R. Jassawalla and Hemant C. Sashittal, "Building Collaborative Cross-Functional New Product Teams," *Academy of Management Review* 13, no. 3 (1999): 50–60.

12. See Travis C. Tubre and Judith M. Collins, "Jackson and Schuler (1985) Revisited: A Meta-Analysis of the Relationships Between Role Ambiguity, Role Conflict, and Job Performance," *Journal of Management* 26, no. 1 (2000): 155–169.

13. Robert L. Kahn, D. M. Wolfe, R. P. Quinn, J. D. Snoek, and R. A. Rosenthal, *Organizational Stress: Studies in Role Conflict and Role Ambiguity* (New York: Wiley, 1964).

14. Daniel C. Feldman, "The Development and Enforcement of Group Norms," *Academy of Management Review*, January 1984, pp. 47–53.

15. "Companies Turn to Peer Pressure to Cut Injuries as Psychologists Join the Battle," *Wall Street Journal*, March 29, 1991, pp. B1, B3.

16. James Wallace Bishop and K. Dow Scott, "How Commitment Affects Team Performance," *HRMagazine*, February 1997, pp. 107–115.

17. Suzy Wetlaufer, "Common Sense and Conflict," *Harvard Business Review*, January/February 2000, pp. 115–125.

18. Kathleen M. Eisenhardt, Jean L. Kahwajy, and L. J. Bourgeois III, "How Management Teams Can Have a Good Fight," *Harvard Business Review*, July/August 1997, pp. 77–89.

19. Robin Pinkley and Gregory Northcraft, "Conflict Frames of Reference: Implications for Dispute Processes and Outcomes," *Academy of Management Journal* 37, no. 1 (1994): 193–205.

20. "How 2 Computer Nuts Transformed Industry Before Messy Breakup," *Wall Street Journal*, August 27, 1996, pp. A1, A10.

21. "Delta CEO Resigns After Clashes with Board," *USA Today*, May 13, 1997, p. B1.

22. "A 'Blood War' in the Jeans Trade," *Business Week*, November 13, 1999, pp. 74–81.

23. Peter Elkind, "Blood Feud," *Fortune*, April 14, 1997, pp. 90–102.

24. "Solving Conflicts in the Workplace Without Making Losers," *Wall Street Journal*, May 27, 1997, p. B1.

Controlling

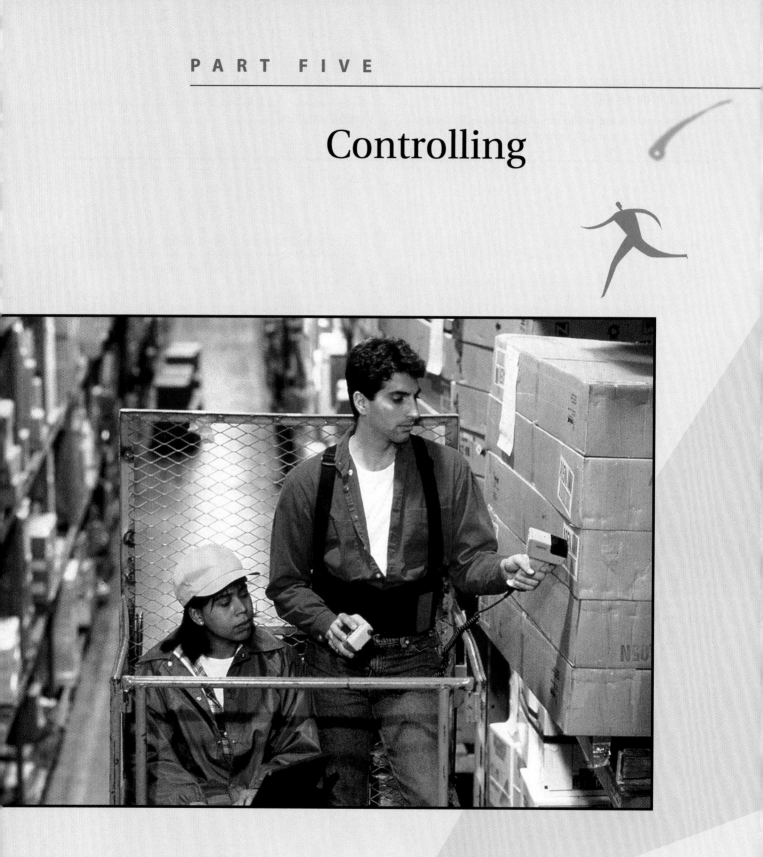

14 Managing the Control Process

Waste Management, started in 1971, is one of the world's largest private waste management companies. The firm does business in the United States, Canada, and Europe and in 1998 earned more than $12 billion in revenues. The company has an excellent reputation for handling trash disposal efficiently and for effectively managing recycling programs. Unfortunately, however, Waste Management's own operations are currently in such disarray that its managers are having to focus most of their energies on sorting out the firm's own waste.

The company's problems first became public in 1997 when an interim CEO took over company reins. As it turned out, massive accounting problems had overstated the firm's earnings for years, and its stock was taking a nosedive. An intensive audit seemed to rectify things, however, and in 1998 senior management at

Waste Management agreed to merge with a smaller, but fast-growing competitor named USA Waste Services. They also agreed to put USA Waste's respected but inexperienced CEO in charge of the new combined company.

For a while everything seemed to be working out well. The new company, which kept the Waste Management moniker, was attracting new business and reporting optimistic business forecasts for future revenues and profit. But in late 1999 everything came crashing down again. As it turned out, the original problems at Waste Management had not been corrected at all, and as a result of the merger, things had quickly gone from bad to worse.

One major problem the firm was experiencing was that, in addition to the big merger between Waste Management and USA Waste, the firm had also acquired literally dozens of

other smaller businesses during a short period of time. But the firm did not appoint a senior executive to oversee the integration of these various businesses, and as a result, some operations were being poorly merged, some were being inexplicably shut down, and others remained in competition with one another.

Costs were also not being closely monitored. For example, even though USA Waste had put down a $2 million nonrefundable deposit for a new $30 million corporate jet for the CEO's use, after the merger, a new $40 million jet was ordered because the merger would result in even more travel demands for the CEO. And, after the firm failed to meet its earning estimates in the second quarter of 1999, no one at

> *"I'm not proud of the fact that, in retrospect, we didn't know what the hell was going on."*
>
> *—Roderick M. Hills,*
> *Waste Management board member*

the company could adequately explain why.

Finally, just as the true nature of the crisis was becoming obvious, the CEO was diagnosed with a serious brain tumor. But, relying on his assurances that he would return to work shortly, Waste Management's board took no action and allowed the firm to continue to drift. Only after it became clear that he would not be able to resume working did the board take any action to reestablish control. So, in early 2000 senior members of the board took control of the firm again and set about straightening out what could only be called a big mess. Indeed, so extensive were the problems at Waste Management that, when new audits were called for, Arthur Andersen assigned 1,160 auditors to the account.

As the numbers started rolling in, Waste Management executives began to recognize the severity of their problems—$211 million in uncollectible bills, $305 million in unrecorded expenses, and $226 million in miscellaneous costs. All told, accounting irregularities resulted in

$1.76 billion in charges. And, finally, Waste Management's board thinks it has identified all the major problems and either corrected them or are at least on the road to recovery. Of course, it is also not the first time they thought they had turned things around, so investors are keeping a wary eye on things.[1]

enior management at Waste Management has failed at one of the most fundamental management responsibilities—control. In general, the CEO did a poor
job of monitoring costs and keeping the organization on track, and the board of directors failed to adequately monitor the performance and activities of the CEO and
other top managers. Effective control helps managers decide where they want
their business to go, point it in that direction, and create systems to keep it on
track. Ineffective control, on the other hand, can result in a lack of focus, weak direction, and poor overall performance.

As we discussed in Chapter 1, control is one of the four basic managerial
functions that provide the organizing framework for this book. In the first section of this chapter, we explain the purpose of control. We then look at types of
control and the steps in the control process. The rest of the chapter examines
the four levels of control that most organizations must employ in order to remain effective: operations, financial, structural, and strategic control. We conclude by discussing the characteristics of effective control, noting why some
people resist control and describing what organizations can do to overcome
this resistance.

The Nature of Control

control The regulation of organizational activities in such a way as
to facilitate goal attainment

Control is the regulation of organizational activities so that some targeted element
of performance remains within acceptable limits. Without this regulation, organizations have no indication of how well they perform in relation to their goals. Control, like a ship's rudder, keeps the organization moving in the proper direction. At
any point in time, it compares where the organization is in terms of performance
(financial, productive, or otherwise) to where it is supposed to be. Like a rudder,
control provides an organization with a mechanism for adjusting its course if performance falls outside of acceptable boundaries. For example, Federal Express has
a performance goal of delivering 99 percent of its packages on time. If on-time deliveries fall to 97 percent, control systems will signal the problem to managers so
that they can make necessary adjustments in operations to regain the target level
of performance. An organization without effective control procedures is not likely
to reach its goals—or, if it does reach them, to know that it has.

The Purpose of Control

As Figure 14.1 illustrates, control provides an organization with ways to adapt to
environmental change, to limit the accumulation of error, to cope with organizational complexity, and to minimize costs. These four functions of control are worth
a closer look.

Adapting to Environmental Change   In today's complex and turbulent business environment, all organizations must contend with change. If managers could
establish goals and achieve them instantaneously, control would not be needed.

Control plays a number of important purposes in organizations. Starbucks, for example, takes pride in the quality of coffees it serves and works to insure that they meet various quality standards for freshness, temperature, taste, and strength. To help uphold these quality standards, coffee tasters like Senior Vice President Mary Williams samples as many as 300 cups of coffee a day for Starbucks. This continuous scrutiny helps the firm catch any problems in roasting, grinding, or brewing that may have inadvertently occurred.

But between the time a goal is established and the time it is reached, many things can happen in the organization and its environment to disrupt movement toward the goal—or even to change the goal itself. A properly designed control system can help managers anticipate, monitor, and respond to changing circumstances. In contrast, an improperly designed system can result in organizational performance that falls far below acceptable levels.

For example, Michigan-based Metalloy, a 46-year-old family-run metal casting company, signed a contract to make engine-seal castings for NOK, a big Japanese auto parts maker. Metalloy was satisfied when its first 5,000-unit production run yielded 4,985 acceptable castings and only 15 defective ones. NOK,

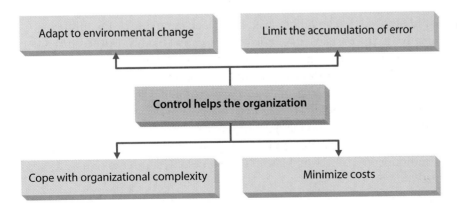

Figure 14.1

The Purpose of Control
Control is one of the four basic management functions in organizations. The control function, in turn, has four basic purposes. Properly designed control systems are able to fulfill each of these purposes.

however, was quite unhappy with this performance and insisted that Metalloy raise its standards. In short, global quality standards are such that many customers demand near perfection from their suppliers. A properly designed control system can help managers like those at Metalloy stay better attuned to rising standards.

Limiting the Accumulation of Error   Small mistakes and errors do not often seriously damage the financial health of an organization. Over time, however, small errors may accumulate and become very serious. For example, Whistler Corporation, a large radar detector manufacturer, once faced such rapidly escalating demand that it essentially stopped worrying about quality. The defect rate rose from 4 percent to 9 percent to 15 percent and eventually reached 25 percent. One day, a manager realized that 100 of the firm's 250 employees were spending all their time fixing defective units and that $2 million worth of inventory was awaiting repair. Had the company adequately controlled quality as it responded to increased demand, the problem would have never reached such proportions. Similarly, Fleetwood Enterprises, a large manufacturer of recreational vehicles, has suffered because its managers did not adequately address several small accounting and production problems years ago. These small problems have now grown into large ones, and the firm is struggling with how to correct them.[2]

Coping with Organizational Complexity   When a firm purchases only one raw material, produces one product, has a simple organization design, and enjoys constant demand for its product, its managers can maintain control with a very basic and simple system. But a business that produces many products from myriad raw materials and has a large market area, a complicated organization design, and many competitors needs a sophisticated system in order to maintain adequate control. In part, this explains what happened at Waste Management—after the firm merged with USA Waste, the new enterprise was so large and complex that the existing control systems were simply inadequate.

Minimizing Costs   When it is practiced effectively, control can also help reduce costs and boost output. For example, Georgia-Pacific Corporation, a large wood products company, learned of a new technology that could be used to make thinner blades for its saws. The firm's control system was used to calculate the amount of wood that could be saved from each cut made by the thinner blades relative to the costs used to replace the existing blades. The results have been impressive—the wood that is saved by the new blades each year fills 800 railcars. As Georgia-Pacific discovered, effective control systems can eliminate waste, lower labor costs, and improve output per unit of input. Similarly, the CEO of Travelers' Insurance decided that the $60,000 cost of repairing a broken fountain in front of company headquarters was excessive and instead spent only $20,000 to have it filled and planted with a low-maintenance tree. And Coca-Cola recently announced that it would lay off 6,000 workers in order to reduce its labor costs.[3]

Types of Control

The examples of control given thus far have illustrated the regulation of several organizational activities, from producing quality products to coordinating complex organizations. Organizations practice control in a number of different areas and at different levels, and the responsibility for managing control is widespread.

Areas of Control   Control can focus on any area of an organization. Most organizations define areas of control in terms of the four basic types of resources they use: physical, human, information, and financial resources.[4] Control of physical resources includes inventory management (stocking neither too few nor too many units in inventory), quality control (maintaining appropriate levels of output quality), and equipment control (supplying the necessary facilities and machinery). Control of human resources includes selection and placement, training and development, performance appraisal, and compensation. Control of information resources includes sales and marketing forecasting, environmental analysis, public relations, production scheduling, and economic forecasting. Financial control involves managing the organization's debt so that it does not become excessive, so that the firm always has enough cash on hand to meet its obligations but does not have excess cash in a checking account, and so that receivables are collected and bills are paid on a timely basis.

In many ways, the control of financial resources is the most important area. This is because financial resources are related to the control of all the other resources in an organization. Too much inventory leads to storage costs; poor selection of personnel leads to termination and rehiring expenses; inaccurate sales forecasts lead to disruptions in cash flows and other financial effects. Financial issues tend to pervade most control-related activities. Indeed, financial issues are the basic problem faced by Waste Management. Various inefficiencies and operating blunders put the company in a position in which it was losing money everywhere but lacked sufficient control to pinpoint specific problems.

Levels of Control   Just as control can be broken down by area, as Figure 14.2 shows, it can also be broken down by level within the organizational system. **Operations control** focuses on the processes the organization uses to transform resources into products or services (quality control is one type of operations control).[5] **Financial control** is concerned with the organization's financial resources (monitoring receivables to make sure customers are paying their bills on time is an example of financial control). **Structural control** is concerned with how the elements of the organization's structure are serving their intended purposes (monitoring the administrative ratio to make sure staff expenses do not become excessive is an example of structural control). Finally, **strategic control** focuses on how effectively the organization's corporate, business, and functional strategies are succeeding in helping the organization meet its goals (for example, if a corporation has been unsuccessful in implementing its strategy of related diversification, its managers need to identify the reasons and either change the strategy or

operations control Focuses on the processes the organization uses to transform resources into products or services

financial control Concerned with the organization's financial resources

structural control Concerned with how the elements of the organization's structure are serving their intended purpose

strategic control Focuses on how effectively the organization's strategies are succeeding in helping the organization meet its goals

Figure 14.2

Levels of Control

Managers use control at several different levels. The most basic levels of control in organizations are strategic, structural, operations, and financial control. Each level must be managed properly if control is to be most effective.

controller A position in organizations that helps line managers with their control activities

renew their efforts to implement it). We discuss these four levels of control more fully later in this chapter.

Responsibility for Control   Traditionally, managers have been responsible for overseeing the wide array of control systems and concerns in organizations. They decide which types of control the organization will use, and they implement control systems and take actions based on the information provided by control systems. Thus ultimate responsibility for control rests with all managers throughout an organization.

Most larger organizations also have one or more specialized managerial positions called "controller." A **controller** is responsible for helping line managers with their control activities, for coordinating the organization's overall control system, and for gathering and assimilating relevant information. Many businesses that use an H-form or M-form organization design have several controllers: one for the corporation and one for each division. The job of controller is especially important in organizations where control systems are complex. As part of its turnaround effort, Waste Management has established controller positions at each of its locations—some 600 in all.

In addition, many organizations are also beginning to use operating employees to help maintain effective control. Indeed, employee participation is often used as a vehicle for allowing operating employees an opportunity to help facilitate organizational effectiveness. For example, Whistler Corporation increased employee participation in an effort to turn its quality problems around. As a starting point, the quality control unit, formerly responsible for checking product quality at the end of the assembly process, was eliminated. Next, all operating employees were encouraged to check their own work and were told that they would be responsible for correcting their own errors. As a result, Whistler has eliminated its quality problems and is now highly profitable once again.

Steps in the Control Process

Regardless of the type or levels of control systems an organization needs, there are four fundamental steps in any control process.[6] These are illustrated in Figure 14.3.

control standard A target against which subsequent performance will be compared

Establish Standards   The first step in the control process is establishing standards. A **control standard** is a target against which subsequent performance will be compared. Employees at Taco Bell fast-food restaurants, for example, work toward the following service standards:

1. A minimum of 95 percent of all customers will be greeted within 3 minutes of their arrival.
2. Preheated tortilla chips will not sit in the warmer more than 30 minutes before they are served to customers.
3. Empty tables will be cleaned within 5 minutes after being vacated.

Figure 14.3

Steps in the Control Process

Having an effective control system can help ensure that an organization achieves its goals. Implementing a control system, however, is a systematic process that generally proceeds through four interrelated steps.

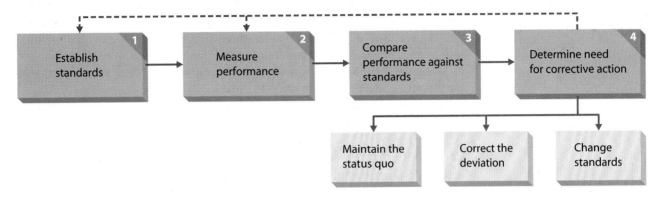

Standards established for control purposes should be expressed in measurable terms. Note that standard 1 has a time limit of 3 minutes and an objective target of 95 percent of all customers. In standard 3, the objective target is implied: "all" empty tables.

Control standards should also be consistent with the organization's goals. Taco Bell has organizational goals involving customer service, food quality, and restaurant cleanliness. A control standard for a retailer like Home Depot should be consistent with its goal of increasing its annual sales volume by 20 percent within five years. A hospital trying to shorten the average hospital stay by a patient will have control standards that reflect current averages. A university reaffirming its commitment to academics might adopt a standard of graduating 80 percent of its student athletes within five years of their enrollment. Control standards can be as narrow or as broad as the level of activity to which they apply and must follow logically from organizational goals and objectives.

A final aspect of establishing standards is to identify performance indicators. Performance indicators are measures of performance that provide information that is directly relevant to what is being controlled. For example, suppose an organization is following a tight schedule in building a new plant. Relevant performance indicators could be buying a site, selecting a building contractor, and ordering equipment. Monthly sales increases are not, however, directly relevant. On the other hand, if control is being focused on revenue, monthly sales increases are relevant, whereas buying land for a new plant is less relevant.

Measure Performance The second step in the control process is measuring performance. Performance measurement is a constant, ongoing activity for most organizations. For control to be effective, performance measures must be valid. Daily, weekly, and monthly sales figures measure sales performance, and production performance may be expressed in terms of unit cost, product quality, or volume produced. Employee performance often may be measured in terms of quality or quantity of output, but for many jobs measuring performance is not so straightforward.

A research and development scientist at Merck, for example, may spend years working on a single project before achieving a breakthrough. A manager who takes over a business on the brink of failure may need months or even years to turn things around. Valid performance measurement, however difficult to obtain, is nevertheless vital in maintaining effective control, and performance indicators usually can be developed. The scientist's progress, for example, may be partially assessed by peer review, and the manager's success may be evaluated by her ability to convince creditors that she will eventually be able to restore profitability.

Compare Performance Against Standards   The third step in the control process is comparing measured performance against established standards. Performance may be higher than, lower than, or identical to the standard. In some cases, comparison is easy. The goal of each product manager at General Electric is to make the product either number one or number two (on the basis of total sales) in its market. Because this standard is clear and total sales easy to calculate, it is relatively simple to determine whether this standard has been met. Sometimes, however, comparisons are less clear-cut. If performance is lower than expected, the question is how much deviation from standards to allow before taking remedial action. For example, is increasing sales by 7.9 percent when the standard was 8 percent close enough?

The timetable for comparing performance to standards depends on a variety of factors, including the importance and complexity of what is being controlled. For longer-run and higher-level standards, comparisons may be appropriate annually. In other circumstances, more frequent comparisons are necessary. For example, a business with a cash shortage may need to monitor its on-hand cash reserves daily.

Determine Need for Corrective Action   The final step in the control process is determining the need for corrective action. Decisions regarding corrective actions draw heavily on a manager's analytic and diagnostic skills. After comparing performance against control standards, one of three actions is appropriate: maintain the status quo (do nothing), correct the deviation, or change the standard. Maintaining the status quo is preferable when performance essentially matches the standard, but it is more likely that some action will be needed to correct a deviation from the standard.

Sometimes performance that is higher than expected may also cause problems for organizations. For example, when DaimlerChrysler first introduced its popular PT Cruiser, demand was so strong that there were waiting lists, and many customers were willing to pay more than the suggested retail price to obtain a car. The company was reluctant to increase production, primarily because it feared demand would eventually drop. At the same time, however, it did not want to alienate potential customers. Consequently, DaimlerChrysler decided to simply reduce its advertising. This curtailed demand a bit and limited customer frustration.

Changing an established standard usually is necessary if it was set too high or too low at the outset. This is apparent if large numbers of employees routinely beat the standard by a wide margin or if no employees ever meet the standard. Also, standards that seemed perfectly appropriate when they were established may need to be adjusted because circumstances have since changed.

Operations Control

One of the four levels of control practiced by most organizations, operations control, is concerned with the processes the organization uses to transform resources into products or services. As Figure 14.4 shows, the three forms of operations control—preliminary, screening, and postaction—occur at different points in relation to the transformation processes used by the organization.

Preliminary Control

Preliminary control concentrates on the resources—financial, material, human, and information—that the organization brings in from the environment. Preliminary control attempts to monitor the quality or quantity of these resources before they enter the organization. Firms like PepsiCo and General Mills hire only college graduates for their management training program, and even then only after applicants satisfy several interviewers and selection criteria. In this way, they control the quality of the human resources entering the organization. When Sears orders merchandise to be manufactured under its own brand name, it specifies rigid standards of quality, thereby controlling physical inputs. Organizations also control financial and information resources. For example, privately held companies like UPS and Mars limit the extent to which outsiders can buy their stock, and television networks attempt to verify the accuracy of news stories before they are broadcast. *Management InfoTech* explains how some businesses today are using electronic purchasing as part of their preliminary control processes.

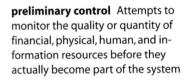

preliminary control Attempts to monitor the quality or quantity of financial, physical, human, and information resources before they actually become part of the system

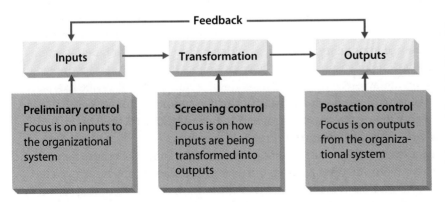

Figure 14.4

Forms of Operations Control

Most organizations develop multiple control systems that incorporate all three basic forms of control. For example, the publishing company that produced this book screens inputs by hiring only qualified persons, typesetters, and printers (preliminary control). In addition, quality is checked during the transformation process such as after the manuscript is typeset (screening control), and the outputs—printed and bound books—are checked before they are shipped from the bindery (postaction control).

E-PURCHASING KEEPS INPUTS UNDER CONTROL

Buying from other businesses is big business. Every year, companies buy more than $7 trillion worth of parts, supplies, and services from suppliers around the world. Not so long ago, purchasing agents and other buyers had to hunt through mountains of supplier catalogues and make dozens of phone calls to track down stock numbers and quotes before writing purchase orders. Now, by using technology to tighten control of the purchasing function, a company can take much of the time and the hassle out of the process of acquiring inputs—and expand its scope to scour the globe for the lowest prices or the quickest delivery times.

On the CheMatch.com web site, for example, buyers can see current market prices and availability for chemicals such as benzene and book orders online with a few keystrokes. On the Petrocosm Marketplace site, buyers for energy companies can instantly compare competitive prices on drilling machinery and other supplies, then place orders online. On FreeMarkets.com, buyers can arrange reverse auctions in which suppliers bid for the right to provide a particular input.

The savings can be enormous, as the following examples show. John Deere's e-purchasing initiative is expected to shave 5 percent off its annual cost of parts and supplies. Over the course of five years, the farm equipment manufacturer will save a total of $1 billion, giving its bottom line a healthy boost. What's more, Deere is achieving these impressive results while reducing the size of its purchasing department by 25 percent. United Technologies, an energy company, has slashed its input expenses by almost $800 million. IBM now uses the web to buy 90 percent of its supplies, streamlining its control of a $45 million supply budget. And online reverse auctions have helped the Naval Supply Systems Command save 22 percent on bunk units purchased for U.S. Navy ships. Tighter control, increased efficiency, and lower costs—the combination makes e-purchasing an attractive technique for businesses of any size.

> *With anonymity, you can move in the market without moving the market. It's a lot easier to click a mouse than call around the world.*
>
> —*Carl McCutcheon, CEO of CheMatch.com**

References: Del Jones, "E-Purchasing Saves Businesses Billions," *USA Today,* February 7, 2000, pp. 1B, 2B (*quote on p. 2B); and "Contract Awarded in NAVSUP's Second Reverse Auction," *NAVICP,* August 3, 2000, http://www.navicp.navy.mil/news/reverseauction2.htm (October 2, 2000).

Screening Control

screening control Relies heavily on feedback processes during the transformation process

Screening control focuses on meeting standards for product or service quality or quantity during the actual transformation process itself. Screening control relies heavily on feedback processes. For example, in a Compaq Computer factory computer system, components are checked periodically as each unit is being assembled. This is done to ensure that all the components that have been assembled up to that point are working properly. The periodic quality checks provide feedback to workers so that they know what, if any, corrective actions to take. Because they are useful in identifying the cause of problems, screening controls tend to be used more often than other forms of control.

More and more companies are adopting screening controls because they are an effective way to promote employee participation and catch problems early in the overall transformation process. For example, Corning adopted screening controls for use in manufacturing television glass. In the past, finished television screens were inspected only after they were finished. Unfortunately, over 4 percent of them were later returned by customers because of defects. Now the glass screens are inspected at each step in the production process rather than at the end, and the return rate from customers has dropped to .03 percent.

Postaction Control

Postaction control focuses on the outputs of the organization after the transformation process is complete. Corning's old system was postaction control—final inspection only after the product was completed. Although Corning abandoned its postaction control system, this method may still be effective in some cases, primarily if a product can be manufactured in only one or two steps or if the service is fairly simple and routine. Although postaction control alone may not be as effective as preliminary or screening control, it can provide management with information for future planning. For example, if a quality check of finished goods indicates an unacceptably high defective rate, the production manager knows that he or she must identify the causes and take steps to eliminate them. Postaction control also provides a basis for rewarding employees. Recognizing that an employee has exceeded personal sales goals by a wide margin, for example, may alert the manager that a bonus or promotion is in order.

Well-established and monitored financial regulations in most of today's developed economies ensure that financial control systems can be easily followed and readily interpreted and evaluated. But less certainty exists in some of today's developing economies. The Almaty stock exchange in Kazakhstan is subject to few rules and has no operating procedures. Not surprisingly, the exchange has had difficulty in attracting foreign investors. But as these economies mature and continue to develop, new controls will be created and investors can have more faith in the financial information they are given.

postaction control Monitors the outputs or results of the organization after the transformation process is complete

Most organizations use more than one form of operations control. For example, Honda's preliminary control includes hiring only qualified employees and specifying strict quality standards when ordering parts from other manufacturers. Honda uses numerous screening controls in checking the quality of components during assembly of cars. A final inspection and test drive as each car rolls off the assembly line are part of the company's postaction control.[7] Indeed, most, successful organizations employ a wide variety of techniques to facilitate operations control.

Financial Control

Financial control is the control of financial resources as they flow into the organization (revenues, shareholder investments), are held by the organization (working capital, retained earnings), and flow out of the organization (expenses). Businesses must manage their finances so that revenues are sufficient to cover cost expenses and still return a profit to the firm's owners. Not-for-profit organizations such as universities have the same concerns: Their revenues (from tax dollars or tuition) must cover operating expenses and overhead. Dickson Poon is a Chinese investor who has profited by relying heavily on financial control. He buys distressed upscale retailers like Britain's Harvey Nichols and the United States' Barney's, implements strict financial control systems, and begins generating hefty profits.[8] A complete discussion of financial management is beyond the scope of this book, but we will examine the control provided by budgets and other financial control tools.

Budgetary Control

budget A plan expressed in numerical terms

A **budget** is a plan expressed in numerical terms. Organizations establish budgets for work groups, departments, divisions, and the whole organization. The usual time period for a budget is one year, although breakdowns of budgets by the quarter or month are also common. Budgets are generally expressed in financial terms, but they may occasionally be expressed in units of output, time, or other quantifiable factors.

Because of their quantitative nature, budgets provide yardsticks for measuring performance and facilitate comparisons across departments, between levels in the organization, and from one time period to another. Budgets serve four primary purposes. They help managers coordinate resources and projects (because they use a common denominator, usually dollars). They help define the established standards for control. They provide guidelines about the organization's resources and expectations. Finally, budgets enable the organization to evaluate the performance of managers and organizational units.

Types of Budgets   Most organizations develop and make use of three different kinds of budgets—financial, operating, and nonmonetary. Table 14.1 summarizes the characteristics of each of these.

A financial budget indicates where the organization expects to get its cash for the coming time period and how it plans to use it. Because financial resources are critically important, the organization needs to know where those resources will be coming from and how they are to be used. The financial budget provides answers to both these questions. Usual sources of cash include sales revenue, short- and long-term loans, the sale of assets, and the issuance of new stock.

For years, Exxon Mobil has been very conservative in its capital budgeting. As a result, the firm has amassed a huge financial reserve but has been overtaken in sales by Royal Dutch/Shell. More recently, Exxon Mobil has decided to loosen its purse strings and begin budgeting more for capital expenditures. For example, although Exxon Mobil's capital budget was less than $8 billion in 1994, managers increased this budget to $9.2 billion in 1996 and to around $11 billion in 2000.[9]

An operating budget is concerned with planned operations within the organization. It outlines what quantities of products or services the organization intends to create and what resources will be used to create them. IBM creates an operating

Type of Budget	What Budget Shows
Financial budget	**Sources and uses of cash**
Cash-flow or cash budget	All sources of cash income and cash expenditures in monthly, weekly, or daily periods
Capital expenditures budget	Costs of major assets, such as a new plant, machinery, or land
Balance sheet budget	Forecast of the organization's assets and liabilities in the event all other budgets are met
Operating budget	**Planned operations in financial terms**
Sales or revenue budget	Income the organization expects to receive from normal operations
Expense budget	Anticipated expenses for the organization during the coming time period
Profit budget	Anticipated differences between sales or revenues and expenses
Nonmonetary budget	**Planned operations in nonfinancial terms**
Labor budget	Hours of direct labor available for use
Space budget	Square feet or meters of space available for various functions
Production budget	Number of units to be produced during the coming time period

Table 14.1

Types of Budgets
Organizations use various types of budgets to help manage their control function. The three major categories of budgets are financial, operating, and nonmonetary budgets. There are several different types of budgets in each category. Each budget must be carefully matched with the specific function being controlled to be most effective.

budget that specifies how many of each version of its personal computer will be produced each quarter.

A nonmonetary budget is simply a budget expressed in nonfinancial terms, such as units of output, hours of direct labor, machine hours, or square-foot allocations. Nonmonetary budgets are most commonly used by managers at the lower levels of an organization. For example, a plant manager can schedule work more effectively, knowing that he or she has 8,000 labor hours to allocate in a week, rather than trying to determine how to best spend $76,451 in wages in a week. Likewise, when planning a new building, a college or university may allocate a certain amount of space to each department and program office.

Developing Budgets   Traditionally, budgets were developed by top management and the controller, and then imposed on lower-level managers. Although some organizations still follow this pattern, many contemporary organizations now allow all managers to participate in the budget process. As a starting point, top management generally issues a call for budget requests, accompanied by an indication of overall patterns the budgets may take. For example, if sales are expected to drop in the next year, managers may be told up front to prepare for cuts in operating budgets.

As Figure 14.5 shows, the heads of each operating unit typically submit budget requests to the head of their division. An operating unit head might be a

Figure 14.5

Developing Budgets in Organizations

Most organizations use the same basic process to develop budgets. Operating units are requested to submit their budget requests to divisions. These divisions, in turn, compile unit budgets and submit their own budgets to the organization. An organizational budget is then compiled for approval by the budget committee, controller, and CEO.

Operating unit budget requests

Division budget requests

Organizational budget
- Prepared by budget committee
- Approved by budget committee, controller, and CEO

department manager in a manufacturing or wholesaling firm or a program director in a social service agency. The division heads might include plant managers, regional sales managers, or college deans. The division head integrates and consolidates the budget requests from operating unit heads into one overall division budget request. A great deal of interaction among managers usually takes place at this stage, as the division head coordinates the budgetary needs of the various departments.

Division budget requests are then forwarded to a budget committee. The budget committee is usually composed of top managers. The committee reviews budget requests from several divisions, and, once again, duplications and inconsistencies are corrected. Finally, the budget committee, the controller, and the CEO review and agree on the overall budget for the organization as well as specific budgets for each operating unit. These decisions are then communicated back to each manager.

Strengths and Weaknesses of Budgeting Budgets offer a number of advantages, but they have weaknesses as well. On the plus side, budgets facilitate effective control. Placing dollar values on operations enables managers to monitor operations better and pinpoint problem areas. Budgets also facilitate coordination and communication between departments because they express diverse activities in a common denominator (dollars). Budgets help maintain records of organizational performance and are a logical complement to planning. That is, as managers develop plans, they should simultaneously consider control measures to accompany them. Organizations can use budgets to link plans and control by first developing budgets as part of the plan and then using those budgets as a part of control.

On the other hand, some managers apply budgets too rigidly. Budgets are intended to serve as frameworks, but managers sometimes fail to recognize that changing circumstances may warrant budget adjustments. The process of developing budgets can also be very time consuming. Finally, budgets may limit innovation and change. When all available funds are allocated to specific operating budgets, it may be impossible to procure additional funds to take advantage of an unexpected opportunity.

Indeed, for these very reasons, some organizations are working to scale back their budgeting system. Although most organizations are likely to continue to use budgets, the goal is to make them less confining and rigid. For example, Xerox, 3M, and Compaq Computer have all cut back on their budgeting systems by reducing the number of budgets they generate and by injecting more flexibility into the budgeting process.

Other Tools of Financial Control

Although budgets are the most common means of financial control, other useful tools are financial statements, ratio analysis, and financial audits.

Financial Statements

A **financial statement** is a profile of some aspect of an organization's financial circumstances. There are commonly accepted and required ways that financial statements be prepared and presented. The two most basic financial statements prepared and used by virtually all organizations are a balance sheet and an income statement.

The **balance sheet** lists the assets and liabilities of the organization at a specific point in time, usually the last day of an organization's fiscal year. For example, the balance sheet might summarize the financial condition of an organization on December 31, 2002. Most balance sheets are divided into current assets (assets that are relatively liquid, or easily convertible into cash); fixed assets (assets that are longer term in nature and less liquid); current liabilities (debts and other obligations that must be paid in the near future); long-term liabilities (payable over an extended period of time); and stockholders' equity (the owners' claim against the assets).

Whereas the balance sheet reflects a snapshot profile of an organization's financial position at a single point in time, the **income statement** summarizes financial performance over a period of time, usually one year. For example, the income statement might be for the period January 1, 2002, through December 31, 2002. The income statement summarizes the firm's revenues less its expenses to report net income (profit or loss) for the period. Information from the balance sheet and income statement is used in computing important financial ratios.

Ratio Analysis

Financial ratios compare different elements of a balance sheet and income statement to one another. **Ratio analysis** is the calculation of one or more financial ratios to assess some aspect of the financial health of an organization. Organizations use a variety of different financial ratios as part of financial control. For example, *liquidity ratios* indicate how liquid (easily converted into cash) an organization's assets are. *Debt ratios* reflect ability to meet long-term financial obligations. *Return ratios* show managers and investors how much return the organization is generating relative to its assets. *Coverage ratios* help estimate the organization's ability to cover interest expenses on borrowed capital. *Operating ratios* indicate the effectiveness of specific functional areas rather than of the total organization. The Walt Disney Company relies heavily on financial ratios to keep its financial operations on track.[10]

Financial Audits

Audits are independent appraisals of an organization's accounting, financial, and operational systems. The two major types of financial audits are the external audit and the internal audit.

---

financial statement A profile of some aspect of an organization's financial circumstances

balance sheet List of assets and liabilities of an organization at a specific point in time

income statement A summary of financial performance over a period of time

ratio analysis The calculation of one or more financial ratios to assess some aspect of the organization's financial health

audit An independent appraisal of an organization's accounting, financial, and operational systems.

External audits are financial appraisals conducted by experts who are not employees of the organization. External audits are typically concerned with determining that the organization's accounting procedures and financial statements are compiled in an objective and verifiable fashion. The organization contracts with certified public accountants (CPAs) for this service. The CPA's main objective is to verify for stockholders, the IRS, and other interested parties that the methods by which the organization's financial managers and accountants prepare documents and reports are legal and proper. External audits are so important that publicly held corporations are required by law to have external audits regularly, as assurance to investors that the financial reports are reliable. An external audit at Enron Corporation recently revealed some serious irregularities in the energy company's financial system. As a result, the firm went from being one of the largest companies in the United States to filing for bankruptcy in a matter of weeks in late 2001.

Some organizations are also starting to employ external auditors to review other aspects of their financial operations. For example, there are now auditing firms that specialize in checking corporate legal bills. An auditor for the Fireman's Fund Insurance Corporation uncovered several thousands of dollars in legal fee errors. Other auditors are beginning to specialize in real estate, employee benefits, and pension plan investments.

Whereas external audits are conducted by external accountants, an *internal audit* is handled by employees of the organization. Its objective is the same as that of an external audit—to verify the accuracy of financial and accounting procedures used by the organization. Internal audits also examine the efficiency and appropriateness of financial and accounting procedures. Because the staff members who conduct them are a permanent part of the organization, internal audits tend to be more expensive than external audits. But employees, who are more familiar with the organization's practices, may also point out significant aspects of the accounting system besides its technical correctness. Large organizations such as Dresser Industries and Ford have internal auditing staffs that spend all their time conducting audits of different divisions and functional areas of the organizations. Smaller organizations may assign accountants to an internal audit group on a temporary or rotating basis.

Structural Control

Organizations can create designs for themselves that result in very different approaches to control. Two major forms of structural control, bureaucratic control and clan control, represent opposite ends of a continuum, as shown in Figure 14.6.[11] The six dimensions shown in the figure represent perspectives adopted by the two extreme types of structural control. That is, they have different goals, degrees of formality, performance expectations, organization designs, reward systems, and levels of participation. Although a few organizations fall precisely at one extreme or the other, most tend toward one end but may have specific characteristics of either.

Figure 14.6

Organizational Control

Organizational control generally falls somewhere between the two extremes of bureaucratic and clan control. NBC Television uses bureaucratic control, whereas Levi Strauss uses clan control.

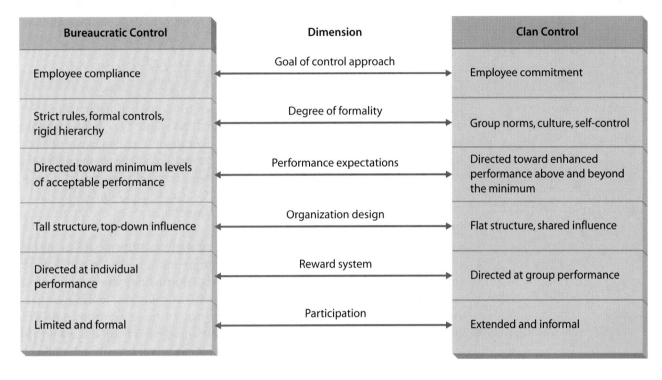

Bureaucratic Control	Dimension	Clan Control
Employee compliance	Goal of control approach	Employee commitment
Strict rules, formal controls, rigid hierarchy	Degree of formality	Group norms, culture, self-control
Directed toward minimum levels of acceptable performance	Performance expectations	Directed toward enhanced performance above and beyond the minimum
Tall structure, top-down influence	Organization design	Flat structure, shared influence
Directed at individual performance	Reward system	Directed at group performance
Limited and formal	Participation	Extended and informal

Bureaucratic Control

Bureaucratic control is an approach to organization design characterized by formal and mechanistic structural arrangements. As the term suggests, it follows the bureaucratic model. The goal of bureaucratic control is employee compliance. Organizations that use it rely on strict rules and a rigid hierarchy, insist that employees meet minimally acceptable levels of performance, and often have a tall structure. They focus their rewards on individual performance and allow only limited and formal employee participation.

NBC television applies structural controls that reflect many elements of bureaucracy. The organization relies on numerous rules to regulate employee travel, expense accounts, and other expenses. A new performance appraisal system precisely specifies minimally acceptable levels of performance for everyone. The organization's structure is considerably taller than those of the other major networks, and rewards are based on individual contributions. Perhaps most significantly, many NBC employees have argued that they have too small a voice in how the organization is managed.

bureaucratic control A form of organizational control characterized by formal and mechanistic structural arrangements

In another example, a large oil company recently made the decision to allow employees to wear casual attire to work. But a committee then spent weeks developing a 20-page set of guidelines on what was and was not acceptable. For example, denim pants are not allowed. Similarly, athletic shoes may be worn as long as they are not white. And all shirts must have a collar. Nordstrom, the department store chain, is also moving toward bureaucratic control as it works to centralize all its purchasing in an effort to lower costs.[12]

Clan Control

clan control An approach to organizational control based on informal and organic structural arrangements

Clan control, in contrast, is an approach to organizational design characterized by informal and organic structural arrangements. As Figure 14.6 shows, its goal is employee commitment to the organization. Accordingly, it relies heavily on group norms and a strong corporate culture, and gives employees the responsibility for controlling themselves. Employees are encouraged to perform beyond minimally acceptable levels. Organizations using this approach are usually relatively flat. They direct reward at group performance and favor widespread employee participation.

Levi Strauss practices clan control. The firm's managers use groups as the basis for work and have created a culture wherein group norms help facilitate high performance. Rewards are subsequently provided to the higher-performing groups and teams. The company's culture also reinforces contributions to the overall team effort, and employees have a strong sense of loyalty to the organization. Levi's has a flat structure, and power is widely shared. Employee participation is encouraged in all areas of operation. Another company that uses this approach is Southwest Airlines. When Southwest made the decision to "go casual," the firm resisted the temptation to develop dress guidelines. Instead, managers decided to allow employees to exercise discretion over their attire and to deal with clearly inappropriate situations on a case-by-case basis as they arise.

■ Strategic Control

Given the obvious importance of an organization's strategy, it is also important that the organization assess how effective that strategy is in helping the organization meet its goals.[13] To do this requires that the organization integrate its strategy and control systems. This is especially true for the global organization.

Integrating Strategy and Control

strategic control Control aimed at ensuring that the organization is maintaining an effective alignment with its environment and is moving toward achieving its strategic goals

Strategic control generally focuses on five aspects of organizations—structure, leadership, technology, human resources, and information and operational control systems. For example, an organization should periodically examine its structure to determine whether or not it is facilitating the attainment of the strategic goals being sought. Suppose a firm using a functional (U-form) design has an established goal of achieving a 20 percent sales growth rate per year. However, performance indicators show that it is currently growing at a rate of only 10 percent per year. Detailed analysis might reveal that the current structure is inhibiting growth in some way (for example, by slowing decision making and inhibiting innovation) and that a divisional (M-form) design would be more likely to bring about the desired growth (by speeding decision making and promoting innovation).

In this way, strategic control focuses on the extent to which implemented strategy achieves the organization's strategic goals. If, as outlined above, one or more avenues of implementation are inhibiting the attainment of goals, that avenue should be changed. Consequently, the firm might find it necessary to alter its structure, replace key leaders, adopt new technology, modify its human resources, or change its information and operational control systems. For example, Ikea, the Swedish furniture manufacturer, has experienced disappointing performance from its internationalization strategy. As a result, the company has announced a major change in how it will manage its international operations.

International Strategic Control

Because of both their relatively large size and the increased complexity associated with international business, global organizations must take an especially pronounced strategic view of their control systems. One very basic question that has to be addressed is whether to manage control from a centralized or a decentralized perspective.[14] Under a centralized system, each organizational unit around the world is responsible for frequently reporting the results of its performance to headquarters. Managers from the home office often visit foreign branches to observe first-hand how the units are functioning.

BP Amoco, Unilever, Procter & Gamble, and Sony all use this approach. They believe centralized control is effective because it allows the home office to keep better informed of the performance of foreign units and to maintain more control over how decisions are made. For example, BP Amoco discovered that its Australian subsidiary was not billing its customers for charges as quickly as were its competitors. By shortening the billing cycle, BP Amoco now receives customer payments five days faster than before. Managers believe that they discovered this oversight only because of a centralized financial control system.

Organizations that use a decentralized control system require foreign branches to report to corporate headquarters less frequently and in less detail. For example, each unit may submit summary performance statements on a quarterly basis and provide full statements only once a year. Similarly, visits from the home office are less frequent and less concerned with monitoring and assessing performance. IBM, Ford, and Shell all use this approach. Because Ford practices decentralized control of its design function, European designers have developed several innovative automobile design features. Managers believe that, if they had been more centralized, designers would not have had the freedom to develop their new ideas.

■ *Managing Control in Organizations*

Effective control, whether at the operations, financial, structural, or strategic level, successfully regulates and monitors organizational activities. To use the control process, managers must recognize the characteristics of effective control and understand how to identify and overcome occasional resistance to control.[15]

Characteristics of Effective Control

Control systems tend to be most effective when they are integrated with planning and when they are flexible, accurate, timely, and objective.

Integration with Planning   Control should be linked with planning. The more explicit and precise this linkage, the more effective the control system will be. The best way to integrate planning and control is to account for control as plans develop. In other words, as goals are set during the planning process, attention should be paid to developing standards that will reflect how well the plan is realized. Managers at Champion Spark Plug Company decided to broaden their product line to include a full range of automotive accessories—a total of 21 new products. As a part of this plan, managers decided in advance what level of sales they wanted to realize from each product for each of the next five years. They established these sales goals as standards against which actual sales would be compared. Thus, by accounting for their control system as they developed their plan, managers at Champion did an excellent job of integrating planning and control.

Flexiblity   The control system itself must be flexible enough to accommodate change. Consider, for example, an organization whose diverse product line requires 75 different raw materials. The company's inventory control system must be able to manage and monitor current levels of inventory for all 75 materials. When a change in product line changes the number of raw materials needed or when the required quantities of the existing materials change, the control system should be flexible enough to handle the revised requirements. The alternative—designing and implementing a new control system—is an avoidable expense. Champion's control system includes a mechanism that automatically shipped products to major customers to keep their inventory at predetermined levels. The firm had to adjust this system when one of its biggest customers decided not to stock the full line of Champion products. Because its control system was flexible, modifying it for the customer was relatively simple.

Accuracy   Managers make a surprisingly large number of decisions based on inaccurate information. Field representatives may hedge their sales estimates to make themselves look better. Production managers may hide costs to meet their targets. Human resource managers may overestimate their minority recruiting prospects to meet affirmative action goals. In each case, the information that other managers receive is inaccurate, and the results of inaccurate information may be quite dramatic. If sales projections are inflated, a manager might cut advertising (thinking it is no longer needed) or increase advertising (to further build momentum). Similarly, a production manager unaware of hidden costs may quote a sales price much lower than desirable. Or a human resource manager may speak out publicly on the effectiveness of the company's minority recruiting, only to find out later that these prospects have been overestimated. In each case, the result of inaccurate information is inappropriate managerial action.

Timeliness   Timeliness does not necessarily mean quickness. Rather, it describes a control system that provides information as often as is necessary. Because Champion has a wealth of historical data on its spark-plug sales, it does not need information on spark plugs as frequently as it needs sales feedback for its newer products. Retail organizations usually need sales results daily, so that they can manage cash flow and adjust advertising and promotion. In contrast, they may require information about physical inventory only quarterly or annually. In general, the more uncertain and unstable the circumstances, the more frequently measurement is needed.

Objectivity   The control system should provide information that is as objective as possible. To appreciate this, imagine the task of a manager responsible for control of his organization's human resources. He asks two plant managers to submit reports. One manager notes that morale at his plant is "okay," that grievances are "about where they should be," and that turnover is "under control." The other reports that absenteeism at her plant is running at 4 percent, that 16 grievances have been filed this year (compared with 24 last year), and that turnover is 12 percent. The second report will almost always be more useful than the first. Of course, managers also need to look beyond the numbers when assessing performance. For example, a plant manager may be boosting productivity and profit margins by putting too much pressure on workers and using poor-quality materials. As a result, impressive short-run gains may be overshadowed by longer-run increases in employee turnover and customer complaints.

Resistance to Control

Managers may sometimes make the mistake of assuming that the value of an effective control system is self-evident to employees. This is not always so, however. Many employees resist control, especially if they feel overcontrolled, if they think control is inappropriately focused or rewards inefficiency, or if they are uncomfortable with accountability.

Overcontrol   Occasionally, organizations try to control too many things. This becomes especially problematic when the control directly affects employee behavior. An organization that instructs its employees when to come to work, where to park, when to have morning coffee, and when to leave for the day exerts considerable control over people's daily activities. Yet many organizations attempt to control not only these but other aspects of work behavior as well. Of particular relevance in recent years is the effort of some companies to control their employees' access to private e-mail and the Internet during work hours. Some companies have no policies governing these activities, some attempt to limit it, and some attempt to forbid it altogether.[16]

Troubles arise when employees perceive these attempts to limit their behavior as being unreasonable. A company that tells its employees how to dress, how to arrange their desks, and how to wear their hair may meet with more resistance. Employees at Chrysler used to complain because, if they drove a non-Chrysler vehicle, they were forced to park in a distant parking lot. People felt that these efforts to control their personal behavior (what kind of car to drive) were excessive. Managers eventually removed these controls and now allow open parking. Some employees at Abercrombie & Fitch argue that the firm is guilty of overcontrol because of its strict dress and grooming requirements—for example, no necklaces or facial hair for men and only natural nail polish and earrings no larger than a dime for women.

Inappropriate Focus The control system may be too narrow, or it may focus too much on quantifiable variables and leave no room for analysis or interpretation. A sale's standard that encourages high-pressure tactics to maximize short-run sales may do so at the expense of goodwill from long-term customers. Such a standard is too narrow. A university reward system that encourages faculty members to publish large numbers of articles but fails to consider the quality of the work is also inappropriately focused. Employees resist the intent of the control system by focusing their efforts only at the performance indicators being used. The cartoon features another example of inappropriately focused control.

Rewards for Inefficiency Imagine two operating departments that are approaching the end of the fiscal year. Department 1 expects to have $5,000 of its budget left over; department 2 is already $3,000 in the red. As a result, department 1 is likely to have its budget cut for the next year ("They had money left, so they obviously got too much to begin with"), and department 2 is likely to get a budget increase ("They obviously haven't been getting enough money"). Thus department 1 is punished for being efficient, and department 2 is rewarded for being inefficient. (No wonder departments commonly hasten to deplete their budgets as the end of the year approaches!) As with inappropriate focus, people resist the intent of this control and behave in ways that run counter to the organization's intent.

Too Much Accountability Effective controls allow managers to determine whether or not employees successfully discharge their responsibilities. If standards are properly set and performance accurately measured, managers know when problems arise and which departments and individuals are responsible. People who do not want to be answerable for their mistakes or who do not want to work as hard as their boss might like therefore resist control. For example, American Express has a system that provides daily information on how many calls each of its customer service representatives handles. If one representative has typically worked at a slower pace and handled fewer calls than other representatives, that individual's deficient performance can now be more easily pinpointed.

Overcoming Resistance to Control

Perhaps the best way to overcome resistance to control is to create effective control to begin with. If control systems are properly integrated with organizational planning and if the controls are flexible, accurate, timely, and objective, the organization will be less likely to overcontrol, to focus on inappropriate standards, or to reward inefficiency. Two other ways to overcome resistance are encouraging participation and developing verification procedures.

Encourage Employee Participation Chapter 7 notes that participation can help overcome resistance to change. By the same token, when employees are involved with planning and implementing the control system, they are less likely to resist it. For instance, employee participation in planning, decision making, and quality control at the Chevrolet Gear Axle plant in Detroit has resulted in increased employee concern for quality and a greater commitment to meeting standards.

Develop Verification Procedures Multiple standards and information systems provide checks and balances in control and allow the organization to verify the accuracy of performance indicators. Suppose a production manager argues that she failed to meet a certain cost standard because of increased prices of raw materials. A properly designed inventory control system will either support or contradict her explanation. Suppose that an employee who was fired for excessive absences argues that he was not absent "for a long time." An effective human resource control system should have records that support the termination. Resistance to control declines because these verification procedures protect both employees and management. If the production manager's claim about the rising cost of raw materials is supported by the inventory control records, she will not be held solely accountable for failing to meet the cost standard, and some action will probably be taken to lower the cost of raw materials.

"You've got to really wonder just how many more cut-backs this department can absorb!"

Cartoon by Bradford Veley

In recent years, many organizations have sought ways to lower their costs through cost-cutting programs. They have reduced their workforce, eliminated perquisites, and outsourced services that independent contractors can do for a lower price. But some experts worry that many organizations have cut too much, increasing pressure and stress on the employees who are left. Although it is doubtful that any organization has gone to the lengths illustrated in this cartoon, many employees nevertheless are feeling the consequences of these cutbacks.

Summary of Key Points

Control is the regulation of organizational activities so that some targeted element of performance remains within acceptable limits. Control provides ways to adapt to environmental change, to limit the accumulation of errors, to cope with organizational complexity, and to minimize costs. Control can focus on financial, physical, information, and human resources, and includes operations, financial, structural, and strategic levels. Control is the function of managers, the controller, and, increasingly, of operating employees.

Steps in the control process are (1) establish standards of expected performance, (2) measure actual performance, (3) compare performance to the standards, and (4) evaluate the comparison and take appropriate action.

Operations control focuses on the processes the organization uses to transform resources into products or services. Preliminary control is concerned with the resources that serve as inputs to the system. Screening control is concerned with the transformation processes used by the organization. Postaction control is concerned with the outputs of the organization. Most organizations need multiple control systems, because no one system alone can provide adequate control.

Financial control focuses on controlling the organization's financial resources. The foundation of financial control is budgets, plans expressed in numerical terms. Most organizations rely on financial, operating, and nonmonetary budgets. Financial statements, various kinds of ratios, and external and internal audits are also important tools that organizations use as part of financial control.

Structural control addresses how well an organization's structural elements serve their intended purpose. Two basic forms of structural control are bureaucratic and clan control. Bureaucratic control is relatively formal and mechanistic, whereas clan control is informal and organic. Most organizations use a form of organizational control somewhere between these two extremes.

Strategic control focuses on how effectively the organization's strategies are succeeding in helping the organization meet its goals. The integration of strategy and control is generally achieved through organization structure, leadership, technology, human resources, and information and operational control systems. International strategic control is also important for multinational organizations. The foundation of international strategic control is whether to practice centralized or decentralized control.

One way to increase the effectiveness of control is to fully integrate planning and control. The control system should also be flexible, accurate, timely, and as objective as possible. Employees may resist organizational controls because of overcontrol, inappropriate focus, rewards for inefficiency, and a desire to avoid accountability. Managers can overcome this resistance by improving the effectiveness of controls, allowing employee participation, and developing verification procedures.

Discussion Questions

Questions for Review

1. What is the purpose of organizational control? Why is it important?
2. What are the steps in the control process? Which step is likely to be the most difficult to perform? Why?
3. What are the similarities and differences between the various forms of operations control? What are the costs and benefits of each form?
4. What are the basic differences and similarities between bureaucratic and clan control?
5. How can a manager understand and overcome resistance and make control effective?

Questions for Analysis

6. How is the controlling process related to the functions of planning, organizing, and leading?
7. Are the differences in bureaucratic control and clan control related to differences in organization structure? If so, how? If not, why not? (The terms do sound similar to those used to discuss the organizing process.)
8. Do you use a budget for your personal finances? Relate your experiences with budgeting to the discussion in the chapter.
9. Have you ever resisted control? Why?
10. Why might control in an international business be more complex and difficult than control in a domestic business?

BUILDING EFFECTIVE *time management* SKILLS

Exercise Overview

Time management skills—a manager's abilities to prioritize work, to work efficiently, and to delegate appropriately—play a major role in the control function. That is, a manager can use time management skills to more effectively control his or her own work. This exercise helps demonstrate the relationship between time management skills and control.

Exercise Background

You are a middle manager in a small manufacturing plant. Today is Monday, and you have just returned from a one-week vacation. The first thing you discover is that your secretary will not be in today. His aunt died, and he is out of town at the funeral. He did, however, leave you the following note:

Dear Boss:
Sorry about not being here today. I will be back tomorrow. In the meantime, here are some things you need to know about:

1. *Ms. Glinski [your boss] wants to see you today at 4:00.*
2. *The shop steward wants to see you ASAP about a labor problem.*
3. *Mr. Bateman [one of your big customers] has a complaint about a recent shipment.*
4. *Ms. Ferris [one of your major suppliers] wants to discuss a change in the delivery schedule.*
5. *Mr. Prescott from the chamber of commerce wants you to attend a breakfast meeting on Wednesday and discuss our expansion plans.*
6. *The legal office wants to discuss our upcoming OSHA inspection.*

7. *Human resources wants to know when you can interview someone for the new supervisor's position.*

8. *Jack Williams, the machinist you fired last month, has been hanging around the parking lot.*

Exercise Task

With the information above as a framework, complete steps 1 through 4.

1. Prioritize the work that needs to be done into three categories: very timely, moderately timely, and less timely.

2. Explain whether importance and timeliness are the same thing.

3. Determine what additional information you need before you can really begin to prioritize this work.

4. Consider how your approach would differ if your secretary had come in today.

BUILDING EFFECTIVE *diagnostic* SKILLS

Exercise Overview

Diagnostic skills enable managers to visualize responses to situations. Given that control focuses on regulating organizational activities, diagnostic skills are clearly important to the determination of what activities should be regulated, how to best assess activities, and how to respond to deviations. This exercise helps demonstrate the nature of this relationship.

Exercise Background

You are the manager of a popular, locally owned restaurant that competes with chains such as Chili's, Bennigan's, and Applebee's. You have been able to maintain your market share in light of increased competition from these outlets by providing exceptional service.

Recently, you have become aware of three trends that concern you. First, your costs are increasing. Monthly charges for food purchases seem to be growing at an exceptionally rapid pace. Second, customer complaints are also increasing. Although the actual number of complaints is still quite small, complaints are nevertheless increasing. And, finally, turnover among your employees is also increasing. Although turnover in the restaurant business is usually very high, the recent increase is in marked contrast to your historical pattern of turnover.

Exercise Task

Using the information presented above, do the following:

1. Identify as many potential causes as possible for each of the three problem areas.

2. Group the causes into two categories: more likely and less likely.

3. Develop at least one potential action that you might take to address each cause.

BUILDING EFFECTIVE *decision-making* SKILLS

Exercise Overview

Decision-making skills refer to the manager's ability to correctly recognize and define problems and opportunities and to then select an appropriate course of action to solve problems and capitalize on opportunities. This exercise enables you to practice your decision-making skills in relation to organizational control.

Exercise Background

Assume that you are the top manager of a medium-sized, family-owned manufacturing company. Family members work in several managerial positions. Because of your own special skills and abilities, you have just been brought in from the outside to run the company. The company has a long-standing tradition of avoiding debt and owns several smaller businesses in related industries.

Over the last few years, the company has lagged in productivity and efficiency and now finds itself in desperate straits. Profits have just

about disappeared, and one of your bigger competitors may be planning an attempt to take over the business. You have hired a consulting firm to help you identify alternatives for turning things around. The primary options are as follows:

1. Issue a public stock offering (IPO) to raise funds.
2. Borrow money from a bank to finance a turnaround.
3. Sell several of the smaller operations to fund a turnaround.
4. Seek a buyer for the entire firm.

Exercise Task

With the background information above as context, do the following:

1. Evaluate each option from a strategic standpoint.
2. Explain how each option relates to control.
3. Select the option that appeals most to you.
4. Describe the barriers you are likely to encounter with the option you have chosen.

SKILLS *self-assessment* INSTRUMENT

Understanding Control

Introduction: Control systems must be carefully constructed for all organizations regardless of their goals. The following assessment surveys your ideas about and approaches to control.

Instructions: You will agree with some of the statements and disagree with others. In some cases, making a decision may be difficult, but you should force a choice. Record your answers next to each statement according to the rating scale.

Rating Scale

4 Strongly agree   **2** Somewhat disagree
3 Slightly agree   **1** Strongly disagree

_____ 1. Effective controls must be unbending if they are to be used consistently.
_____ 2. The most objective form of control is one that uses measures such as stock prices and rate of return on investment (ROI).
_____ 3. Control is restrictive and should be avoided if at all possible.

_____ 4. Controlling through rules, procedures, and budgets should not be used unless measurable standards are difficult or expensive to develop.

_____ 5. Overreliance on measurable control standards is seldom a problem for business organizations.

_____ 6. Organizations should encourage the development of individual self-control.

_____ 7. Organizations tend to try to establish behavioral controls as the first type of control to be used.

_____ 8. The easiest and least costly form of control is output or quantity control.

_____ 9. Short-run efficiency and long-run effectiveness result from the use of similar control standards.

_____ 10. ROI and stock prices are ways of ensuring that a business organization is responding to its external market.

_____ 11. Self-control should be relied on to replace other forms of control.

_____ 12. Controls such as ROI are more appropriate for corporations and business units than they are for small groups or individuals.

_____ 13. Control is unnecessary in a well-managed organization.

_____ 14. The use of output or quantity controls can lead to unintended or unfortunate consequences.

_____ 15. Standards of control do not depend on which constituency is being considered.

_____ 16. Controlling through the use of rules, procedures, and budgets can lead to rigidity and a loss of creativity in an organization.

_____ 17. Different forms of control cannot be used at the same time. An organization must decide how it is going to control and just do it.

_____ 18. Setting across-the-board output or quantity targets for divisions within a company can lead to destructive results.

_____ 19. Control through rules, procedures, and budgets are generally not very costly.

_____ 20. Individual self-control can lead to integration and communication problems.

For interpretation, see Interpretations of Skills Self-Assessment Instruments.

Source: Adapted Charles W. L. Hill and Gareth R. Jones, *Strategic Management,* Fourth Edition. Copyright © 1998 by Houghton Mifflin Company. Used by permission.

EXPERIENTIAL EXERCISE

Learning About "Real" Control

Purpose: The purpose of this exercise is to give you additional insights into how organizations deal with fundamental control issues.

Instructions:

Step 1: Working individually, interview a manager, owner, or employee of an organization. The individual can be a local entrepreneur, a manager in a larger company, or an administrator in your college or university, among other choices. If you currently work, interviewing your boss would be excellent.

Using your own words, ask these general questions:

1. In your organization, what are the most important resources to control?
2. Who is primarily responsible for control?

3. Which level of control is most important to your organization? (Briefly describe the three levels of operations control.)
4. Do you use budgets? If so, what kinds and in what ways?
5. Which of these types of control does your organization most typically use? (Briefly describe bureaucratic and clan control.)
6. Have you had any instances in which employees resisted control? Can you explain why and what you did about it?

Step 2: Form small groups of four or five. Then do the following:
1. Have each member describe the organization and manager interviewed and the interview findings.
2. Identify as many commonalities across findings as possible.
3. Summarize the differences you found.
4. Select one group member to report your group's experiences to the rest of the class.

CHAPTER CLOSING CASE

CONTROL KEEPS SIEBEL SYSTEMS ON THE FAST TRACK

Control is paying off for Siebel Systems, a fast-growing U.S. company that rings up $1.6 billion in annual sales of sophisticated software to such corporations as British Telecom and Sun Microsystems. Siebel's software helps corporate customers better manage sales and other critical functions, allowing more effective monitoring and control of activities and results. Inside Siebel, Tom Siebel, the founder and CEO, is a strong believer in control. He enforces standards for almost everything in the organization, from employee performance, to customer service, to service response. This helps him maintain control over operations, finances, structure, and strategy covering 5,200-plus employees in 100 offices worldwide.

Siebel needs peak performance day in and day out to fuel the company's torrid rate of growth, which is more than 117 percent a year. So, every six months, the company ranks the employees in each department. Those who fall in the lowest 5 percent are terminated, whereas top performers are rewarded. Still, Siebel's turnover is lower than that of other high-tech firms. This control process will help Siebel maintain high performance while doubling its global workforce to more

than 10,000 and adding 2 million square feet of office space in the coming years.

Operations are another area where Siebel exerts strict control. Too often, software companies announce plans to introduce updated or new programs, then miss the launch date by months or even years. Not Siebel. Customers know that the company can be depended on to release updated versions of its software every spring. They also know they can get speedy, knowledgeable help if they have problems installing or operating some of the complex programs Siebel sells. The CEO and his management team set an example for all employees by spending considerable time working with customers. Seibel, for example, devotes about 60 percent of his working day meeting with customers, learning about their problems, offering advice, and showing how his firm's products can provide solutions.

Wall Street appreciates public companies with strong financial controls, so it is not surprising that investors have flocked to Siebel. The company's habit of beating analysts' expectations every quarter since the company first offered its stock in 1996—and the upward trend of its stock price—have definitely pleased investors. Although some competitors have been caught up in accounting scandals through the years, Siebel's tight controls have kept its finances running smoothly, another reason for its investor appeal. Until recently, the CEO was the only manager who could sign off on expenses over $10,000; now two senior managers have been given the authority to approve expenses up to $50,000, with higher amounts going to Siebel's desk for review and approval.

Unlike many high-tech firms, Siebel has an unwritten dress code mandating professional business wear at work. Male employees are expected to appear in suits and ties; female employees are expected to wear skirt or pants suits. This dress code supports the air of professionalism that pervades the entire company. Every Siebel office is decorated in the same way, with blue carpeting and off-white walls, gray desktops, and maple furniture. Every desk is neat, with no empty soda cans or empty pizza cartons (eating at the desk is forbidden). In another departure from Silicon Valley norms, Siebel doesn't allow the basketball games and beer blasts that are so common in many high-tech firms. In short, Siebel is all business, an approach that impresses customers and adds in a small way to Siebel's ability to compete against Oracle, PeopleSoft, Baan, and other rivals.

As CEO, Siebel holds tight rein on his company, but he has lately begun sharing some control with other top executives. For example, he appointed a chief operating officer to oversee day-to-day issues in marketing and sales, engineering, and services. Still, he expects managers and employees to move quickly when he asks questions or requests action. After Siebel met with a customer one Friday, he promised a complete proposal by Monday—impossible for many companies, but a normal reaction time for the people at Siebel.

Case Questions

1. Identify as many forms of control as possible in this case.

2. What are the advantages and disadvantages of concentrating control in the hands of one top manager?

3. Does Siebel sound like a good working environment for you? Why or why not?

Case References

Melanie Warner, "Confessions of a Control Freak," *Fortune*, September 4, 2000, pp. 130–140.

CHAPTER NOTES

1. "Star Rescuers Took on Waste Management—And Ended up Tarnished," *Wall Street Journal*, February 29, 2000, pp. A1, A8; and *Hoover's Handbook of American Business 2001* (Austin, TX: Hoover's Business Press, 2001), pp. 1522–1523.

2. "Fleetwood: Not a Happy Camper Company," *Business Week*, October 9, 2000, pp. 88–90.

3. "Coke to Lay off 6,000 Workers," *USA Today*, January 27, 2000, p. 1B.

4. Mark Kroll, Peter Wright, Leslie Toombs, and Hadley Leavell, "Form of Control: A Critical Determinant of Acquisition Performance and CEO Rewards," *Strategic Management Journal* 18, no. 2 (1997): 85–96.

5. Sim Sitkin, Kathleen Sutcliffe, and Roger Schroeder, "Distinguishing Control from Learning in Total Quality Management: A Contingency Perspective," *Academy of Management Review* 19, no. 3 (1994): 537–564.

6. Edward E. Lawler III and John G. Rhode, *Information and Control in Organizations* (Pacific Palisades, CA: Goodyear, 1976).

7. "An Efficiency Guru Refits Honda to Fight Auto Giants," *Wall Street Journal*, September 15, 1999, p. B1.

8. "Luxury's Mandarin," *Newsweek*, August 25, 1997, p. 43.

9. "The Tiger Is on the Prowl," *Forbes*, April 21, 1997, pp. 42–43.

10. "Mickey Mouse, CPA," *Forbes*, March 10, 1997, pp. 42–43.

11. William G. Ouchi, "The Transmission of Control Through Organizational Hierarchy," *Academy of Management Journal*, June 1978, pp. 173–192; and Richard E. Walton, "From Control to Commitment in the Workplace," *Harvard Business Review*, March/April 1985, pp. 76–84.

12. "Nordstrom Cleans out Its Closets," *Business Week*, May 22, 2000, pp. 105–108.

13. Peter Lorange, Michael S. Scott Morton, and Sumantra Ghoshal, *Strategic Control Systems* (St. Paul, MN: West, 1986). See also Joseph C. Picken and Gregory G. Dess, "Out of (Strategic) Control," *Organizational Dynamics*, Summer 1997, pp. 35–45.

14. See Hans Mjoen and Stephen Tallman, "Control and Performance in International Joint Ventures," *Organization Science*, May–June 1997, pp. 257–265.

15. See Diana Robertson and Erin Anderson, "Control System and Task Environment Effects on Ethical Judgment: An Exploratory Study of Industrial Salespeople," *Organization Science*, November 1993, pp. 617–629, for a recent study of effective control.

16. "Workers, Surf at Your Own Risk," *Business Week*, June 12, 2000, pp. 105–106.

15 Managing Operations, Quality, and Productivity

Young Joseph Hartmann immigrated to the United States from Bavaria in 1877. Soon after arriving, he started a small trunk-making company, using the skills he had learned in his homeland. Today, Hartmann Luggage, a division of Brown-Forman Corporation and based in Lebanon, Tennessee, is among the most respected names in the luggage industry.

The firm makes a full line of luggage products, ranging from business cases to suitcases to computer cases. Hartmann bags are also among the most expensive in the industry, with even a small bag costing hundreds of dollars. So why are consumers willing to pay such a premium price for a suitcase? Among other reasons is the quality that characterizes Hartmann bags. Hartmann luggage has a lifetime guarantee—the company will repair or replace any damaged product for as long as it is in the possession of its original owner. It honors warranties even when it is apparent that product damage is attributable to owner neglect.

Why is the firm able to offer such a strong guarantee? In large part it is due to the quality construction used to make the bags and the rigorous testing to which they are subjected before being placed on the market. For example, virtually all of the work on a Hartmann bag is done by hand, by trained workers who excel at their craft. The company also uses only the highest-quality materials, ranging from industrial-strength belting leather to the strongest cloth and metal hinges. And its manufacturing systems are among the most efficient in the industry.

But it is in the quality control testing lab that Hartmann truly excels. For example, every new case or bag that Hartmann intends to make is first tested for a lifetime of use before being placed in production. And most of this testing is done with special machines that Hartmann managers have conceptualized and constructed, which are a fundamental part of its operations systems.

One of its machines, for example, is call the "tumble tester." This large machine resembles a Ferris wheel with a cage. A bag is put inside the cage, and the wheel slowly begins to turn. The bag tumbles like a towel in a clothes dryer, crashing against metal protrusions made to resemble the baggage handling system in an airport. The machine simulates the treatment the bags will receive in just such an airport. Each

"We have repaired or refurbished bags that are 40 years old."

—*Gail Jamison, Hartmann repair section chief**

LEARNING OBJECTIVES

After studying this chapter, you should be able to

- Describe and explain the nature of operations management.

- Identify and discuss the components involved in designing effective operations systems.

- Discuss organizational technologies and their role in operations management.

- Identify and discuss the components involved in implementing operations systems through supply chain management.

- Explain the meaning and importance of managing quality and total quality management.

- Explain the meaning and importance of managing productivity, productivity trends, and ways to improve productivity.

test run is for 7,000 turns, simulating five years' worth of bouncing.

Another machine Hartmann uses lifts a briefcase up and down every few seconds, as many as 100,000 times in all. This machine assesses the wear-and-tear that lifting creates on the briefcase handle. If the wear is excessive, stronger leather will be used. Another machine tests the amount of energy or tension needed to pull apart the stitches that hold a bag together. Among the most interesting machines Hartmann uses is a treadmill-like device that simulates asphalt, tile, and carpet—testing how a bag holds up to being dragged or pulled from an airport to a parking lot. Other machines test wheel strength or the durability of shoulder straps, or how well a bag holds up to ultraviolet rays, rain, humidity, heat, and ice.

Given the extensive battery of tests that Hartmann bags must pass, it is little wonder that the firm backs them with such a praiseworthy guarantee. And there is little wonder that consumers who can afford to pay the price are eager to own the firm's products.[1]

Managers at Hartmann Luggage have made quality a hallmark of their company's operations. This quality, in turn, has allowed them to charge premium prices and earn superior profits. But, to be successful with this strategy, the firm also must have the confidence that its products can withstand the demands of consumers and hold up to the rigors of daily and business use. And they must effectively use operations management as part of their overall strategy.

In this chapter we explore operations management, quality, and productivity. We first introduce operations management and discuss its role in general management and organizational strategy. The next three sections discuss designing operations systems, organizational technologies, and implementing operations systems. We then introduce and discuss various issues in managing for total quality. Finally, we discuss productivity, which is closely related to quality.

The Nature of Operations Management

operations management The total set of managerial activities used by an organization to transform resource inputs into products, services, or both

Operations management is at the core of what organizations do as they add value and create products and services. But what exactly are operations? And how are they managed? **Operations management** is the set of managerial activities used by an organization to transform resource inputs into products and services. When Dell Computer buys electronic components, assembles them into PCs, and then ships them to customers, it is engaging in operations management. When a Pizza Hut employee orders food and paper products and then combines dough, cheese, and tomato paste to create a pizza, he or she is engaging in operations management.

The Importance of Operations

Operations is an important functional concern for organizations, because efficient and effective management of operations goes a long way toward ensuring competitiveness and overall organizational performance, as well as quality and productivity. Inefficient or ineffective operations management, on the other hand, will almost inevitably lead to poorer performance and lower levels of both quality and productivity. Indeed, *Management InfoTech* illustrates how Hershey Foods learned what can happen when operations go awry.

In an economic sense, operations management creates value and utility of one type or another, depending on the nature of the firm's products or services. If the product is a physical good, such as a Harley-Davidson motorcycle, operations creates value and provides form utility by combining many dissimilar inputs (sheet metal, rubber, paint, combustion engines, and human skills) to make something (a motorcycle) that is more valuable than the actual cost of the inputs used to create it. The inputs are converted from their incoming forms into a new physical form. This conversion is typical of manufacturing operations and essentially reflects the organization's technology.[2]

In contrast, the operations activities of American Airlines create value and provide time and place utility through its services. The airline transports passen-

MANAGEMENT INFOTECH

MANAGING OPERATIONS MANAGEMENT SYSTEMS

Hershey Foods got quite a scare during one recent Halloween candy-selling season. Over the summer months, Hershey had installed new software and computers to manage its ordering and fulfillment functions. By fall, however, the system was still not running as it should. Stores waited and waited for the Reese's Peanut Butter Cups, Hershey's Kisses, and other varieties of Hershey's 3,300 candies they had ordered for the trick-or-treat set. As Halloween approached, Hershey was quoting a 12-day turnaround on orders—twice as long as its usual fulfillment period—and filling only part of most orders.

Even when shipments moved out of its warehouses, Hershey could not find out from the new system what had been shipped or where; sales representatives wound up calling customers to find out what they had received. To fulfill orders placed by larger customers, such as Kmart, Hershey sent some shipments by truck and some by air, absorbing the extra cost to get its candies onto store shelves as quickly as possible. Meanwhile, worried retailers began placing extra orders with other candy manufacturers to fill their shelves and meet consumer demand. By the time Halloween arrived, Hershey's sales were $100 million lower than expected, and its profits were down by 19 percent.

Hershey's experiences point up the challenges of implementing state-of-the-art operations systems. Although detailed planning and exhaustive testing will smooth the way toward successful implementation, software bugs and even the small-

est incompatibilities can derail a system. Fear of system slowdowns or breakdowns haunt many organizations. The two computers that process electronic payments between the world's banks at the New York Clearing House, for example, run on software that is as bug free as humanly possible, because a breakdown would disrupt the entire international financial network. Thanks to constant vigilance, the computers have been operational an astounding 99.99 percent of the time. Not every organization requires this level of quality, but because companies are increasingly dependent on automated systems for managing purchasing, inventory, and other key operations, managers must use extra care and allow extra time when upgrading or installing operations systems software.

> *Improvements in some quarters are followed by increased risks in others. And new systems introduce more problems than the systems they replace.*
>
> —*Peter G. Neumann, a computer scientist with SRI International**

References: Peter Galuszka, "Just-in-Time Manufacturing Is Working Overtime," *Business Week,* November 8, 1999, pp. 36–37; Emily Nelson and Evan Ramstad, "Trick or Treat: Hershey's Biggest Dud Has Turned out to Be New Computer System," *Wall Street Journal,* October 29, 1999, pp. A1, A6; and Neil Gross, Marcia Stepanek, and Otis Port, "Software Hell," *Business Week,* December 6, 1999, pp. 87–89 (*quote on p. 88).

---

gers and freight according to agreed-upon departure and arrival places and times. Other service operations, such as a Coors Brothers Beer distributorship or The Gap retail chain, create value and provide place and possession utility by bringing the customer and products made by others together. Although the organizations in these examples produce different kinds of products or services, their operations processes share many important features.[3]

Manufacturing and Production

Because manufacturing once dominated U.S. industry, the entire area of operations management used to be called *production management.* **Manufacturing** is a

manufacturing A form of business that combines and transforms resource inputs into tangible outcomes

form of business that combines and transforms resources into tangible outcomes that are then sold to others. The Goodyear Tire and Rubber Company is a manufacturer because it combines rubber and chemical compounds, and uses blending equipment and molding machines to create tires. Broyhill is a manufacturer because it buys wood and metal components, pads, and fabric, and then combines them into furniture.

During the 1970s, manufacturing entered a long period of decline in the United States, primarily because of foreign competition. U.S. firms had grown lax and sluggish, and new foreign competitors came onto the scene with better equipment and much higher levels of efficiency. For example, steel companies in the Far East were able to produce high-quality steel for much lower prices than were U.S. companies like Bethlehem Steel and U.S. Steel (now USX Corporation). Faced with a battle for survival, many companies underwent a long and difficult period of change, by eliminating waste and transforming themselves into leaner and more efficient and responsive entities. They reduced their work forces dramatically, closed antiquated or unnecessary plants, and modernized their remaining plants. In the last decade, their efforts have started to pay dividends, as U.S. business has regained its competitive position in many different industries. Although manufacturers from other parts of the world are still formidable competitors, and U.S. firms may never again be competitive in some markets, the overall picture is much better than it was just a few years ago. And prospects continue to look bright.

Service Operations

service organization An organization that transforms resources into services

During the decline of the manufacturing sector, a tremendous growth in the service sector kept the U.S. economy from declining at the same rate. A **service organization** is one that transforms resources into an intangible output and creates time or place utility for its customers. For example, Merrill Lynch makes stock transactions for its customers, Avis leases cars to its customers, and your local hairdresser cuts your hair. In 1947 the service sector was responsible for less than half of the U.S. gross national product (GNP). By 1975, however, this figure reached 65 percent, and by 1999 it was over 75 percent. The service sector was responsible for almost 90 percent of all new jobs created in the United States during the 1990s. Managers have come to see that many of the tools, techniques, and methods that are used in a factory are also useful to a service firm. For example, managers of automobile plants and hair salons each have to decide how to design their facility, identify the best location for it, determine optimal capacity, make decisions about inventory storage, set procedures for purchasing raw materials, and set standards for productivity and quality.

The Role of Operations in Organizational Strategy

It should be clear by this point that operations management is very important to organizations. Beyond its direct impact on such things as competitiveness, quality, and productivity, it also directly influences the organization's overall level of effectiveness. For example, the deceptively simple strategic decision of whether to stress high quality regardless of cost, lowest-possible cost regardless of quality, or some combination of the two has numerous important implications. A highest-possible-quality strategy will dictate state-of-the-art technology and rigorous control of product design and materials specifications. A combination strategy might call for lower-grade technology and less concern about product design and materials specifications. Just as strategy affects operations management, so, too, does operations management affect strategy. Suppose that a firm decides to upgrade the quality of its products or services. The organization's ability to implement the decision is dependent in part on current production capabilities and other resources. If existing technology will not permit higher-quality work, and if the organization lacks the resources to replace its technology, increasing quality to the desired new standards will be difficult.

Designing Operations Systems

The problems, challenges, and opportunities faced by operations managers revolve around the acquisition and utilization of resources for conversion. Their goals include both efficiency and effectiveness. A number of issues and decisions must be addressed as operations systems are designed. The most basic ones involve product-service mix, capacity, and facilities.

Determining Product-Service Mix

A natural starting point in designing operations systems is determining the **product-service mix.** This decision flows from corporate, business, and marketing strategies. Managers have to make a number of decisions about their products and services, starting with how many and what kinds to offer.[4] Procter & Gamble, for example, makes regular, tartar-control, gel, and various other formulas of Crest toothpaste and packages them in several different sizes of tubes, pumps, and other dispensers. Similarly, workers at Subway sandwich stores can combine different breads, vegetables, meats, and condiments in hundreds of different kinds of sandwiches. Decisions also have to be made regarding the level of quality desired, the optimal cost of each product or service, and exactly how each is to be designed. GE, for example, recently reduced the number of parts in its industrial circuit breakers from 28,000 to 1,275. The whole process was achieved by carefully analyzing product design and production methods.

product-service mix How many and what kinds of products or services (or both) to offer

Capacity Decisions

The **capacity** decision involves choosing the amount of products, services, or both that can be produced by the organization. Determining whether to build a factory capable of making 5,000 or 8,000 units per day is a capacity decision. So, too, is deciding whether to build a restaurant with 100 or 150 seats, or a bank with five or ten teller stations. The capacity decision is truly a high-risk one because of the uncertainties of future product demand and the large monetary stakes involved. An organization that builds capacity exceeding its needs may commit resources

capacity The amount of products, services, or both that can be produced by an organization

(capital investment) that will never be recovered. Alternatively, an organization can build a facility with a smaller capacity than expected demand. Doing so may result in lost market opportunities, but it may also free capital resources for use elsewhere in the organization.

A major consideration in determining capacity is demand. A company operating with fairly constant monthly demand might build a plant capable of producing an amount each month roughly equivalent to its demand. But, if its market is characterized by seasonal fluctuations, building a smaller plant to meet normal demand and then adding extra shifts staffed with temporary workers or paying permanent workers extra to work more hours during peak periods might be the most effective choice. Likewise, a restaurant that needs 150 seats for Saturday night but never needs more than 100 at any other time during the week would probably be foolish to expand to 150 seats. During the rest of the week, it must still pay to light, heat, cool, and clean the excess capacity.

Facilities Decisions

facilities The physical locations where products or services are created, stored, and distributed

location The physical positioning or geographic site of facilities

Facilities are the physical locations where products or services are created, stored, and distributed. Major decisions pertain to facilities location and facilities layout.

Location   **Location** is the physical positioning or geographic site of facilities and must be determined by the needs and requirements of the organization. A company that relies heavily on railroads for transportation needs to be located close to rail facilities. GE decided that it did not need six plants to make circuit breakers, so it invested heavily in automating one plant and closed the other five. Different organizations in the same industry may have different facilities requirements. Benetton uses only one distribution center for the entire world, whereas Wal-Mart has several distribution centers in the United States alone. A retail business must choose its location very carefully to be convenient for consumers.

layout The physical configuration of facilities, the arrangement of equipment within facilities, or both

product layout A physical configuration of facilities arranged around the product; used when large quantities of a single product are needed

process layout A physical configuration of facilities arranged around the process; used in facilities that create or process a variety of products

Layout   The choice of physical configuration, or the **layout**, of facilities is closely related to other operations decisions. The four entirely different layout alternatives shown in Figure 15.1 help demonstrate the importance of the layout decision. A **product layout** is appropriate when large quantities of a single product are needed. It makes sense to custom-design a straight-line flow of work for a product when a specific task is performed at each workstation as each unit flows past. Most assembly lines use this format. For example, Dell's personal computer factories use a product layout.

Process layouts are used in operations settings that create or process a variety of products. Auto repair shops and health-care clinics are good examples. Each car and each person is a separate "product." The needs of each incoming job are diagnosed as it enters the operations system, and the job is routed through the unique sequence of workstations needed to create the desired finished product. In a process layout, each type of conversion task is centralized in a single workstation or department. All welding is done in one designated shop location, and any car that requires welding is moved to that area. This setup is in contrast to the product layout, in which several different workstations may perform welding operations if

Figure 15.1

Approaches to Facilities Layout

When a manufacturer produces large quantities of a product (such as cars or computers), it may arrange its facilities into an assembly line (product layout). In a process layout, the work (such as patients in a hospital or custom pieces of furniture) moves through various workstations. Locomotives and bridges are both manufactured in a fixed-position layout. Cellular layouts are used when families of products can follow similar flow paths.

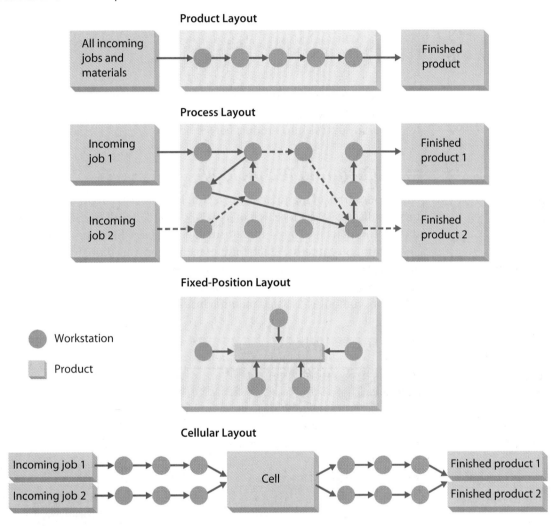

the conversion task sequence so dictates. Similarly, in a hospital all X-rays are done in one location, all surgeries in another, and all physical therapy in yet another. Patients are moved from location to location to get the services they need.

The **fixed-position layout** is used when the organization is creating a few very large and complex products. Aircraft manufacturers like Boeing and shipbuilders like Newport News use this method. An assembly line capable of moving a 747 would require an enormous plant, so instead the airplane itself remains stationary and people and machines move around it as it is assembled.

The cellular layout is a relatively new approach to facilities design. **Cellular layouts** are used when families of products can follow similar flow paths. A clothing

fixed-position layout A physical configuration of facilities arranged around a single work area; used for the manufacture of large and complex products, such as airplanes

cellular layout A physical configuration of facilities used when families of products can follow similar flow paths

manufacturer, for example, might create a cell, or designated area, dedicated to making a family of pockets, such as pockets for shirts, coats, blouses, and slacks. Although each kind of pocket is unique, the same basic equipment and methods are used to make all of them. Hence, all pockets might be made in the same area and then delivered directly to different product layout assembly areas, where the shirts, coats, blouses, and slacks are actually being assembled.

■ *Organizational Technologies*

technology The set of processes and systems used by organizations to convert resources into products or services

One central element of effective operations management is technology. In Chapter 6 we defined **technology** as the set of processes and systems used by organizations to convert resources into products or services.

Manufacturing Technology

Numerous forms of manufacturing technology are used in organizations. In Chapter 6 we discussed the research of Joan Woodward. Recall that Woodward identified three forms of technology—unit or small batch, large batch or mass production, and continuous process.[5] Each form of technology was thought to be associated with a specific type of organization structure. Of course, newer forms of technology not considered by Woodward also warrant attention. Three of these are automation, computer-assisted manufacturing, and robotics.

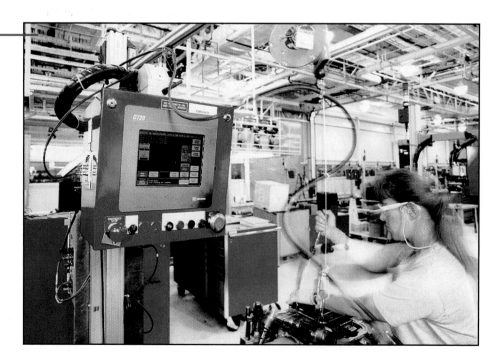

Manufacturing technology continues to become increasingly sophisticated. Take this DaimlerChrysler automobile factory in Indiana, for instance. The machinist is using traditional assembly-line technology and equipment to perform a basic job. In addition, though, the PC monitor is also providing the machinist with information about how well the job is being performed. This allows the machinist to do both faster and higher-quality work.

Automation **Automation** is the process of designing work so that it can be completely or almost completely performed by machines. Because automated machines operate quickly and make few errors, they increase the amount of work that can be done. Thus automation helps to improve products and services, and it fosters innovation. Automation is the most recent step in the development of machines and machine-controlling devices. Machine-controlling devices have been around since the 1700s. James Watt, a Scottish engineer, invented a mechanical speed control to regulate the speed of steam engines in 1787. The Jacquard loom, developed by a French inventor, was controlled by paper cards with holes punched in them. Early accounting and computing equipment was controlled by similar punched cards.

Automation relies on feedback, information, sensors, and a control mechanism. Feedback is the flow of information from the machine back to the sensor. Sensors are the parts of the system that gather information and compare it to some preset standards. The control mechanism is the device that sends instructions to the automatic machine. Early automatic machines were primitive, and the use of automation was relatively slow to develop. These elements are illustrated by the example in Figure 15.2. A thermostat has sensors that monitor air temperature and compare it to a preset low value. If the air temperature falls below the preset value, the thermostat sends an electrical signal to the furnace, turning it on. The furnace heats the air. When the sensors detect that the air temperature has reached a value higher than the low preset value, the thermostat stops the furnace. The last step (shutting off the furnace) is known as *feedback*, a critical component of any automated operation.

The big move to automate factories began during World War II. The shortage of skilled workers and the development of high-speed computers combined to bring about a tremendous interest in automation. Programmable automation (the use of computers to control machines) was introduced during this era, far outstripping conventional automation (the use of mechanical or electromechanical devices to control machines). The automobile industry began to use automatic machines for a variety of jobs. In fact, the term *automation* came into use in the 1950s in the

automation The process of designing work so that it can be completely or almost completely performed by machines

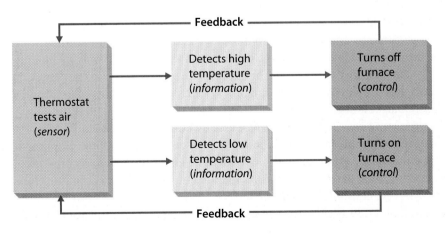

Figure 15.2

A Simple Automatic Control Mechanism

All automation includes feedback, information, sensors, and a control mechanism. A simple thermostat is an example of automation. Another example is Benetton's distribution center in Italy. Orders are received, items are pulled from stock and packaged for shipment, and invoices are prepared and transmitted with no human intervention.

automobile industry. The chemical and oil-refining industries also began to use computers to regulate production. During the 1990s, automation became a major element in the manufacture of computers and computer components such as electronic chips and circuits. It is this computerized, or programmable, automation that presents the greatest opportunities and challenges for management today.

The impact of automation on people in the workplace is complex. In the short term, people whose jobs are automated may find themselves without jobs. In the long term, however, more jobs are created than are lost. Nevertheless, not all companies are able to help displaced workers find new jobs, so the human costs are sometimes high. In the coal industry, for instance, automation has been used primarily in mining. The output per miner has risen dramatically from the 1950s on. The demand for coal, however, has decreased, and productivity gains resulting from automation have lessened the need for miners. Consequently, a lot of workers have lost their jobs, and the industry has not been able to absorb them. In contrast, in the electronics industry, the rising demand for products has led to increasing employment opportunities despite the use of automation.[6]

Computer-assisted Manufacturing   Current extensions of automation generally revolve around computer-assisted manufacturing. **Computer-assisted manufacturing** is technology that relies on computers to design or manufacture products. One type of computer-assisted manufacturing is *computer-aided design (CAD)*—the use of computers to design parts and complete products, and to simulate performance so that prototypes need not be constructed. Boeing uses CAD technology to study hydraulic tubing in its commercial aircraft. Japan's automotive industry uses it to speed up car design. GE used CAD to change the design of its circuit breakers, and Benetton uses CAD to design new styles and products. Oneida Ltd., the table flatware firm, used CAD to design a new spoon in only two days.[7] CAD is usually combined with *computer-aided manufacturing (CAM)* to ensure that the design moves smoothly to production. The production computer shares the design computer's information and is able to have machines with the proper settings ready when production is needed. A CAM system is especially useful when reorders come in, because the computer can quickly produce the desired product, prepare labels and copies of orders, and send the product out to where it is wanted.

Closely aligned with this approach is *computer-integrated manufacturing (CIM)*. In CIM, CAD and CAM are linked together, and computer networks adjust machine placements and settings automatically to enhance both the complexity and the flexibility of scheduling. In settings that use these technologies, all manufacturing activities are controlled by the computer network. Because the network can access the company's other information systems, CIM is both a powerful and a complex management control tool.

Flexible manufacturing systems (FMS) usually have robotic work units or work stations, assembly lines, and robotic carts or some other form of computer-controlled transport system to move material as needed from one part of the system to another. FMS like the one at IBM's manufacturing facility in Lexington, Kentucky, rely on computers to coordinate and integrate automated production and materials-handling facilities. And Ford Motor Company recently used FMS to

computer-assisted manufacturing A technology that relies on computers to design or manufacture products

transform an English factory producing Ford Escorts into a Jaguar plant making its new Jaguar X-Type luxury cars. Using traditional methods, the plant would have been closed, its workers laid off, and the facility virtually rebuilt from the ground up. But by using FMS Ford was able to keep the plant open and running continuously while new equipment was being installed and its workers were being retrained in small groups.[8]

These systems are not without disadvantages, however. For example, because they represent fundamental change, they also generate resistance. Additionally, because of their tremendous complexity, CAD systems are not always reliable. CIM systems are so expensive that they raise the breakeven point for firms using them. This means that the firm must operate at high levels of production and sales to be able to afford the systems.

Robotics   Another trend in manufacturing technology is computerized robotics. A **robot** is any artificial device that is able to perform functions ordinarily thought to be appropriate for human beings. Robotics refers to the science and technology of the construction, maintenance, and use of robots. The use of industrial robots has steadily increased since 1980 and is expected to continue to increase slowly as more companies recognize the benefits that accrue to users of industrial robots.[9]

robot Any artificial device that is able to perform functions ordinarily thought to be appropriate for human beings

Welding was one of the first applications for robots, and it continues to be the area for most applications. In second place and close behind is materials handling. Other applications include machine loading and unloading; painting and finishing; assembly; casting; and machining applications, such as cutting, grinding, polishing, drilling, sanding, buffing, and deburring. DaimlerChrysler, for instance, recently replaced about 200 welders with 50 robots on an assembly line and increased productivity about 20 percent. The use of robots in inspection work is increasing. They can check for cracks and holes, and they can be equipped with vision systems to perform visual inspections.

Robots are also beginning to move from the factory floor to all manner of other applications. The Dallas police used a robot to apprehend a suspect who had barricaded himself in an apartment building. The robot smashed a window and reached with its mechanical arm into the building. The suspect panicked and ran outside. At the Long Beach Memorial Hospital in California, brain surgeons are assisted by a robot arm that drills into the patient's skull with excellent precision. Some newer applications involve remote work. For example, the use of robot submersibles controlled from the surface can help divers in remote locations. Surveillance robots fitted with microwave sensors can do things that a human guard cannot do, such as "seeing" through nonmetallic walls and in the dark. In other applications, automated farming (agrimation) uses robot harvesters to pick fruit from a variety of trees.

Robots are also used by small manufacturers. One robot slices carpeting to fit the inside of custom vans in an upholstery shop. Another stretches balloons flat so that they can be spray-painted with slogans at a novelties company. At a jewelry company, a robot holds class rings while they are engraved by a laser. These robots are lighter, faster, stronger, and more intelligent than those used in heavy manufacturing and are the types that more and more organizations will be using in the future.

Service Technology

Service technology is also changing rapidly. And it, too, is also moving more and more toward automated systems and procedures. In banking, for example, new technological breakthroughs have led to automated teller machines and made it much easier to move funds between accounts or between different banks. Many people now have their paycheck deposited directly into a checking account from which many of their bills are then automatically paid. And credit card transactions by Visa customers are recorded and billed electronically.

Hotels use increasingly sophisticated technology to accept and record room reservations. Universities use new technologies to electronically store and provide access to all manner of books, scientific journals, government reports, and articles. Hospitals and other health-care organizations use new forms of service technology to manage patient records, dispatch ambulances, and monitor vital signs. Restaurants use technology to record and fill customer orders, order food and supplies, and prepare food. Given the increased role that service organizations are playing in today's economy, even more technological innovations are likely to be developed in the years to come.[10]

Implementing Operations Systems Through Supply Chain Management

After operations systems have been properly designed and technologies developed, they must then be put into use by the organization. Their basic functional purpose is to control transformation processes to ensure that relevant goals are achieved in areas such as quality and costs. Operations management has a number of special purposes within this control framework, including purchasing and inventory management. Indeed, this area of management has become so important in recent years that a new term—*supply chain management*—has been coined. Specifically, **supply chain management** can be defined as the process of managing operations control, resource acquisition and purchasing, and inventory so as to improve overall efficiency and effectiveness.[11]

supply chain management The process of managing operations control, resource acquisition, and inventory so as to improve overall efficiency and effectiveness

Operations Management as Control

One way of using operations management as control is to coordinate it with other functions. Monsanto Company, for example, established a consumer products division that produces and distributes fertilizers and lawn chemicals. To facilitate control, the operations function was organized as an autonomous profit center. Monsanto finds this effective because its manufacturing division is given the authority to determine not only the costs of creating the product but also the product price and the marketing programs.

In terms of overall organizational control, a division like the one used by Monsanto should be held accountable only for the activities over which it has decision-making authority. It would be inappropriate, of course, to make operations accountable for profitability in an organization that stresses sales and market share over quality and productivity. Misplaced accountability results in ineffective organizational control, to say nothing of hostility and conflict. Depending on the strategic role of operations, then, operations managers are accountable for different kinds of results. For example, in an organization using bureaucratic control, accountability will be spelled out in rules and regulations. In a clan system, it is likely to be understood and accepted by everyone.

Within operations, managerial control ensures that resources and activities achieve primary goals, such as a high percentage of on-time deliveries, low unit-production cost, or high product reliability. Any control system should focus on the elements that are most crucial to goal attainment. For example, firms in which product quality is a major concern (as it is at Rolex), might adopt a screening control system to monitor the product as it is being created. If quantity is a pressing issue (as it is at Timex), a postaction system might be used to identify defects at the end of the system without disrupting the manufacturing process itself.

Purchasing Management

Purchasing management is concerned with buying the materials and resources needed to create products and services. In many ways, purchasing is at the very heart of effective supply chain management. The purchasing manager for a retailer like Sears, Roebuck is responsible for buying the merchandise the store will sell. The purchasing manager for a

Businesses are continuously looking for new ways to improve their supply chain management technology so as to be more efficient and more competitive. Take Aeroquip, for example. The Ohio firm makes a variety of metal connectors, fittings, adapters, and rubber hoses. Aeroquip has improved its effectiveness dramatically in recent years by changing its whole approach to inventory management and control. This 210,000-square-foot distribution center adjoins Aeroquip's main factory. A combination of human labor and automation can get parts to their needed locations in the factory within just a few minutes of an order being placed. This speed, in turn, allows the plant to supply many high-priority orders to customers within four hours.

purchasing management Buying materials and resources needed to produce products and services

manufacturer buys raw materials, parts, and machines needed by the organization. Large companies like GE, IBM, and Siemens have large purchasing departments.[12] The manager responsible for purchasing must balance a number of constraints. Buying too much ties up capital and increases storage costs. Buying too little might lead to shortages and high reordering costs. The manager must also make sure that the quality of what is purchased meets the organization's needs, that the supplier is reliable, and that the best financial terms are negotiated.

Many firms have recently changed their approach to purchasing as a means to lower costs and improve quality and productivity. In particular, rather than relying on hundreds or even thousands of suppliers, many companies are reducing their number of suppliers and negotiating special production delivery arrangements.[13] For example, the Honda plant in Marysville, Ohio, found a local business owner looking for a new opportunity. They negotiated an agreement whereby he would start a new company to mount car stereo speakers into plastic moldings. He delivers finished goods to the plant three times a day, and Honda buys all he can manufacture. Thus he has a stable sales base, Honda has a local and reliable supplier, and both companies benefit.

Inventory Management

inventory control Managing the organization's raw materials, work-in-process, finished-goods, and in-transit inventories

Inventory control, also called *materials control,* is essential for effective operations management. The four basic kinds of inventories are *raw materials, work-in-process, finished-goods,* and *in-transit* inventories. As shown in Table 15.1, the sources of control over these inventories are as different as their purposes. Work-in-process inventories, for example, are made up of partially completed products that need further processing; they are controlled by the shop-floor system. In contrast, the quantities and costs of finished-goods inventories are under the control of the overall production scheduling system, which is determined by high-level planning decisions. In-transit inventories are controlled by the transportation and distribution systems.

Like most other areas of operations management, inventory management changed notably in recent years. One particularly important breakthrough is the **just-in-time (JIT) method**. First popularized by the Japanese, the JIT system reduces the organization's investment in storage space for raw materials and in the materials themselves. Historically, manufacturers built large storage areas and filled them with materials, parts, and supplies that would be needed days, weeks, and even months in the future. A manager using the JIT approach orders materials and parts more often and in smaller quantities, thereby reducing investment in both storage space and actual inventory. The ideal arrangement is for materials to arrive just as they are needed—or just in time.[14]

just-in-time (JIT) method An inventory system that has necessary materials arriving as soon as they are needed (just in time) so that the production process is not interrupted

Recall our example about the small firm that assembles stereo speakers for Honda and delivers them three times a day, making it unnecessary for Honda to carry large quantities of the speakers in inventory. In an even more striking example, Johnson Controls makes automobile seats for DaimlerChrysler and ships them by small truckloads to a DaimlerChrysler plant 75 miles away. Each shipment is scheduled to arrive two hours before it is needed. Clearly, the JIT approach requires high levels of coordination and cooperation between the company and its suppliers. If shipments arrive too early, DaimlerChrysler has no place to store

Table 15.1

Inventory Types, Purposes, and Sources of Control

JIT is a recent breakthrough in inventory management. With JIT inventory systems, materials arrive just as they are needed. JIT therefore helps an organization control its raw materials inventory by reducing the amount of space it must devote to storage.

Type	Purpose	Source of Control
Raw materials	Provide the materials needed to make the product	Purchasing models and systems
Work-in-process	Enable overall production to be divided into stages of manageable size	Shop-floor control systems
Finished-goods	Provide ready supply of products on customer demand and enable long, efficient production runs	High-level production scheduling systems in conjunction with marketing
In-transit (pipeline)	Distribute products to customers	Transportation and distribution control systems

them. If they arrive too late, the entire assembly line may have to be shut down, resulting in enormous expense. When properly designed and used, the JIT method controls inventory very effectively.

■ *Managing Total Quality*

Quality and productivity have become major determinants of business success or failure today and have become central issues in managing organizations. But, as we will see, achieving higher levels of quality is not an easy accomplishment. Simply ordering that quality be improved is about as effective as waving a magic wand. The catalyst for its emergence as a mainstream management concern was foreign business, especially Japanese. And nowhere was it more visible than in the auto industry. During the energy crisis in the late 1970s, many people bought Toyotas, Hondas, and Nissans because they were more fuel-efficient than U.S. cars. Consumers soon found, however, that not only were the Japanese cars more fuel-efficient, they were also of higher quality than U.S. cars. Parts fit together better, the trim work was neater, and the cars were more reliable. Thus, after the energy crisis subsided, Japanese cars remained formidable competitors because of their reputation for quality.

The Meaning of Quality

The American Society for Quality Control defines **quality** as the totality of features and characteristics of a product or service that bear on its ability to satisfy stated or implied needs.[15] Quality has several different attributes. Table 15.2 lists eight basic dimensions that determine the quality of a particular product or service. For example, a product that has durability and is reliable is of higher quality than a product with less durability and reliability.

Quality is also relative. For example, a Lincoln is a higher-grade car than a Ford Taurus, which in turn is a higher-grade car than a Ford Focus. The difference in

quality The totality of features and characteristics of a product or service that bear on its ability to satisfy stated or implied needs

---

1. **Performance.** A product's primary operating characteristic. Examples are automobile acceleration and a television's picture clarity.
2. **Features.** Supplements to a product's basic functioning characteristics, such as power windows on a car.
3. **Reliability.** A probability of not malfunctioning during a specified period.
4. **Conformance.** The degree to which a product's design and operating characteristics meet established standards.
5. **Durability.** A measure of product life.
6. **Serviceability.** The speed and ease of repair.
7. **Aesthetics.** How a product looks, feels, tastes, and smells.
8. **Perceived quality.** As seen by a customer.

Source: Reprinted by permission of *Harvard Business Review*. Exhibit from "Competing on the Eight Dimensions of Quality," by David A. Garvin, November/December 1987. Copyright © 1987 by Harvard Business School Publishing Corporation, all rights reserved.

Table 15.2

Eight Dimensions of Quality
These eight dimensions generally capture the meaning of quality, which is a critically important ingredient to organizational success today. Understanding the basic meaning of quality is a good first step to managing it more effectively.

quality stems from differences in design and other features. The Focus, however, is considered a high-quality car relative to its engineering specifications and price. Likewise, the Taurus and Lincoln may also be high-quality cars, given their standards and prices. Thus quality is both an absolute and a relative concept.

Quality is relevant for both products and services. Although its importance for products like cars and computers was perhaps recognized first, service firms ranging from airlines to restaurants have also come to see that quality is a vitally important determinant of their success or failure. Service quality, as we will discuss later in this chapter, has thus also become a major competitive issue in U.S. industry today.

The Importance of Quality

Malcolm Baldrige Award Named after a former secretary of commerce, this prestigious award is given to firms that achieve major quality improvements

To help underscore the importance of quality, the U.S. government created the **Malcolm Baldrige Award**, named after the former secretary of commerce who championed quality in U.S. industry. The award, administered by an agency of the Department of Commerce, is given annually to firms that achieve major improvements in the quality of their products or services. That is, the award is based on changes in quality, as opposed to absolute quality.

Recent winners of the Baldrige Award include Motorola, the Cadillac Division of General Motors, and divisions of Texas Instruments, AT&T, Xerox, and Ritz-Carlton. In addition, numerous other quality awards have also been created. For example, the Rochester Institute of Technology and *USA Today* award their Quality Cup award not to entire organizations but to individual teams of workers within organizations. Quality is also an important concern for individual managers and organizations for three very specific reasons: competition, productivity, and costs.[16]

Competition   Quality has become one of the most competitive points in business today. Ford, DaimlerChrysler, General Motors, and Toyota, for example, each argues that its cars and trucks are higher in quality than the cars and trucks of the others. And American, United, and Continental airlines each claims that it provides the best and most reliable service. Indeed, it seems that virtually every U.S. business has adopted quality as a major point of competition. Thus a business that fails to keep pace may find itself falling behind not only foreign competition but also other U.S. firms.

Productivity   Managers have also come to recognize that quality and productivity are related. In the past, many managers thought that they could increase output (productivity) only by decreasing quality. Managers today have learned the hard way that such an assumption is almost always wrong. If a firm installs a meaningful quality enhancement program, three things are likely to result. First, the number of defects is likely to decrease, causing fewer returns from customers. Second, because the number of defects goes down, resources (materials and people) dedicated to reworking flawed output will be decreased. Third, because making employees responsible for quality reduces the need for quality inspectors, the organization is able to produce more units with fewer resources.

Costs   Improved quality also lowers costs. Poor quality results in higher returns from customers, high warranty costs, and lawsuits from customers injured by faulty products. Future sales are lost because of disgruntled customers. An organization with quality problems often has to increase inspection expenses just to catch defective products. We noted in an earlier chapter, for example, how Whistler Corporation was using 100 of its 250 employees just to fix poorly assembled radar detectors.[17]

Total Quality Management

Once an organization makes a decision to enhance the quality of its products and services, it must then decide how to implement this decision. The most pervasive approach to managing quality has been called **total quality management**, or **TQM** —a real and meaningful effort by an organization to change its whole approach to business, to make quality a guiding factor in everything the organization does.[18] Figure 15.3 highlights the major ingredients in TQM.

Strategic Commitment   The starting point for TQM is a strategic commitment by top management. Such commitment is important for several reasons. First, the organizational culture must change to recognize that quality is not just an ideal but is instead an objective goal that must be pursued.[19] Second, a decision to pursue the goal of quality carries with it some real costs—for such expenditures as new equipment and facilities. Thus, without a commitment from top management, quality improvement will prove to be just a slogan or gimmick, with little or no real change.

Employee Involvement   Employee involvement is another critical ingredient in TQM. Virtually all successful quality enhancement programs involve making the person responsible for doing the job responsible for making sure it is done right.[20] By definition, then, employee involvement is a critical component in improving quality. Work teams, discussed in Chapter 13, are common vehicles for increasing employee involvement.

Technology   New forms of technology are also useful in TQM programs. Automation and robots, for example, can often make products with higher precision and better consistency than can people. Investing in higher-grade machines

total quality management (TQM)
A strategic commitment by top management to change its whole approach to business to make quality a guiding factor in everything it does

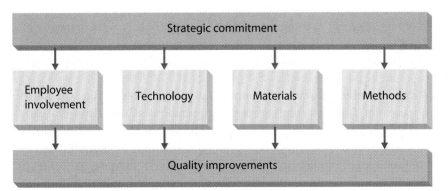

Figure 15.3
Total Quality Management
Quality is one of the most important issues facing organizations today. Total quality management, or TQM, is a comprehensive effort to enhance an organization's product or service quality. TQM involves the five basic dimensions shown here. Each is important and must be addressed effectively if the organization truly expects to increase quality.

capable of doing jobs more precisely and reliably often improves quality. For example, Nokia has achieved notable improvements in product quality by replacing many of its machines with new equipment. Similarly, most U.S. auto and electronics firms have all made significant investments in technology to help boost quality.

Materials   Another important part of TQM is improving the quality of the materials that organizations use. Suppose that a company that assembles stereos buys chips and circuits from another company. If the chips have a high failure rate, consumers will return defective stereos to the company whose nameplate appears on them, not to the company that made the chips. The stereo firm then loses in two ways: refunds back to customers and a damaged reputation. As a result, many firms have increased the quality requirements they impose on their suppliers as a way of improving the quality of their own products. Recall from our opening incident that Hartmann uses only high-quality materials in its luggage.

Methods   Improved methods can improve product and service quality. Methods are operating systems used by the organization during the actual transformation process. American Express Company, for example, has found ways to cut its approval time for new credit cards from 22 to only 5 days. This results in improved service quality.

TQM Tools and Techniques

Beyond the strategic context of quality, managers can also rely on several specific tools and techniques for improving quality. Among the most popular today are benchmarking, outsourcing, speed, ISO 9000, and statistical quality control.

benchmarking The process of learning how other firms do things in an exceptionally high-quality manner

Benchmarking   **Benchmarking** is the process of learning how other firms do things in an exceptionally high-quality manner. Some approaches to benchmarking are simple and straightforward. For example, Xerox routinely buys copiers made by other firms and takes them apart to see how they work. This enables the firm to stay abreast of improvements and changes its competitors are making. When Ford was planning the newest version of the Taurus, it identified the 400 features customers identified as being most important to them. It then found the competing cars that did the best job on each feature. Ford's goal was to equal or surpass each of its competitors on those 400 features. Other benchmarking strategies are more indirect. For example, many firms study how L. L. Bean manages its mail-order business, how Disney recruits and trains employees, and how Federal Express tracks packages for applications they can employ in their own businesses.

outsourcing Subcontracting services and operations to other firms that can perform them more cheaply or better

Outsourcing   Another innovation for improving quality is outsourcing. **Outsourcing** is the process of subcontracting services and operations to other firms that can provide them more cheaply or better. If a business performs each and every one of its own administrative and business services and operations, it is almost certain to be doing at least some of them in an inefficient or low-quality manner. If those areas can be identified and outsourced, the firm will save money and realize a higher-quality service or operation.[21] For example, until recently Eastman Kodak handled all of its own computing operations. Now, however, those operations are subcontracted to IBM, which handles all of Kodak's computing. The result is higher-quality computing systems and operations at Kodak for less money than it was spending before.

Speed   A third popular TQM technique is speed. **Speed** is the time needed by the organization to get something accomplished, and it can be emphasized in any area, including developing, making, and distributing products or services. A good illustration of the power of speed comes from General Electric. At one point the firm needed six plants and three weeks to produce and deliver custom-made industrial circuit breaker boxes. By emphasizing speed, the same product can now be delivered in three days, and only a single plant is involved. Table 15.3 identifies a number of basic suggestions that have helped companies increase the speed of their operations. For example, GE found it better to start from scratch with a remodeled plant. GE also wiped out the need for approvals by eliminating most managerial positions and set up teams as a basis for organizing work. Stressing the importance of the schedule helped Motorola build a new plant and start production of a new product in only 18 months.

ISO 9000   Still another useful technique for improving quality is ISO 9000. **ISO 9000** refers to a set of quality standards created by the International Organization for Standardization. There are five such standards, numbered 9000 to 9001. They cover such areas as product testing, employee training, record keeping, supplier relations, and repair polices and procedures. Firms that want to meet these standards apply for certification and are audited by a firm chosen by the

© Ros Chast 2000 from cartoonbank.com. All rights reserved.

Effective total quality management requires major commitments from an organization. Thorough and rigorous quality checks and inspections are often a fundamental part of quality management. But managers who pay only lip service to inspections, such as the managers illustrated here checking water quality, should not be surprised later when they discover major quality problems throughout their organization. Only by using objective and rigorous statistical quality control measures can the firm be assured of high-quality products and services.

speed The time needed by the organization to get its activities, including developing, making, and distributing products or services, accomplished

---

1. Start from scratch (it's usually easier than trying to do what the organization does now faster).
2. Minimize the number of approvals needed to do something (the fewer people who have to approve something, the faster approval will get done).
3. Use work teams as a basis for organization (teamwork and cooperation work better than individual effort and conflict).
4. Develop and adhere to a schedule (a properly designed schedule can greatly increase speed).
5. Don't ignore distribution (making something faster is only part of the battle).
6. Integrate speed into the organization's culture (if everyone understands the importance of speed, things will naturally get done quicker).

Source: Reprinted by permission from Brian Dumaine, "How Managers Can Succeed Through Speed," *Fortune*, February 13, 1989, pp. 54–59. © 1989 Time Inc. All rights reserved.

Table 15.3

Guidelines for Increasing the Speed of Operations

Many organizations today are using speed for competitive advantage. Listed in the table are six common guidelines that organizations follow when they want to shorten the time they need to get things accomplished. Although not every manager can do each of these things, most managers can do at least some of them.

ISO 9000 A set of quality standards created by the International Organization for Standardization

organization's domestic affiliate (in the United States, this is the American National Standards Institute). These auditors review every aspect of the firm's business operations in relation to the standards. Many firms report that merely preparing for an ISO 9000 audit has been helpful. Many firms today, including General Electric, Du Pont, Eastman Kodak, British Telecom, and Philips Electronics are urging—or in some cases requiring—that their suppliers achieve ISO 9000 certification.[22]

statistical quality control (SQC) A set of specific statistical techniques that can be used to monitor quality; includes acceptance sampling and in-process sampling

Statistical Quality Control   A final quality control technique is **statistical quality control (SQC)**. As the term suggests, SQC is concerned primarily with managing quality. Moreover, it is a set of specific statistical techniques that can be used to monitor quality. *Acceptance sampling* involves sampling finished goods to ensure that quality standards have been met. Acceptance sampling is effective only when the correct percentage of products that should be tested (for example, 2, 5, or 25 percent) is determined. This decision is especially important when the test renders the product useless. Flash cubes, wine, and collapsible steering wheels, for example, are consumed or destroyed during testing. Another SQC method is *in-process sampling*. In-process sampling involves evaluating products during production so that needed changes can be made. The painting department of a furniture company might periodically check the tint of the paint it is using. The company can then adjust the color as necessary to conform to customer standards. The advantage of in-process sampling is that it allows problems to be detected before they accumulate.

■ *Managing Productivity*

Although the current focus on quality by American companies is a relatively recent phenomenon, managers have been aware of the importance of productivity for several years. The stimulus for this attention was a recognition that the gap between productivity in the United States and productivity in other industrialized countries was narrowing. This section describes the meaning of productivity and underscores its importance. After summarizing recent productivity trends, we suggest ways that organizations can increase their productivity.

The Meaning of Productivity

productivity An economic measure of efficiency that summarizes what is produced relative to resources used to produce it

In a general sense, **productivity** is an economic measure of efficiency that summarizes the value of outputs relative to the value of the inputs used to create them.[23] Productivity can be and often is assessed at different levels of analysis and in different forms.

Levels of Productivity   By "level of productivity" we mean the units of analysis used to calculate or define productivity. For example, aggregate productivity is the total level of productivity achieved by a country. Industry productivity is the total productivity achieved by all the firms in a particular industry. Company productivity, just as the term suggests, is the level of productivity achieved by an individual company. Unit and individual productivity refer to the productivity achieved by a unit or department within an organization and the level of productivity attained by a single person.

Forms of Productivity There are many different forms of productivity. Total-factor productivity is defined by the following formula:

$$\text{Productivity} = \frac{\text{Outputs}}{\text{Inputs}}$$

Total-factor productivity is an overall indicator of how well an organization uses all of its resources, such as labor, capital, materials, and energy, to create all of its products and services. The biggest problem with total-factor productivity is that all the ingredients must be expressed in the same terms—dollars (it is difficult to add hours of labor to number of units of raw materials in a meaningful way). Total-factor productivity also gives little insight into how things can be changed to improve productivity. Consequently, most organizations find it more useful to calculate a partial productivity ratio. Such a ratio uses only one category of resource. For example, labor productivity could be calculated by this simple formula:

$$\text{Labor productivity} = \frac{\text{Outputs}}{\text{Direct Labor}}$$

This method has two advantages. First, it is not necessary to transform the units of input into some other unit. Second, this method provides managers with specific insights into how changing different resource inputs affects productivity. Suppose that an organization can manufacture 100 units of a particular product with 20 hours of direct labor. The organization's labor productivity index is 5 (or 5 units per labor hour). Now suppose that worker efficiency is increased (through one of the ways to be discussed later in this chapter) so that the same 20 hours of labor result in the manufacture of 120 units of the product. The labor productivity index increases to 6 (6 units per labor hour), and the firm can see the direct results of a specific managerial action.

The Importance of Productivity

Managers consider it important that their firms maintain high levels of productivity for a variety of reasons. Firm productivity is a primary determinant of an organization's level of profitability and, ultimately, of its ability to survive. If one organization is more productive than another, it will have more products to sell at lower prices and have more profits to reinvest in other areas. Productivity also partially determines people's standards of living within a particular country. At an economic level, businesses consume resources and produce goods and services. The goods and services created within a country can be used by that country's own citizens or exported for sale in other countries. The more goods and services the businesses within a country can produce, the more goods and services the country's citizens will have. Even goods that are exported result in financial resources' flowing back into the home country. Thus the citizens of a highly productive country are likely to have a notably higher standard of living than are the citizens of a country with low productivity.

Productivity Trends

The United States has the highest level of productivity in the world. For example, Japanese workers produce only about 76 percent as much as U.S. workers, whereas German workers produce about 84 percent as much.[24] But in recent years other countries have been closing the gap.[25] This trend was a primary factor in the decisions made by U.S. businesses to retrench, retool, and become more competitive in the world marketplace. For example, General Electric's dishwasher plant in Louisville has cut its inventory requirements by 50 percent, reduced labor costs from 15 percent to only 10 percent of total manufacturing costs, and cut product development time in half. As a result of these kinds of efforts, productivity trends have now leveled out, and U.S. workers are generally maintaining their lead in most industries.[26]

One important factor that has hurt U.S. productivity indices has been the tremendous growth of the service sector in the United States. While this sector grew, its productivity levels did not. One part of this problem relates to measurement. For example, it is fairly easy to calculate the number of tons of steel produced at a Bethlehem Steel mill and divide it by the number of labor hours used; it is more difficult to determine the output of an attorney or a certified public accountant. Still, virtually everyone agrees that improving service sector productivity is the next major hurdle facing U.S. business.[27]

Figure 15.4 shows manufacturing productivity growth since 1970 in terms of annual average percentage of increase. As you can see, that growth was slow during the 1970s but began to rise again in the mid-1980s. Some experts believe that productivity both in the United States and abroad will continue to improve at even more impressive rates. Their confidence rests on the potential ability of technology to improve operations. For example, Ford Motor Company has unveiled plans for a comprehensive purchasing network that it calls Auto-Xchange. This system will replace all of its current purchasing arrangements, eliminating the need for personal contracts, paper and telephone ordering, and the like—saving billions of dollars and sharply boosting productivity in the process. Ford projects that this part of its business may well achieve annual productivity growth rates of up to 10 percent.[28]

Figure 15.4

Manufacturing and Service Productivity Growth Trends (1970–2000)

Both manufacturing productivity and service productivity in the United States continue to grow, although manufacturing productivity is growing at a faster pace. Total productivity, therefore, also continues to grow.

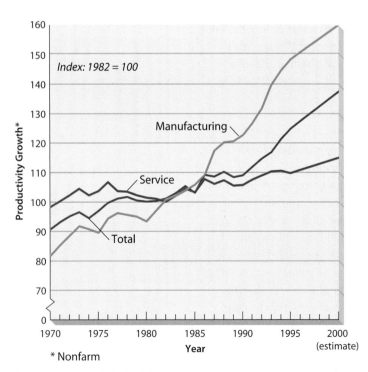

*Nonfarm

Source: U. S. Bureau of Labor Statistics.

Improving Productivity

How does a business or industry improve its productivity? Numerous specific suggestions made by experts generally fall into two broad categories: improving operations and increasing employee involvement.

Improving Operations   One way that firms can improve operations is by spending more on research and development. R&D spending helps identify new products, new uses for existing products, and new methods for making products. Each of these contributes to productivity. For example, Bausch & Lomb almost missed the boat on extended-wear contact lenses because the company had neglected R&D. When it became apparent that its major competitors were almost a year ahead of Bausch & Lomb in developing the new lenses, management made R&D a top-priority concern. As a result, the company made several scientific breakthroughs, shortened the time needed to introduce new products, and greatly enhanced both total sales and profits—and all with a smaller workforce than the company used to employ. Even though other countries are greatly increasing their R&D spending, the United States continues to be the world leader in this area.[29]

Another way in which firms can boost productivity through operations is by reassessing and revamping their transformation facilities.[30] We noted earlier how one of GE's modernized plants does a better job than six antiquated ones. Just building a new factory is no guarantee of success, but IBM, Ford, Caterpillar, and many other businesses have achieved dramatic productivity gains by revamping their production facilities.[31] Facilities refinements are not limited to manufacturers. Most McDonald's restaurants now have drive-through windows, and many have moved soft-drink dispensers out to the restaurant floor so that customers can get their own drinks. Each of these moves is an attempt to increase the speed with which customers can be served and thereby to increase productivity.

Increasing Employee Involvement   The other major thrust in productivity enhancement has been toward employee involvement. We noted earlier that participation can enhance quality. So, too, can it boost productivity. Examples of this involvement are an individual worker's being given a bigger voice in how she does her job, a formal agreement of cooperation between management and labor, and total involvement throughout the organization. GE eliminated most of the supervisors at its one new circuit breaker plant and put control in the hands of workers.

Another method popular in the United States is increasing the flexibility of an organization's workforce by training employees to perform a number of different jobs. Such cross-training allows the firm to function with fewer workers because workers can be transferred easily to areas where they are most needed. For example, the Lechmere department store in Sarasota, Florida, encourages workers to learn numerous jobs within the store. One person in the store can operate a forklift in the stockroom, serve as a cashier, or provide customer service on the sales floor. At one Motorola plant, 397 of 400 employees have learned at least two skills under a similar program.

Rewards are essential to making employee involvement work. Firms must reward people for learning new skills and using them proficiently. At Motorola, for example, workers who master a new skill are assigned for five days to a job requiring them to use that skill. If they perform with no defects, they are moved to a higher pay grade, and then they move back and forth between jobs as they are needed. If there is a performance problem, they receive more training and practice. This approach is fairly new, but preliminary indicators suggest that it can increase productivity significantly. Many unions resist such programs because they threaten job security and reduce a person's identification with one skill or craft.

Summary of Key Points

Operations management is the set of managerial activities that organizations use in creating their products and services. Operations management is important to both manufacturing and service organizations. It plays an important role in an organization's strategy.

The starting point in using operations management is by designing appropriate operations systems. Key decisions that must be made as part of operations systems design relate to product and service mix, capacity, and facilities.

Technology also plays an important role in quality. Automation is especially important today. Numerous computer-aided manufacturing techniques are widely practiced. Robotics is also a growing area. Technology is as relevant to service organizations as to manufacturing organizations.

After an operations system has been designed and put in place, it must then be implemented. Major areas of interest during the use of operations systems are purchasing and inventory management.

Quality is a major consideration for all managers today. Quality is important because it affects competition, productivity, and costs. Total quality management is a comprehensive, organizationwide effort to enhance quality through a variety of avenues.

Productivity is also of major concern to managers. Productivity is a measure of how efficiently an organization is using its resources to create products or services. The United States still leads the world in individual productivity, but other industrialized nations are catching up.

Discussion Questions

Questions for Review

1. What is quality? Why is it so important today?
2. How can an organization go about trying to increase the speed of its operations?
3. What are some of the basic TQM tools and techniques that managers can use to improve quality?
4. What is productivity? How can it be increased?
5. What is the relationship of operations management to overall organizational strategy? Where do productivity and quality fit into that relationship?

Questions for Analysis

6. How might the management functions of planning, organizing, and leading relate to the management of quality and productivity?
7. Some people argue that quality and productivity are inversely related: As one goes up, the other goes down. How can that argument be refuted?
8. Is operations management most closely linked to corporate-level, business-level, or functional strategies? Why or in what way?
9. Consider your college or university as an organization. How might it go about developing a TQM program?
10. Think of a product or service you purchased recently that subsequently failed to meet your expectations regarding quality. How could the product or service have been improved to make it of higher quality?

BUILDING EFFECTIVE *conceptual* SKILLS

Exercise Overview

A manager's conceptual skills are her or his ability to think in the abstract. As this exercise demonstrates, there is often a relationship between the conceptual skills of key managers in an organization and that organization's ability to implement total quality initiatives.

Exercise Background

Conceptual skills may help managers see opportunities for learning how to improve some aspect of their own operations from observations or experiences gleaned from dealings with other organizations.

To begin this exercise, carefully recall the last time you ate in a restaurant that involved some degree of self-service. Examples might include a fast-food restaurant like McDonald's, a cafeteria, or even a traditional restaurant with a salad bar. Recall as much about the experience as possible and develop some ideas as to why the restaurant is organized and laid out as it is.

Now carefully recall the last time you purchased something in a retail outlet. Possible examples might be an article of clothing from a specialty store, a book from a bookstore, or some software from a computer store. Again recall as much about the experience as possible and develop some ideas as to why the store is organized and laid out as it is.

Exercise Task

Using the two examples you developed above, do the following:
1. Identify three or four elements of the service received at each location that you think most directly influenced—either positively or negatively—the quality and efficiency of your experience there.
2. Analyze the service elements from one organization and see whether they can somehow be used by the other.
3. Now repeat the process for the second organization.

BUILDING EFFECTIVE *diagnostic* SKILLS

Exercise Overview

As noted in this chapter, the quality of a product or service is relative to price and expectations. A manager's diagnostic skills—the ability to visualize responses to a situation—can be useful in helping to best position quality relative to price and expectations.

Exercise Background

Think of a recent occasion in which you purchased a tangible product. For example, think about clothing, electronic equipment, luggage, or professional supplies that you subsequently came to feel to be of especially high quality. Now recall another product that you evaluated as having appropriate or adequate quality

and a third that you felt had low or poor quality.

Next, recall parallel experiences involving purchases of services. Examples might include an airline, train, or bus trip; a meal in a restaurant; a haircut; or an oil change for your car.

Finally, recall three experiences in which both products and services were involved. Examples might include having questions answered by someone about a product you were buying or returning a defective or broken product for a refund or warranty repair. Try to recall instances in which there was an apparent disparity between product and service quality (for example, a poor-quality product accompanied by outstanding service or a high-quality product with mediocre service).

Exercise Task

Using the nine examples identified above, do the following:

1. Assess the extent to which the quality you associated with each was a function of price and your expectations.
2. Consider whether the quality of each item could be improved without greatly affecting its price. If so, how?

3. Consider whether high-quality service can offset only adequate or even poor product quality. Similarly, consider whether outstanding product quality can offset only adequate or even poor-quality service.

BUILDING EFFECTIVE *technical* SKILLS

Exercise Overview

Technical skills are the skills necessary to accomplish or understand the specific kind of work being done in an organization. This exercise helps you see how technical skills relate to quality, productivity, and operations management.

Exercise Background

Select a product that you use on a regular basis. Examples might include computers, compact disks, books, or apparel. Next, do some research to learn as much as you can about how the product you chose is designed, produced, and distributed to consumers.

Assume that you have decided to go into business to make the product selected. Create two columns on a sheet of paper. In one col-umn, list all the relevant activities that you know how to do (for example, install software on a computer, sew two pieces of fabric together). In the second column, list the activities that you do not know how to do.

Exercise Task

With the background information above as context, do the following:

1. Specify where people might learn the skills necessary to perform all the activities for the product you intend to make.
2. Rank-order the importance of the skills regarding the product.
3. Determine how many people you will likely need to employ to have a full skill set available.

SKILLS *self-assessment* INSTRUMENT

Defining Quality and Productivity

Introduction: *Quality* is a complex term whose meaning has no doubt changed over time. The following assessment surveys your ideas about and approaches to quality.

Instructions: You will agree with some of the statements and disagree with others. In some cases, making a decision may be difficult, but you should force a choice. Record your answers next to each statement according to the rating scale:

Rating Scale

4 Strongly agree   **2** Somewhat disagree

3 Slightly agree   **1** Strongly disagree

_____ 1. Quality refers to a product's or service's ability to fulfill its primary operating characteristics, such as providing a sharp picture for a television set.

_____ 2. Quality is an absolute, measurable aspect of a product or service.

_____ 3. The concept of quality includes supplemental aspects of a product or service, such as the remote control for a television set.

_____ 4. Productivity and quality are inversely related, so that, to get one, you must sacrifice the other.

_____ 5. The concept of quality refers to the extent to which a product's design and operating characteristics conform to certain set standards.

_____ 6. Productivity refers to what is created relative to what it takes to create it.

_____ 7. Quality means that a product will not malfunction during a specified period of time.

_____ 8. Quality refers only to products; it is immeasurable for services.

_____ 9. The length of time that a product or service will function is what is known as quality.

_____ 10. Everyone uses exactly the same definition of quality.

_____ 11. Quality refers to the repair ease and speed of a product or service.

_____ 12. Being treated courteously has nothing to do with the quality of anything.

_____ 13. How a product looks, feels, tastes, or smells is what is meant by quality.

_____ 14. Price, not quality, is what determines the ultimate value of service.

_____ 15. Quality refers to what customers think of a product or service.

_____ 16. Productivity and quality cannot both increase at the same time.

For interpretation, see Interpretations of Skills Self-Assessment Instruments.

Source: Adapted from Chapter 21, especially pp. 473–474, in David D. Van Fleet and Tim O. Peterson, *Contemporary Management*, Third Edition. Copyright © 1994 by Houghton Mifflin Company.

EXPERIENTIAL EXERCISE

Preparing the Fishbone Chart

Purpose: The fishbone chart is an excellent procedure for identifying possible causes of a problem. It provides you with knowledge that you can use to improve the operations of any organization. This skill exercise focuses on the *administrative management model*. It helps you develop the *monitor role* of the administrative management model. One of the skills of the monitor is the ability to analyze problems.

Introduction: Japanese quality circles often use the fishbone "cause-and-effect" graphic technique to initiate the resolution of a group work problem. Quite often the causes are clustered in categories such as materials, methods, people, and machines. The fishbone technique is usually accomplished in the following six steps:

1. Write the problem in the "head" of the fish (the large block).
2. Brainstorm the major causes of the problem and list them on the fish "bones."

3. Analyze each main cause and write in minor subcauses on bone subbranches.
4. Reach consensus on one or two of the major causes of the problem.
5. Explore ways to correct or remove the major causes.
6. Prepare a report or presentation explaining the proposed change.

Instructions: Your instructor will provide you with further instructions.

The fishbone will look something like this:

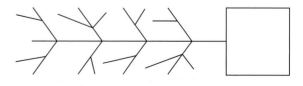

Source: Adapted from Burton, Gene E., *Exercises in Management*, Fifth edition. Copyright © 1996 by Houghton Mifflin Company. Used with permission.

BUILDING BETTER CARS IN BRAZIL

Better in Brazil? DaimlerChrysler, Volkswagen, Ford, General Motors, and Toyota are just some of the auto manufacturers that have opened factories in Brazil to turn out cars, vans, and trucks. These automakers and their suppliers have been pioneering productivity-boosting methods that save money and streamline the assembly process.

One innovation is the combination of just-in-time and just-in-sequence methods. Here's how Daimler-Chrysler and its suppliers are using these methods to make Dakota pickup trucks in a manufacturing center south of São Paulo. Dana Corporation, a key supplier, is responsible for procuring 205 parts from 67 suppliers to build chassis subassemblies (complete with fuel tank, brakes, suspension, and wheels). Dana's trucks haul three subassemblies down the road to the Chrysler factory a few miles away every 42 minutes. The subassemblies arrive in time to be combined with engines and incorporated into the pickup truck cabs rolling down the assembly line at that moment. Thanks to JIT and JIS methods, a new Dakota truck rolls off the end of the line every 14 minutes. DaimlerChrysler saves space because the subassemblies are put together in Dana's facility. It also saves time and effort because Dana, not Daimler-Chrysler, has to locate and purchase all the parts for the subassemblies.

The Dakota plant is home to another money-saving idea: outsourcing an activity performed on the premises. Supplier PPG Industries provides the paints as well as the employees to prime and paint each Dakota truck within DaimlerChrysler's factory. As a result, DaimlerChrysler does not have to invest in raw materials or hire employees for this part of the manufacturing process—and it benefits from PPG's expertise in developing new paints and painting practices.

Even the assembly lines look different. In the newer VW-Audi and Mercedes factories in Brazil, for example, cars move through the first half of the assembly line mounted on large wooden platforms. Workers stand on these platforms and complete their assembly tasks, then dismount and walk back to the car behind to go through the routine again. In contrast, workers in tradi-tional plants generally have to work as they walk to keep up with cars moving down the assembly lines. VW-Audi also tracks vehicles as they progress through the factory, posting a transmitter on each car's roof and monitoring the signals to identify slowdowns and keep output on schedule.

Suppliers like Dana Corporation play a critical role in maintaining productivity in these plants. Johnson Controls, which makes car seats, instrument panels, and other components, has five production centers in Brazil and is thinking of building additional facilities to give its factory customers what they want, when they want it. Yet suppliers still have to juggle their own purchasing, inventory, and production functions to achieve productivity goals by minimizing costs while maximizing output. Dana, for example, needs sufficient capacity to keep up with its customers' manufacturing capacity; anticipating future demand, the Dana facility has excess capacity right now, as does the Dakota plant it serves. And locating near a particular plant to provide JIT and JIS benefits effectively ties the supplier to that customer, which can cause problems if the customer reduces output or withdraws from the market.

Competitive pressures also affect what suppliers decide to do in Brazil. After all, no supplier wants to say no to a customer—and then watch as a rival says yes and takes away a significant chunk of business. At the same time, suppliers are making hefty investments in plant, equipment, and personnel to accommodate their automaker customers. Although experts are projecting increased demand for cars and other vehicles, which should translate into higher sales for automakers and their suppliers, an economic downturn or a currency crisis could hurt. On the other hand, with little increase in demand in the United States, Japan, and Europe, the automakers are looking toward South American markets for future growth—and advances in productivity.

Case Questions

1. What issues do operations managers for the automakers and their suppliers face in Brazil?

2. What total quality management tools and techniques are being applied in these Brazilian operations?

3. Which of the three approaches to facilities layout do the automakers appear to be applying in Brazil? Why is this an appropriate approach?

Case References

Philip Siekman, "Building 'Em Better in Brazil," *Fortune,* September 6, 1999, pp. 246c–246v; and Philip Siekman, "Where 'Build to Order' Works Best," *Fortune,* April 26, 1999, pp. 160c–160v.

CHAPTER NOTES

1. *Hoover's Handbook of American Business 2001* (Austin, TX: Hoover's Business Press, 2001), pp. 284–285; and "The Quest for Quality Is in the Bag(gage)," *USA Today,* September 23, 1997, p. 12E (*quote on p. 12E).
2. See "Keep Your Eye on the Factory Floor," *Business Week,* April 23, 2001, pp. 115–116.
3. Paul M. Swamidass, "Empirical Science: New Frontier in Operations Management Research," *Academy of Management Review,* October 1991, pp. 793–814.
4. For an example, see Robin Cooper and Regine Slagmulder, "Develop Profitable New Products with Target Costing," *Sloan Management Review,* Summer 1999, pp. 23–34.
5. Joan Woodward, *Industrial Organization: Theory and Practice* (London: Oxford University Press, 1965).
6. See "Tight Labor? Tech to the Rescue," *Business Week,* March 20, 2000, pp. 36–37.
7. "Computers Speed the Design of More Workaday Products," *Wall Street Journal,* January 18, 1985, p. 25.
8. "New Plant Gets Jaguar in Gear," *USA Today,* November 27, 2000, p. 4B.
9. "Thinking Machines," *Business Week,* August 7, 2000, pp. 78–86.
10. James Brian Quinn and Martin Neil Baily, "Information Technology: Increasing Productivity in Services," *Academy of Management Executive* 8, no. 3 (1994): 28–37.
11. See Charles J. Corbett, Joseph D. Blackburn, and Luk N. Van Wassenhove, "Partnerships to Improve Supply Chains," *Sloan Management Review,* Summer 1999, pp. 71–82; and Jeffrey K. Liker and Yen-Chun Wu, "Japanese Automakers, U.S. Suppliers, and Supply-Chain Superiority," *Sloan Management Review,* Fall 2000, pp. 81–93.
12. See "Siemens Climbs Back," *Business Week,* June 5, 2000, pp. 79–82.
13. See M. Bensaou, "Portfolios of Buyer-Supplier Relationships," *Sloan Management Review,* Summer 1999, pp. 35–44.
14. "Just-in-Time Manufacturing Is Working Overtime," *Business Week,* November 8, 1999, pp. 36–37.
15. Ross Johnson and William O. Winchell, *Management and Quality* (Milwaukee, WI: American Society for Quality Control, 1989). See also Carol Reeves and David Bednar, "Defining Quality: Alternatives and Implications," *Academy of Management Review* 19, no. 3 (1994): 419–445; and C. K. Prahalad and M. S. Krishnan, "The New Meaning of Quality in the Information Age," *Harvard Business Review,* September/October 1999, pp. 109–120.
16. W. Edwards Deming, *Out of the Crisis* (Cambridge, Mass.: MIT Press, 1986).
17. Joel Dreyfuss, "Victories in the Quality Crusade," *Fortune,* October 10, 1988, pp. 80–88.
18. Thomas Y. Choi and Orlando C. Behling, "Top Managers and TQM Success: One More Look After All These Years," *Academy of Management Executive* 11, no. 1 (1997): 37–48.
19. James Dean and David Bowen, "Management Theory and Total Quality: Improving Research and Practice Through Theory Development," *Academy of Management Review,* 19, no. 3 (1994): 392–418.
20. Edward E. Lawler, "Total Quality Management and Employee Involvement: Are They Compatible?" *Academy of Management Executive* 8, no. 1 (1994): 68–79.
21. See James Brian Quinn, "Strategic Outsourcing: Leveraging Knowledge Capabilities," *Sloan Management Review,* Summer 1999, pp. 8–22.
22. Ronald Henkoff, "The Hot New Seal of Quality," *Fortune,* June 28, 1993, pp. 116–120. See also Mustafa V. Uzumeri, "ISO 9000 and Other Metastandards: Principles for Management Practice?" *Academy of Management Executive* 11, no. 1 (1997): 21–28.
23. John W. Kendrick, *Understanding Productivity: An Introduction to the Dynamics of Productivity Change* (Baltimore: Johns Hopkins, 1977).
24. "The Productivity Payoff Arrives," *Fortune,* June 27, 1994, pp. 79–84.
25. "Study: USA Losing Competitive Edge," *USA Today,* April 25, 1997, p. 9D.
26. "Why the Productivity Revolution Will Spread," *Business Week,* February 14, 2000, pp. 112–118.
27. Michael van Biema and Bruce Greenwald, "Managing Our Way to Higher Service-Sector Productivity," *Harvard Business Review,* July/August 1997, pp. 87–98.
28. See "Yank the Supply Chain," *Fortune,* November 15, 2000, pp. 152–159.
29. Gene Bylinsky, "Look Who's Doing R&D," *Fortune,* November 27, 2000, pp. 232c–232f.
30. "Better Machine Tools Give Manufacturers Newfound Resilience," *Wall Street Journal,* February 15, 2001, pp. A1, A8.
31. Cf. "The Soul of a New Machine," *Forbes,* June 11, 2001, pp. 66–70.

Tools for Planning and Decision Making

This appendix discusses a number of the basic tools and techniques that managers can use to enhance the effectiveness of planning and decision making. We first describe forecasting, an extremely important tool, and then discuss several other planning techniques. Next we discuss several tools that relate more to decision making. We conclude by assessing the strengths and weaknesses of the various tools and techniques.

Forecasting

To plan, managers must make assumptions about future events. But, unlike wizards of old, planners cannot simply look into a crystal ball. Instead, they must develop forecasts of probable future circumstances. **Forecasting** is the process of developing assumptions or premises about the future that managers can use in planning or decision making.

forecasting The process of developing assumptions or premises about the future that managers can use in planning or decision making

Sales and Revenue Forecasting

As the term implies, **sales forecasting** is concerned with predicting future sales. Because monetary resources (derived mainly from sales) are necessary to finance both current and future operations, knowledge of future sales is of vital importance. Sales forecasting is something that every business, from Exxon to a neighborhood pizza parlor, must do. Consider, for example, the following questions that a manager might need to answer:

sales forecasting The prediction of future sales

1. How much of each of our products should we produce next week? next month? next year?
2. How much money will we have available to spend on research and development and on new-product test marketing?
3. When and to what degree will we need to expand our existing production facilities?
4. How should we respond to union demands for a 5 percent pay increase?
5. If we borrow money for expansion, when can we pay it back?

None of these questions can be answered adequately without some notion of what future revenues are likely to be. Thus sales forecasting is generally one of the first steps in planning.

Unfortunately, the term *sales forecasting* suggests that this form of forecasting is appropriate only for organizations that have something to sell. But other kinds of organizations also depend on financial resources, and so they also must forecast. The University of South Carolina, for example, must forecast future state aid before planning course offerings, staff size, and so on. Hospitals must forecast their future income from patient fees, insurance payments, and other sources to assess their ability to expand. Although we will continue to use the conventional term, keep in mind that what is really at issue is **revenue forecasting**.

revenue forecasting The prediction of future revenues from all sources

Several sources of information are used to develop a sales forecast. Previous sales figures and any obvious trends, such as the company's growth or stability, usually serve as the base. General economic indicators, technological improvements, new marketing strategies, and the competition's behavior all may be added together to ensure an accurate forecast. Once projected, the sales (or revenue) forecast becomes a guiding framework for various other activities. Raw materials expenditures, advertising budgets, sales commission structures, and similar operating costs are all based on projected sales figures.

Organizations often forecast sales across several time horizons. The longer-run forecasts may then be updated and refined as various shorter-run cycles are completed. For obvious reasons, a forecast should be as accurate as possible, and the accuracy of sales forecasting tends to increase as organizations learn from their previous forecasting experience. But the more uncertain and complex future conditions are likely to be, the more difficult it is to develop accurate forecasts. To partially offset these problems, forecasts are more useful to managers if they are expressed as a range rather than as an absolute index or number. If projected sales increases are expected to be in the range of 10 to 12 percent, a manager can consider all the implications for the entire range. A 10 percent increase could dictate one set of activities; a 12 percent increase could call for a different set of activities.

Technological Forecasting

technological forecasting The prediction of what future technologies are likely to emerge and when they are likely to be economically feasible

Technological forecasting is another type of forecasting used by many organizations. It focuses on predicting what future technologies are likely to emerge and when they are likely to be economically feasible. In an era when technological breakthrough and innovation have become the rule rather than the exception, it is important that managers be able to anticipate new developments. If a manager invests heavily in existing technology (such as production processes, equipment, and computer systems) and the technology becomes obsolete in the near future, the company has wasted its resources.

The most striking technological innovations in recent years have been in electronics, especially semiconductors. Home computers, electronic games, and sophisticated communications equipment are all evidence of the electronics explosion. Given the increasing importance of technology and the rapid pace of technological innovation, it follows that managers will grow increasingly concerned with technological forecasting in the years to come.

Other Types of Forecasting

Other types of forecasting are also important to many organizations. Resource forecasting projects the organization's future needs for and the availability of human resources, raw materials, and other resources. General economic conditions are the subject of economic forecasts. For example, some organizations undertake population or market-size forecasting. Some organizations also attempt to forecast future government fiscal policy and various government regulations that might be put into practice. Indeed, almost any component in an organization's environment may be an appropriate area for forecasting.

Forecasting Techniques

To carry out the various kinds of forecasting we have identified, managers use several different techniques.[1] Time-series analysis and causal modeling are two common quantitative techniques.

Time-Series Analysis The underlying assumption of **time-series analysis** is that the past is a good predictor of the future. This technique is most useful when the manager has a lot of historical data available and when stable trends and patterns are apparent. In a time-series analysis, the variable under consideration (such as sales or enrollment) is plotted across time, and a "best-fit" line is identified.[2] Figure A.1 shows how a time-series analysis might look. The dots represent the number of units sold for each year from 1994 through 2002. The best-fit line has also been drawn in. It is the line around which the dots cluster with the least variability. A manager who wants to know what sales to expect in 2003 simply extends the line. In this case, the projection would be around 8,200 units.

Real time-series analysis involves much more than simply plotting sales data and then using a ruler and a pencil to draw and extend the line. Sophisticated mathematical procedures, among other things, are necessary to account for seasonal and cyclical fluctuations and to identify the true best-fit line. In real situations data seldom follow the neat pattern found in Figure A.1. Indeed, the data points may be so widely dispersed that they mask meaningful trends from all but painstaking, computer-assisted inspection.

time-series analysis A forecasting technique that extends past information into the future through the calculation of a best-fit line

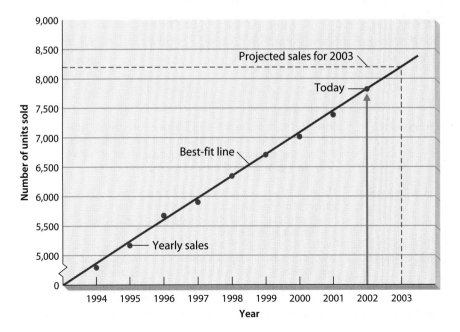

Figure A.1

An Example of Time-Series Analysis

Because time-series analysis assumes that the past is a good predictor of the future, it is most useful when historical data are available, trends are stable, and patterns are apparent. For example, it can be used for projecting estimated sales for products like shampoo, pens, and automobile tires. (Of course, few time-series analyses yield such clear results, because there is almost always considerably more fluctuation in data from year to year.)

causal modeling A group of different techniques that determine causal relationships between different variables

regression model An equation that uses one set of variables to predict another variable

Causal Modeling   Another useful forecasting technique is **causal modeling**. Actually, the term *causal modeling* represents a group of several techniques. Table A.1 summarizes three of the most useful approaches. **Regression models** are equations created to predict a variable (such as sales volume) that depends on several other variables (such as price and advertising). The variable being predicted is called the *dependent variable*; the variables used to make the prediction are called *independent variables*. A typical regression equation used by a small business might take this form:

$$y = ax_1 + bx_2 + cx_3 + d$$

where

y = The dependent variable (sales in this case)

x_1, x_2, and x_3 = Independent variables (advertising budget, price, and commissions)

a, b, and c = Weights for the independent variables calculated during development of the regression model

d = A constant

To use the model, a manager can insert various alternatives for advertising budget, price, and commissions into the equation and then compute y. The calculated value of y represents the forecasted level of sales, given various levels of advertising, price, and commissions.[3]

econometric model A causal model that predicts major economic shifts and the potential impact of those shifts on the organization

Econometric models employ regression techniques at a much more complex level. **Econometric models** attempt to predict major economic shifts and the potential impact of those shifts on the organization. They might be used to predict various age, ethnic, and economic groups that will characterize different regions of the United States in the year 2010 and also to predict the kinds of products and services these groups may want. A complete econometric model may consist of hundreds or even thousands of equations. Computers are almost always necessary to apply them. Given the complexities involved in developing econometric mod-

Table A.1

Summary of Causal Modeling Forecasting Techniques

Managers use several different types of causal models in planning and decision making. Three popular models are regression models, econometric models, and economic indicators.

Regression models	Used to predict one variable (called the dependent variable) on the basis of known or assumed other variables (called independent variables). For example, we might predict future sales based on the values of price, advertising, and economic levels.
Econometric models	Make use of several multiple-regression equations to consider the impact of major economic shifts. For example, we might want to predict what impact the migration toward the Sun Belt might have on our organization.
Economic indicators	Various population statistics, indexes, or parameters that predict organizationally relevant variables such as discretionary income. Examples include cost-of-living index, inflation rate, and level of unemployment.

els, many firms that decide to use them rely on outside consultants specializing in this approach.

Economic indicators, another form of causal model, are population statistics or indexes that reflect the economic well-being of a population. Examples of widely used economic indicators include the current rates of national productivity, inflation, and unemployment. In using such indicators, the manager draws on past experiences that have revealed a relationship between a certain indicator and some facet of the company's operations. Pitney Bowes Data Documents Division, for example, can predict future sales of its business forms largely on the basis of current GNP estimates and other economic growth indexes.

Qualitative Forecasting Techniques   Organizations also use several qualitative techniques to develop their forecasts. A **qualitative forecasting technique** relies more on individual or group judgment or opinion rather than on sophisticated mathematical analyses. The Delphi procedure, described in Chapter 4 as a mechanism for managing group decision-making activities, can also be used to develop forecasts. A variation of it—the *jury-of-expert-opinion* approach—involves using the basic Delphi process with members of top management. In this instance, top management serves as a collection of experts asked to make a prediction about something—competitive behavior, trends in product demand, and so forth. Either a pure Delphi or a jury-of-expert-opinion approach might be useful in technological forecasting.

The *sales-force-composition* method of sales forecasting is a pooling of the predictions and opinions of experienced salespeople. Because of their experience, these individuals are often able to forecast quite accurately what various customers will do. Management combines these forecasts and interprets the data to create plans. Textbook publishers use this procedure to project how many copies of a new title they might sell.

The *customer evaluation* technique goes beyond an organization's sales force and collects data from customers of the organization. The customers provide estimates of their own future needs for the goods and services that the organization supplies. Managers must combine, interpret, and act on this information. This approach, however, has two major limitations. Customers may be less interested in taking time to develop accurate predictions than are members of the organization itself, and the method makes no provision for including any new customers that the organization may acquire. Wal-Mart helps its suppliers use this approach by providing them with detailed projections regarding what it intends to buy several months in advance.

Selecting an appropriate forecasting technique can be as important as applying it correctly. Some techniques are appropriate only for specific circumstances. For example, the sales-force-composition technique is good only for sales forecasting. Other techniques, like the Delphi method, are useful in a variety of situations. Some techniques, such as the econometric models, require extensive use of computers, whereas others, such as customer evaluation models, can be used with little mathematical expertise. For the most part, selection of a particular technique depends on the nature of the problem, the experience and preferences of the manager, and available resources.[4]

economic indicator A key population statistic or index that reflects the economic well-being of a population

qualitative forecasting technique One of several techniques that rely on individual or group judgment rather than on mathematical analyses

Other Planning Techniques

Of course, planning involves more than just forecasting. Other tools and techniques that are useful for planning purposes include linear programming, breakeven analysis, simulations, and PERT.

Linear Programming

linear programming A planning technique that determines the optimal combination of resources and activities

Linear programming is one of the most widely used quantitative tools for planning. **Linear programming** is a procedure for calculating the optimal combination of resources and activities. It is appropriate when there is some objective to be met (such as a sales quota or a certain production level) within a set of constraints (such as a limited advertising budget or limited production capabilities).

To illustrate how linear programming can be used, assume that a small electronics company produces two basic products—a high-quality cable television tuner and a high-quality receiver for picking up television audio and playing it through a stereo amplifier. Both products go through the same two departments, first production and then inspection and testing. Each product has a known profit margin and a high level of demand. The production manager's job is to produce the optimal combination of tuners (T) and receivers (R) that maximizes profits and uses the time in production (PR) and in inspection and testing (IT) most efficiently. Table A.2 gives the information needed for the use of linear programming to solve this problem.

The *objective function* is an equation that represents what we want to achieve. In technical terms, it is a mathematical representation of the desirability of the consequences of a particular decision. In our example, the objective function can be represented as follows:

Maximize profit = $\$30X_T + \$20X_R$

where

R = Number of receivers to be produced

T = Number of tuners to be produced

The $30 and $20 figures are the respective profit margins of the tuner and receiver, as noted in Table A.2. The objective, then, is to maximize profits.

However, this objective must be accomplished within a specific set of constraints. In our example, the constraints are the time required to produce each product in each department and the total amount of time available. These data are also found in Table A.2 and can be used to construct the relevant constraint equations.

$10T + 6R \leq 150$

$4T + 4R \leq 80$

That is, we cannot use more capacity than is available, and of course,

$T \geq 0$

$R \geq 0$

Department	Number of Hours Required per Unit		Production Capacity for Day (in hours)
	Tuners (*T*)	Receivers (*R*)	
Production (*PR*)	10	6	150
Inspection and testing (*IT*)	4	4	80
Profit margin	$30	$20	

Table A.2

Production Data for Tuners and Receivers

Linear programming can be used to determine the optimal number of tuners and receivers an organization might make. Essential information needed to perform this analysis includes the number of hours each product spends in each department, the production capacity for each department, and the profit margin for each product.

The set of equations consisting of the objective function and constraints can be solved graphically. To start, we assume that production of each product is maximized when production of the other is at zero. The resultant solutions are then plotted on a coordinate axis. In the production department, if $T = 0$, then

$$10T + 6R \leq 150$$

$$10(0) + 6R \leq 150$$

$$R \leq 25$$

In the same department, if $R = 0$, then

$$10T + 6(R) \leq 150$$

$$10T + 6(0) \leq 150$$

$$T \leq 15$$

Similarly, in the IT department, if no tuners are produced,

$$4T + 4R \leq 80$$

$$4(0) + 4R \leq 80$$

$$R \leq 20$$

and, if no receivers are produced,

$$4T + 4R \leq 80$$

$$4T + 4(0) \leq 80$$

$$T \leq 20$$

The four resulting inequalities are graphed in Figure A.2. The shaded region represents the feasibility space, or production combinations that do not exceed the capacity of either department. The optimal number of products will be defined at one of the four corners of the shaded area—that is, the firm should produce 20 receivers only (point *C*), 15 tuners only (point *B*), 13 receivers and 7 tuners (point *E*), or no products at all. With the constraint that production of both tuners and receivers must be greater than zero, it follows that point *E* is the optimal solution. That combination requires 148 hours in PR

Figure A.2

The Graphical Solution of a Linear Programming Problem

Finding the graphical solution to a linear programming problem is useful when only two alternatives are being considered. When problems are more complex, computers that can execute hundreds of equations and variables are necessary. Virtually all large firms, such as General Motors, Texaco, and Sears, use linear programming.

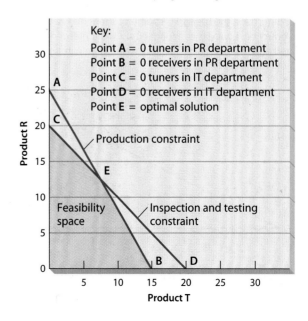

Key:
Point **A** = 0 tuners in PR department
Point **B** = 0 receivers in PR department
Point **C** = 0 tuners in IT department
Point **D** = 0 receivers in IT department
Point **E** = optimal solution

and 80 hours in IT, and yields $470 in profit. (Note that, if only receivers were produced, the profit would be $400; producing only tuners would mean $450 in profit.)

Unfortunately, only two alternatives can be handled by the graphical method, and our example was extremely simple. When there are other alternatives, a complex algebraic method must be employed. Real-world problems may require several hundred equations and variables. Clearly, computers are necessary to execute such sophisticated analyses. Linear programming is a powerful technique, playing a key role in both planning and decision making. It can be used to schedule production, select an optimal portfolio of investments, allocate sales representatives to territories, or produce an item at some minimum cost.

Breakeven Analysis

Linear programming is called a *normative procedure* because it prescribes the optimal solution to a problem. Breakeven analysis is a *descriptive procedure*, because it simply describes relationships among variables; then it is up to the manager to make decisions. We can define **breakeven analysis** as a procedure for identifying the point at which revenues start covering their associated costs. It might be used to analyze the effects on profits of different price and output combinations or various levels of output.

breakeven analysis A procedure for identifying the point at which revenues start covering their associated costs

Figure A.3 represents the key cost variables in breakeven analysis. Creating most products or services includes three types of costs: fixed costs, variable costs, and total costs. *Fixed costs* are costs that are incurred regardless of what volume of output is being generated. They include rent or mortgage payments on the building, managerial salaries, and depreciation of plant and equipment. *Variable costs* vary with the number of units produced, such as the cost of raw materials and direct labor used to make each unit. *Total costs* are fixed costs plus variable costs. Note that, because of fixed costs, the line for total costs never begins at zero.

Other important factors in breakeven analysis are revenue and profit. *Revenue*, the total dollar amount of sales, is computed by multiplying the number of units sold by the sales price of each unit. *Profit* is then determined by subtracting total costs from total revenues. When revenues and total costs are plotted on the same axes, the breakeven graph shown in Figure A.4 emerges. The point at which the lines representing total costs and total revenues cross is the breakeven point. The company represented in Figure A.4 sells more units than are represented by point *A*, it will realize a profit; selling below that level will result in a loss.

Mathematically, the breakeven point (expressed as units of production or volume) is shown by the formula

$$BP = \frac{TFC}{P - VC}$$

Figure A.3

An Example of Cost Factors for Breakeven Analysis

To determine the breakeven point for profit on sales for a product or service, the manager must first determine both fixed and variable costs. These costs are then combined to show total costs.

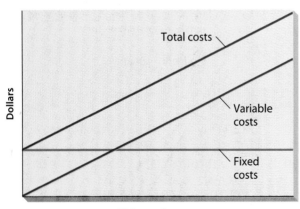

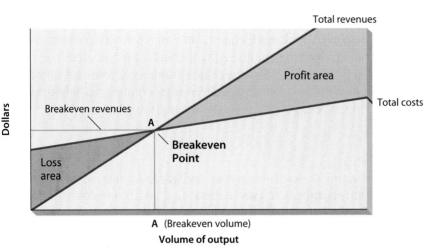

Total revenues

Profit area

Total costs

Breakeven revenues

A

Breakeven Point

Loss area

Dollars

A (Breakeven volume)

Volume of output

Figure A.4

Breakeven Analysis

After total costs are determined and graphed, the manager then graphs the total revenues that will be earned on different levels of sales. The regions defined by the intersection of the two graphs show loss and profit areas. The intersection itself shows the breakeven point—the level of sales at which all costs are covered but no profits are earned.

where

BP = Breakeven point

TFC = Total fixed costs

P = Price per unit

VC = Variable cost per unit

Assume that you are considering the production of a new garden hoe with a curved handle. You have determined that an acceptable selling price will be $20. You have also determined that the variable costs per hoe will be $15, and you have total fixed costs of $400,000 per year. The question is: How many hoes must you sell each year to break even? Using the breakeven model, you find that

$$BP = \frac{TFC}{P - VC}$$

$$BP = \frac{400,000}{20 - 15}$$

$$BP = 80,000 \text{ units}$$

Thus you must sell 80,000 hoes to break even. Further analysis would also show that if you could raise your price to $25 per hoe, you would need to sell only 40,000 to break even, and so on.

The state of New York used a breakeven analysis to evaluate seven variations of prior approvals for its Medicaid service. Comparisons were conducted of the costs involved in each variation against savings gained from efficiency and improved quality of service. The state found that only three of the variations were cost effective.[5]

Breakeven analysis is a popular and important planning technique, but it also has noteworthy weaknesses. It considers revenues only up to the breakeven point, and it makes no allowance for the time value of money. For example, because the funds used to cover fixed and variable costs could be used for other purposes (such as investment), the organization is losing interest income by tying up its money prior to reaching the breakeven point. Thus managers often use breakeven analysis as only the first step in planning. After the preliminary analysis has been completed, more sophisticated techniques (such as rate-of-return analysis or discounted-present-value analysis) are used. Those techniques can help the manager decide whether to proceed or to divert resources into other areas.

Simulations

organizational simulation A model of a real-world situation that can be manipulated to discover how it functions

Another useful planning device is simulation. The word *simulate* means "to copy" or "to represent." An **organizational simulation** is a model of a real-world situation that can be manipulated to discover how it functions. Simulation is a descriptive, rather than a prescriptive, technique. Northern Research & Engineering Corporation is an engineering consulting firm that helps clients plan new factories. By using a sophisticated factory simulation model, the firm recently helped a client cut several machines and operations from a new plant and save more than $750,000.

To consider another example, suppose the city of Houston wants to build a new airport. Issues to be addressed might include the number of runways, the direction of those runways, the number of terminals and gates, the allocation of various carriers among the terminals and gates, and the technology and human resources needed to achieve a target frequency of takeoffs and landings. (Of course, actually planning such an airport would involve many more variables than these.) A model could be constructed to simulate these factors, as well as their interrelationships. The planner could then insert several different values for each factor and observe the probable results.

Simulation problems are in some ways similar to those addressed by linear programming, but simulation is more useful in very complex situations characterized by diverse constraints and opportunities. The development of sophisticated simulation models may require the expertise of outside specialists or consultants, and the complexity of simulation almost always necessitates the use of a computer. For these reasons simulation is most likely to be used as a technique for planning in large organizations that have the required resources.

PERT

PERT A planning tool that uses a network to plan projects involving numerous activities and their interrelationships

A final planning tool we will discuss is PERT. **PERT**, an acronym for Program Evaluation and Review Technique, was developed by the U.S. Navy to help coordinate the activities of 3,000 contractors during the development of the Polaris nuclear submarine, and it was credited with saving two years of work on the project. It has subsequently been used by most large companies in different ways. The purpose of PERT is to develop a network of activities and their interrelationships and thus highlight critical time intervals that affect the overall project. PERT follows six basic steps.

1. Identify the activities to be performed and the events that will mark their completion.
2. Develop a network showing the relationships among the activities and events.

3. Calculate the time needed for each event and the time necessary to get from each event to the next.
4. Identify within the network the longest path that leads to completion of the project. This path is called the *critical path*.
5. Refine the network.
6. Use the network to control the project.

Suppose that a marketing manager wants to use PERT to plan the test marketing and nationwide introduction of a new product. Table A.3 identifies the basic steps involved in carrying out this project. The activities are then arranged in a network like the one shown in Figure A.5. In the figure, each completed event is represented by a number in a circle. The activities are indicated by letters on the lines connecting the events. Notice that some activities are performed independently of one another and that others must be performed in sequence. For example, test production (activity a) and test site location (activity c) can be done at the same time, but test site location has to be done before actual testing (activities f and g) can be done.

The time needed to get from one activity to another is then determined. The normal way to calculate the time between activities is to average the most optimistic, most pessimistic, and most likely times, with the most likely time weighted by 4. Time is usually calculated with the following formula:

$$\text{Expected time} = \frac{a + 4b + c}{6}$$

where

a = Optimistic time

b = Most likely time

c = Pessimistic time

Activities		Events	
		1	Origin of project.
a	Produce limited quantity for test marketing.	2	Completion of production for test marketing.
b	Design preliminary package.	3	Completion of design for preliminary package.
c	Locate test market.	4	Test market located.
d	Obtain local merchant cooperation.	5	Local merchant cooperation obtained.
e	Ship product to selected retail outlets.	6	Product for test marketing shipped to retail outlets.
f	Monitor sales and customer reactions.	7	Sales and customer reactions monitored.
g	Survey customers in test-market area.	8	Customers in test-market area surveyed.
h	Make needed product changes.	9	Product changes made.
i	Make needed package changes.	10	Package changes made.
j	Mass-produce the product.	11	Product mass-produced.
k	Begin national advertising.	12	National advertising carried out.
l	Begin national distribution.	13	National distribution completed.

Table A.3

Activities and Events for Introducing a New Product
PERT is used to plan schedules for projects, and it is particularly useful when many activities with critical time intervals must be coordinated. Besides launching a new product, PERT is useful for projects like constructing a new factory or building, remodeling an office, or opening a new store.

Figure A.5

A PERT Network for Introducing a New Product

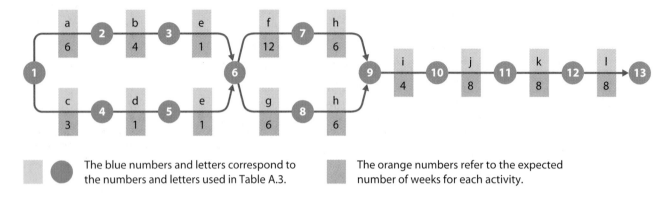

The blue numbers and letters correspond to the numbers and letters used in Table A.3.

The orange numbers refer to the expected number of weeks for each activity.

critical path The longest path through a PERT network

The expected number of weeks for each activity in our example is shown in the orange boxes along each path in Figure A.5. The **critical path**—or the longest path through the PERT network—is then identified. This path is considered critical be-cause it shows the shortest time in which the project can be completed. In our ex-ample, the critical path is 1-2-3-6-7-9-10-11-12-13, totaling 57 weeks. PERT thus tells the manager that the project will take 57 weeks to complete.

The first network may be refined. If 57 weeks to completion is too long a time, the manager might decide to begin preliminary package design before the test products are finished. Or the manager might decide that 10 weeks rather than 12 is a sufficient time period to monitor sales. The idea is that, if the critical path can be shortened, so, too, can the overall duration of the project. The PERT network serves as an ongoing framework for both planning and control throughout the project. For example, the manager can use it to monitor where the project is rela-tive to where it needs to be. Thus, if an activity on the critical path takes longer than planned, the manager needs to make up the time elsewhere or live with the fact that the entire project will be late.

■ *Decision-Making Tools*

Managers can also use a number of tools that relate more specifically to decision making than to planning. Two commonly used decision-making tools are payoff matrices and decision trees.

Payoff Matrices

payoff matrix A decision-making tool that specifies the probable value of different alternatives de-pending on different possible out-comes associated with each

A **payoff matrix** specifies the probable value of different alternatives, depending on different possible outcomes associated with each. The use of a payoff matrix requires that several alternatives be available, that several different events could occur, and that the consequences depend on which alternative is selected and on which event or set of events occurs. An important concept in understanding the payoff matrix, then, is probability. A **probability** is the likelihood, expressed as a percentage, that a particular event will or will not occur. If we believe that a particular event will occur 75 times out of 100, we can say that the probability of its occurring is 75 percent, or .75. Probabilities range in value from 0 (no chance of occurrence) to 1.00 (certain occurrence—also referred to as 100 percent). In the business world, there are few probabilities of either 0 or 1.00. Most probabilities that managers use are based on subjective judgment, intuition, and historical data.

The **expected value** of an alternative course of action is the sum of all possible values of outcomes due to that action multiplied by their respective probabilities. Suppose, for example, that a venture capitalist is considering investing in a new company. If he believes there is a .40 probability of making $100,000, a .30 probability of making $30,000, and a .30 probability of losing $20,000, the expected value (EV) of this alternative is

$$EV = .40(100,000) + .30(30,000) + .30(-20,000)$$

$$EV = 40,000 + 9,000 - 6,000$$

$$EV = \$43,000$$

The investor can then weigh the expected value of this investment against the expected values of other available alternatives. The highest EV signals the investment that should most likely be selected.

For example, suppose another venture capitalist wants to invest $20,000 in a new business. She has identified three possible alternatives: a leisure products company, an energy enhancement company, and a food-producing company. Because the expected value of each alternative depends on short-run changes in the economy, especially inflation, she decides to develop a payoff matrix. She estimates that the probability of high inflation is .30, and the probability of low inflation is .70. She then estimates the probable returns for each investment in the event of both high and low inflation. Figure A.6 shows what the payoff matrix

probability The likelihood, expressed as a percentage, that a particular event will or will not occur

expected value When applied to alternative courses of action, the sum of all possible values of outcomes from that action multiplied by their respective probabilities

		High inflation (*probability of .30*)	Low inflation (*probability of .70*)
Investment alternative **1**	Leisure products company	−$10,000	+$50,000
Investment alternative **2**	Energy enhancement company	+$90,000	−$15,000
Investment alternative **3**	Food-processing company	+$30,000	+$25,000

Figure A.6

An Example of a Payoff Matrix

A payoff matrix helps the manager determine the expected value of different alternatives. A payoff matrix is effective only if the manager ensures that probability estimates are as accurate as possible.

might look like (a minus sign indicates a loss). The expected value of investing in the leisure products company is

$$EV = .30(-10{,}000) + .70(50{,}000)$$

$$EV = -3{,}000 + 35{,}000$$

$$EV = \$32{,}000$$

Similarly, the expected value of investing in the energy enhancement company is

$$EV = .30(90{,}000) + .70(-15{,}000)$$

$$EV = 27{,}000 + (-10{,}500)$$

$$EV = \$16{,}500$$

And, finally, the expected value of investing in the food-processing company is

$$EV = .30(30{,}000) + .70(25{,}000)$$

$$EV = 9{,}000 + 17{,}500$$

$$EV = \$26{,}500$$

Investing in the leisure products company, then, has the highest expected value.

Other potential uses for payoff matrices include determining optimal order quantities, deciding whether to repair or replace broken machinery, and deciding which of several new products to introduce. Of course, the real key to using payoff matrices effectively is making accurate estimates of the relevant probabilities.

Decision Trees

decision tree A planning tool that extends the concept of a payoff matrix through a sequence of decisions

Decision trees are like payoff matrices because they enhance a manager's ability to evaluate alternatives by making use of expected values. However, they are most appropriate when there are several decisions to be made in sequence.

Figure A.7 illustrates a hypothetical decision tree. The small firm represented wants to begin exporting its products to a foreign market, but limited capacity restricts it to only one market at first. Managers feel that either France or China would be the best place to start. Whichever alternative is selected, sales for the product in that country may turn out to be high or low. In France, there is a .80 chance of high sales and a .20 chance of low sales. The anticipated payoffs in these situations are predicted to be $20 million and $3 million, respectively. In China, the probabilities of high versus low sales are .60 and .40, respectively, and the associated payoffs are presumed to be $25 million and $6 million. As shown in Figure A.7, the expected value of shipping to France is $16,600,000, whereas the expected value of shipping to China is $17,400,000.

The astute reader will note that this part of the decision could have been set up as a payoff matrix. However, the value of decision trees is that we can extend the model to include subsequent decisions. Assume, for example, that the company begins shipping to China. If high sales do in fact materialize, the company will soon reach another decision situation. It might use the extra revenues to (1) increase

Figure A.7

An Example of a Decision Tree

A decision tree extends the basic concepts of a payoff matrix through multiple decisions. This tree shows the possible outcomes of two levels of decisions. The first decision is whether to expand to China or France. The second decision, assuming that the company expands to China, is whether to increase shipments to China, build a plant close to China, or initiate shipping to France.

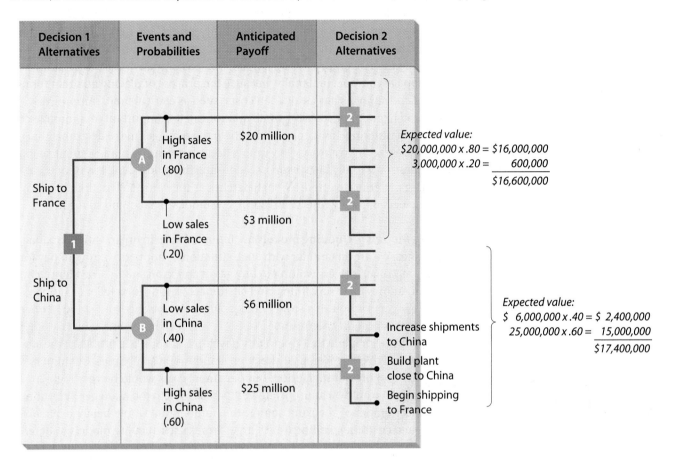

shipments to China, (2) build a plant close to China and thus cut shipping costs, or (3) begin shipping to France. Various outcomes are possible for each decision, and each outcome will have both a probability and an anticipated payoff. It is therefore possible to compute expected values back through several tiers of decisions all the way to the initial one. As it is with payoff matrices, determining probabilities accurately is the crucial element in the process. Properly used, however, decision trees can provide managers with a useful road map through complex decision situations.

Other Techniques

In addition to payoff matrices and decision trees, a number of other quantitative methods are also available to facilitate decision making.

inventory model A technique that helps managers decide how much inventory to maintain

just-in-time (JIT) An inventory management technique in which materials are scheduled to arrive in small batches as they are needed, eliminating the need for resources such as big reserves and warehouse space

queuing model A model used to optimize waiting lines in organizations

distribution model A model used to determine the optimal pattern of distribution across different carriers and routes

game theory A planning tool used to predict how competitors will react to various activities that an organization might undertake

Inventory Models **Inventory models** are techniques that help the manager decide how much inventory to maintain. Target Stores uses inventory models to help determine how much merchandise to order, when to order it, and so forth. Inventory consists of both raw materials (inputs) and finished goods (outputs). Polaroid, for example, maintains a supply of the chemicals that it uses to make film, the cartons it packs film in, and packaged film ready to be shipped. For finished goods, both extremes are bad: Excess inventory ties up capital, whereas a small inventory may result in shortages and customer dissatisfaction. The same holds for raw materials: Too much inventory ties up capital, but if a company runs out of resources, work stoppages may occur. Finally, because the process of placing an order for raw materials and supplies has associated costs (such as clerical time, shipping expenses, and higher unit costs for small quantities), it is important to minimize the frequency of ordering. Inventory models help the manager make decisions that optimize the size of inventory. New innovations in inventory management such as **just-in-time**, or **JIT**, rely heavily on decision-making models. A JIT system involves scheduling materials to arrive in small batches as they are needed, thereby eliminating the need for a big reserve inventory, warehouse space, and so forth.[6]

Queuing Models **Queuing models** are intended to help organizations manage waiting lines. We are all familiar with such situations: shoppers waiting to pay for groceries at Kroger, drivers waiting to buy gas at an Exxon station, travelers calling American Airlines for reservations, and customers waiting for a teller at Citibank. Take the Kroger example. If a store manager has only one checkout stand in operation, the store's cost for checkout personnel is very low; however, many customers are upset by the long line that frequently develops. To solve the problem, the store manager could decide to keep 20 checkout stands open at all times. Customers would like the short waiting period, but personnel costs would be very high. A queuing model would be appropriate in this case to help the manager determine the optimal number of checkout stands: the number that would balance personnel costs and customer waiting time. Target Stores uses queuing models to determine how many checkout lanes to put in its retail stores.

Distribution Models A decision facing many marketing managers relates to the distribution of the organization's products. Specifically, the manager must decide where the products should go and how to transport them. Railroads, trucking, and air freight have associated shipping costs, and each mode of transportation follows different schedules and routes. The problem is to identify the combination of routes that optimizes distribution effectiveness and distribution costs. **Distribution models** help managers determine this optimal pattern of distribution.

Game Theory **Game theory** was originally developed to predict the effect of one company's decisions on competitors. Models developed from game theory are intended to predict how a competitor will react to various activities that an organization might undertake, such as price changes, promotional changes, and the introduction of new products. If Wells Fargo Bank were considering raising its prime lending rate by 1 percent, it might use a game theory model to predict whether Citicorp would follow suit. If the model revealed that Citicorp would do so, Wells Fargo would probably proceed; otherwise, it would probably maintain the current interest rates. Unfortunately, game theory is not yet as useful as it was originally expected to be. The complexities of the real world combined with the limitations of the technique itself restrict its applicability. Game theory, however, does provide a useful conceptual framework for analyzing competitive behavior, and its usefulness may be improved in the future.

Artificial Intelligence   A fairly new addition to the manager's quantitative tool kit is **artificial intelligence (AI)**. The most useful form of AI is the expert system.[7] An expert system is essentially a computer program that attempts to duplicate the thought processes of experienced decision makers. For example, Hewlett-Packard has developed an expert system that checks sales orders for new computer systems and then designs preliminary layouts for those new systems. HP can now ship the computer to a customer in components for final assembly on site. This approach has enabled the company to cut back on its own final-assembly facilities.

artificial intelligence (AI) A computer program that attempts to duplicate the thought processes of experienced decision makers

Strengths and Weaknesses of Planning Tools

Like all issues confronting management, planning tools of the type described here have several strengths and weaknesses.

Weaknesses and Problems

One weakness of the planning and decision-making tools discussed in this appendix is that they may not always adequately reflect reality. Even with the most sophisticated and powerful computer-assisted technique, reality must often be simplified. Many problems are also not amenable to quantitative analysis because important elements of them are intangible or nonquantifiable. Employee morale or satisfaction, for example, is often a major factor in managerial decisions.

The use of these tools and techniques may also be quite costly. For example, only larger companies can afford to develop their own econometric models. Even though the computer explosion has increased the availability of quantitative aids, some expense is still involved, and it will take time for many of these techniques to become widely used. Resistance to change also limits the use of planning tools in some settings. If a manager for a retail chain has always based decisions for new locations on personal visits, observations, and intuition, she or he may be less than eager to begin using a computer-based model for evaluating and selecting sites. Finally, problems may arise when managers have to rely on technical specialists to use sophisticated models. Experts trained in the use of complex mathematical procedures may not understand or appreciate other aspects of management.

Strengths and Advantages

On the plus side, planning and decision-making tools offer many advantages. For situations that are amenable to quantification, they can bring sophisticated mathematical processes to bear on planning and decision making. Properly designed models and formulas also help decision makers "see reason." For example, a manager might not be inclined to introduce a new product line simply because she or he doesn't think it will be profitable. After seeing a forecast predicting first-year sales of 100,000 units coupled with a breakeven analysis showing profitability after only 20,000, however, the manager will probably change her or his mind. Thus rational planning tools and techniques force the manager to look beyond personal prejudices and predispositions. Finally, the computer explosion is rapidly making sophisticated planning techniques available in a wider range of settings than ever before.

The crucial point to remember is that planning tools and techniques are a means to an end, not an end in themselves. Just as a carpenter uses a handsaw in some situations and an electric saw in others, a manager must recognize that a particular model may be useful in some situations but not in others that may call for a different approach. Knowing the difference is one mark of a good manager.

Summary of Key Points

Managers often use various tools and techniques as they develop plans and make decisions. Forecasting is one widely used method. Forecasting is the process of developing assumptions or premises about the future. Sales or revenue forecasting is especially important. Many organizations also rely heavily on technological forecasting. Time-series analysis and causal modeling are important forecasting techniques. Qualitative techniques are also widely used.

Managers also use other planning tools and techniques in different circumstances. Linear programming helps optimize resources and activities. Breakeven analysis helps identify how many products or services must be sold to cover costs. Simulations model reality. PERT helps plan how much time a project will require.

Other tools and techniques are useful for decision making. Constructing a payoff matrix, for example, helps a manager assess the expected value of different alternatives. Decision trees are used to extend expected values across multiple decisions. Other popular decision-making tools and techniques include inventory models, queuing models, distribution models, game theory, and artificial intelligence.

Various strengths and weaknesses are associated with each of these tools and techniques, as well as with their use by a manager. The key to success is knowing when each should and should not be used and knowing how to use and interpret the results that each provides.

APPENDIX NOTES

1. For a classic review, see John C. Chambers, S. K. Mullick, and D. Smith, "How to Choose the Right Forecasting Technique," *Harvard Business Review*, July/August 1971, pp. 45–74.

2. Charles Ostrom, *Time-Series Analysis: Regression Techniques* (Beverly Hills, CA: Sage Publications, 1980).

3. Fred Kerlinger and Elazar Pedhazur, *Multiple Regression in Behavioral Research* (New York: Holt, 1973).

4. Chambers, Mullick, and Smith. See also J. Scott Armstrong, *Long-Range Forecasting: From Crystal Ball to Computers* (New York: Wiley, 1978).

5. Edward Hannan, Linda Ryan, and Richard Van Orden, "A Cost-Benefit Analysis of Prior Approvals for Medicaid Services in New York State," *Socio-Economic Planning Sciences* 18 (1984): 1–14.

6. Ramon L. Alonso and Cline W. Fraser, "JIT Hits Home: A Case Study in Reducing Management Delays," *Sloan Management Review*, Summer 1991, pp. 59–68.

7. Beau Sheil, "Thinking about Artificial Intelligence," *Harvard Business Review*, July/August 1987, pp. 91–97; and Dorothy Leonard-Barton and John J. Sviokla, "Putting Expert Systems to Work," *Harvard Business Review*, March/April 1988, pp. 91–98.

Interpretations of Skills Self-Assessment Instruments

Chapter 1: Self-Awareness

Total your scores for each skill area.

Skill Area	Items	Score
Self-disclosure and openness to feedback from others	1, 2, 3, 9, 11	_____
Awareness of own values, cognitive style, change orientation, and interpersonal orientation	4, 5, 6, 7, 8, 10	_____
Now total your score:		_____

To assess how well you scored on this instrument, compare your scores to three comparison standards. (1) Compare your scores with the maximum possible (66). (2) Compare your scores with the scores of other students in your class. (3) Compare your scores to a norm group consisting of five hundred business school students. In comparison to the norm group, if you scored

55 or above, you are in the top quartile.
52 to 54, you are in the second quartile.
48 to 51, you are in the third quartile.
47 or below, you are in the bottom quartile.

Chapter 2: Global Awareness

All the statements are true. Thus, your score should be close to 40. The closer your score is to 40, the more you understand the global context of organizational environments. The closer your score is to 10, the less you understand the global context. For developmental purposes, you should note any particular items for which you had a low score and concentrate on improving your knowledge of those areas.

Chapter 3: Are You a Good Planner?

According to the author of this questionnaire, the "perfect" planner would have answered: (1) Yes, (2) No, (3) Yes, (4) Yes, (5) Yes, (6) Yes, (7) Yes, and (8) No.

Chapter 4: Decision-Making Styles

Generally there are three decision-making styles: reflexive, consistent, and reflective. To determine your style, add up your score by totaling the numbers assigned to each response. The total will be between 10 and 30. A score of between 10 and 16 indicates a reflexive style, 17 to 23 indicates a consistent style, and 24 to 30 indicates a reflective style.

Reflexive Style: A reflexive decision maker likes to make quick decisions (to shoot from the hip) without taking the time to get all the information that may be needed and without considering all alternatives. On the positive side, reflexive decision makers are decisive; they do not procrastinate. On the negative side, making quick decisions can lead to waste and duplication when the best possible alternative is overlooked. Employees may see a decision maker as a poor supervisor if he or she consistently makes bad decisions. If you use a reflexive style, you may want to slow down and spend more time gathering information and analyzing alternatives.

Reflective Style: A reflective decision maker likes to take plenty of time to make decisions, gathering considerable information and analyzing several alternatives. On the positive side, the reflective type does not make hasty decisions. On the negative side, he or she may procrastinate and waste valuable time and other resources. The reflective decision maker may be viewed as wishy-washy and indecisive. If you use a reflective style, you may want to speed up your decision making. As Andrew Jackson once said, "Take time to deliberate; but when the time for action arrives, stop thinking and go on."

Consistent Style: Consistent decision makers tend to make decisions without rushing or wasting time. They know when they have enough information and alternatives to make a sound decision. Consistent decision makers tend to have the best record for making good decisions.

Chapter 5: An Entrepreneurial Quiz

If most of your marks are in the first column, you probably have what it takes to run a business. If not, you are likely to have more trouble than you can handle by yourself. You should look for a partner who is strong on the points on which you are weak. If most marks are in the third column, not even a good partner will be able to shore you up. Now go back and answer the first question on the self-assessment.

Chapter 6: How Is Your Organization Managed?

0–9 10–19 20–29 30–39	Bureaucratic System 1
40–49 50–59 60–69 70–79	Mixed Systems 2 and 3
80–89 90–100	Organic System 4

High scores indicate a highly organic and participatively managed organization. Low scores are associated with a mechanistic or a bureaucratically managed organization.

Chapter 7: Innovative Attitude Scale

To determine your score, simply add the numbers associated with your responses to the twenty items. The higher your score, the more receptive to innovation you are. You can compare your score with that of others to see if you seem to be more or less receptive to innovation than a comparable group of business students.

Score	Percentile*
39	5
53	16
62	33
71	50
80	68
89	86
97	95

*Percentile indicates the percentage of the people who are expected to score below you.

Chapter 8: Diagnosing Poor Performance and Enhancing Motivation

Skill Area	Item	Rating
Diagnosing performance problems	1	_____
	11	_____
Establishing expectations and setting goals	2	_____
	12	_____
Facilitating performance (enhancing ability)	3	_____
	13	_____
	20	_____
Linking performance to rewards and discipline	5	_____
	14	_____
	6	_____
	15	_____
Using salient internal and external incentives	7	_____
	16	_____
	8	_____
	17	_____
Distributing rewards equitably	9	_____
	18	_____
Providing timely and straightforward performance feedback	4	_____
	10	_____
	19	_____
Total score:		_____

To assess how well you scored, compare your score to three comparison standards: (1) Compare your score with the maximum possible (120). (2) Compare your score with the scores of other students in your class. (3) Compare your score to a norm group consisting of five hundred business school students. In comparison to the norm group, if you scored

101 or above, you are in the top quartile.
94 to 100, you are in the second quartile.
85 to 93, you are in the third quartile.
84 or below, you are in the bottom quartile.

The higher your score, the better you are at identifying performance problems and the more skillful you are at taking steps to correct them. You can compare your score with that of others to see whether you seem to be more or less skillful than a comparable group of business students.

Chapter 9: Assessing Your Mental Abilities

Research spanning fifty years has identified ten primary mental abilities. The higher your score on each statement, the more you see yourself as having the corresponding mental ability. The mental abilities associated with each statement are as follows:

1. Flexibility and speed of closure
2. Originality/fluency
3. Inductive reasoning
4. Associative memory
5. Span memory
6. Number facility
7. Perceptual speed
8. Deductive reasoning
9. Spatial orientation and visualization
10. Verbal comprehension

Chapter 10: Assessing Your Needs

This set of needs was developed in 1938 by H. A. Murray, a psychologist, and operationalized by another psychologist, J. W. Atkinson. These needs correspond one-to-one to the items on the assessment questionnaire. Known as Murray's Manifest Needs because they are visible through behavior, they are:

1. Achievement
2. Affiliation
3. Aggression
4. Autonomy
5. Exhibition
6. Impulsivity
7. Nurturance
8. Order
9. Power
10. Understanding

Although little research has evaluated Murray's theory, the different needs have been researched. People seem to have a different profile of needs underlying their motivations at different ages. The more any one or more are descriptive of you, the more you see yourself as having that particular need active in your motivational makeup. For more information, see H. A. Murray, *Explorations in Personality* (New York: Oxford University Press, 1938) and J. W. Atkinson, *An Introduction to Motivation* (Princeton, NJ: Van Nostrand, 1964).

Chapter 11: Managerial Leader Behavior Questionnaire

These statements represent twenty-three behavior categories that are identified by research as descriptive of managerial leadership. Not all twenty-three are important in any given situation. Typically less than half of these behaviors are associated with effective performance in particular situations; thus, there is no "right" or "wrong" set of responses on this questionnaire. The behavior categories are

1. Emphasizing performance
2. Showing consideration
3. Career counseling
4. Inspiring subordinates
5. Providing praise and recognition
6. Structuring reward contingencies
7. Clarifying work roles
8. Goal setting
9. Training-coaching
10. Disseminating information
11. Encouraging decision participation
12. Delegating
13. Planning
14. Innovating
15. Problem solving
16. Facilitating the work
17. Monitoring operations
18. Monitoring the environment
19. Representing the unit
20. Facilitating cooperation and teamwork
21. Managing conflict
22. Criticism
23. Administering discipline

In military organizations at war, inspiring subordinates, emphasizing performance, clarifying work roles, problem solving, and planning seem most important. In military organizations during peacetime, inspiring subordinates, emphasizing performance, clarifying work roles, showing consideration, criticism, and administering discipline seem most important. In business organizations, emphasizing performance, monitoring the environment, clarifying work roles, goal setting, and sometimes innovating seem to be most important. In each of these instances, however, the level of organization, type of technology, environmental conditions, and objectives sought help determine the exact mix of behaviors that will lead to effectiveness. You should analyze your particular situation to determine which subset of these behavior categories is most likely to be important and then strive to develop that subset.

Chapter 12: Sex Talk Quiz

1. **False**—According to studies there is no truth to the myth that women are more intuitive than men. However, research has shown that women pay greater attention to "detail." Linguist Robin Lakoff in her classic book, *Language and Woman's Place* (Harper Colophon, 1975), confirms this and states that women tend to use finer descriptions of colors.
2. **True**—Men are listened to more often than women. In "Sex Differences in Listening Comprehension," Kenneth Gruber and Jacqueline Gaehelein (*Sex Roles*, Vol. 5, 1979) found that both male and female audiences tended to listen more attentively to male speakers than to female speakers.

3. **False**—Contrary to popular stereotype it is men—not women—who talk more. Studies like the one done by linguist Lynnette Hirshman showed that men far outtalk women ("Analysis of Supportive and Assertive Behavior in Conversations." Paper presented at the Linguists Society of America, July 1974).

4. **False**—Although several studies show that women talk more rapidly than men, women don't necessarily talk extremely fast.

5. **False**—Numerous studies show that women, not men, tend to maintain more eye contact and facial pleasantries. Dr. Nancy Henley in her chapter "Power, Sex, and Non-Verbal Communication" in *Language and Sex: Difference and Dominance* (Newbury House Publishers, 1975), shows that women exhibit more friendly behavior such as smiles, facial pleasantries, and head nods than men.

6. **True**—Studies show that women are more open in their praise and give more "nods of approval" than men. They also use more complimentary terms throughout their speech according to Peter Falk in his book *Word-Play: What Happens When People Talk* (Knopf, 1973).

7. **True**—Donald Zimmerman and Candace West showed that 75 percent to 93 percent of the interruptions were made by men. ("Sex Roles, Interruptions and Silences in Conversation," in *Language and Sex: Difference and Dominance*, edited by B. Thorne and N. Henley, Newbury House Publishers, 1975.)

8. **False**—Men use more command terms or imperatives, which makes them sound more demanding. In essence, several researchers have concluded that women tend to be more polite in their speech.

9. **False**—Men and women definitely differ in their sense of humor. Women are more likely to tell jokes when there is a small, non-mixed sex group, and men were more likely to tell jokes in a larger, mixed sex group.

10. **False**—In a survey conducted for the Playboy Channel, people were asked what they wanted to hear when making love. In general, women wanted to be told they were beautiful and loved, and men wanted to hear how good they were in bed and how they pleased their women.

11. **True**—Deborah Tannen in her book, *You Just Don't Understand: Women and Men in Conversation* (William Morrow, 1990), found that men usually will not ask for help by asking for directions while women will.

12. **False**—Several surveys and numerous psychotherapists' observations have indicated that women tend to be more self-critical and more apt to blame themselves than men. Deborah Tannen's findings confirm this as she states that women also tend to use more "apologetic phrases" in their conversations such as, "I'm sorry," "I didn't mean to," or "Excuse me."

13. **True**—Naturalist Charles Darwin stated that making oneself appear smaller by bowing the head to take up less space can inhibit human aggression. Other researchers found that women tend to inhibit themselves by crossing their legs at the ankles or knees or keeping their elbows to their sides.

14. **False**—As mentioned earlier, women tend to be more detailed and more descriptive than men in what they say and in how they explain things. As Robin Lakoff's research shows (see Item 1), women tend to use more description in word choices.

15. **False**—Men tend to touch more than females. According to several researchers, women are more likely to be physically touched by men who guide them through the door, assist them with jackets and coats, and help them into cars.

16. **False**—Women, not men, appear to be more attentive when listening. Studies consistently show that women exhibit greater eye contact and express approval by smiling and head-nodding as a form of attentiveness and agreement.

17. **True**—Men and women are equally emotional when they speak. However, women appear to sound more emotional according to researchers such as Robin Lakoff (see item 1) because they use more psychological-state verbs: I *feel,* I *hope,* and I *wish.*

18. **False**—In general, men tend to bring up less personal topics than women. Women tend to discuss people, relationships, children, self-improvement, and how certain experiences have affected them. Men, on the other hand, tend to be more "outer directed" as they originate discussions about events, news, sports-related issues, and topics related to more concrete physical tasks.

19. **False**—Even though men do not bring up as many subjects of conversation as women, men interrupt more which ultimately gives them control of the topics that are raised by women.

20. **False**—Even though there are many progressive and socially enlightened parents in the modern world, parents still treat their male children differently than their female children. They tend to communicate differently to their children according to their sex, which, in turn, induces sex-stereotyped behaviors.

21. **True**—Even though men make more direct statements, a recent survey indicated that women tend to confront and bring up a problem more often than men. Even though women bring up a problem more often, they tend to be more indirect and polite, as Deborah Tannen relates in her book.

22. **False**—In several studies, it was determined that women are more animated and livelier speakers than men. Studies also show that women make more eye contact, use more body movement, use more intonation, have a more varied pitch range, and use more emotionally laden words and phrases than men.

23. **False**—Just as women bring up more topics of conversation, they also ask more questions. According to researchers, this is usually done to facilitate the conversation.

24. **False**—Men and women usually talk about different things. Studies indicate that women enjoy talking about diet, personal relationships, personal appearance, clothes, self-improvement, children, marriages, personalities of others, actions of others, relationships at work, and emotionally charged issues that have a personal component. Men, on the other hand, enjoy discussing sports, what they did at work, where they went, news events, mechanical gadgets, latest technology, cars, vehicles, and music.

25. **True**—A recent Gallup poll survey commissioned for Lillian Glass, *He Says, She Says,* found that women rather than men were more likely to introduce the topics of AIDS testing and safe sex.

Chapter 13: Using Teams

Based on research conducted by J. Richard Hackman and others, all the statements are false.

1. An emphasis on individual accountability essentially undermines any effort to develop a team.

2. Complete authority is likely to lead to anarchy. Limits should be set.

3. Teams should be kept small, have clear boundaries, and have an enabling structure that ensures member motivation.
4. Teams need coaching, counseling, and support at certain intervals during their functioning.
5. The start-up period is critical, which is why managers must spend time and energy coaching and counseling the team during this period. Once the team gets going, the manager should pull back until it reaches a natural break or completes a performance cycle.
6. Training is absolutely critical and should be done before the team is assembled or shortly thereafter. If the needed skills and knowledge change, management should be ready to assist in training to help the team quickly learn the new skills and knowledge.
7. Providing support for teams is difficult. A reward system must recognize and reinforce team performance, an educational system must provide needed skills and knowledge, an information system must provide necessary information, and physical and fiscal resources must be available as needed.
8. Teams need some structure to work effectively.
9. The opposite is true. Managers should set the direction and establish wide limits on constraints with the means to the end determined by the team.
10. Teams cannot effectively be used in organizations that have strong individualistic cultures.

Chapter 14: Understanding Control

The odd-numbered items are all false, and the even-numbered ones are all true. Thus, you should have positive responses for the even-numbered items and negative responses for the odd-numbered ones. If you agreed strongly with all of the even ones and disagreed strongly with all of the odd ones, your total score would be zero.

Examine your responses to see which items you responded to incorrectly. Focus your attention on learning why the answers are what they are.

Chapter 15: Defining Quality and Productivity

The odd-numbered items are all true; they refer to eight dimensions of quality (see Table 15.2). Those eight dimensions are performance, features, reliability, conformance, durability, serviceability, aesthetics, and perceived quality. The even-numbered statements are all false. Thus, you should have positive responses for the odd-numbered items and negative responses for the even-numbered ones. If you agree strongly with all of the odd-numbered ones and disagree strongly with all of the even-numbered ones, your total score is zero.

Examine your responses to see which items you responded to incorrectly. Focus your attention on learning why the answers are what they are. Remember that the American Society for Quality Control defines quality as the *total* set of features and characteristics of a product or service that bears on its ability to satisfy stated or implied needs of customers.

Credits

Part One: pp. 2–3: Jason Fulford; *Chapter 1:* p. 5: Carol Lundeen; p. 11: Jean-Francois Campos/Agence VU; p. 16: Property of AT&T Archives. Reprinted with permission of AT&T; *Chapter 2:* p. 33: Spencer Grant/Photoedit; p. 34: Radhika Chalasani/SIPA; p. 46: AP/Wide World Photos; *Part Two:* pp. 62–63: Gail Albert Halaban/SABA; *Chapter 3:* p. 65: Leslie Hugh Stone/The Image Works; p. 67: Alex Tehrani; p. 73: Volkswagen of America, Inc.; p. 90: From Ricky Griffin, *Management*, Fourth edition © 1993 by Houghton Mifflin Co. Reprinted with permission of the publisher; *Chapter 4:* p. 95: Carol Lundeen; p. 99: Karen Kuehn/Matrix; p. 109: Stone/Getty Images; *Chapter 5:* p. 121: David Grahm; p. 124: Chris Usher/Corbis Sygma; p. 132: Republished with permission of Globe Newspaper Company, Inc., from the May 10, 2000, issue of the *Boston Globe* © 2000; *Part Three:* pp. 152–153: © Robert Wright 2000; *Chapter 6:* p. 155: AFP/Corbis; p. 157: Eli Reichmann; p. 169: Photographed by Lloyd Wolf for the U.S. Census Bureau; *Chapter 7:* p. 185: Will Hart/Photoedit; p. 187: Richard Baker/Matrix; p. 193: Steven Ahlgren; *Chapter 8:* p. 213: AP/Wide World Photos; p. 220: Erin Patrice O'Brien; p. 223: © Kenny Braun; *Part Four:* pp. 242–243: Ki Ho Park/Kistone; *Chapter 9:* p. 245: Mark Richards/Photoedit; p. 251: Reuters/Archive Photo; p. 262: Sarah A. Friedman; *Chapter 10:* p. 275: Kristine Larsen; p. 280: Mark Richards; p. 290: Pham Van Quang; *Chapter 11:* p. 303: Mark Wilson/Newsmakers/Getty News; p. 309: Michael O'Neill/Corbis Outline; p. 320: Todd Warshaw/ICON SMI Media; *Chapter 12:* p. 333: PhotoDisc, Inc./Getty Images; p. 338: © Peter Ross 2001; p. 343: © Fritz Hoffmann All Rights Reserved; *Chapter 13:* p. 361: Courtesy of Fastener Supply Company; p. 362: Phillippe Diederich; p. 372: AP/Wide World Photos; *Part Five:* pp. 388–389: Chuck Savage/CORBIS Stockmarket; *Chapter 14:* p. 391: PhotoDisc, Inc./Getty Images; p. 393: Starbucks Coffee Company; p. 401: Nikolai Ignatiev/Network/SABA Press Photos; *Chapter 15:* p. 423: Courtesy of Hartmann Luggage; p. 430: Bernd Auers; p. 435: Louis Psihoyos/Matrix.

Name Index

Robinson, Sandra L., 273n
Rockefeller, John D., 13
Rocks, David, 10
Rodgers, T. J., 175, *376f*
Roethlisberger, Fritz J., 31n
Rohwer, Jim, 93n
Rollins, John D., 359n
Rosen, Benson, 387n
Rosenman, R. H., 273n
Rosenthal, R. A., 387n
Rosenzweig, James E., 31n
Rosenzweig, Mark, 273n
Ross, Jerry, 119n
Rotter, J. B., 273n
Rubin, Elaine, 128
Rubin, Harriet, 31n
Rubinstein, Laila, 142
Rumelt, Richard, 93n
Ryan, Linda, 471n
Ryan, Lori V., 119n
Rynes, Sara L., 31n

Sackett, Paul R., 241n
Salter, Chuck, 150n
Sampler, Jeff, 166
Sandling, Heidi, 210n
Sanford, R. N., 273n
Sant, Marta, 221
Sarnoff, Nancy, 150
Sashittal, Hemant C., 387n
Sashkin, Marshall, 29
Sawyer, John E., 273n
Scandura, Terri A., 331n
Scarborough, Norman M., 151n
Schaubroeck, John, 273n
Schendel, Dan, *78f*
Scherer, F. M., 150n
Schlender, Brent, 210, 240
Schlesinger, Leonard A., 210n
Schmidt, Frank L., 241n
Schneider, Benjamin, 211n
Schrank, Robert, 387n
Schrempp, Jurgen, 302
Schriesheim, Chester A., 331n
Schroeder, Roger, 420n
Schultz, Howard, 6, 94–95, 105
Schweiger, David M., 119n, 359n
Schwenk, Charles R., 119n
Scott, K. Dow, 301n, 387n
Scott, Susanne G., 60n
Selye, Hans, 273n
Senge, Peter, 183n
Serwer, Andy, 151n
Shalley, Christina E., 273n
Sharkey, Thomas W., 331n
Shaw, Marvin E., 387n
Sheil, Beau, 471n
Sheremata, Willow A., 211n
Siebel, Tom, 419–420
Siekman, Philip, 451
Siemens, Werner von, 154
Simon, Herbert A., 106, 119n
Simons, Tony, 119n
Sims, Henry P., Jr., 331n

Singer, Andrew, 60n
Singer, Thea, 151n
Sitkin, Sim, 420n
Skinner, B. F., 300n
Slagmulder, Regine, 451n
Slocum, John W., 183n
Smith, D., 471n
Smith, Ken A., 119n
Smith, Page, 31n
Smith, Patricia C., 273n
Smith, Peter B., 273n
Snoek, J. D., 387n
Snow, Charles C., 183n
Snyderman, Barbara, 300n
Sonnack, Mary, 211n
Spendolini, Michael J., 183n
Stajkovic, Alexander D., 300n
Stalker, G. M., 168, 183n
Starke, Mary, 241n
Starr, Martin K., 119n
Staw, Barry M., 119n
Steers, Richard M., 300n
Stepnanek, Marcia, 425
Sternberg, Robert J., 330n
Stewart, Martha, 174
Stewart, Thomas A., 210, 211n
Stogdill, Ralph M., 331n
Stoka, Ann Marie, 31n
Strauss, J. Perkins, 273n
Sutcliffe, Kathleen, 273n, 420n
Sviokla, John J., 471n
Swaiij, Michael van, 71
Swamidass, Paul M., 451n

Tabak, Filiz, 273n
Tallman, Stephen, 421n
Taylor, Frederick W., 14, *14f*, 19, 22, 31n
Tepper, Bennett J., 330n, 331n
Tetrault, Linda A., 331n
Thomke, Stefan, 211n
Thompson, James, 183n
Thompson, Jane, 70
Thompson, Kenneth R., 93n
Thompson, Paul, 357
Thoreson, Carl J., 273n
Thornton, Emily, 273n
Todor, William D., 183n
Toombs, Leslie, 420n
Trank, Christine Quinn, 31n
Tubre, Travis C., 387n
Tully, Shawn, 60n, 183n
Tushman, Michael L., 331n

Urwick, Lyndall, 15
Useem, Jerry, 119n, 183n, 241n
Uzumeri, Mustafa V., 451n

Van Biema, Michael, 451n
Vanderbilt, Cornelius, 13
Vander Houwen, Boyd A., 359n
Van de Ven, Andrew H., 119n
Van Fleet, David D., 183n, 300n, 328, 449
Van Orden, Richard, 471n
Van Wassenhove, Luk N., 451n

Vavelas, A., 359n
Vest, Michael J., 301n
Victor, Bart, 183n
Vishwanath, Vijay, 119n
Von Hippel, Eric, 211n
Von Pierer, Heinrich, 154–155
Vroom, Victor H., 300n, 311, 316–318, *317f*, *318f*, 331n

Wager, Deidra, 6
Wagner, Jenny, 7
Wallace, Charles P., 119n
Walton, Richard E., 420n
Walton, Sam, 5, 52
Wanous, John P., 210n
Warner, Melanie, 420
Watson, Bill, 387n
Watson, James L., 182
Watt, James, 431
Webb, Susan, 124
Weber, Max, 15, 31n, 164–165, 183n
Weinberg, Neil, 200
Weir, Cheryl, 67
Weis, Richard M., 31n
Welch, Jack, 5, 209, 210, 321
Wetlaufer, Suzy, 387n
Wexner, Leslie, 4–5, 22
Whetten, D., 28, 239
Whyte, Glen, 119n
Wigdor, Lawrence A., 300n
Wilkins, Alan L., 31n
Williams, Eric J., 331n
Williams, Larry J., 273n
Williams, Margaret, 273n
Williams, Mary, 393
Williams, Robert, 183n
Williams, Venus, 251
Williamson, Oliver E., 93n, 183n
Winchell, William O., 451n
Wofford, J. C., 331n
Wofford, Jerry, 359n
Wolfe, D. M., 387n
Wong, Anny, 343
Woodman, Richard W., 273n
Woodward, Joan, 167, 169, 183n, 430, 451n
Worthy, James C., 183n
Wozniak, Steve, 202
Wrege, Charles D., 31n
Wren, Daniel, 31n
Wren, Worth, Jr., 182
Wright, Patrick, 241n
Wright, Peter, 420n
Wu, Yen-Chun, 451n

Yetton, Philip H., 331n
Young, Mary, 359n
Yukl, Gary A., 328, 330n

Zander, Alvin, 387n
Zellner, Wendy, 150n
Zesinger, Sue, 61n
Zetsche, Dieter, 302–303, 304
Zimmerer, Thomas W., 151n

Organization and Product Index

Subject Index